Heights of Reflection

Mountains have always stirred the human imagination, playing a crucial role in the cultural evolution of peoples around the globe and becoming infused with meaning in the process. Beyond their geographical-geological significance, mountains affect the topography of the mind, whether as objects of peril or attraction, of spiritual enlightenment or existential fulfillment, of philosophical contemplation or aesthetic inspiration. This volume challenges the oversimplified assumption that human interaction with mountains is a distinctly modern development, one that began with the empowerment of the individual in the wake of Enlightenment rationalism and Romantic subjectivity. These essays by European and North American scholars examine the lure of mountains in German literature, philosophy, film, music, and culture from the Middle Ages to the present, with a focus on the interaction between humans and the alpine environment. The contributors consider mountains not as mere symbolic tropes or literary metaphors, but as constituting a tangible reality that informs the experiences and ideas of writers, naturalists, philosophers, filmmakers, and composers. Overall, this volume seeks to provide multiple answers to questions regarding the cultural significance of mountains as well as the physical practice of climbing them.

Studies in German Literature, Linguistics, and Culture

Heights of Reflection

Mountains in the German Imagination from the Middle Ages to the Twenty-First Century

Edited by
Sean Ireton and Caroline Schaumann

Rochester, New York

Copyright © 2012 by the Editors and Contributors

All Rights Reserved. Except as permitted under current legislation,
no part of this work may be photocopied, stored in a retrieval system,
published, performed in public, adapted, broadcast, transmitted,
recorded, or reproduced in any form or by any means,
without the prior permission of the copyright owner.

First published 2012 by Camden House
Transferred to digital printing 2016
Reprinted in paperback 2017

Camden House is an imprint of Boydell & Brewer Inc.
668 Mt. Hope Avenue, Rochester, NY 14620, USA
www.camden-house.com
and of Boydell & Brewer Limited
PO Box 9, Woodbridge, Suffolk IP12 3DF, UK
www.boydellandbrewer.com

Hardcover ISBN-13: 978-1-57113-502-5
Hardcover ISBN-10: 1-57113-502-2
Paperback ISBN-13: 978-1-57113-987-0
Paperback ISBN-10: 1-57113-987-7

Library of Congress Cataloging-in-Publication Data

Heights of reflection : mountains in the German imagination from the middle
  ages to the twenty-first century / edited by Sean Ireton and Caroline
  Schaumann.
    p. cm. — (Studies in German literature, linguistics, and culture)
  Includes bibliographical references and index.
  ISBN-13: 978-1-57113-502-5 (hardcover: alk. paper)
  ISBN-10: 1-57113-502-2 (hardcover: alk. paper)
    1. German literature — History and criticism. 2. Philosophy of nature
  — Germany — History. 3. Mountains in literature. 4. Mountains in
  motion pictures. 5. Literature and society — Germany. I. Ireton, Sean
  Moore. II. Schaumann, Caroline, 1969–

PT139.H45 2012
830.9'36—dc23

2011051732

This publication is printed on acid-free paper.
Printed in the United States of America.

Contents

Acknowledgments — ix

Introduction: The Meaning of Mountains: Geology, History, Culture — 1
   Sean Ireton and Caroline Schaumann

Prelude: Classical Mountain Landscapes and the Language of Ascent — 20
   Dan Hooley

Part I: First Forays: Mountain Exploration and Celebration from the Middle Ages to the Eighteenth Century

Terra Incognita? Mountains in Medieval and Early Modern German Literature — 35
   Albrecht Classen

From Meadows to Mountaintops: Albrecht von Haller's "Die Alpen" — 57
   Caroline Schaumann

Interlude: Geo-Poetics: The Alpine Sublime in Art and Literature, 1779–1860 — 77
   Anthony Ozturk

Time and Narrative in the Mountain Sublime around 1800 — 98
   Sean Franzel

Faust's Mountains: An Ecocritical Reading of Goethe's Tragedy and Science — 116
   Heather I. Sullivan

Spectacular Scenery and Slippery Descents: Narrating the Mountains of Tropical Polynesia — 134
   Sabine Wilke

Part II: Beckoning Heights: Summits Near and Far in the Nineteenth Century

Fascinating Voids: Alexander von Humboldt and the Myth of Chimborazo   153
Oliver Lubrich

From Eros to Thanatos: Hiking and Spelunking in Ludwig Tieck's *Der Runenberg*   176
Peter Arnds

Geology, Mountaineering, and Self-Formation in Adalbert Stifter's *Der Nachsommer*   193
Sean Ireton

"An Apparition from Another World": The Mountains of the Moon and Kilimanjaro from the Perspective of Nineteenth-Century Germany   210
Christof Hamann

Part III: Modern Expeditions and Evocations: Climbing from the Twentieth into the Twenty-First Century

Leaving the Summit Behind: Tracking Biographical and Philosophical Pathways in Richard Strauss's *Eine Alpensinfonie*   231
Peter Höyng

Elevation and Insight: Thomas Mann's *Der Zauberberg*   248
Johannes Türk

"The Essence of the Alpine World Is Struggle": Strategies of *Gesundung* in Arnold Fanck's Early Mountain Films   267
Wilfried Wilms

"Mountain of Destiny": The Filmic Legacy of Nanga Parbat   285
Harald Höbusch

Spatial Orientation and Embodied Transcendence in Werner Herzog's Mountain Climbing Films   302
Roger Cook

W. G. Sebald's Magic Mountains   320
Scott Denham

Conflicting Ascents: Inscriptions, Cartographies, and
Disappearance in Christoph Ransmayr's *Der fliegende Berg*   334
    Olaf Berwald

Works Cited   349

Notes on the Contributors   379

Index   385

Acknowledgments

Like any successful mountain expedition, the present volume is not only the outcome of sustained collaboration among a devoted and close-knit group of climbing partners; it also rests on the groundwork and assistance of key supporters back at basecamp, all of whom deserve mention. The Alexander von Humboldt Foundation provided each of us with a research fellowship in 2009–10, enabling us to scope out our objective. At the annual conferences of the German Studies Association, Rocky Mountain Modern Language Association, and Pacific and Ancient Modern Language Association from 2008 to 2011, several members were able to meet and discuss strategies of the ascent. Expedition leader Jim Walker was a fortress of encouragement from start to finish. The Emory College of Arts and Science and the Laney Graduate School as well as the University of Missouri Research Council generously provided the funds for essential supplies, equipment, and hardware. Simon Roth at the Médiathèque Valais-Sion kindly made available the cover image for which we are grateful. The anonymous reviewers offered helpful suggestions and critical feedback in decisive, do-or-die moments. Sue Innes's meticulous copyediting ensured a flawless and relatively painless summit day. Our families bestowed much-needed sustenance, keeping us focused on getting down in one piece and offering a warm home upon our return. And, finally, we extend our deepest thanks to the mountains themselves, which continue to rise ever majestically, imparting their guidance and inspiration, reminding us of many summits to come.

Introduction: The Meaning of Mountains: Geology, History, Culture

Sean Ireton and Caroline Schaumann

"MOUNTAIN" IS A RELATIVE and variable concept, not only across the diverse cultures of the world but also in geoscientific terms. As products of tectonic, volcanic, glaciological, gravitational, and meteorological forces, mountains continually form and deform all over the globe. What were once the highest summits on the planet are now reduced to weathered mounds, as attested for instance by the Appalachians or the even older Laurentians. On the other hand, geologically younger ranges such as the Alps, Andes, and Himalayas continue to rise. While mountain elevations are generally determined from sea level, the Hawaiian Islands contain the tallest peaks in the world if one measures them from the ocean floor. Mauna Kea officially stands at 4,205 meters or 13,796 feet above sea level but rises over 10,000 meters or 33,000 feet from its base in the Pacific Ocean; it therefore surpasses Mt. Everest (8,848 m/29,029 ft.) in height. The neighboring Mauna Loa (4,170 m/13,680 ft.), the largest volcano on earth in terms of sheer mass, has depressed the sea floor some five miles, thus attaining approximately 17,000 meters or 56,000 feet in total elevation. It can therefore be considered the frontrunner in long-standing debates about mountain altitudes. But nothing is clear-cut when it comes to the earth's complex geomorphology. Owing to the imperfect sphere of our planet or its so-called "equatorial bulge," the summit of Chimborazo (6,310 m/20,702 ft.), located only one degree south of the equator, is farther removed from the earth's center than either Everest or the Hawaiian volcanoes. These submarine and subterranean considerations aside, Kilimanjaro (5,895 m/19,330 ft.) remains the highest freestanding mountain, towering more than 5,000 meters (16,000 ft.) over the East African plains. Beyond these geophysical criteria, the human perception of what qualifies as the loftiest world summit has changed throughout history. While Westerners first believed that the Alps were home to the high points of the world, European exploration and colonization of the Americas revealed even more towering peaks in the Andes. Chimborazo was consequently thought to top the list from the sixteenth to the early nineteenth century, when yet higher mountains were discovered in the Himalayas. The honor then fell to Dhaulagiri, and finally, in the 1850s, to Everest.

Given this confusion as to what precisely constitutes the highest mountain in the world, one cannot but question the contingency of this geological concept and anthropological construct. It thus comes as no surprise that there exists no universal definition of "mountain" in terms of elevation, volume, or gradient. In the cultural history of the Alps, for instance, one notes a tradition of conflating mountains and their surrounding terrain. The Middle High German *Albe* or *Alpe* (from the Latin *albus*: "white") refers to a snow-capped mountain as well as to a high-altitude pasture (compare the modern German *Alm*). Both of these terms aptly describe the Alps or *Alpen*, which even at lower elevations remain under snow throughout much of the year; but they also indicate that pastoral meadows were at least equally important as peaks in the minds of local inhabitants. Indeed, up until the eighteenth century, *Alpen* was an appellation that encompassed not only summits and meadows but also mountain passes, which were commonly viewed as a topographical amalgam of peak *and* valley. Since pilgrims, traders, and war leaders considered routes of passage infinitely more vital than the peaks themselves, maps of the Alps identified only the St. Gotthard Pass, leaving out the names, location, and height of Alpine mountains. In sum, definitions and designations of mountains are closely related to their historical, cultural, and economic significance and function.

Trigonometric and topographical measurements notwithstanding, diverse cultures have fundamentally different ways of defining and relating to mountains. As Hartmut Böhme has observed, the mountain is an "absolute metaphor." An "Urphänomen," or primordial phenomenon, like water or light, mountains are inherently symbolic and play a crucial role in the cultural evolution of peoples around the globe. They are infused with "Bedeutungscluster," or clusters of meaning, and these in turn "strukturieren die Topographie des Geistes" (structure the topography of the mind).[1] These clusters are readily discernible in the contrasting perceptions of mountains in Western and Eastern cultures. To the Western world, forests, deserts, and mountains were inhospitable places unsuited for cultivation and thus deemed of no value. Etymologically speaking, this "wilderness" was an uninhabited and undeveloped place where "wildeor" (wild beasts) roamed. This long-standing tradition of opposing *wild* (denoting "useless," "disordered," "alien") and *civilized* (denoting "cultivated," "fertile," "flat") terrain also has its roots in the Judeo-Christian belief system. The Hebrew word for "wilderness" is *midbar*, which not only connotes a forbidding place full of dangerous animals ("that great and terrible wilderness, wherein were fiery serpents, and scorpions, and droughts . . ."; Deut. 8:15) but also, in a more geographical or ecological sense, a transitional zone between the infertile, uninhabited desert and arable regions of human settlement (see Num. 21:13–18).[2] Whereas they have an originary presence in many Eastern religions, mountains go unmentioned in the

Hebrew story of Creation. Paradise was an abundant, well-groomed, and peaceful garden antithetical to the savage and threatening nature looming outside its confines (*pairidaêza* means "an enclosed garden or park" in the early Indo-Iranian language of Avestan). In the Garden of Eden, Adam and Eve enjoyed plentiful water, edible plants, and domesticated animals, in contrast to the "wilderness" (the English term first appeared in a fourteenth-century translation of the Latin Bible) that comprised the accursed "thirsty" land of "thorns and thistles" east of Eden. This stark contrast, already evinced at the dawn of Western culture, reverberates to this day. As Roderick Nash explains:

> Today dictionaries define wilderness as uncultivated and otherwise undeveloped land. The absence of men and the presence of wild animals is assumed. The word also designates other non-human environments, such as the sea and, more recently, outer space. Of equal importance to these actualities are the feelings they produce in the observer. Any place in which a person feels stripped of guidance, lost, and perplexed may be called wilderness.[3]

It is no surprise, then, that Western civilizations busied themselves with clearing and burning down forests, domesticating animals, and raising crops in an attempt to eliminate "wilderness" and thereby better steer the course of their own existence.[4]

With specific respect to mountains, the Judeo-Christian tradition — somewhat paradoxically — tends to accord a privileged status to such desolate and elevated territory. In the Old Testament, Noah's ark came to rest on Mount Ararat; Abraham bore Isaac to a mountaintop for sacrifice; Moses received the Ten Commandments on Mount Sinai; and Elijah triumphed over the followers of Baal on Mount Carmel. As for the New Testament, one need only mention a few critical stations in the life and teachings of Jesus: the Mount of Temptation, the Sermon on the Mount, the Mount of Transfiguration, the Mount of Olives, and Golgotha. All of these physical heights function as symbolic sites of spirituality, sacrifice, and transcendence. But such spiritually enlightened views did not always carry over in full to the popular (Christian) mentality. Throughout much of human history in the West, mountains exuded both fear and fascination: while often regarded as the domain of dark spirits, demons, and dragons, they also attracted a great deal of curiosity. A case in point is Mount Pilatus (2,120 m/6,955 ft.) near Lucerne, Switzerland. According to legend, the Roman prefect Pontius Pilate — the very man who is said to have sent Jesus to Golgotha — was interred at the top, and the City Council of Lucerne barred any citizen from climbing the mountain for fear that it would unleash the wrath of Pilate. In 1387, six clergymen were jailed because they attempted to ascend the peak, which remained unclimbed until 1518, when professor of medicine

*Fig. 1. "Images of Dragons," by Johann Jakob Scheuchzer, 1723.
From* Itinera per Helvetiae Alpinas Regiones.
Copyright: VIATICALPES / Bibliothèque Cantonale et Universitaire Lausanne.

Vadianus was issued a special permit to scale Pilatus and failed to encounter any supernatural beings. As late as the eighteenth century, mountains were believed to house terrestrial forces of evil, and in his four-volume *Itinera per Helvetiae Alpinas Regiones Facta Annis 1702–1711* (Travels through the Alpine regions of Switzerland made in the years 1702–1711), the Swiss professor of physics and mathematics Johann Jakob Scheuchzer compiled sightings, descriptions, and illustrations of dragons (fig. 1), distinguishing winged from unwinged, and footed from nonfooted species.

By most accounts, this long-reigning superstition precluded any large-scale exploration of mountains up until the 1800s, when advances in the sciences and a shifting mental paradigm brought scholars, poets, and climbers into contact with Alpine terrain. This book, however, challenges what we see as the oversimplified assumption that human interaction with mountains is a distinctly modern development, one that began with the empowerment of the individual, whether in the wake of Enlightenment rationalism or Romantic subjectivity. The 1991 discovery of Ötzi, the Ice Man, a remarkably well-preserved mummy dating back to around 3,300 BCE, which two climbers stumbled upon at 3,210 meters or near 11,000 feet in the Ötztal Alps of Tyrol, testifies that Neolithic man frequented the high mountains — and these of course were even more glaciated at the time. Based on the arrowhead buried in his shoulder (presumably the cause of his death), blood from another human on his clothes, and a rudimentary backpack made of animal skins stretched over a wooden frame, scientists conclude that Ötzi had traveled across this section of the Alps, possibly as a trader or shepherd, and that had he had encountered other people — including his own killers — high above the realm of human habitation.[5]

In the Americas, numerous peaks from the Rockies to the Andes also display signs of human presence. Stone circles or so-called "enclosures" in Nevada and Wyoming (the highest such structure is located on the sub-summit of the Grand Teton) suggest that Amerindians climbed to remote heights in order to experience visions, an important rite of passage in many tribes. Arrowheads have been found on some of the highest reaches in the Rockies and Sierra Nevada. One furthermore finds pre-Columbian traces on more soaring heights in Mexico and South America, for instance structural ruins 1,200 feet below the Mexican summit of Popocatépetl (5,452 m/17,887 ft.) and an Incan burial site atop Llullaillaco (6,739 m/22,110ft.) along the Chilean-Argentinian border. Again, it is important to note here that mountains have not always been utter terra incognita throughout anthropological history. They have, rather, borne witness to human activity — whether worship, hunting, exploration, or passage — on various continents and among a wide array of premodern cultures.

As intimated above in the examples drawn from Native America, non-Western civilizations tend to revere rather than fear mountains. Mount Meru occupies the center of the universe in Hindu and Buddhist cosmologies, while in Taoism the Kunlun Mountains form the cosmogonical origin of the "ten thousand things" that make up the world. Pilgrimages to high elevations for the sake of illumination have a long tradition that continues into the present. Famous examples include Mount Fuji (3,776 m/12,389 ft.), one of three holy mountains in Japan, whose symmetrical cone-summit is celebrated for its beauty in mythology, poetry, and painting, and was climbed as early as 663 CE; and Tai Shan, one of the Five Sacred Mountains in ancient China from whose relatively low-lying summit (1,533 m/5,029 ft.)

Confucius is said to have gained insight into the insignificance of the world below him. Today both Fuji and Tai Shan draw tens of thousands of visitors and pilgrims annually; over the course of its history, the latter peak has in fact been ascended by seventy-two emperors as well as Mao Zedong. Other prominent holy peaks and their respective worshippers around the world include Mount Emei (Buddhists), Ayers Rock (Aboriginal Australians), Mount Kenya (the Kikuyu people), Kilimanjaro (the Chaga people), Ol Doinyo Lengai or "The Mountain of the God" (the Masai people), and Adam's Peak in Sri Lanka, whose rocky summit contains an indentation attributed to the footprint of Buddha, Shiva, or Adam, depending on one's religious perspective. Moreover, two major prophets, Zoroaster and Mohammed, are identified with mountain topography: whereas the latter received his first revelation from the Angel Gabriel in the remote Hira Cave on Jebel-an-Nur ("The Mountain of Light") just outside Mecca, the former is believed to have dwelled and elaborated his religious doctrines in the rugged heights of ancient Persia.[6]

This volume, however, is firmly rooted in European — more specifically, German — cultural history. Within this area, the subject of mountains has received little scrutiny, at least in any concentrated or sustained form, which seems curious given the (widely perceived) German penchant for both thorough scholarship and mountain climbing.[7] Yet, as this volume shows in sixteen chronologically arranged chapters, references to mountains abound in the broader German-speaking humanistic tradition. Given the intellectual "tyranny of Greece over Germany," to allude to E. M. Butler's study of the modern German fascination with Hellenic culture,[8] we begin with a prelude that addresses the role of mountains in the classical imagination. As Dan Hooley argues in "Classical Mountain Landscapes and the Language of Ascent," mountains have always mattered, whether as objects of peril or attraction, of spiritual enlightenment or existential fulfillment, of philosophical contemplation or aesthetic inspiration. His opening contribution covers much historical and authorial terrain (Pindar, Euripides, Horace, Vergil, Seneca, Petrarch, and others) and helps to establish the discursive ground for the chapters that follow. Hooley's discussion of Petrarch is of particular importance from the standpoint of mountaineering history. In April 1336, Petrarch decided to climb Mont Ventoux (1,912 m/6,273 ft.) in southern France, ostensibly for no other reason than the sheer desire to experience nature in all its fullness. Choosing his brother as companion and ignoring a local shepherd's warning, Petrarch eventually reached the top of the "Giant of Provence," where he marveled at the panoramic view that stretched from the Pyrenees to the Alps. Though Petrarch's epistolary account of his climb is stylized, perhaps nothing more than a literary construct,[9] many regard it as testimony of the first premodern example of mountain climbing for climbing's sake. Petrarch, that is, seeks the summit of Ventoux based on individualistic, non-utilitarian motives. In his classic study *Die Kultur der Renaissance in Italien* (The civilization of the Renaissance in Italy, 1860), Jacob Burckhardt famously called Petrarch "einer der frühsten völlig modernen Menschen" (one of the earliest completely modern human beings), in large part because of his "planloses Bergsteigen" (mountain climbing without plan).[10] Petrarch's aesthetic summit delight in the horizontal and vertical space below, and his simultaneous inward turn to a moral experience reinforce this fundamental connection between mountains and intellectual history.

The cultural importance of mountains increased during the Middle Ages, when their resources of copper and iron were increasingly needed for coinage, armor, and weapons. These material reserves underwent various literary-metaphorical transformations, resulting in fantasies of magnetism, water reservoirs, precious minerals, and treasure troves. Albrecht Classen's "Terra Incognita? Mountains in Medieval and Early Modern German Literature" offers a survey of perceptions and evocations of mountains from the early to late Middle Ages. He shows that poets often focus on the depths rather than the heights of mountains; heroes do not so much climb peaks as explore their cavernous interiors. On a psychological level, this interiorization of geophysical terrain may be interpreted as a response to the harsh if not fatal mountainous environment looming on the horizon. Courtly culture was of course based in regions close to the Alps (Swabia, Bavaria, and Austria), and this major mountain range posed a formidable barrier — both physical and mental — to pilgrims, clergymen, and political officials on their way to and from Rome, the religious capital of the Holy Roman Empire of the German Nation. Nevertheless, in early modern woodcuts mountains rise to artistic prominence, intimating the beginnings of an artistic concern with the landscape: Alpine scenes become dominant background motifs, whether in Maximilian I's *Theuerdank* of 1517 or in contemporary *vedute* of cities located both close to (Salzburg) and far from (Strasbourg and even Constantinople) the Alps.

Historical records reveal a number of intriguing ascents during the late medieval and early modern eras. These climbing milestones attest to both an intellectual interest and a physical participation in mountain landscapes well before the birth of Alpinism and the age of Romanticism in the latter half of the eighteenth century. Though it is not possible to discuss all of these landmarks in the present context, several deserve mention, again, if only to show that mountains were not altogether shunned by premodern Europeans or signified a *locus horribilis*.[11] In 1358, a knight by the name of Bonifacio Rotario D'Asti climbed Rocciamelone (3,538 m/11,607 ft.), a steep and partially glaciated mountain in the Graian Alps of Italy. While Columbus was making preparations to sail the Atlantic in late June of 1492, King Charles VIII of France summoned a party of seven led by Antoine de Ville to attain the summit of what was known back then as "Mons

Inascensibilis" (2,086 m/6,843 ft.), a relatively low-lying yet sheer peak in the French Dauphiné. Using ropes, ladders, and iron bars driven into the rock, the party (including three clerics) reached the top, after which they sang prayers, erected three crosses, and christened it Mont Aiguille (*aiguille* = "needle" or "spire"). Perhaps more importantly, de Ville drew up a notarized protocol of the ascent, which has become known as the "Magna Carta of Alpinism," an early form of guidebook in which he documented the difficulties of the climb. Leonardo da Vinci made various sketches of mountain landscapes and in 1511, at the age of sixty, scaled a peak by the name of Monboso. The primary motivation of his undertaking, however, differed from the pure joy in climbing that propelled Petrarch up Mont Ventoux. As an artist and scientist, Leonardo was more interested in studying light filtration, atmospheric conditions, and geological structures, and his descriptions of higher altitudes have been shown to possess vivid imagination. The first recorded ascent of an Alpine peak by a woman occurred in 1552, when Regina von Brandis and her daughter Katharina Botsch summited the Laugenspitze (2,433 m/7,982 ft.) in South Tyrol.

Mountain fascination and interaction is a recurrent theme in the life and work of Zurich botanist and physician Conrad Gesner, who climbed Mount Pilatus in 1555 and recorded his ascent in *Descriptio Montis Fracti juxta Lucernam* (Description of the jagged mountain near Lucerne), in which he dismissed the presence of Pilate or his ghost on the summit. To Gesner, mountains were blessed rather than cursed, a sentiment he expressed as early as 1541 in a letter to his friend, the physician Jakob Vogel, under the telling title *De montium admiratione* (On the admiration of mountains).[12] The following passage, albeit lengthy, offers insight into Gesner's passion with respect to a physical terrain that most people of that era failed to appreciate:

> Ich habe mir vorgenommen, sehr geehrter Vogel, fortan, so lange mir Gott das Leben gibt, jährlich mehrere, oder wenigstens *einen* Berg zu besteigen; und zwar, wenn die Pflanzen in Blüte sind, teils um diese kennen zu lernen, teils um den Körper zu stärken und den Geist zu ergötzen. Denn welche Lust ist es, welche Wonne dem ergriffenen Geist, die gewaltige Masse der Gebirge zu bewundern und das Haupt gleichsam zu den Wolken zu erheben. Ich weiss nicht, auf welche Weise durch diese unbegreiflichen Höhen das Gemüt erschüttert und hingerissen wird zur Bewunderung des erhabenen Baumeisters. Die aber, deren Geist stumpf ist, wundern sich über nichts. Sie brüten in ihren Stuben und sehen das gewaltige Schauspiel des Weltalls nicht; in ihren Winkel verkrochen wie die Siebenschläfer im Winter, denken sie nicht daran, dass das Menschengeschlecht auf die Welt gesetzt wurde, um aus ihren Wundern etwas Höheres, ja das höchste Wesen selbst zu begreifen. Soweit geht ihr Stumpfsinn, dass sie wie die Schweine immer zu Boden schauen und nie mit erhobenem Antlitz gen Himmel blicken, niemals ihr Auge aufheben zu den Sternen.

Mögen sie sich wälzen im Dreck, mögen sie kriechen, verblendet von Gewinn und knechtischer Streberei! Die Jünger der Weisheit aber mögen fortfahren, die Erscheinungen dieses irdischen Paradieses mit den Augen des Leibes und des Geistes zu betrachten, worunter die hohen und steilen Firste der Berge nicht die geringsten sind, mit ihren unzugänglichen Wänden, himmelanstrebenden ungeheuren Flanken, rauhen Felsen und schattigen Wäldern.[13]

[I made the plan, esteemed Dr. Vogel, from now on and as long as God grants me life, to ascend several or at least *one* mountain a year, when the vegetation is in bloom, partly to get to know the latter, partly to strengthen my body and delight my mind. What joy it is, what bliss to admire the mighty mass of mountains and to lift one's head into the clouds, so to speak. I do not know by what means these unfathomable heights stir the soul and cause one to gaze at them in admiration of the sublime master builder. But those whose minds are dull do not wonder at anything. They brood in their parlors and neglect to see the grand spectacle of the universe, holed up in their corners like dormice in winter, and they do not consider that humankind was put on this world to grasp, from its wonders, something higher, indeed the highest Being itself. Their dullness goes so far that they always look to the ground like pigs and never lift their head to look at the sky, never lift their eyes to look at the stars. May they roll in the dirt, may they crawl, blinded by profit and menial conceit! The disciples of wisdom, on the other hand, with the eyes of their body and their mind, may continue to observe the phenomena of this earthly paradise. Among them are not least the high and steep ridges of mountains, with their inaccessible walls, their enormous flanks reaching to the sky, their rugged cliffs, and shadowy forests.]

The first detailed maps of the High Alps were printed in Gesner's time, publicizing and eventually popularizing these seemingly indomitable mountains with such evocative names as Schreckhorn (horn of terror), Gross-Grünhorn (great green horn), Jungfrau (virgin), Mönch (monk), and Eiger (ogre). Woodcuts and illustrations depict villages amid hilly landscapes or in pastoral valleys at the foot of towering peaks; the wilderness in the background looks increasingly accessible through the presence of pathways, chapels, and hospices. Later the Swiss scholar Scheuchzer followed Gesner's example: he was among the first to haul thermometers, barometers, and graphometers into the mountains, collecting and analyzing an abundance of material from twelve Alpine excursions undertaken between 1694–1711. In 250 manuscripts, Scheuchzer recorded his observations on a wide range of natural and cultural phenomena, from Swiss dialects and customs to flora, fauna, rocks, and minerals, even foehn winds and avalanches. In fact, his *Natur-Histori des Schweizerlands* (Natural History of Switzerland, 1716–18) later served Schiller as a prime reference work for the many cultural and geographical details in *Wilhelm Tell* (1804).

Scheuchzer greatly contributed to Alpine geology, history, meteorology, and cartography,[14] and viewed the Alps as a product of divine benevolence (despite his still lingering belief in the existence of dragons), emphasizing the ineffable diversity of Swiss mountain terrain:

> Bald steigen sie gemächlich in die Höhe / bald sind sie rauh / steil / gähstotzig / und fast unersteiglich. Wer wollte alle Verschiedentheiten der äusseren Form erzehlen?[15]
>
> [Sometimes they rise leisurely upward / sometimes they are rugged / steep / precipitous / and almost unclimbable. Who could recount all the differences in their external appearance?]

The notion of mountains as God's beautiful creation was perpetuated by the Swiss physiologist, anatomist, botanist, and poet Albrecht von Haller, who made numerous trips to the Alps to collect plant specimens. His poem "Die Alpen" (The Alps, 1732), inspired by his impressions from an excursion to Switzerland during the summer of 1728, signals a major turning point in the history of Alpine discourse, insofar as it celebrates the beauty of the mountains as well as the moral virtues of its citizens. As Caroline Schaumann's chapter "From Meadows to Mountaintops: Albrecht von Haller's 'Die Alpen'" relates, Haller combines his critique of civilization with aesthetic and scientific reflections on Alpine flora and minerals, thereby creating a lasting literary topos of mountain veneration. He thus helped transform the previously regnant paradigm of mountainous landscapes as a *locus horribilis* into the new and influential construct of a *locus amoenus*. Texts set in the Alps, for instance Haller's poem and Jean-Jacques Rousseau's novel *Julie, ou la nouvelle Héloïse* (Julie, or the new Heloise, 1761), led to a gradual popularization of the range that culminated in the ascent of its highest peak, Mont Blanc (4,810 m/15,782 ft.). This mountaineering feat owes a great deal to the initiative of Horace-Bénédict de Saussure, a Swiss aristocrat, naturalist, botanist, and geologist, who became intimately acquainted with the Alps in 1760 while on a botanical mission directed by Haller. The two soon became friends, in large part because of their mutual enthrallment with the Alpine world. But in contrast to the less adventurous Haller, de Saussure engaged in mountaineering and became particularly obsessed with Mont Blanc. He put out a reward for its first ascent, and on 8 August 1786 the Chamonix natives Dr. Michel-Gabriel Paccard and Jacques Balmat cashed in on the prize. A year later de Saussure reached the summit, its third official ascent, having his eighteen guides transport bulky scientific instruments, appropriate reading material (Homer), and lavish provisions to the top. His scientific observations and ecstatic descriptions of this and other outings were published in the eight-volume *Voyages dans les Alpes* (1779–96), a book that was translated into English and Italian and that laid the foundation for his later reputation as the father of Alpinism.

Although the essays in this volume focus on conceptions and representations of mountains rather than on the history of Alpinism per se, there is an underlying connection between mountaineering practice and aesthetic theory. Accordingly, the chapters on texts of the eighteenth and nineteenth centuries probe the tenuous relationship between actual mountaineering experiences and aesthetic conceptualization. Just as de Saussure and many others in his wake were scaling peaks previously believed to be inaccessible, sublime painting and literature began to disrupt the conventional sense of balance with respect to the dimensions of depth and space, thereby calling for new categories of aesthetics. Anthony Ozturk's "Geo-Poetics: The Alpine Sublime in Art and Literature, 1779–1860" serves as an interlude to situate the subsequent discussion of mountains in the German cultural and aesthetic tradition within a greater framework of Western European discourses. Concentrating on notions of the Alpine sublime in the works of William Coxe, Louis-François Ramond de Carbonnières, Helen Maria Williams, William Wordsworth, and John Ruskin, among others, Ozturk examines the fusion of aesthetic, ethical, political, metaphysical, and geomorphological concerns during the period of Revolution and Romanticism. He subsumes these wide-ranging concerns under the concept "geo-poetics." As Ozturk suggests, the Helvetic myth emerging in accounts of British and Continental European travelers in the late eighteenth century is imbued with malleable, interdependent paradoxes such as conservative nostalgia (Coxe), geological inquiry (Ramond de Carbonnières), feminized revolutionary vision (Williams), romantic imagination (Wordsworth), and finally, mountain reverence (Ruskin). In a similar vein, Sean Franzel's "Time and Narrative in the Mountain Sublime around 1800" more specifically considers discourses of the sublime in the context of theories of narration. Contrasting dynamic movement with quiet contemplation, Franzel contends that the new paradigm of an Alpine sublime destabilizes not only existing spatial and temporal frames but also narrative logic. He compares the idealist aesthetics of Kant, Schiller, and Fichte — all of whom posit a dynamism that evokes mental and moral transcendence — with Goethe's description of the Alpine landscape, which is characterized by a more direct human engagement with the natural environment. In contrast to both these approaches, Franzel finds the conventional narrative sequence of the sublime disrupted in Hegel's travel descriptions of the Bernese Alps. For Hegel, Alpine scenery is both monotonous and meaningless, a landscape of privation that can offer only an epistemologically unproductive experience of boredom. Franzel's analysis brings a fresh, unsentimental, and critical perspective to sublime mountain veneration. Heather Sullivan's chapter, "Faust's Mountains: An Ecocritical Reading of Goethe's Tragedy and Science," continues this approach by pointing to the material dimensions of *Faust*, which have received little attention in scholarship. Using theories of ecocriticism to question both idealized concepts of nature and environmental rhetoric, Sullivan argues that Faust's transformations are always rooted in concrete reality and often hindered by physical or bodily limitations. She examines three mountain ascents that take place in *Faust I* and *II*, suggesting that mountains do not figure as sites of heroic or moral transformation but rather of material interventions.

As evidenced above, some of the essays in this book focus on representations or interpretations of mountains in works by canonical writers, while others examine nonfictional accounts of mountaineering expeditions. This juxtaposition of distinct narrative and generic modes not only allows for a reading of literary works in conjunction with actual mountaineering history and vice versa, but also expands the field of inquiry by pointing toward multifaceted, interdisciplinary connections. In her chapter "Spectacular Scenery and Slippery Descents: Narrating the Mountains of Tropical Polynesia," Sabine Wilke discusses George Forster's 1773 and 1774 scientific explorations of Tahiti (at first glance an unlikely site for mountain climbers), delineating the intersections of such discourses as mountaineering, colonialism, ecocriticism, and tropicalization. Wilke argues that Forster's narrative is characterized by an intermingling of these discourses, from mountaineering's models of (colonial) conquest to tropical tropes of fecundity and superabundance. Forster is thus a pivotal figure in transferring the mentality of early Alpinism to a topographically exotic locale, where "conquering" a mountain is integrally tied to the larger project of colonialism. Turning to Forster's friend and even more renowned explorer Alexander von Humboldt, Oliver Lubrich's "Fascinating Voids: Alexander von Humboldt and the Myth of Chimborazo" examines the mythical and literary aftermath of Humboldt's celebrated climb of Mount Chimborazo in 1802. While Humboldt failed to reach the Ecuadorean volcano's summit, Lubrich proposes that it is precisely Humboldt's nuanced response to this abortive undertaking that captures the essence of a self-reflective pioneer in the realms of both geographical and intellectual exploration. Humboldt's narratives of Chimborazo offer, in the end, an innovative, if not postmodern, poetics of failure.

Later in the nineteenth century, the fascination with another distant equatorial summit would also elicit a variety of discursive practices and narrative techniques. Mount Kilimanjaro, whose existence — at least in the European imagination — had long been conflated with the fabled Mountains of the Moon, is the principal object of scrutiny in Christof Hamann's "'An Apparition from Another World' — Kilimanjaro and the Mountains of the Moon from the Perspective of Nineteenth-Century Germany." Using his own novel *Usambara* (2007) as a point of departure, Hamann examines assorted fictional and nonfictional encounters with the African volcano, beginning with mid-century missionary reports, then turning to Hans Meyer's classic travelogue *Ostafrikanische Gletscherfahrten* (Across East African glaciers, 1890), and concluding with a discussion of

Wilhelm Raabe's *Abu Telfan oder die Heimkehr vom Mondgebirge* (Abu Telfan, or The return from the Mountains of the Moon, 1867). Hamann shows that the normally separate provinces of fact and fiction tend to overlap in nineteenth-century discourses about Kilimanjaro, which had only recently been "discovered" by Europeans, and the Mountains of the Moon, a nebulous geographical construct that had been mythologized since Ptolemy. Indeed, Hamann's *Usambara*, which blends the narratives of Meyer, Raabe, and his own semi-fictionalized journey to Africa's rooftop, gives perfect testimony to these blurred lines between fact and fable.

Two other chapters that deal with nineteenth-century texts do not venture to distant continents but remain grounded in German-Austrian mountain terrain — if not soil. "From Eros to Thanatos: Hiking and Spelunking in Ludwig Tieck's *Der Runenberg*," by Peter Arnds picks up precisely on this historically problematic metaphor of *Boden* or soil, drawing a sweeping interpretive arc that encompasses Heidegger, Nietzsche, Euripides, and Freud. As Arnds illustrates through his multiperspectival approach, Tieck's tale typifies the Romantic attraction to mountainous landscapes, both to their precipitous heights, as expressed through the activity of mountain climbing or *Bergsteigen*, and to their hidden depths, as evidenced in frequent allusions to mining or *Bergbau*. A vast psychological dimension, if not abyss, is laid bare in the subtext of *Der Runenberg* (Rune Mountain, 1802), one that is closely tied to mountain discourse and German etymologies, for example *Berg* (mountain), *bergen* (to rescue, recover) *Bergung* (rescue, recovery), *verbergen* (to conceal) and *Verborgenheit* (concealment). Tieck's paradigmatic Romantic text is thus replete with mountain images and metaphors, which it playfully exploits on numerous semantic levels. Sean Ireton's "Geology, Mountaineering, and Self-Formation in Adalbert Stifter's *Der Nachsommer*" interprets the semantic levels of a different word, *Bildung* (formation). This term, along with its many lexical variants, permeates the pages of Stifter's colossal novel, which is commonly classified as a Bildungsroman. Published in 1857, at the height of European Alpinism, *Der Nachsommer* (Indian Summer) draws a sustained analogy between the inner formation of its main character, Heinrich Drendorf, and the geological formations that comprise its principal setting: the Austrian Alps. Drendorf is, moreover, largely modeled on Stifter's friend Friedrich Simony, a professional geologist and accomplished mountaineer who published widely on his Alpine explorations, whether on his groundbreaking scientific discoveries or his equally impressive climbing feats. Stifter's novel is thus not only a literal brand of Bildungsroman, one that capitalizes on the multi-faceted notion of *Bildung*, but is solidly grounded in the nineteenth-century discourse and practice of mountaineering.

During the "Age of Empire," to borrow from the title of Maurice Isserman and Stewart Weaver's recent history of Himalayan climbing, mountaineering became inextricably connected with male conquest and national competition on the one hand and flight from urbanity on the other. As Isserman and Weaver point out, the emerging Himalayan expeditions espoused colonial and military strategies, while simultaneously attracting individual climbers who sought to escape the conventional principles of their respective societies.[16] Even though Germany had no colonial presence in India, nationalists traced their ethnic history back to Indo-European origins and a mythic Aryan homeland. In Europe, the construction of railroads and tunnels, the opening of numerous health resorts, and the development of skiing contributed to an unprecedented tourist boom in Switzerland, spurring debates about Alpine development and exclusivity. Some essays in this book reflect these tensions and ideological turns while examining diverse representations of climbing in both textual and nontextual forms. Peter Höyng's "Leaving the Summit Behind: Tracking Biographical and Philosophical Pathways in Richard Strauss's *Eine Alpensinfonie*" retraces the steps of Strauss's own *Bergpartie* (mountain tour) during the summer of 1879 in the Bavarian Alps, but this autobiographical approach forms only one strand in Höyng's argument. Strauss's musical composition grew from a life-long personal experience of the Alpine world yet also pays tribute to the composer's late friend, the artist and climber Karl Stauffer, as well as to the works of Friedrich Nietzsche, in particular *Der Antichrist*. Höyng fuses these various approaches in his effort to interpret Strauss's musical Alpine journey as a composition that is at once rooted in Nietzsche's critique of modernity and in the modern appropriation of the Alpine landscape. The Swiss resort town of Davos epitomizes the growing touristic infrastructure that took hold of the Alps around the turn of the century, and it is here that *Der Zauberberg* (The magic mountain, 1924) is set. As Johannes Türk demonstrates in "Elevation and Insight: Thomas Mann's *Der Zauberberg*," this modern novel breaks with the traditional tripartite structure of mountaineering narratives, which are generally oriented around ascent, summit arrival, and descent. Mann's novel dilates this trajectory to such a degree that the plot turns into an erring digression, typified by the famous "Schnee" chapter. Within this narrative configuration, Türk focuses on the physiological processes of life and disease, grounding his analysis in the broader medical discourse of infection and immunity. High altitudes, Türk argues, require an adaptation — or, more accurately, acclimatization — that challenges bourgeois physiology, and over the course of his extended stay in this foreign Alpine environment the lowlander Hans Castorp continually gains new insight into human existence and mortality.

Castorp's Alpine sojourn also serves as a point of departure for Scott Denham, who contends that any mountain journey in modern German literature inevitably harkens back to Castorp's dangerous, aimless, yet liberating wanderings in the snow. In his chapter "W. G. Sebald's Magic

Mountains," Denham urges us to read Sebald's pervasive and iconic representations of mountains in the wake of Castorp's near-death experience, and with the same degree of irony. Sebald's characters encounter the romantic sensibility of the sublime in the mountains, but what they take away from this potentially transformative moment remains ambiguous. The mountain is imagined as the precipice of both life and death, the sublime and the macabre, and is imbued with the potential to provide existential knowledge about the human condition. Sebald's characters, however, are not always able to live up to this potential. This quest, straddling the polarities of conquest and dissolution, also informs the book's final chapter, Olaf Berwald's "Conflicting Ascents: Inscriptions, Cartographies, and Disappearance in Christoph Ransmayr's *Der fliegende Berg*." Berwald uncovers the multiple metaphorical dimensions of the titular "flying mountain," as manifested in the text's lyrical prose and free verse, which mirror both surrender to and mastery of nature, and in the diametrical characters who seek to immerse themselves in and ultimately appropriate the mountain. Yet Berwald's examination reveals that both of these seemingly irreconcilable modes of ascent overlap and ultimately hinder existential insight: Liam's geodetic computer simulations fail to give an adequate sense of the mountain's power and leave the brothers in a state of helplessness; consequently, the narrator ignores the danger of solo glacier travel, falling into a crevasse and barely escaping with his life. Though he later makes it to the summit with his brother via a less dangerous route, their descent during a snowstorm results in failure: Liam dies and it can be argued that the narrator does too.

A further strand of essays examines the ways in which German cinema, from the early *Bergfilm* to Werner Herzog's portrayals of contemporary climbers, has transposed and primed the mountainscape for public consumption, as well as mediated a particular set of national-cultural values associated with it. The *Bergfilm*, an exclusively German genre pioneered by Arnold Fanck in the 1920s, remains one of the most important and successful artistic homages to Alpine sports to this day, promoting the Alps as a destination where men can seek refuge from frenzied life in the Weimar Republic and find greater physical and spiritual meaning in a monumental setting. As Fanck himself explains:

> Und all diese Schönheit einer Bergwelt, allen Jubel und alles Leid, das wir als Jugend einst selbst da hinaufgetragen, nunmehr den großen Massen in den Städten zu zeigen und mitzuteilen — das war die Aufgabe, die mir übrigblieb, nachdem der Tod aller Jugendfreunde (Walter Schaufelberger und Hans Rohde) dem eigenen Bergglück ein Ende gesetzt hatte.[17]

> [To show and convey to the urban masses all this beauty of the Alpine world, all the jubilation and suffering that we took up there with us

back in our youth — this was the task left to me after the death of all my childhood friends [Walter Schaufelberger and Hans Rohde] had put an end to my own mountains bliss.]

More recently, the two big-budget German film productions *Nordwand* (dir. Philipp Stölzl, 2008) and *Nanga Parbat* (dir. Joseph Vilsmaier, 2010) can be interpreted as contemporary variations on the *Bergfilm*. *Nordwand* dramatizes the ideologically laden story of Toni Kurz and Anderl Hinterstoißer's fatal attempt to climb the Eiger North Face in the summer of 1936 but manages to transform the two German climbers into opponents of the Nazi regime. While Stölzl decidedly rejects the *Bergfilm's* ideological implications, his film recalls both Fanck's innovative camera work and editing and the genre's problematic division of the Alpine environment and civilized society. *Nanga Parbat*, which fictionalizes the 1970s Messner-brothers' ascent of the mountain that ended in Günther Messner's death, attempts a similar balancing act. While the film's overly dramatic plot emphasizes brotherhood, heroism, and the struggle for survival, Vilsmaier lends the story an unequivocally anti-Nazi spin by heralding Messner as a postwar child who, in the spirit of 1968, rails against his antiquated and restrictive mountaineering leader. Both films seem to continue the *Bergfilm's* dichotomist structures, carrying on the genre's ambivalent legacy.

In "'The Essence of the Alpine World is Struggle': Strategies of *Gesundung* in Arnold Fanck's Early Mountain Films," Wilfried Wilms departs from the much-contested notion of the *Bergfilm* as prefascist premonition to understand the genre as a product of war and defeat in 1918. Drawing on the theoretical underpinnings of the social philosopher Georg Simmel and the chairman of the Munich Alpine Club, Gustav Müller, Wilms contends that the icy heights of the Alps were fashioned into a corrective for a nation suffering from the consequences of a lost war, heights that offered remedies for *Gesundung* (recuperation). Fanck's early films can likewise be read within this context, promoting national redemption and deliverance by staging a process of affective stabilization on a collective and individual level while outlining a vital generational and gender identity. Harald Höbusch's "'Mountain of Destiny': The Filmic Legacy of Nanga Parbat" furthers this premise, interpreting the German missions to Nanga Parbat in terms of national renewal. Höbusch investigates the filmic documentations of the 1934, 1937, and 1953 expeditions, exposing the militaristic and mythical undertones of the 1934 and 1937 films. While Hans Ertl's *Nanga Parbat 1953* seeks to distance itself from the previous (National Socialist-sponsored) productions, Höbusch emphasizes some core continuities pertaining both to Ertl himself, who began as an assistant to Arnold Fanck and continued as a cameraman under Leni Riefenstahl, and to the ideological values propagated in the earlier films. *Nanga Parbat*

1953 thus straddles a fine line between embracing the capitalistic market doctrine of the postwar decade and perpetuating the language of the Nazi past.

Finally, Roger Cook's chapter, "Spatial Orientation and Embodied Transcendence in Werner Herzog's Mountain Climbing Films," also considers the impact of visual media on its audience. Cook, however, focuses not on ideological messages but on spatial orientation. Examining Herzog's television documentary *Gasherbrum — Der leuchtende Berg* (The dark glow of the mountains, 1985), which relates Reinhold Messner's and Hans Kammerlander's unprecedented climb of two 8,000-meter peaks in succession, Cook suggests that the film not only visually presents the mountain landscape in images meant to stir the viewer's own imagination but also seeks to physically track the very climbing experience itself. To explain such different visualizations of space, Cook distinguishes two modes of spatial orientation, cognitive mapping and proprioception. Contrasting Herzog's *Gasherbrum* with his later feature film, *Cerro Torre: Schrei aus Stein* (Cerro Torre: Scream of stone, 1991), Cook elucidates the ways in which the former engages both modes of spatial orientation, enabling the viewer to share in the mind-body experience of the climber.

In sum and true to its title, *Heights of Reflection: Mountains in the German Imagination from the Middle Ages to the Twenty-First Century* focuses on conceptions and representations of mountains in the German-speaking intellectual tradition over the course of approximately one thousand years. "Reflection" here implies philosophical and aesthetic contemplation and, more literally, artistic replication. This volume of essays thus seeks to provide multiple answers to questions regarding the meaning of mountains as well as of climbing them, questions expressed for instance in typically provocative fashion by Thomas Bernhard, who spent much of his life in the shadow of the Austrian Alps: "Was ist das schon, das Bergsteigen? Was ist für ein Unterschied, ob ich dreihundert Meter hoch oben bin oder dreitausend?"[18] (What is it, really, mountain climbing? What difference does it make whether I'm three hundred meters high up or three thousand?) As evidenced in the wide-ranging chapters that comprise this volume, mountains acquire meaning through a variety of dynamic perspectives, including philosophy, literature, aesthetic theory, music, politics, film, and fine arts.[19] In response to Bernhard and in further allusion to the main title of this book, *Heights of Reflection*, the crucial "difference" in understanding mountains lies not in their objectively measurable height but in one's own chosen mode of interpretive reflection.

Notes

[1] Hartmut Böhme, "Berg," in *Wörterbuch der philosophischen Metaphern*, ed. Ralf Konersmann (Darmstadt: Wissenschaftliche Buchgesellschaft, 2007), 46–49.

[2] Quoted from the Authorized King James Version of the Bible. For this observation, we are indebted to Max Oehlschlaeger, *The Idea of Wilderness: From Prehistory to the Age of Ecology* (New Haven, CT: Yale UP, 1991), 356–57.

[3] Roderick Frazier Nash, *Wilderness and the American Mind*, 4th ed. (New Haven, CT: Yale UP, 2001), 3.

[4] For a detailed study of Western views of wilderness and its gradual eradication over millennia, see Oehlschlaeger, *The Idea of Wilderness*.

[5] Other theories propose that Ötzi may have been sacrificed after an asteroid crashed in present-day Austria, or that he might have been killed at a lower elevation and placed upon a burial platform at higher altitude. In any case, the proof remains that Chalcolithic man frequented regions long thought inhabitable and inhospitable.

[6] Nietzsche exploits this geographical detail in *Also sprach Zarathustra* (Thus spoke Zarathustra, 1883–85), a work whose central idea of eternal recurrence he conceived in an ideal Alpine setting: 6,000 feet above sea level at the foot of a massive rock on the shores of Lake Silvaplana in the heart of the Swiss Alps. See Friedrich Nietzsche, *Ecce homo*, in *Werke: Kritische Gesamtausgabe*, section 6, vol. 3, ed. Giorgio Colli and Mazzino Montinari (Berlin: de Gruyter, 1969), 333.

[7] An exception is the recent volume of essays entitled *"Über allen Gipfeln . . .": Bergmotive in der deutschsprachigen Literatur des 18. bis 21. Jahrhunderts*, ed. Edward Bialek and Jan Pacholski (Dresden/Wroclaw: Neisse, 2008). While this voluminous collection deals with the role of mountains in German literature in a fairly comprehensive fashion, most of the essays regard the textual presence of mountains as mere literary motifs or symbolic backdrops rather than as a fundamental interactive landscape that informs the deeper thematic core of the works in question.

[8] See E. M. Butler, *The Tyranny of Greece over Germany: A Study of the Influence Exercised by Greek Art and Poetry over the Great German Writers of the Eighteenth, Nineteenth, and Twentieth Centuries* (London: Cambridge UP, 1935).

[9] See Peter Grupp, *Faszination Berg: Die Geschichte des Alpinismus* (Cologne: Böhlau, 2008), 26.

[10] Jacob Burckhardt, *Die Kultur der Renaissance in Italien*, in *Gesammelte Werke*, vol. 3 (Basel: Benno, 1955), 200, 201. Burckhardt also points to the importance of Dante, whom he considers one of the first individuals since antiquity to climb mountains with the express purpose of gaining a summit vista (200).

[11] For some of the following historical facts and figures, we are indebted to Grupp, *Faszination Berg*; Gabriele Seitz, *Wo Europa den Himmel berührt: Die Entdeckung der Alpen* (Munich: Artemis, 1987); and Aurel Schmidt, *Die Alpen — schleichende Zerstörung eines Mythos* (Zurich: Benziger, 1990).

[12] Conrad Gesner, *On the Admiration of Mountains, the Prefatory Letter Addressed to Jacob Avienus, Physician, in Gesner's Pamphlet "On Milk and Substances Prepared from Milk,"* trans. H. B. D. Soulé (San Francisco: Grabhorn, 1937).

[13] Quoted in Peter F. Kopp, "Natur und Berge — erforscht, erlebt und angebetet," in *Natur: Ein Lesebuch*, ed. Rolf Peter Sieferle (Munich: C. H. Beck, 1991), 279–80. All translations in this chapter are our own.

[14] In this respect, his work was anticipated by Josias Simler, who never set foot in the Alps yet wrote about them with great detail and sensitivity in such texts as *Vallisiae descriptio* (Description of the Valais Alps) and *De Alpibus commentarius* (An Alpine commentary), both written in 1574. Here Simler describes, much like Scheuchzer, a wide range of natural phenomena (including storms, glaciers, and avalanches) as well as human-made devices for the exploration of this mountainous environment (ropes, alpenstocks, crampons, and snowshoes).

[15] Johann Jakob Scheuchzer, quoted in Robert Felfe, *Naturgeschichte als kunstvolle Synthese: Physikotheologie und Bildpraxis bei Johann Jakob Scheuchzer* (Berlin: Akademie Verlag, 2003), 87.

[16] Maurice Isserman and Stewart Weaver, *Fallen Giants: A History of Himalayan Mountaineering from the Age of Empire to the Age of Extremes* (New Haven, CT: Yale UP, 2008), xi.

[17] Arnold Fanck, "Die Zukunft des Naturfilms (1928)," in *Berge, Licht und Traum: Dr. Arnold Fanck und der deutsche Bergfilm*, ed. Jan-Christopher Horak and Gisela Pichler (Munich: Bruckmann, 1997), 143.

[18] Thomas Bernhard, *Frost* (Frankfurt am Main: Suhrkamp, 1972), 133.

[19] Though we have tried to incorporate as many different academic discourses and artistic media as possible, some inevitably remain neglected, whether for reasons of space or because they have received sufficient attention elsewhere. One will of course note a glaring omission of pre-filmic visual arts, particularly the mountain paintings of Caspar Wolf, Caspar David Friedrich, and Joseph Anton Koch. However, Bettina Hausler's *Der Berg: Schrecken und Faszination* (Munich: Hirmer, 2008), a voluminous book that features numerous reproductions, cannot be surpassed in the scope of its art history and presentation of images. An adequate treatment of mountain landscapes in the realm of painting and other graphic media requires precisely this kind of pictorial approach, which one more readily finds in studies from fields such as art history.

Prelude: Classical Mountain Landscapes and the Language of Ascent

Dan Hooley

> *Let it be yours to walk in this time to the heights*
> — Pindar, *Olympian 1*

A PAGE OR TWO INTO HIS *When Men and Mountains Meet* (1946), the great British mountaineer of the early-mid twentieth century H. W. ("Bill") Tilman allowed himself a rare, almost lyrical passage:

> This would be my sixth visit to the Himalaya, and though occasionally I had qualms about such indulgence, I had so far managed to stifle them without any severe struggle. The appetite grows as it is fed. Like the desire for drink or drugs, the craving for mountains is not easily overcome, but a mountaineering debauch, such as six months in the Himalaya, is followed by no remorse. . . . Having once tasted the pleasure of living in high, solitary places with a few like spirits, European or Sherpa, I could not give it up. The prospect of what is euphemistically termed "settling down," like mud to the bottom of a pond, might perhaps be faced when it became inevitable, but not yet awhile.[1]

Readers of mountain literature will recognize, through the laconic wit of this post-Edwardian sensibility, one of those maddening passages that hints at but never quite explains the urge to climb. Instead, we hear the play of analogy — addiction *versus* muddy stagnation — to rationalize his abandonment of all good prudence: indulgence, appetite, drink, drugs, debauch, craving, relapse ("my sixth visit to the Himalaya"), remorse, pleasure. The last term distills the rest and entails much unspoken: the rise of the mountaineering "movement" in the Alps particularly since 1750, and the entailed enthusiasms of precedent (getting there first), conquest, nationalism (and national alpine clubs), exploration; the rise of the "sublime" (or various sublimes) in European aesthetics (Shaftesbury, Burke, Kant, Schopenhauer) and Romanticism and American transcendentalism in literature; the metamorphosis of climbing from research and exploration to something like sport. These factors, to be discussed in the essays that follow with respect to the German tradition, inform the mountaineer's pleasure but do not, as they are often said to do, explain it. Repeatedly we are told that climbing as a pleasure-oriented activity begins as Enlightenment sensibility melds into Romanticism; that, earlier, "primitive" and agrarian, societies saw mountains as barriers, hazards, and inconveniences rather than attractions. And there is some truth to the notion, particularly in respect to the related late Romantic fascination with frozen places, the Frankenstein monster's natural habitat,[2] and the race for the poles. But the absurdity of the broad claim is evident in the play of any child scrambling up a rock or tree.[3]

Of course, it's more complicated than this. Scott's decision to take on the commission of the Royal Geographic Society to be the first to reach the South Pole had nothing to do with pleasure, or, for that matter, with any particular competence in polar travel.[4] And the obsessive and often unscrupulous competition of alpinists literally to plant their flags first on alpine summits, much less the Nazi drive to claim conquest of the Eigerwand, can have had little to do with pleasure in any ordinary sense. National politics, personal ambition, self-justification, and compensation for failure elsewhere have all driven the climber up, and down to death. The mystery of climbing lies in this elusive connection of these and other factors more and less admirable — with the deep, addictive urge Tilman hints at. In that connection something "chemical" happens, perhaps; discrete elements meld into a focused, nearly imperative urgency, maybe not far from the transgressive pleasure Lacan called *jouissance*. Lyotard writes of the mind's *aporia* before the sublime, which is not quite the same as the Socratic *aporia*, but Plato's rendering of the mind's helpless paralysis, or more crucially its inability to grasp and formulate something viscerally *there*, is near the truth. Climbing as a serious, life-risking proposition, because so strange to most, requires explanation; people always ask. Yet those who are in the best position to know the answers are most often aphasiac. They evade, say the silly things Mallory did about "why," or reveal, as Tilman has, just a little: "Having once tasted the pleasure of living in high, solitary places. . . ."

"Pleasure," "high," "solitary": the collocation implies that this mountaineer's pleasure is lonely and in this regard unlike that of game or sport. The experience of being "up" and "away" from the rest of us is naturally isolating and that complicates things, paradoxically by simplifying them. Once removed from the distracting noise of quotidian life, attention naturally turns inward. The ascent's physical demands and the climber's exposure to frequently mortal hazards — to rockfall, avalanche, storm, cold, crevasse, an untimely slip or broken hold, the caprices of an indifferent mountain — prompt self-assessment and, frequently, radical interrogation of priorities. The mountain thus can be the locus of meditation, as it long has been in divers religious traditions. This is true even when the mountain itself is not a sacred site, as in the case of Petrarch's famous 1336 description of his ascent of Mt. Ventoux.[5]

> To-day I made the ascent of the highest mountain in this region, which is not improperly called Ventosum [windy]. My only motive was the wish to see what so great an elevation had to offer. I have had the expedition in mind for many years; . . . the mountain, which is visible from a great distance, was ever before my eyes, and I conceived the plan of some time doing what I have at last accomplished to-day. The idea took hold upon me with especial force when, in re-reading Livy's *History of Rome*, yesterday, I happened upon the place where Philip of Macedon, the same who waged war against the Romans, ascended Mount Haemus in Thessaly, from whose summit he was able, it is said, to see two seas, the Adriatic and the Euxine. Whether this be true or false I have not been able to determine, for the mountain is too far away, and writers disagree. Pomponius Mela, the cosmographer — not to mention others who have spoken of this occurrence — admits its truth without hesitation; Titus Livius, on the other hand, considers it false. . . .[6]

He then proceeds to describe the climb: his brother, partner for the occasion, takes a straight route up the ridge, while Petrarch, wearying, turns off to apparently easier approaches that take him down or away from his goal. As he reflects on his error, the climb quickly becomes figurative:

> But nevertheless in the end, after long wanderings, thou must perforce either climb the steeper path, under the burden of tasks foolishly deferred, to its blessed culmination, or lie down in the valley of thy sins. . . . These thoughts stimulated both body and mind in a wonderful degree for facing the difficulties which yet remained. Oh, that I might traverse in spirit that other road for which I long day and night, even as to-day I overcame material obstacles by my bodily exertions![7]

Standing at the summit in wonder, "like a man dazed," he contemplates the distant Alps, the Pyrenees, and himself — his past, his education, his attachments, and his soul. He thinks to consult his Augustine, conveniently to hand on this peak, and opens the book to this: "And men go about to wonder at the heights of the mountains, and the mighty waves of the sea, and the wide sweep of rivers, and the circuit of the ocean, and the revolution of the stars, but themselves they consider not." Upon reading which, Petrarch renounces his summit view in favor of tendance within, something the Stoics would call *anachoresis*, a "retreat into the self," a generic recourse to which we will return later.

Now, scholarship has had its way with this supposed "first European ascent of a mountain for pleasure," noting the obvious allegorical elements of the report and suggesting that the climb may never have occurred[8] — though Petrarch was undeniably a lover of nature ("Would that you could know with what delight I wander free and alone among the mountains, forests, and streams"[9]). To those weighing the place of this account in the mountaineering literature, the climb's historicity is not of crucial import, while its allegory surely is. For it is a curious fact that, in the case of the Alps, an accidental folding of the earth's superficial crust at a tectonic impact zone during the Oligocene and Miocene epochs matters, prepossessingly, to the human mind. As Petrarch demonstrates, and as the essays to follow will illustrate, mountains are always significant. They are not always loved, they are not always beautiful, but they do always stand above us in ways more than topographic. They "look down" upon us, they intimidate, they inspire fear and, paradoxically, draw us to them. Once attaining their high ridges and summits, one gains perspective; one sees more and farther — and further too, for there is always something metaphysical in that view. The mountain experience, then, is nearly always invested with significance. Petrarch's allegory invests his mountain as deeply, for him, as possible: it is the "place" where life's journey, quest, ambition, conflict, disappointment, grief, loss, hope, sin, and triumph are staged. It is perhaps the only place it could be staged so effectively.

The climb thus *means*, and what and how it means depends on the intellectual and cultural gestalt that informs it. For Petrarch, that mental calibration is an early humanist recursion to Graeco-Roman bearings: hence his reference to Philip's climb of Haemus in Livy, classical discussion of *its* historicity, and finally a turn to Augustine, presiding genius of that late antique *mentalité* that reprocessed classical learning for a new Christian world. Just as Petrarch is a pivotal Renaissance figure, Augustine is a transitional and transformative figure; they both stand at the threshold of something excitingly new, and both look back. Petrarch thus reflects on this matter of ascending mountains or "mountains" in multiple ways: through his classical books, through his Christian identity, through Augustine's similar situation and authority, and through the renunciatory lens of Augustine's own regard of his once-beloved classics. Figures like Petrarch are important to us because, precisely in speaking of more than the climb, they address the infrastructure of its significance.

Historians of mountaineering, who naturally enough look to mountains as the site of a particular, rather narrowly defined activity, sometimes forget this. Seeing the activity as they do, they are bound to observe that sporting ascents began late in European history, perhaps Antoine de Ville's 1492 ascent of Mt. Aiguille being the real "first" (though even that was commissioned by his king), and that earlier, from "primitive" through classical and most of early modern European history, mountains were viewed as obstacles, defenses, or dangers — anything but objects of fascinated attention. The single exception to that common wisdom is the wide recognition that mountains have always been the haunts of the gods. This seems true of the preponderance of heights of relative significance (a "mountain" need not be high) in virtually all cultures. In the Americas, the intact remains of Machu Picchu with its sacred rock stand as a conspicuous example of the inclination to sanctify high peaks. Explorers in the northern hemisphere routinely discovered traces of native peoples' ceremonial presence on mountain tops, and even to this day vertical features remain sacred to First Americans: Baboquivari Peak, Bear Lodge (Devil's Tower), Rainy Mountain, Bear Butte, and many others, from the relatively tiny Pilot Knob in Minnesota to the vast eminence of Denali.[10] Egeria's famous fourth-century pilgrimage to the top of Sinai, perhaps our earliest "route description," along with longstanding fascination with Nebo, the Carmel range, and Ararat reflect the same tendency in the Hebrew and Christian traditions. In Asia, Tai Shan in China, Fuji in Japan, Chomolungma (Qomolangma, Sagarmatha, Everest) on the edge of Tibet and Nepal — all are sacred. In Greece, Helicon, Cithaeron, Ida, Dicte, Cyllene, and of course Olympus among many more figure in myth as divine habitat. Gods are born on mountains, they glide nimbly across their peaks, they occasionally entrap or seduce human interlopers, and they look down from their heights with bemused indifference on human folly, striving, and dying. While all mythologies have divinity located in groves, deserts, seas, forests, or rivers, mountains uniquely represent a physio-spatial and ontological separation between human and divine spheres.

This human ascription of divinity to high places cannot be separated from contingent conceptual semantics. Mountains' visual perspective, their proximity to sources of nonhuman power, sky and water in particular, and their topographical abnormality articulate terms of human orientation and thought. Where they impede linear progress or stand as distant bearings, mountains require adjustment, response, and are thus frequently the physical stuff of which humans make meaning. Richard Buxton in his structuralist study of Greek imaginary mountains describes them as those places that stand in opposition to the polis and the domesticated plain,[11] thus describing a characteristic triangulation of sea, polis, and mountain to orient foundational ideas. The well-defended polis makes sense in opposition to the sea, which is dangerously fickle and the locus of necessary trespass for trade and food, and to the mountain, where human incursion, again necessary for timber and transhumance, is perilous. The Greek polis per se could not have existed as a relatively independent political entity were it not for the mountain-riven geography of Greece; its several experiments in governance, including the radical democracy of Athens, could scarcely have arisen.

But if the domesticated life of polis and plain, in contradistinction to sea and mountain, is the ground from which forbidding boundary conditions are observed, transgression of those frontiers, imaginary or real, is a regular occurrence. In their studies of Greek topography, Buxton, A. R. Burn, and W. K. Pritchett have described several customary uses of real mountain terrain in Greece: pasturage, and exploitation of material resources, particularly wood and charcoal; the hunt, travel, defense, ambush, and battle; sanctuaries and temples; scientific research; (perhaps) infant exposure.[12] Buxton continues into imaginative territory (that is to say, literature), noting "three primary aspects to the mythical image of the *oros*" (mountain): first, mountains are wild places inhabited by wild creatures (centaurs, the sphinx) and sites of wild violence; second, "mountains are before," originary habitations of men and gods; third, mountains are places for reversals, where humans come into contact with the divine ("almost any hunter or herdsman on an imaginary Greek mountain will probably meet a god"), and where normal social relationships are reversed.[13] In this last regard, the uncharacteristic presence of women on mountains is emblematic of dangerous anomaly: Atalanta, Procris and others, the goddess Artemis, the bacchantes of Euripides raving in their madness.[14] In Euripides' eyes, Cithaeron is the locus of a dark power that eclipses any merely administrative or coercive attempts to contain it.

> At this we fled
> and barely missed being torn to pieces by the women.
> Unarmed, they swooped down upon the herds of cattle
> grazing there on the green of the meadow. And then
> you could have seen a single woman with bare hands
> tear a fat calf, still bellowing with fright,
> in two, while others clawed heifers to pieces. . . .
> Like invaders they swooped on Hysiae
> and on Erythrae in the foothills of Cithaeron.
> Everything in sight they pillaged and destroyed.[15]

If women's presence in mountainscapes is anomalous for Greeks — while at the same time a recognition of the deep necessity for the liberating inversions of normative social custom — mountains are themselves also conceptually apart from *nomos* (custom, law). Mountains are outlaw landscapes, where real brigands often lurked to waylay travelers. They also persistently escape human efforts to chart or control them. They resist us, and they move. And precisely because they are places where the laws of men and human nature do not apply, they are landscapes where miracles can occur, and where, as Euripides' chorus sings (of Dionysus), ecstasy is possible:

> He runs to the mountains of Phrygia, to the mountains
>   of Lydia he runs! . . .
> And he cries, as they cry, Evohé —
>   On, Bacchae!
>   On, Bacchae!
> Follow, glory of golden Tmolus,
>   hymning god
>   with a rumble of drums,
> with a cry, Evohé! to the Evian god,

> with a cry of Phrygian cries,
> when the holy flute like honey plays
> the sacred song of those who go
> *to the mountain!*
>   *to the mountain!*
> — Then, in ecstasy, like a colt by its grazing mother
> the Bacchante runs with flying feet, she leaps![16]

Though less disposed to such transports, the Romans also went to the mountains for timber, for the views, hunted their ridges, grazed herds on their flanks, and of course waged war around and over them. Petrarch, as we have seen, pointed out Livy's description of the Macedonian Philip's climb of Mt. Haemus, and both Livy and Polybius write of the epic crossing of the Pyrenees and Alps by Rome's great enemy Hannibal. The dread that Hannibal provoked in the Roman mind came not just from his having terrorized Italy for years but also from the superhuman act of having surpassed Italy's mountainous fortifications. In the literary landscape, since Rome was almost inseparably Greece's cultural debtor, the same gods inhabit the same mountains. Olympus still rules in the Roman world, the muses still dwell on Helicon and Parnassus. In the case of the latter two mountains particularly, Rome's cultural sophistication is enfigured by Greek mountainscapes. The great literary efflorescence at the cusp of the late Republic and early Empire is largely driven by aesthetic ideas inherited from the Greek Hellenistic period, which fostered a taste for smaller, recherché, non-mainstream literary works. The figurative reflex for invoking these literary values was reference to the pure Castalian spring, which runs down from the snows of Parnassus. So too, the springs of poetic inspiration, Aganippe and Hippocrene, flow from the top of Helicon. The clarity of mountain spring water, its proximity to the divine (Apollo and the Muses), and the narrow defile leading to it, draw out and refocus Greek ideas about the art and nature of poetry; in Rome nearly every poet climbs a Greek mountain.[17]

> What man or hero, Clio, will you take up
> to celebrate on lyre or clear flute?
> Or what god? Whose name will witty
>   echo play
> in Helicon's shady reaches
> over Pindus, or frigid Haemus,
> where the forest once moved
> to hear Orpheus sing.[18]

Yet Horace's ode on Mt. Soracte, a limestone extrusion of only a few hundred meters just north of Rome in the Tiber valley, conveys something subtly different about certain Roman mountains.

> See how Soracte stands, gleaming with deep drifts,
> and how the trees, struggling, cannot any longer
> bear their snowy burdens, and how
> its rivers stand still in frozen ice.[19]

Whether Soracte was ever this forbiddingly arctic is less important than the counterpoint Horace constructs with the image in the remainder of the poem: dissolve this cold, throw logs on the fire, drink aged Sabine wine, think not about the future (its frozen image is there, right outside the window), but about friends and sweet love now. The mountain here operates symbolically, a multivalent image that structures the poem's larger meanings. For the purposes of this volume, we can observe that a mountain functions (for the first time?) as an object of meditation quite apart from its material, mythological, or ritual "uses" in the world. It stands as both an ineluctably real thing, like the cold death it is meant to suggest, and as a psychic reality or knowledge that bears meaning in the frame of the poem. Horace is still a long way from wanting to "go up there" but his deft sketch of the physical features of the peak registers an aesthetic appreciation that prefigures characterizations of the sublime in the eighteenth and nineteenth centuries.

Not unrelated is the feeling of other-worldly power latent in mountainscapes. The natural scientist Pliny the Elder wrote long books on Greek and Italian geography, mentioning mountains with fair frequency. Often they serve merely to locate inhabitants or to characterize topography. But he was particularly taken with volcanic mountains, and writes of the terrible wonders of fire, lava, and fume emerging from Etna, Mt. Chimaera, the "mountains of Hephaestus," and others.[20] Commenting on the sometimes fatal, sometimes intoxicating emanations (inspiring prophets at Delphi, for instance) to be found in such volcanic landscapes, he writes: "What other cause could any mortal infer but that the divine power of nature breaks out now and then in this or that place."[21] Pliny's interest in the subject was to lead to his death when he sailed across the Bay of Naples to witness the eruption of Vesuvius close up in 79 CE. That death, accepted with philosopher-scientist's calm, is described by his nephew the younger Pliny in a letter to Tacitus that is still commonly read today. Several peaks in the region are volcanic, and their ominous power was a source of mythological elaboration and simple human curiosity. Etna, into whose active crater the pre-Socratic philosopher Empedocles was said to have cast himself, became a kind of tourist attraction. Diogenes Laertius claims that Plato himself traveled there to see the crater, and the emperor Hadrian is said to have slogged up the peak before dawn to witness the multi-colored sunrise at the summit in 125 CE.[22] Yet more colorful are the literary descriptions of the seething energy of the volcanic mountain, as for instance where Vergil's Cyclopes hammer in their subterranean smithies.

> The Cyclopes were working iron in the vast cave, Brontes, Steropes and Pyragmon, with bare arms. They had in their hands a rough thunderbolt, partially polished, which in great numbers the Father of Gods and Men casts down onto the earth.... Now they were forging together in the work terrifying fires and thunder and fear and wrath with pursuing flames.[23]

Those who have witnessed or seen images of the pyrotechnics of electrical storms around erupting volcanoes will know this is less fanciful a description than it may seem.

The first century CE Stoic philosopher and writer Seneca also expressed an interest in Etna in a letter to his friend Lucilius (Epistle 79):

> If you will write me a full account of these matters [Lucilius' tour of Sicily], I shall then have the boldness to ask you to perform another task, — also to climb Aetna at my special request. Certain naturalists have inferred that the mountain is wasting away and gradually settling, because sailors used to be able to see it from a greater distance. The reason for this may be, not that the height of the mountain is decreasing, but because the flames have become dim and the eruptions less strong and less copious, and because for the same reason the smoke also is less active by day.... But let us postpone this discussion, and look into the matter when you have given me a description just how far distant the snow lies from the crater, — I mean the snow which does not melt even in summer, so safe is it from the adjacent fire.... Now if Aetna does not make your mouth water, I am mistaken in you. You have for some time been desirous of writing something in the grand style and on the level of the older school. For your modesty does not allow you to set your hopes any higher; this quality of yours is so pronounced that, it seems to me, you are likely to curb the force of your natural ability, if there should be any danger of outdoing others; so greatly do you reverence the old masters. Wisdom has this advantage, among others, — that no man can be outdone by another, except during the climb. But when you have arrived at the top, it is a draw; there is no room for further ascent, the game is over.... Men who have attained wisdom will therefore be equal and on the same footing.... I do not know whether this Aetna of yours can collapse and fall in ruins, whether this lofty summit, visible for many miles over the deep sea, is wasted by the incessant power of the flames; but I do know that virtue will not be brought down to a lower plane either by flames or by ruins. Hers is the only greatness that knows no lowering; there can be for her no further rising or sinking. Her stature, like that of the stars in the heavens, is fixed. Let us therefore strive to raise ourselves to this altitude.[24]

This and related passages in Seneca have been studied by scholars, most recently Sylvia Montiglio, by way of addressing Seneca's attitude toward travel: that is, whether he deems it good, as a means of increasing knowledge, or bad, as a distraction from the Stoic's quest for wisdom within.[25] Montiglio argues against others that the case is not clear cut, that Seneca frequently deplores travel for the sake of learning, but nearly as frequently yields, as in the quoted passage, to the yearning to know what is out there. Her assessment is persuasive, but for the present purposes it is helpful simply to note that the debate was an active and lively one in the ancient world, and Seneca's ambivalence is not unusual. Horace, in a famous line from *Epistles* 1.11 writes that "those who sail across the sea change their sky, not their minds."[26] Yet elsewhere he too writes less negatively of travel. There was a long tradition of travel for learning's sake that goes back at least to Herodotus, and later proponents looked to the Homeric model of Odysseus, who became a model for the restless searcher after new knowledge. We know the image from Tennyson ("I cannot rest from travel; I will drink / Life to the lees. . ."[27]) and Nikos Kazantzakis's modern epic poem, but both Greeks and Romans were fascinated with this figure of the traveler encountering the often perilous wonders of the world. Indeed, the understanding that the world was full of wondrous spectacles, literally, things to be seen — in distant lands, on the mountains, on the seas — was widespread.

Seneca writes fully aware of that fascination, aware of its dangers and distractions too, and in this passage he prefigures Petrarch's own reaction upon arriving at the top of Mt. Ventoux. For both writers in the end, the ascent of Mt. Virtue displaces any value a merely physical climb may entail. Yet . . . Seneca *does* want to know; he has thought about that glacier at the summit, wonders about its integrity, will have heard of the strangely colored sunrises that drew Hadrian, knew the mythology associated with the mountain and Empedocles' apocryphal end there, and remembers that Plato, too, once looked on the storied peak. Other traditions would call it a place of power. For Seneca it is a thing to be seen and learned about. He wants a full account from Lucilius, and asks for it in its proper register, "something in the grand style and on the level of the older school," a register the aesthetician "Longinus" (first-to-third century CE, dates and identity uncertain) would call the sublime. The emotional impact of the presentation of events is at the heart of Longinus's treatise, *Peri hypsous* (*On the sublime*), and this too Seneca, tragedian as well as philosopher, understood. Burke and others in the eighteenth and nineteenth centuries would read Longinus and develop their own theories of aesthetic and psychological sublimity, which directly informed the mountaineering and polar quests of the period. The first phase of those climbs too, with their barometers, thermometers, and other scientific instruments stuffed into rucksacks or porters' loads, participates in the tradition of scientific inquiry known to Seneca and his contemporaries. It is interesting that as the Alpine climbing movement grew in the later nineteenth century, the gathering of scientific data increasingly became otiose, a mere pretext, a few instruments hauled along for the sake of appearances. The appeal of simply getting to the top by increasingly technical and dangerous routes overshadowed the quest for more data. Yet now, in the age of climate change, science is again emerging as one good reason to go to the tops of the world and document what is happening there. The two appeals have always been linked in shifting imbalance; both sublimity and knowledge seem to reside up high.

Which is why ascetics, hermits, priests, monks, and holy men have always gone there: Meteora, the monasteries on Athos, the Skelligs in Ireland, among many others. The precisely arranged Amerindian ritual stones discovered by John Wesley Powell mark, exactly, this conjunction of knowledge and dangerous, extraordinary access to greater-than-human forces. But, as any mountaineer will be quick to add, the Skelligs, Athos, and their like are not among the exceptionally high places on this planet, and on the latter one does not live. As the Greeks understood, these are places where trespass is just that. A serious mountain peak offers to the lucky and skilled a momentary access to rare knowledge — call it that or simply access to *something* not found elsewhere — a singularity of experience too precarious and dangerous to savor for more than a few minutes before the climber's retreat. In descent, there is always loss, and of the summit moment only ghostly memory remains; it cannot be "brought back" to ordinary life. This ephemerality is surely part of the addictive chemistry that draws some, as it did Tilman, to go back. He never stopped going back ("not yet awhile . . .") to mountains, and then cold seas, disappearing in his eightieth year while sailing to the Falklands.

Yet for others, the thing to be valued is often *not* the summit but the climbing itself, the process of getting up. A. F. Mummery put it prosaically but effectively looking back on his own brilliant nineteenth-century climbing career: "The essence of the sport lies, not in ascending a peak, but in struggling with and overcoming difficulties."[28] The statement would not make sense were such difficulties simply a matter of a job to be done; but in the context of the climb it is where one's response to the mountain's complex meanings, as invested by centuries of human engagement, is most manifest. The upward movement becomes a heuristic process, sorting the business out for oneself, enacting significance, just as Petrarch's divagations from the direct route were meant to signify. And here too Seneca informs. "Now if Aetna does not make your mouth water, I am mistaken in you," he writes to Lucilius, meaning, we may think, both getting up there to see the sight and writing some account appropriate to its scale and significance. Then, shifting focus from literary ambition and achievement to moral attainment, he slips into the perennial language of ascent: *nemo ab altero potest vinci, nisi dum ascenditur. Cum ad summum perveneris, paria sunt, non est incremento locus, statur* (No man can be outdone by another, except during the climb. But when you have arrived at the top, it is a draw; there is no room for further ascent: the game is over).[29]

Notes

[1] H. W. Tilman, *When Men and Mountains Meet*, in *The Seven Mountain-Travel Books* (Seattle: The Mountaineers, 1983), 277.

[2] The Frankenstein monster in Mary Shelley's gothic novel retreats to the mountains after killing young William and makes for the North Pole for his final immolation.

[3] Garrett Soden makes the argument that humans are in fact hardwired for climbing and/or controlled falling. Early primate evolution fitted out the ancestors of "Lucy" with tools for tree-life (grip, body-shape, balance, eye placement) that of course stayed with the species as it moved down from the trees to flat land. The capacity and instinct to climb remained. See Garrett Soden, *Falling* (New York: Norton, 2003), 205–19. Thanks to Caroline Schaumann for this reference.

[4] On polar travel and the Romantic sublime see Francis Spufford's superb *I May Be Some Time: Ice and the English Imagination* (London: Faber & Faber, 1996). Recent studies that reexamine Scott's sometime damaged reputation as explorer and leader include (from an active explorer's perspective) Sir Ranulph Fiennes, *Race to the Pole: Tragedy, Heroism, and Scott's Antarctic Quest* (New York: Hyperion, 2005); Ross D. E. MacPhee, *Race to the End: Amundsen, Scott, and the Attainment of the South Pole* (New York: Sterling Innovation, 2010); and with particular emphasis on Scott's scientific contributions, Edward J. Larson, *An Empire of Ice: Scott, Shackleton, and the Golden Age of Antarctic Science* (New Haven, CT: Yale UP, 2011).

[5] Petrarch, *Epistolae familiares*, 4.1. In English, *Petrarch: The First Modern Scholar and Man of Letters*, trans. James Harvey Robinson (New York: Putnam, 1898), 308–9.

[6] Robinson, *Petrarch*, 307–8.

[7] Robinson, *Petrarch*, 312–13.

[8] See, among others, Lyell Asher, "Petrarch at the Peak of Fame," *PMLA* 108, no. 5 (1993): 1050–63.

[9] Robinson, *Petrarch*, 297.

[10] On mountains in a Native American context Matthew Hooley writes, *per litteras*, "a mountain differentiates itself not necessarily by any objective topographical metric, but in the ways that people are forced to 'read' it differently. Try to turn the Rocky Mountains into townships (as in the Northwest Ordinance). Allotment (based on making squares for tilling and growing) just doesn't *stick* in certain places . . . mountains." Others to whom I owe thanks for their ideas for this short essay are David Schenker, Anatole Mori, Caroline Schaumann, and Sean Ireton.

[11] Richard Buxton, "Imaginary Greek Mountains," *Journal of Hellenic Studies* 112 (1992): 1–15; revised version printed in *Imaginary Greece: The Contexts of Mythology* (Cambridge: Cambridge UP, 1994), 80–96.

[12] A. R. Burn, "Helikon in History: A Study in Greek Mountain Topography," *Annual of the British School at Athens* 44 (1949): 313–23; W. K. Pritchett, *Studies in Ancient Greek Topography 1* (Berkeley: U of California P, 1965).

13 Buxton, "Imaginary Greek Mountains," 8–9.
14 Buxton, "Imaginary Greek Mountains," 9.
15 Euripides, *Bacchae*, trans. William Arrowsmith, in *Euripides V* (Chicago: U of Chicago P, 1959), 186–87.
16 Euripides, *Bacchae*, 160–61.
17 Michael Comber, "Reading Propertius Reading Pound," *Journal of Roman Studies* 88 (1998): 44n47, observes "for the symbolic correlation of the height of water with height of literary genre, see Virgil, *Eclogues* 6 (with Clausen). There Gallus is first shown as an erotic elegist wandering (*errantem*) by the Permessus at the foot of the mountain. He then goes higher up Helicon in connection with his learned, aetiological elegy on the Grynaean Grove (vv. 64–73)."
18 Horace, *Odes* 1.12.1–8. *Q. Horati Flacci Opera*, ed. Fredericus Klingner (Leipzig: Teubner, 1970), 14.
19 Horace, *Odes* 1.9.1–4.
20 Pliny, Book 2. 110. *Natural History*, trans. H. Rackham (Cambridge, MA; Harvard UP, 1938, rev. 1949), 363.
21 Pliny, 2, 95; *Natural History*, 339.
22 "Hadrian," *The Scriptores Historiae Augustae*, vol. 1, trans. David Magie (Cambridge: Harvard UP, 1967), 40/41.
23 R. A. B. Mynors, ed., *P. Virgili Maronis Opera* (Oxford: Oxford UP, 1969. *Aeneid* 8, 424–32.
24 L. Annaeus Seneca, *Ad Lucilium epistulae morales II*, trans. Richard M. Gummere (Cambridge, MA: Harvard UP, 1958); my ellipses.
25 Silvia Montiglio, "Should the Aspiring Wise Man Travel? A Conflict in Seneca's Thought," *American Journal of Philology* 127 (2006): 553–86. See Montiglio for related bibliography, notably Giovanna Garbarino, "Secum peregrinari: Il tema del viaggio in Seneca," in *De tuo tibi: Omaggio degli allievi a Italo Lana* (Bologna: Pàtron, 1996), 263–85.
26 "Caelum, non animum mutant, qui trans mare currunt." Klingner, *Horatius Opera*, Ep. 1.11.27.
27 Alfred Tennyson, "Ulysses," (vv. 6–7), *Selected Poems* (London: Penguin, 2007), 49.
28 A. F. Mummery, *My Climbs in the Alps and Caucasus* (London: Scribners, 1895), 326.
29 Seneca, *Ad Lucilium*, epistle 79, 205.

Part I: First Forays: Mountain Exploration and Celebration from the Middle Ages to the Eighteenth Century

Terra Incognita? Mountains in Medieval and Early Modern German Literature

Albrecht Classen

IN THE MIDDLE AGES wild nature outside the courtly, aristocratic precinct, where it was delicately tamed and regulated in the garden,[1] always seems to have represented a dangerous, uncivilized, uncanny, if not threatening territory. We hardly ever hear of any poet expressing his or her delight in simple nature scenes, unless these provided safe haven for lovers, such as the delightful meadow at the edge of the forest in Walther von der Vogelweide's famous poem "Under der linden" (Under the linden tree, ca. 1200). In Gottfried von Straßburg's romance *Tristan* (ca. 1210),[2] Tristan and Isolde escape to their love cave when their existence at King Mark's castle has become intolerable, but that utopian space is situated in a remote forest where dangerous animals roam and human existence is possible only because the two lovers can withdraw into that magical grotto, nourished only by their mysterious love.[3] The forest proves to be the space of lawlessness, the domain of robbers, giants, dwarfs, and other uncanny creatures.[4] The same applies to the mountain, about which poets rarely reported positive aspects, and which appears to have evoked primarily negative feelings even among chroniclers and artists. Not surprisingly, we often observe the metaphoric use of the mountain as a space of hostility and extra-territoriality, hence as a threat to and danger for human existence.

However, research has hardly begun to investigate this topic, and we are therefore still subject to many modern assumptions about mental attitudes toward mountains as they were represented in the past. Gottfried's account, for instance, is not completely devoid of references to a mountain: when young Tristan tries to find his way to a human settlement after having been dropped off by the Norwegian merchants, he espies some considerable elevations in the distance. At first he climbs a mountain to gain some orientation (2522–25), then he discovers a small country road and follows it down into the valley, which ultimately will bring him into contact with the monks, and later with the king's hunters. Since there is no trodden path up to the peak, Tristan has to make his own way, crawling up the slope on his hands and feet:

> über stoc und über stein
> wider berc er allez clam,
> unz er ûf eine hoehe kam (2568–70)
>
> [over branches and rocks
> he climbed up the mountain
> until he reached the top.]

This example indicates how careful we will have to be in our assessment of what mountains constituted in the Middle Ages, because the references to them are sparse and often vague. Such references serve a variety of purposes but hardly reflect a "true" concern with nature.

Although mountains did not arouse significant interest in the medieval world, at least not at first sight, they have often left a considerable impact on people's minds.[5] To what extent this was also the case in medieval and early modern German literature will be the topic of this chapter. After all, mountains are of major presence in geophysical terms: they are often unavoidable and daunting, and simply have to be confronted, particularly by travelers and merchants. The Alps, for instance, represented a significant barrier between northern and southern Europe, and yet merchants, diplomats, scholars, and clerics crossed them on a regular basis. Every German ruler who wanted to pursue his claim on Italy had to face the Alps as the first major hurdle.[6] Whether poets, as spokespersons of their society and as influential sources for the formation of a people's mentality, embraced mountains as intriguing, fascinating, aesthetically pleasing entities or instead regarded them with fear — depends on many different factors.[7] To be sure, encyclopedists and chroniclers since at least the twelfth century have referred to mountains as they knew them, discussing their origin and appearance, passages across their passes, and resting places in their midst.[8] The critical question here will be, however, to what extent vernacular authors not only were aware of the existence of mountains but also had their protagonists operate in those regions while traversing them, getting lost in them, hiding in them, or searching for their secrets.

One of the most significant examples of a literary hero dealing with the difficulties presented by a mountain proves to be the pre-courtly, or *goliardic*, epic poem *Herzog Ernst*, extant in many different manuscripts, probably composed first around 1170 (ms. A), and most comprehensively recorded ca. 1220 or even 1230 (ms. B). After years of bitter warfare with his father-in-law, Emperor Otte, Ernst has to escape from Germany because he has exhausted his resources and cannot accept the growing suffering of the people in his dukedom of Bavaria. Although he intends to go on a crusade, stopping first in Constantinople, he soon loses his orientation and enters a world of adventures and monsters. Ultimately he regains his old self and previous power, leaves the monstrous peoples behind, continues on to Jerusalem, achieves great triumphs, and returns home to

Germany. Although it proves to be extremely difficult, he eventually strikes up friendship with the emperor again, who forgives him for everything that stood between them in the past and reinstalls him as the Duke of Bavaria.⁹

His first adventure involves an encounter with the crane people of Grippia, but the protagonists survive. Thereafter they run into new difficulties, and this time their ship is attracted to the Magnetic Mountain, from which there is no escape unless by a miracle or an intelligent strategy. This mountain consists of a huge rock formation, at the bottom of which countless other ships have already been stranded, unable to set sail again because of the magnetic force emanating from the geological mass. Since the hero and his men can observe the mighty mountain ("kreftigen berc," 3895) from a long distance, and thus also all the masts from the abandoned ships, they believe they have reached a populated country where they might find a respite from their journey. As soon as they get closer, however, they realize the power of the mountain's magnetic force and are unable to prevent their ship from crashing into the other ships, making it impossible for them to leave again. To find a way out, they climb to the top of the mountain, where they realize that they are stranded on a completely isolated island:

> der berc stuont wîten in dem mer
> dâ muosen die helde âne wer
> vil jâmerlîchen ersterben (4077–79)
>
> [the mountain stood far away in the sea /
> and the heroes would have to die there a miserable death
> without being able to protect themselves. (Translation my own)]

Indeed, one man after the other starves to death, and the mountain itself thus literally turns into a graveyard, a threatening barrier, or prison for Ernst and his companions.¹⁰ Nevertheless, when they are about to despair, they find a solution, observing how the griffins carry away their dead companions. Instead of waiting for their own death, they now pretend to be corpses wrapped in animal skins, and are thus transported by the birds to their nests, apparently on tall trees in a distant land. Having rescued themselves in this manner from the island mountain, they kill the young griffins and climb down the tree. Yet they are still trapped in this new mountainous region until they come across a river that disappears into the rocks, obviously making its way out again on the other side, because the water is not dammed up in any way. Here we get a somewhat more detailed description of the entire setting, the one side of the river blocked by huge piles of small stones, the other by the towering wall of the mountain, "daz sich ûf gên den wolken zôch" (4382; which rose up to the clouds).

In fact, the mountain seems to block their way wherever they turn, as if to keep them prisoners. Finally Ernst and his men find a new escape route by building a raft and managing to ride the water through the tunnel, although, as the narrator comments, the waves often threaten to capsize them (4438–41). Some scholars have perceived this description as a psychological metaphor of death and rebirth,[11] but in our context we can content ourselves with the observation that the narrator conceives the mountain as a natural phenomenon of great significance in the protagonist's life. Ernst even manages to break off a luminescent gemstone, a white opal, which he will later hand over to the emperor as a gesture of friendship and honor. This shining stone thus, according to this literary legend, becomes the centerpiece of the German imperial throne, associating it with the deep inner forces hidden in a mountain that separates the known world of the West from an Orientalized East. We need to pay close attention to the origin of the opal that comes, so to speak, from the heart of a mountain that is insurmountable yet opens itself up at its base in the form of a tunnel. This allows Ernst to reach, not only a new world where monsters live, but also a world where he can discover himself.[12] The small company has to rely completely on the assumption that the river will exit the mountain again through an opening big enough for them to fit through, and they do indeed experience a frightful journey, one that transpires totally in the dark, except for light given off by some of the luminous gems.

As threatening as this mighty mountain and the Magnetic Mountain may actually be, in the end all dangers posed by the physical barriers also prove to be the decisive catalysts that enable Ernst and his followers to leave their old existence behind and enter a new one, which is a significant metaphor for the essential transformation of human life over the course of time. Fittingly, as soon as the men have left the tunnel, they enter a pleasant landscape and can find enough food to survive, although they have also stepped into a world of monsters. From that time onwards we no longer hear of any references to a mountain, but the symbolic significance of such a huge geophysical barrier has become clear.[13]

The powerful magnetism exerted by the loadstone mountain on the island forces the protagonist into its domain and thus demonstrates how much such rocky barriers have to be considered as critical in human life. This is underscored even further by the second mountain. Without his ability to discover a way through the mountain, Ernst would have failed and simply perished. In other words, the mountain emerges in this text as a catalyst for the hero's individual development and growth into the leader of his people because he knows how to overcome its challenge, a feat that later poets did not find so fascinating. In the *Kudrun* (ca. 1220–50), for instance, there is only a brief reference to the Magnetic Mountain, but the sailors are able to leave it safely behind.[14]

Heroic epic poetry is often, though only loosely, associated with mountains, for instance in the *Nibelungenlied* (Song of the Nibelungs, ca. 1200) and the *Eckenlied* (The Song of Ecke, ca. 1250).[15] In the former work we hear of a mountain, but only in Hagen's report about Siegfried's adventures. As Hagen relates, Siegfried had encountered the two warriors Schilbunc and Nibelung at the edge of a mountain, where they were trying to divide a vast treasure among themselves, a treasure that had been carried out of the depths of the earth (stanza 89, 1–3). After he had slaughtered all those who dared to oppose him, Siegfried became lord of the treasure and hence also of the inner mountain kingdom. Later, when he returns to the Nibelungen land, he has to fight first against the guardsman, then against the king of the dwarfs, Alberich, whom he had already defeated once. Then, however, he frees both and is accepted as their lord. The entire scene, which takes place on a mountain where the castle is located, underscores Siegfried's might and yet also connects him, once again, to the underworld, a common and important motif in Old Norse and Germanic poetry, whether with regard to a burial mound or a cave harboring a treasure hoard where a dragon also resides.[16] Whereas we normally associate a mountain with height, in this heroic epic it is connected with depth, a place where dwarfs rule and dragons sometimes have their lair.

In the *Eckenlied*, the protagonist Dietrich is regularly found spending time in the mountains as his personal territory of retreat. But he is challenged by giants and their kin and barely manages to overcome them all. As the other protagonist Egge (Ecke) confirms, heroic battles take place primarily in mountainous areas (15, 8); dragons live in caverns and devour their victims there (21, 11); Egge turns to the "gebirge" (37, 1) to find Dietrich and is later directed by Hiltebrand toward Tyrol (48, 10). At this point the narrative becomes more concrete, including specific references to the town of Trento and the mountain Nones (51), but then the geographical details lose their profile again, except when we are given a time marker in relation to the mountain: "Die sunne an das gebirge gie" (110, 1; The sun set behind the mountains).

Truly noteworthy and sustained references to a mountain can be found in The Stricker's *Daniel von dem Blühenden Tal* (Daniel of the Flowering Valley, ca. 1220),[17] albeit at first sight only in a rather fleeting and negative manner. Nevertheless, just as in *Herzog Ernst*, the narrative account is determined at several occasions by mountains that play a significant role particularly because of their size and inaccessibility. In other words, The Stricker offers a remarkable perspective on mountainous landscapes that constitute a challenge, though mostly in a negative sense.

The knights of the Round Table still enjoy a great reputation, but they are mostly ineffectual and generally sidelined by Daniel, who employs skill and cunning, wit and rationality to overcome his many opponents, some of whom are learned in necromancy and can create machine-like creatures.[18] Two of these were built by the so-called Riesenvater, the father of the giants, whom Daniel overcomes, but only with the greatest of difficulties, relying on magical objects that powerful female figures had granted him after he had rescued them from their own predicaments. While everyone is enjoying the courtly festivities, the Old Man suddenly appears and demands to see the highest ranking person, who is, of course, King Arthur, but in reality he intends to kidnap the king, whom he can easily seize with his bare hands and carry away without anyone able to follow him and rescue the king. The Old Man turns to a high mountain and manages to climb to the lofty summit "dâ sie hin niht mohten jagen" (7006; where they could not chase after him). The narrator illustrates the steepness of the rocky peaks by using a comparison with a monkey, an animal known for its climbing skills. As he comments, even such an animal would hesitate to follow the Old Man to such heights (7016–18). Several archers get ready to kill the Old Man with their arrows, but everyone is afraid that the king would subsequently die on the mountain because the Old Man is holding the captive by his hands and would take him down into the abyss should he be hit (7022–26). The narrator emphasizes how alarming the situation is for King Arthur, who is precariously perched up on the mountain (7031–36). Only the Old Man knows how to make this dangerous climb, so eventually he leaves the king all by himself, returning to the courtly company. There he explains that he had abducted the king in revenge for the death of his "children," the mechanical giants (7056–63), hoping thus to rob the company of all their joy as well.

Once again, the people wish to kill the Old Man, shooting at him with arrows, but Daniel holds them back, since King Arthur can be retrieved from his dangerous spot only with the help of the Old Man; otherwise he would fall to his death (7070). But the Old Man has sinister thoughts and intends to bring the entire court to the mountaintops, where they would all die, helplessly caught on those perilous cliffs (71095–119). This kind of death would give him even more satisfaction than to kill his opponent/s with conventional weapons (7120–22). He then dares the group to try to overcome him in regular combat, though without sword or shield, which then allows him to capture Parzival, whom he also abducts and takes to the top of the mountain. The victim tries to defend himself so vigorously that the Old Man finally loses his temper and simply smashes Parzival against a rock, whereupon the latter loses consciousness (7209–15).

Once more Daniel realizes how much he needs to resort to cunning, as in the cases with the Old Man's mechanical sons and some of the monsters who had challenged him along the way. He thus returns to one of the ladies whom he had helped before, and quickly reappears with a magical net. In the meantime the Old Man has waited for his real opponent, Daniel, but has not counted on his intelligence and wit. Soon enough, the

Old Man is caught in the net and cannot get out of it, because its magical powers are stronger than his own (7463–86). This finally provides Daniel with the long-awaited opportunity to enter into a discussion with the Old Man and to explain why he had to kill the giants simply in defense of his king and the honor of Arthur's court. The Old Man, who quickly realizes how much he had been left in the dark, begs for pardon, promises to forego his wrath (7765), and so becomes a good friend of the entire courtly company. When the lady of the green meadow, the owner of the net and of a salve that makes the net visible, promises to grant him both objects as a gift, he is so delighted that he runs up the mountain and rescues the prisoners.

Arthur expresses deep horror about the enormous elevation, which he would never have escaped without the Old Man's help (7869–73). Soon enough, though, the court festivities resume, and in the process Arthur also offers the Old Man any gift of his choice. The latter, however, only requests to be enfeoffed with a land beyond the peculiar mountain, land that itself is surrounded by other mountains. No person would ever be able to enter or leave it because of magic arts that only he, the Old Man, knows how to use. He has brought everything into that land that can delight him and only wants to be the lord of that mysterious territory (8365–82), a wish that Arthur happily grants (8395), pleased that he does not have to live there himself.

This scene offers an intriguing perspective on medieval attitudes regarding mountains, which are portrayed, at least in this context, as dangerous and impenetrable. The Old Man does not belong to the world of courtly society, so it is only fitting that he disappears at the end into his own mountainous kingdom. The Stricker is thus the first to incorporate mountains as significant elements on the mental horizon of his narrative, allowing their fearsome and menacing rocky heights to function as a threat to the well-being of King Arthur and his court. The mountains are clearly the ultimate limits for Daniel and all other knights, whose physical strength is useless in face of the necromantic capacities of the Old Man.

Although medieval poets normally refrain from extensive discussions of the natural environment, in one case at least we find specific allusions to mountains that had a great, though not quite welcome, relevance in an autobiographical context. Oswald von Wolkenstein (1376/77–1445) specifically includes the term "mountain" many times in his poetry, which should not surprise us considering his origin, South Tyrol, where he also wrote for most of his life.[19] Nevertheless, he does not project the mountains explicitly into his oeuvre but rather tends to include them only as one aspect of the larger picture of nature's renewal in spring, for instance: "Grün ist der wald, perg, au, gevild und tal" (Kl. 100, 7; forest, mountain, field, and valley are turning green). Similarly, we hear in his dawn song "Ich spür ain lufft" (Kl. 16):

> Die voglin klingen überal,
> galander, lerchen, zeisel, droschel, nachtigal,
> auf perg, in tal hat sich ir gesangk erschellet (7–9)
>
> [Everywhere the birds are singing,
> crested larks, skylarks, siskins, thrushes, nightingales,
> their melody echoes from the mountains and the valleys. (68)]

In fact, for Oswald the mountains form an integral part of his life, even if he refers to them only fleetingly and in topical formulas:

> Perg, au und tal, forscht, das gevild
> sich schon erzaigt aus grundes mild.
>
> [Mountains, meadow, valley, forest and field
> present themselves most splendidly thanks to the earth's mercifulness. (82)][20]

But in his "Von trauren möcht ich werden taub" (Kl. 104), a melancholic song about his personal misfortunes drastically reflected in the cold winter landscape, we hear more specifically of the Alpine world in its cold, unpleasant manifestation. Whereas the poet had once spent exciting times in some of the great imperial cities in the flatlands (61–63), the present situation leaves much to be desired: "Dorumb das ich von ebner wis / dick hausen müss auf hohen berg" (65–66; since I have had to live on the high mountain for so long / instead of on the low-lying plains [meadow]; 185).[21]

Most remarkably, in "Durch Barbarei, Arabia" (Kl. 44) we are confronted with an impressive image of Oswald's "personal" feelings about being "locked up," so to speak, in his own castle located high up in the South Tyrolean Alps:

> In Races vor Saleren,
> daselbs belaib ich an der e,
> mein ellend da zu meren
> vast ungeren.
> Auf ainem runden kosel smal,
> mit dickem wald umbfangen,
> vil hoher berg und tieffe tal,
> stain, stauden, stöck, snee stangen,
> der sich ich teglich ane zal. (18–26)
>
> [In Ratzes below Castle Schlern
> I am caught in marriage,
> which increases my misery
> very much against my will,
> caught on a round, small hill,
> encircled by thick forest.

Every day I see countless
tall mountains and deep valleys,
rocks, bushes, tree stumps, and snow sticks. (126)]

Since medieval poets usually originated from the nobility and/or composed their songs for an aristocratic audience, we cannot expect much more from them in terms of attention to the mountainous regions, since these were for the most part populated by peasants and shepherds. But then, most castles were situated on hills and mountaintops for military protection, a fact that hardly receives any mention in courtly romances, a genre whose protagonists typically have to struggle against enemies and prove themselves individually, though these trials do not involve climbing physical heights. Oswald represents an exception, because he created his songs primarily for his own personal interest and was not dependent on a patron. This provided him with the opportunity to formulate his own thoughts and ideas as they were relevant for him alone. Nevertheless, even he harbored no particular liking for the mountains and regarded them only as part of the landscape in which his own castle was situated. For him, living in such an environment proved to be a hardship after his glorious time in the service of Emperor Sigismund, during which he had been afforded numerous opportunities to travel all over the known world. Thus it comes as no surprise that Oswald projects his personal unhappiness and frustration onto the wintry mountains and the rural population.

One of the first poets ever to mention the Alps by name was the so-called Mönch von Salzburg, a contemporary of Oswald, whose identity has not been clearly determined. He was the most popular poet of his time; his religious songs were particularly celebrated.[22] In W 19, "Wier, wier der fünfczehent an der schar," a group of fifteen courtiers address the women at court whom they have fallen in love with and from whom they hope to receive a response. They insist on the absolute value of "stät" (16; constancy) and severely criticize those who do not subscribe to that ideal. They denounce disloyalty and unsteady love, chastising those who are guilty of "pöse[-] lust" (36; evil lust), whereas they greatly praise those who have demonstrated a constant heart (39). As a group, these men pledge that they will keep their promise of constant love, which they have sworn to the imperial court that was held "hoch auf der alben in herbsts frist" (43; high up in the Alps during the Fall season). We might, of course, suffer from a misreading of the term "alben" here, which older scholarship associated with the Nuremberg castle.[23] In reality, the Mönch alludes to the Alps, and perhaps to a hunting episode involving the emperor. He does not offer any other reference, but at least he reminds us that Austrian poets were familiar with that name and could easily refer to that mountain range for specific purposes.

However, in a number of other earlier verse narratives, mountains already figured quite prominently and were identified with the term "Alps," whether the poets had those specific mountains in mind or merely used the term generically.[24] In *Dietrichs Flucht* (from the second half of the thirteenth century), for instance, the anonymous poet alludes to Alpine snowfall in order to illustrate the intensity with which the warriors exchange fatal sword blows:

> Und wart iu dehein sne bechant,
> als er von den alben gat,
> noch dicher vielen an der stat
> die leute tot dar nidere. (9395–98)

> [If you are familiar with the snow
> that is coming down from the Alps,
> [then you can imagine] that even more
> people fell down dead. (Translation my own)]

This imagery was used quite often, for instance in *Kudrun* (861, 2–3), whereas Rudolf von Ems in his *Alexander* mentions the "alben" only in order to identify a mountain range from which an ice-cold river flows (a river in which Alexander takes a bath to cool down and almost dies from a heart attack).[25] Similarly, we hear of the impenetrably high country near the Caucasus that would make it difficult, if not impossible, for Alexander to cross (13670–74). In another passage we are told of the river Gôzâ that runs through the country of Caspîâ, which cannot be easily conquered because it is surrounded by "wilden alben" (16807; wild mountains), a formulation that finds an echo in a later description of an equally "fortified" territory:

> daz gebirge ist sô verhagt
> mit hôhen wilden alben
> mit wälden allenthalben
> al umbe an allen sîten
> daz ez nie man erstrîten
> mit deheinen listen mac
> unz ûf die erde tage ein tac. (18010–16)

> [the mountain range is so fenced in
> with high, wild peaks,
> with forests everywhere
> on all sides
> that no man can conquer it by means of fighting,
> or with the help of any kind of cunning
> until the last day of time. (Translation my own)]

But the poet in this context seems to emphasize more the property of inaccessibility than the economic aspect.

When we turn to late-medieval travelogues, we might expect to witness a different approach, since their authors traversed the mountainous borders of various lands. However, although some of these accounts provide astonishingly detailed reports of villages, towns, cities, rivers, castles, and bridges, the Alpine landscape hardly figures in concrete terms. The same applies to countless pilgrimage accounts, perhaps because to them mountains represented nothing but a hindrance and bother, a space without much meaning. The Cologne pilgrim-traveler Arnold von Harff, for instance, left home in 1496 and returned in 1498 after having seen all three major pilgrimage sites: Rome, Jerusalem, and Santiago de Compostela. His report contains astounding details of the various countries, cities, and landscapes, including extensive vocabulary lists of some exotic languages. But when it comes to his journey through the Alps, we find only the briefest possible description, which sounds like a protocol of stations and distances that he covered on his journey. He informs us, for example, about South Tyrol in the following way:

> Moran is eyn kleyn fijn steetgen licht in eyme schoynen dalle; daer boeuen off die lyncke hant licht eyn schoyn berchsloss Tyroil genant eyn graeffschafft gehoert yetzont der koenynclicher maiestaet zoe. Hie zo Moran synt gar vil geboren gecken, as man myr waerlich dae saichte. . . . Item van Moran zo Eppen eyn dorff iij mijlen. lanxt eyn berchsloss heyscht dat nuwe huyss, dae scheydent sich tzwene wege, der eyne off die lyncke hant geyt nae Praytz eyn stat; die ander geyt off die rechte hand nae Eppe lanxt eyn hoyge berchsloss heyscht hogen Epp.[26]

> [Meran is a little pretty town located in a delightful valley; on the left-hand side on the hill is an impressive mountain castle called Tirol; it is a dukedom that presently belongs to the royal house. Here in Meran are many feeble-minded people, as I was told as truth. From Meran to the village Eppan the route consists of three miles, passing a mountain castle called Neuhaus. There the road splits, one leads on the left side to the city of Bozen, the other on the right side leads to Eppan, passing a highly situated mountain castle called High Epp. (Translation my own)]

The mountains themselves do not play any particular role, because von Harff demonstrates interest only in urban settlements, villages, castles, and the actual road through the Alps. Even at a later moment, when the pilgrim and his companions have arrived at Mount Sinai to visit the St. Catherine monastery, which is situated at a relatively high elevation, the mountain itself does not leave much of an impression on von Harff (121).

The same observation can be made with regard to the fascinating anonymous prose novel *Fortunatus* (first printed in Augsburg in 1509).

The protagonist traverses virtually all parts of Europe, later also parts of the Middle East and India, but mountains are not mentioned anywhere, whereas distances, cities, and monasteries dominate and dot the landscape. Fortunatus crosses the Pyrenees twice, for instance, but we are told only of the major stops on the route, nothing of the mountains (448).[27] Other authors also include references to mountains where giants rule, fairies exist, and the protagonists struggle to overcome their opponents, such as in Thüring von Ringoltingen's *Melusine* (1456).[28] But overall, the interest in mountains, as expressed by Albrecht von Haller in his epic poem "Die Alpen" (1729), did not find any noteworthy parallels in medieval and early modern German literature. This is not to say that mountains did not emerge on the mental horizon, but they prove to be a fleeting background, locations for castles or monsters, and they certainly do not attract greater interest unless the protagonist is invited to enter their depths and take control of unheard of treasures, such as in the *Nibelungenlied*.

Our investigation has unearthed a number of specific examples in which the protagonist operates on or near a mountain and must cope with it as a barrier or a challenge. Since even late medieval pilgrims and other travelers did not express opinions about mountains and limited their attention mostly to towns and cities on their route south across the Alps, we could not expect a radically different approach by the vernacular poets and writers. Some reveal, however, a clear awareness of what life in a mountainous region means in specific terms, and others obviously mystified mountains for the entertainment of their audiences.

Of course, a true literary focus on mountains such as in Haller's case had not yet emerged in the Middle Ages or in the early modern era. Nevertheless, and this might be the most important conclusion of our investigation, medieval poets and writers were not blithely ignorant of mountains and did not deliberately ignore them.[29] Indeed, we could find many more references to mountains in encyclopedias, scientific texts, and maps, but suffice it here to observe that medieval German authors made some remarkable preliminary attempts to experiment with mountains as signifiers and firm entities. In the tradition of heroic poetry, which also includes the so-called *Dietrich* epics, the protagonists often prove to be uncannily associated with the world of mountains because of their connection with the dwarfs that dwell in their depths. Thus it is not the mountain peak but its inner core and foundation that attract the most attention, perhaps because the heroic protagonists also need to find their strength within themselves. Both dwarfs and magnetic forces apparently provided the most fitting metaphors for this quest. In The Stricker's *Daniel*, mountains suddenly assume forces of their own; here automatons rule and a sorcerer — or rather a master of quasi-magic mechanisms — wants to retire to find peace from the rest of the world. Travelogue authors sometimes take note of mountains, but then only in passing.

Nevertheless, by the end of the fifteenth century, mountains gained in significance for the background of woodcuts, as we can observe in Hartmann Schedel's famous *Liber chronicarum* (World chronicle) dating from 1493.[30] The city veduta of Salzburg, for instance, contains the typical elements of late medieval woodcuts, yet it also reveals a remarkable depth of perception. The image is divided onto two pages (156v and 157r), both featuring a castle or palace situated on the top of a hill. The city itself is located at the bottom, and the Salzach River runs through the valley. In the distance the craggy Alpine mountains rise up, apparently free of any forest. The artist's interest in them, however, still seems to be rather limited. The same applies to Ravenna (952r), where the architectural design dominates almost the entire scene, while in the background some mountains are visible, but only as a convenient backdrop to mark the contrast between city and country. After all, Ravenna is a coastal city far away from the Alps, but the artist incorporated the mountains anyway to conform to a schematic design characteristic of most of the woodcuts included here. So we can confirm that these geophysical heights were present in the late medieval mentality and considered important reference points.

In the case of Strasbourg (139v and 140r), where we would also not expect any mountains because the city is located in the Rhine valley, the left part reveals a hilly landscape which appears to be devoid of trees. Intriguingly, these hills appear almost inviting and are certainly accessible to any citizen interested in a walk or hike. We encounter a different type of cityscape in the case of Constantinople (249r); in this image the entire city is built on a mountainous slope. Beyond the city walls ever higher hills and mountains rise and strongly profile the background. But we also recognize numerous buildings, perhaps castles, perched on some of the peaks, indicating the extent to which even mountains could already be regarded as habitable locations. Basel (243v and 244r), by contrast, appears to be situated right next to pointed and rocky mountains that lean steeply toward the city and nearly hang over the towers of the city wall. For Breslau (233v and 234r) the artist chose, for the left image, a rather pastoral landscape with rolling hills that eventually turn into higher mountains, below which we can still recognize fields and a church tower. Similarly, the city of Ulm (190v and 191r) is situated in a mixed landscape, with roads leading up to a church on a hill right behind the city. And on both edges the eye is allowed to wander into the distance, where mountains rise above the landscape.

On folio 281 (see fig. 1) the artist/s portray the entire territory of Hesse: "Wischen Westfaln vnd Franckenland ligt das Hessenland ein pirgige gegent, die sich vom Rhein gein mitternacht streckende an Thueringen stoesset" (Between Westphalia and France there is Hesse, a mountainous region that extends from the Rhine in the West [from midnight] to Thuringia). In order to confirm this impression, we are presented with an

Fig. 1. Hartmann Schedel, Liber chronicarum *(World Chronicle), by Hartmann Schedel, 1493, folio 281. Bayerische Staatsbibliothek.*

enormous rocky mountain on the left side rising to the edge of the image, underneath which a wealthy city with an impressive wall and many houses and churches, and where what appears to be a cathedral are located. The mountain itself is free of vegetation, which is intended to underline its height. On the opposite side another mountain parallels the first one, but its elevation is not the same, and a couple of buildings top it off. In the background, before another major city with a two-towered church, a third mountain extends, seemingly more rounded than the mountains in the foreground, which signals the distance to us viewers. Schedel does not comment on the details of the woodcut and limits himself to remarks on the dynastic family of the Landgrave of Hesse. The artist/s, by contrast, apparently delighted in the opportunity provided by Hesse, a region of Germany that is actually characterized by a wide variety of landscapes, including low-lying mountains and river valleys.

The artist/s no doubt found it most effective to frame many of the cities not only by rivers or other bodies of water, or by a simple landscape with forests and fields, but increasingly also by hills and mountains. This technique allowed the spectator's eyes to wander more easily from one vantage point to another and also helped profile the cityscape more markedly by way of contrast. We do not yet recognize specific elements that characterize these elevations, but they prove to be integral elements of the entire city veduta and do not appear as threatening or fear-inducing, as was still the case with the mythical Magnetic Mountain.

Finally, in a major text from 1517, Emperor Maximilian I's *Theuerdank*,[31] we literally observe the impressive rise of mountains both in the distance and, metaphorically speaking, in the protagonist's life, even though all this does not necessarily transform the mountains into positively charged aspects of early modern landscapes in literary and art-historical terms. The emperor commissioned this work as a highly representative reflection of himself and his life as a young man pursuing his love and eventual wife, Mary of Burgundy. Several authors were involved, one of whom was the private scribe Marx Teitzsaurwein, but then also the emperor himself. The final redaction was carried out by the Nuremberg scholar Melchior Pfinzing. This massive (auto)biographical and panegyrical account features 118 large-sized colored woodcuts by Hans Burgkmair, Hans Schäufelin, and Hans Beck, which contain numerous mountainscapes similar to those found in Hartmann Schedel's famous *Liber chronicarum* from 1493, but they are much more lively and dramatic in their setup.

Theuerdank, or Maximilian, is seeking the hand of Lady Ehrenreich (rich in honor), or Mary, heiress of the duchy of Burgundy, which is a historical fact. But the chivalric novel is strongly determined by allegorical figures, for instance when Theuerdank has to overcome the evil spirit by means of reason, virtue, and divine teachings; and when he must cross three mountain passes, at each of which malicious allegorical characters try to prevent him from reaching his goal. The protagonist has to face a long series of dangerous adventures, many of which take place in the mountains while he is hunting, then in fires, on staircases, with false medical doctors, and in various other hostile situations. Eventually, however, he triumphs over all perils and defeats every one of his opponents, which then clears the path for him to marry his beloved.

Many episodes take place in the mountains, but not because they are attractive in and of themselves. Instead Maximilian, here personified by Theuerdank, in fact enjoyed hunting in the mountains, which made them a favored backdrop for the various authors as well as artists contributing to this chivalric novel in verse. Each episode begins with a woodcut, and many of them are dominated by images of mountains rising up in the background, topped off by craggy peaks beyond the treelines. These scenarios typically indicate the danger that the young hero quickly finds himself in as an expression of his youthful attitude and behavior. Nevertheless, the woodcuts clearly signal a new interest in the Alpine landscape, although the artists mostly depict the mountains in a rather fanciful manner, overdramatizing their height and threatening appearance. The motifs mainly follow the same pattern, placing two or three people in the foreground next to some trees representing the wild forest, behind which emerge mountain peaks. Sometimes we see a few animals, probably chamois, which Maximilian enjoyed hunting, and other times a lonely monastery or castle. In several cases the woodcuts show life-threatening avalanches of huge boulders, such as the illustration from chapter 36, or other dangers that can occur in the mountains, such as in chapter 55, where Unfallo hurls stones at Theuerdank (see fig. 2).[32] Image and text support each other powerfully, and both signal the developing change with regard to the general attitude toward mountains in the premodern world. The hunt takes the protagonist to high peaks, and here he also meets perils that force him to prove his skills and abilities as a hiker, but then also in terms of character and intelligence, when he risks falling or being killed by an avalanche of rocks. The mountains continue to represent danger, but they also begin to exude a certain allure, which the royal hunter cannot withstand because there he finds the critical opportunity for personal growth and self-realization.

We might conclude that the specific approaches to mountains, either as threats or as fascinating territory, can well serve as indicators of individual paradigm shifts in the history of mentality. Medieval German poets were not blind to mountains and occasionally describe their protagonists as intimately associated with these physical barriers, when they force them to change the course of their lives. However, in effect we do not discover any specific interest in mountains per se during the Middle Ages. In the early sixteenth century, however, Emperor Maximilian can be credited with having been one of the first authors in the history of German litera-

Wolt weyter fahen mit dem Held
Dardurch Er ein mal wurd gefelt
Fand gar bald einen anndern list
Wie der hernach geschriben ist.

Wieder Edel Tewrdannck durch anweysung des val
schn Vnfalo auf einem Gembsen ieid abermale ein geferli
cheit überstunnd dann Im ein stein nach vber abgeslagen
het

Fig. 2. From chapter 55 of Theuerdank, *by Emperor Maximilian I, 1517. Bayerische Staatsbibliothek.*

ture to situate his protagonist, Theuerdank, many times in the mountains, where he proves his personal strength and superior character. The numerous artists of the woodcuts included in Schedel's *World Chronicle* and in *Theuerdank* can likewise be credited with having been highly noteworthy forerunners in the intellectual exploration and treatment of mountains as a major frontier of medieval and early modern society.[33] Certainly, nothing similar to the collection of names of mountains along with their detailed description as published by Boccaccio in his *De montibus, silvis, fontibus, lacubus, fluminibus, stagnis seu paludibus, et de nominibus maris* (ca. 1350–60) seems to have existed north of the Alps during the Middle Ages and Renaissance.[34] This does not mean, however, that mountains were ignored altogether. On the contrary, as our analysis has demonstrated, traveling through and underneath a mountain (*Herzog Ernst*) was regarded as transformative for the individual. Mythical forces and powers were presumably hidden in mountains (*Nibelungenlied*), or protagonists were associated with mountains as their home and source of their strength (*Dietrichepik*). In other cases mountains mark the absolute limits of the courtly world (*Daniel von dem Blühenden Tal*), where no one except magicians or necromancers can operate to their advantage. Mountains also serve as a kind of testing ground for young princes (*Theuerdank*). Finally, late medieval artists increasingly enjoyed framing their images with mountainous heights and thus reveal a considerable shift in attitude toward the natural world.

Considering that most medieval texts hardly ever focus on the natural environment, the number of references to mountains proves in the end to be quite impressive. We can be certain that mountains were as much a geophysical reality for medieval people as they are for us, but this did not necessarily mean that they would have commented on them with any frequency. Our evidence, however, suggests that in a number of texts mountains do exhibit a noticeable presence, reflecting important staging grounds where the respective protagonists experience their transformation or face their ultimate challenge.

Notes

[1] Sylvia Landsberg, *The Medieval Garden* (Toronto: U of Toronto P, 2003).
[2] Gottfried von Straßburg, *Tristan und Isolde*. All translations from this romance are my own.
[3] See Ludolf Kuchenbuch and Joseph Morsel, "Naturräume," in *Enzyklopädie des Mittelalters*, ed. Gert Melville and Martial Staub, 2:246–48 (Darmstadt: Wissenschaftliche Buchgesellschaft, 2008); for a bibliography, see 476–77. They do not, however, deal with the topic of the "mountain" per se. See also Harry Kühnel together with Peter Dinzelbacher, "Natur/Umwelt: Mittelalter," in

Europäische Mentalitätsgeschichte: Hauptthemen in Einzeldarstellungen, ed. Peter Dinzelbacher, 2nd revised and expanded ed., Kröners Taschenausgabe 469 (Stuttgart: Kröner, 2008), 648–68. Cf. also Derek Pearsall and Elizabeth Salter, *Landscapes and Seasons of the Medieval World* (London: Paul Elek, 1973), although they do not deal with mountains either.

[4] See the contributions to Josef Semmler, ed., *Der Wald in Mittelalter und Renaissance*, Studia humaniora 17(Düsseldorf: Droste Verlag, 1991); and Corinne J. Saunders, *The Forest of Medieval Romance: Avernus, Broceliande, Arden* (Cambridge: D. S. Brewer, 1993).

[5] René Jantzen, *Montagne et symboles* (Lyon: Presses Universitaires de Lyon, 1988); Claude Thomasset and Danièle James-Raoul, eds., *La montagne dans le texte médiévale: Entre mythe et réalité*, Cultures et Civilisations Médiévales 19 (Paris: Presses de l'Université de Paris-Sorbonne, 2000).

[6] See the contributions to *Le Alpi porta d'Europa: Scritture, uomini, idee da Giustiniano al Barbarossa; Atti del convegno di studio (Cividale del Friuli, 5–7 ottobre 2006)*, ed. Laura Pani and Cesare Scalon (Spoleto, Italy: Editoriali Fondazione Cisam, 2009).

[7] Claire-Eliane Engel, *La littérature alpestre en France et en Angleterre aux XVIIIe et XIXe siècles* (Chambéry: Dardel, 1930).

[8] See the contributions by Joëlle Ducos, "Entre terre, air et eau: la formation des montagnes" (19–51) and by Chantal Connochie-Bourgne, "Quelques notes sur l'orogenèse chez les encyclopédistes de langue française au XIIIe siècle" (53–60), in Thomasset and James-Raoul, *La montagne dans le texte médiévale*.

[9] *Herzog Ernst: Ein mittelalterliches Abenteuerbuch*. In the Middle High German version B in accordance with the Karl Bartsch edition, together with the fragments of version A, translated, and with notes and an epilogue by Bernhard Sowinski (Stuttgart: Reclam, 1970).

[10] The Magnetic Mountain, which has appeared in many different ancient and medieval texts since the time of Pliny the Elder, has been discussed numerous times. See, for instance, Claude Lecouteux, "La Montagne d'Aimant," in Thomasset and James-Raoul, *La montagne dans le texte médiévale*, 167–86; Claude Lecouteux, "Die Sage vom Magnetberg," in *Burgen, Länder, Orte*, ed. Ulrich Müller and Werner Wunderlich, Mittelalter Mythen 5 (Constance: UVK Verlagsgesellschaft, 2008), 529–39.

[11] David Malcolm Blamires, *Herzog Ernst and the Underworld Voyage: A Comparative Study*, Publications of the Faculty of Arts at the University of Manchester (Manchester: U of Manchester P, 1979), 24; Albrecht Classen, "Medieval Travel into an Exotic Orient: The *Spielmannsepos Herzog Ernst* as a Travel into the Medieval Subconsciousness," in *Lesarten: New Methodologies and Old Texts*, ed. Alexander Schwarz (Frankfurt am Main: Peter Lang, 1990), 103–24.

[12] Albrecht Classen, "Multiculturalism in the German Middle Ages? The Rediscovery of a Modern Concept in the Past: The Case of *Herzog Ernst*," in

Multiculturalism and Representation: Selected Essays, ed. John Rieder and Larry E. Smith (Honolulu: U of Hawaii P, 1996), 198–219.

[13] Alexandra Stein, "Die Wundervölker des *Herzog Ernst (B)*: Zum Problem körpergebundener Authentizität im Medium der Schrift," in *Fremdes wahrnehmen — fremdes Wahrnehmen: Studien zur Geschichte der Wahrnehmung und zur Begegnung von Kulturen in Mittelalter und früher Neuzeit*, ed. Wolfgang Harms and C. Stephen Jaeger, together with Alexandra Stein (Stuttgart: S. Hirzel, 1997), 21–48.

[14] *Kudrun*, edited by Karl Stackmann in accordance with the Karl Bartsch edition, Altdeutsche Textbibliothek 115 (Tübingen: Max Niemeyer, 2000), stanza 1135.

[15] *Das Nibelungenlied*. Middle High German / New High German. Translated into New High German from the text by Karl Bartsch and Helmut de Boor, with a commentary by Siegfried Grosse (Stuttgart: Reclam, 1997). Francis B. Brévart, ed., *Das Eckenlied: Sämtliche Fassungen*, 3 parts, Altdeutsche Textbibliothek 111 (Tübingen: Niemeyer, 1999). See also *Dietrichs Flucht: Textgeschichtliche Ausgabe*, ed. Elisabeth Lienert and Gertrud Beck. Texte und Studien zur mittelhochdeutschen Heldenepik 1 (Tübingen: Niemeyer, 2003).

[16] Joyce Tally Lionarons, "The Otherworld and Its Inhabitants in the *Nibelungenlied*," in *A Companion to the Nibelungenlied*, ed. Winder McConnell (Columbia, SC: Camden House, 1998), 157.

[17] Der Stricker, *Daniel von dem Blühenden Tal*, ed. Michael Resler, 2nd ed., Altdeutsche Textbibliothek 92 (1983; repr., Tübingen: Niemeyer, 1995).

[18] Markus Wennerhold, *Späte mittelhochdeutsche Artusromane: "Lanzelet," "Wigalois," "Daniel von dem Blühenden Tal," "Diu Crône"; Bilanz der Forschung, 1960–2000*. Würzburger Beiträge zur deutschen Philologie 27 (Würzburg: Königshausen & Neumann, 2005), 129–81.

[19] Karl Kurt Klein, ed., *Die Lieder Oswalds von Wolkenstein*, 3rd, revised and enlarged edition ed. Hans Moser, Norbert Richard Wolf, and Notburga Wolf. Altdeutsche Textbibliothek 55 (Tübingen: Niemeyer, 1987); In English, Albrecht Classen, *The Poems of Oswald von Wolkenstein: An English Translation of the Complete Works (1376/77–1445)*, The New Middle Ages (New York: Palgrave Macmillan, 2008). Further references to these works are given in the text using page and line numbers.

[20] Klein, *Lieder Oswalds*, 21, 16–17; See also 50, 1–3; 26, 1–2.

[21] For a solid commentary, see Werner Marold, *Kommentar zu den Liedern Oswalds von Wolkenstein*, ed. and revised by Alan Robertshaw, Innsbrucker Beiträge zur Kulturwissenschaft, Germanistische Reihe 52 (Innsbruck: Institut für Germanistik, 1995), 249–51.

[22] *Die weltlichen Lieder des Mönchs von Salzburg: Texte und Melodien*, ed. Christoph März, Münchener Texte und Untersuchungen zur deutschen Literatur des Mittelalters 114 (Tübingen: Niemeyer, 1999); see also Christian Schneider, *Hovezuht: Literarische Hofkultur und höfisches Lebensideal um Herzog Albrecht III. von Österreich und Erzbischof Pilgrim III. von Salzburg (1365–1396)*, Beiträge zur älteren Literaturgeschichte (Heidelberg: Universitätsverlag Winter, 2008); Albrecht

Classen, "Schwellenphänomen, Paradigmenwechsel, Popularitätserfolg: Hybridisierung und Konkretisierung des spätmittelalterlichen Liebeslieds als Erfolgsrezept beim Mönch von Salzburg," *Studia Neophilologica* 81 (2009): 69–86.

[23] See the commentary by März, *Die weltlichen Lieder des Mönchs von Salzburg*, 421, although he does not know exactly what to make out of the term "alben."

[24] In the Alemannic-Swabian region the word "Alpen" generally refers to the last area in the mountains where some agriculture is still possible (cf. "Alm," which is otherwise the common term). See K. Fehn, "Alm," in *Aachen bis Bettelordenskirchen*, vol. 1 of *Lexikon des Mittelalters* (Munich: Artemis, 1980), 443.

[25] Rudolf von Ems, *Alexander: Ein höfischer Versroman des 13. Jahrhunderts*, ed. Victor Junk (Darmstadt: Wissenschaftliche Buchgesellschaft, 1970), 5716.

[26] Eberhard von Groote, ed., *Die Pilgerfahrt des Ritters Arnold von Harff von Cöln durch Italien, Syrien, Aegypten, . . . wie er sie in den Jahren 1496 bis 1499 vollendet*, ed. E. von Groote (Cologne: J. M. Heberle, 1860); *Rom — Jerusalem — Santiago: Das Pilgertagebuch des Ritters Arnold von Harff (1496–1498)*, trans. from the text of the Eberhard von Groote edition, with a commentary and introduction by Helmut Brall-Tuchel and Folker Reichert (Cologne: Böhlau, 2007).

[27] See Jan-Dirk Müller, ed., *Romane des 15. und 16. Jahrhunderts*, Bibliothek der Frühen Neuzeit 1 (Frankfurt am Main: Deutscher Klassiker Verlag, 1990). Albrecht Classen, *The German Volksbuch: A Critical History of a Late-Medieval Genre*, Studies in German Language and Literature 15 (Lewiston, NY: Edwin Mellen, 1995), 163–83.

[28] Müller, *Romane des 15. und 16. Jahrhunderts*. See, for instance, the description of Melusine's sister Palantine: "Darnach will ich fürbaß sagen von Palantina der schoenen junckfrawen / die zuo Konitsche auff dem berg in Arrogon gelegen inbeschlossen was Die selb Palantina als ir vor mer gehoert habent darzuo von irer muotter Presina geordnet vnd gesant was das sy da beschlossen vnd ein huetterinires vatters schaczes sein solt . . ." (165).

[29] Claude Thomasset, "Conclusion," *La montagne dans le texte médiéval*, 327–29; here 329.

[30] For a completely digitized version of the chronicle, see online at: http://www.obrasraras.usp.br/obras/000192/ and http://mdz1.bib-bvb.de/~mdz/kurzauswahl.html?url=http://mdz1.bib-bvb.de/cocoon/bsbink/Exemplar_S-199,1.html; for print editions, see *The Nuremberg Chronicle: A Facsimile of Hartmann Schedel's Buch der Chroniken; Printed by Anton Koberger in 1493* (New York: Arno, 1979); see also Elisabeth Rücker, *Hartmann Schedels Weltchronik: Das größte Buchunternehmen der Dürer-Zeit; Mit einem Katalog der Städteansichten*. (Munich: Prestel, 1988); see also Hartmann Schedel, *Weltchronik: Nachdruck [der] kolorierten Gesamtausgabe von 1493*, with an introduction and commentary by Stephan Füssel (Augsburg: Weltbild, 2004).

[31] Kaiser Maximilian I., *Theuerdank, 1517*, with an epilogue by Horst Appuhn (Dortmund: Harenberg Kommunikation, 1979); Jan-Dirk Müller, *Gedechtnus: Literatur und Hofgesellschaft um Maximilian I.*, Forschungen zur Geschichte der

älteren deutschen Literatur, vol. 2 (Munich: Fink, 1982); Stephan Füssel, *Kaiser Maximilian und die Medien seiner Zeit: Der Theuerdank von 1517, eine kulturhistorische Einführung* (Cologne: Taschen, 2003).

[32] For excellent images online, see http://special.lib.gla.ac.uk/exhibns/month/feb2005.html. A sixteenth-century copy, beautifully colored, is in the Universitätsbibliothek Rostock, mostly available now online at: http://rosdok.uni-rostock.de/metadata/DocPortal_codice_000000000002 (both last accessed on 12 Aug. 2009). See also the entry in *Wikipedia*: http://de.wikipedia.org/wiki/Theuerdank.

[33] *Kaiser Maximilian I. (1459–1519) und die Hofkultur seiner Zeit*, ed. Sieglinde Hartmann and Freimut Löser, Jahrbuch der Oswald von Wolkenstein-Gesellschaft 17 (Wiesbaden: Reichert, 2009).

[34] Giovanni Boccaccio, *Dizionario geografico: De montibus* . . ., trans. Nicolò Luburnio, with a preface by Gian Franco Pasini (Turin: Fògola Editore, 1978); see also Wojciech Iwańczak, *Die Kartenmacher: Nürnberg als Zentrum der Kartographie im Zeitalter der Renaissance*, trans. Peter Oliver Loew (2005; Darmstadt: Primus Verlag, 2009), 56–57.

From Meadows to Mountaintops: Albrecht von Haller's "Die Alpen"

Caroline Schaumann

IN 1732 THE ANONYMOUS POEM "Die Alpen" was published along with nine other poems in a slim volume entitled the *Versuch Schweizerischer Gedichten*[1] (Attempt at Swiss poems). Written in German and crafted in 490 alexandrine verses, the elaborate poem already had some impact in its handwritten form, after Haller had written the piece in March 1729, drawing on the impressions of his trip through Switzerland with his friend Johannes Gessner.[2] After its publication, however, the work enjoyed immediate success with the intellectual elite. A second edition appeared in 1734, issued this time under Haller's name; nine more editions followed during his lifetime, each featuring further revisions, commentary, and addenda (the final edition contained thirty-one poems). The volume was also translated into French, English,[3] Italian, and Latin, making Haller famous as a poet even before he became a recognized scholar and scientist.

While "Die Alpen" builds on the works of Swiss naturalists and writers who had already collected vast knowledge about the region (Josias Simler, Johann Jakob Scheuchzer,[4] and Beat Ludwig von Muralt), it represents a pivotal turn in the conception of the Alps insofar as Haller invokes the classical trope of the pastoral and extends it to the high peaks, introducing a discourse that had both immediately tangible and long-term paradigmatic effects. In contrast to earlier representations, Haller's poem endows the mountains with moral qualities, exuberantly celebrating the simple, rural life in preference to the decadence and turmoil that prevailed in courtly society. Along with such adulation, Haller adds an astonishing amount of botanical and mineralogical detail, making a case for the meticulous scientific study of the Alpine environment. What is more, Haller's poem was among the first literary documents in the German language to associate the high mountains with a mixture of fear and awe typical of later definitions of the sublime. While it is widely acknowledged that Haller's seminal representation of the Alps signals a landmark paradigm shift in eighteenth-century thinking, the curious blend of fact and fantasy, of science, ethics, and wonderment has been less closely explored. Moreover, the specific causes, conditions, and consequences of Haller's mountain-idealization deserve further inquiry.

In his veneration of unspoiled nature and peasant life, Haller creates an effective counterimage to the society of his time. In order to define this Alpine myth, he drew on his experiences in the lowlands and thereby delineated a utopian Other from afar. Thus Haller's journeys between 1725 and 1728 to the rapidly expanding metropolises of Western Europe, notably London and Paris, were as important to his idealization of the high country and its people as was his actual visit to the Alpine realm in 1729. In this vein, Haller's work draws on the well-established discourse of the pastoral and applies it to the decidedly un-pastoral, harsh mountainous landscape. With "Die Alpen," Haller deliberately conflates the word's double meaning of mountain meadow and mountaintop to construct a utopian space that is pitted against the artificially regimented aristocratic life in the cities. If the rising upper-middle class of Haller's time faced difficulties in moving up into the aristocracy, Haller's poem insinuates the possibility of an elevated existence in the mountains.[5] As Burghard Dedner recognizes:

> Hallers Alpenbauern sind nicht nur Gegenbilder zum Städter und Höfling, sie sind zugleich auch Gegenbilder zu den Gestalten der konventionellen Schäferpoesie und zu dem herkömmlichen Ideal des goldenen Zeitalters.[6]
>
> [Haller's Alpine peasants are not only counterimages to the townsfolk and courtiers; they are at the same time counterimages to conventional bucolic poetry and the traditional ideal of a golden age.]

This creation of an enthralling and untainted Alpine location makes Haller's verses resonate in the works of figures from Rousseau to Wordsworth to Ruskin. Yet the success of Haller's poem is also rooted in practical applications that go beyond its stated moral lessons. With its botanical details and enigmatic depictions of sublime mountain peaks, the poem contributed to a growing aesthetic and scientific curiosity about the mountain world. Addressing the aesthete as well as the intellectual, the scientist, the spectator, and the future climber, Haller's poem feeds into a rationale for Alpine travels that ultimately turned the Alps into a tourist destination for the middle class.

Haller's veneration of the Swiss Alps began in absentia, when in 1723, as a fifteen-year-old student, he left Bern for Tübingen to study medicine and anatomy. Two years later Haller continued his studies in Leiden in the Netherlands, conducting anatomical experiments on human corpses in order to dispute the existence of a separate salivary duct. During this time he befriended several Swiss scholars, most prominently Johannes Gessner (1709–90), who was a student of the well-known Zurich natural scientist Johann Jakob Scheuchzer, and who piqued Haller's interest in botany. Haller studied the first descriptive volumes on the Alps written by Swiss scholars and wrote his own nostalgic verses praising his native country.⁷ As Greg Garrard points out, the trope of the pastoral can acquire either nostalgic or utopian character: "We can set out three orientations of pastoral in terms of time: the *elegy* looks back to a vanished past with a sense of nostalgia; the *idyll* celebrates a bountiful present; the *utopia* looks forward to a redeemed future."⁸ In Haller's oeuvre, all three of these dimensions come into play, beginning with nostalgia. "Sehnsucht nach dem Vaterlande" (Longing for the fatherland, 1726), one of Haller's few early poems that survived his self-censorship,⁹ does not explicitly mention Switzerland or the Alps but can be seen as the starting point for his mythical re-creation of his native land. Marveling at the Bernese countryside — at the "beliebter Wald" (*VSG*, 5 and 8; beloved forest), "angenehmes Feld" (*VSG*, 8; pleasant field), "kleinen Wasser-Güssen" (*VSG*, 6; small waterfalls), and "väterlichen Hügeln" (*VSG*, 7; fatherly hills), — Haller evokes a lush and cultivated countryside. The young narrator, however, has been displaced from this veritable Garden of Eden, "entfernt vom Land, wo ich begann zu leben" (far away from the land where I began to live; *VSG*, 6), and can only yearn for both a lost time and a lost home. The nostalgic look back follows the traditional markers of the pastoral by employing what Greg Garrard calls its "two key contrasts": "the spatial distinction of town (frenetic, corrupt, impersonal) and country (peaceful, abundant), and the temporal distinction of past (idyllic) and present ('fallen')."¹⁰ Correspondingly, the poem begins with a description of peaceful nature that then leads into general reflections on the human condition (loneliness, infelicity, death). Haller thus conveniently employs a trope of pastoral beauty that has been entrenched not only in the Graeco-Roman tradition but also in the Judeo-Christian notion of a lost paradise.

The accompanying vignette added to the ninth edition of Haller's poems (1762), however, introduces an odd contrast: while the focus of "Sehnsucht nach dem Vaterlande" lies on the bountiful lowland, the illustration shows a different, more majestic landscape. Instead of the poem's hills we see snow-capped peaks; instead of creeks, raging waterfalls; instead of rural fields, alpine forests. The image positions the observer at the level of the mountains, above the clouds, looking down into an Alpine valley (fig. 1). Though incongruent with the subject matter of the poem itself, this illustration directly ties into the verses and illustration of "Die Alpen," signaling a change in focus from low to high country and an extension of the conventional use of the pastoral.

After graduating from Leiden University in 1727, Haller embarked on an educational journey with extended stays in London, Paris, and Strasbourg. Ensconced in the European centers of science, art, and medicine, he visited places of interest and met with renowned scholars and scientists; in Paris he also attended university lectures. He subsequently spent a year with Gessner in Basel, resuming his anatomical experiments

Fig. 1. Head vignette to "Sehnsucht nach dem Vaterlande."

while listening to lectures in mathematics and beginning studies in botany. During this time, in the summer of 1728, Haller and Gessner (who later became a professor of mathematics and physics at the University of Zurich) went on a botanical excursion, first through the foothills of the Jura and Lake Geneva environs, then to the mountainous regions of the Valais, the Bernese Oberland, and Central Switzerland. Though Haller initially undertook this trip to obtain botanical and mineralogical knowledge, he became captivated with the beauty of the landscape, which inspired him to work on his poem "Die Alpen." The following year he returned to Bern to establish himself as a practicing physician.

Both "Sehnsucht nach dem Vaterlande" and "Die Alpen" were thus the result of Haller's travels, but they were composed in the urban environments of Leiden and Basel respectively. Overcome by longing for his home, Haller even called his poetic drive an "illness," as he explained in his preface to the fourth edition (1748):

> Nach meinen Reisen, und hauptsächlich zu Basel, befiel mich die poetische Krankheit wieder, nachdem ich mehrere Jahre nichts mehr von dieser Art gewagt hatte.
>
> [Following my travels, and mainly in Basel, I was afflicted again by the poetic sickness after I hadn't dared anything of its kind for several years.][11]

This type of nostalgic yearning is central to the main motif of the "Heldengedicht" (heroic poem), which was the original subtitle of "Die Alpen,"[12] but the poem also delineates Haller's critique of urban society and his utopian vision of life in the mountains.

"Die Alpen" consists of forty-nine stanzas, each comprising ten alexandrine verses. Following the poetic meter (iambic hexameter), each line consists of either twelve or thirteen syllables (ending with a stressed or unstressed syllable respectively) and contains an obvious caesura after the third foot that lends the verse an antithetical character. Originating in twelfth-century heroic epics about Alexander the Great, the meter gained popularity in France during the sixteenth and seventeenth centuries and in German baroque poetry. Haller chose to write "Die Alpen," like all of his major poems, in alexandrines, and he adhered strictly to its metric rules. He found the straightforward, symmetrical, and antithetical structure ideal, since it does not seek a dazzling rhetorical effect but rather underscores the poem's purpose: each stanza introduces a new theme, which is developed and contrasted in the stanza's first eight lines, and condensed into a moral message in the last two. According to Haller's preamble (added in the fourth edition), this tight structure made the writing of the poem infinitely difficult. The self-imposed constrictions in form, however, underscore Haller's agenda. Not only does the poem's somewhat forced overall composition favor repetition and contrast over metaphorical and stylistic perfection, but the rigid organization of each stanza also lends itself to a concluding didactic message. Rather than seeking to expand the potential of the alexandrine form, Haller relies on the meter in order to emphasize tradition, convention, and conscientious labor.

Utilizing repeated and manifold oppositions, the poem is framed by the contrast between the simple life of the Alpine peasants and the decadent, wasteful existence of the aristocracy in the cities. It commences with a call to action: "Versuchts, ihr Sterbliche, macht euren Zustand besser" (*VSG*, 25; Try, mortals, if you will, improve your earthly lot, *TA*, 41). The first stanza (which was not added until the second edition) outlines the cultivation of the mountainous landscape, concluding with the poem's repeated credo: "Ihr werdet arm im Glück, im Reichthum elend bleiben" (*VSG*, 26; In wealth you still shall want, and in your plenty pine! *TA*, 41). The contrast between poverty (*Armut*) and wealth (*Reichthum*) is the overriding theme of the poem's first part; indeed, both words are repeated three times each. The next two stanzas describe the cornucopia, both in material goods and natural abundance. Material wealth, as the second stanza reminds us, leads to greed, envy, false friendships, and mental distress. And, as the third stanza explains, the paradisiacal gifts of ever-flowing milk and honey propagate excess and avarice. According to Haller, the Alps' greatest advantage is dearth and isolation: they fence in its rural inhabitants and fend off worldly influence. In contrast to the fruitful garden that provides pleasure, the harsh mountainous environment does not offer its rewards in such abundance as to spoil its inhabitants. Here Haller reverses the prevailing ideal of fertile nature. Making a Biblical argument in favor of the Alpine landscape, he cleverly transforms this seeming *locus horribilis* (as mountains were long known in the European mind) into a useful training ground and promising *locus amoenus*.

Far away from the world's stage, with its pursuit of prosperity, fame, and petty amusement, the Alpine peasants remain protected from the moral decline of lowland society. Thanks to the remoteness and desolation of the mountainous terrain, they are guided toward a life of modesty and virtue. Haller develops a vision of self-production and self-proficiency: Alpine peasants breathe fresh air, drink pure spring water, wear the skins of their animals, and live happily amid the ripening crops in their fields. Farmers till their fields, milk their cows, and spin their wool, thus being independent and unaffected by the agricultural mechanization that was beginning to take hold in Europe. To illustrate this point, the concluding vignette of the poem's ninth edition (1762) depicts various agricultural tools: a scythe, rake, fork, shovel, and flail, next to a couple of (alp) horns.

Haller's emphasis on farming and cultivation reinforces the conventional ideal of manicured gardens and tilled fields, but he was among the first authors to apply this pastoral trope to the rugged mountainous landscape. This emphasis is all the more logical because Haller and his friend Gessner did not climb any peaks on their botanical trip but mainly traveled through the Alpine valleys. However, by crossing various mountain passes (the highpoint of their trip being the Gemmi Pass (2,346 m/7,592 ft.), they got a good sense of the inaccessibility of the Bernese Alps. With its baroque poetic meter, references to antiquity ("Zephirs Hauch," *VSG*, 56; zephyrs blow, *TA*, 77), and literary clichés ("weichen Rasen," *VSG*, 56; "yielding turf, *TA*, 77), the poem evokes a bucolic idyll and transfers this idyll to the high country, creating a new locus of pastoral allure.

Nevertheless, the reality was that most Alpine peasants lived in impoverished conditions far different from Haller's interpretation. The poet's plea for a rural existence came at a time when traditional farming was beginning to change, when more frequent crop rotation, enclosure, mechanization, and selective breeding led to an unprecedented increase in agricultural productivity that fueled the Industrial Revolution, a process that began in Britain in the late-eighteenth century. Since the steep Alpine terrain made the adoption of such innovations difficult, farmers witnessed an increased imbalance between lowland and highland cultivation in terms of labor expended and harvest earned.[13] Haller's depiction of agricultural production idealizes a type of workmanship that was economically untenable, as Alpine peasant life was no longer able to keep pace with technological advances, and farmers increasingly moved to the cities. Haller's readers, though, were not fooled by the fact that the poem obscured the harsh realities of rural labor. It is not surprising that Haller's tribute to the Alpine farmers had little effect on slowing the growth of urbanization or converting city inhabitants into rural dwellers. Instead, his vision influenced the intellectual elite seeking a temporary respite from urban life and merged with the late eighteenth- and nineteenth-century notion of traveling that solidified rather than reversed urbanization. In other words, Haller's response to the economical, cultural, and political tensions of his time delivered an incongruous, evocative, and effective trope of country and mountain living that enjoys currency to this day.

The idealized image of "Die Alpen" not only offers a glimpse into Haller's concerns about the deep-seated changes taking place during his lifetime but also reveals much about his dissatisfaction with his own lowland life. Rather than seeking peaceful constancy, he was restless in his drive for new insights and experiences.[14] Throughout his life Haller went through periods of contemplation, anxiety, and depression, partly because he had difficulty establishing himself in public service in Bern: the Bernese Council refused to create a professorship for him, and so in 1736 he accepted an appointment as Professio Anatomiae et Botanices at the newly established Georgia Augusta Universität in Göttingen,[15] still, however, keeping alive his hopes of eventually returning to Bern. Finally, in 1753, Haller was chosen by lot to serve in a Bernese cantonal minor office as a *Rathausammann* (Cantonal Secretary), but ran nine times for a seat in the Swiss Small Council (*Kleiner Rat*), each time unsuccessfully. Haller also mourned the loss of two wives and increasingly battled with ill health: headaches, fever, and eye infections beginning in 1729, and dysentery in 1734 forced him to cancel two more Alpine excursions with Gessner, and chronic urinary-tract infections robbed him of restful sleep and led to his later addiction to opium.

Not only his compromised health but also his economic situation and physical surroundings could not have been more different from what he preaches in "Die Alpen." While Haller knew little about Alpine peasant life, he was intimately familiar with the affluent urban lifestyle, thanks to his many travels before composing "Die Alpen." In London he visited the Chelsea Botanic Garden and was introduced to the Royal Society, where his scientific ambitions were fueled by the work of other anatomists and physicists. In Paris he came to know French fashion, which dominated upper-class life in European cities during the eighteenth century. Upon his arrival in the French capital, he reportedly wasted no time visiting a barber and a tailor and spent many hours (and francs) at Parisian cafes, regularly visited the Comédie Française and the Opera, bought luxury items such as silk stockings and silver buckles,[16] and began to write French verses (even though, in the spirit of the German Enlightenment, he later criticized the predominance of the French language and the generally stilted French style). He likely had to leave town because of his private (and illegal) anatomical experiments on human corpses.[17] In Bern, where the powerful positions in the *Kleiner* and *Grosser Rat* increasingly converged around a few influential families, an oligarchic and corrupt aristocracy impeded Haller's appointment to a public office.[18] Yet he patriotically waited it out, favoring the unappreciated public service in his hometown over scholarly opportunities in Göttingen and several lucrative job offers: a professorship in medicine, physiology, and anatomy in Göttingen (1755); the presidency of the university in Halle (1755); and finally, the presidency of the Georgia Augusta Universität Göttingen (1764 and 1768).[19] In 1749, Kaiser Franz I elevated Haller to the nobility, making him a member of the class he so frowned upon in the poem.

Haller's didactic description of a harmonious Alpine world thus functions as an effective counterargument to courtly idleness and stagnation. By referring to antiquity in references to Seneca and Horace, he invokes not only a bucolic idyll but also the decline of the Roman Empire. For Haller the high mountains are more than a mere backdrop, as he repeatedly lauds their use and value within a divine order. Not even Haller could have known that his poem would be instrumental in creating a topos that would eventually extend into a general archetype of nature in its raw, unsullied form that resonates to this day as a powerful critique of modernity and civilization.

The poem's first seven stanzas call for humans to prosper in an environment that is decidedly no Garden of Eden. In the next ten stanzas, Haller elaborates on the different aspects of the simple and modest Alpine way of life, using the existence of the aristocracy for contrast. These verses are especially interesting because they combine Haller's youthful political vision, playful rumination, serious concern, and philosophical reflection in a surprising and even contradictory manner. For instance, the footnote to the poem's tenth stanza advocates the equality of Alpine citizens, who live without governmental oppression:

> Man sieht leicht, daß dieses Gemählde auf die vollkommne Gleichheit der Alpenleute geht, wo kein Adel, und so gar kein Landvogt ist, wo keine möglichen Beförderungen eine Bewegung in den Gemühtern erwecken, und die Ehrsucht keinen Nahmen in der Landsprache hat. (*VSG*, 31)
>
> [One immediately recognizes that this image refers to the complete equality among the Alpine citizens who know no nobility and no bailiff, whose minds are not moved by chances of promotion, and who have no word for ambition in the local language.]

While Haller briefly ponders the envy and discontent caused by social inequality, the poem first and foremost advocates the peaceful cheerfulness of the Alpine people. Moreover, the stanza to which the footnote was appended arrives at a different, somewhat unexpected, conclusion by advocating equality in the Alpine *lifestyle* rather than in societal structure:

> Hier macht kein wechselnd Glück die Zeiten unterschieden,
> Die Thränen folgen nicht auf kurze Freudigkeit:
> Das Leben rinnt dahin in ungestörtem Frieden,
> Heut ist wie gestern war, und morgen wird wie heut.
> Kein ungewohnter Fall bezeichnet hier die Tage,
> Kein Unstern mahlt sie schwarz, kein schwülstig Glücke roth.
> Der Jahre Lust und Müh ruhn stets auf gleicher Waage,
> Des Lebens Staffeln sind nichts als Geburt und Tod.
> Nur hat die Fröhlichkeit bisweilen wenig Stunden
> Dem unverdrossnen Volk nicht ohne Müh entwunden.
> (*VSG*, 30–31)

> [Here no capricious chance disrupts time's steady flow,
> And hours of joy do not to sudden tears give way;
> The days with equal pace and calm demeanour go,
> Today as yesterday, tomorrow as today.
> No brief sensation can this sheltered life assail
> To mark with red or black their days on this calm earth.
> Labour and pleasure both lie balanced on the scale,
> The milestones of their fate are only death and birth,
> While they with steadfast step move uncomplaining on,
> Though pleasure's favoured hours are short and swiftly gone.
> (*TA*, 47)]

As John Van Cleve points out, however, for a middle class susceptible to economic and social fluctuations, such assurance of continuity and peace functions as a utopian promise.[20] While Haller refrains from radical political conclusions, his polarized characterization is brimming with social critique. And if the plea for such uniformity of life is beginning to sound monotonous and unappealing, Haller enlivens it by turning next to Alpine celebrations and games. His vivid depiction of wrestling, shot-putting, ball games, dancing, and flirting is sure to make Alpine life enticing, especially since it is followed by five stanzas on courtship, marriage, and lovemaking.

Haller's thoughts on love and marriage contain the poem's most radical ideas, conveying his critique of aristocratic society. He emphatically argues in favor of a free partner choice that is not determined by class, political power, or wealth, and does not necessitate a dowry or a father's blessing:

> Man wiegt die Gunst hier nicht für schwere Kisten hin,
> Die Ehrsucht theilet nie, was Werth und Huld verbunden,
> Die Staatssucht macht sich nicht zur Unglücks-Kupplerin:
> Die Liebe brennt hier frey, und scheut kein Donner-Wetter,
> Man liebt für sich selbst, und nicht für seine Vätter.
> (*VSG*, 32)

[Favour cannot be bought with money's shameful bait,
Ambition severs not what feeling once has bound,
No joyless yokes are forged by high affairs of state.
Love fears no consequence but speaks out free and frank,
Each loves in his own right, and not for class and rank.
(*TA*, 51)]

In contrast to arranged marriages based on material wealth or political influence, the Alps offer unbridled courtship and free love. To Van Cleve, these lines express the poet's hope of breaking away from the middle-class practice of rising in wealth and status through marriage, a conflict later expressed in the *Bürgerliches Trauerspiel* (bourgeois tragedy).[21] According to Haller, the ease of finding a suitable partner rids lovers of false pride and chasteness, and encourages true passion found outdoors rather than in frilly beds. Amid the poem's general emphasis on morality and modesty, here the young Haller comes to surprisingly free-minded and liberated, if not libertine, conclusions.

Die holde Nachtigall grüßt sie von nahen Zweigen,
Die Wollust deckt ihr Bett auf sanft-geschwollnes Mooß,
Zum Vorhang dient ein Baum, die Einsamkeit zum Zeugen,
Die Liebe führt die Braut in ihres Hirten Schooß.
O dreymahl selig Paar! Euch muß ein Fürst beneiden,
Dann Liebe balsamt Gras und Eckel herrscht auf Seiden.
(*VSG*, 33)

[Their bed's a bank of moss beyond the leafy brake,
The rustic nightingale their music does provide,
Their witness is the tree whose boughs their curtains make
When love untutored brings the bridegroom to the bride.
Thrice happy pair! For this a prince would crowns abjure,
Since grass so gracious is, and silks so oft impure!
(*TA*, 51)]

While these lines expand on a well-known literary motif of outdoor love found in medieval poetry from Walther von der Vogelweide to Carmina Burana (which, in turn, reinforces the classical bucolic idyll of lust and labor found in Theocritus), Haller goes a step further by claiming that such healthy and uninhibited sexuality can actually prevent unfaithfulness and sexually transmitted diseases. According to this logic, Haller proclaims "Hier bleibt das Ehbett rein" (*VSG*, 34; Here the marriage bed remains pure), and then elaborates on the Alpine peasants' excellent health. This is clearly the future physician in Haller responding to urgent issues of his time in order to convey a note of caution. In contrast to the decadent idleness and excessive consumption of the court, Haller advises his readers that the remote Alpine world remains free of the influence of French food and wine ("fremder Wein"; foreign wine), welscher Koch (*VSG*, 35; French cooks," *TA*, 53), of lewd pus ("geiles Eiter," *VSG*, 35; hidden abscess, *TA*, 53), and of inbred genetic diseases ("erblich Gift von siechen Vätern" (*VSG*, 34; poison, left by their fathers' sins, *TA*, 53).

In this context the teetotaler Haller (who apparently gave up alcohol after some excessive drinking bouts as a student in Tübingen[22]) makes an emphatic if somewhat surprising plea against grape production and wine consumption.

> Zwar bekränzt der Herbst die Hügel nicht mit Reben,
> Man preßt kein jährend Naß gequetschten Beeren ab.
> Die Erde hat zum Durst nur Brünnen hergegeben,
> Und kein gekünstelt Saur beschleunigt unser Grab.
> Beglückte, klaget nicht; Ihr wuchert im verlieren;
> Kein nöhtiges Getränk, ein Gift verlieret ihr.
> Die gültige Natur verbietet ihn den Thieren,
> Der Mensch allein trinkt Wein, und wird dadurch ein Thier.
> (*VSG*, 38)

> [On these green hills, 'tis true, no purple grapes are grown,
> And no fermenting sap is from the clusters pressed.
> The earth, to quench their thirst, has given them springs alone,
> No artificial draught to speed them to their rest.
> Complain not, happy race, thus of an evil rid!
> No needful drink you lose, but poison at the least,
> That Nature's sapient laws to hapless beast forbid;
> For man alone drinks wine, and so becomes a beast.
> (*TA*, 57)]

Yet Haller saw reason to address an obvious contradiction in a later footnote. There he explains that while the low-lying valleys produce some of the strongest wines, his description focuses on the highlands and the Bernese valleys, where viniculture does not exist. There still remains a contradiction, though, since the previous stanza elaborates on the cultivation of fruit trees, which are likewise limited to the lower valleys, a fact that puts into question Haller's distinction between low and high country. While Haller links wine to moral decline, he favors water and "der süsse Schaum der Euter" (*VSG*, 36; the sweet foam of udders), devoting an entire stanza to the description of cheese- and butter-making.

After describing various kinds of food production (animal husbandry, agriculture, fruit cultivation, hunting, and dairy farming) throughout the seasons, Haller turns from physical to mental activities. He lauds the peasants' hard-won respite, their intelligent conversation, unadorned song, and free-flowing verses (which stand in odd contrast to the measured poem). Yet Haller seamlessly inserts into the pastoral idyll more radical political positions, which he later revised in favor of a more conservative stance expressed in his novels. Haller's political opinions in the poem, however, serve once again to reinforce the contrast he creates between courtly and rural society. His praise of Wilhelm Tell's fight against tyranny is largely directed at France as the new imperialist yoke:

> Wie eitler Fürsten Pracht den Mark der Länder frißt:
> Wie Tell mit kühnem Muth das harte Joch zertretten,
> Das Joch, das heute noch Europens Helfte trägt:
> Wie um uns alles darbt, und hungert in den Ketten,
> Und Welschlands Paradies nur nackte Bettler hegt.
>
> (*VSG*, 42–43)

> [And let vain princes' pomp consume their heritage;
> How Tell's high-hearted deed once trod this yoke to earth,
> The yoke that even yet half Europe's lands must bear,
> How all around us still must languish in their dearth,
> And France's paradise spawns beggars everywhere.
>
> (*TA*, 63)]

Haller's apparent critique of princedom and social inequality thus romanticizes the notion of a classless society rather than functioning as a political call to action. "Die Alpen" does not pursue this political perspective in further detail but instead turns to yet another topic. After praising the peasants' eloquence, wisdom, song, poetry, and steadfastness, Haller asserts that they are natural meteorologists who have learned from experience how to predict the weather (stanza 27) and born herbologists who recognize and enumerate valuable plants (stanza 31). Haller thereby makes a transition to the second half of the poem, setting up an effective argument for his own work as a scientist.

In the second part of the poem, Haller increasingly includes more details on the Alpine topography and its flora. Filled with adverbs of place such as "here" and "there," his visual impressions in stanzas 32 to 44 contain an unprecedented amount of data regarding specifically named herbs, flowers, tree species, and even rocks and crystals. He describes the appearance of gentian and snapdragon, the visual effect of dew and rain on leaves and meadows, and the lakes and rivers feeding from the Schreckhorn, but also ruminates about the insides of mountains, referring to the salt mine near Bevieux, the crystal mine by the Grimsel River, and even gold particles in the Aar River (which, characteristically, the virtuous shepherd ignores). These stanzas later gave Lessing, in his treatise *Laokoon oder über die Grenzen der Malerei und der Poesie* (Laocoon: An essay on the limits of painting and poetry, 1766), reason to disparage Haller's poetic scope.[23] In the fourth edition of *Versuch Schweizerischer Gedichte* (1748), after Haller had published the results of his botanical findings in the comprehensive volume *Enumeratio methodica stirpium Helvetiae indigenarum* (Systematic catalogue of the native

Swiss flora, 1742), he meticulously added footnotes with each plant's scientific name as well as information on its appearance, habitat, and usage. Providing the specific page numbers in his *Enumeratio Helvetica*, Haller creates a convenient reference that introduces and bolsters his work as a scientist.

Yet Haller cleverly combines his detailed botanical descriptions with sentiments beyond scientific observation. On the one hand, his comments on Alpine crystal mines serve once more to sustain his practice of city-bashing, and effectively constitute a jab against the Parisian elite:

> O Reichthum der Natur! verkriecht euch, welsche Zwerge:
> Europens Diamant blüht hier und wächst zum Berge!
> (*VSG*, 50)
>
> [Oh riches of Nature! Hide away, you French midgets:
> Here Europe's diamonds bloom and grow up the mountains.
> (my translation)]

On the other hand, Haller introduces a quixotic characterization of the inhospitable mountain tops that transcends the summits' practical value and thus anticipates a notion of the sublime espoused in later philosophical definitions. In accordance with the previous gist of the poem, Haller first attempts to make an argument for the practical usage of mountain cliffs:

> Der Berge wachsend Eiß, der Felsen steile Wände
> Sind selbst zum Nutzen da und tränken das Gelände.
> (*VSG*, 44)
>
> [Even the icy peaks, the steeps that round them stand
> Serve useful ends, since they water the outspread land.
> (*TA*, 65)]

A footnote to these verses names the major rivers such as the Rhine, Rhône, and Aar that originate from the mountain glaciers. The following three stanzas, however, do not elaborate on the value or usefulness of rock faces but instead give the reader an impression of the grandeur and austerity of the high mountains. Stanza 39 continues:

> Wenn Titans erster Strahl der Felsen Höh' vergüldet
> Und sein verklärter Blick die Nebel unterdrückt,
> So wird, was die Natur am prächtigsten gebildet,
> Mit immer neuer Lust von einem Berg erblickt;
> Durch den zerfahrnen Dunst von einer dünnen Wolke
> Eröfnet sich zugleich der Schauplatz einer Welt,
> Ein weiter Aufenthalt von mehr als einem Volke
> Zeigt alles auf einmahl, was sein Bezirk enthält:

> Ein sanfter Schwindel schließt die allzuschwachen Augen,
> Die den zu breiten Kreis nicht durchzustrahlen taugen.
> (*VSG*, 44–45)

> [When once the sun's first rays have reached the snowy heights
> And from the brightening earth the creeping mists have banned,
> Then all the proud array of Nature's fairest sights
> Can from a mountain-top with rising joy be scanned.
> Through the last thinning haze touched by the heavens' sheen
> Appears a far-flung world of sunlight and of shade,
> More than one people's home in one extensive scene,
> Outspread to where its hems on far horizons fade.
> A gentle vertigo now drowns the swooning sense,
> Too feeble to absorb the scene's magnificence.
> (*TA*, 65)]

Even though Haller describes a view of mountains from below rather than from the summit, the zest of the beholder and his keen interest in the changing light, fog, and cloud formations introduce a completely different vocabulary to describe the mountainous terrain. The last two verses of the stanza, in particular, begin to delineate the curious mixture of fear and awe that has come to define the sensation of the sublime. According to Haller, the human eye is not capable of absorbing the entire mountain panorama, which leads the spectator to close his eyes in vertigo. Such an experience, one that shows the limits of human perception and understanding, prefigures later definitions of the sublime experience when an all-encompassing view transcends humans' intellectual capacity.

Haller devotes the following three stanzas to the literal view of mountains, reinforcing the previous sentiments expressed in the poem. What he aestheticizes here are not pastoral meadows and flourishing flowers but a natural world beyond human control and the limited power of intellect: bleak rocks, steep cliff bands, sheets of ice, foaming rivers, thunderous waterfalls, and fierce weather. Departing from the familiar discourses on mountain valleys, Haller paints a picture of the high peaks that fuels a sense of awe and wonder in the observer. This transition to later discourses on the sublime is further evidenced by the fact that Haller replaced a chamois witnessing the spectacular mountain scenery in the poem's first two editions with a human wanderer in the editions thereafter:

> Ein Wandrer sieht erstaunt im Himmel Ströme fliessen,
> Die aus den Wolken fliehn, und sich in Wolken giessen.
> (*VSG*, 46)

> [The wanderer sees, amazed, streams in the heavens now
> That, fleeing from the clouds, pour into clouds below.
> (*TA*, 67)]

Haller ostensibly made the substitution after criticism by his patrons.[24] Yet by inserting a human witness to nature's wonders, he makes a direct case for mountain hiking and climbing. By his own admission, Haller's hiker stands below the Staubbach Falls near Lauterbrunnen, one of the highest unbroken waterfalls in Europe. Waterfalls in general and the Staubbach Falls in particular came to define the sublime as epitomes of austerity and grandeur. Haller's sense of awe in observing the falls ("Den Regenbogen habe ich gesehn und bin stundenlang stillegestanden, die seltene Erscheinung zu betrachten" (This rainbow I saw and stopped for hours to observe the rare event), added in a footnote to stanza 36 in the 1773 edition) directly corresponds to Albert Bierstadt's painting "Staubbach Falls near Lauterbrunnen" more than a century later.

Haller does not conclude his poem with grand views of nature but returns again to the honorable Alpine citizens. Resuming the initial challenge of "Versuchts, ihr Sterbliche" (Try, mortals, if you will), stanza 45 gives first a negative answer to the challenge at hand. While colorful metaphors such as "güldne Ketten" (*VSG*, 54; golden chains, *TA*, 75), "Gift-geschwollne Neid" (*VSG*, 54; poisoned greed, *TA*, 75), "geile Wollust" (*VSG*, 55; carnal lust, *TA*, 75), and "Der Laster schwarze Brut" (*VSG*, 55; the sable brood of vice, *TA*, 77) underscore the venoms of courtly city life, the poem concludes with the triumph of modesty. The attempt has been successful, the temptation conquered:

> O selig! Wer wie Ihr mit selbst-gezognen Stieren
> Den angestorbnen Grund von eignen Aeckern pflügt:
> Den reine Wolle deckt, belaubte Kränze zieren,
> Und ungewürzte Speis' aus süsser Milch vergnügt:
> Der sich bey Zephirs Hauch, und kühlen Wasser-Fällen,
> In ungesorgtem Schlaf, auf weichen Rasen streckt:
> Den nie in hoher See das Brausen wilder Wellen,
> Noch der Trompeten Schall in bangen Zelten weckt;
> Der seinen Zustand liebt, und niemals wünscht zu bessern,
> Gewiß der Himmel kan sein Glücke nicht vergrössern.
> (*VSG*, 55–56)

> [O happy you who here, with steers of your own rearing,
> Plough your ancestral fields and tend paternal leas,
> Who wear your flocks' warm wool, no wintry weather fearing.
> And live on unspiced food of milk and country cheese;
> Who, when soft zephyrs blow, upon the yielding turf
> Can soon be lulled to sleep by some cool waterfall;
> Who never wake to hear the raging ocean's surf
> Nor yet in troubled times the shrilling trumpet's call;
> Who would not seek to change, who live the life you love!
> Lo, Fortune has no gifts that could your state improve.
> (*TA*, 77)]

Fig. 2. Head vignette to "Die Alpen."

Haller's didactic emphasis and the concluding plea for contentment and humility sustains rather than departs from the natural discourses that had prevailed since antiquity. On the one hand, the poem celebrates a pastoral landscape marked by gentle meadows and fertile fields. By way of visual demonstration, the head vignette of the ninth edition (1762) features a fertile and relatively flat landscape abundant with pasture, creeks, brush, and trees. The human potential and yield of this land is emphasized by the presence of a young shepherd resting in the tranquil landscape with his alpenhorn. The majestic, unrealistically steep, and snow-covered Alpine peaks are pushed to the very background of the scene, providing a fitting and picturesque backdrop to the viewer more on a level with meadowlands and pine trees (fig. 2).

On the other hand, Haller also marvels at landscape characterized by barren cliffs, ice chasms, and raging torrents. He thus draws on the existing paradigm of a cultivated (garden) landscape but transfers the pastoral ideal to a terrain considered inhospitable and perilous. This shift is most obvious in the poem's title. According to Grimm's dictionary, "Alpe" or "Albe," meaning "white," refers both to a high peak in an area of permanent snow *and* to a pasture located below high peaks. Martin Scharfe further complicates definitions of "Alpen" by claiming that until the eighteenth century the word designated summits and pastures, as well as mountain passes, which were confusingly regarded both as a peak *and* a valley.[25] Haller's conflation of pastoral and non-pastoral topography exploits the double meaning of this term, attesting to both the appeal and the pliancy of the pastoral trope. In this way, Haller was instrumental in opening up a new locus of the pastoral at the cusp of the ensuing Industrial Revolution that would send Europeans in search of unspoiled lands.

Haller's critique of modern civilization at the beginning and end, as well as his striking description of the high mountains in the middle of the poem, likely inspired Jean-Jacques Rousseau's descriptions of the Alps in *La nouvelle Héloïse* (Julie, or the new Heloise, 1761) three decades later. For Rousseau's autobiographical protagonist, the middle-class teacher Saint-Preux, the Savoy mountains near Lake Geneva become the only place where he finds peace and solace during and after his failed affair with Julie d'Etange, the daughter of an aristocrat. Both Haller and Rousseau stress the soothing and purifying influences of nature over the souls of men, deploring what they see as the artificial and false manners of civilization. Yet both writers employ the language and imagery of the pastoral trope to arrive at radically different political ends. Rousseau's liberal political, religious, educational, and philosophical views informed both the American and French Revolutions. Haller attacked Rousseau as a "Musicanten von Genf" (hack musician of Geneva[26]), published theological essays that refuted a liberal interpretation of the Christian faith, and in the 1770s wrote three political novels that each idealized a different form of absolutism and sought to refute Rousseau's writings.

Haller continuously incorporated into "Die Alpen" the results of his scientific research in details that go far beyond the explicit message of the poem. "Die Alpen" hence reflects the impressive quantity of Haller's oeuvre: as a man of science and a representative of the Enlightenment situated at the very hub of an extensive network of scholarly communication, he wrote nearly 17,000 letters. Moreover, he published one of the most important volumes of eighteenth-century poetry, 24 monographs, 9,000 reviews, and 200 encyclopedia entries.[27] "Die Alpen" contains an unprecedented amount of information on Alpine plants and crystals, and Haller not only expanded upon this information in the footnotes to later editions but also continued to work meticulously on stylistic improvement. He judicially replaced the Swiss dialect expressions with high-German, rid his poem of what he called "Sprachfehler" (*VSG*, 5; language flaws), and perfected the metric structure. Moreover, he continued to rework imagery and muted the religious and political jibes.[28] In the fourth edition (1748), Haller also included preliminary notes to many of his poems, which provide information concerning the poem's date and origin and justify its inclusion in the collection.

The distinct combination of scientific observation and aesthetic representation, of landscape description, travel report, field analysis, cultural criticism, and bucolic entertainment proved to be groundbreaking in the representation of mountains in the eighteenth century and beyond. Introducing the location, language, and imagery of an extremely pliable ideal of unspoiled nature, the poem helped both popularize and mythologize the Alps just as Alpine tourism began to flourish. "Die Alpen" thus provides the general moral grounds as well as the specific arguments for Alpine scientific exploration that, in the nineteenth century, turned the Alps into a major tourist destination. Haller offered an emergent middle class an essential paradigm of approaching and experiencing the mountain landscape that has prevailed to this day.

Notes

[1] This text was published by Haller's older brother, Nikolaus Emanuel Haller, in Bern. The spelling of "Gedichten" was a dialect variation that Haller omitted beginning with the third edition.

[2] The original poem consisted of forty-eight stanzas, since Haller added the first stanza only in the second edition of 1734.

[3] On the English translation that appeared in 1794 by amateur botanist Mrs. J. Howorth, see Alison E. Martin's article "Natural Effusions: Mrs J. Howorth's English translation of Albrecht von Haller's *Die Alpen*," in *Translation Studies* 5.1 (2012): 17–32.

[4] According to Renato G. Mazzolini, Scheuchzer even used the term nostalgia "to describe homesickness as a specific Swiss malady." "Haller and the Swiss Scientific Movement," in *Albrecht von Haller: Leben — Werk — Epoche*, ed. Hubert Steinke, Urs Boschung, and Wolfgang Proß (Göttingen: Wallstein, 2008), 478.

[5] Many thanks to both Sean Ireton and Heather Sullivan, whose insightful feedback informs the core of my argument.

[6] Burghard Dedner, "Vom Schäferleben zur Agrarwirtschaft: Poesie und Ideologie des 'Landlebens' in der deutschen Literatur des 18. Jahrhunderts," in *Europäische Bukolik und Georgik*, ed. Klaus Garber (Darmstadt: Wissenschaftliche Buchgesellschaft, 1976), 351. All translations in this chapter are my own, unless otherwise noted.

[7] Albrecht von Haller, *Versuch Schweizerischer Gedichte*, 9th ed. (1762; repr., Bern: Herbert Lang, 1969). Further references to this work are cited in the text using the abbreviation *VSG* and the page number. Translations are from Stanley Mason, *The Alps: An English Translation* (Dübendorf, Switzerland: Walter Amstutz De Clivo Press, 1987), hereafter *TA*. Where no *TA* reference is given, the translation is my own, since in that case the published translation does not reflect the original's wording.

[8] Greg Garrard, *Ecocriticism* (London: Routledge, 2004), 37.

[9] At the age of twelve Haller had already begun to write verses, but by his own admission he burned, in 1729, all of his poems composed between 1721–23.

[10] Garrard, *Ecocriticism*, 35.
[11] The somewhat sarcastic term, "poetische Krankheit," indicates that Haller saw the creative process as both a consequence of, and remedy for, inner uneasiness. Quite literally, Haller's poetry was also produced in times of illness, as physical ill-being often afforded him the time to write. See Haller, "Vorrede," *VSG*, 4.
[12] See Urs Boschung, "Ein Berner Patriot: Hallers Lebensstationen," in *Albrecht von Haller im Göttingen der Aufklärung*, ed. Norbert Elsner and Nicolaas A. Rupke (Göttingen: Wallstein, 2009), 31.
[13] See Jon Mathieu, *Geschichte der Alpen, 1500–1900: Umwelt, Entwicklung, Gesellschaft* (Vienna: Böhlau, 1998), 69–70.
[14] See Karl S. Guthke, *Die Entdeckung des Ich: Studien zur Literatur* (Tübingen: Francke, 1993), 99.
[15] For further information on Haller in Göttingen, see Peter Hanns Reill, "'Pflanzengarten der Aufklärung': Haller und die Gründung der Göttinger Universität," 47–69; and Ulrich Joost, "'Trübselige kleine Stadt in einem trüb-seligen Land'? Hallers Göttingen," in Elsner and Rupke, *Albrecht von Haller im Göttingen der Aufklärung*, 71–105.
[16] See Haller's diary of his trip, especially the list of expenses, in Erich Hintzsche, ed., *Albrecht Hallers Tagebuch seiner Studienreise nach London, Paris, Straßburg und Basel, 1727–1728* (Bern: Hans Huber, 1968).
[17] See Reimer Eck, ed., *Albrecht von Haller in Göttingen*, exhibition catalogue (Göttingen: Institut für Wissenschaftsgeschichte, 2008), 6.
[18] For further information on Haller's difficulties in Bern, see François de Capitani, "Hallers Bern," in Steinke, Boschung, and Proß, *Albrecht von Haller: Leben — Werk — Epoche*, 83–97.
[19] For further context on the Bernese bourgeoisie society and Haller's rising-middle-class background, see John Van Cleve's excellent article "Social Commentary in Haller's 'Die Alpen,'" *Monatshefte* 72, no. 4 (Winter 1980): 379–88, esp. 380–81.
[20] Van Cleve, "Social Commentary in Haller's 'Die Alpen,'" 384.
[21] Van Cleve, "Social Commentary in Haller's 'Die Alpen,'" 385.
[22] In his early student days at Tübingen, Haller (who may or may not have been involved) and others were fined when they caused a night guard to drink so much alcohol that he died. Haller's expenses for wine consumption can be traced until 1727. See Urs Boschung, "Leben und Umfeld," in Steinke, Boschung, and Proß, *Albrecht von Haller: Leben — Werk — Epoche*, 21–22.
[23] For further detail, see Geoffrey Atherton, "'Poetische Mahlerey': Placing Albrecht von Haller's 'Enzian' Portrait in a Georgic Gallery," *German Quarterly* 71, no. 4 (Fall 1998): 353.
[24] See Haller's footnote to line 359, *VSG*, 46.
[25] See Martin Scharfe, "Was ist ein Berg? Was ein Tal?" in *Berg-Sucht: Eine Kulturgeschichte des frühen Alpinismus, 1750–1850* (Vienna: Böhlau, 2007), 184–86.

[26] Florian Gelzer and Béla Kapossy, "Roman, Staat und Gesellschaft," in Steinke, Boschung, and Proß, *Albrecht von Haller: Leben — Werk — Epoche*, 172.

[27] Hubert Steinke and Martin Stuber have put numbers to Haller's impressive publication output: "Haller hat diese Ebenen der Wissensproduktion effizient eingesetzt und so ein riesiges Oeuvre geschaffen von 24 monographischen Werken in 50 Bänden, 136 Abhandlungen, 200 *Encyclopédie*-Artikeln, 25 Vorreden, 9.000 Rezensionen, 25 Bänden mit Überarbeitungen eigener Schriften und weiteren 10 von ihm herausgegebenen Werken in 52 Bänden" (Haller efficiently employed these levels of scientific production and thus created an enormous oeuvre of 24 monographs in 50 volumes, 136 essays, 200 encyclopedia articles, 25 preambles, 9,000 reviews, 25 volumes of his own writings, and furthermore 10 edited works in 52 volumes.). Hubert Steinke und Martin Stuber, "Haller und die Gelehrtenrepublik," in Steinke, Boschung, and Proß, *Albrecht von Haller: Leben — Werk — Epoche*, 398.

[28] Karl Zagajewski's *Albrecht von Hallers Dichtersprache* (Strasbourg: Trübner, 1909) offers a detailed analysis of Haller's revisions.

Interlude: Geo-Poetics: The Alpine Sublime in Art and Literature, 1779–1860

Anthony Ozturk

"THERE IS NOTHING IN NATURE MORE SHAPELESS and ill-figur'd than an old Rock or Mountain. . . . They are the greatest Examples of Confusion that we know in Nature; no Tempest or Earthquake puts things into more Disorder."[1] This account of the Alps by Thomas Burnet in *The Sacred Theory of the Earth* (1684) typifies seventeenth-century impressions of mountains as spectacles of horror and chaos, or as excrescences of a cursed upheaval consequent to the expulsion from Eden. In Milton's *Paradise Lost* (1667) the fallen angels roam an infernal Alpine topology:

> Through many a dark and dreary dale
> They pass'd, and many a region dolorous
> O'er many a frozen, many a fiery alp;
> Rocks, caves, lakes, fens, bogs, dens, and shades of death.[2]

More equivocal post-medieval imaginations had fathomed mountains either as abyssal diabolic chasms or holy summits for ascetic purification.[3] From mountain purgatories to John Ruskin's notion of Alpine *paradiso terrestre* there is a radical perceptual and conceptual leap. The pinnacles that are in Ruskin's redaction "the beginning and the end of all natural scenery" affirm vertiginous virtue in the scale of the beauty and moral quality of art, architecture, and society. His aesthetics of the Alpine sublime may be summed up in the architectonic formula: "Mountains are the cathedrals of the earth."[4]

Ironically, mountain *mentalité* begins to shift in the very apocalyptic rhapsodies of Burnet's *The Sacred Theory*, for in reconciling his elation to disgust, theology to science, and geology to Genesis, Burnet posits the Alps an "inchanted Country" in terms that anticipate the sublime:

> There is something august and stately in the Air of these things, that inspires the mind with great thoughts and passions [because] for whatsoever hath but the shadow and appearance of INFINITE, as all things have that are too big for our comprehension, they fill and overbear the mind with their Excess, and cast it into a pleasing kind of stupor and admiration.[5]

To rationalize this cosmogony, he concludes that the "wild, vast and undigested Heaps of Stones" must be the "ruins of a broken world" left by the receding waters of the flood. They have to be post-Noachian, for of course Genesis records no orogeny (or mountain formation). There are reminiscences of Burnet in Burke, Wordsworth, Coleridge, and Shelley, all of whom contribute to changing attitudes toward mountains during the Romantic period, retaining a recurrent if vestigial ethical dimension in the "aesthetics of the infinite."[6]

The classical concept of the "sublime" is revived and extended by Edmund Burke in *A Philosophical Enquiry into Our Ideas of the Sublime and the Beautiful* (1757).[7] This influential treatise structures ocular and epistemic encounters with nature along physiological and psychological lines. While images of beauty rest on pleasurable sensations, Burke declares, sublimity is defined by feelings of "astonishment" in terror, real or imagined, irresistible force, obscurity, the privations of solitude, silence, loudness (such as in cataracts), ruggedness, immensity, and mountain vastness:

> No passion so effectually robs the mind of all its powers of acting and reasoning as fear, for fear being an apprehension of pain and death, it operates in a manner that resembles actual pain. Whatever therefore is terrible, with regard to sight too is sublime, whether this cause of terror be endured with greatness of dimension or not.[8]

These ingredients were evident in the sensations that travelers, painters, and writers experienced among summits. However, the Augustan theories postulated by William Gilpin opposed Burke's psychological distinctions by incorporating the tensions of beauty and sublimity in a blend of correspondent if contradictory qualities, in which the sublime is absorbed into the picturesque.[9] Telluric (i.e. earth-related) receptions of the sublime are therefore first shaped through the distensions and perplexities of the picturesque, and the word "sublime" itself is diffused, overused, and exchanged everywhere to the extent that, like the "picturesque," it could be pressed into almost any unfocused connotation.[10] I use the term "geo-poetics" to define a particular kind of sublime, a fervent cult of orographic sensibility in the cultural landscapes of the Swiss and Savoyard Alps. This notion of *terribilità* demands a fusion of ethics and aesthetics and intuits a paradoxical dynamic between metaphysics and natural science. These responses derive from subjective and objective interventions in nature to elicit or absorb mountains as the chief vehicle of psychological experience. Out of Alpine rootstock grows the transformation from landscape to inscape, where apprehensions of the visible dissolve into the invisible by harnessing spiritual instinct and physical faculty. The geo-poetic archetype results from an interpenetration of matter and psyche, in which earthly reality unveils divine essences that take on idealist or Neoplatonic features. And classical stylistics of unity, proportion, and coherence are disrupted by the aesthetics of disharmony or fragmentation.

That *sublimis* denotes "uplifting" and "lofty," makes for a ready affinity between mountains and the sublime, especially as *altitudo* implies both height and depth. In this new sensibility, politics are glossed with the Romantic validation of nature, and nature itself aestheticized in symbolic archetypes. The period between 1789 and 1800 marks a watershed in apprehensions of nature: while the French Revolution is enacted in the name of reason and nature, Burke's *Reflections of the Revolution in France* (1790) imports sublime nature into the idea of the State. Mountain power and "otherness," whether of transcendental or geomorphic origin, are deployed to sanction and authorize identity and ideology. The Alpine sublime is interpreted by writers and artists in ways that affect both radical and conservative politics.

The enduring prestige of verbal and visual texts testifies to geo-poetic veneration during the period of Revolution and Romanticism. Ruskin is the most incisive exponent of the Alpine sublime for the Anglo-American nineteenth century. After German and English Romantic poets, and Turner and Ruskin, the Alps become a natural and aesthetic trope for physical and mental heights. As a contrast to Turner, I consider the pictorial language of Caspar David Friedrich, whose sublimity of the mind's eye evinces various Romantic themes in early nineteenth-century German political culture. Turner and Friedrich are contemporaries, both are antagonistic to naturalism, but they approach mountains from opposite though revealing directions that illustrate the triangulation of the intellect, corporeal nature, and the Godhead inherent in theories of the sublime. In Turner, the mountain antedates symbol, the natural object acquiring subjective values; in Friedrich, symbolic meaning precedes the mountain, where mystery is subjectively schematized in the object of nature. Turner's visceral scrutiny aspires to capture nature's *energeia*, that is, its capacity for endless change overlaying the eternal; Friedrich's still-life symmetries are imbued with the sublime of the "Jetztzeit," the everlasting now beyond time, where eternity becomes a permanent present in the union of man and earth. On the margins of vision and history, his world is a domain beyond itself. For Turner and Ruskin, Alpine communion is not a passive reception but an active conception of the entelechy of nature. Geo-poetics are inscribed in the reciprocal motion of the subject and object, the transcendental and the immanent.

I shall begin my examination of this renewal of mountain perception with *Sketches of the Natural, Civil, and Political State of Swisserland* (1779) by William Coxe and conclude with Ruskin's *Modern Painters*, published between 1843 and 1860.[11] Additionally, I will show how the Helvetic mythos, from which geo-poetics emerge is composed through the genetic texts of Albrecht von Haller and Jean-Jacques Rousseau, who endorse the picturesque landscape of moral sentiment, and through Horace-Bénédict de Saussure, whose work distils the geomorphology of the Alpine sublime. Indeed, de Saussure's influence runs like a major leitmotiv through late eighteenth- and nineteenth-century images of Switzerland.

That Switzerland becomes a cynosure of primitive sublimity, and the Alps the focus of a metamorphic charisma, is telling. The Grand Tour evolves into a sacred quest for Helvetia, textually conjectured as "classic ground" for the stylistics of discovery, reinvention, and appropriation by traveler-writers. Between 1770 and 1800 thousands of descriptive sketches, poetic travelogues, *veduti*, Alpine itineraries, relations, personal narratives, journals, tracts, guidebooks, reportage, *vade mecums*, and annotated folio plates of prospects were published in English, German, and French, and frequently translated. So pivotal is the fashion of these "dithyrambes helvetiques," refracted through the prism of epistolary texts among wayfarers and cultural pilgrims, that Johannes Bürkli declares with irony in 1793 that "Gleich als ob es ein Verbrechen wäre zu sterben, ohne die Schweiz gesehen zu haben." (It were as though a crime to die without having seen Switzerland.)[12]

It was on the canvas of this reinvented country that the landscape of the sublime was drawn. Coxe's *Travels in Switzerland* (1790), a three-volume synoptic compendium that Turner read before his tour of 1802, famously applied picturesque theories to Swiss topography. However, it was another handbook by Coxe, *Sketches of the Natural, Civil, and Political State of Swisserland*, published in 1779 (the same year as the first volume of de Saussure's *Voyages dans les Alpes*[13]) that helped to establish Helvetic mythography. Through its translation into French, and paratextual insertions, this book made the most significant impact on the epoch for the Alpine sublime among both British and European voyagers.

The impetus of the French Revolution in these circuits ramified and problematized European travel writing and literature from observations of "living manners" into political contentions and the dislocation of religious and secular hierarchies. The acclamations of sentiment, satire, and sex that travel afforded writers about Switzerland change after 1789 into metonyms more tragic and elegiac, whereby the picturesque yields to images with a revolutionary edge. The original admiration for the "dream republic" is sublimated toward the idea of an absolute landscape, in which the association of nature and ideology mutates from conservative to revolutionary nostalgia, and geo-poetics implicate geo-politics. Second, as an adjunct of the Romantic reaction, individual transcendence replaces revolutionary disorder with conditions of wonder.

Swiss liminal spaces are first classicized and then romanticized in seamless transitions that construct an iconography of the sublime. The forms and functions of the Alpine landscape claim a new ontology where and when geology extends the artist or traveler's repertoire of sensation beyond the canons of the picturesque. The mythopoesis of Alpine topography develops through a nexus of literary and visual images. While sublimity reaches for the immanence of earthly passions, textual semiotics address Alpine realities. Some of these key writings include Coleridge's "Hymn before Sun-rise, in the Vale of Chamouni" (1802); Byron's poetic travelogue *Childe Harold's Pilgrimage* (1812–18) and *Manfred* (1817); and Shelley's "Mont Blanc: Lines Written in the Vale of Chamouni" (1817), *Alastor* (1816), and *Prometheus Unbound* (1820). From Goethe's three trips, including a visit to de Saussure in 1779, came *Die Leiden des jungen Werthers* (The sorrows of young Werther, 1774), *Briefe aus der Schweiz* (*Letters from Switzerland*, 1796), dramatic monologues in part 2 of *Faust* (1832), and sections of *Dichtung und Wahrheit* (Poetry and truth, 1775).

Poets and painters viewed nature in a chain of images, interpreting topography and ethnography through a mosaic of pictures and popular prints that received wide circulation around Europe. These included the engravings by Abraham Wagner's *Merkwürdige Prospekte aus den Schweizer-Gebürgen und derselben Beschreibung*, circulated widely as *Vues remarquables des montagnes de la Suisse* (Notable views of the mountains of Switzerland, 1776), edited by Haller and based on his writings, and the *Tableaux topographiques, pittoresques, physiques, historiques, moraux, politiques, littéraires de la Suisse* (Topographic, picturesque, physical, historical, moral, political, and literary scenes of Switzerland, 1780–86) by Jean-Benjamin de Laborde and Baron Zurlauben. Haller's didactic eclogue, "Die Alpen," first published in 1732, is a precursor of Alpine sublimity.[14] It refigures *Alpes Helveticae* in a marriage of poetry and science, shifting its viewpoint from the chasms of a post-Deluge fallen world to a "paradis montagne," where the glacial *topos horribilis* conjoins the *locus amoenus*, the "happy garden" of orchards and shepherds of the valleys and foothills. Haller's natural idyll embraces the pivotal argument that the Golden Age has survived and flourishes in the noble stoicism of a pastoral ecology. This redemptive landscape, inseparable from political freedom and natural ethics, derides and denies luxury and civilization. The savage precipices that alarmed the tourist shield the honest, placid, industrious mountain people from perdition. Atavistic, autochtonous verities of the terrain embody a self-reflexive allegory weighted with moral philosophy. They unfold a divine presence in the deformed bleakness of a country dismissed by Johann Georg Zimmermann in 1755 as a "mountain with thirteen cantons 'to right and left, like chamois, on the cliffs.'"[15] After Haller's didactic synthesis, the earlier sylvan and satiric panoramas of Arcadia transform into bucolic preeminence. It is important to note, however, that in Haller, while mountains shape the "gifts of Nature," they have yet to achieve a sublime teleology. Such geomorphic emphasis would arrive with de Saussure. Similarly, for earlier travelers to Mont Blanc, mountains were not themselves the primary objects;

indeed they were barely noticed except as unimportant details of the picturesque setting. The strangeness of altitude and glacier were certainly beguiling, but these travelers lacked insight into the geo-poetic sublimity of what they surveyed. Interestingly, Kant asserts that Haller's depiction of the sublime falls short of the "transcendental ideal."[16]

Haller's Alpine purism is, however, no less exotically transformative for adventurers than are transoceanic expeditions around the globe, and it carries over into notions of perfect harmony for the international Grand Tourist, absorbing the Helvetic periphery into the European core. On Goethe's recommendation, for instance, Alexander von Humboldt voyages across Switzerland before journeying to South America. Wordsworth's *Descriptive Sketches* (1793) and the Alpine spiritual catharsis in book 6 of *The Prelude* (1805) are but two other inflections of Haller, transfused through Coxe, Ramond de Carbonnières, and de Saussure, visualizing Wordsworth's first reception of Switzerland as an innocent wilderness, akin to images of ethnographic virtue perceived in the New World.[17]

Haller's portrayal of simple, frugal folk, unfettered by civility and unsullied by vileness, foreshadows Rousseau's primitivist theories and the "noble savage." The Swiss exceptionalism that Rousseau nurtured in exile and propagated in *Julie: ou la nouvelle Héloïse* (Julie: or the new Heloise, 1781) derived its categories from the Zeitgeist of the Natural Man as *homo alpinus*: "their manner of living, their simplicity, their equanimity, and that peaceful tranquillity that makes them happy through freedom from pain rather than taste for pleasures."[18] Rousseau's conjugation of exhilaration and eroticism in the Valais is astoundingly potent for British writers and travelers in Switzerland, for having assimilated English literary influences, including the "jardin anglais" (English garden), *La nouvelle Héloïse* reflects them back in creating a pre-Alpine mise-en-scène for moral and political discourses.[19] Indeed, this novel's conjunctions of "Anglomanie" and Helvetomania, in a pastoral picturesque ethos, emphasized its appeal to such travel writers as Coxe and satisfied the expectations of British readers. Rousseau's descriptions avoid geological details of glacier and crag; he is more concerned with natural anthropology, and the regional topography in his *Confessions* or the *Letter to M. d'Alembert* on the theater is equally vague and formless. The sublime is for him an emotional response to mountains held in the mind. Overwhelmed by feeling, reason cannot comprehend what it knows. Through such panaromic ethereal ecstasies as St. Preux displays in part 1, letter 23, Rousseau helps to foster in individuals who survey mountains a sentimental savoir-vivre, which lifts them above "base earthly sentiments" toward imperishable purity: "high in the mountains where air is pure and subtle, one breathes more freely, one feels lighter in the body, more serene of mind; pleasures there are less intense, passions more moderate. Meditations there take on an indescribably grand and sublime character."[20] Rousseau speaks thus of the devastating sensations associated with sublime heights: "The spectacle has something indescribably magical, supernatural about it that ravishes the spirit and the senses; you forget everything, even yourself, and do not even know where you are."[21] In the interplay between novels, itineraries, and poem-travelogues, orographic experience assumes a ritual of reality and nostalgia, where Anglo-German and Latin spirits comingle. Switzerland marks the borderline between Northern approaches and yearning for the "cult of the South" born of a persistent *fatigue du nord*.

Another dimension to an understanding of the sublime may be gathered from Schiller, whose explanation of the "sentimental" as the lost oneness of man and nature shapes Goethe's spiritual landscapes. As a solitary wanderer among the Alps, Goethe finds in mountain prospects the means to restore that moral union. The division between "Vorstellungen" (representations) and "Empfindungen" (perceptions) in Schiller's essay *Über naive und sentimentalische Dichtung* (On naive and sentimental poetry, 1795) is resolved in the aesthetics of the sublime, in which nature's vital powers instil in the "traveler of perception" a cognitive integrity through a state of marvel.[22] In a burst of Sturm und Drang sensibility, Goethe reaches for this exalted sense of the Godhead in *Die Leiden des jungen Werthers*, bewilderment transposed from philosophy into a locus of physical substance:

> Ungeheure Berge umgaben mich, Abgründe lagen vor mir, und Wetterbäche stürzten herunter die Flüsse strömten unter mir, und Wald und Gebirg erklang; und ich sah sie wirken und schaffen ineinander in den Tiefen der Erde, alle die unergründlichen Kräfte.[23]
>
> [Stupendous mountains encompassed me; precipices were before my feet; torrents fell by the side of me; impetuous rivers ran through the plain; rocks and mountains resounded from afar; and in the depths of the earth I saw innumerable powers in motion, multiplying to infinity.][24]

Coxe's *Sketches of the Natural, Civil and Political State of Swisserland* (1779) uses *La nouvelle Héloïse* as a travelogue, noting the "wonderful and sublime works of nature" marked with ardor and despair.[25] The *Sketches* both drew attention to the Alpine and rustic ethos and, more importantly, linked it to a cogent account of the Swiss *res publica*. English writers had for a century admired the country as an example of resistance to tyranny. And, in the manner of Haller, Coxe reads Swiss topography in classical terms, for here, as in Britain, ancient Roman virtues still abide. Consciously or not, this refers to Joseph Addison's essay, where Helvetia's "paradise amid the wildness" allegorizes the "landscape of freedom." Pulling together the underlying connections between the ineffable "picturesque" terrain and its primordial democrats, Coxe avers that "Nature designed Switzerland for the seat of freedoms."[26] With Coxe, the Helvetic "classic ground" is identified with the "British ground" of patriotic and Protestant attitudes and values.

The French translation of the *Sketches* as *Lettres de M. William Coxe à M. W. Melmoth, sur l'Etat politique, civil et naturel de la Suisse* in 1781 by Louis-François Ramond de Carbonnières makes a significant contribution to the mystique of the Alpine sublime.[27] Ramond was himself a mountain traveler and an accomplished writer on the existential power of the Pyrenees, whose optical and sensuous effects testified that "deep time" is embedded in mountains beyond any calibration of human history. Ramond's translation of Coxe is remarkable for his own augmented paratextual relation smuggled into the *Sketches* through extensive commentary and "Notes du traducteur" (remarks by the translator). Ramond replaces Coxe's anecdotal observations with percipient Romantic expression, his discussion of mountain topography overlaying Coxe's extempore classicizing platitudes with the descriptive beauty and orogeny that de Saussure brought to the sublime in his *Voyages dans les Alpes*. In a long segment of "Observations du traducteur sur les glacières et les glaciers,"[28] he acknowledges de Saussure's theories and, with ironical intelligence and far-sightedness prefiguring later nineteenth-century debates, examines Alpine glaciation with a sense of realism. In contrast to Hallerian eclogues about the mountains, he highlights for the traveler the hazardous actualities of ice and avalanche. Ramond inquires whether nature has an active, purposive *physis* underlying its normative forms and thereby anticipates the traveler-aesthete's restatement of the Swiss idyll toward the geo-poetic sublime. The redeeming qualities of liberty and virtue defined by Rousseau linger, but Ramond reworks Coxe's travelogue beyond its picturesque limitations and the conventional British outlook on mountains.[29] Ramond's work is part of a self-conscious artistic search to refine a new ideal from the truer perception of geological realities and their unearthly sensations. The historiography of mountain perception describes a full circle, for the self-same heights that terrified the wayfarer in search of picturesque "stations" have now been redeemed as ecstatic extensions of God's grandeur. As Claire-Eliane Engel argues, Ramond was the first Romantic poet of mountains and stands with de Saussure in the reorientation that announces a new age.[30] Cuthbert Girdlestone baptized this hybrid "Coxe-Ramond," but "Ramond-Coxe" seems more apposite, for it was the translator's antithetical and philosophical rewriting of the original, and not Coxe's original work, that most impinged upon the era. Girdlestone is closer to the mark in saying that Ramond is "un romantique allemand de langue française, le seul qui ait existé" (a German romantic in the French language, the only one of his kind that existed).[31]

Dissatisfied with the Swiss "Elysium," Helen Maria Williams offers an insurgent and feminizing counterpoint, adapting the Alpine sublime to her own revolutionary purposes. Williams appends to *A Tour in Switzerland* (1798)[32] her translation, *Observations on the Glacières, and the Glaciers, by*

M. Ramond, as a geological coda to the book's political and cultural survey. Williams's *Tour*, which almost coincides with the French invasion of Switzerland in 1798, projects yearning and opprobrium in equal measure toward the Swiss Confederation, insisting on a different kind of "translation" from male to female scrutiny, and from eulogy to critique. A mélange of *Realpolitik* and sentiment, *A Tour in Switzerland* runs counter to the received idealization of the Helvetic cultural landscape, and even to her own previous acceptance of the Swiss idyll gained through the texture of travel writers, including John Moore's *A View of Society and Manners in France, Switzerland and Germany*.[33] The first volume declares her intention to repose her "wearied spirit on those sublime objects":

> to sooth my desponding heart with the hope that the moral disorder I have witnessed shall be rectified, while I gaze on nature in all her admirable perfections; and how delightful a transition shall I find in the picture of social happiness which Switzerland presents! I shall no longer see liberty profaned and violated; here she smiles upon the hills, and decorates the vallies [*sic*], and finds, in the uncorrupted simplicity of this people, a firmer barrier than in the cragginess of their rocks, or the snows of their Glaciers! (1:4–5)

This initial innocence finds its experiential climax of "visionary architecture" always "at the foot of an Alpine hill, [where] a torrent stream rolls invisibly past the dwelling, and an enormous glacier lifts its snows in the neighbourhood" (2:277). However, in between these two exultations, Williams is much disappointed. While the geography of Valais remains unaltered, virtuous enlightenment has perished into ignorance, injustice, avarice, superstition, immorality, and oligarchical despotism: "All in nature is still romantic, wild, and graceful, as Rousseau has painted it; but the soothing charm associated with moral feeling, is in some sort dissolved" (2:180). Her contention is that Switzerland is in need of the "general resurrection to liberty" (1:119) that the French occupation would soon impose anyway when revolutionary élan was deflected into Bonapartist conquest. Although British opinion generally saw the invasion as a violation of the "region of liberty," Williams sets out to vindicate Napoleon's motives in trying to install a puppet regime. In order to countervail conservative panegyrics to the civic probity of the cantons, she mocks Coxe's accolades of its political culture and attacks Burke's hyperbolic comment in *Reflections on the Revolution in France* "that the Republic of Berne is one of the happiest, most prosperous, and best governed countries on earth" (2:205).

The narrative of the "Natural History in Switzerland" in the second volume is a prolonged political propaganda which promotes the release and liberation of consciousness. Williams opposes what travel writers had before identified as the topographical and moral virtues of Switzerland. Just as intertextual inferences to the wretchedness of the inhabitants and their oppressive polity deconstruct the Swiss political fabric, so Ramond's work is appended to subvert bucolic platitudes through the coded republican (and autocratic) austerity of glacier and crag. The precipitous power of cataracts and torrents provides natural figurations of radical energies. As Theresa Kelley has noted in writing about the motif of Alpine cascades in Wordsworth's work, contemporaries would have caught the inferential association of the French Revolution as a "torrent révolutionnaire."[34] In 1796 Napoleon had addressed his Army of Italy on entering Milan thus: "You have precipitated yourselves, like a torrent, from the heights of the Apennines; you have overthrown and scattered all that opposed your march."[35] Within the same synchronic and diachronic moment, it is the power of the earth itself that traces for Williams the correspondence between a lost past and a better future. Ramond is part of a perceptual shift brought about by the impact of geological science, and by using his writings Williams places natural and cultural toponyms at the service not only of political revolution but of a Romantic Neoplatonism.[36] Seemingly, high mountains at once arrest and drive the forces of history. For those who fled the terror of Robespierre's "mountain" in France for the consolation of the Alps, the sempiternal sublimity of geology attests to nature's endurance over the mutabilities of politics in Paris or Geneva. Geo-poetics recuperate nature as "feeling" from the wreck of revolutionary longings. This metaphysical search for radical affirmation provides an aesthetic context for the disruptions of the Alpine sublime.

Turner further illustrates the amorphous boundary between geo-poetics and the political history of mountains. His impressionistic masterpiece *Snowstorm: Hannibal and His Army Crossing the Alps* (1812) is more than a landscape: it speaks to the analogies of the Revolutionary wars. The classical motif of Hannibal's traverse of the Alps was imported into the myth of Napoleon as an invincible, irresistible force, especially after in his transalpine exploits and invasion of Switzerland and Tyrol. Numerous French poems and pictures portrayed Napoleon as Hannibal's avatar. However, Turner's sublime treatment of the subject creates a modern perspective beyond heroic history painting. Turner had privately viewed Jacques-Louis David's epic *Napoleon at the St Bernard Pass* (1800–1801), and his painting associates ironically the two vanquished conquerors, the mountains silently witnessing their daring, vainglorious endeavors that are doomed to failure in an image of history and transience.[37]

Less historicist than Turner, Friedrich looks upon Napoleon as the Anti-Christ incarnate, and the invader of his native Pomerania. In his work, nature's divine immanence is summoned to defy imperial hubris and signal a German national resurgence through victory over the French.[38] Friedrich's allegorical version of the sublime in *Der Watzmann* (1824–25) pits the form of timeless mountain against the evanescence of human power. And the *Riesengebirgslandschaft mit aufsteigendem Nebel* (1820)

(Riesengebirge landscape with rising mist) probably alludes to the earthly paradise in Genesis: "Aber ein Nebel ging auf von der Erde und feuchtete alles Land" (But there went up a mist from the earth, and watered the whole face of the ground).[39] Unlike Turner, who engaged directly with material nature, Friedrich did not paint his mountain landscapes, for all the sharpness of their external drama, from nature in the Alps, but from the "Stimmung" (mood) within himself, and possibly from sketches supplied by Carl Gustav Carus. *Der Watzmann*, for example, was painted from a watercolor.[40] Their esoteric, elegiac bleakness articulates a compelling theater of a specifically German-Christian culture, offering a composite "Gefühl" (reverential perception) of organic forms, what Carus calls in Letter VIII the "Erdleben-Bildkunst," or earth-life paintings.[41] The transactions between the subjective mind and objective nature are grounded and fulfilled in the divine.

An important and representative inheritor of the Alpine sublime is Wordsworth, who on his pedestrian Continental journey of 1790 carries the "Ramond-Coxe" version as his guide. His notes to *Descriptive Sketches* report his debt to this work, including the sentence: "For most of the images in the next sixteen verses I am indebted to M. Raymond's interesting observations annexed to his translation of Coxe's Tour in Switzerland." Adapted from the "Observations du traducteur" on mountain mysteries, the lines in question include:

> 'Tis his with fearless step at large to roam
> Thro' wastes, of Spirits wing'd the solemn home
> Thro vacant worlds where Nature never gave
> A brook to murmur or a bough to wave,
> Which insubstantial Phantoms sacred keep;
> Thro' worlds where Life and Sound, and Motion sleep;
> Where Silence still her death-like reign extends,
> Save when the startling cliff unfrequent rends:
> In the deep snow the mighty ruin drown'd,
> Mocks the dull ear of Time with deaf abortive sound[42]

After his crossing the Alps, Wordsworth's discovery of the sublime, recorded in *The Prelude* as the "types and symbols of eternity,"[43] at once marks a redirection from republican idealism toward a natural revolution, and his overthrowing of the tyranny of the picturesque. In their revolutionary energies, mountain topologies signify the paradoxical epitome of liberty and authority, while the Alpine destination itself engenders its own paradigm.[44] His note to the poem indicates how it was first conceived of as "Picturesque Sketches," but that "the Alps are insulted" by that term, for, "Whoever, in attempting to describe their sublime features, should confine himself to the cold rules of painting would give his reader but a very imperfect idea of those emotions which they have the irresistible power of communicating to the most impassive imagination."[45]

For Wordsworth the quintessence of orographic nature is therefore infused with a mind in search of a mountain adequate to its idea of the sublime.[46] Despite the poem's ambivalences, natural and republican values are in 1790 commensurate with Wordsworth's self-inscribed, if unintentional, rite of passage through the Simplon Pass. According to Arthur Beatty, Ramond's essays were "the ruling ideas and the general ordering of the poem,"[47] and formulate the poet's attempt to invoke a natural basis for the French Revolution. In retrospect, the "Crossing of the Alps" announces his revisionist transposition into another mode of existence and religion for which mountains hold eternal truths cognate with reason.[48] Ramond had stated that nothing distracts or misleads the mind gazing on the colossal magnitude and eternal silence of these sublime objects that were beyond the abyss of time. "The Imagination seizes hold where Reason falls, and in that long succession of epochs, glimpses an image of eternity which it enters with religious terror."[49] For Wordsworth such immensities become transcendent; he writes in Book 13 of the revised *Prelude* of the mist dissolving to show the Wanderer the mysterious life that underlies ordinary existence:

> A meditation rose in me that night
> Upon the lonely mountain when the scene
> Had passed away, and it appeared to me
> The perfect image of a mighty mind,
> Of one that feeds on infinity.[50]

These words share both the Romantic *topoi* and the symbolic aura that exudes from Friedrich's *Der Wanderer über dem Nebelmeer* (Wanderer above a sea of fog, 1818). As Koerner shows, it is Wordsworth's poetry that most closely approaches Friedrich's work in its "dual emphasis on the radical specificity of nature, and the constitutive role of an intervening subjectivity."[51] In his second letter on landscape painting, Carus epitomizes this geognostic conjunction of the Alpine sublime: "Climb to the topmost mountain peak, gaze across long chains of hills," he writes, and "There is a silent reverence within you; you lose yourself in infinite space; silently, your whole being is purified and cleansed; your ego disappears. *You are nothing; God is all.*"[52]

In early-nineteenth-century art, the paintings of Turner and Friedrich exemplify the intersubjective tensions of geo-poetics. After his Swiss tour of 1802 during the French incursion, Turner takes the pictorial sublime beyond Burkean subjectivism toward psychology and orography. We can locate the grandeur and desolation of geo-poetics in Turner's *The Passage at Mount St. Gotthard* (1804), where the anti-picturesque lack of foreground plunges the onlooker into a brooding abyss (fig. 1). The truth to

Fig. 1. J. M. W. Turner, The Passage at Mount St. Gotthard (Taken from the Centre of the Teufels Brücke) *1804. Abbot Hall Art Gallery, Kendal, UK.*

nature is rooted in the sheer materiality of landscape.[53] Friedrich also banishes the conventional foreground in *Der Wanderer über dem Nebelmeer* (fig. 2) but toward a vastly different conclusion. This picture is iconic for the "Rückenfigur" (back view) of the Kantian image of a man isolated in existential vertigo. He stands on the mountain summit, contemplating with rapt awe the infinite spaces between the sandstone peaks and swirling

Fig. 2. Caspar David Friedrich, Der Wanderer über dem Nebelmeer, *1818. Kunsthalle, Hamburg, Germany.*

clouds. But if for Kant the sublime is the perception of nature in process, the figure in *Der Wanderer* represents the spectator in the process of perceiving the sublime in nature. Expressive of the mood's moment, melancholy and fugitive, the sublime is composed vicariously in the viewer's imagination. It is a stylistic paradox that Friedrich's linear clarity and exactitude of treatment cultivate an indeterminacy of "Stimmung," one that oscillates between subject and object, the noumena and phenomena. *Der Wanderer* orders "harmonically" the multiplicity and cognitive randomness of nature, while the imagination acts on the nebulous in pursuit of illumination. Indeed, this painting objectifies, for such latecomers as Nietzsche, psychological mountain criteria for transformative joy in the Dionysian self-realization of the will. A passage in *Also sprach Zarathustra* (1883–85) echoes the self-sublimation in Friedrich's painting: "Ich bin ein Wanderer und ein Bergsteiger, sagte er zu seinem Herzen, ich liebe die Ebenen nicht und es scheint, ich kann nicht lange still sitzen." (I am a wanderer and mountain climber, he said to his heart, I do not love the plains, and it seems I cannot long sit still.)[54] And changing standards of stylistic taste would later redeem Friedrich's metaphysics (and Turner's elemental geo-poetics) as Romantic forerunners of twentieth-century expressionist art in Europe and the United States.[55]

Ruskin would assert of Turner's pictures of the Alpine sublime that the artist had "made them before geology existed; but it is only by help of geology that I can prove their power" (26:102). Friedrich is uninterested in geological intricacies, preferring an allegorical formulation of "die romantische Stimmungslandschaft" (the landscape of Romantic mood) where topology is imagined as typology. If Turner's desolate sublime is detached from humanity, Friedrich's *Kreuz im Gebirge* (Crufix in the mountains, 1812) construes topography as itself the sacred object, its poignant "Weltgefühl" (communion with the created world) reflected through the soul, primal nature the vehicle for the supernatural. Interestingly, by making the cathedral in the painting into a mountain, its Gothic iconography echoing natural forms, Friedrich reverses Ruskin's dictum that "mountains are the cathedrals of the earth."[56]

Initially impelled by the lyrical theorems of de Saussure's *Voyage dans les Alpes*, Ruskin is the period's most fervent propagator of geo-poetics, and *Modern Painters* (1843–60) registers a climax in the cultural geography of Helvetica.[57] The optical asphyxia of mountain fever, which Ruskin inherits from Turner and the poets, reaches beyond the banalities of "sublimity tourism" toward the convergence of social and divine prospects. In an exegesis of God's hieroglyphs, geo-poetics predicate a moral force in accordance with what the age demands. *Modern Painters* proposes architecture as an index of the sanity of civilization, and in the dialectics of Ruskin's design, geomorphology becomes *Kulturmorphologie*. The Alps are no longer a secret Romantic place, but in Ruskin the theistic sublimation of mountain into architecture is taken beyond Romanticism, and his subtle vision of geology and human society affirms a singular moral imagination. (35:115) The Alpine sublime is continuous and contiguous with the Venetian Gothic, his architectural ideal, while the perceived is elevated to the conceptual and Ruskin constantly yearns for glimpses of a *civitas dei*. Mont Blanc and Venice are metonyms for the transvaluation of all aesthetics, and are made tangible in geo-poetic temples and templates of lucid stillness: "these great cathedrals of the earth, with their gates of rock, pavements of cloud, choirs of streams and stone, altars of snow, and vaults of purple traversed by the continual stars" (6:425).[58]

Indeed, Alpine-Venetian affinities predicate Ruskin's semiotics of *natura naturans*, the palpable rendering of visual geo-poetics. As he argues in the case of Turner's pictures, nature herself composed the Gothic architecture of Venice. Their abstract lines are not duplicates but *doubles* of Alpine heights because natural designs compel human imitations through their connection to eternal truths. Alpine epiphany meets architectural quintessence and provides a true touchstone for understanding the Venetian Gothic and creating geomorphic patterns for construction in Europe and North America.[59]

Ruskin's moral vista on the Alpine sublime also recognizes how it may be occluded by human vanity, the vulgarity of popular tourism, and a lewd contemporary paganism. What is implicit in "Mountain Gloom" of *Modern Painters* foreshadows the recent Swiss calamities that are beginning to rival the Bacchanalian disaster of Venice. There is a disjuncture between the aesthetics and the ethics of a lost Eden. He writes in *Sesame and Lilies*: "The French Revolutionists made stables of the Cathedrals of France; you have made race-courses of the cathedrals of the earth . . . the Alps themselves, which your own poets used to love so reverently, you look upon as soaped poles in a bear-garden, which you set yourselves to climb and slide down again, with 'shrieks of delight'" (18:89–90). Equivalent to the hedonism of art-for-art's-sake is nature-for-distraction's-sake. "Mountain Glory" acidly predicts in 1851 the decline of the Alpine sublime into macabre cosmopolitan chaos, simultaneously "atheistical, brutal and profane" (4:200).

> and I can foresee, within the perspective of but few years, the town of Lucerne consisting of a row of symmetrical hotels round the foot of the lake, its old bridges destroyed, an iron one built over the Reuss, and an acacia promenade carried along the lake-shore, with a German band playing under a Chinese temple at the end of it, and the enlightened travelers, representatives of European civilization, performing before the Alps, in each afternoon summer sunlight, in their modern manner, the Dance of Death. (6:456)

Beauty conjures tragedy in the face of accelerated social corrosion and moral degradation. The once-acute disparity between the "divine permanence" of mountains and the picturesque mouldering of human construction is blurred, response to natural landscape blunted, the redemptive motif of geo-poetics violated. The impious mentality of the Alpine Club substituted conquest for the sublime. And mountain reverence was eventually despoiled by the earth sciences, which eliminated the numinous from nature and separated natural theology from geology. Nevertheless, despite these vicissitudes and depredations, an after-life of the Alpine sublime and its cultural history still persisted. When the frames of reference of sublimity no longer served contemporary psychological or political needs, the mountain archetype of interdependent paradoxes, through the writings and visual images of Ruskin and his followers, triumphed and transferred into the nineteenth-century Gothic revival, whose arts and architecture continued to bear the geo-poetic imprint.

Notes

[1] Thomas Burnet, *The Sacred Theory of the Earth*, 4th ed. (London: John Hooke, 1719), 1:198. (The Latin version first appeared in 1681 as *Telluris Theoria Sacra*.)

[2] John Milton, *Paradise Lost*, ed. Alastair Fowler (London: Longman, 1972), 118–19.

[3] See Marjorie Hope Nicolson, *Mountain Gloom and Mountain Glory* (1959; repr., Seattle: U of Washington P, 1997).

[4] E. T. Cook and Alexander Wedderburn, eds., *The Works of John Ruskin* (London: George Allen, 1903–12), 6:425 and 6:457. All in-text references are to this 39 volume edition.

[5] Burnet, *The Sacred Theory*, 191–92.

[6] Coleridge envisaged turning the prose poetry of *The Sacred Theory* into epic verse. Wordsworth included Burnet in his notes to *The Excursion*. Shelley's *Prometheus Unbound* (act 4) contains echoes of Burnet. See also John Wyatt, *Wordsworth and Geologists* (Cambridge: Cambridge UP, 2005), 45–50.

[7] Edmund Burke, *A Philosophical Enquiry into the Origin of Our Ideas of the Sublime and Beautiful*, new ed. (London: J. Dodsley, 1757).

[8] Burke, *A Philosophical Enquiry into the Origin of Our Ideas of the Sublime and Beautiful*, 42. Burke asserts here that the sublime is "the strongest emotion which the mind is capable of feeling."13.

[9] William Gilpin, *Observations, Relative Chiefly to Picturesque Beauty, Made in the Year 1772, on Several Parts of England; Particularly the Mountains and Lakes of Cumberland and Westmoreland*, 2 vols., 2nd ed. (London: R. Blamire, 1788). And *Three Essays: On the Picturesque Beauty; On Picturesque Travel; and On Sketching Landscape; to which is added a Poem, On Landscape Painting*, 3rd ed. (London: T. Cadell & W. Davies, 1808).

[10] Some modern accounts of the picturesque include Christopher Hussey, *The Picturesque: Studies in a Point of View* (London: Frank Cass, 1967); J. R. Watson, *Picturesque Landscape and English Romantic Poetry* (London: Hutchinson, 1970); and Sidney K. Robinson, *Inquiry into the Picturesque* (Chicago: U of Chicago P, 1991). Cf. George Landow, *The Aesthetic and Critical Theories of John Ruskin* (Princeton, NJ: Princeton UP, 1974). The complexities of the eighteenth-century

sublime are analyzed in Andrew Wilton, *Turner and the Sublime* (London: British Museum, 1980).

[11] William Coxe, *Sketches of the Natural, Civil and Political State of Swisserland* (London: J. Dodsley, 1779).

[12] *Gedichte über die Schweiz und über Schweizer* (Bern: Galler, 1793), vol. 1, i–ii. See also Stanley Mason, *The Alps: An English Translation* (Dübendorf, Zurich: De Clivo Press, 1986), 23.

[13] Horace-Bénédict de Saussure, *Voyages dans les Alpes: Précédés d'un essai sur l'histoire naturelle des environs de Genève*, 4 vols. (Neuchâtel, Switzerland: Fauche, 1779–96).

[14] It was first rendered into English by J. Howorth, *The Poems of Baron Haller* (London: J. Bell, 1794). Another contemporary version by Henry Barrett, *The Alps: A Moral and Descriptive Poem of the Great Haller* (London: Parsons) appeared in 1796. In 1710 Addison anticipated Haller by locating in the Alpine *locus desertus* the "happy fields" of a *hortus conclusus*. Joseph Addison, "Dream of the Region of Liberty," *Tatler*, 20 April, 1710, 291.

[15] Cited in Mason, *The Alps: An English Translation*, 22–23.

[16] Immanuel Kant, *Critique of Pure Reason,* part 2, trans. F. Max Müller (London: Macmillan, 1881), 526.

[17] William Wordsworth, *The Prelude: or Growth of a Poet's Mind* (1805 Text), ed. Ernest de Selincourt, revised by Stephen Gill (Oxford: Oxford UP, 1970), 97.

[18] Jean-Jacques Rousseau, *Julie: or the New Héloïse: Letters of Two Lovers Who Live in a Small Town at the Foot of the Alps*, trans. and annotated by Philip Steward and Jean Vache, *Collected Works of Rousseau*, vol. 6 (Hanover: UP of New England, 1997), 65. Cf. Walter Stutzer, *Jean-Jacques Rousseau und die Schweiz: Zur Geschichte des Helvetismus* (Zurich: Tages-Anzeiger, 1950), 65.

[19] Joseph Texte and J. W. Matthews highlight this theme in *Jean-Jacques Rousseau and the Cosmopolitan Spirit in Literature: A Study of the Literary Relations between France and England during the Eighteenth Century* (London: Duckworth, 1899).

[20] Rousseau, *Julie, or the New Héloïse*, 85–86.

[21] Rousseau, *Julie, or the New Héloïse*, 65.

[22] Friedrich Schiller, *On Naïve and Sentimental Poetry*, in *German Aesthetic and Literary Criticism: Winckelmann, Lessing, Hamann, Herder, Schiller, Goethe*, ed. H. B. Nisbet (Cambridge: Cambridge UP, 1985), 196.

[23] *Die Leiden des jungen Werthers*, in Goethe, *Werke*, vol. 12 (Stuttgart: J. G. Cotta, 1817), 76.

[24] Johann Wolfgang Goethe, *The Sorrows of Werter [sic]: A German Story*, trans. Daniel Malthus, new edition (London: J. Dodsley, 1784), vol. 1:141–42. This was the first English translation of *Werther*.

[25] William Coxe, *Sketches of the Natural, Civil and Political State of Swisserland*, 315.

[26] William Coxe, *Travels in Switzerland and in the Country of Grisons* (Basel: Decker, 1802), 53. Joseph Addison, "Dream of the Region of Liberty," 291–92.

[27] Louis-François Ramond de Carbonnières, trans., *Lettres de M. William Coxe à M. W. Melmoth, sur l'état politique, civil et naturel de la Suisse*, new edition (Paris: Belin, 1782).

[28] His own footnote draws the distinction: "I call *glacières* those mountain-points where snows gather: the term *glaciers* is given to the ice sheets that branch from that apex." Ramond de Carbonnières, *Lettres de M. William Coxe*, 2:96 (my translation).

[29] See Claire-Eliane Engel, *La littérature alpestre en France et en Angleterre au XVIIIe et XIXe Siècles* (Chambéry, France: Librairie Dardel, 1930), 80–81.

[30] See Engel, *La littérature alpestre*, 95.

[31] Cuthbert Girdlestone, *Poésie, Politique, Pyrénées: Louis-Francois Ramond, 1755–1827* (Paris: Minard, 1968), 60. See also 86–110. Coxe and Ramond are discussed in Simon Schama, *Landscape and Memory* (London: Harper Collins, 1995), 483–89; and Claude Reichler, "Ramond de Carbonnières avec et contre William Coxe," in *Le second voyage ou le déja-vu: Etudes réunies*, ed. François Moureau (Paris: Klinksieck, 1996), 39–40.

[32] Helen Maria Williams, *A Tour in Switzerland, or A View of the Present State of the Government and Manners of Those Cantons*, 2 vols. (London: G. G. & R. Robinson, 1798). All in-text references are to this edition.

[33] For example, Williams glorified Swiss "natural liberty" in the poem "An Epistle to Dr Moore, Author of A View of Society and Manners in France, Switzerland, and Germany" (1796).

[34] Theresa M. Kelley, *Wordsworth's Revolutionary Aesthetics* (Cambridge: Cambridge UP, 1988), 182. For Williams, see also Elizabeth A. Bohls, *Women Travel Writers and the Language of Aesthetics, 1716–1818* (Cambridge: Cambridge UP, 2004), 115; and Katherine Turner, *British Travel Writers in Europe, 1750–1800: Authorship, Gender and National Identity* (London: Ashgate, 2001), 223–24.

[35] *Napoleon's Addresses: Selections from the Proclamations, Speeches and Correspondence of Napoleon Bonaparte*, ed. Ida M. Tarbell (Boston: Joseph Knight, 1897), 36.

[36] For Shelley, too, in "Mont Blanc: Lines Written in the Vale of Chamouni" (1817), the politics of geomorphic Romanticism would supplant the failure of revolutionary hopes and Napoleonic dreams.

[37] See Lynn R. Matteson, "The Poetics and Politics of Alpine Passage: Turner's *Snowstorm: Hannibal and His Army Crossing the Alps*," *Art Bulletin*, 62, no. 3 (September 1980): 395. Andrew Wilton discusses Turner's fascination with Napoleon in a sublime context in *Turner and the Sublime*, 72–77. For another analysis of Turner, see Gerald E. Finley, "The Genesis of Turner's 'Landscape Sublime,'" in *Zeitschrift für Kunstgeschichte* 42, 2–3 (1979): 141–65.

[38] Schama, *Landscape and Memory*, 238–39.

[39] Genesis 2:6 in *Die Bibel: oder die ganze, Heilige Schrift des Alten und Neuen Testaments nach der deutschen Übersetzung D. Martin Luthers* (Halle: Druck und Verlag der Cansteinschen Bibelanstalt, 1900), 2. The English translation is from

the King James version, *The Holy Bible Containing the Old and New Testaments* (Cambridge: Cambridge UP, 1977), 2.

[40] In his memoirs Carus discusses Friedrich's working methods. See Carl Gustav Carus, *Nine Letters on Landscape Painting*, intro. Oskar Bätschmann, trans. David Britt (Los Angeles: Getty Research Institute, 2002), 33–36. Cf. Joseph Leo Koerner, *Caspar David Friedrich and the Subject of Landscape* (London: Reaktion, 2009), 219–20; and Sigrid Hinz, *Caspar David Friedrich in Briefen und Bekenntnissen* (Munich: Rogner and Bernhard, 1968), 202. Since he never visited Mont Blanc, the mountain in Coleridge's "Hymn before Sunrise, in the Valley of Chamouni" is similarly a textual sensation in the mind.

[41] Carus, *Nine Letters on Landscape Painting*, 131.

[42] William Wordsworth, *Descriptive Sketches: In Verse; Taken during a Pedestrian Tour in the Italian, Grison, Swiss, and Savoyard Alps* (London: J. Johnson, 1793). Also in E. de Sélincourt and E. Darbishire, eds., *The Poetical Works of William Wordsworth*, vol. 1 (Oxford: Oxford UP, 1963), 64. Cf. Duncan Wu, *Wordsworth's Reading, 1770–1799* (Cambridge: Cambridge UP, 1993).

[43] William Wordsworth, *The Prelude; or Growth of a Poet's Mind* (1805 Text), 100.

[44] See Keith Hanley, "Wordsworth's Grand Tour," in *Romantic Geographies: Discourses of Travel, 1775–1844*, ed. Amanda Gilroy (Manchester: Manchester UP, 2000), 71–92.

[45] Cf. Wordsworth's later comments in *A Complete Guide to the Lakes, Comprising Minute Directions for the Tourist with Mr Wordsworth's Description of the Scenery* (Kendal, UK: J. Hudson, 1846), passim.

[46] See also Geoffrey H. Hartman, "Wordsworth's *Descriptive Sketches* and the Growth of a Poet's Mind," *PMLA* 76, no. 5 (Dec. 1961): 519–27.

[47] Wordsworth, William, *Wordsworth: Representative Poems*, ed. Arthur Beatty (New York: Doubleday, 1937), 34.

[48] Kelley, *Wordsworth's Revolutionary Aesthetics*, 170–92; and Wyatt, *Wordsworth and the Geologists*, 54–56.

[49] Ramond, *Lettres de M. William Coxe à M. W. Melmoth*, vol. 2, 138. My translation.

[50] William Wordsworth, *The Prelude; or Growth of a Poet's Mind* (1805 Text), 230–31.

[51] Koerner, *Caspar David Friedrich*, 214. Wordsworth read William Taylor's translation of Goethe's eclogue "Der Wandrer" (1774) in 1798. See Wu, *Wordsworth's Reading*, 68.

[52] Carus, *Nine Letters on Landscape Painting*, 87.

[53] See David Hill, *Turner in the Alps: The Journey through France and Switzerland in 1802* (London: George Philip, 1992); and Ian Warrell, *Through Switzerland with Turner: Ruskin's First Selection from the Turner Bequest* (London: Tate Gallery, 1995). Cf. T. S. R. Boase, "English Artists and the Val d'Aosta," *Journal of the Warburg and Courtauld Institutes*, 19, nos. 3–4 (Jul.-Dec. 1956): 286–88.

⁵⁴ Friedrich Nietzsche, *Also sprach Zarathustra: Ein Buch für Alle und Keinen* (Leipzig: C. G. Naumann, 1899), 223.

⁵⁵ See Robert Rosenblum, *Modern Painting and the Northern European Tradition: Friedrich to Rothko* (New York: Harper & Row, 1977). Anna Jameson describes Friedrich in 1834 as one of the "most *poetical* of the German landscape painters": "He is rather a mannerist in color, like Turner, but in the opposite excess. His genius revels in gloom, as that of Turner revels in light." Anna Jameson, *Visits and Sketches at Home and Abroad*, vol. 1 (London: Saunders and Otley, 1834), 144. See also Charles Sala, *Caspar David Friedrich: The Spirit of Romantic Painting* (Paris: Terrail, 1994), 55–67.

⁵⁶ Friedrich's technique falls into what Ruskin condemned as the "pathetic fallacy," that is, the loss of nature's truth through the subjective attribution of fanciful emotions to its forms. He dismissed "German dullness and English affectation" for spreading "two of the most objectionable words that were ever coined by the troublesome of metaphysicians, — namely, 'Objective,' and 'Subjective.'" Ruskin, *Works*, 5:201.

⁵⁷ The key text here is *Modern Painters*, containing the sections "Of the Sculpture of Mountains," "The Mountain Gloom," and "The Mountain Glory." Ruskin, *Works*, vol. 4.

⁵⁸ See Anthony Ozturk, "Geo-Aesthetics: Venice and the Architecture of the Alps," in *John Ruskin and Nineteenth Century Cultural Travel*, ed. Keith Hanley and Emma Sdegno (Venice: Le Bricole: Università Ca' Foscari, 2010), 187–211.

⁵⁹ Virginia L. Wagner discusses Ruskin's transatlantic influences in "John Ruskin and Artistical Geology in America," *Winterthur Portfolio* 23 (1988): 151–67. See also Andrew Wilton and Tim Barringer, eds., *American Sublime: Landscape Painting in the United States, 1820–1880* (London: Tate Gallery, 2002).

Time and Narrative in the Mountain Sublime around 1800

Sean Franzel

THIS ESSAY TAKES a simple observation as its point of departure, namely that the traversal of mountain landscapes manifests a series of events that lend themselves to being ordered in chronological sequence.[1] Ascending and descending, lingering at striking sights, weathering a storm in a tent or cabin, imagining rocks as they formed over millions of years or witnessing their repositioning in a matter of seconds in a violent avalanche — all these activities involve the experience and often conscious perception of time. Viewed in this light, the notion that mountains are locations in which different events unfold in time might be considered in the more general context of theories of narration. Narrative characteristically represents the unfolding of events or states of being[2] by negotiating the transition from A to B, thus establishing logics of temporal sequence.[3] Todorov, for example, classically defines narrative as the shift "from one equilibrium to another . . . separated by a period of imbalance."[4] Transposed into the context of mountain or rock climbing, this minimalist account of narrative serves as a fitting allegory of the climb itself. In the following, I use concepts of the Alpine sublime as a lens for exploring how the mountain landscape operates as a site for experimentation with narrative logics of eventfulness and temporal sequence. I argue that the discourse of the sublime gripped the imagination around 1800 in part because it enabled new ways of narrating human experience; that is, of situating experience in spatial and temporal frames of reference.[5]

A certain affinity inheres between the aesthetics of the sublime and mountain narratives, not least because striking vistas are highlights of Alpine travel. It is the particular obsession of eighteenth- and nineteenth-century poets, philosophers, tourists, explorers, and natural scientists to seek out encounters with overwhelmingly large and dynamic phenomena. Part of the thrill of sublime objects — jagged peaks, glaciers, waterfalls, oceans, storms, and so on — lies in a two-part conceptual/affective movement: the realization that "rude," "unruly," or "uncontrollable" natural forces could destroy human life and the resulting elevation achieved by envisioning these forces at more and less safe remove. Relatedly, a variety of literary, philosophical, and scholarly texts frequently render the encounter with sublime nature as a transformative moment that offers the individual new insights into self and world. The discourse of the sublime drives depictions of shifting emotional and geographical landscapes forward.[6]

This essay's exploration of narrative logics at work in the aesthetics of the sublime occurs against the backdrop of other recent studies of time in eighteenth- and nineteenth-century literature, philosophy, and natural science. As scholars have argued, this is an era that "temporalizes" nature in new ways and "bursts" previous notions and representations of time.[7] Though many studies of mountain sublimity have focused on the imagination of physical space rather than of time, others have explored how reflections on deep geological time resonate widely throughout science and literature.[8] This essay complements and augments these studies, examining issues of time, narrative, and the mountain sublime in three steps. First I explore descriptions of aesthetic experience in which the sublime is described as bringing about dynamic movement (*Bewegung*). Concepts of spatial and temporal agitation typify canonical accounts of the sublime from Mendelssohn, Burke, and Kant to Goethe and Jean Paul; notions of agitation are instrumental in construing the sublime as an experience that destabilizes states of equilibrium and ushers in new ones (to recall Todorov's structuralist definition of narrative).

Related to the concept of *Bewegung* is the figuration of transitions from one emotional or mental state to another. The idealist aesthetics of Kant, Schiller, and Fichte frequently invoke the sublime as a vehicle for transcending the natural world and entering into a realm of reason and moral calling. Questions of time and the mountain sublime play an important role in narrating these and other transformative experiences. Here it is instructive to contrast Schiller and Fichte with Goethe's description of an Alpine landscape in his 1779 Swiss travelogue. Goethe's narrative of mental and emotional transition relies less on the idealist conceit of transport to a realm of reason and attends more to concrete features of the natural environment.

In a third and final step, I turn to Hegel's journal of a 1796 trip through the Bernese Alps as a point of contrast to previous aesthetic constellations under consideration, for Hegel rejects the mountain sublime as a compelling object of aesthetic experience. Echoing earlier accounts of mountain landscapes as expressly boring, Hegel shows where the narrative potential of the sublime might meet its limits. For narrative to function, sequences of events must be organized by principles of meaningful succession and differentiation: event B followed event A, for X reason. In contrast to this narrative logic, Hegel views the encounter with Alpine landscapes as a repetitive cycle of meaningless natural phenomenality that is ultimately uninteresting to the human observer. In putting forth what one might call an anti-narrative account of the sublime, Hegel can be read as responding to contemporaneous narratives of mountain temporality characteristic of late-eighteenth-century aesthetic theory.

The Temporality of Aesthetic Experience and *Bewegung*

Aesthetic theories repeatedly return to the question of the temporal unfolding of aesthetic experience. In contrast to the placid, lasting sensation of harmonious order associated with the beautiful, the sublime is often seen to shock, interrupt, or unsettle the observer. Take Moses Mendelssohn's account of the effects of an especially large object:

> Das Unermesslichgroße befestigt die Achtsamkeit des Geistes, und schwächt alle ungleichartigen Nebenbegriffe dergestalt, daß die Seele keinen Übergang zu andern Gegenständen findet, sondern diesen eine Weile anstaunt.[9]

> [the immeasurably immense [object] seizes the mind's attention and weakens all secondary concepts, such that the soul is not able to turn to view any other object and instead gazes at it with astonishment.]

For Mendelssohn, the sublime object generates astonishment (*Erstaunen*) that interrupts other frames of cognition, thwarts perception, and can even elicit "Eine Art von Betäubung, ein Mangel des Bewusstseins" (a type of stupor, an absence of consciousness).[10]

The duration of sublime effects becomes an especially salient question in the attempt to theorize auditory sensations, which paradigmatically unfold in time. Edmund Burke, for example, associates "excessive loudness" and "sudden beginning or sudden cessation of sound" with the sublime: "the shouting of multitudes ... amazes and confounds the imagination" and produces a "staggering, and hurry of the mind."[11] In rhetoric and music the departure from rules, "bold strokes," "daring flights," and the "sudden transitions in mood, texture, tempo, or volume" were all seen as sublime, as were certain authors and composers — one critic even called Handel a "Man-Mountain."[12] The analogy between the structure of aesthetic objects and the experience of the observer was common: an unruly piece of music, a thunderous storm, or a loud public event are all capable of creating a dynamic "hurry of the mind" (Burke) in the viewer or listener.

The question of what followed unexpected sublime moments was likewise always close at hand. Mendelssohn, for example, claims that the sublime is "mit einem Blitze zu vergleichen, der in einem Augenblicke uns blendet und wieder verschwindet" (comparable to a lightning bolt, which blinds us in one moment and disappears in the next).[13] The Swiss aesthetician J. G. Sulzer disagreed, writing that even though the sublime seizes the observer immediately, it achieves its effect "anhaltend; je länger man dabei verweilet und je näher man es betrachtet, je nachdrücklicher empfindet man seine Würkung" (continuously; the longer one lingers with it and the more closely one observes it, the more forcibly one feels its effect).[14] Whether as interruption or sustained elevation, narrating the sequence of sublime effects helped writers explore liminal experiences of self and other.

A notion of dynamic movement or *Bewegung* played a central role in depicting the agitation of the observer by sublime objects. Like other theorists, Kant contrasts the sublime's conceptual and affective *Bewegung* with the quiet contemplation of the beautiful.[15] In the judgment of the sublime, the object of consciousness forces the subject to search in vain for the right concepts with which to process it: "Diese Bewegung kann (vornehmlich in ihrem Anfange) mit einer Erschütterung verglichen werden, d.i. mit einem schnellwechselnden Abstoßen und Anziehen eben desselben Objekts" (This movement [especially in its inception] may be compared to a convulsion, that is, to a rapidly alternating repulsion from and attraction to one and the same object).[16] The conceptual frames that normally organize the phenomenal world are "erschüttert," shaken in their foundations. The object's dynamism finds its correlation in an imaginary spatial and temporal manipulation performed by aesthetic judgment (the mind's eye moves the object "toward" and "away from" itself in a kind of hurried, shaking motion).

Goethe likewise uses the figure of *Bewegung* (among others) to describe the experience of the sublime. His short piece entitled "Granit II" (1784) situates a narrative voice in an abstract mountain landscape, staging the human heart's encounter with ancient rocks:

> Ich fürchte den Vorwurf nicht daß es ein Geist des Widerspruches sein müsse der mich von Betrachtung und Schilderung des menschlichen Herzens, des jüngsten mannigfaltigsten beweglichsten veränderlichsten, erschütterlichsten Teiles der Schöpfung zu der Beobachtung des ältesten, festesten, tiefsten, unerschütterlichsten Sohnes der Natur geführt hat.[17]

> [I don't fear the reproach that it must have been a spirit of contradiction that led me from the consideration and depiction of the human heart — the youngest, most manifold, most dynamic, most inconstant, most shakable part of creation — to the observation of the oldest, most solid, deepest, most unshakeable son of nature.]

From beginning to end, "Granit II" interlocks modes of observing self and natural other. The above passage gains much of its pathos from the effusive piling up of adjectives that contrast human ephemerality and rocky permanence. Heightened insight into the human heart is accorded by the encounter with the sublime; the flitting *Bewegung* of the heart stands in contrast to the rocks' sublime immovability — "ihr ältesten würdigsten Denkmäler der Zeit" (you oldest, most dignified monuments of time)[18]— but also to the subject's intimation of the overwhelming forces that created them. The scene of sublime experience helps Goethe juxtapose the temporal unfolding of self-observation with imagined durations of non-human modes of becoming.

In addition to contrasting the temporality of inner life to that of nature, writers sometimes also implicated human history in the aesthetics of the sublime. Like Burke, Jean Paul writes in his *Vorschule der Ästhetik* (School for aesthetics, 1804) that listening — rather than seeing — is the primary medium of perceiving the dynamic sublime.[19] But Jean Paul invokes the auditory sublime in order to describe more than just the overwhelming force of sense data when he stages a scene of historical recollection amid a deafening rainstorm in his novel *Titan* (1800). Here the reader finds the main character Albano in modern Rome as a tourist, reflecting on the greatness of Ancient Rome:

> So war ihm, als sei die Vergangenheit von den Toten auferstanden und er schiffe im zurücklaufenden Strome der Zeit; unter den Strömen des Himmels hört' er die alten sieben Bergströme rauschen, die einst von Roms Hügeln kamen und mit sieben Armen die Welt aus dem Boden aufhoben.[20]

> [It seemed to him as if the past had risen from the dead and he was boating in the backward-moving stream of time; amidst the streams [of rain] from the sky he heard the seven ancient mountain streams which had once come from Rome's hills and with seven arms lifted the world out of the ground.]

Conjuring up an image of unrestrained torrents of water, this passage figures ancient Rome as an imaginary object of sublime desire. Albano's auditory hallucination mixes spatial and temporal frames. The "streams from heaven" of rainwater ("Ströme des Himmels") simultaneously suggest, first, a kind of imaginary river of time ("Strom der Zeit") that allows Albano to "boat" back through history to imagine ancient Rome in the first place; second, the mountain rivers ("Bergströme") that converged to form ancient Rome's topography; and third, these rivers metaphorized as "arms" that cradled and elevated human culture. The reader is presented with an intricate if not confusing collection of imaginary spatial and temporal motion backward and forward as well as up and down, movements linked to the concrete visual and auditory image of rain pouring from the sky. The storm's sublimity enables the imaginary correlation of disjunctive temporal frames, including the rise and fall of Rome, historical memory, the difference between ancients and moderns, and the storm's duration.

Whether in British sensualism or German idealism, or in accounts of geological or historical time, writers take the sublime as an occasion for narrating the eventfulness of human perception and natural phenomena. In turn, these writers juxtapose different temporal frames of reference that track flitting human emotion and geological processes; momentary weather patterns and historical memory; sudden interruptions and lasting duration. The encounter with the sublime stands out as eventful in part because it occasions attempts to account for its meaningfulness in and through time.

Sublime Transitions and Turns (Schiller, Fichte, Goethe)

Related to the notion of *Bewegung* is a concept of transition or transport from one state of being into another. Philosophical and literary narratives of individual transformation frequently dwell on the temporality of subjective experience, and mountain experience is routinely invoked as the catalyst of this transformation.

For post-Kantian idealist thinkers such as Schiller and Fichte, the senses' difficulty in grasping a sublime object signals the transition to a higher realm of human freedom. The individual subject is accorded a new sense of self by affirming his unity as abstracted from the phenomenal world. As Schiller puts it in "Über das Erhabene" (On the sublime, 1801):

> Das Erhabene verschafft uns also einen Ausgang aus der sinnlichen Welt, worin uns das Schöne gern immer gefangenhalten möchte. Nicht allmählich (denn es gibt von der Abhängigkeit keinen Übergang zur Freiheit), sondern plötzlich und durch eine Erschütterung reißt es den selbstständigen Geist aus dem Netze los, womit die verfeinerte Sinnlichkeit ihn umstrikte.[21]

> [The sublime thus allows us to exit the sensuous world in which the beautiful would forever imprison us. It is not little by little (for there is no slow transition from dependence to freedom), but suddenly and by a shock that the sublime tears the independent spirit free from the net that sophisticated sensuousness has cast around it.]

Echoing Mendelssohn's and Kant's descriptions of the abruptness of sublime effects, Schiller describes aesthetic judgment as a moment of transition to a higher plane of consciousness. The metaphor of "tearing" the mind or spirit free from the netting of sense perception highlights the eventfulness and temporality of this transformation. For Kant, as for Schiller, the transcendental realm of freedom both exists separate from the empirical world and ultimately conditions it. Schiller takes the imagination's difficulties in apprehending sublime natural objects as a sign that a complete understanding of nature cannot depend solely on empiricist laws of natural science:

> Dieser Abfall der Natur von den Erkenntnisregeln . . . macht die absolute Unmöglichkeit sichtbar, durch *Naturgesetze* die *Natur selbst* zu erklären . . . das Gemüt wird also unwiderstehlich aus der Welt der Erscheinungen heraus in die Ideenwelt, aus dem Bedingten ins Unbedingte getrieben.[22]

> [This deviation of nature from the rules of knowledge . . . makes visible the absolute impossibility of explaining nature itself according to nature's laws . . . in this way, the mind is driven out of the phenomenal world into the world of ideas, from the conditioned to the unconditioned or the absolute.]

Here, the subject's self-perception rather than its discernment of concrete empirical laws accords ultimate meaning to nature. Schiller elevates the "world" of aesthetic "ideas" over scientific perception, suggesting a fundamental incompatibility between empiricist and transcendental perspectives on nature. In Schiller's narrative of the subject arriving at its self-determination as rational being (a narrative that he fleshes out in philosophical-historical terms in other works), the sublime operates as a central hinge experience.

It is no accident that Schiller's drama *Wilhelm Tell* draws heavily on the symbolism of the Alpine sublime in staging moral and political self-determination. Set in the canton of Uri in the central Swiss Alps (where Wilhelm Tell is thought to have hailed from), the drama's defining actions — the formation of political community, resistance to foreign oppressors, and tyrannicide — are set in landscapes overflowing with the mountain sublime. As detailed by extensive stage directions, the play opens with an image of towering, cloud-draped mountain peaks surrounding Lake Lucerne.[23] The famous "Rütli" oath that seals the secret agreement by the Swiss men to resist foreign subjugation likewise occurs in an environment deliberately coded as sublime:

> Eine Wiese von hohen Felsen und Wald umgeben. Auf den Felsen sind Steige, mit Geländern, auch Leitern, von denen man nachher die Landleute herabsteigen sieht. Im Hintergrunde zeigt sich der See. . . . Den Prospekt schließen hohe Berge, hinter welchen noch höhere Eisgebirge ragen. Es ist völlig Nacht auf der Szene, nur der See und die weißen Gletscher leuchten im Mondenlicht.[24]

> [A meadow surrounded by high cliffs and forest. On the rocks are steep paths, with railings and ladders, by which the peasants are afterwards seen descending. In the background the lake shows itself. . . . The prospect is closed by lofty mountains, with even higher icy peaks rising behind them. It is complete night on the stage, but the lake and glaciers glisten in the moonlight.]

This Alpine landscape helps to underline the eventfulness of this and other key actions throughout the drama, associating important transitional moments in the play's dramatic arc with the suggestive form and structure of mountains, glaciers, and bodies of water. The Swiss men's command over the natural surroundings is allegorized by their facility in navigating sublime rock formations. Typical of the period's fascination with Swiss freedom, *Wilhelm Tell* associates ideals of individual and national self-assertion with this region, linking the iconic scenery of the Alps to philosophical-historical and national-political narratives dominant in subsequent centuries.

Like Schiller, Fichte stages a scene of the transition from empirical necessity to transcendental freedom, and he also takes up the question of the (mountain) sublime's relationship to temporal frames of orientation. In his 1794 *Einige Vorlesungen über die Bestimmung des Gelehrten* (A few lectures concerning the scholar's vocation), Fichte describes the life of the scholar as a social and ethical activity of the highest order where one commits — through teaching and research — to entering into relation with other subjects *qua* autonomous selves. Fichte dramatizes the embrace of scholarly vocation as a confrontation of phenomenal and noumenal realms, where the mortal temporality of the embodied self runs up against the immortality of abstract interpersonal relations:

> O! es ist der erhabenste Gedanke unter allen . . . ich kann nie aufhören *zu wirken* und mithin nie aufhören *zu seyn*. Das, was man Tod nennt, kann mein Werk nicht abbrechen; denn mein Werk soll vollendet werden, und es kann in keiner Zeit vollendet werden, mithin ist meinem Daseyn keine Zeit bestimmt, — und ich bin ewig. . . . Ich hebe mein Haupt kühn empor zu dem drohenden Felsengebirge, und zu dem tobenden Wassersturz, und zu den krachenden, in einem Feuermeer schwimmende Wolken, und sage: ich bin ewig, und ich trotze eurer Macht! Brecht alle herab auf mich, und du Erde und du Himmel, vermischt euch im wilden Tumulte, und ihr Elemente alle, schäumet und tobet, und zerreibt im wilden Kampfe das letzte Sonnenstäubchen des Körpers, den ich mein nenne; — mein Wille . . . soll kühn und kalt über den Trümmern des Weltalls schweben, denn ich habe meine Bestimmung ergriffen, und die ist dauernder, als ihr.[25]

> [Oh! and this is the most sublime thought of all: . . . I can never cease *to have an effect*, and thus I can never cease *to be*. That which is called death cannot interrupt my work; for my work should be completed and it cannot be completed in any time, thus no time determines my existence, — and I am eternal. . . . I lift my head boldly to the threatening bouldery heights, to the roaring cataract, and to the crashing clouds in their fire-red sea, and say: I am eternal and I defy your power! Rain down, all of you, upon me, and you earth and you heaven, mingle in wild tumult, and all of you elements foam and roar, and in savage combat pulverize the last dust mote of that body which I call my own; — . . . my will shall hover boldly and indifferently

above the wreckage of the universe. For I have seized my vocation, and it is more permanent than you.]

Quoting Kant's description of natural sublimity almost word for word,[26] Fichte dramatizes the stakes of embracing a life of scholarship. He establishes a narrative voice that submits itself to a nearly apocalyptic experience of sublime force, thus contrasting the infinite process of enlightenment with the life cycle of the human body. The juxtaposition of these temporal frames serves to characterize the endless project of scholarly communication *qua* social and ethical progress, a key principle organizing philosophies of history around 1800. Like Goethe, Fichte imagines a confrontation between short-term human impermanence and a realm of infinite becoming; here the narrative "I" voices its aspiration to preserve itself from the vagaries of human embodiment by embracing the calling to rational knowledge. This dramatization of Kant's rather matter-of-fact listing of sublime phenomena exhibits the narrative potential inherent in idealist aesthetics of the sublime, such that the event of transformative self-determination lends itself to being situated in various spatial and temporal landscapes.

Goethe's letters to Charlotte von Stein from a 1779 trip to the Swiss Alps likewise cast the encounter with the sublime as a moment of transition (these letters were later published in Schiller's *Horen* journal in 1796 as *Briefe aus der Schweiz* [Letters from Switzerland]). This Swiss travelogue narrates Goethe's ascent into the Alps, culminating at the Gotthard Pass. In the first letter Goethe sets out from Basel to Biel, following the scenic Birs River valley on a route popular and well traveled at least since the Romans. Opening with a description of a rocky mountain pass leading to the small town of Moutier (*Münster*), Goethe decidedly sets this travel narrative in the musical key of the mountain sublime:

> Mir machte der Zug durch diese Enge eine grosse ruhige Empfindung. Das Erhabene giebt der Seele die schöne Ruhe, sie wird ganz dadurch ausgefüllt, fühlt sich so gros als sie seyn kann und giebt ein reines Gefühl, wenn es bis gegen den Rand steigt ohne überzulaufen. Mein Aug und meine Seele konnte die Gegenstände fassen, und da ich rein war, diese Empfindung nirgends falsch wiedersties, so würkten sie was sie sollten.[27]

> [Traveling through this pass gave me a grand, quiet feeling. The sublime gives the soul beautiful quietude; it is filled by it completely, feels itself as large as it can be and gives a pure feeling when it approaches the edge without spilling over. My eye and my soul could grasp the objects and because I was pure, because this feeling was never misplaced, the objects had their proper effects.]

Here the mountain environment is not disruptive or violent; it instead elicits a sense of quiet dynamism, increased attentiveness, and emotional purity. Evocative descriptions of the river valley — "das über Felsstücke rauschende Wasser und der Weg . . . neben einander . . . machen an den meisten Orten die ganze Breite des Passes" (in most places, the water rushing over boulders and the path, next to each other, form the entire width of the passage-way) — and of Goethe's movement through gorges formed by drastic rock structures — "Grosse Klüfte spalten sich aufwärts und Platten von Mauerstärke haben sich von dem übrigen Gesteine losgetrennt" (great chasms split upwards and slabs with the strength of walls have separated themselves from the rest of the stone) — contribute to this effect, symbolizing the transition from one existential state to another (*BS*, 196). Marking differences between this region and flatter environs back in central Germany, Goethe casts this landscape as one of "greatness" or "magnitude" ("Großheit") out of which he hopes to draw "nourishment" ("Nahrung"; *BS*, 197). Contrasting his emotional state with the petty distractions of everyday life back home, Goethe describes his feeling as pervasive and ongoing rather than fleeting or momentary: it "approaches the edge without spilling over" and occasions heightened perception of both self and landscape. This elevated sentiment colors the entirety of this opening experience, leaving the reader to wonder how long a sublime tone will resonate before shifting into secondary emotional keys.

The rest of the letter continues to sketch the interpenetration of mountain landscape and heightened self-awareness. As if consciously experimenting with self-observation, Goethe returns to the same pass once more alone:

> Am Ende der Schlucht stieg ich ab und kehrte einen Theil alleine zurük. Ich entwikelte mir noch ein tiefes Gefühl . . . Man ahndet im Dunkeln die Entstehung und das Leben dieser seltsamen Gestalten. . . . Was für Revolutionen sie nachhero bewegt, getrennt, gespalten haben, so sind auch diese auch nur einzelne Erschütterungen gewesen und selbst der Gedanke einer so ungeheuren Bewegung gibt ein hohes Gefühl von ewiger Festigkeit. Die Zeit hat auch gebunden an die ewigen Gesetze, bald mehr bald weniger auf sie gewirkt. (*BS*, 197)
>
> [At the end of the gorge I dismounted and turned to go back a bit on my own. I developed another deep feeling in myself . . . one has a vague sense of the creation and the life of these strange forms. . . . Whatever revolutions later moved them, separated them, split them, these were only single convulsions, and the thought itself of such a massive movement lends [the observer] an elevated feeling of eternal solidity. Time, bound to the laws of eternity, had sometimes more, sometimes less effect upon them.]

Reflections on the age of these massive rocks invoke several common markers of sublimity, including force, "convulsion" (Erschütterung), and temporal permanence. The trope of "turning" or "revolving" juxtaposes contrasting human and geological temporalities: the author's own turning back to the gorge stands in drastic contrast to the "revolutions" of the formation of ancient rocks.[28] Imagining this "massive movement" makes the author's brief yet ponderous turn back to the edge of the gorge all the more insignificant in its momentariness. Continuing with the predominant sense of quietude established earlier (as opposed to the violent upheaval frequently associated with the sublime), Goethe intimates an "Alles langsam bewegendes, ewiges Gesetz" (*BS*, 198; an eternal law that slowly moves everything), a lawful frame of temporal movement. Barring more detailed scientific research, the subject's intimation of this frame relies on the depth and purity of a sense of sublimity — that is, on the workings of aesthetic imagination rather than any kind of objective measurement. For Goethe, however, the experience of the sublime enables a subjective transformation that makes the individual more open to concrete natural laws than before, in contrast to the increasing indifference to empirical nature championed by Schiller and Fichte's evocations of the natural sublime. The figure of the turn is characteristic of Goethe's keener attention to natural phenomena. The individual does not "tear through" sense perception (Schiller) or "hover indifferently above the wreckage of the universe" (Fichte). Rather, he ponderously turns around to observe before continuing his journey.[29]

Each of these writers embeds aesthetic vision in processes of temporal unfolding through transitional events turning back, away, or toward the sublime. The figuration of these events lends narrative coherence and import to cognitive and affective activities. At the same time, these narratives indicate something of the sublime's central role in each writer's larger narratives of philosophical-historical progress.

Hegel: Alpine Time as *Langeweile*

In the texts considered thus far, the sublime operates as a narrative motor that propels observations of self and other forward. Descriptions of the temporal unfolding of Alpine experience (going out into the mountains, reflecting on their natural formation, being threatened by the elements, and so on) frequently complement and give definite form to narratives of subjective agitation and transformation. Turning now to one final account of the mountain sublime, I am interested in how Hegel's journal of a 1796 trip through the Bernese Alps decidedly undermines the linkage of mountain aesthetics and robust narrative temporality.[30] Hegel stands in a long line of premodern writers who described mountains, oceans, and other purportedly sublime objects as boring (*langweilig*). That said, I want to argue that Hegel's engagement with aesthetic debates of the 1790s inflect earlier notions of boredom in new ways, probing the limits of the aesthetics of the sublime at the height of its celebration.

Hegel's notes show the philosopher as a twenty-six-year-old traveler, guide in hand, reflecting on his own and previous visitors' reactions to iconic tourist attractions such as the Reichenbach Falls, the Aar Gorge, the Jungfrau and its glaciers, and even the Rütli mountain in Uri Canton, which Schiller would highlight in *Wilhelm Tell* just a few years later. Hegel's journal engages with key features of the aesthetic constellation considered thus far. For example, he finds ample proof of the unrelenting laws of nature at work in Alpine landscapes, a commonplace of the idealist imagination. Describing the "raging" and "anger" (*RT*, 481) of a waterfall, for example, Hegel comments that nowhere else does one get such a pure sense of the "*Müssen* der Natur" (*RT*, 481) (the *necessity*, the "*must*" of nature). However, even while rehearsing typical notions of the sublime as necessary *Bewegung*, Hegel just as frequently concludes that mountains do not deliver on the promise of elevation and transport, at one point complaining that they did not awaken the sense of sublime magnitude that he had expected (*RT*, 474–75).

One particular reaction to the Grindelwald Glacier near the Jungfrau indicates a source of Hegel's underastonishment, namely the inability of Alpine scenery to generate human interest:

> Ihr Anblick bietet weiter nichts Interessantes dar. Man kann es nur eine *neue Art von Sehen* nennen, *die aber dem Geist schlechterdings keine weitere Beschäftigung gibt,* als daß ihm etwa auffällt, sich in der stärksten Hitze des Sommers so nahe bei Eismassen zu befinden. (*RT*, 475)

> [Its sight does not offer anything of interest. One can call it *a new form of seeing, yet one that does not give the spirit any form of activity*, save that it is struck by finding itself so close to ice masses in the fiercest heat of summer.]

While acknowledging that aesthetic vision becomes implicated in something of a narrative projection (the glacier-sun interaction, as well as the intimation of the glacier's slow and steady movement), Hegel nevertheless denies that this glacier has any relevance for human meaning-making, the purview of *Geist*. The most Hegel's *Geist* can take away from this sight is the curious fact that the glacier seems to resist the melting powers of the sun.

A later description of the Reichenbach Waterfall (a well-known tourist attraction detailed by Hegel's travel guides)[31] likewise serves as an interesting reflection on aesthetic vision and temporality, a central preoccupation of Romantic writers and painters such as Caspar David Friedrich and J. M. W. Turner.[32] Hegel watches the water as it thrusts

> durch eine enge Felsenkluft . . . [und] fällt dann . . . in Wellen, die den Blick des Zuschauers beständig mit sich niederziehen und die er doch nie fixiren, nie verfolgen kann, denn ihr Bild, ihre Gestalt, lös't sich alle Augenblicke auf, wird in jedem Moment von einem neuen

verdrängt, und *in diesem Falle sieht er ewig das gleiche Bild, und sieht zugleich, daß es nie dasselbe ist.* (*RT,* 478)

[through a narrow fissure in the rock . . . [and] falls . . . in waves that constantly pull the observer's vision down with them, yet which he can never fix, never completely follow, because their image, their form dissipates at every moment, it is repressed at every moment by a new image; *in this waterfall [the observer] perpetually sees the same image and at the same time sees that it is never the same.*]

Here Hegel reflects on the temporal unfolding of perception: How does vision process an incessantly shifting sight? How does it condense infinite multiplicity into a unified image? He goes on to affirm previous travelers' comments that it would be impossible to depict the waterfall's dynamism in a static painting (*RT,* 479). In contrast to a person viewing the falls on sight, a painting does not allow the imagination to temporally extend the object being depicted (*RT,* 479). For Hegel, the imagination's ability to "extend" (*ausdehnen*) an image of the waterfall forward and backward in time is key for capturing its visual richness. It is the imagination's play with space and time that accords aesthetic pleasure. The painting, in contrast, can only capture a single freeze frame (*RT,* 479), a contention that draws on longstanding debates about differences between spatial and temporal media since Lessing.[33]

Hegel's analysis of the paradox of capturing a dynamic phenomenon in a static image represents little more than a philosophical fantasia on a cliché of the tourist trade: you have to see it to believe it or enjoy it. That said, his reflections on spatial and temporal phenomenality bear little trace of the excitement to which so many Alpine tourists testify. Despite manifesting phenomenal complexity, the waterfall does not present a sequence of events representative of significant transition or meaningful dynamism. Even if the perception of the waterfall as "eternally the same" and simultaneously "never the same" is compelling on some level, it is not significant or eventful in the final analysis. For Hegel, the micro-temporality of the Reichenbach Falls correlates on a macro level to his feeling about his Alpine travels as a whole, namely that they are a tedious series of subtle modifications of the same.

This convergence of temporal difference in the eternal recurrence of the same is perhaps most evident in Hegel's notes about the Aar Gorge (to this day a popular tourist attraction), which he describes as a "öde, traurige Steinwüstenei" (*RT,* 482; desolate, sad stone desert):

Weder das Auge noch die Einbildungskraft findet auf diesen formlosen Massen irgend einen Punkt, auf dem jenes mit Wohlgefallen ruhen . . . könnte. Der Mineralog allein findet Stoff, über die Revolutionen dieser Gebirge unzureichende Muthmaßungen zu wagen. Die Vernunft findet in dem Gedanken der Dauer dieser Berge oder in der Art von Erhabenheit, die man ihnen zuschreibt, nichts, das ihr imponiert, das ihr Staunen und Bewunderung abnöthigte. Der Anblick dieser ewig todten Massen gab mir nichts als die einförmige und in die Länge langweilige Vorstellung: *es ist so.* (*RT*, 483)

[Neither the eye nor the imagination finds any point on these form- less masses to alight with [viewing] pleasure . . . Only the mineralogist can find material with which to make inadequate conjectures about the revolutions of these mountains. Reason finds nothing that strikes it or that could command astonishment and admiration in the thought of the permanence of these mountains or in the kind of sub- limity that people ascribe to them. The sight of these eternally dead masses offered me nothing but the unchanging and persistently bor- ing idea: *this is the way it is.*]

Like Goethe, Hegel contemplates the deep geological time of rocks — their "permanence" and "revolutions" — and yet for Hegel this expan- sive unhuman temporality is not at all thrilling; it elicits neither Mendelssohn's "astonishment" nor a bracing contextualization of the human. Hegel's imagination finds no aesthetic pleasure in the overlay of different, contrasting temporalities; he views sublimity as a touristic cliché rather than a quasi-divine manifestation of eternity that can transport the subject. Sublimity becomes a reported phenomenon much more than a technology of the self,[34] something that it is fashionable to observe rather than something that actually intervenes in essential human thought. In addition to suggesting a kind of existential mood affecting the entirety of Hegel's Alpine travels, it would seem that this extended repetition of the same — *Langeweile,* drawn out "in die Länge" — limits the aesthetic vision of the natural sublime *tout court.*

One might be tempted to read Hegel's rejection of the eventfulness of unhuman, natural temporalities as an implicit turn to a different kind of temporality, namely to the expressly historical time of Reason and Spirit. Parallel to the nascent disciplines of the natural sciences and their explora- tion of the spatial and temporal extensions of natural phenomena, the philosophical, philological, and historical exploration of the rise and fall of cultures became ever more prominent over the course of the nineteenth century. In Hegel's groundbreaking account of the unfolding of human culture and thought, it would seem that the only time of philosophical interest is that of the historically manifested idea; his repudiation of natural beauty in his later aesthetic theory is just one symptom of this attitude.[35] This view seems to already be in place in this 1796 travel journal, where mountains represent little more than a landscape of lack: nature is "form- less," "effectless," "powerless," and so on. Seen in the light of issues of time and narrative, much of Hegel's rejection of the sublime becomes clear. The deep time of prehuman history is of little relevance in the nar- ratives that Hegel wants to tell.

The Sublime as Narrative Motor?

This essay has tracked certain implications of a simple observation, namely that mountains are often viewed as places where different events unfold in time. The mountain sublime proved to have an extremely long shelf life, both as eventful highlight and as prototype for narrating the interrelation of distinct events. The sublime might well be seen as a condensed moment of narrative potentiality that came to be elaborated in diverse ways throughout the eighteenth and nineteenth centuries. As narrative motor, the sublime has hummed, roared, and sputtered in philosophies of historical progression; theories of geological formation; narratives of global travel, trade, and colonial expansion; figurations of the emergence of political community; patriotic depictions of *Heimat*; accounts of the micro-temporality of individual perception; or descriptions of the macro-temporality of evolution.

Hegel's account of the temporality of nature and perception helps us gain perspective on both the allure and the limitations of the mountain sublime. Even while according a certain legitimacy to scientific accounts of mountain time, Hegel nonetheless repudiates both the stylization of the mountain sublime as a site of personal or philosophical transformation and the linkage of moral and aesthetic insight to sublime *Bewegung*. However much Hegel himself rejects the sublime, one might still view his encounter with the Alpine sublime as productive in terms of generating new paradigms for narrating human experience. If the encounter with the sublime entails the juxtaposition of different temporal frames of reference, might one not view Hegel's groundbreaking exploration of human, historical time as a result of the philosophical confrontation of human with non-human temporalities? That is to say, does not the dynamic dance of human history to the tune of reason achieve much of its narrative power by being contrasted with uneventful, non-human temporalities? Or to pose a related question, might one not wonder what would have happened to Hegel's narrative of the human idea's emergence out of ahistorical nature had he been a slightly more engaged Alpine tourist?

Notes

[1] Many thanks to Roger Cook for his remarks on an earlier version of this essay.

[2] Abbott calls narrative the "representation of an event or a series of events." See H. Porter Abbott, *The Cambridge Introduction to Narrative* (Cambridge: Cambridge UP, 2002), 12.

[3] Sequentiality "involves changes of state in the represented world and thereby implies the presence of temporality, which is a constitutive aspect of narration and distinguishes it from other forms of discourse such as description or argumenta-

tion." Wolf Schmid, "Event and Eventfulness," in *Handbook of Narratology*, ed. Peter Hühn, John Pier, Wolf Schmid, and Jörg Schönert, 80–97 (Berlin: de Gruyter, 2009), 80.

[4] Tzvetan Todorov, "Structural Analysis of Narrative," *NOVEL: A Forum on Fiction* 3, no. 1 (Autumn, 1969): 75.

[5] One might say that the sublime operates as as what Bender and Wellbery call a "chronotype," a term they introduce in the context of understanding "temporal construction as a function of narrative formation" and define as "a model or pattern through which time assumes practical or conceptual significance." John Bender and David Wellbery, "Introduction," in *Chronotypes: The Construction of Time*, ed. Bender and Wellbery (Stanford, CA: Stanford UP, 1991), 3 and 4.

[6] On eighteenth-century aesthetics of the sublime in relation to mountain landscapes (in German and British traditions respectively) see Brad Prager, *Aesthetic Vision and German Romanticism: Writing Images* (Rochester, NY: Camden House, 2007); and Noah Heringman, *Romantic Rocks, Aesthetic Geology* (Ithaca, NY: Cornell UP, 2004).

[7] Among many other recent examples of this literature, see Peter Matussek, ed., *Goethe und die Verzeitlichung der Natur* (Munich: Beck, 1998); Martin Rudwick, *Bursting the Limits of Time: The Reconstruction of Geohistory in the Age of Revolution* (Chicago: U of Chicago P, 2005); and Andrew Piper, "Mapping Vision: Goethe, Cartography, and the Novel," in *Spatial Turns: Space, Place, and Mobility in German Literary and Visual Culture*, ed. Jaimey Fisher and Barbara Mennel (Amsterdam: Rodopi, 2010), 27–52.

[8] See Heringman, *Romantic Rocks, Aesthetic Geology*, on the symbiotic relationship of the aesthetics of the sublime and nascent geological sciences. See also Heather I. Sullivan's work on geology and literature in the eighteenth and nineteenth centuries: "Ruins and the Construction of Time: Geological and Literary Perspectives in the Age of Goethe" *Studies in Eighteenth-Century Culture* 30 (2001): 1–30; and "Collecting the Rocks of Time: Goethe, the Romantics, and Early Geology," *European Romantic Review* 10 (1999): 341–70.

[9] This and all subsequent quotes are from Mendelssohn's "Über das Erhabene und Naïve in den schönen Wissenschaften" (On the sublime and naive in the fine sciences, 1758) in *Schriften zur Philosophie, Aesthetik und Apologetik* (Hildesheim: Olms, 1968), 177. All translations are my own, except where otherwise noted.

[10] Mendelssohn, "Über das Erhabene und Naïve," 178.

[11] Edmund Burke, "A Philosophical Enquiry into the Sublime and Beautiful" (1757), in *A Philosophical Enquiry into the Sublime and Beautiful and Other Pre-Revolutionary Writings* (London: Penguin, 1998), 123.

[12] Claudia L. Johnson, "'Giant HANDEL'? and the Musical Sublime," *Eighteenth-Century Studies* 19, no. 4 (1986): 518 and 526.

[13] Mendelssohn, "Über das Erhabene und Naïve," 198.

[14] This is taken from Sulzer's encyclopedia of aesthetics: Johann Georg Sulzer, "Erhaben," in *Allgemeine Theorie der schönen Künste*, 97–114 (Leipzig: Weidemann & Reich, 1771–74), 97.

¹⁵ Immanuel Kant, *Kritik der Urteilskraft*, in *Werkausgabe*, vol. 10, ed. W. Weischedel (Frankfurt am Main: Suhrkamp, 1957), 181.

¹⁶ Kant, *Kritik der Urteilskraft*, 181.

¹⁷ Johann Wolfgang Goethe, "Granit II," in *Schriften zur allgemeinen Naturlehre, Geologie und Mineralogie*, ed. Wolf von Engelhardt and Manfred Wenzel, vol. 25 of *Sämtliche Werke: Briefe, Tagebücher und Gespräche* (Frankfurt am Main: Deutscher Klassiker Verlag, 1989), 313–14. This posthumously published text was written in 1784. On Goethe's geological studies, see recent essays by Powers and Sullivan: Elizabeth Powers, "The Sublime, 'Über den Granit,' and the Prehistory of Goethe's Science," *Goethe Yearbook* 15 (2008): 35–56; and Sullivan "Ruins and the Construction of Time" and "Collecting the Rocks of Time."

¹⁸ Goethe, "Granit II," 313.

¹⁹ "Das Ohr ist der unmittelbare Gesandte der Kraft und des Schreckens, man denke an den Donner der Wolken, der Meere, der Wasserfälle, der Löwen, etc." (The ear is the immediate messenger of power and fear, as in the thunder of clouds, of the sea, of waterfalls, or of lions.") Jean Paul Richter, *Vorschule der Ästhetik* (Hamburg: Meiner, 1990), 106.

²⁰ Jean Paul Richter, *Titan*, vol. 2 (Berlin: Aufbau, 1986), 252.

²¹ Friedrich Schiller, "Über das Erhabene," in *Gedichte, Prosa*, ed. Benno von Wiese (Cologne: Kiepenheuer & Witsch, 1959), 673–74.

²² Schiller, "Über das Erhabene," 678.

²³ Friedrich Schiller, *Wilhelm Tell*, in *Dramen IV*, ed. Matthias Luserke, in *Werke und Briefe* (Frankfurt am Main: Deutscher Klassiker Verlag, 1996), 388.

²⁴ Schiller, *Wilhelm Tell*, 421.

²⁵ Johann Gottlieb Fichte, *Einige Vorlesungen über die Bestimmung des Gelehrten* (1794), in *Gesamtausgabe der Bayerischen Akademie der Wissenschaften*, vol. 1,3, 1–74 (Stuttgart: Frommann-Holzboog, 1966), 50. English translation (with minor adaptations by author) from "Some Lectures on the Vocation of the Scholar," *Fichtes Early Philosophical Writings*, ed. and trans. Daniel Breazeale, 137–84 (Ithaca, NY: Cornell UP, 1988), 168–69.

²⁶ Kant, *Kritik der Urteilskraft*, 185.

²⁷ Johann Wolfgang Goethe, "Brief an Charlotte von Stein, 3.10.1779," in *Das erste Weimarer Jahrzehnt: Briefe, Tagebücher und Gespräche vom 7. November 1775 bis 2. September 1786*, ed. Hartmut Reinhardt, in *Sämtliche Werke: Briefe, Tagebücher und Gespräche* (Frankfurt am Main: Deutscher Klassiker Verlag, 1997), 196. Further references to this work are cited in the text using the abbreviation *BS* and the page number.

²⁸ To be sure, this is a notion of revolution not as radical rupture but rather cyclical turning-over. On early modern and modern notions of revolution, see Reinhart Koselleck, "Historische Kriterien des neuzeitlichen Revolutionsbegriffs," in *Vergangene Zukunft: Zur Semantik geschichtlicher Zeiten* (Frankfurt am Main: Suhrkamp, 1988), 67–86.

²⁹ In a longer discussion of aesthetic vision and figures of turning, one would surely have to deal with the beginning of *Faust II*, which has Faust awaken in an

Alpine landscape and turn from beholding the rising sun to a sublime waterfall. Needless to say, issues of narrative structure and temporality are of considerable importance in this passage.

[30] "Reisetagebuch Hegels durch die Berner Oberalpen, 1796," in *G. W. F. Hegels Leben*, ed. Karl Rosenkranz (Darmstadt: Wissenschaftliche Buchgesellschaft, 1963), 470–90. Further references to this work are given in the text using the abbreviation *RT* and the page number.

[31] Throughout his journey Hegel makes frequent reference to Christoph Meiners's popular Alpine travelogue. See Christoph Meiners, *Briefe über die Schweiz* (Berlin: Spena, 1785–91).

[32] J. M. W. Turner painted iconic images of the Reichenbach Falls *qua* sublime in 1804 and 1810.

[33] For an outline of these debates, see Prager, *Aesthetic Vision and German Romanticism*, esp. 17–33.

[34] Ashfield and de Bolla use this term to describe the discourse of the sublime. See Andrew Ashfield and Peter de Bolla, "Introduction," in *The Sublime: A Reader in British Eighteenth-Century Aesthetic Theory* (Cambridge: Cambridge UP, 1996), 1–16.

[35] Hegel departs from Kant in arguing that natural phenomena are not proper objects of aesthetic theory, a position with which Adorno takes issue at great length. See Theodor Adorno, *Ästhetische Theorie* (Frankfurt am Main: Suhrkamp, 1973), esp. 97–134.

Faust's Mountains: An Ecocritical Reading of Goethe's Tragedy and Science

Heather I. Sullivan

ECOCRITICISM'S ENVIRONMENTAL PERSPECTIVE views human beings, bodies, and culture as participants in ecological interactions and exchanges with the rest of the energetic and material world, including both biotic and abiotic forms. This ecocritical essay assesses how Goethe portrays Faust's mountain experiences in both part I and part II (1808, 1832) of the tragedy as engagements with physical matter rather than with spiritual inspiration. Indeed, by using ecocriticism to study Goethe's science as the context for the play, we see that Faust's many mountains are more than a setting; they actively destabilize his — and our — assumptions about "passive matter" and recontextualize human endeavors in their physical environment. Faust's mountains inspire the desire to "ascend," but they also offer a glimpse into the massive geological changes occurring through deep time even as they radically alter the climatic systems of the biosphere on a daily basis. In other words, scientists in the Age of Goethe recognized that the apparent solidity of mountains is actually a short-term illusion; mountains instead embody and enact climatic and geological flows in which we human beings are not the only active forces. Goethe's *Faust* documents such issues, though this is often overlooked in readings celebrating human ingenuity and action as the supreme, spiritual, and/or modern force shaping our world for the "better," regardless of so-called "collateral damage" such as murder, colonialism, piracy, and the final putrid swamp. In contrast, viewing the tragedy through ecocriticism and Goethe's science offers a possible environmental stance acknowledging humanity's position within these many physical processes rather than as transcendental beings who dominate at whim and without long-term costs. Previous ecocritical readings of *Faust* include Jost Hermand's assertion that the play is a "green-leaning" critique of modernity, and, conversely, Kate Rigby's condemnation of both Faust and Goethe himself as advocates of modern development celebrating the taming of the sea and creating "new land."[1] My work straddles these two views, noting that while the play does not offer an overtly green agenda, it nevertheless highlights the environmental surroundings against which Faust and Mephistopheles strive but which they fail to escape. Indeed, Goethe's *Faust* ends, not in heaven, but rather with Mephistopheles overcome with physical desire as Faust's remains float passively through the "mountain gorges," as if part of the natural flux.

Mountains are, indeed, the setting and actors in many aspects of Goethe's *Faust*. In addition to the debates about their formation, the economic pursuit of their resources, and military battles in their heights, the tragedy also stages multiple ascents. While the mountain scenes in *Faust* may appear as the typically metaphorical site for encounters with the divine, diabolical, or sublime, they function more as a space of transformation, where seemingly transcendental events take on rather earthly qualities. In fact, Faust's own three major forays up the mountains present just such a Goethean transformation; what might have been a heroic climb is instead rendered ironically ambiguous, or even comically focused on bodily challenges and limitations. On his "Walpurgis Night" hike up the Brocken in part I, for example, Faust yields to Mephistopheles' complaints about the strain of continuing on foot and the dangers of walking in the dark, and they famously stop halfway up and miss the satanic ritual on the peak. Then, in part II, act 4, Faust does not climb up the "High Mountains" but rather is carried there by a cloud — an anomalous mode of travel that demands further exploration in relation to Goethe's atmospheric studies on clouds. Once he lands, Mephistopheles joins him and again grumbles about the perils and vexation of contending with mountainous terrain. Finally, after his death in act 5 Faust is also borne upward through the "Mountain Gorges," though this time by swirling angels, who, not coincidentally, flow upward much like clouds. Faust's three mountain ascents are, in other words, either cut short or else occur with no actual effort on his part as he is transported upward.[2] Mostly billed as an epic drama of a man who ceaselessly strives (for knowledge, power, or simply for the sake of ongoing action), Goethe's *Faust* actually features a remarkably indolent character in terms of his physical experiences on mountains.

In contrast, Goethe himself is well-known for his extensive climbs, particularly his solitary winter ascent of the Brocken in 1777 — he was the first to accomplish this feat — and his various adventures in the Swiss and Italian mountains.[3] In fact, many of Goethe's literary, autobiographical, and scientific works refer to his heroic escapades with high-altitude sublimity; he refers to himself in almost superhuman terms when portraying his own mountain ascents, such as in his famous poem, "Harzreise im Winter" (Winter journey in the Harz), which describes his journey up the Brocken. The marked contrast between Goethe's own experiences documented in his writings and his protagonist in *Faust* should draw our attention to how very unimpressive Faust's actual mountaineering accomplishments are, despite the proliferation of mountain references and settings in the drama. Besides the abbreviated hike up the Brocken, these references also include Mephistopheles' promise to the kaiser of vast quantities of gold hidden in mountain lodes ("Bergesadern"), which will be the reserves for modern paper money. Additionally, multiple figures debate the formation and alteration of mountains through time, including Mephistopheles and Faust as they stand atop the "High Mountains." Finally, the last scene in the play is labeled "Mountain Gorges" (rather than "heaven,") which is the setting for Faust's third and final ascent. Goethe's geological and meteorological writings shed light on the fact that Faust's mountain experiences — and his actions more broadly — play out within the context of larger, uncontrollable forces. Mountains are hence neither symbols of permanence nor of the conquering hero with an unflinching will, but rather of the tenuous, fluid, and constantly changing world around us. While the forces influencing Faust may seem divine, such as the "Lord's" gamble with Mephistopheles and the battle between devils and angels, I argue that they are primarily physical or environmental factors. This may well be the drama's most radical characteristic: Goethe takes an overtly spiritual tale and reconfigures it as a portrayal of humans grappling with the concrete materiality of their physical environment.[4] As Astrida Tantillo notes, "a scientific, naturalistic understanding of the world replaces a religious one" in *Faust*.[5] *Faust* is a very "modern" tragedy in that it dethrones the "Übermensch" and relegates humanity to the earth's geological, climatic, and biotic developments despite, or even because of, our strivings.[6]

Reading *Faust* through the lens of ecocriticism brings our attention to the drama's frequent references to mountains, not just as background or sublime site but rather as central features of Faust's material framework. Kate Rigby's 2004 ecocritical study, *Topographies of the Sacred: The Poetics of Place in European Romanticism*, offers one of the few in-depth discussions of mountains in *Faust*.[7] These she reads in terms of the Romantic susceptibility for "Promethean temptation when high (if never high enough) in the mountains."[8] She studies Goethe's mining, alpine climbs, and poetry, and documents his desire to ascend beyond the mere human, and to control nature's course. Faust, she notes, acts as a "modern developer," whose Promethean desires drive him to intervene and fight against the water. Rigby condemns both Faust and Goethe for wanting to conquer nature, particularly within the drama's final act of building a large dike to claim land from the sea. Her analysis lays the groundwork for a thorough rereading of Goethe's radical revisions of nature, one in which nature is the context and not merely the optional backdrop to human life. This essay follows Rigby's work critiquing Faust's efforts at development, though I see the overall play, if not its protagonist, as offering an alternative view. This view has ecocritical potential, because it insists on the materiality of both mountains and human beings.[9]

Particularly applicable for this "material" study of *Faust* is Dana Phillips's work critiquing the tendency in much of environmental rhetoric to seek primarily aesthetic, holistic, or idealized abstractions of nature. Phillips prefers to avoid views about nature that are laden with heavy-handed "reverence, awe, and piety," for these "are antiseptic responses to nature; one might even say that they are *unnatural* responses, in that they are incompatible with what we know about the earthy flavor, by which I mean to suggest not only the randiness, but the rawness and rankness as well, of most biological processes."[10] Above all, Phillips keeps us on the ground — no rhapsodizing about becoming one with nature as if it were primarily pure alpine sublimity and lovely blossoms. He eschews idealized and pious approaches to nature even as he advocates his views from a staunchly environmental perspective. Similarly, I suggest that we approach Faust's mountains without excessive reverence and piety and look at them with a grounded, material stance. Despite his best efforts, Faust remains mired in the "rankness," "randiness," and "rawness" of his natural and material environment.

Since Goethe worked on *Faust* throughout his life, a brief description of his changing perspectives on mountains is essential for following their different meanings in his tragedy. Goethe documents many of his own exhilarating climbs, in which he experienced the sublimity of the peaks and the feeling of achieving a superhuman status. Yet with his dedication to re-opening the Ilmenau mine near Weimar once he began working at the court as an administrator for the young prince Carl August in 1776, his writings in this regard become much more concretely material. He traveled through Germany studying mines, minerals, and mountains, delving into questions about their formation and history. Following the renowned instructor at the Freiberg mining academy, Abraham Gottlob Werner, Goethe found Neptunism's emphasis on gradual developments in water more compelling than the Vulcanist theories, which considered sudden disasters and fiery eruptions as the primary causes of changes to the earth's surface.[11] Goethe's work with the mine made such inquiries eminently practical, of course, since he and all mining officials wanted to understand the earth's formations in order to locate valuable material resources. This was the era of the burgeoning Industrial Revolution in Germany, and the practical discussions of mining, resources, and the earth's development led to heated debates with serious implications for theology and science alike. During this time early geologists came to realize that the earth had a real material history of eons beyond imagination rather than the 6,000 years suggested biblically. Furthermore, they were beginning to understand that mountains and all other geological formations had been changing and developing through time, repeatedly undergoing major upheavals.[12] This is the "material" context for Goethe's own fascination with mountains and minerals. Indeed, granite became an obsession for Goethe because he thought it was the oldest solid material that first consolidated out of the cosmic "ur-soup" before the earth's surface separated into land and sea. He believed he touched the ancient core of the planet when standing atop a granite peak. Goethe's view of mountains thus developed from his earliest pleasure in high-altitude superiority to a practical study of the composition of mountains; but then his perspective changed again toward the end of his life, when he began to understand them within the context of air flows, water cycles, and weather patterns.

Goethe's later meteorological studies laid a specific emphasis on mountains, because they offered a broader view of the shifting pressure systems. In order to see and understand clouds, he writes that the view from above is essential:

> Alle atmosphärische [sic] Erscheinungen haben in dieser Gebirgsgegend einen andern Charakter als im niederen Lande und drücken sich viel entschiedener aus. Nur muß man . . . sich entschließen aus der Karlsbader Schlucht heraus zu gehen und die Höhen zu ersteigen, wo man nach dem Egerkreis und den sächsischen Gebirgen hinsieht. Alles was man in der Enge nur einzeln und mißmutig gewahr wird übersieht sich sodann mit Vergnügen und Belehrung.[13]

> [All atmospheric phenomena have a different character in this mountainous region than in the lowlands and present themselves much more decisively. One must only . . . decide to go out of the Carlsbad valley and to climb up into the heights, where one looks out toward the Eger region and the mountains of Saxony. Everything that one can only see individually and with irritation when in the narrow (valley), can then be overseen with pleasure and learning (my translation).]

Furthermore, in his studies of air-pressure changes, Goethe concentrated on the more rapid fluxes occurring at high altitudes. He incorrectly believed that the cause of such barometric changes is the "inhalation and exhalation" of the earth, which first draws the air more strongly toward it and then releases it (causing high- and low-pressure shifts). Through a view from above, he gained greater insight into tumultuous air-pressure shifts, the water cycles, and the fluid formations of clouds. As Leland Phelps notes: "Goethe saw the panorama of weather in the Alps as a large scale [sic] battle involving the winds, clouds, and atmosphere. He stated that one tended to overlook the play of natural forces involved in atmospheric processes except when one was surrounded by them in the mountains."[14] The mountains in *Faust* are thus not surprisingly the sites of battles both atmospheric and military, and they provide essential clues for understanding the play's significant move into materiality. This materiality represents a participation in nature's flows, changes, and conflicts that draw us in — and "onward," as in the final word of the play — whether we recognize it or not. Goethe's shift in interest from the minerals and the history of mountains toward atmospheric studies marks an important development in his thinking about mountains and science more generally: his earlier polarity of water and fire as the forces shaping the earth's surface is transformed into a more complex emphasis on multiple *relations* among earth's attraction (gravity), water flow, air-pressure fluctuations, and temperature. Instead of the old Neptunist-versus-Vulcanist debate, he studied the energized interactions of multiple forces in the earth's atmosphere and thought about how this plays out within human experiences as well.

In *Faust* we see right from the beginning a desire for the materiality of physical nature. Faust declares in his first monologue a desire to "know" nature (actually, nature's "breasts") physically:

Wo fass' ich dich, unendliche Natur?
Euch Brüste, wo? Ihr Quellen alles Lebens

[How, boundless Nature, seize you in my clasp?
You breasts where, all life's sources twain
(455–56)]

This craving leads him to make a wager with Mephistopheles, and then to experience the physical world by flying to a tavern filled with drunken students, visiting the witch's kitchen where he drinks a rejuvenation potion, and seducing Gretchen. Most relevant for our discussion, he leaves Gretchen after impregnating her and hikes up into the Harz mountains on "Walpurgis Night" with Mephistopheles, yet their climb is truncated. The famously excised scene atop the Brocken describes Satan's ceremony with a new recruit into the world of sex and money, and it occurs on the very site where Goethe himself ascended the Brocken, alone, in the middle of the winter. There he decided that fate was smiling upon him and leading him to the heady heights of court at Weimar.[15] Most readers believe that Goethe self-censored the scene with Satan because of its controversial nature; he instead leaves Mephistopheles and Faust halfway up the mountain, where they dance with witches and watch satirical theater. However, there is another practical explanation if we simply listen to Mephistopheles. While he wants to seduce Faust with his devilish offers, he does not wish to expend much physical effort in the process. Magic is no match for physical fatigue, it seems, and the body's needs — even of such a figure as Mephistopheles — override supernatural events. Their climb has hardly begun when Mephistopheles voices his complaint about how he would rather fly. Then he refuses to walk any higher. Since he is therefore the one who prevents Faust from completing this ascent, perhaps it is his reluctance to continue the strenuous hike that ends the heroic quest to reach the top of the Brocken on "Walpurgis Night." This is one of the key moments where the spiritual world is overwritten by simple physical realities, an example, in other words, of Goethe's switch from potential moments of sublimity or transcendence to the material body and its surroundings. *Faust* the tragedy repeatedly enacts quests to leave the physical realm, but these quests are just as often undone, ironically, by mundane physical demands such as fatigue, or later, sexual desire. Most readers see the quest and possibly the destruction left in its wake, but they overlook its failure and inevitable return to the body. This is what makes the play environmentally relevant: regardless of their efforts, Faust and Mephistopheles are overcome by the body and the elements of water, fire, air, and earth. Even Faust's final ascent needs reassessment as an occurrence *within* the mountain gorges, the air flow, and the water cycle, as I argue below.

Another example of Goethe's bent for shifting from cosmic reflections and claims of sublimity to the material realm, particularly in his discussions of mountains, is found in his 1785 text "Granit II." Here he waxes poetic about standing on a granite peak as the "oldest eternal altar" that connects directly to the vast depths of creation. His soul feels its own sublimity and longs for the heavens — only to be called back by hunger and thirst to material human needs. Note the abrupt switch:

> Hier auf dem ältesten ewigen Altare der unmittelbar auf die Tiefe der Schöpfung gebaut ist bring ich dem Wesen aller Wesen ein Opfer. Ich fühle die ersten festesten Anfänge unsers Daseins, ich überschaue die Welt ihre schrofferen und gelinderen Täler und ihre fernen fruchtbaren Weiden, meine Seele wird über sich selbst und über alles erhaben und sehnt sich nach dem nähern Himmel. Aber bald ruft die brennende Sonne Durst und Hunger [die] menschlichen Bedürfnisse zurück.[16]

> [Here on the oldest, eternal altar that is built directly on top of the depths of creation, I bring the being of all beings a sacrifice. I feel the first, most solid beginnings of our existence, I look over the world's more rugged and gentler valleys and the distant fruitful meadows; my soul is sublime beyond itself and everything, and it longs for the nearer heavens. But soon the burning sun calls back the human needs of thirst and hunger. (my translation)]

The sublime transcendence of the soul lifting itself on high while standing atop the ancient granite is interrupted by the material body, much like the seemingly mythological moments in *Faust* that move into descriptions of the flows of physical matter. In other words, where one expects the divine, one finds instead "nature."[17] *Faust* hereby provides an ecocritical model.

Mephistopheles is often the catalyst for the interruption of potential transcendence. There are, in fact, three occasions in *Faust* when Mephistopheles frets specifically about having to climb or hike. On their first hike on "Walpurgis Night" he vociferously complains about the strenuous walk in the dark, longing to fly instead of continuing on foot:

> Verlangst du nicht nach einem Besenstiele?
> Ich wünschte mir den allerderbsten Bock.
> Auf diesem Weg sind wir noch weit vom Ziele.
>
> [Would you not have a broomstick rather?
> I wish I rode a buck, however tough.
> Our route will take us yet a good way farther.
> (3835–37)]

And then he bemoans the dim moonlight, in which he stumbles into rocks and trips over tree roots:

> Wie traurig steigt die unvollkommne Scheibe
> Des roten Mondes mit später Glut heran,
> Und leuchtet schlecht, daß man bei jedem Schritte
> Vor einen Baum, vor einen Felsen rennt!
>
> [How drearily the moon-disk's ragged cinder
> Swims up with its belated reddish glow,
> And shines so poorly that one risks collision
> At every step with crag or rooted snare!
> (3851–54)]

Faust, on the other hand, keeps marching boldly onwards, wanting to enjoy the thrill of the walk. He keeps asking Mephistopheles why they do not continue upward to the devilish spectacle above rather than stopping midway to entertain themselves with witches and theater:

> Doch droben möcht' ich lieber sein!
> Schon seh' ich Glut und Wirbelrauch.
> Dort strömt die Menge zu dem Bösen;
> Da muß sich manches Rätsel lösen.
>
> [I'd rather be up over there!
> I spy a glow and fumes awhirl.
> There flocks the crowd to Evil-kind;
> There many a riddle should unfurl.
> (4037–40)]

Mephistopheles emphasizes the fact that staying is easier and requests that Faust be kind and remain below.

> Seid freundlich, nur um meinetwillen;
> Die Müh ist klein, der Spaß ist groß.
>
> [Be sociable, just for my sake;
> It's lots of fun and little ache.
> (4048–49)]

Social entertainment replaces the arduous climb up the mountain in the dark for the apparently rather delicate devil figure.

Mephistopheles similarly laments the physical exertion and mountainous dangers while climbing on two other occasions. During the "Classical Walpurgis Night," he separates from Faust and the Homunculus, scrambling upwards on his own, across from them, "an der Gegenseite kletternd" (climbing on the opposite side). Once again he fumes about the strain and the tree roots with distinct echoes of the previous hike,

> Da muß ich mich durch steile Felsenstreppen
> Durch alter Eichen starre Wurzeln schleppen!
>
> [Here I must toil up stairs of slanting rocks,
> Across unyielding roots of ancient oaks!
> (7951–52)]

And on the third occasion, he complains as he and Faust arrive on the "High Mountains" in act 4, Faust by cloud-transport, and Mephistopheles with the help of seven-mile boots. Warning Faust of the cliffs' dangers, Mephistopheles demands to know why they are landing in the awful heights. Mephistopheles dislikes the wild landscape, and he prefers the magical strides of his boots over tedious hiking:

> Das heiß ich endlich vorgeschritten!
> Nun aber sag, was fällt dir ein?
> Steigst ab in solcher Gräuel Mitten,
> Im gräßlich gähnenden Gestein.
>
> [Now that was rapid transport for us!
> But tell me, what are you about?
> Debarking in the midst of horrors,
> In grimly yawning rock redoubt?
> (10067–70)]

Mephistopheles stresses his concern, and his fussiness and fatigue limit Faust's mountain excursions.

Faust's flight to the "High Mountains" in act 4 has specific connections to both the hike in part 1 on "Walpurgis Night" and to his third and final ascent with the cloud-angels from the "Mountain Gorges" in part 2. In the first and second ascents, we see Mephistopheles' hesitation to climb, his complaints about both the exertion and the dangers, and his concern about Faust's safety. There are also extensive geological descriptions and discussions in both the "Walpurgis Night" climb and the "High Mountains." In the former scene, he warns Faust to heed the deep cracks in the rocks, describing the glowing fire visible in the abyss of the cliffs. This description attests to Goethe's increasing interest in geological forces and mining, though it is described by Mephistopheles as being "Lord Mammon's fabulous palace."

Faust describes at length the glowing light and steaming vapors emerging from below, which means that rather than gazing upward at the peak or into the valley, he remains mesmerized by the glimpse into the mountain's interior. The potentially sublime moment is instead a mix of geological description and ominous evocation of hellish glimmerings.

> Wie seltsam glimmert durch die Gründe
> Ein morgenrötlich trüber Schein!
> Und selbst bis in die tiefen Schlünde
> Des Abgrunds wittert er hinein.
>
> [How strangely in the vales it glimmers,
> As of a lurid sunrise sheen,
> And probes with summer-lightening shimmers
> The deepest clefts of the ravine!
> (3916–19)]

As Faust gazes downwards into the depths, Mephistopheles remains the cautious, worrying guide instructing his companion to hold tightly to the cliffs lest he plummet into the yawning chasms. It seems Mephistopheles fears that the steep rocks and gleaming lights may lead Faust to a premature fall; it is odd that a devilish figure seeking the soul's capture in Hell would dedicate so much time to fearful admonitions about avoiding descent into "Mammon's palace." It is as if he actually sees the physical risk as a greater threat than the moral gamble with the soul. Again, the play insists on the physical body even in scenes where one expects the supernatural.

Similarly, in the "High Mountains," during Faust's second mountain ascent, Mephistopheles worries about his companion's wellbeing and describes the mountain as the "Grund der Hölle" (pit of Hell) that was deep in the earth until raised up by tremendous volcanic forces. The imagery he uses is once again simultaneously geological and diabolical, so that the reader is confronted with how this seemingly spiritual moment is as much a material description of mountain formation as it is a sublime view of transcendence. Faust and Mephistopheles echo here the debate between Thales and Anaxagoras in the "Classical Walpurgis Night" about whether the earth's surface is shaped primarily by violent, fiery upheavals or rather the long, slow processes of consolidation out of the watery chaos into solid form, views with which Goethe himself struggled for years. Mephistopheles claims to have been there through the entire process, and to have witnessed the wild transformations of the earth's surface when "down became up."

> Was ehmals Grund war ist nun Gipfel.
> Sie gründen auch hierauf die rechten Lehren
> Das Unterste ins Oberste zu kehren.
>
> [What was the base one time, is now the peak.
> On this the proper recipes are grounded
> By which the top and bottom are confounded.
> (10088–90)]

Standing on high peaks in Goethe's *Faust* provides the reader with *material* insights into earth's historical processes much more than with *spiritual* insights. It is a physical realm that confounds expectations of time and space. In sum, Faust's first and second mountain ascents share concrete geological details of the earth's active processes, and both these experiences feature Mephistopheles' complaints about hiking, his preference for flying, and his fears about mountain dangers.

In contrast, the second and third ascents share the significant feature of Faust's cloud-travel. His trip into the "High Mountains" on the cloud demonstrates that in Faust's world, one *can* travel on clouds, physically.[18] Flying is also possible with the help of Mephistopheles' magic mantle and horses. Yet the cloud trips in acts 4 and 5 present a new dimension, not of magic, but rather of atmospheric processes — this is where geology joins meteorology. The first misty (rather than mystical) flight into the high mountains after his love affair with Helen is, in other words, the preamble for Faust's final ascent with the clouds at the conclusion of the tragedy. It establishes cloud travel as a "real" possibility (rather than just a metaphor for the spirit's journey to the Lord above) and it thereby links Faust's physical acts and movements with the water cycle. Additionally, act 3 continues after Faust's and Helen's departure; significantly, it concludes with the chorus of female spirits who refuse to return to Hades because they desire to remain on the earth's surface as various forms of water. They transform into mountain streams, the juice of fruits that feed the hungry and make wines for the thirsty, and the creeks bringing life-giving water to meadows, forests, and to farmers' cultivated fields. The trajectory here moves once again from the mythological (the chorus and Helen) to various forms of water, or from the ephemeral and literary into more concrete and material forms.

Faust's development at this point seems to be the opposite of the chorus: the female spirits of the chorus become part of the water cycles, while Faust decides he must intervene and control the flow of water by building a dike against the sea. Yet his final ascent with the clouds through the mountains at the end of the play demonstrates that he, just like the chorus, becomes part of the water cycles. Believing that he can control the sea water, he dies with the delusion of success. However, his final flight through the mountains occurs as his remains are carried upward by cloud-like angels, whose rising path follows the same swirling motions that Goethe describes in his atmospheric studies. Faust's trajectory hence moves from love story to cloud story, or from mythology to meteorology. Perhaps the play is a "tragedy" as the subtitle claims, because Faust's life is inescapably pushed, pulled, and drawn onward not only by the "eternal feminine" as in the final line in the play, but also by the "eternal material" such as bodily desire, pregnancies, and the weather flows. He succumbs, unwittingly and ironically, to the very forces against which he dedicates his final battle against the sea.

Before he can vanquish the waves with a grandiose dike, however, Faust must first obtain political support. Hence he joins the wars in the "High Mountains" in act 4, helping the Kaiser to gain victory. The next step is financing his land-development project, which Faust easily manages with the aid of his minions, who engage in colonialism, piracy, and murder. This strategy is successful, and act 5 of *Faust* features the dike, but also a putrid swamp where there was supposed to be free land. Faust's best efforts to counter nature's mutability fail and he does not realize that his workers, the lemurs, are actually digging his grave ("Grab") instead of channels ("Graben") to drain the excess water. We never learn the fate of this land, but we witness Faust's death, the ensuing battle over his remains, and his final ascent into the clouds. The earth-air battle between the devils (wanting to pull Faust into the earth) and the angels (wanting to pull him upward into the air) begins when Mephistopheles calls his devilish helpers to come and transport Faust's remains to Hell, only to watch helplessly as the cloud-like angels emerge from the air, grabbing Faust's remains and fluttering distracting rose petals everywhere. The devils blow fire in order to protect themselves from the lurid blossoms, but the heated air from the burning petals only serves to help the angels as they ascend upward on the drafts with Faust's remains. Though this victorious flight is usually understood as an affirmation of Faustian striving and forgiveness by God, I read it as being also an ironic enactment of the meteorological battles between the earth and the air that Goethe describes in his analyses of weather. As he writes in his cloud essay describing this conflict: "Die mittlere Region ist die des Kumulus; in ihr wird eigentlich der Konflikt bereitet, ob die obere Luft oder die Erde den Sieg erhalten soll" (The mid-region is that of the cumulus; this is where the conflict is actually prepared: the battle to decide whether the upper air or the earth will be victorious).[19] This final scene in *Faust* contains many precise details of Goethe's "Witterungslehre" (meteorological study), of which I mention here only several for the sake of brevity. For example, in both the scientific essay and the play, Goethe describes three air regions through which the water vapor (or Faust's remains) must travel as they ascend; a main consideration in both texts is the air's ability to "carry" water or "elements" upward; and

Goethe presents the movement upward in both instances as a battle between the earth and the air for preeminence.

The final ascent through the "Mountain Gorges" is famously laden with imagery and terms taken from the Bible and, equally, from Goethe's meteorological studies. Yet the vast majority of readings follow only the biblical path and see Faust's flight with clouds as a redemptive ascent to heaven. In such readings, Faust's many deeds are forgiven and accepted as merely the collateral damage of a heroic and "spiritual" quest that is accepted by God. In contrast, I build on the readings by John McCarthy and Gernot Böhme, among others, who focus on the material and meteorological aspects of this journey (and the play more broadly).[20] The material framework for this scene deserves at least the same amount of attention as the Christian terminology. Furthermore, with particular relevance for our discussion of mountains, the landscape here is concretely rugged: "Bergschluchten, Wald, Fels," (mountain gorges, forest, cliffs). The scenery sets the stage for Faust's final flight upward with the misty angels, whose qualities are as heavenly as those of water vapor, shifting in shape, size, and content as they progress through the three regions of air (the lower, middle, and upper realm). To assume that this scene depicts only transcendence is to ignore all of the mountain discussions throughout Goethe's play that enact the transformation from the apparently divine or sublime into the concretely material. It also means ignoring, as people are so often wont to do, the physical environment, even when the climatic events dramatically reshape events, as in the final scene of the play, but also more broadly today.

Taking climate seriously in Goethe's *Faust* requires noting that the battle between the devils and angels at the end is an ironic enactment of what Goethe saw as a battle between the "Anziehungskraft," or the pull of the earth on air, and the "Erwärmungskraft," or warming power that causes expansion, "Ausdehnung." According to Goethe, all atmospheric interactions are caused by "telluric," or earthly, not heavenly or astrological, forces. He makes this assertion repeatedly in his weather writings: he declares "die Hauptbedingungen der Witterungslehre für tellurisch" (the primary conditions of the weather theory to be telluric); these forces emerge from a "veränderlichen pulsierenden Schwerkraft der Erde" (shifting, pulsing gravitational pull of the earth).[21] Claiming the actions of the heavenly planets as a cause for weather is unsupportable. McCarthy also reads *Faust* alongside Goethe's meteorological essays, asserting that "the entire opus of *Faust* is framed by telluric explanations."[22] Following McCarthy and accepting that one must seek earthly, not heavenly, causes in *Faust* has significant implications for the final scenes, in which the angels and devils battle over Faust's remains until the former victoriously ascend. In this battle, the devils blow fire and the angels take advantage of the inevitable rising of hot air that also carries

Faust's remains. Mephistopheles rages against the fire (one must note the irony):

> Mir brennt der Kopf, das Herz, die Leber brennt,
> Ein überteuflisch Element!
>
> [My liver burns, my heart, my head as well,
> Some super-devilish element!
> (11753–54)]

The angels, on the other hand, sing happily of the holy flames that rise up and cleanse the air:

> Heilige Gluten!
> Wen sie umschweben
> Fühlt sich im Leben
> Selig mit Guten.
> Alle vereinigt
> Hebt euch und preist,
> Luft ist gereinigt
> Atme der Geist.
>
> [Sheltered by glows
> All-holiest, mightiest,
> Bliss with the righteous
> Living, he knows.
> In unison fair
> Soar now and quire,
> In purified air
> May the spirit respire!
> (11817–24)]

And the clouds carry him off, upwards, "Wolkengewande / Tragt ihn empor" (Cloud garments / Carry him upward)[23] through the mountains as Mephistopheles is left below, bemoaning his loss and brief fall into desire. This experience shares much with Goethe's description of the changes in air pressure and the impact on water vapor or precipitation in his barometer essay: either the earth draws the water vapor toward itself and precipitation occurs (during low barometric pressure) or else the vapor is "carried upwards" and dispersed (during high barometric pressure):

> Hoher Barometerstand hebt die Wasserbildung auf, die Atmosphäre vermag die Feuchte zu tragen, oder sie in ihre Elemente zu zersetzen; niederer Barometerstand läßt eine Wasserbildung zu, die oft grenzenlos zu sein scheint. Nach unserer Terminologie würden wir also sagen: zeigt die Erde sich mächtig, vermehrt sie ihre Anziehungskraft, so überwindet sie die Atmosphäre, deren Inhalt ihr nun ganz ange-

hört; was allenfalls darin zu Stande kommt muß als Tau, als Reif herunter . . .

[High barometric pressure eliminates precipitation, since the atmosphere is able to carry the moisture or to reduce it to its elements; low barometric pressure allows a precipitation, which can often seem endless. In our terminology, we would thus say: when the earth shows its power and increases its pull (gravity), then it overcomes the atmosphere and claims its content, this must then fall to form dew or frost . . . (my translation)][24]

When the atmosphere, rather than the earth, reigns supreme, then water vapor is lifted up, much like in *Faust*, as the titular hero spirals upwards with the angels. Of course, as Goethe notes in virtually every weather essay he writes, any water vapor that rises will eventually return to the earth as precipitation — this is a true cycle, one that implies a potential return to the earth and not just the linear path "upward" with a conclusive ending in heaven.

Fittingly, the final ascent in *Faust* has no moment of actual arrival. That is, Goethe excised a concluding scene in which Faust would be tried by Mary and the angels. As J. M. van der Laan writes, Faust "never leaves the earthly confines of the mountain gorges, never rises above the mountain peaks. While there are strong indications that Faust continues to ascend and develop in the afterlife, his passivity, unconsciousness, even obliviousness negate such a conclusion."[25] Faust does not complete his ascent at the end of part II, nor does he gain access to the devil atop the mountain in part I, rather, he's still moving in both — spiraling onward in the one and dancing (and watching theater) in the other. This symmetry of incomplete mountain ascents is relevant for understanding how the play enacts materiality as our inescapable environment. Stuart Atkins notes, "if there is a 'beyond,' it can only be part of the non-transcendental continuum in which Faust's mortal existence was lived."[26] If we consider Faust's final flight with the cloud angels as an enactment of movement through the three regions of air described in Goethe's weather studies, then it is reasonable to assume that he might continue to follow the water vapor, "precipitate" and — in perfect symmetry — fall again to earth. Rather than achieving ephemeral transcendence, Faust is rendered material, bodily, and still participating (albeit passively since he is carried by cloud-angels) in earthly flows. He remains part of earth.

By thus delineating our human strivings within nature's processes despite Faust's grandiose and hubristic efforts to the contrary, Goethe's tragedy is an important document for ecocriticism. Furthermore, Faust's three mountain ascents — one on foot, two by cloud — evoke the landscape of modernity as Goethe sees it with all of its delusions of grandeur and efforts to manipulate and control on a grand scale the elements around us. Yet these ascents also provide quite modern insights into our material existence. That is, the most ephemeral and transcendent moments in *Faust* abruptly — or simultaneously — appear to be the most material. Hence when Faust ascends carried by swirling cloud angels, that ethereal moment is also the most concretely meteorological description in the play. Weather and mountains are the cosmic frame in Goethe's tragedy; they provide access to dreams of divinity that transform before our eyes, like shape-shifting clouds, into material flows. Faust resists and then succumbs to the modern human fate: he believes that he can move beyond matter, but he remains, of course, fully within environmental materiality, no matter how poetically garbed that realm may appear.

Notes

[1] See Jost Hermand, *Im Wettlauf mit der Zeit: Anstöße zu einer ökologiebewußten Ästhetik* (Berlin: Sigma Bohn Verlag, 1991); and Kate Rigby, *Topographies of the Sacred: The Poetics of Place in European Romanticism* (Charlottesville: U of Virginia P, 2004).

[2] There is one other "ascent" of sorts in the play, when Faust and Mephistopheles are on the "high mountain" in act 4 of part II. They decide to help the Kaiser's war efforts in order to fund Faust's dike-building venture. Hence, "they climb over the low mountain range" (sie steigen über das Mittelgebirg herüber; stage directions after line 10296). This climb, however, is actually more of a *descent* from the high mountain, and there is no discussion of it in the play's dialogue. All German citations from *Faust* are based on Johann Wolfgang Goethe, *Faust: Texte*, ed. Albrecht Schöne (Frankfurt am Main: Deutscher Klassiker Verlag, 1994); English citations are from Johann Wolfgang von Goethe, *Faust: A Tragedy*, trans. Walter Arndt, ed. Cyrus Hamlin (New York: Norton, 2001). Further references are given in the text with references to the line numbers from the play.

[3] For more details of Goethe's "impossible climb" up the Brocken, as well as many of his other excursions, see Nicholas Boyle, *Goethe: The Poet and the Age*, vol. 1, *The Poetry of Desire* (Oxford: Oxford UP, 1992).

[4] Even the "Prologue in Heaven," when the Lord speaks to Mephistopheles, is framed by nature's ongoing processes such as the sun's course across the skies and the eternal struggles between the ocean and the cliffs. Jane Brown similarly notes that "Goethe's modernity would thus seem to lie in his emphasis on nature over the divine order." Jane Brown, *Goethe's* Faust: *The German Tragedy* (Ithaca, NY: Cornell UP, 1986), 44.

[5] Astrida Orle Tantillo, "Damned to Heaven: The Tragedy of *Faust* Revisited," *Monatshefte* 99, no. 4 (2007): 455.

[6] I describe Faust's final ascent in terms of Goethe's weather studies in Heather I. Sullivan, "Ecocriticism, the Elements, and the Ascent/Descent into Weather in Goethe's *Faust*," *Goethe Yearbook* 17 (2010): 55–72.

⁷ Considering the number of studies on Goethe's geology and the universal acknowledgement of its reverberations in *Faust*, it is surprising that there is not more discussion of the play's mountains. Even the thorough volume by Wilhelm Emrich, *Die Symbolik von Faust II* (Bonn: Athenäum, 1957), which includes much on geology, has little to say about mountains. Typically, the vast scholarship on both *Faust* and Goethe's geology tends to be *either* literary *or* scientific rather than both together. Even the recent and insightful study by Margrit Wyder, "Goethes geologische Passionen: Vom Alter der Erde," *Goethe Jahrbuch* 125 (2008): 136–46, brings in citations from *Faust* primarily as documentation of Goethe's interest in geology rather than as part of literary analysis. For the most extensive testimony of Goethe's geological themes in literature and science, see Wolf von Engelhardt, *Goethe im Gespräch mit der Erde: Landschaft, Gesteine, Mineralien und Erdgeschichte in seinem Leben und Werk* (Weimar: Böhlau, 2003).

⁸ Rigby, *Topographies of the Sacred*, 165.

⁹ For introductions to ecocriticism, see Greg Garrard's *Ecocriticism* (London: Routledge, 2004); Cheryll Glotfelty and Harold Fromm, eds., *The Ecocriticism Reader* (Athens: U of Georgia P, 1996); and Lawrence Buell, *Writing for an Endangered World: Literature, Culture, and Environment in the U.S. and Beyond* (London: Belknap, 2001).

¹⁰ Dana Phillips, *The Truth of Ecology: Nature, Culture, and Literature in America* (Oxford: Oxford UP, 2003), 209.

¹¹ Many have claimed that Goethe's preference for non-violent and long, slow development on earth (both geological and political) meant that he was a "Neptunist." His actual position was more complex and involved the incorporation of aspects of Vulcanism into Neptunism. See Gabrielle Bersier, "Goethe's Geology in Flux: Vulcanism and Neptunism in the Translation of Richard Payne Knight's *Expedition into Sicily* and the *Italian Journey*," in *Goethe, Chaos, and Complexity*, ed. Herbert Rowland (Amsterdam: Rodopi, 2001), 35–45; and Ingrid Dzialas, *Auffassung und Darstellung der Elemente bei Goethe* (Berlin: Ebering, 1939).

¹² For discussions of early geology, the dawning recognition of the earth's immense age, and the ongoing alterations of mountains, see, for example, Claude C. Albritton, *The Abyss of Time: Changing Conceptions of the Earth's Antiquity after the Sixteenth Century* (San Francisco: Freeman, Cooper, 1980); G. S. Rousseau and Roy Porter, eds., *The Ferment of Knowledge: Studies in the Historiography of Eighteenth-Century Science* (Cambridge: Cambridge UP, 1980); Nicholas A. Rupke, "Caves, Fossils and the History of the Earth," in *Romanticism and the Sciences*, ed. Andrew Cunningham and Nicholas Jardine (Cambridge: Cambridge UP, 1990), 241–59; and Heinz-Dieter Weber, ed., *Vom Wandel des neuzeitlichen Naturbegriffs* (Constance: Konstanz UP, 1989). Regarding Goethe specifically, see Peter Matussek, ed. *Goethe und die Verzeitlichung der Natur* (Munich: Beck, 1998).

¹³ Johann Wolfgang Goethe, "Karlsbad, Anfang September 1819," in *Schriften zur allgemeinen Naturlehre, Geologie und Mineralogie*, ed. Wolf von Engelhardt and

Manfred Wenzel, vol. 25 of *Sämtliche Werke: Briefe, Tagebücher und Gespräche* (Frankfurt am Main: Deutscher Klassiker Verlag, 1989), 210.

[14] Leland Phelps, "Goethe's Meteorological Writings," *Monatshefte* 48, no. 6 (1956): 318.

[15] See the discussion in Boyle, *Goethe: The Poet and the Age*, 299–301.

[16] Johann Wolfgang Goethe, "Granit II," in *Schriften zur allgemeinen Naturlehre, Geologie und Mineralogie*, 314–15.

[17] Many scholars agree that Goethe puts "nature" where God had been before; John Gearey states, for example: "Where an earlier age might have seen God or an unfathomable universal design behind what the eye could not perceive, he saw physical occurrences and physical laws." John Gearey, *Goethe's Other* Faust*: The Drama, Part II* (Toronto: U of Toronto P, 1992), 93.

[18] For an excellent discussion of Faustian clouds as both physical and spiritual, see Edith Anna Kunz, "'Luftige Welten' — Zur Poetik von Rauch und Wasserdampf in Goethes *Faust*," *Colloquia Germanica* 39, no. 1 (2006): 43–56.

[19] Johann Wolfgang Goethe, "Wolkengestalt: Nach Howard," in Engelhardt and Wenzel, *Schriften zur allgemeinen Naturlehre, Geologie und Mineralogie*, 231.

[20] John McCarthy's exemplary study of *Faust* in terms of Goethe's science and chaos theory thoroughly grounds the play in terms of materiality. See John McCarthy, *Remapping Reality: Chaos and Creativity in Science and Literature (Goethe — Nietzsche — Grass)* (Amsterdam: Rodopi, 2006). See also Gernot Böhme, "'Mir läuft ein Schauer übern ganzen Leib': Das Wetter, die Witterungslehre und die Sprache der Gefühle," *Goethe Jahrbuch* 124 (2007): 133–41.

[21] Johann Wolfgang Goethe, "Witterungslehre 1825," in *Schriften zur allgemeinen Naturlehre, Geologie und Mineralogie*, 300.

[22] McCarthy, *Remapping Reality*, 184.

[23] This quotation from *Faust* is included in the Klassiker edition but has no numbering (it is inserted between lines 11831 and 32) and follows logically with the final scene's cloud-thematic (as noted in the comments to this edition). See Albrecht Schöne, *Johann Wolfgang Goethe. Faust; Kommentare* (Frankfurt am Main: Deutscher Klassiker Verlag, 1994), 776. (My translation, since the Norton edition excludes it.)

[24] Johann Wolfgang Goethe, "Über die Ursache der Barometerschwankungen," in *Schriften zur allgemeinen Naturlehre, Geologie und Mineralogie*, 259.

[25] J. M. van der Laan, *Seeking Meaning for Goethe's* Faust (London: Continuum, 2007), 140.

[26] Stuart Atkins, *Essays on Goethe*, ed. Jane K. Brown and Thomas P. Saine (Columbia, SC: Camden House, 1995), 316.

Spectacular Scenery and Slippery Descents: Narrating the Mountains of Tropical Polynesia

Sabine Wilke

COMPARED TO THE HEROIC TALES of mountaineering in the Alps, the Himalayas, or the Andes, the narratives about climbing volcanoes in the Pacific do not even come close in drama. Most tourists today fly to Hawaii and other tropical islands to lie on the beach, surf the waves, snorkel in the pristine waters, enjoy the sunshine, and smell the tropical flowers, but not to exert themselves on strenuous hikes. The Pacific is, after all, "a place of dreams," as Rod Edmond recently reminded us.[1] Travel guides caution even the physically fit visitor about summiting peaks in the Pacific during the heat of the day. Climbers posting online at summitpost.org, for example, characterize Tahitian mountains as wet and rainy. One climber "came to the more accurate conclusion that small things can also come in terrifying packages. . . . Holding on to a rope while descending wet rock covered with slick mud having the consistency of glazed snot, while dangling over a 370 meter/1,200 foot void in the rain does not inspire confidence."[2] Mt. Orohena, the highest peak in Tahiti, rises an impressive 2,241 m/7,352 ft. above sea level and is a challenging climb by any measure. In their trip reports, climbers seem to distinguish between the stunning views from the summits of Tahitian mountains and the actual ascent and descent. It is this bifurcation that characterizes mountaineering discourses in tropical Polynesia, a trope that was first articulated by German explorer and scientist George Forster in the latter half of the eighteenth century.[3]

George Forster was the oldest son of Johann Reinhold Forster, a naturalist and pastor, who had taken his ten-year-old son on assignment to Russia, where they researched the German colony on the Volga. Upon their return from Russia, the Forster family settled in England, where the father took a teaching post. In 1772 Johann Reinhold became a member of the Royal Society. When Captain Cook decided to replace Joseph Banks with another scientist (because Banks demanded too much room on the ship) the British admiralty asked Johann Reinhold to take Bonks's place. George was only seventeen years old when he and his father left on their voyage with Captain Cook. George Forster's travel narrative, *A Voyage round the World* (1777), offers a detailed reflection on the nature and the anthropology of the places that he and his father visited during Captain Cook's second expedition to the Southern Hemisphere (1772–75), a mission that aimed to verify the location of a southern continent.[4] Forster first composed his travelogue in English for the British admiralty, then translated it into German and significantly revised it, adding a new preface explaining the history and circumstances of the publication. While the ethnography of Forster's travelogue and the philosophical approach to his topic has been critically analyzed by many scholars from a variety of viewpoints, the narration of the mountain scenery, specifically the passages in which he talks about his forays into the highlands of Tahiti, have not received the same amount of critical attention. Through a close analysis of select passages from the expedition's first and second visit to Tahiti in 1773 and in 1774 respectively, I discuss the specific parameters of the discourse on mountaineering in the Pacific, which forms part of a larger discourse of tropicalization. Forster stands at the very beginning of the formation of this discourse, whose chief tropes are fertility and superabundance. While Forster's depictions of tropical plants and mountain scenery adhere to the aesthetic of tropicalization, the narrative descriptions of the actual ascents and descents also reflect the difficulty of conquest. Climbing the tropical mountains of the Pacific is a unique experience that cannot be easily told using the typical discursive models of mountaineering conquest. The undoing of these discursive models is the flipside of that tradition and can be effectively studied through the example of Forster's report.

Summiting the peaks of tropical islands and narrating their ascent and descent has little to do with the classic mountaineering adventure narratives of the nineteenth and twentieth centuries, which tend to focus on the heroic masculine figure, often in a context of national pride and imperial identity — a tendency that was heightened in the polar discourses from the turn of the century. Peter Bayers argues that "Everest and Denali offered white men particularly unique symbolic spaces on which to enact their masculine fantasies, figuratively elevating their supposed masculine virtues to 'new' height."[5] This process of "elevating" the virility of the imperial male body in order to master the challenges of the natural environment frequently led to naming these spaces after European figures, usurping these mountains from the local mythological imagination of the indigenous populations, and inscribing them with a Romantic aura of distance that would forever heighten the achievement of conquest to a level that future generations of climbers would find difficult to surpass.[6] Mountaineering in the Pacific, especially as practiced by the Forsters in the later eighteenth century, is never an activity performed for conquest alone. It is usually an activity that has a specific purpose (botanizing), one that is often undertaken in groups, before or after pleasurable picnic stops and after an extended period of engaging in transactions with the local population in the lowlands before the climb, frequently in tropical heat or rainfall and in slippery, foggy conditions. Forster's botanizing trips to the peaks of Tahiti led him through thick virgin forests without paths, culminating (if luck was on their side) in a climactic experience at the top where, when the fog lifted, the most beautiful panoramic views of the island could be enjoyed. Bringing insights from colonial and postcolonial studies of the Pacific to bear on this material, we are able to understand Forster's descriptions of the Tahitian mountains not only as tropicalized objects in a Western aesthetic frame, but also as physical places of contact that are difficult to conquer and that assert their specificity over climbers from a temperate climate. Nowadays Tahiti's bays and scenic valleys have become part of the discourse that constitutes the nature of tropical paradise: its foggy mountaintops still engage today's hiker in an interactive experience with the tropical environment, which frequently delays or even denies a satisfactory summit experience. Tropical nature, it seems, is even more elusive than the typical rugged Alpine peak. It is the physical counterpart of the Pacific muse, the exotic female that lures men with "intoxicating color, movement, and hospitality without peer."[7]

The sensory aspect of mountain climbing is still an important part of the brochures that frame celebrations of mountaineering culture such as the annual mountain film festival in Telluride, Colorado, which aspires to deliver a "six-senses experience of art, adventure, culture and the environment."[8] The festival features a symposium, special events, film screenings, and, of course, the chance to hike the trails and summit the nearby peaks. It is a celebration of a relationship that the modern Euro-American subject has developed vis-à-vis mountainous environments, a discourse that was formed in the context of nineteenth- and twentieth-century Alpinism and discussed in the introduction as well as the previous chapters on Haller, geo-poetics, and the mountain sublime. As Clemens Wimmer has shown, the Alps appear first as places of farming and mining, but over a period of time were transformed into the last bastion against industrialization, as the quintessential location of beauty and the sublime.[9] This essay seeks to position the discourse of Pacific mountaineering that emerges in Forster's travelogue within a discussion located at the intersection of ecocriticism, postcolonialism, tropicalization, and the critique of globalization. While environmental perspectives on culture tend to stress global issues, postcolonial orientations in scholarship pay attention to local issues.[10] In response to this challenge, some scholars have identified the need to bring together ecocriticism's concern for nature with a postcolonial critique of dominant culture.[11] "Greening" postcolonialism is a process that refers to the fact that "postcolonial criticism has effectively renewed, rather than belatedly discovered, its commitment to the environment, reiterating its insistence on the inseparability of current crises of ecological mismanagement from historical legacies of imperialistic exploitation and authoritarian abuse."[12] On the other hand, a postcolonial perspective within ecocriticism effectively reduces the risk of first-world environmentalism "turning itself into another, late-capitalist form of ecological imperialism" by insisting that overpopulation (especially in the third world) is the greatest threat to our environment, rather than blaming first-world consumption.[13] George Forster's narrative of his botanizing trips in Tahiti can be positioned at the borderline of postcolonial and environmental engagements, as it presents "a western white male subject in his claims to a new environmental and epistemological territory."[14] At the same time, Forster wrestles with the ideal of hybridity and cross-culturation, writing local history and developing more diverse models of writing the environmental experience.[15] Forster's discourse on mountaineering in the tropics pulls the rug out from under postcolonial criticism's claim that a universalist conceit of the European male is a limited conception of the natural universe.[16] The historian Richard Grove has recently made the controversial claim that "while European instrumentalist attitudes to the environment and the corporate exploitation of land continue . . . it was in the colonized areas of the world that European naturalists, scientists and administrators first apprehended the need for conservation measures and, in recognizing the finitude of lands, flora and fauna, began to implement strategies of preservation."[17] He was extending to environmental discourse what Franz Fanon had claimed for colonial discourse, namely that it demonstrates the fact that Europe is the product of its encounter with the other. Forster's travelogue shapes this discourse of ecological imperialism and at the same time points to its erasure by paying close attention to local specimens and their indigenous context. Forster describes mountain ascents and descents as concrete physical engagements with tropical nature, underscoring the belief that "direct experience has the power to transform content and is not fully restricted by codes or discursive paradigms."[18] Alfred W. Crosby defined ecological imperialism as the biological expansion of Europe between 900 and 1900, a time in which Europeans established homes far away from their native continent and "leapfrogged around the globe," creating Neo-Europes in temperate regions that produce food surpluses.[19] Part of this ecological imperialism is the act of writing an illustrated natural history of such a colonized region, such as Mark Catesby's work on the southeastern coastal regions of the United States.[20] Forster's job on Cook's team was to collect and draw plant and animal species. He completed this task systematically and passionately by following the principles of close observation and direct representations, as famously depicted in Jean Francis Rigaud's painting from 1780 and the widely circulating 1781 engraving of the image that shows father and son in New Zealand engaged in drawing a tropical bird.[21] In fact, Rigaud's painting was recently acquired by the National

Portrait Gallery of Australia, where it was unveiled next to James Webber's portrait of Captain Cook on 29 September 2009 in a ceremony honoring the development of Australia's colonies in the context of European enlightenment. Forster's plant and animal drawings are catalogued in the botany and zoology libraries of the Natural History Museum in London. The Forster collection in the botany library consists of about 200 drawings, drafts, and engravings mounted on cupboard frames and stored in boxes.[22] While the animal drawings are typically characterized by a sense of drama — birds are depicted as they land or as they catch prey and usually within a context such as sitting on a bush or atop a tree that is typical for their environment — Forster's representations of plants closely follow the system of plant classifications established by Carl Linnaeus. Donald Worster explains how the "artificial" system of biological taxonomy that underlay these many writings took all Europe by storm and soon were taught both to advanced scholars in universities and to young ladies in their gardens: "The system was an accurate reflection of Linnaeus's economical, arranging mind: one simply counted the number of stamens and pistils to determine where a plant belonged in the divine scheme. A few such calculations, and all living nature could be organized into neat rows of shelves and boxes."[23] The universalizing impetus behind such classifications is evidence of the colonial mindset that characterizes the travelogues of these early explorers — including Forster's — and their attempt to narrate colonial nature. From a postcolonial perspective, they "must be critiqued for their propensity to project European fears, hopes, or expectations in the place of the native."[24]

To be sure, such a general colonial attitude toward his subject matter characterizes Forster's narrative as well, but he transcends it at the level of local description. Russell Berman even suggests that "Forster stands for a capacity within the Enlightenment to recognize and appreciate other cultures, not because he represents some sort of exception to an otherwise domineering rationalism, but because this emancipatory possibility was and remains a potential for the Enlightenment and its exploration of the world."[25] Anja Hall argues that the spatial perception of approaching mountainous islands on ships is comparable to the topographical "monarch-of-all-I-survey" view that is so characteristic of colonial gazing into virgin space from a privileged angle.[26] It is a viewpoint that imposes order and structure on its otherwise chaotic material. Forster's famous passage relating the Resolution's approach to Tahiti on 16 August 1773 shares many features of this privileged view, which moves from describing a broad overview of the island to a physical sensation (faint breeze and a delicious scent), then to the mountains lit by the morning sun, from there to a lower range of hills and, finally, to the plain with its fertile landscape. This choice of narrative sequence reflects Forster's debt to the European aesthetic of landscape that characterizes his prose:

> It was one of those beautiful mornings which the poets of all nations have attempted to describe, when we saw the isle of O-Taheitee, within two miles before us. The east wind which had carried us so far, was entirely vanished, and a faint breeze only wafted a delicious perfume from the land, and curled the surface of the sea. The mountains, clothed with forests, rose majestic in various spiry forms, on which we already perceived the light of the rising sun: nearer to the eye a lower range of hills, easier of ascent, appeared, wooded like the former, and coloured with several pleasing hues of green, soberly mixed with autumnal browns. At their foot lay the plain, crowned with its fertile bread-fruit trees, over which rose innumerable palms, the princes of the grove. (*V*, 143)

The first perception is that of the sweet scent that pervades the Tahitian air. The mountains of the tropical seas are "clothed" and they rise from sea level in majestic "spiry" forms in very dramatic fashion, as seen through the filter of sunrise. Forster refers to a gaze that is trained in looking at paintings of European landscapes and describing them according to a certain pattern, usually from background to middle ground to foreground in increasingly telescopic fashion, from nature to anthropology, commenting on composition and on color.[27] The passage continues to dwell on the peacefulness of the scene and finally progresses to a description of the homes among the trees, the canoes hauled up along the beaches, and the security of the harbor, and ends with an affirmation of the theatrical nature of the colonial scenery: "The sun beginning to illuminate the plains, its inhabitants arose, and enlivened the scene" (*V*, 143). The native islanders of Tahiti are perceived as part of this landscape. The description of the indigenous context is eclipsed for a prioritized view of the scene as landscape. Forster's framing of the description of Aitepeha Harbour establishes the blueprint for a metaphoric engagement with the land, a reading of colonial nature with the help of established European aesthetic models. The passage continues with a focus on the physical features of their surroundings, retracing the initial narrative sequence from a description of the harbor back to the plain, the slopes of lower hills, and, finally, ending with another set of comments on the interior mountains, all of which exhilarate the spirits of the European voyagers.

> The harbour in which we lay was very small, and would not have admitted many more vessels besides our own. The water in it was as smooth as the finest mirror, and the sea broke with a snowy foam around us upon the outer reef. The plain at the foot of the hills was very narrow in this place, but always conveyed the pleasing ideas of fertility, plenty, and happiness. . . . The slopes of the hills, covered with woods, crossed each other on both sides, variously tinted according to their distances; and beyond them, over the cleft of the valley, we saw the interior mountains shattered into various peaks

> and spires, among which was one remarkable pinnacle, whose summit was frightfully bent to one side, and seemed to threaten its downfall every moment. The serenity of the sky, the genial warmth of the air and the beauty of the landscape united to exhilarate our spirits. (*V*, 150)

It is the eye of the European observer trained in ekphrastic language that constructs this telescopic detail of a mountain panorama complete with a frightful pinnacle, a reflecting body of water to heighten the effect of the scene, and almost as an afterthought some indication of native life, people or animals, to show scale. While generally betraying a Eurocentric focus, such close attention to the physical features of the landscape can also function as a location in the narrative where the colonial mindset is undermined by careful attention to local specificities. Barbara Stafford's research on the illustrated travel account is helpful in this context. She maintains that the landscape elements in European travel accounts from that time period attest to a more empirical attitude toward nature and a growing belief in the legibility of matter. In fact, they give testimony to "specific ways in which the legacy of the factual travel narrative forged during the second half of the eighteenth century shaped nineteenth-century attitudes toward landscape representation."[28] For the eighteenth-century traveler "nature comes to be looked upon pictorially — that is, as a series of pictures created to stimulate automatic aesthetic enjoyment,"[29] a point also emphasized by Michael Jacobs, who agrees that "well into the nineteenth century, the European vision of Nature continued to be influenced by such artistic concepts as the Picturesque and the Sublime" but that "by the mid-nineteenth century a more scientific attitude toward the representation of Nature had undoubtedly developed among artists," which led to a more balanced attitude toward the object of description.[30]

This scientific attitude toward nature motivates the European explorer to go on botanizing trips.[31] On Thursday, 19 August 1773, George Forster and his father went ashore for the first time "in pursuit of botanical discovery" (*V*, 153). They meet a group of native women who are beating the fibrous bark of the mulberry tree to manufacture tapa cloth and observe how Tahitians cook breadfruit. When the European party wanders further away from shore into the countryside, the native islanders seem to express some uneasiness:

> When they saw us persist in our expedition, the greatest part of them dispersed into their different habitations, and only a few of them attended to us, who made it their business to act as our guides. . . . We came to the foot of the hills, where we left the huts and plantations of the natives behind us, and ascended on a beaten path, passing through an uncultivated shrubbery mixed with several tall timber-trees. Here we searched the most intricate parts, and found several plants and birds hitherto unknown to natural historians. With these

little acquisitions we returned towards the sea, at which our friends the natives expressed their satisfaction. (*V*, 155–56)

Forster's botanizing trips on Tahiti follow a pattern of entry into the tropical forest from the lush inhabited foothills on beaten paths, then continue through virgin brush with the aim of collecting plant specimens, and eventually return to the foothills and to the ship, at times with the accompaniment of a few native guides. In Forster's description of the plants and birds that they encountered, "hitherto unknown to natural historians," local people's knowledge of the flora and fauna of the island is generally discounted. The islanders also do not appear to enjoy the hiking part of these trips to the same degree as the Europeans and the decision, on the part of the Europeans, to discount indigenous knowledge and cultural preferences displays their colonial mindset. The scientific yield of these trips is altogether disappointing to Forster, who compensates for this loss by including observations about the native culture in his field notes (see *V*, 160). Affirming his party's resolution toward discovery, Forster confirms that "we were not to be diverted from our purpose" (*V*, 160) and proceeds to describe his first mountainous ascent, leaving the natives behind, collecting new plant species, marveling at the beauty of a waterfall, and focusing on the panorama that unfolds to the European spectator who looks down onto a pastoral landscape from an elevated position: "This spot, where we had a prospect of the plain below us, and of the sea beyond it, was one of the most beautiful I had ever seen, and could not fail of bringing to remembrance the most fanciful descriptions of poets, which it eclipsed in beauty" (*V*, 160). Narrating Pacific mountaineering experiences always also means engaging the classics and following in their trace. There is never an original experience that precedes the discursive framing. Climbing Tahitian mountains and telling us about it is an activity that happens in a discursive field. Vergil is a must on Forster's packing list.

One of the plant drawings that Forster completed on his botanizing trips to Tahiti is that of "barringtonia speciosa." Forster's illustration reinforces what I call the aesthetics of theatrical display, which is an important part of the aesthetics of the panorama.[32] In this image we can see how Forster gives a view of the adult plant in full display. In other depictions of plants found in Tahiti, Forster records the different developmental stages of the fruit. These are scientific drawings that adhere to the aesthetic of display that characterizes the Western preference for theatrical spectacles. Colonial nature is thus framed twice, scientifically through the Linnean impulse for structured order and aesthetically through the lens of the panorama.

Forster's account of the transactions in Matavai Bay continues to feature his interest in the local cultures, but also contains descriptions of mountain ascents and descents. A visit with King O-Too, for example, is followed by intense descriptions of the many interactions between native islanders and the European crew, including the exchange of women for gifts, something that Forster mentions frequently and disapprovingly. On 29 August 1773, Forster's party left the ship in the early morning hours to explore the island. They observed how the inhabitants of the island rise and then perform their "customary ablutions" (*V*, 186) in the Matavai river. They then visited a family in their dwelling before getting ready to climb a mountain. Forster's narration of his botanizing trips always begins with a description of life and transactions in the lowlands before he proceeds to tell us about the mountainous slopes. On the one hand, this distinct feature of his account is in line with those mountaineering narratives that typically set the scene by discussing ordinary life down below only to establish the mountaineer as an individual who rises above ordinary people, rather than with those that tend to focus on the action above the tree line. At the same time, a gradual intensification in his outdoor endeavors comes across in his narrative. Unfortunately, no undiscovered plant species were found on this particular trip, but Forster and his party were able to observe a large flock of wild ducks rise right before their eyes. The party then crossed a hillside where all the bushes and ferns had been burnt. From there they descended into a lush valley with a picturesque stream running through it. While on the lookout for rare plant species, the Forsters encountered, for the first time in their stay on Tahiti, the challenges of mountaineering in the tropics as they were trying to collect plant specimen in extremely slippery terrain: "On the sides of the hills we gathered several new plants, sometimes at the risk of breaking our necks, on account of the pieces of rock which rolled away under our feet" (*V*, 187). Finally they came to a steep hill and decided to climb to the top despite the difficulties this posed and against the recommendation of the local guide:

> Our Taheitian friend laughed at us, when he saw us faint with fatigue, and sitting down every moment to recover our breath. We heard him blow or breathe slowly but very hard, with open mouth, as he walked behind us; we therefore tried the same experiment, which nature had probably taught them, and found it answered much better than our short panting, which always deprived us of breath. (*V*, 191)

When they made it to the top thanks to their newly acquired breathing technique that made it possible for them to climb this steep and arduous mountain, they were rewarded with a breathtaking view down the Matavai valley, "while the meridian sun threw a steady and calm light on the whole landscape" (*V*, 191). It is this aesthetic experience that gives meaning to the strenuous climb for Forster and his team. Just as he alluded to classical poetry in the description of his earlier climb, here it is a scene of nature lit in the panorama style of landscape painting that makes it all worthwhile.

After a brief sojourn on the top, their native guide then led them back down safely, which turned out to be an even harder and more difficult project than the climb itself and explains the fact that Forster's mountaineering discourse often dwells on the descent more than on the ascent:

> We began to descend therefore, but found it more dangerous than when we came up: we stumbled every moment, and in many places were obliged to slide down on our backs. Our shoes were rather a disadvantage to us, being made extremely slippery by the dry grasses over which we had walked, while the native with his bare feet was surprisingly surefooted. In a short time we gave him our fowling-pieces, to enable us to make use of our hands, and at last we resumed them again, and letting him go before, leaned on his arm in the most difficult places. (*V*, 192)

The guide then called for help, and a Tahitian family approached with refreshing drinks and the promise of a soothing massage for aching leg muscles. Discourses on Tahitian mountaineering originate in and return to a scene of pleasure, keeping in line with the nature of European projections about the Pacific and the filter of tropicalization that shapes these passages. This tendency toward gratification of the senses sets them apart from discourses of Alpine-style mountaineering, which focus on manly climax and summit conquest.

In April 1774 Cook's party returned to Tahiti and revisited many of these scenes. After observing the Tahitian war fleet in action, both Forsters and the Swedish naturalist Dr. Andreas Sparrman once again felt the urge to summit a nearby mountain.[33] As indicated above, Forster's narrative dwells at length on the transactions in the lowlands that precede their actual climb. He observes how they "had a great number of canoes about us all this time, and in them there were always some chiefs of different districts, who brought on board their hogs, and their most valuable possessions, in order to exchange them for red feathers, on which they placed an extravagant value (*V*, 360). After many more distractions of this kind, Johann Reinhold Forster and Dr. Sparrman finally began their botanizing trip, even though the Tahitian guide cautioned them about penetrating further into the tropical forest. But the Forsters and Dr. Sparrman were resolute about climbing the mountain and decided to drop their gear and walk on their own to the summit, where the clouds eventually broke and they had the most delightful views down the valley — if only for a short moment. On the way down, Johann Reinhold Forster injured his leg quite seriously and was only able to return to the boat with the help of the guide. Although the trip was successful from the perspective of collecting new plant species and obtaining a brief view from the summit, Tahitian mountaineering continued to be a dangerous affair because of the steep terrain and slippery ground.

Fig. 1. William Hodges, Tahiti Revisited *(1766).*
National Maritime Museum, Greenwich.

While the Forsters went on their botanizing trips and George later sketched many of the plants as part of his mission to record the whole range of botanical species found on the tropical islands, the painter who accompanied the expedition, William Hodges, drew many mountain scenes and later finished them in oil in his studio in London. The most famous of these scenes is called *Tahiti Revisited* (1766; see fig. 1) and refers to a shore excursion on 2 May 1774, when Forster had "recommended it to Mr. Hodges to visit the cascade which [he] had found in the valley" (*V*, 369). This painting combines, in characteristic fashion, the aesthetic of the panorama with Alpine-style snow-capped mountains in the background and a group of bathing native women in the foreground, framed in the tradition of biblical scenes and deemphasizing their otherness. The only markers of otherness are the basalt pillars to the side of the bay.[34] Bernhard Smith has further analyzed this painting and commented on the replacement of conventional classical motifs with such typical Tahitian elements as the bread-fruit tree, the coconut palm, and the Tahitian girls.[35] The effect of this process is the creation of an eroticized sublime landscape.[36] The terrain is high and mountainous but covered with trees and shrubs. Jagged mountain summits rise up in the distance — painted in the style of Alpine peaks — and in the middle distance a hut is visible by the bank of the river. While Forster's narrative of these climbs reflects concrete and local descriptions of their botanizing trips, always situating the scene of the climb in local transactions, underscoring the group experience at the summit, and acknowledging indigenous help, Hodge's panorama emphasizes the sublimity of the mountainous scene as opposed to the lushness of valley life. Tropical nature as it appears in Hodge's painting is filtered through the tradition of the sublime spectacle first seen in the work of Salvator Rosa, the seventeenth-century Italian Baroque painter who was instrumental in shaping the more dramatic and extravagant style of landscapes that would later become popular in the Romantic era.[37] Forster often refers to Rosa's style of painting when describing rugged nature scenes.

In an analysis of the racial dimension of colonial writing with respect to mountainous Africa, Hermann Wittenberg argues that the picturesque rather than the sublime became the dominant mode of colonial "white writing" and that a postcolonial theory of the sublime needs to emphasize that the sublime is not merely a purely aesthetic category but a rhetorical style that rests on a mode of domination "in which a male subject asserts his rational supremacy over an excessive and unrepresentable experience, leading to a triumphantly enhanced sense of identity."[38] That landscapes are ideological-spatial formations is an important point. But as opposed to the classical colonial mountains that shape imperial discourses, the foggy summits of Tahiti often disappoint the intense European desire for mastery. While it is true that the Forsters and the members of their botanizing parties exhibited "a pervasive and deep interest in mountains" and that they most likely believed that the summits "are privileged places to experience 'a new freedom, a great exhilaration, an exaltation of the body,'"[39] the experience and the narration of mountainous ascents and descents in tropical Polynesia is not immune to effeminizing effects that undercut the fascination with colonial mountains and emphasize the entanglement with an ideology of racial and sexual difference.[40]

Part of this ambivalence has to do with the relation between George Forster's narration of tropical mountain climbing — his emphasis on local transactions and indigenous knowledge, the gradual intensification of his engagement with the mountain slopes, and his emphasis on the dangerous and slippery descent — and the discourse of tropicalization that shapes his travelogue. David Arnold argues that tropicalization is a process that refers to "the idea of the tropics — warm, fecund, luxuriant, paradisiacal and pestilential — that was in many respects the most influential source of inspiration and innovation and had the most prodigious effect upon scenic appraisal and scientific practice."[41] Tropicalization shaped European responses to an unfamiliar landscape in a number of ways. Frequently this response took the shape of a hyperbolic misinterpretation of tropical fecundity. Elizabeth DeLoughrey and others claim with respect to Caribbean nature that "since Columbus's early journals, Europeans marveled at the 'variety and newness' of the islands' flora and fauna, their 'eternal greenness,' the lack of deciduous trees, and the staggering absence, to European eyes, of a dormant winter season."[42] The process of picturing and narrating tropical nature rests on the idea of "creating an impression of a world of nature that is different from, or alien to, nature in the temperate world," where the vegetative existence belongs to an older, more primitive world, where plants can be found that are from the era in which dinosaurs roamed.[43] Nancy Stepan argues further that "our idea of tropical nature as a particular kind of place or space, with its own characteristic ensembles of plants and animals (as well as peoples and diseases), represented via a repertoire of images that we can immediately identify as 'tropical,' is fundamentally a modern one, belonging, that is, to our post-Enlightenment era."[44]

Forster stands at the very beginning of a process that would eventually result in the formation of the discourse of tropicalization: a discourse in which the tropes of fertility and superabundance characterize the narrative patterns used for the discursive framing of tropical mountains. Forster's travelogue lays the foundation for an aesthetics that organizes "a landscape for a spectator from a distance or from height, as though it were a fine painting."[45] But he also narrates his engagement with a nature that is difficult to conquer and that may not afford the visitor a perspective of mastery and a feeling of conquest. While his depictions of tropical plants and the narration of mountain scenes adhere to the aesthetic of display and theatrical panorama that are reinforced by the process of tropicalization, his descriptions of actual mountaineering experiences also incorporate aspects of the encounter with tropical nature that cannot be attributed neatly to this process. Johann Reinhold's leg injury and the physical exhaustion felt by both Forsters on their way down from the summits of Tahiti are not necessarily offset by the subsequent enjoyment of a soothing massage. Climbing the tropical mountains of the Pacific and then writing about this experience points us to the failure of language to adequately capture the actual event. Narrating mountain climbing never covers the entire physical and spiritual experience. Pacific mountaineering emerges as a specific instance in which the failure of language is made particularly obvious. Tropical nature is at the same time both part of the space created for nature in the European tradition and outside that space. This ambivalent position is experienced by the Forsters during their strenuous climbs in search of rare botanical species and it leads to a characteristic bifurcation in the discourse of tropical mountaineering. Successful ascents promise panoramic views and a masterly gaze. They can also lead to frustration and sheer exhaustion or, worse, injury. Slippery descents undercut all feelings of mastery and pleasure. The undoing of the discourse of heroic mountaineering and climactic summit experiences is part of that tradition.

Notes

[1] Rod Edmond, *Representing the South Pacific: Colonial Discourse from Cook to Gaugin* (Cambridge: Cambridge UP, 1997), 6.
[2] SummitPost.org, www.summitpost.org, accessed 5 March 2009.
[3] George Forster published his travelogue under his English name first and, in the English-speaking world, is generally referred to as "George" — a tradition that I follow in this essay.
[4] George Forster, *A Voyage round the World*, ed. Nicholas Thomas and Oliver Berghof (Honolulu: U of Hawaii P, 2000). Further references to this work are cited in the text using the abbreviation *V* and the page number.
[5] Peter L. Bayers, *Imperial Ascent: Mountaineering, Masculinity, and Empire* (Boulder: U of Colorado P, 2003), 5.
[6] See Bayers, *Imperial Ascent*, 6.
[7] Patty O'Brien, *The Pacific Muse: Exotic Femininity and the Colonial Pacific* (Seattle: U of Washington P, 2006), 3.
[8] Mountainfilm in Telluride, www.mountainfilm.org, accessed 4 July 2009.
[9] See Clemens Wimmer, "Die Alpen: Vom Garten Europas zum Stadion Europas," in *Mit den Bäumen sterben die Menschen: Zur Kulturgeschichte der Ökologie*. ed. Jost Hermand (Cologne: Böhlau, 1993), 103.
[10] See Susie O'Brien, "Articulating a World of Difference: Ecocriticism, Postcolonialism, and Globalization," *Canadian Literature* 170–71 (2001): 143.
[11] See Scott Slovic, "Editor's Note," *ISLE* 14 (2007): v.
[12] Graham Huggan, "'Greening' Postcolonialism: Ecocritical Perspectives," *Modern Fiction Studies* 50 (2004): 702.
[13] Huggan, "'Greening' Postcolonialism," 702.
[14] Cara Cilano and Elizabeth DeLoughrey, "Against Authenticity: Global Knowledges and Postcolonial Ecocriticism," *ISLE* 14 (2007): 72.
[15] See Rob Nixon, "Environmentalism and Postcolonialism," in *Postcolonial Studies and Beyond*, ed. Ania Loomba, Suvir Kaul, Matti Bunzl, Antoinette Burton, and Jed Esty (Durham, NC: Duke UP, 2005), 23.
[16] See Elizabeth DeLoughrey, "Quantum Landscapes: A 'Ventriloquism of Spirit,'" *Interventions* 9 (2007): 63–64.
[17] Cited in Graham Huggan and Helen Tiffin, "Editorial," *Interventions* 9 (2007): 3.
[18] Russell A. Berman, *Enlightenment or Empire: Colonial Discourse in German Culture* (Lincoln: U of Nebraska P, 1998), 27.
[19] Alfred W. Crosby, *Ecological Imperialism: The Biological Expansion of Europe, 900–1900* (Cambridge: Cambridge UP, 1986), 3.
[20] See Amy R. W. Meyers and Margaret Beck Pritchards, eds., *Empire's Nature: Mark Catesby's New World Vision* (Chapel Hill: U of North Carolina P, 1998), 5.
[21] A digital image of Daniel Beyel and John Francis Rigaud, "Ioh. Reinhold Forster und George Forster, Vater und Sohn," is available online through the picture library of the National Australia Library (nla.pic-au945835).

[22] Many of Forster's plant and animal drawings are now available online through the picture library of the National Historical Museum.

[23] Donald Worster, *Nature's Economy: A History of Ecological Ideas* (Cambridge: Cambridge UP, 1977), 32.

[24] Alex Calder, Jonathan Lamb, and Bridget Orr, eds., *Voyages and Beaches: Pacific Encounters, 1769–1840* (Honolulu: U of Hawaii P, 1999), 5.

[25] Berman, *Enlightenment or Empire*, 64. See also Harry Liebersohn, *The Traveler's World: Europe to the Pacific* (Cambridge: Harvard UP, 2006), 1.

[26] Anja Hall, *Paradies auf Erden? Mythenbildung als Form von Fremdwahrnehmung — Der Südsee-Mythos in Schlüsselphasen der deutschen Literatur* (Würzburg: Königshausen & Neumann, 2008), 76.

[27] See Rüdiger Joppien and Bernhard Smith, *The Art of Captain Cook's Voyages*, 2 vols. (New Haven, CT: Yale UP, 1985), 1:146.

[28] Barbara Maria Stafford, *Voyage into Substance: Art, Science, Nature, and the Illustrated Travel Account, 1760–1840* (Cambridge: MIT Press, 1984), xxi.

[29] Stafford, *Voyage into Substance*, v.

[30] Michael Jacobs, *The Painted Voyage: Art, Travel, and Exploration, 1564–1875* (London: British Museum Press, 1995), 12 and 14. See also Marshall Sahlins, *Islands of History* (Chicago: U of Chicago P, 1985), viii, and Lynne Whitey, *Voyages of Discovery: Captain Cook and the Exploration of the Pacific* (Berkeley: U of California P, 1987), 10.

[31] See Winfried Volk, *Die Entdeckung Tahitis und das Wunschbild der seligen Insel in der deutschen Literatur* (Heidelberg: Kranz & Heinrichmöller, 1934), 21.

[32] See "Barringtonia speciosa, barringtonia tree. No. 266" from the botanical drawings George Forster made during Cook's second voyage, 1772–75, available through the picture library of the National History Museum, London; illustration annotated with the number 191.

[33] Forster's narrative of the display of the Tahitian war fleet emphasizes its staged character as performance. The show that Cook and his scientists observed is similar in function and style to displays of foreign cultures in zoos and ethnographic shows at the turn of the century or even contemporary shows that emphasize "foreignness," such as the night show at the Polynesian Cultural Center in Hawaii.

[34] See William Hodges, Oaitepeha Bay, Tahiti, © National Maritime Museum, Greenwich, London; the image is also available online from the Ministry of Defense Art Collection.

[35] See Bernhard Smith, *European Vision and the South Pacific* (New Haven, CT: Yale UP, 1985), 64.

[36] O'Brien, *The Pacific Muse*, 38.

[37] See Gordon M. Sayre, "If Thomas Jefferson Had Visited Niagara Falls: The Sublime Wilderness Spectacle in America, 1775–1825," in *The ISLE Reader: Ecocriticism 1993–2003*, ed. Michael P. Branch and Scott Slovic (Athens: U of Georgia P, 2003), 103.

[38] Hermann Wittenberg, "The Sublime, Imperialism and the African Landscape" (PhD. thesis, U of the Western Cape, 2004), 1.

[39] Wittenberg, "The Sublime, Imperialism and the African Landscape," 6.
[40] Wittenberg, "The Sublime, Imperialism and the African Landscape," 8.
[41] David Arnold, *The Tropics and the Traveling Gaze: India, Landscape, and Science, 1800–1856* (Seattle: U of Washington P, 2006), 7.
[42] Elizabeth DeLoughrey, Renée K. Gosson, and George B. Handley, eds., *Carribean Literature and the Environment: Between Nature and Culture* (Charlottesville: U of Virginia P, 2005), 7.
[43] Nancy Stepan, *Picturing Tropical Nature* (Ithaca, NY: Cornell UP, 2001), 11.
[44] Stepan, *Picturing Tropical Nature*, 15.
[45] Stepan, *Picturing Tropical Nature*, 37.

Part II: Beckoning Heights: Summits Near and Far in the Nineteenth Century

Fascinating Voids: Alexander von Humboldt and the Myth of Chimborazo

Oliver Lubrich

WHEN ALEXANDER VON HUMBOLDT reached the village of Calpi in the Andes on 22 June 1802, he was greeted with reverence and enthusiasm. Triumphal arches adorned with cotton, cloth, and silver decorated his path. The natives performed a dance in festive dress. A singer praised the explorer's expedition, which had departed three years earlier from the Spanish port of La Coruña. Like Odysseus on the isle of the Phaeacians, the traveler listened to a local rhapsodist singing about his heroic deeds.[1] Before his adventure ended, it had already spun a popular myth.

This episode, which Humboldt recorded in his diary, occurred at a significant moment. One day later, the "Second Discoverer of America"[2] rose to even greater fame on an excursion marking in more ways than one the *climax* of his enterprise. Humboldt set out to climb Chimborazo (6,310 m/20,702 ft.), the mountain then thought to be the highest in the world. He was accompanied by the French botanist Aimé Bonpland (1773–1858) and the Creole nobleman and future activist Carlos Montúfar (1780–1816), as well as native guides and assistants. They climbed to heights never reached before, setting a new record and catapulting Humboldt to fame on both continents.

Myths

The ascent of Chimborazo had a great symbolic significance. A man of the Enlightenment reaching uncharted altitudes inspired contemporary artists such as Friedrich Georg Weitsch (1810) and Karl von Steuben (1812/21) to paint Humboldt in promixity to the mountain.[3] Even in Humboldt's very last portrait, Julius Schrader (1859)[4] sets him in front of the famous volcano, the ice-capped peak elegantly corresponding to the ninety-year-old's snow-white hair. Depicted at the foot of Chimborazo in the first picture, Humboldt is at eye level with its summit in the second one, and even surpasses it in the third. The proportion between man and mountain thus shifts iconographically. Fantasies of Humboldt's American journey merged in this sensational episode such that Chimborazo came to symbolize him, his life, and his work.

The hike reverberated in literature as well as in history. In 1822, at the pinnacle of his revolutionary struggle, Simón Bolívar allegedly climbed Chimborazo as well, and composed a visionary prose-poem: "Mi delirio sobre el Chimborazo" (My delirium on Chimborazo).[5] As a culmination of his "marcha de la libertad," the ascent became an allegory of the liberation from the Spanish Empire as well as a foundational myth of a freed continent, surveyed from its peak — from the very perspective that Humboldt had previewed. The *Libertador* "followed," as he wrote, "daringly" in Humboldt's footsteps ("Busqué las huellas . . . de Humboldt; seguílas audaz, nada me detuvo"; I looked for the traces . . . of Humboldt; I followed them daringly and perseveringly), before he ultimately "surpassed them" ("dejé atrás las huellas de Humboldt"; I left Humboldt's traces behind) in order to set foot on new land. He experienced a revelation, hearing the voices of the demon of Colombia and the spirit of Time. Taking possession of the mountain's highest point for an independent Latin America, he concludes the work of his German mentor, whose critique of colonialism, as legend has it, inspired him.

The Venezuelan artist Tito Salas interpreted Bolívar's lyrical meditation on canvas (1929–30).[6] His painting depicts the "liberator" on top of the mountain, embraced by a white-bearded man with angel wings. Today it is on display in the *Casa Natal del Libertador* in Caracas, consecrating the connection between Bolívar, Chimborazo, and Humboldt in the politics of public remembrance. The Salas painting also served as the frontispiece for an epic poem *in memoriam* about Simón Bolívar, *The Spirit of Chimborazo Speaks* (1930), by Jordan Herbert Stabler.[7] It frames Bolívar's campaign in two mountain scenes, placing the *Libertador* in the footsteps left by his predecessor in the eternal snow of the Andean volcano. Stabler associates Bolívar's literal climb ("up the Humboldt trail he trod," 7) as well as his imagined deification ("he mounts up the Humboldt path again," 20) with the explorer's historical ascent. By referring to the peak as a "crest" (7), he underlines the emblematic significance of Chimborazo for Latin America's cultural identity. Upon Bolívar's arrival, the geological summit becomes a heraldic symbol. (Chimborazo has figured in Ecuador's national coat of arms since 1848.)

Two volcanoes also frame the political drama *Humboldt und Bolivar oder Der neue Continent* (1980) by East German playwright Claus Hammel.[8] They connect the encounter of the protagonists in Napoleon's Paris in 1804 with the ascent of Chimborazo in 1802 and with the *Independencia* of the 1820s. The play opens with a colonial allegory, in which Humboldt's voyage prefigures Bolívar's revolution. Humboldt, Bonpland, and Montúfar examine the riches of the "New Continent" that six figures (embodying the traveled lands) carry into the crater. As they reemerge, they transport dead rebels instead of resources. The epilogue complements this prelude in a scene relating the last meeting between Humboldt and Bolívar, on Mount Vesuvius, in 1805. "Ich werde Völker aus den Kratern erloschener Vulkane schleudern" (I shall cast entire peoples out of the craters of dormant volcanoes), says Bolívar. "Auf dem Thron, den ich errichte, werden zwei Plätze frei sein" (The throne I shall erect will have two seats). Bolívar's last words are: "Humboldt! — Humboldt! — Humboldt!" The volcano is a metonym for Humboldt's American voyage, a metaphor for the American revolution, and an allegory linking the two.

Eduardo Galeano introduces a new element to the Chimborazo mythology. The second volume of his monumental *Memoria del fuego* (Memory of fire, 1985), a chronological series of prose miniatures on Latin American history, includes twelve episodes about Humboldt. One of them conjures up a fantasy about the explorer on Chimborazo. It bears the evocative title "En las cumbres del mundo" (On the summits of the world).[9] Galeano discretely links Humboldt with Bolívar by using the word "delirio" (delirium) from the title of his mysterious prose-poem. The Uruguayan writer stages the peregrination, once again, as a near-mystical experience, this time, however, not as an apotheosis, but as a moment of illumination ("plenitud de luz"; plenitude of light), and, moreover, the onset of mythopoiea. Galeano's Humboldt is seized by an irresistible desire to tell his story: "siente tremendas ganas de contárselo ya mismo al hermano Goethe, allá en su casa de Weimar" (he feels a tremendous urge to tell it to his brother Goethe at his distant home in Weimar).

What makes the resonance of Humboldt's climb so extraordinary, however, beyond its interpretation by painters such as Weitsch, Steuben, Schrader, and Salas and writers such as Bolívar, Stabler, Hammel, and Galeano, are two aspects that none of these artists made explicit. Humboldt *failed* to reach the summit. And he chose *not* to tell the story himself. Odysseus burst into tears when Demodokos sang about his adventures, but eventually he told his own tale, which constitutes the main part of the *Odyssey*. Humboldt, however, did not report to "Goethe in Weimar," as Galeano put it, in the sense of presenting the glorious episode to the literary public. For many years he resisted the temptation to capitalize on his adventure. When he finally did give his account, his narrative took on surprising forms.

Representations

In more than five decades as a travel writer, scientific author, and artist Humboldt represented his ascent of Chimborazo in diverse narrative and pictorial genres: his field journal, letters, book chapters, and essays, as well as landscape drawing, allegory, and geographic diagram. In the following, I reconstruct the rhetoric and the poetics as well as the implicit discursive strategies of Humboldt's accounts in order to analyze his innovative way of coming to terms with the most famous of his achievements. When and how did Humboldt describe his ascent of Chimborazo? And how do his own representations compare with the versions invented by others?

On 25 November 1802, five months after the mountain excursion, Humboldt wrote a letter to his brother Wilhelm from Lima.[10] The passage relating to the climb up the volcano is loaded with dramatic rhetoric. In a few lines he mentions sickness ("malaise") and suffering ("nous souffrions"), horror ("horriblement") and murder (the Indios fear "que nous avions intentions de les tuer"; that we intended to kill them), an ulcerating wound ("pied ulcéré") and the danger of falling into terrible abysses ("abîmes affreux"). In vivid language, he calls attention to the mountain's huge size, its impressive height, and the sadness and darkness of the landscape, as well as its eerie loneliness, which came from the lack of living beings on its slopes. But the prospect of reaching the peak justifies all of these sacrifices. Should the volcano reignite, it could devastate an entire province ("si ce volcan se rallumait, ce colosse détruirait toute la province"). In this personal letter, climbing Chimborazo and reaching the top is a matter of life and death.

Yet Humboldt chose not to publish an account in this vein. His letters inspired many reports, which circulated widely. After his return, he spoke about America in Parisian salons, at the Prussian court, and in academic circles. His most famous adventure, however, is missing in his published writings. He kept his diary entries to himself. His *Relation historique* (Personal narrative, 1814–31) breaks off before the expedition reaches the Andes. Nor does the mountain play a prominent role in *Ansichten der Natur* (Views of nature, 1808, 1826, 1849), a book that would have lent itself splendidly to its description and that even includes a chapter "On the structure and mode of action of volcanoes." Reduced to references and displaced in footnotes, faint trails of Chimborazo interlace Humboldt's works, for example his *Kosmos*, but the volcano is never their epicenter.

Some years after the voyage, two short essays on Chimborazo appeared in *Vues des Cordillères* (Views of the Cordilleras, 1810–13, chapters 16 and 25). Each comments on one of the sixty-nine images included in this illustrated volume.[11] A mere seventeen lines in chapter 16 are dedicated to the entire event of 23 June 1802. They consistently downplay the importance of such enterprises: "These tedious excursions, the accounts of which generally excite the interest of the public, offer only a very small number of results that are useful for scientific progress" (*VC*, 106). Instead Humboldt cautions travelers to question common "illusions": not to underestimate the elevation of the plains, misjudge the dimension of the summits, or mistake individual peaks for independent mountains (see *VC*, 103–5).

Fig. 1. Vues des Cordillères, *plate 16: "Vue du Chimborazo et du Carguairazo"* (1810).

While chapter 16 has thus at least briefly summed up the expedition, chapter 25 refrains from narrative altogether. Humboldt provides five additional arguments that further diminish the significance of his ascent: the balloonist Gay-Lussac attained greater altitudes; the neighbouring peak El Altar had probably been higher before it collapsed; the Himalayan mountains might be more prominent; it would not surprise him if even greater peaks were discovered elsewhere; and the "true geologist" should attend to "formations" instead of "absolute heights" (*VC*, 201–2).

Neither of the images illustrating these texts presents Chimborazo on the day of the ascent. Humboldt visualized the volcano in two opposing conditions: *before* the climb, with minimal precipitation, showing the lower limit of the eternal snow (plate 16, sketched in Riobamba-Nuevo, *VC*, 200, 104 [fig. 1]); and *after* the excursion, when the heavy snowfall had already settled (plate 25, sketched in Licán, *VC*, 200, 202 [fig. 2]). Unlike Bolívar after him, Humboldt localizes his aesthetic experience *below* rather than *on* the mountain. The view from afar is a surrogate for the panoramic gaze from the top. From a secure distance, the observer contemplates the awe-inspiring presence of Chimborazo as if it were a work of art. Humboldt evokes the perspective of someone who has *not* reached the summit.[12] Like a Greek tragedy, in which the actual climax occurs behind the scenes, Humboldt's volcanic aesthetics concentrate on a "pregnant moment."

Humboldt sets the mountain apart from its surroundings both in aesthetic and historical terms. Chimborazo rises above the Andes, he writes, like the Renaissance art of Michelangelo over the monuments of Ancient Rome: "comme ce dôme majestueux, ouvrage du génie de Michel-Ange, sur les monumens antiques qui environnent le Capitole"

Fig. 2. Vues des Cordillères, *plate 25: "Le Chimborazo, vu depuis le plateau de Tapia"* (1811).

(*VC*, 107; like this majestic dome, work of the genius of Michelangelo, above the ancient monuments that surround the Capitole).The volcano becomes an allegory of modernity — and the attempt to ascend it, a journey into the future.

In the allegorical frontispiece of Humboldt's *Atlas géographique et physique*, the illustrator François Gérard turned Chimborazo, as the *Vues des Cordillères* depicted it in two of its plates (16 and 25), into a setting for a historico-philosophical modernization. The title reads: "L'Amérique relevée de sa ruine par le Commerce et par l'Industrie" (America rises from its misery with the aide of trade and industry, 1814).[13] Against the backdrop of the volcano, Hermes helps a bowing Aztec onto his feet, while Athena hands him an olive branch. The "New World" is resurrected out of the spirit of liberalism (fig. 3).

In a way that is compatible with Gérard's vision of American history, Germaine de Staël cites Humboldt's representations of the mountain as a philosophical simile that visualizes global Enlightenment. Referring to his famous cross-sections of the Andes, she concludes her *Considérations sur les principaux événemens de la Révolution françoise* (Considerations on the principal events of the French Revolution, 1818) with a botanical metaphor. As in Humboldt's vertical layering of bio-zones, "freedom-loving people" all over the world inhabit "a certain height of thinking." Madame de Staël assumed that higher education correlates with progressive political

Fig. 3. François Gérard, "*L'Amérique relevée de sa ruine par le Commerce et par l'Industrie*" (1814).

attitudes, independent of nationality, ethnicity, and culture.[14] And Chimborazo serves as their scale.

In dealing with the volcano, Humboldt developed original modes of aesthetic perception and philosophical reflection along with new forms of representation. The most notable result is his mountain profile, which he published in different forms. His *Essai sur la géographie des plantes* (Essay on the geography of plants, 1807) contains a drawing he sketched in Ecuador in 1803: A "tableau" of the Andes, presenting vertical zones of vegetation and climate.[15] In this cross-section, the mountain has a graphic *and* a textual dimension. By using both modes to determine the location of certain plants and relate them to scientific data, Humboldt merges science and art. Goethe, by contrast, created a purely pictorial version of this image: "Höhen der alten und neuen Welt bildlich verglichen" (Altitudes of the old and new world compared pictorially, 1807, 1813). His concept is realistic; it has three dimensions and a traditional perspective. He marginalized the informational elements, separating image and text.[16]

Humboldt's cross-section reappeared in his *Nova genera et species plantarum* (New genres and species of plants), under the title "Geographiae plantarum lineamenta" (Outlines of plant geography, 1816).[17] The mountain profile takes on the easily recognizable form of a pictogram that stands for a major innovation in the presentation of knowledge and signifies Humboldt's innovative multidisciplinary method. Though he contributed to the taxonomic system of natural history by adding "new" species collected in America, he set the static classification in motion by tracing their geographical migration and distribution. Humboldt thus dynamized Linnean botany. Günter Herburger commented on the artistic quality of Humboldt's motif in the eponymous story of *Humboldt* (2001), his collection of travel novellas. Herburger remarks that the profile is more than a representation of quantitative science. The numerous plant names, which Humboldt inscribed "in tiny script," adhere to methods of classification, yet they also create an aesthetic impression: "ähnlich Schneegestöber," like snowfall.[18]

Another variant of this pictorial-textual hybrid appeared in Humboldt's *Atlas géographique et physique des régions équinoxiales du Nouveau Continent* (Geographical and physical atlas of the equinoctial regions of the new continent), which Gérard's allegory served to illustrate. The title of this third version of his profile is not descriptive but narrative. It refers to the "voyage" that was "attempted" merely "toward" the mountain top: "Voyage vers la cime du Chimborazo, tenté le 23 Juin 1802" (1825).[19] The new presentation inspires a poetics of failure. This takes on a particularly striking form when Humboldt finally attempted to give an account of his famous endeavour.

In 1837, Alexander von Humboldt published a longer essay, which appeared under a somewhat strange title: "Ueber zwei Versuche den

Chimborazo zu besteigen" (On two attempts to ascend Chimborazo).[20] Why did it take him thirty-five years to present his most celebrated experience? And which "*two* attempts" is he referring to? The text appeared after Humboldt's legendary world record from 1802 had been broken by Jean Baptiste Boussingault in 1831, a feat that Humboldt acknowledges at the beginning of his text. A few years before his death, Humboldt republished this essay as "Ueber *einen* Versuch den *Gipfel* des Chimborazo zu *er*steigen" (On *one* attempt to *reach* the *peak* of Chimborazo, 1853, emphasis added). Though the text has only minor revisions and its title has been altered but slightly, the differences are significant.[21] The second version of the title specifies that Humboldt's original goal was not just to climb up the mountain but to arrive at its summit. He changed the word "*be*steigen" (to climb) to "*er*steigen" (to reach), with the German prefix *er-* suggesting determination, effort, and ultimate achievement.[22] And he now speaks of just *one* attempt, instead of *two*, marking only his own enterprise a failed one.[23]

Humboldt encoded the program of his writing in his paratexts. Details such as titles, subtitles, and dedications matter. The first version of the essay appeared in the *Jahrbuch für 1837* (Yearbook for 1837). This account of an enterprise of international public interest, which remained a sensational achievement in the collective memory of the era, was not only postponed from 1802 to 1837, but when he finally published it, he placed it in a periodical under an unspecific title ("Yearbook") and under someone else's name: "edited by H. C. Schumacher." It is as if Humboldt intended to hide the text, foisting it upon another man, whose name obfuscates his own authorship.

Humboldt placed the second version of the article among a collection of pieces defined by the title as marginal: *Kleinere Schriften* (Minor writings, 1853). The climb of Chimborazo is thus downgraded in relation to the rest of his travel writing. The subtitle, *Geognostische und physikalische Erinnerungen* (Geognostic and physical memoirs), hardly describes the volume in a more specific or popular fashion. In a manner characteristic of Humboldt's works, the subtitle claims an intermediate position between science (geognosy, physics) and literature (autobiography, narrative). The Chimborazo text is located among writings on volcanology, mountain studies, meteorology, and acoustics. Within this multidisciplinary context, the account of his legendary ascent appears as a chapter like any other.

The book is dedicated to Leopold von Buch, the "greatest geognost of our times." Humboldt conspicuously understates his own specific expertise in the field of geology (which includes his studies of a volcano) through his superlative remarks about his colleague. This tribute creates inter- as well as intra-textual references. As an allusion to Buch's *Physicalische Beschreibung der canarischen Inseln* (Physical description of the Canary Islands, 1825), it recalls Humboldt's own layover in Tenerife in 1799, where he stopped on his expedition to America, and which he understood as a microcosm of the "New World." Hiking up Teide (3,718 m/12,198 ft.), the highest point on the island, anticipates the ascent of Chimborazo. When describing the Andean volcano, Humboldt refers back to its Canarian counterpart. His dedication to Buch and the reference to Teide lessen his own accomplishments even further. Published by Schumacher, surpassed by Boussingault, and perfected by Buch, Humboldt's achievement becomes an understated trifle.

Appended to *Kleinere Schriften* is an *Atlas* (which the title page refers to) containing *Umrisse von Vulkanen aus den Cordilleren und Mexico: Ein Beitrag zur Physiognomik der Natur* (Outlines of volcanoes from the Cordilleras and Mexico: A contribution to the physiognomy of nature). Humboldt, who frequently supplemented his texts with images (sketches, engravings, allegories, profiles), presents twelve views of volcanoes, among them Chimborazo and Carguairazo.[24] He unnecessarily relegates them to an inferior category: *Minor Writings* are illustrated with mere *Outlines*. The addition "Erster Band" (first volume) to a singular piece that was never to be followed by a second volume, indicates that this book, like most by Humboldt, is a fragment. Incompleteness expresses his understanding of research as a contingent process. He relinquishes all claims to totality and systematicity. Knowledge is always historical, every insight is relative, results are provisional, and their publications fragmentary. Traveling to unexplored regions in high altitude, Humboldt exclaimed: "Man ist hier überall zuerst" (*KS*, 146; We are the first here, wherever we go). He knew, however, that others would follow, advance farther, and explore deeper. Recognizing the extent to which every contribution is indebted to its predecessors and is bequeathed to future researchers, Humboldt acknowledges Benzoni (1565), La Condamine (1742), and Boussingault (1831).[25]

The first noun in the essay's title, "Versuch" (attempt), is particularly programmatic: this acknowledgment of limited knowledge and ultimate failure leads us to the center of Humboldt's understanding of science and his concept of travel literature. "Versuch" spells out both the tentative nature of his project and its empirical character. It depends on sensory perception and personal experience; it assembles results from zoological and meteorological observations, botanical and mineralogical collections, from measurements of altitudes, temperatures, and humidity. The mountain climb is a large-scale experiment. As a young man Humboldt had already conducted studies on his own muscle and nerve fiber, and years later the explorer's body continues to be the subject as well as the instrument of investigation. The findings consist of Humboldt diagnosing on himself the symptoms of *soroche* or altitude sickness: breathlessness, nausea, headaches, dizziness, and bleeding of his lips, gums, and eyes.

In another sense, the term "Versuch" describes the literary form in which the explorer's experience translates into language. Humboldt's

"Versuch" is both an *experiment* and an *essay*. The author had previously published two *Essais politiques* about the Kingdom of New Spain (1808–11) and the Island of Cuba (1826). In his "Versuch den Gipfel des Chimborazo zu ersteigen," Humboldt uses the most legendary of his "deeds" in order to experiment with this form, which he adapted in different ways in most of his works. "Ueber einen *Versuch* den Gipfel des Chimborazo zu ersteigen" is as much an autobiographical narrative and a treatise on natural sciences as it is a reflection on the essay as form.

From this point of view, the text constitutes a search for an appropriate mode of communicating the journey and the knowledge it generated. The implied questions are of far-reaching importance: How can an expedition be narrated? How should a field journal be used? What role should the explorer play? How might the traveled regions and cultures be adequately represented? The form, Humboldt seems to suggest, is as important as the content. Completeness is illusory (hence the fragment). The point is not to reach a goal (hence the essay). A venture that has shaken off its teleological intention, the ascent of Chimborazo is a symbol, not of a totalizing vision, but of a tentative and fragmented experience. It represents the caution of the self-reflective scholar and anticipates the journey of the (post) modern traveler.

In his "Versuch," Humboldt takes care to avoid the epic genre, indeed any type of closed form. The ascent of Chimborazo would have been ideally suited for the traditional format of travel literature. It would have fulfilled the expectations of those readers who demanded a dramatic story recounting dangers heroically overcome, presenting breath-taking vistas and concluding with a panorama from the highest point of the world. From a postcolonial perspective, such a Eurocentric celebration of the imperial subject, surveying American nature from a central perspective and thereby displaying discursive claims of appropriation, would have rightly merited criticism as a conquest narrative. Humboldt rejects this conventional format. His project is not a *conquista*, not even a scientific one.[26] Nothing would be more absurd than to imagine Humboldt planting the Prussian flag on Mount Chimborazo.[27]

What he reaps, instead, is an aesthetic benefit far greater than heroic objectives and imperial intentions to cover and conquer a *terra incognita*. His narrative tells the story of a "marvelous *dis*possession."[28] What might have been a colonial feat goes awry. Bad weather on the day of the hike almost entirely clouds any potential aesthetic experience. In a wonderful epiphany of the sublime, Chimborazo finally appears, if only for a brief moment: "It was a solemn, grand sight" as the fog "suddenly" dispersed and the "dome-shaped summit" became visible (*KS*, 150). Immediately after this revelation (inflated in Bolívar's "delirio," Stabler's "spirit," Galeano's "plenitud de luz," and Hammel's opening crater), the expedition reaches an abyss and is forced to turn back. In conformity with the graphic representations in *Vues des Cordillères*, depicting the *before* and the *after* instead of the climb itself, Chimborazo "erschien uns" (appeared) a second time, just when the mountaineers returned to base camp, "in seiner ganzen Pracht, ich möchte sagen in der stillen Größe und Hoheit, die der Naturcharakter der tropischen Landschaft ist" (*KS*, 157; in its complete majesty, I should say in the quiet grandeur and dignity that is the natural character of the tropical landscape). Even though the weather improved and there were other routes to try, no further attempt was made. The aesthetic experience took place when Humboldt recognized and accepted the fact that his objective had failed. Thereafter, the failure was of no further significance, because it spawned new, original forms.

Paratextually and formally, rhetorically and narratively, Humboldt devalues his adventure. Not only did he postpone its publication (from 1802 to 1837/1853) and displace it within his works (from the *Voyage* to the *Jahrbuch* and *Kleinere Schriften*), but he also downplays the meaning of the episode in two parallel comments at the beginning of his essay. His climb was "von geringem wissenschaftlichen Interesse" (*KS*, 133; of little scientific interest), as "Unternehmungen dieser Art" (ventures of this type) usually offer "den Wissenschaften" only "wenigen Gewinn" (*KS*, 158; little value to science). And even as a story, it promises "wenig dramatisches Interesse" (*KS*, 135; little dramatic interest). The text therefore begins with two disclaimers. But why describe it at all, if the event was of such limited scientific and literary import? Humboldt's artistic answer is a rhetoric of disenchantment, demystifying both his climb as well as the Enlightenment, which it symbolized. A series of direct and indirect comments seem to suggest that climbing Chimborazo is nothing special. The hike lasted only three and a half hours (*KS*, 154) and the mountain was so enshrouded in clouds that Humboldt felt "wie in einem Luftballon isolirt" (*KS*, 152; isolated, as if in an air balloon). The landscape was dismal, a wasteland: "Wir blieben kurze Zeit in dieser traurigen Einöde" (*KS*, 152; We stayed only a short while in this sad desolation). Condors avoided the inhospitable mountain, and not even insects or grasses were there "freiwillig" (*KS*, 152–53; voluntarily). Hardly any plants grow at high altitude. The deep cover of snow makes it impossible to collect rocks. It would not even have been necessary to climb the mountain in order to establish its altitude and location. On the contrary, the trigonometric calculations that were carried out in the surrounding highlands were more accurate than the barometric measurements on the summit itself, since these are influenced by local factors. Mountain climbers tend to overestimate the height they attain and to express "Verdruß" (*KS*, 147; annoyance) when they are confronted with correct measurements. As to the question whether the mountain has a volcanic crater — a question that, in his letter to Wilhelm, was of the utmost importance and that might indeed be answered by reaching the top — Humboldt remarks in a casual aside: Chimborazo has none (see *KS*, 162).

None of the botanical, mineralogical, or climatological elements that could be studied on the mountain are unusual enough to warrant thorough investigation. The grasses "gehören, der größten Zahl nach, nordeuropäischen Geschlechtern an" (belong for the most part to the northern European genera), Humboldt states. "Es ist fast die Steppennatur, die ich in dem dürren Theile des nördlichen Asiens gesehen habe" (*KS*, 142; It is almost the same steppe climate that I saw in the arid parts of northern Asia). At certain altitudes and certain latitudes the air temperature "gewöhnlich" (typically) remains within predictable extremes. The average temperature for the whole year reminds the traveler of the German provincial town of Lüneburg (*KS*, 142). What, then, remains from the journey? Humboldt foresaw that Europeans would ask him for "ein kleines Stück vom Chimborazo" (*KS*, 153; a small piece of Chimborazo). Rocks may indeed make popular gifts, though bringing them home is in fact rather absurd. The mining and mineralogy scholar emphasized on various occasions that the earth went through the same upheavals everywhere, so that regions that seem, on cultural, botanical, and zoological grounds, to be vastly different, were in fact geologically quite similar. Humboldt consistently refuted proponents of the immaturity of the "New World," for example Buffon and Hegel, with observations such as these.[29] Bringing back ordinary rocks is, in fact, ironic. Their auratic quality as souvenirs could not have stood in starker contrast to their scientific significance.

On Chimborazo Humboldt failed in meaningful and productive ways. The ascent into the icy heights of the Andes demonstrates that science can be self-reflexive and aware of its weaknesses, false assumptions, and blind spots. The Enlightenment takes a dialectic turn. Venturing into unknown territory, the scholar is surrounded by fog and overcome by dizziness. The extreme situation makes him experience his limits all the more clearly, both those of his body and those of his intellect. But at the same time compensations emerge: these very insights and their new artistic and literary representations.

The programmatic implications of Humboldt's poetics are as evident in his published works as they are in his handwritten records. His notes from 1802 (later joined by annotations) may be considered the foundational *Ur*-version of all texts about Chimborazo.[30] Humboldt misleadingly refers to his essay of 1837 and 1853 as a mere "Fragment eines Tagebuchs" (*KS*, 136; excerpt from a diary), taken "aus einem ungedruckten Reisejournale" (from an unprinted travelogue) that is "einfach mitgetheilt" here (*KS*, 162; simply conveyed). Though some features of his writing remained constant for over fifty years (1802–53), Humboldt's journal entry connected the failure of the ascent with his concept of writing and his scientific agenda in a truly creative way.

Here again, the title is telling: "Voyage au Chimborazo."[31] This might be translated as "Voyage *to* Chimborazo" or "Voyage *at* Chimborazo," but certainly not as "Ascent *to the top* of Chimborazo" (Dy 33, 21r). After five densely written pages, more than 300 lines with additions, comments, and side notes, the narrative breaks off. Humboldt refers to a later resumption: "v. la Continuation p. 45." There he resumes with the corresponding words: "Continuation du Voyage de Chimborazo" (Dy 38, 23v; 45, 31r). What is strange about this process is not only *that* the writer interrupts the account of his adventurous climb, but even more so, *when* and *how* he does this.

Humboldt's story is one of adverse conditions, limited sight, painstaking measurements, disloyalty of Indian assistants, dangerous abysses, painful hardships, and an altitude sickness that steadily worsens. Humboldt did not expect to reach the summit. "Nous montions très haut, plus que je l'espérais." (Dy 38, 23v; We climbed very high, higher than I expected). But just before he discontinues his account, he becomes hopeful: "Il nous vint une lueur d'espérance de parvenir à la Cime." (Dy 38, 23v; Suddenly there was a glimmer of hope that we might reach the top). "Mais une grande Cre-. . ." Here, his entry ends. "But a large cre-. . ." The cut-off occurs at the geographic and narrative climax. At the dramatic peripety, the traveler and his companions reach a *crevasse*, which abruptly ends their ascent and forces them to turn back. In the middle of the word "crevasse," Humboldt suspends his narrative, and refers to the page where it continues.

In the interim pages (Dy 39–44), several digressions — or more accurately, insertions — provide information about collected stones ("Roches rapportés de Chimborazo," "Roches de Yanaurcu," "roches de Tunguragua"), measurements of the terrain ("Mesure géométrique de Tunguragua"), Jesuit missionaries ("Jésuites"), a volcanic eruption ("Éruption de la Moya de Pelileo"), and glaciers ("Glaciers Tunguragua"), and present a captivating interview with an Indian chief who is a direct descendant of the last Inca ("Notions données par Don Leandro Zepla, Grand Apu de Quito, Otavalo, la Ville d'Ibarra, Gouverneur de Lican"). Humboldt filled the linear account of his ascent with mineralogical, geological, volcanic, geographic, meteorological, political, social, historical, and ethnographic observations. Narrative and digression, which alternate in the essay of 1837/1853, are separated in the diary of 1802, or more accurately: all the digressions are inserted into the narrative at the decisive moment.

This extravagant trick serves many purposes. It slows the progress of the report and creates suspense, quite literally, with a *cliffhanger*. Humboldt *performs* the word "cre/vasse." He compensates for the frustration of his ascent by filling the abyss that caused it with the numerous yields of his research — and, furthermore, by developing an original way to narrate the climb. Just as he covered the mountain in his profiles with text, Humboldt literally *inscribes* meaning into his failed excursion, pro-

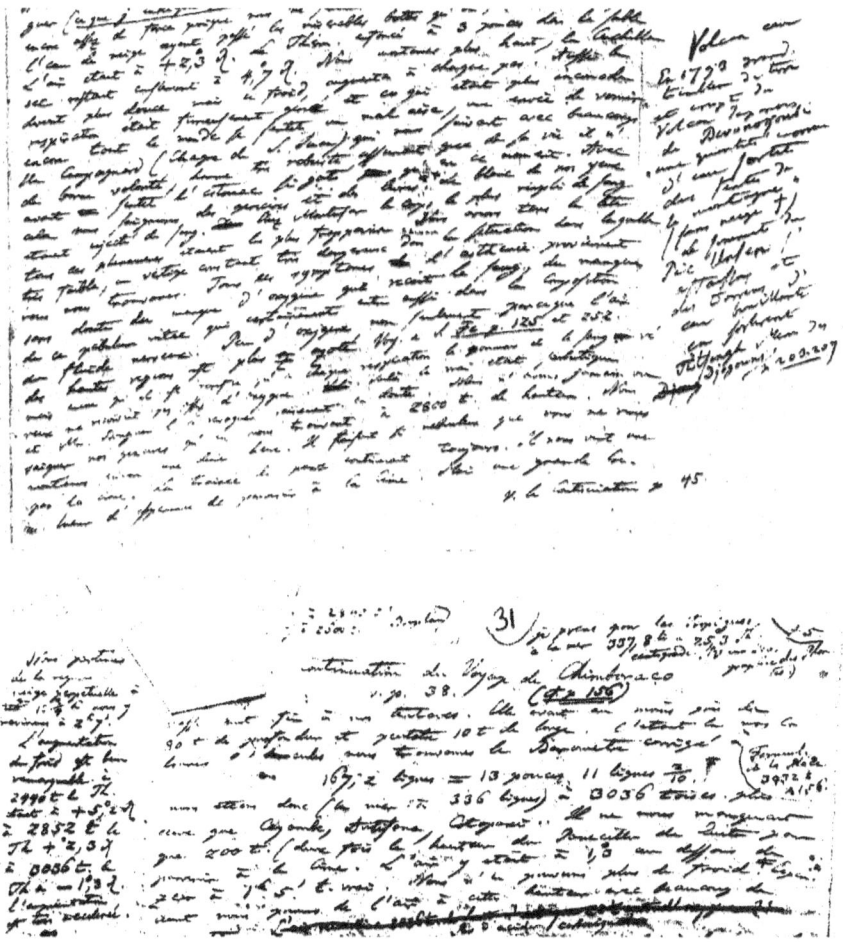

Fig. 4. "Mais une grande Cre- / v. la Continuation p. 45." (Diary 1802, 23v) and "Continuation du Voyage de Chimborazo / v. p. 38 / -vasse mit fin à nos tentatives." (Diary 1802, 31r).

viding a miniature of his multi-discipline research that connects travel, science, and anthropology. After this disruption and interval, the sentence continues: ("Mais une grande Cre-...") "....-vasse mit fin à nos tentatives" ([But a large cre-...] ...-vasse put an end to our attempts; see fig. 4).

Humboldt's creativity is particularly striking in contrast with the diary of Carlos Montúfar. While Humboldt interweaves different types of texts, his companion Montúfar narrates in a conventional, chronological manner. Of the twenty-nine handwritten pages of his *Diario del año de 1802: Biage de Quito á Lima* (Diary of the year 1802: Voyage from Quito to Lima), only three contain a brief account of the Chimborazo climb. Although the future revolutionary uses a term that underscores the disruptive nature of the crevasse (*quebrada*, literally "the break"), no disruption is reflected in his narrative. The moment of turning back has no poetic consequence. "No pudimos pasar adelante por una profundissima quebrada . . ." (We were not able to pass because of a deep chasm . . .).[32]

Irony

Alexander von Humboldt's writings revolve around the void of an unattainable summit with little explorational value, except perhaps an empty crater that had long since disappeared. His ascent reached its climax in a void of another kind, a chasm of insurmountable nothingness that forced him to give up and return to his point of departure. For many years he omitted this episode in his publications, leaving a strange literary void. And when he finally did publish a series of "attempts," they had so many narrative voids that other writers felt compelled to fill them.

Humboldt's attitude was clearly provocative. It was as puzzling as if the first person on the moon were to declare, upon his return to earth, that he saw nothing special and could just as well have stayed at home. The explorer himself was a fascinating void, and his writing marked a degree zero of mythology. While he himself chose not to make a myth of his expedition, numerous fantasies sprang up from this episode. Many authors supplemented what Humboldt left out and left open to interpretation. They replaced and reconfigured his long-awaited but disappointing accounts in order to reestablish the heroic story he had denied them. The ascent of Chimborazo thus became a legend in the literal sense of the word. Humboldt's understatement, his openness, and his originality made it *legible* in multiple ways. The episode became the topic of numerous literary and cinematic adaptations (though, curiously enough, hardly ever a subject of literary criticism[33]).

Jules Verne displays prevalent expectations and popular notions, which Humboldt's texts disappointed and denied (this time referring to Teide, in the Canary Islands): the ascent of the peak, the panoramic gaze, the exhaustive research, the complete description. In *Les enfants du Capitaine Grant* (The children of Captain Grant, 1868), Verne's travelers despair when they learn that Humboldt had already investigated a volcano before they had the chance to do so themselves:

> Le gravir! Le gravir, mon cher capitaine, à quoi bon, je vous prie, après MM. de Humboldt et Bonpland? Un grand génie, ce Humboldt! Il a fait l'ascension de cette montagne; il en a donné une description qui ne laisse rien à désirer. . . . C'est au sommet du piton même qu'il

a posé le pied, et là, il n'avait même pas la place de s'asseoir. Du haut de la montagne, sa vue embrassait un espace égal au quart de l'Espagne. Puis il a visité le volcan jusque dans ses entrailles, et il a atteint le fond de son cratère éteint. Que voulez-vous que je fasse après ce grand homme, je vous le demande?[34]

[Oh, ascend it! ascend it, my dear captain! What would be the good after Humboldt and Bonpland! That Humboldt was a great genius. He made the ascent of this mountain, and has given a description of it, which leaves nothing unsaid. . . . He set his foot on the very summit, and found that there was not even room enough to sit down. The view from the summit was very extensive, stretching over an area equal to a fourth part of Spain. Then he went right down into the volcano, and examined the extinct crater. What could I do, I should like you to tell me, after that great man?[35]]

Humboldt's divergence from conventional travel narratives becomes obvious when we juxtapose his accounts of the expedition with the fictional adventures reconstructed by others. In the "Historical Novel" (subtitle) *Der Entdecker* (The explorer, 2001) by Mattias Gerwald, for example, the mountaineers fall into snow-covered depths (from which they were spared in 1802) and free themselves from an icy fissure (which was in reality not the case) while condors circle above their heads (the very birds that Humboldt had looked for in vain).[36]

In his feature film *Die Besteigung des Chimborazo* (The ascent of Chimborazo, 1989),[37] East German director Rainer Simon contributed existential, intercultural, and political interpretations. Simon portrays the ascent as a human aspiration to reach higher goals. When the chasm, at the end of the film, forces him to return, Alexander von Humboldt looks toward the summit with an expression that is supposed to signify, according to the script: "Nicht deine Höhe, sondern die meines Selbstanspruchs ist mir das Maß!" (Not your height, but that of my own standards is my measure!)[38] Furthermore, the scenes with native Ecuadorians performing as extras alongside European professional actors give the film an ethnographic and documentary quality. The German-Ecuadorian cooperation pays tribute to Humboldt's collaboration with the local *indígenas* two centuries ago. When Simon describes the production in his journal[39] and in his autobiography,[40] he superimposes Humboldt's account over his own intercultural experience as a director on the set. Finally, the movie is a comment on German history. It was released in the GDR in September 1989, just weeks before the Berlin Wall fell. The story of an eccentric traveler, whom he shows as a youthful rebel, prompted Simon to question East Germany's travel restrictions and censorship. When he has to seek permission from the Spanish ruler to enter his colonies, a furious Humboldt protests: "I do not accept that I must ask a king where I can travel to."

In his poem "A. v. H. (1769–1859)," Hans Magnus Enzensberger, on the other hand, presents Humboldt's projects as slightly crazy enterprises:

> Er steigt auf
> in die höchsten Luftschichten, und er taucht, in einer eisernen Glocke,
> mit einem wahnwitzigen Engländer namens Brunel auf den Grund der
>   Themse.
>
> [He mounted
> to the highest layers of air, and, in an iron bell,
> with a lunatic Briton named Brunel, he dived to the bottom of the
>   Thames.][41]

Tankred Dorst adds an even stronger satirical touch to the story when he displaces the volcano to the border between the two Germanys. In his comedy *Auf dem Chimborazo* (On Chimborazo, 1974) the mountain becomes a metaphor for the divided country. An elevation on the West side offers a view of the East. Chimborazo, which is reduced to a mere hill, stands for the assumed destination of many East Germans who want to go to the West. "Wenn ich an die armen Leute denke" (when I think of the poor people), one character says, "die da drüben im Osten sitzen" (who are over there in the East), "sie sehen unseren schönen Berg an und er ist unerreichbar für sie" (they look at our beautiful mountain, and it is unreachable for them). An indirect reference to Humboldt reads: "Chimborazo! Weißt Du noch, 'der Chimborazo' hast Du immer gesagt als Kind. Da hattest du so ein Abenteuerbuch gelesen." (Chimborazo! Do you remember, 'Chimborazo' you used to say as a child. You had read about it in some adventure book.)[42]

What Humboldt wrote was anything but "so ein Abenteuerbuch." Instead, his failure was the occasion for a literary game in which absurdity and sarcasm play important parts. While some authors chose titles — "Mi delirio sobre el Chimborazo" (My delirium on Chimborazo, Bolívar), "En las cumbres del mundo" (On the summits of the world, Galeano), *Die Besteigung des Chimborazo* (The ascent of Chimborazo, Simon) — that suggest a successful venture (which is how it entered the collective memory), others accentuate the deficiency. There is a certain irony in the fact that those who perpetuate the legend (Gerwald) as well as those who attempt to critique it (Dorst) both seem to assume that Humboldt had written just "some adventure book," which can be either affirmed or subverted. Those who emphasize Humboldt's shortcomings, unknowingly, come closer to his own humorous deflation.

The most recent text to satirize the ascent became a bestseller. In Daniel Kehlmann's *Die Vermessung der Welt* (Measuring the world, 2005), Humboldt and Bonpland deal with the "crevasse" in a way that is strikingly un-Humboldtian. When they realize that they have to turn back, they are tempted to fill the void with a triumphant lie: "Man könnte . . . auch einfach behaupten, man wäre oben gewesen." — "Überprüfen könne es ja keiner." (We could simply say that we were at the top — no one could disprove it).[43]

Notes

This essay is an abridged and revised English version of a keynote address delivered at the Biannual Conference of the Latin American German Studies Association in Havana on 13 March 2006; *Akten des XXII. ALEG-Kongresses* (Havana/Leipzig: ALEG/CD, 2006), 1–70.

[1] Homer, *Odyssee*, trans. Johann Heinrich Voss, ed. Peter Von der Mühll (Zurich: Diogenes, 1980), VIII, lines 72–95, 250–369, 471–586.

[2] The epithet "segundo descubridor" — a modified quote from Simón Bolívar on Humboldt as the "true discoverer" of America — is generally attributed to the Cuban José de la Luz y Caballero (1800–1862). Cf. Ingo Schwarz, "Acerca de la historia de la dedicatoria 'Al segundo descubridor de Cuba. La Universidad de la Habana, 1939' en el monumento a Alejandro de Humboldt en Berlín," in *Alejandro de Humboldt en Cuba*, ed. Frank Holl (Augsburg: Wissner, 1997), 103–9.

[3] Friedrich Georg Weitsch, *Alexander von Humboldt und Aimé Bonpland in der Ebene von Tapia am Fuße des Chimborazo* (ca. 1810, Berlin, Schloss Charlottenburg). Cf. Halina Nelken, *Alexander von Humboldt: His Portraits and Their artists* (Berlin: Dietrich Reimer, 1980), 70–73. Karl von Steuben, *Alexander von Humboldt am Chimborazo* (ca. 1812–21, destroyed in 1945, black-and-white reproductions remain). Cf. Nelken, *Alexander von Humboldt*, 80–83.

[4] Julius Schrader, *Alexander von Humboldt* (1859, New York, Metropolitan Museum of Art). Cf. Nelken, *Alexander von Humboldt*, 163–69.)

[5] Simón Bolívar, "Mi delirio sobre el Chimborazo" [1822], in *Papeles de Bolívar*, ed. Vicente Lecuna (Caracas: Litografía del Comercio, 1917), 233–34; in English, "My Delirium on Chimborazo" in *Writings of Simón Bolívar*, trans. Frederick Fornoff, ed. David Bushnell (Oxford: Oxford UP, 2003), 135–36.

[6] Tito Salas, *Mi delirio sobre el Chimborazo* (1929–30, Caracas, Casa Natal del Libertador).

[7] Jordan Herbert Stabler, *Bolívar: The Spirit of Chimborazo Speaks* (Caracas: Vargas, 1930).

[8] Claus Hammel, *Humboldt und Bolivar oder Der neue Continent* (Berlin, GDR: Aufbau, 1980), 9–12 (scene 1) and 122–37 (scene 21).

[9] Eduardo Galeano, *Memoria del fuego*, vol. 2: *Las caras y las máscaras* (Montevideo: Chanchito, 1987), 114.

[10] Letter to Wilhelm von Humboldt, dated Lima, 25 November 1802, in *Annales du Muséum national d'histoire naturelle* 2 (1803), 322–37, here 329–31.

11 *Vue du Chimborazo et du Carguairazo* (plate 16), from a sketch by Humboldt, drawn by Gmelin, engraved by Arnold; *Le Chimborazo, vu depuis le plateau de Tapia* (plate 25), after a sketch from Humboldt, drawn by Thibaut, engraved by Bouquet, in Alexander von Humboldt, *Vues des Cordillères et monumens des peuples indigènes de l'Amérique* (Paris: Schoell, 1810[–13]), 102–7 and 200–202. Further references to this edition of Humboldt's *Vues des Cordillères* are given in the text, using the abbreviation VC.

12 Humboldt, *Vues des Cordillères*, 102, "servi de signa[l]" (served as a signal); 103, "de loin" (from afar); 104, "projeté[] sur la voûte azurée du ciel" (projected on the sky's azure vault); 105, "vue . . . magnifique" (magnificent sight); 106, "forme . . . majestueuse" (majestic form); 107, "comme un nuage à l'horizon: il se détache" (like a cloud on the horizon: it stands out); 200, "scène imposante" (imposing scene); 201, "se présente de loin comme un tapis d'un jaune doré" (looks from afar like a golden-yellow carpet); and 202, "le contour" (the contour).

13 François Gérard, "L'Amérique relevée de sa ruine par le Commerce et par l'Industrie" (1814), in *Atlas géographique et physique des régions équinoxiales du Nouveau Continent* (Paris: Gide, 1814–38).

14 Germaine de Staël, *Considérations sur les principaux événemens de la Révolution françoise* (Paris: Delaunay, Bossange & Masson, 1818), 3:389–91.

15 *Essai sur la géographie des plantes, accompagné d'un tableau physique des régions équinoxiales. . . . Avec une planche* (Paris: Schoell; and Tübingen: Cotta, 1807); illustration: *Géographie des plantes équinoxiales. Tableau physique des Andes et Pays voisins. Dressé d'après des Observations & des Mesures prises Sur les Lieux. . . .* The subtitle explains that it was "sketched" and "redacted" by Humboldt, drawn by Schönberger and Turpin in Paris in 1805 and engraved by Bouquet. In his preface Humboldt explains: "C'est au pied du Chimborazo . . . que j'ai rédigé la plus grande partie de cet ouvrage" (vii).

16 When Goethe received the German edition, *Geographie der Pflanzen* (1807), dedicated to him, without the illustration (which was not finished yet), he conceived a sketch on his own and sent a copy to Humboldt (with pencil, pen, and water colors). Six years later he published an engraving of it: *Höhen der alten und neuen Welt bildlich verglichen*, in *Allgemeine Geographische Ephemeriden* 41 (1813): 3–8. The rock in the foreground bears a dedication to Humboldt; on the side Goethe indicated the height that his friend had reached on Mount Chimborazo. Where Humboldt turned back, a small figure can be detected.

17 Humboldt, *Geographiae plantarum lineamenta* (illustration to the "Prolegomena," from a sketch from Humboldt, drawn by Marchais, engraved by Coutant), in *Nova genera et species plantarum*, 7 vols. (Paris: Librairie Grecque-Latine-Allemande, 181[6]–2[6]), 1:3–58. (The first of the three images shows South America with Chimborazo.)

18 Günter Herburger, *Humboldt: Reise-Novellen* (Munich: A1 Verlag, 2001), 20.

19 Humboldt, *Atlas géographique*, illustration 9: *Voyage vers la cime du Chimborazo, tenté le 23 Juin 1802 par Alexandre de Humboldt, Aimé Bonpland et Carlos*

Montúfar. . . . Dessiné par A. de Humboldt à Mexico 1803, par F. Marchais à Paris 1824.

[20] Humboldt, "Ueber zwei Versuche den Chimborazo zu besteigen," in *Jahrbuch für 1837*, ed. H. C. Schumacher (Stuttgart: Cotta, 1837), 176–206.

[21] *Kleinere Schriften*, vol. 1, *Geognostische und physikalische Erinnerungen: Mit einem Atlas, enthaltend Umrisse von Vulkanen aus den Cordilleren von Quito und Mexico* (Stuttgart: Cotta, 1853), 133–74. Further references to this version of Humboldt's "Ueber einen Versuch den Gipfel des Chimborazo zu ersteigen" will be given in the text, using the abbreviation *KS*.

[22] As in the verbs "*er*arbeiten" (work), "*er*lernen" (learn), "*er*ringen" (struggle), "*er*reichen" (reach) or "*er*klimmen" (climb).

[23] Humboldt published Boussingault's account in a separate chapter following his own: "Auszug aus einem Briefe von J. B. Boussingault an A. v. Humboldt, über einen wiederholten Versuch auf den Gipfel des Chimborazo zu gelangen," in Humboldt, *Kleinere Schriften*, 175–205. In contrast to Humboldt, Boussingault points out adventurous dangers and scientific exploits, turning his point of return into the site of a triumphal record and a grandiose view.

[24] *Chimborazo (20.100 Par. Fuss) und Carguairazo (14.700 Par. Fuss) gesehen über der Hochebene von Tapia (8.900 F.)*, after a sketch from Humboldt, drawn by Hildebrandt, engraved by Riegel. This corresponds to illustration 16 of *Vues des Cordillères* but was executed by different artists.

[25] The first man to reach the summit was Edward Whymper in 1880.

[26] Humboldt's report does not conform to general assumptions of post-colonial theory; for example, that European travelers displayed their imperial designs by subjecting American landscapes to their sovereign gaze from mountain peaks. In a contribution that dominates Humboldt scholarship in the United States, Mary Louise Pratt spoke of "monarch-of-all-I-survey scenes;" and she claimed that the scientist 'naturalized' America by excluding its inhabitants from his narratives. However, not only his notebooks but also many of his published articles contain countless accounts of encounters with natives: Mary Louise Pratt, "Alexander von Humboldt and the Reinvention of América," in *Imperial Eyes: Travel Writing and Transculturation* (London: Routledge, 1992), 111–43. On Alexander von Humboldt and post-colonial criticism see, for example: Oliver Lubrich, "Welche Rolle spielt der literarische Text im postkolonialen Diskurs?" *Archiv für das Studium der neueren Sprachen und Literaturen* 157, no. 242 (2005/1): 16–39; "Postcolonial Studies," in *Literaturtheorien des 20. Jahrhunderts*, ed. Ulrich Schmid (Stuttgart: Reclam, 2010), 351–76; "In the Realm of Ambivalence: Alexander von Humboldt's Discourse on Cuba," *German Studies Review* 26, no. 1 (2003): 63–80; and "Alexander von Humboldt: Revolutionizing Travel Literature," *Monatshefte* 96, no. 3 (2004): 360–87.

[27] Like Hans Meyer, who did indeed plant the German flag on the summit of Kilimanjaro in 1890.

[28] Stephen Greenblatt, *Marvelous Possessions: The Wonder of the New World* (Chicago: U of Chicago P, 1992)

²⁹ Cf. Hugo Loetscher, "Humboldt und die Rehabilitierung eines Kontinentes," in *Du* 30 (1970): 666; and Antonello Gerbi, *La disputa del Nuovo Mondo: Storia di una polemica, 1750–1900* (Milan: Riccardo Ricciardi, 1983).

³⁰ Alexander von Humboldt's notes were published unabridged for the first time in a collection of his writings on Chimborazo: *Ueber einen Versuch den Gipfel des Chimborazo zu ersteigen*, ed. Oliver Lubrich and Ottmar Ette (Berlin: Eichborn, 2006).

³¹ Alexander von Humboldt, *Diaries*, 7:33–53 (sheets 21–38). All further references will appear parenthetically in the main text, in the form Dy 33, 21r, where 21 is the sheet number and r is recto, the front side; correspondingly, v is verso, the backside. I thank Ulrich and Christine von Heinz for their generous permission to consult the original manuscript at Schloss Tegel; and Ingo Schwarz for allowing me to use the photocopy and the transcription at the Alexander von Humboldt Research Center, Berlin. I am also grateful to Rex Clark, Michael Gruenbaum, and the Department of Germanic Languages and Literatures at the University of Kansas, where I presented an early version of this essay.

³² Carlos Montúfar, *Diario del año de 1802: Biaje de Quito á Lima* [9 June–10 September 1802], The Lilly Library, Indiana U, Bloomington: Manuscripts Department, Latin American Mss. — Peru.

³³ Without taking into account the Diaries or *Kleinere Schriften*, Juan Pimentel suggests that Humboldt himself theatricalized his ascent and stylized the volcano as "sublime" in order to advertise his achievements and promote his fame. Pimentel, *Testigos del mundo: Ciencia, literatura y viajes en la Ilustración* (Madrid: Marcial Pons, 2003), 179–210.

³⁴ Jules Verne, *Les enfants du Capitaine Grant, voyage autour du monde* (Paris: Hetzel, 1868), 72–73.

³⁵ Jules Verne, *A Voyage round the World*, 3 vols. [no translator is named] (London: George Routledge & Sons, 1876), 1:76.

³⁶ Mattias Gerwald, *Der Entdecker: Historischer Roman über Alexander von Humboldt* (Bergisch Gladbach: Lübbe, 2001), 327–67.

³⁷ Rainer Simon, dir., *Die Besteigung des Chimborazo*, GDR/FRG/Ecuador: DEFA, 1989.

³⁸ Rainer Simon and Paul Kanut Schäfer, *Die Besteigung des Chimborazo: Eine Filmexpedition auf Alexander von Humboldts Spuren* (Cologne: vgs, 1990), 110.

³⁹ Rainer Simon, "Meine Chimborazo-Tagebücher," in Simon and Schäfer, *Die Besteigung des Chimborazo*, 120–57.

⁴⁰ Rainer Simon, *Fernes Land: Die DDR, die DEFA und der Ruf des Chimborazo* (Berlin: Aufbau, 2005), 21–25 and 244–86.

⁴¹ Hans Magnus Enzensberger, "A. v. H. (1769–1859)," in *Mausoleum. Siebenunddreißig Balladen aus der Geschichte des Fortschritts* (Frankfurt am Main: Suhrkamp, 1975), 56–58, here 57; in English, "A. v. H. (1769–1859)," in *Mausoleum: Thirty-seven Ballads from the History of Progress*, trans. Joachim Neugroschel (New York: Urizen, 1976), 62–66, here 64.

⁴² Tankred Dorst, *Auf dem Chimborazo* (Frankfurt am Main: Suhrkamp, 1974), 49.

⁴³ Daniel Kehlmann, *Die Vermessung der Welt* (Reinbek: Rowohlt, 2005), "Der Berg," 163–80; here 177–78.

From Eros to Thanatos: Hiking and Spelunking in Ludwig Tieck's *Der Runenberg*

Peter Arnds

As MICHEL FOUCAULT TELLS US, "the disciplinary space is always basically cellular" as "solitude [is] necessary to both body and soul, according to a certain asceticism."[1] Martin Heidegger was well aware of this as he took refuge in his mountain hut in Todtnauberg, whose solitude far away from the city was deeply connected to the harmony of his work world and essential to his roots in the Alemannic-Swabian soil. Heidegger saw the link between the German *Volk* and its home soil as deeply rooted in the autochthony, the *Bodenständigkeit*, of ancient Greece. To his mind, these chthonic roots of Greek antiquity constituted the very being of its people in the city of Athens. He understood Athens, the *polis*, as etymologically derived from *pelein*, being.[2] He also regarded his own roots and those of Germany as connected specifically with the Black Forest. In this regard he differed substantially from Greek perceptions of places outside the city (especially the mountains) as a *locus daemonis*, an uncivilized space in which the *Sein* (*pelein*) of human *Dasein* loses its contours.

In the wake of German Enlightenment and its various forms of bourgeois self-constraint based on rationality and rationalism, the mountains are a terrain in which subconscious, repressed (*verborgene*) desires are unearthed (*geborgen*) and come to the surface. This occurs especially in Romantic literature, where the repressed emerges from the subterranean domain of the mountains, their cavernous interior, mineshafts, and caves. One might best express this revealing-concealing tendency as follows in German: "Das im Berg Verborgene wird geborgen" (what lies hidden in the mountain is being revealed). There seems to be a particular connection between Romanticism's insistence on a mythological dimension in the mountain landscape and Heidegger's discussion of subterranean rootedness in myth, which he tries to wed to the Nazi-style Germanic blood-and-soil ideology. Yet while Heidegger identified his Black Forest hills with a sense of rootedness, post-Enlightenment literature in the wake of eighteenth-century fears of uncivilized nature associates mountains with a loss of roots. Mountains in nineteenth-century literature provide the possibility of an escape from the nation-state as the location in which the individual's poetry of the heart, as Hegel once called it, has to be given up for the prose of circumstances.[3] Especially for the hero of Romantic literature the journey into the mountains becomes a way of rekindling the poetry of his heart.

Fear and fascination thus determine the nineteenth century's attitude toward mountains. By way of Ludwig Tieck's *Der Runenberg* (Rune Mountain, 1802), in this chapter I demonstrate Romantic literature's acute interest in the mountain terrain, with the ascent of peaks and the descent into their interior as a reflection of the soul's journey from lofty jubilation to its dark abysmal recesses. The very topography of the mountains in Romantic literature, and in Tieck's novella in particular, is tied to the notion of *Verborgenheit* (concealment) of the repressed and its *Bergung*, its unearthing. Although the Romantics predate psychoanalytic theories, the theme of mountains — climbing them and exploring their depths — testifies to the deep awareness of a psychological dimension attached to this landscape. At the same time, Romantic literature remains well aware of Enlightenment's (and subsequently Classicism's and Biedermeier's) fear and distrust of the mountains as a location topographically reflecting the abysses of the soul. Rather than suppressing the perils that the Enlightenment associates with the mountain landscape — the danger to bourgeois society posed by individualism, loneliness, mental and sexual transgression, and the threat of homelessness — Romantic literature is playful with them.

The mountains are both a *locus amoenus* and *locus daemonis* where transgression takes place, where the individual experiences intoxication and a fragmentation of the *principium individuationis*.[4] The fragmentation of individuality can be a prerequisite for the individuation process, or in other terms, for regaining the totality of one's soul, a return to those blissful ancient times (Tieck's "Wunder aus der alten Zeit"; miracles from days gone by)[5] that Nietzsche and Lukács believed went missing in modernity. Nietzsche discusses this phenomenon of the fragmentation of the soul and mind in the context of Dionysus, a mythological figure that, in the spirit of Romanticism, has the potential to disintegrate personalities but may also, strangely enough, contribute to the completion of the individuation process. Dionysus, who tears to pieces and is torn to pieces, who fragments and is fragmented,[6] is part of the archaic, pre-Socratic world of *mythos* rather than of the post-Socratic *logos*, which ousts him. The Dionysian, anti-Classicist dimension that Nietzsche sees represented in Wagner's music appears in Romantic literature as a variety of characters whose function is primarily to abduct young men (and women) from the bourgeois path of reason, self-restraint, and moderation. In Jungian terms, these Dionysian figures are part of the "wild woman" and "wild man" archetypes in which the contours between genders become uncannily blurred. The mountain terrain as traditionally male is no longer valid. Instead, it is a topography in which the gender lines are obfuscated to the point of shapeshifting and androgyny, and in which femininity rules. We encounter these manifestations of Dionysian femininity in Tieck's titanic woman in *Der Runenberg*, but also in E. T. A. Hoffmann's mountain queen in *Die Bergwerke zu Falun* (The mines of Falun, 1819), a work closely modeled after Tieck's story. But an effeminate Dionysus also appears in the male figure of the *Spielmann* (piper) with whom we are familiar from the *Pied Piper of Hamelin* legend, and who is associated with the Venus Mountain in Tieck's tale *Der getreue Eckart und der Tannhäuser* (Loyal Eckart and Tannhauser, 1799) from the *Phantasus* collection. Like the maenads in Euripides' play *The Bacchae* (circa 405 BCE) — the women in the mountains who have turned mad under the spell of Dionysus — these post-Enlightenment Dionysian figures are marginalized. In literature, this repressed subconscious is represented as wilderness, as a forest landscape or the mountains, and within the latter primarily as a subterranean dimension, an environment located well beyond the confines of the *polis*, where the contours of *pelein*, of being, dissolve.

Dionysus is the mythological paradigm that breaks through repression. In philosophical terms and in keeping with the Greek *Weltbild*, he shatters the layers of *lethe* — *lethe* in the sense of forgetting, concealment, and repression — for a glimpse of *aletheia*, the Greek concept of truth, or literally emergence from concealment. These concepts, upon which Heidegger elaborates in his Parmenides lectures, of the winter semester 1942/43, trying to merge them with the nationalist thinking of his times, complement Nietzsche's philosophical but also Sigmund Freud's psychoanalytical theories. Specifically, Freud's notion of *das Heimliche* (as the secret that is concealed and repressed) and the Uncanny, *das Unheimliche*, echo Heidegger's *lethe* and *aletheia* as well as Nietzsche's Apollinian (as semblance and concealment through form) and the Dionysian disruption of that semblance through intoxication. These theoretical paradigms shed light on Tieck's *Kunstmärchen* (unlike the folktale, a fairy tale invented by the writer), specifically on Christian's psychological journey through the mountain landscape, a journey that initially leads him away from his sheltered home, with its "Ebene, d[em] Schloß de[m] kleine[n] beschränkte[n] Garten meines Vaters mit den geordneten Blumenbeeten" (the plain, the castle, my father's constricted garden with its orderly flower beds), a narrow world that he hates: "alles ward mir noch betrübter und verhaßter" (it depressed me and I hated it, *Ph*, 188). From here his journey leads up to the top of Rune Mountain with its erotically charged vision of the beautiful giantess who hands him the *Runentafel*, a strange jewel-bedecked slab, so that he will always remember her. He immediately represses this vision and its inherent spiritual renewal into his subconscious as he returns to the plains on the other (southern) side of the mountains.[7] Back in the lowlands he leads a bourgeois life full of repressed desires until he starts returning to the mountains, initially to visit his parents, and then again for the third time during what one might call a full-blown midlife crisis. With this third sojourn in the mountains, Christian gives up his wife Elisabeth and their child, and instead runs after the vision of his youth, the beautiful giantess, that mythical figure who bears qualities ranging from a demonic shapeshifter to a hermaphrodite. It is during this third outing that he also descends into the mountains' interior with the intention of unearthing hidden treasures, a quest that ultimately leads to insanity.

Although in themselves concealing, mountains in Romanticism are a space that also allow for the undoing of concealment, of the layers of *lethe*, for a glimpse of *aletheia*. The mountains are a realm in which repression, because of being *heimisch* (at home) and *heimlich* (secretive) in the civilized domain, gives way to *das Unheimliche*, and in which this *Unheimliche* unfolds as myth in the form of Dionysian intoxication as the cloak of repression is lifted. As Freud points out, *das Heimliche* and *das Unheimliche* are not necessarily antonyms. When *heimlich* has the meaning of "secretive," as it does in German (apart from the secondary meanings of "familiar," "home-like," and "cozy,"), then it can be *unheimlich* at the same time; the term "uncanny" (*unheimlich*) then "sei alles, was ein Geheimnis, im Verborgenen bleiben sollte und hervorgetreten ist" (applies to everything that was intended to remain secret, hidden away, and has come into the open).[8] This coming into the open of the secret corresponds precisely to the ancient Greek notion of *aletheia*, which implies something emerging into the open from the field (it is literally a "field" or "expanse" in Greek mythology) of *lethe*. *Aletheia* is then tied to *das Unheimliche* as it is to Dionysian intoxication. *Das Unheimliche* reveals itself during Dionysian intoxication as a moment of *aletheia*. At first glance, Tieck's text displays the Freudian notion of *das Unheimliche* and the Greek concept of unconcealment, *aletheia*, only in the three-dimensional mountain landscape, while *lethe* as repression is located in the two-dimensional plains, in the confinement of the parental home on one side of the mountains, and that of married life on the other. During his first hike Christian tries to leave behind the confinement of the parental home and its garden by escaping to the mountain peak, where "eine neue Welt [ihm] aufgeschlossen [war]" (a new world opened up to him, *Ph*, 188). His trek along ever steeper terrain ("der Steig ward mit jedem Schritte schmaler, und der Jüngling mußte sich an vorragenden Steinen fest halten, um nicht hinunter zu stürzen" (the trail grew narrower with each step and the young man had to hold on to protruding rocks so he would not slip and fall, *Ph*, 190) functions both as a foreshadowing of his ensuing sexual intoxication upon seeing the beautiful giantess at the top, but also as a reminder — very much in Enlightenment and Biedermeier fashion — of the dangers of such licentiousness. The peril of falling from the mountain into an abyss (a physical and emotional *Abgrund*) can thus be equated with bourgeois warnings against too much passion. The fact that Christian senses a deeply rooted intimation of this bourgeois constraint becomes clear in his initial emotional reaction to the mountain terrain, that "einsamste[s] Gebirge" (loneliest of mountain ranges) which fills him with sadness and despair: "Am Abend wurde mir heut so traurig zu Sinne, wie noch niemals in meinem Leben, ich kam mir so verloren, so ganz unglückselig vor" (in the evening today I became as sad as never before in my life, I felt so lost and unhappy, *Ph*, 189). The conjunction of *das Unheimliche* and *aletheia* first occurs in Christian's vision of the beautiful giantess. This scene is a highly graphic emergence from *das Heimliche*, from *lethe* as concealment, as she undresses in front of him on the top of Rune Mountain:

> Dann löste sie das Gewand des Busens, und der Jüngling vergaß sich und die Welt im Anschauen der überirdischen Schönheit. Er wagte kaum zu athmen, als sie nach und nach alle Hüllen löste; nackt schritt sie endlich im Saale auf und nieder, und ihre schweren, schwebenden Locken bildeten um sie her ein dunkel wogendes Meer, aus dem wie Marmor die glänzenden Formen des reinen Leibes abwechselnd hervorstrahlten. (*Ph*, 192)
>
> [Then she opened the gown over her bosom, and the young man forgot himself and the world at the sight of her heavenly beauty. He dared not breathe as she dropped her garments, one after another; she stepped back and forth in the hall naked, her heavy floating curls forming a dark undulating sea around her, from which shone forth the radiant curves of her body like marble.]

Although this act constitutes a moment of *aletheia* and is uncanny in the sense of a secret being revealed, Dionysian intoxication does not yet develop its full potential during Christian's climb up the mountain. This scene is Dionysian insofar as it occurs under a moon equipped with horns (*Ph*, 189), thus linking the Christian iconography of the satanic to the lunar Venus cult, while repression is a day-time phenomenon under Apollo, in line with Nietzsche's argument that the Apollinian implies semblance ("Die Sonne schien dem betäubten Schläfer auf sein Gesicht"; the sun shone onto the face of the unconscious sleeper, *Ph*, 193). That he is "betäubt" (unconscious) signals Christian's immediate repression of his erotic vision into the realm of *lethe*, his subconscious, as he leaves the mountains again for a bourgeois life in the village community on the plains. Yet he subsequently suffers from a neurotic compulsion to repeat his trip to the mountains. His erotic vision and experience of an excessive passion has allowed him to partake of an illicit knowledge that has been associated with the satanic in Christian societies but has also triggered an insatiable yearning for a renewal of this heightened sensation.[9] Christian is essentially doomed from the moment he sees the giantess. As Rüdiger Safranski points out referring to Nietzsche's concept of *Verzückungsspitzen* (pinnacles of elation), there are moments in life that are so ecstatic that they cannot be duplicated, a phenomenon that easily leads to repression and depression.[10] Ironically, contrary to psychoanalysis's dictum that the return of the repressed is a step toward healing, it is during his final trip to the mountains that he fully overcomes bourgeois repression and that the Dionysian *Rausch* (intoxication) of his insanity reaches its maximum momentum, and his *principium individuationis* is now completely destroyed and no longer restorable.

In his travels and travails in the mountains, Christian advances from *eros* on their summits to *thanatos* within their depths. His psychic development is thus closely tied to the spatiality of the mountain landscape, to its verticality or depth-dimension. In Freudian terms, Christian's initial hike to the peak is governed by the pleasure principle, which is displaced by the reality principle that reigns in the plains. During his final return to the mountains, the pleasure principle merges with a death drive. The reality principle can be defined as having

> die Aufgabe . . . zwischen den Ansprüchen des Es und dem Einspruch der realen Außenwelt zu vermitteln. . . . Einerseits beobachtet es . . . die Außenwelt, um den günstigen Moment für schadlose Befriedigung zu erhaschen, andererseits beeinflußt es das Es, zügelt dessen Leidenschaften, veranlaßt die Triebe, ihre Befriedigung aufzuschieben.[11]
>
> [the task to mediate between the demands of the id and the external world. On the one hand, the pleasure principle observes the external world in order to avail itself of the opportune moment for harmless gratification, on the other hand, it influences the id, curbs its passions and induces its instincts to postpone their desire for satisfaction. (my translation)]

In the nineteenth-century context of *Bildung*, the Freudian pleasure principle can be equated with what Hegel calls the "poetry of the heart," while the reality principle corresponds to his "prose of circumstances."[12] The protagonist of the classical Bildungsroman has to learn to give up the poetry of his heart for the prose of circumstances. The Romantic hero, in contrast, develops in the other direction. Christian renounces the prose of circumstances to rekindle the poetry of his heart. The fact that his psychic and physical return to the pleasure principle is linked to both a sexual drive and a death drive is indicated through his eventual spiritual marriage with the *Waldweib* (woman of the forest), who is sometimes young and beautiful, sometimes old and ugly, thus uniting *eros* and *thanatos* in herself:

> Ein altes Weib von der äußersten Häßlichkeit kam auf ihn zu . . . wandte sie sich um, und Christian glaubte, zwischen den Bäumen den goldenen Schleier, den hohen Gang, den mächtigen Bau der Glieder wieder zu erkennen. (*Ph*, 204)

[An extremely ugly old woman approached him . . . when she turned around he thought he saw the golden veil, her proud walk, her mighty build between the trees.]

But the union between the sexual and the death drive also manifests itself in the act of spelunking (the exploration of caves, from Latin "spelunca," Greek "spelynx"); that is, in Christian's penetration into Mother Earth's surface, and his search for rocks and minerals. His obsessive digging efforts, his merging with the stony terrain, reflects this Freudian death drive, "dem die Aufgabe gestellt ist, das organische Lebende in den leblosen Zustand zurückzuführen" (which is charged with the task of causing animate organisms to revert to an inanimate state; *EP*, 388), to that state of *being* before birth and to primordial *being* at the dawn of humankind. "Ich bin dir so gut wie gestorben" (I am as good as dead to you), says Christian to his wife Elisabeth the very last time they meet, and that "dort im Walde wartet schon meine Schöne, die Gewaltige, auf mich" (there in the forest the Beautiful one, the Powerful one is waiting for me, *Ph*, 208). This confession expresses a complete merging of the pleasure principle, his sexual drive, with the death drive, of *eros* and *thanatos*, which may indeed lie in close proximity if one considers that there is an "Ähnlichkeit des Zustandes nach der vollen Sexualbefriedigung mit dem Sterben" (the state that ensues upon full sexual gratification is similar to dying, *EP*, 393). If we argue, however, that Christian's sexual drive merges with the death drive during his final journey to the mountains, and that this dual drive as organic life's return to inanimate life is an attempt to return to the prenatal state, then it would follow that Christian's descent into mineshafts symbolizes his desire to reenter the channel through which he had once been born. This desire to return to the womb as the gateway to the state of pre-conception, his penetration of Mother Earth's vagina, as it were, is densely Oedipal and establishes a close link between the mountain terrain and the mother, which are metaphorically alluded to in the giantess, the Venus figure.[13]

The fear-cum-longing inscribed into this amalgamation of the sexual and the death drive is foreshadowed in Christian's second journey to the mountains with the (conscious) intention to visit his parents, whom he has not seen for many years. Subconsciously, however, "[s]eine Angst nahm zu, indem er sich dem Gebirge näherte," (his fear increased upon approaching the mountains, *Ph*, 197), a fear stemming from his Oedipal complex. This becomes clear if one looks at the sequence of motifs during this trip: the anxiety that he experiences in the proximity of the mountains is due to the fact that they contain and conceal (*verbergen*) his Oedipal secret. Christian's Oedipal fear is then also subconsciously linked to his father's authority on the other side of the range, to the threat of castration and the loss of his mother to the father. The Oedipal plot thickens when, still in the mountains, Christian encounters his father, who is looking for him and holding a rare flower in his hands. As a gardener, his father stands for the reality principle of cultivation, or *Bildung*, but by pulling this plant out of the maternal mountain terrain his father destroys the pleasure principle that exists between mother and son, and reasserts his paternal authority over the latter, whose subconscious fear of castration is inscribed into the very image of tearing out the flower.[14] The father is not surprised to see his son; in fact he has expected him. He tells him of the death of his mother, thus shattering his son's hopes of ever seeing her again. As an embodiment of the reality principle, he strengthens his authority even more by moving in with his son and Elisabeth, and exercising control over their lives in the village, a place traditionally ruled by paternal morality and Christian values.

Christian's movement in the mountain landscape — the upward versus downward movement, the peaks versus the abysses — reflects the spatiality of consciousness outlined in Freud's "Das Ich und das Es" (see *EP*, 378). Repression surfaces from the id into the ego, and Christian's descent into the mineshafts echoes the psychoanalyst's reaching down into the lower levels of consciousness. The ego as the reality principle is located in the plains suppressing the drives; the id, which contains the repressed, lies below the plains in the subterranean passages of the mountain landscape. The sexual drive's ability to project itself upward, well beyond the ego's control, is represented as erotic heights, as in the vision on the mountain peak. The direct link between the repressed surfacing into the ego's space and well beyond to unknown heights is suggested by the image of the abyss connecting the realm of the beautiful giantess on top of the mountains and the world deep down. This is where the stranger lives, whom Christian encounters time and again, and who is an uncanny double of the giantess:

> "Unser Weg trennt sich hier," sagte der Fremde, "ich gehe in diese Tiefe hinunter, dort, bei jenem alten Schacht ist meine Wohnung: die Erze sind meine Nachbarn, die Berggewässer erzählen mir Wunderdinge in der Nacht, dahin kannst du mir doch nicht folgen." (*Ph*, 189)
>
> ["Our paths diverge here," said the stranger. "I will climb down to those depths; my abode is right by that old mineshaft: the ores are my neighbors, the mountain's waters tell me wondrous things, and you cannot follow me there."]

"Dahin kannst du mir *noch* nicht folgen" (You cannot follow me *yet*), the stranger might as well say, for Christian's scramble to the top, his adolescent discovery of the pleasure principle, is but a stage in his journey toward experiencing how this principle can, in typical Romantic fashion, join the death drive that will eventually take him into the underworld.

Tieck's landscape is thus a mirror of the psyche. It stands for the workings, the very spatiality of consciousness. In its dichotomy of ego and id, the landscape of plains and mountains is highly gendered. It follows old patterns: the division also outlined in Euripides' *The Bacchae*, where the mountains are maternal terrain (Agave) associated with irrational femininity, the city with masculine rationality (Pentheus). In Euripides and Tieck, pleasure and reality remain divided along these gender lines. By tearing her son Pentheus's head off, Agave enacts the Dionysian pleasure principle, decapitating the reality principle, whereas in Tieck's story Christian's father does the opposite: he persistently points to the reality principle, thus trying to castrate his son, who is so eager to pursue the pleasure principle. In Tieck the *polis* on the plain is male, patriarchal, ruled by Christianity; it represents the ego, the reality principle, and is populated by rational bourgeois citizens (indeed, the name of the protagonist refers to this reality principle that his father wants him to adhere to). The mountains, in contrast, are female, matriarchal, mythical, and pagan; they represent the id, the pleasure principle, and are the domain of the Venus. Tieck's *Waldweib* is an incarnation of the mythical Venus as the Great-Mother archetype, a fact that becomes understandable through the duality of *eros* and *thanatos* that both share. While the mythical Venus morphs between the forces of life — youth and beauty — on the one hand, and the forces of death in the form of old age and ugliness on the other, the Mother too is associated with the drive to give life (the sexual drive) and the death drive (the son's Oedipal quest to return to the womb). Incestuous desire thus becomes equivalent to the death drive, and it is because of this Oedipal death-drivenness that the female in Venus Mountain becomes demonized in patriarchal societies throughout the ages.

In such societies sexualized woman is repressed into a realm of forgetting and concealment, into a lofty or subterranean dimension closely linked to the mountainous landscape. In this process of patriarchal repression of women, the female body and the mountain can even become reflections of one another: "Aber siehe dort den Runenberg mit seinem schroffen Mauerwerke, wie schön und anlockend das alte Gestein zu uns herblickt!" (But look at the Rune Mountain with its jagged cliffs; how beautifully its old rocks lure us! *Ph*, 189) Later on in his life, when Christian runs back toward the mountains, they seem to him even more merged with the appearance of the giantess:

> "Sehe ich nicht schon Wälder wie schwarze Haare vor mir? Schauen nicht aus dem Bache die blitzenden Augen nach mir her? Schreiten die großen Glieder nicht aus den Bergen auf mich zu?" (*Ph*, 197)
>
> ["Are those forests ahead of me not like black hair? Are those sparkling eyes not coming from the stream, are those mighty limbs not walking toward me from the mountains?"]

Women in the mountains and mountains in the shape of women — these are motifs we encounter in various locales, for instance the Tetons in

Wyoming, the Pats in Killarney, the Sleeping Witch near Berchtesgaden. From a general physical equation of the female body with mountains it is only a step to their association with sexuality, procreation, birth — but also inaccessibility and impenetrability.[15]

Romantics like Tieck (and E. T. A. Hoffmann) thus stand in a patriarchal Enlightenment tradition by connecting unrestrained femininity with mountains and a subterranean dimension as raw, uncultured, pre-civilized female territory. Not surprisingly then, in Romantic literature the impressionable young man is often warned against female wantonness by male father figures. Tieck's *Der getreue Eckart* reflects masculine, patriarchal resistance to the danger of unrestrained female sexuality in the figure of the titular hero, and just as Eckart alerts youth at the portal of Venus Mountain to the dangers inside, Christian is warned by his father not to return to the mountains that tempt him with sexual and excessive material longing. In Freudian terms, Loyal Eckart is charged with the power to castrate Oedipally driven young men. Eros is encapsulated in the mountain, locked away as a secret, the Oedipal drive placed well under control.

But Romantic *Entgrenzung* (delimitation), the embrace of infinity and the universe, implies the return and release of the repressed, even of incestuous drives. Romantic transgression is not limited to the different regions of the landscape in these texts but is also reflected in the transgression of bodies beyond their own confines. What Foucault discusses as the docile bodies of the rising bourgeois age, the Age of Confinement as he calls it, contrasts with the more open, chaotic body of earlier periods. The Venus's open body, signaled by Tieck's erotic scene of the giantess in the process of undressing, manifests a less restrained perception of physicality than in earlier, pre-bourgeois periods. The human structure of desire and instincts implies archaic needs that are part of the "chaotic body." In the eighteenth century such needs became subject to forms of "policing." In line with Foucault, Hartmut Böhme has argued that such policing does not accept what it perceives to be mental aberration as constituting a part of one's subjectivity, and hence disciplines and punishes the chaotic body and mind within institutions of power (clinic, city, state).[16]

In the Romantic period the mountains function as a refuge from the reach of the emerging nation-state and its power structures. Homelessness resides in the mountains as a location where not only unrestrained femininity is not suppressed but where also men are allowed to turn wild, explore their deeper consciousness, even their femininity. Christian, who emerges from the mountains disheveled, insane, and equipped with a sapling as staff, regresses from a domesticated sedentary man into one who is nomadic and wild. He appears in torn clothes, with a wreath of leaves in his hair, and leaning on a young spruce (see *Ph*, 207). The wreath indicates his Dionysian impulses, while the spruce staff belongs to the paraphernalia of the legendary wild man. In the post-Freudian era, this archetype may refer to a complete surrender to sexual and incestuous impulses, but the archetype reaches back to the beginnings of human evolution, to the Paleolithic Age and its hunting and gathering nomads, who in the Neolithic phase developed into sedentary farmers. In the Bible, this transition from a nomadic to an agrarian culture is symbolically reflected in the story of Cain, the farmer, who kills — that is, replaces — Abel, the shepherding nomad. By regressing from a sedentary lifestyle in the plains to a nomadic one in the mountains, Christian gives up the lifestyle of Cain for that of Abel, the hunter and gatherer.

The fact that his regression into the woods and mountains is considered heathen, even demonic or satanic, by his religious-minded family and agrarian community, has its roots in the imagination of the Middle Ages, where the wild man archetype signifies godlessness and is a relative of the fool (in carnival rituals) and the devil. Especially the *Wollust* (lust, *Ph*, 192) that Christian experiences in the mountains was identified by Sebastian Brant in his late medieval work *Das Narrenschiff* (The ship of fools, 1494) as one of the great follies, and indeed a sin because it is directed toward terrestrial, earthly pleasures.[17] In Tieck's novella, *Wollust* reveals itself in Christian's obsession with ores, stones, and metals — earth's subterranean treasures. His *Wollust* is sexualized, but on a different level it also stands for greed and is thus a reflection of the rising capitalism of the early-nineteenth century. His lust and greed are associated with music, with woeful and gleeful melodies (see *Ph*, 192), a motif that evokes the medieval iconography of Satan as piper or drummer and the Pied Piper, whose music also has a direct relationship with the phenomenon of bourgeois greed and avarice.

In the Middle Ages the knight was the model of society and in literature was often pitted against his opposite, giants and wild men whom he had to overpower. To overcome these wild men in the Early Modern Age was then the task of miners exploiting the subterranean world. At the beginning of this era the wild men become the keepers of earthen treasures, a role that had earlier been attributed to the dwarfs and underground gnomes (see the tale of Snow White, for example, in the oral tradition). Christian's obsession with ores and metals is in line with this development of the wild-man archetype as a keeper of treasures at a time when mountains were no longer *terra incognita* to be feared and avoided but increasingly becoming the focus of an exploitation of their resources. Tieck's novella thus metaphorically illustrates this process of industrialization and exploitation of nature.

Christian's Dionysian intoxication is sexual and material, and as such it is a transgression of the boundaries of rationalism in an emotive and economic sense. Like the Romantics, Nietzsche defines this transgression of rational boundaries in the Dionysian state as a dissolution of the usual barriers and limits of existence, in Heideggerian terms a destruction of *pelein* itself. This supports the idea of the Freudian death drive as a return from the animate to the inanimate world in Christian's descent into the mountain. Nietzsche further stresses that this experience is not necessarily liberation from all constraints but that it also contains a *lethargic* element in which the individual's past is submerged.[18] Here it becomes clear that *lethe* and *aletheia* constitute a pseudo-dichotomy, as the moment of *aletheia*, in which truth is glimpsed in the state of Dionysian intoxication, submerges all past experiences and therefore in turn leads to lethargy, to *lethe*. *Lethe* is addressed in *Der Runenberg* especially at times when Christian thinks "wie habe ich mein Leben in einem Traume verloren" (I have lost my life in a dream, *Ph*, 203), and when he recognizes the depression that throttles his life outside the mountains: "Ich kann auf lange Zeit, auf Jahre, die wahre Gestalt meines Innern vergessen" (I can forget the true nature of my soul for a long time, even for years, *Ph*, 201). The despair and lethargy Christian experiences in the village are clearly symptoms of repression and its companion, depression. Romanticism seems to be acutely attuned to this clinical condition, as the motif of escape from a bourgeois life is ubiquitous in its literature. The Romantics went to extremes in order to free themselves from depression and mourning; one only need think of Novalis consciously willing himself to die in pursuit of his deceased beloved, Sophie von Kühn.

The parallel of *lethe* and *aletheia* with the lowlands versus the mountains is therefore not consistent. *Lethe* occurs in both domains, in the community as a repression of deeper impulses and instincts, and in the mountains where reason is forgotten and unrestrained femininity is removed and concealed from the patriarchal community. Consequently, Christian's midlife journeys into the mountains as a social drop-out or *Aussteiger*, are not necessarily trips away from *lethe*. His ultimate intoxication with the *Waldweib* leads to the kind of lethargy that Nietzsche addresses and to a merging of what Christian perceives as *aletheia*, "die wahre Gestalt [s]eines Innern" (the true nature of my soul, *Ph*, 201), with what could also be seen as *lethe*, his former life submerged in the subterranean realm of the mountains, *lethe* as death, lethality. Euripides' play already contained this ambivalence: at the moment of *aletheia*, when Pentheus sees the maenads in their Dionysian *Rausch* (intoxication), he dies.

In Romanticism, however, death is not complete annihilation; it is not tied to finality. The mountains draw Christian from stagnation and depression, although in the process of becoming one with the mythological world he appears insane and thus indeed dead to bourgeois visions of reason. Although a symptom of the new bourgeois age, the material greed that coincides with his insanity is more of a union with nature than the attempt to exploit it for utilitarian purposes. It is a kind of *Bergtod* (mountain death), *lethe* in the sense of the Romantics' self-effacement from the bourgeois world, not least because of the Oedipal impulse the bourgeoisie represses into the realm of *lethe*.[19]

Christian's *Bergtod* ("ich bin dir so gut wie gestorben"; I am as good as dead to you, *Ph*, 208), the obliteration of his former identity, is not final.[20] His death drive converges with the drive to preserve life, a process that manifests itself in his rejuvenation, his illusory forgetting of the aging process. Death as the preservation of an eternal youth is a typically Romantic idea, and Novalis's early end is an effort in that spirit, for by dying young he saw himself eternally connected to Sophie von Kühn, their youth forever preserved. Christian's repeated journeys into the mountains are triggered by a midlife crisis, that is, a sense of having lost his youth. He consequently tries to forget his aging process by rejuvenating himself with the eternal *Waldweib*. In her faculty of appearing old at times and then young again, she reflects how illusory Christian's moment of *jouissance* really is, and that his depression is never fully healed but that his trip back into the mountains is in itself an act of repression of life as such and the passage of time. Tieck seems to be acutely aware of this vicious circle of joy and misery, youth and old age, life and death, *eros* and *thanatos* — binaries that are physically inscribed into the *Waldweib*.

The power of rejuvenation is an integral part of the Venus cult, while Christianity embraces the aging process as a portal to the afterlife. Time seems to stand still in Venus Mountain. It does so for E. T. A. Hoffmann's Elis Fröbom, whose dead body does not decompose until unearthed from the mines of Falun. It also does so for Rip van Winkle in the Catskills, for Australia's Hanging Rock into which a group of girls allegedly disappeared on Valentine's Day in 1900,[21] and for Hans Castorp on the Magic Mountain. In contrast, Foucault points out that the bourgeois disciplinary methods "reveal a linear time . . . evolutive time" and that "the administrative and economic techniques of control reveal a social time of a serial, oriented, cumulative type: the discovery of an evolution in terms of progress."[22] Christian's accumulation of rocks, the treasures of the earth, is a parody of the signs of his times. By the same token, his insanity contains an aspect of timelessness, his Oedipal *Rausch* pointing to the eternity of the Mother archetype as a life-giving force.

Lethe can never be seen in separation from its pseudo-opposite *a-letheia*, the revelation or *Unverborgenheit*, the "un-concealment" of truth, literally its being carried forth from the mountains, a process indicated by the privative "a-."[23] The mountains in *Der Runenberg* are the landscape of *aletheia* in the Heideggerian sense of bringing into *Unverborgenheit* Christian's true nature: "bei allen eckigen Figuren . . . will dann die inwohnende Gestalt entbinden und zur Geburt befördern" (with all angular figures the inner *gestalt* wants to be unleashed and born, *Ph*, 202). The a- in *a-letheia* denotes the truth as something that is torn or stolen from concealment. The Dionysian experience in the mountains ultimately implies *lethe* as a forgetting of the rational world that is left behind. But the *aletheia* of the Dionysian experience, this unearthing of a forbidden truth — be it the Oedipus complex or some other repressed material — Nietzsche's "grauenhafte Wahrheit" (terrible truth)[24] that accompanies Dionysian intoxication, also implies breaking through the field of *lethe* that the rational world has created by excluding that forbidden knowledge. "For mad Bacchic possession brings considerable prophetic skill,"[25] says Teireseas, Apollo's blind prophet in Euripides' play. It is this prophetic skill that the Middle Ages associated with the satanic and the figure of the fool. In his innocent idiocy, the fool possesses a knowledge that is inaccessible to the rational mind. Foucault concedes that this forbidden wisdom "must be torn from the bowels of the earth."[26] In Romanticism, as Christian's folly — his illusion of eternal youth — shows us, this forbidden wisdom must be *geborgen* from the *Berg* in which it lies *verborgen*. In Freudian terms, *das Heimliche*, which is withdrawn from knowledge, unconscious, is revealed as *das Unheimliche* in a terrain that is *un-heimlich* (un-homely), subterranean and mountainous. As *das Heimliche* and *das Unheimliche* coincide in the mountain landscape, Freud's dichotomy becomes as much a pseudo-dichotomy as the Heideggerian notions of *lethe* and *aletheia*.

Heidegger, who sought in myth the chthonic power to root the Germans, understood myth as related to the chthonic or telluric, the earth, especially to what lies concealed in its subterranean dimension, a philosophical construct no doubt partly derived from Romanticism. His notion of "being," *Sein*, is central to this understanding of dwelling and its loss due to the gradual destruction of the planet since the Enlightenment. Such destruction commences on a large scale in the age of industrialization during the late eighteenth and early nineteenth centuries. Tieck's *Der Runenberg* engenders this process of material rationalization and subsequent loss of dwelling. The mountains conceal and reveal femininity as well as nature's hidden resources in the male age of reason. In the collective subconscious these resources are intrinsically connected to Mother Nature, that is to the feminine, and it is this tension between exploiting and loving Mother Nature that triggers Christian's obsessive-compulsive behavior, his treatment of Venus as his great mistress while he is eager to rob her hidden treasures. In the Oedipus complex, loving and exploiting are the same: the suckling son exploits his mother for her milk, which is why she consequently becomes a sexual object for him. The son's exploitation of the mother as a food source triggers his Oedipal drive. Christian's insanity resulting from this Oedipal tension may foreshadow modernity's homelessness. One will need to keep in mind, however, that the Romantics still felt very much at home in their metaphysical homelessness, and despite what the community perceives to be Christian's *Bergtod*, this ostensible "mountain death" is no less than his homecoming: his *Rückkehr in den Berg ist eine Heimkehr* (my coinage: his return into the mountain is a homecoming).

Notes

[1] Michel Foucault, *Discipline and Punish: The Birth of the Prison* (New York: Random House, 1995), 143.
[2] Cf. Martin Heidegger, *Parmenides*, trans. André Schuwer and Richard Rojcewicz (Bloomington: Indiana UP, 1992), 94–97.
[3] G. W. F. Hegel, *Vorlesungen über die Ästhetik III* (Frankfurt am Main: Suhrkamp, 1970), 393.
[4] See Friedrich Nietzsche, *Die Geburt der Tragödie*, in *Sämtliche Werke, Kritische Studienausgabe*, vol. 1, ed. Giorgio Colli and Mazzino Montinari (Munich: dtv/de Gruyter, 1999); In English, *The Birth of Tragedy and Other Writings*, ed. Raymond Geuss and Ronald Speirs (Cambridge: Cambridge UP, 1999).
[5] Ludwig Tieck, *Schriften in 12 Bänden*, vol. 6, *Phantasus*, ed. Manfred Frank (Frankfurt am Main: Deutscher Klassiker Verlag, 1985), 190. Further references to this work are given in the text using the abbreviation *Ph* and the page number. All translations in this chapter are my own unless otherwise noted.
[6] Cf. James Fraser, *The Golden Bough* (London: Penguin, 1996), 472.
[7] Although the mountains in this story are never specified, Tieck may have had the Fichtelgebirge of Franconia in mind, where he hiked with Wackenroder during the summer of 1793. Cf. Rüdiger Safranski, *Romantik: Eine deutsche Affäre* (Frankfurt am Main: Fischer, 2009), 99.
[8] Sigmund Freud, *Das Unheimliche: Aufsätze zur Literatur*, ed. Klaus Wagenbach (Hamburg-Wandsbek: Fischer doppelpunkt, 1963), 51. In English, *The Uncanny*, trans. David McLintock (London: Penguin, 2003), 132.
[9] Cf. also Robert Macfarlane, *Mountains of the Mind* (New York: Pantheon, 2003), 159–60: "Romanticism fused into the imagination of altitude a new element of attractiveness: that one was almost guaranteed enlightenment — spiritual or artistic epiphany — by getting high. The mountain-top and the viewpoint became accepted sites of contemplation and creativity: places where you were brought to see further both physically and metaphysically."
[10] See Safranski, *Romantik*, 103.
[11] Sigmund Freud, *Elemente der Psychoanalyse*, in *Werkausgabe in zwei Bänden*, ed. Anna Freud and Ilse Grubrich-Simitis, vol. 1 (Frankfurt am Main: Fischer, 1978), 419. Further references to this edition of Freud's works are given in the text using the abbreviation *EP* with the volume and page number.
[12] Eine der gewöhnlichsten und für den Roman passendsten Kollisionen ist deshalb der Konflikt zwischen der Poesie des Herzens und der entgegenstehenden Prosa der Verhältnisse . . . ein Zwiespalt, der sich entweder tragisch und komisch löst oder seine Erledigung darin findet, dass . . . die der gewöhnlichen Weltordnung zunächst widerstrebenden Charaktere das Echte und Substantielle in ihr anerkennen lernen, mit ihren Verhältnissen sich aussöhnen und wirksam in dieselben eintreten. (Hegel, *Vorlesungen über die Ästhetik III*, 393)

[One of the most common and typical collisions in the novel is the conflict between the poetry of the heart and the prose of external conditions, of reality, a conflict that is resolved either tragically or comically, or in such a way that the characters, who are initially opposed to the world order, learn to recognize its genuine and substantial aspects, learn to become reconciled with its conditions, and to be integrated effectively into this order.]

[13] Cf. Hartmut Böhme, "Romantische Adoleszenzkrisen: Zur Psychodynamik der Venuskult-Novellen von Tieck, Eichendorff und E. T. A. Hoffmann," in *Literatur und Psychoanalyse*, ed. Klaus Bohnen, Sven Aage Jørgensen, and Friedrich Schmoë (Copenhagen: Text & Kontext, 1981), esp. 143–49.

[14] Cf. Harry Vredeveld, "Ludwig Tieck's *Der Runenberg*: An Archetypal Interpretation," *Germanic Review: Literature, Culture, Theory* 49, no. 3 (1974): 204: "The predominance of the father in Christian's development means that the masculine side of his psyche is growing at the expense of the feminine, for the father is a symbol of the conscious, just as the mother symbolizes the unconscious and irrational side of being."

[15] The ancient burial mound of Newgrange, Ireland, for example, is a tomb in the shape of a womb, thus testifying to the significance of the goddess and the eternal cycle of life, death, rebirth, but also to the symbolism of the mound's or mountain's entrance as Mother Earth's vagina. After all, the *Venusberg* is derived from the *mons veneris*, the fatty cushion of flesh in human females situated at the junction of the pubic bones. The Irish Sheela na Gig, a pre-Christian figure of fertility found on rocks and portals of churches, is pointing at her pudenda, a pose that can be read as a cultural echo of Venus Mountain. These motifs of female sexual liberty and their physical openness were outlawed by patriarchal Christianity. Freud identifies them as secret places of the body ("heimliche Orte am menschlichen Körper, pudenda," Freud, *Das Unheimliche*, 52; *The Uncanny*, 133), as *heimlich*. Their emergence into the open points to them as *unheimlich*, uncanny.

[16] Böhme, "Romantische Adoleszenzkrisen," 134–35.

[17] Cf. the 50th chapter in Sebastian Brant, *Das Narrenschiff* (Stuttgart: Reclam, 2006), 179. This edition is a facsimile of Karl Goedeke's edition, Leipzig 1872.

[18] Nietzsche, *Die Geburt der Tragödie*, 56; *The Birth of Tragedy*, 40.

[19] Heather I. Sullivan even argues, quoting Susan Sontag's *The Volcano Lover* (1992), that collecting rocks is "an act of self-annihilation and yet a linking of the individual to greater forces and energies." Heather I. Sullivan, "Collecting the Rocks of Time: Goethe, the Romantics, and Early Geology," *European Romantic Review* 10 (1999): 343.

[20] This is also argued by Ralph W. Ewton, Jr. in "Life and Death of the Body in Tieck's *Der Runenberg*," *Germanic Review: Literature, Culture, Theory* 50 (1975): 19–33.

[21] This event has inspired Joan Lindsay's 1967 novel *Picnic at Hanging Rock* and Peter Weir's 1975 film adaptation.

[22] Foucault, *Discipline and Punish*, 160.
[23] Heidegger, *Parmenides*, 14.
[24] Nietzsche, *Die Geburt der Tragödie*, 57; *The Birth of Tragedy*, 40.
[25] Euripides, *The Bacchae and Other Plays* (Oxford: Oxford UP, 2008), 52.
[26] Michel Foucault, *Madness and Civilization: A History of Insanity in the Age of Reason* (New York: Random House, 1988), 22.

Geology, Mountaineering, and Self-Formation in Adalbert Stifter's *Der Nachsommer*

Sean Ireton

ADALBERT STIFTER'S COLOSSAL three-volume novel *Der Nachsommer* (Indian Summer) appeared in 1857 at the apogee of Alpinism's Golden Age, a period of intense summit pursuits that began around 1850 and culminated in 1865 with the first ascent of the Matterhorn. In a unique and oblique way, the novel provides literary testimony to numerous facets of mountaineering history. Throughout the text, Alpine peaks present physical challenges, inspire feelings of awe, and form the principal object of scientific inquiry. Although often categorized as a Bildungsroman (novel of education or self-formation), this book might just as well bear Hermann Broch's label of a *Bergroman* (mountain novel), for mountains constitute the matrix of its setting, plot, and deeper thematics.[1] Indeed, the idea of *Bildung* is inextricably linked with the activity of climbing. Moreover, the main character, Heinrich Drendorf, is largely modeled on Stifter's friend Friedrich Simony, a geologist and mountaineer who made exploring the Alps, particularly the Salzkammergut of Austria, his life-long project. Here Simony conducted countless geoscientific studies, many of which are faithfully reproduced in Heinrich's semi-fictionalized sojourns. Heinrich thus proves to be an atypical protagonist within the tradition of the German Bildungsroman. His development is predicated less on artistic aspirations and human relationships than on his interaction with mountains as age-old geophysical formations — or *Bildungen*. With *Der Nachsommer* Stifter thus creates a new and literal brand of Bildungsroman, one that is rooted in the discourse and practice of mountaineering during the nineteenth century.

Heinrich's Alpine education begins in his childhood. His father, who enforces a subtle yet systematic pedagogical regimen, introduces Heinrich to various forms of exercise, including swimming, hiking, and mountain climbing. This emphasis on physical fitness and "naturgemäß[e] Entfaltung" or "natural development"[2] of the body will later play a crucial role in Heinrich's deep-seated urge to be outdoors. In the second chapter of the novel, significantly entitled "Der Wanderer" (The wanderer), Heinrich reveals what else draws him to the high country: "Ich war nur im Allgemeinen in das Gebirge gegangen, um es zu sehen" (4,1:39; I generally just went to the mountains in order to see them, *IS*, 26 [translation modified]). This notion of "seeing" is central to the novel. Over the course of some 800 pages (nearly 1,400 in the print of the original edition), Heinrich scrutinizes nature, and indeed the verbs *sehen* (to see), *beobachten* (to observe), and especially *betrachten* (to view) permeate the narrative like leitmotifs, underscoring this basic optical perception of reality. Heinrich constantly strives to detect *Naturbildungen* (natural formations), an externally oriented effort that mirrors his own internal cultivation. The classical German idea of *Bildung* (compare Herder, the Humboldts, and especially Goethe) as an organic process that operates in the parallel realms of nature and human existence looms large throughout the novel. To employ some helpful German here (my own, not Stifter's): "Heinrich *bildet* sich an den *Bildungen* der Natur." In other words, his *formation* occurs through extended contact with the variegated *forms* of nature. And these he studies on two levels. First, he examines what readily presents itself to him, namely the surface manifestations of natural phenomena, whether botanical structures, geological configurations, glacial patterns, or cloud shapes. He then probes more deeply, collecting, measuring, and analyzing data, all in a concerted effort to fathom the inner dynamics of nature. This act of "fathoming" becomes especially apparent, if not literalized, in his ongoing project of plumbing the Lautersee in order to measure its depths and map its underwater basin. However, of all the natural phenomena that he investigates in a morphological manner it is geological formations that captivate him the most. And these of course can best be studied in the mountains, whose outward appearances bear direct witness to geological, glaciological, and meteorological processes. Moreover, Heinrich pursues his scientific research not only at the base or on the flanks of mountains but also on top of them, so that hiking and climbing inevitably become part of his education. Mountains thus offer optimal insight into the notion of *Bildung* in all its dimensions.

Heinrich seeks out mountaintops in order to observe the geophysical totality of the region. In the midst of the Austrian Alps he is able to grasp the interconnectivity and history of nature from a panoramic height of reflection:

> Ich habe schon gesagt, daß ich gerne auf hohe Berge stieg, und von ihnen aus die Gegenden betrachtete. Da stellten sich nun dem geübteren Auge die bildsamen Gestalten der Erde in viel eindringlicheren Merkmalen dar, und faßten sich übersichtlicher in großen Theilen zusammen. Da öffnete sich dem Gemüte und der Seele der Reiz des Entstehens dieser Gebilde, ihrer Falten und ihrer Erhebungen, ihres Dahinstreichens und Abweichens von einer Richtung, ihres Zusammenstrebens gegen einen Hauptpunkt und ihrer Zerstreuungen in die Fläche. (4,1:43)

[I already said that I liked to climb high mountains and observe the landscape from there. From these vantage points the formable configurations [*die bildsamen Gestalten*] of the earth were much more obvious to the practiced eye, and the salient features could be surveyed much more comprehensively. My heart and soul were captivated by these formations, their origin, their depressions and elevations, their chains extending in one direction and going off in another, their coming together into one high point and then dissipating into the flatlands. (*IS*, 28)]

This comprehensive and contemplative vantage of a summit vista is of course a topos that goes back to Petrarch (as mentioned in the introduction and prelude) and can further be found in the works of modern contemporaries of Stifter such as Alexander von Humboldt, Goethe, Thoreau, and John Muir.[3] Also important is the fact that this elevated view inspires feelings of awe. From his lofty perch, Heinrich is overcome by "das große und erhabene Ganze" (4,1:44; the great and sublime whole, *IS*, 29 [translation modified]) of nature. He goes on to describe this totalistic effect in comparative terms. Drops of water freeze on a windowpane and create on its surface heterogeneous designs, which subsequently break apart and become reconfigured as a result of fluctuations in weather (frost, wind, thaw, refreezing). Mountains, he claims, have been shaped by the same climatic factors, only on a monumental scale. (Later in the novel he will develop a more precise geological understanding of these factors, realizing that mountains exist in their present form as a result of volcanic activity, glaciation, and erosion.) Thanks to this initial yet decisive experience in the Alps, he finds a new object of interest, one that appeals to both his emotions and his intellect:

> Ich begann, durch diese Gefühle und Betrachtungen angeregt, gleichsam als Schlußstein oder Zusammenfassung aller meiner bisherigen Arbeiten die Wissenschaft der Bildung der Erdoberfläche und dadurch vielleicht der Bildung der Erde selber zu betreiben. (4,1:44)
>
> [Inspired by these feelings and observations, I began to study the formation of the Earth's surface, almost as a keystone or summary of my studies up to now, and then perhaps, I would proceed to the formation of the Earth itself. (*IS*, 29; translation modified)]

Heinrich's budding scientific curiosity concerns both the outward form of the planet and the process of its formation. In an added signification, he too will undergo crucial formative experiences through his tireless geological fieldwork. His inner development is, in other words, congruent with outer reality. Like "die bildsamen Gestalten der Erde" (4,1:43; formable configurations of the Earth, *IS*, 28) that he observes from any given summit, he himself is *bildsam* and caught up in a continual process of *Bildung*.

Stifter develops an entire vocabulary, if not a complex of motifs around the idea of *Bildung*. His novel is replete with such variants as *bilden* (to form), *bildsam* (formable), *Bild* (image), *Bildung* (formation), and especially *Gebilde* (shape, pattern). Even the negatively connoted *verbildet* (deformed) surfaces once (4,3:179; *IS*, 419).[4] Also recurring are the terms *Gestalt* (form, shape) and *Gestaltung* (structure). Stifter thus capitalizes on the linguistic potential of the German morpheme *Bild*. This recourse should not be surprising in a text widely considered to be a Bildungsroman. In the *Wilhelm Meister* novels, Goethe operates with his own creative arsenal of terms and concepts that underscore his fundamental tenet of *Bildung*,[5] but Stifter is without parallel in this regard. He devises a comprehensive semiotic system that fortifies the thematic foundation of his novel. Heinrich's self-formation, his *Bildung*, is intertwined with the geophysical formations — the *Gebilde, Bildungen, Gestalten*, and *Gestaltungen* — that he encounters on a daily basis. Both Heinrich and his outside world are formable, subject to a constant yet gradual state of development. Gradualism is a major operating principle in *Der Nachsommer*. As in Charles Lyell's influential theory, it applies to the slow geological processes that have occurred over millennia and hence to the very object of Heinrich's research. Indeed, Stifter's long and plodding novel contains its own sluggish geological tempo, thus serving as literary attestation of Lyellean gradualism and its "aesthetics of inordinate slowness."[6] The parallelism between humanity and geohistory is further evident in some of the books that Heinrich notices in Risach's library, particularly the classic study by Karl Ritter with the revealing title: *Die Erdkunde im Verhältnis zur Natur und Geschichte des Menschen* (Geography in relation to the nature and history of humankind, published in 21 volumes between 1822 and 1859). Stifter's view of social progress is symbolically coded in the geological discourse that pervades the text; however, this is not the place to examine his stubbornly Restorative perspective on history.[7] Important for my argument here is that Heinrich's development unfolds at a decelerated pace analogous to that of the mountainous formations in whose midst he wanders, climbs, and *gradually* comes of age.

Heinrich's mountain climbing follows a steady, logical progression. Throughout the novel he oscillates between two environmental extremes in accordance with the model of self-development that Goethe likened to systole and diastole, or contraction and expansion. This pattern of evolution is emblematically stated in the first two chapter headings: "Die Häuslichkeit" (Domesticity) and "Der Wanderer" (The wanderer). Heinrich's childhood education is restricted to the domestic sphere, yet when he becomes a teenager his pedagogue father sends him farther away from home every summer. Heinrich thus travels ever deeper — and higher — into the Austrian countryside. At first he chooses routes that lead through fields and vineyards; then he sets foot on remote paths that wind through dense forests and often disappear in their depths; finally, he opts to hike off-trail through whatever type of landscape he encounters. He thus makes an important developmental transition from the accessible cultivated landscape to the remote backwoods, and upon his return home from these excursions he finds himself "stets gereifter" (4,1:34; always... more mature, *IS*, 23). During the following summer he pays his first visit to the Alps, which he had previously discerned only on the horizon. He crosses high passes, climbs several peaks, and generally makes a concerted effort to keep to the crest of the range. In other words, he wants to spend as much time as possible up high. The next summer brings an "expansion" of mountaineering; now he hires professional guides to take him onto glaciers and reach the highest peaks. At this point his newly discovered pastime becomes an enduring passion, and Stifter makes the following sentence into a single programmatic paragraph: "Ich ging von nun an jeden Sommer in das Gebirge" (4,1:40; From now on I spent every summer in the mountains, *IS*, 26).

True to the principles of expansion and contraction, Heinrich continually broadens his Alpine explorations and unfailingly returns home to concentrate on other aspects of his education, such as reading, drawing, and attending the theater. He soon establishes a routine whereby he spends spring and summer in the Alps, autumn and winter back home in the city (which remains nameless but is obviously Vienna). Sometimes the borders between these otherwise distinct realms overlap such that Heinrich, the now seasoned mountaineer accustomed to physical exertion, feels the need to take long walks through the urban environs or inhale cold autumn air as a substitute for the rarefied mountain variety. One has the sense that Heinrich, deep down, is more attracted and attuned to one pole of his existence than the other. By the end of the first volume he is in fact so familiar with the mountains of Upper Austria that even the locals consider him "fast der Bewandertste" (4,1:307; almost the best informed, *IS*, 177). He can identify all the peaks, their subsidiary summits, the valleys, snowfields, and even the topological boundaries that separate individual massifs and subranges. He is well versed in regional geography precisely because he is well traveled — or as the German implies, "well wandered." At the beginning of the second volume, in a chapter bearing the indicative title "Die Erweiterung" (Broadening the Horizons), he extends the parameters of his seasonal routine by remaining in the mountains well into autumn and beyond the first snowfall (see 4,2:35; *IS*, 182). In the third volume he expresses a desire to view the high country in winter (see 4,3:21; *IS*, 332) and before long embarks on a multiday glacier tour during the middle of January (see 4,3:98–111; *IS*, 375–82). Early on Heinrich declares two major goals: "'Mein Zweck ist, soweit meine Kräfte reichen, wissenschaftliche Bestrebungen zu verfolgen, und nebenbei, was ich auch nicht für unwichtig halte, das Leben in der freien Natur zu genießen'"

(4,1:65; my purpose is, as far as my ability permits, to pursue scientific matters and also enjoy life in the great outdoors, something I do not consider unimportant, *IS*, 41). He accomplishes both these objectives less through the contracting experience of domestic life than through his ever-expanding forays into the Austrian hinterland. Stifter consistently describes how Heinrich visits the mountains in pursuit of these twin ambitions; however, I will restrict my focus to two episodes, both of which exemplify certain historical features of mountaineering as they function within the pedagogical program of the novel.

During one of his annual Alpine pilgrimages, Heinrich forgoes lodging at the Ahornwirtshaus (Maple Inn), his habitual base of operations, and takes up residence deeper in the mountains. Here he has quicker access to the rock masses that form the object of his geological studies. Nevertheless, when he and his crew finish their work at a given site, they waste no time before engaging in an aspect of mountaineering that, by the end of the nineteenth century, would replace the previously dominant motive of scientific research: climbing for pure pleasure or sport. As Heinrich states in this regard: "Ich suchte auch gerne auf die Gipfel hoher Berge zu gelangen, wenn mich selbst eben meine Beschäftigung nicht dahin führte" (4,2:186; I also enjoyed scaling the higher peaks, even if my projects didn't necessarily take me there, *IS*, 277). These words reflect a mid-century shift in Alpinism that one historian has characterized as "die Suspension des wissenschaftlichen Interesses" (the suspension of scientific interest).[8] Although Heinrich never truly "suspends" his geological investigations, he is able to balance intellectual inquiry with physical play, which is another way of saying that he also practices climbing for climbing's sake. This combination of interests emerges, for example, in the following passage:

> In die wildesten und abgelegensten Gründe führte uns so unser Plan, auf die schroffsten Grate kamen wir, wo ein scheuer Geier oder irgendein unbekanntes Ding vor uns aufflog, und ein einsamer Holzarm hervor wuchs, den in Jahrhunderten kein menschliches Auge gesehen hatte. . . . Meine Leute waren in einer gesteigerten Freude und Empfindung, wenn wir mit dem Hammer und Meißel theils Stufen in die glatten Wände schlugen, theils Löcher machten, unsere vorräthigen Eisen eintrieben, auf solche Weise Leitern verfertigten, und auf einen Standort gelangten, auf den zu gelangen eine Unmöglichkeit schien. Wir kamen oft eine Reihe von Tagen nicht in unser Tannwirthshaus hinab. (4,2:185–86)

> [And so our plans often led us to the wildest and most remote areas; we ventured onto the most precipitous ridges, where a shy buzzard or some other unidentifiable bird flew up at our approach, where a lonely gnarled arm of wood, never beheld by the eye of man over the centuries, was growing out of the cliff face. . . . My people were in a

heightened state of euphoria whenever we hammered and chiseled steps, or bored holes, or drove our spare iron into the sheer rock walls and in this manner fashioned ladders that enabled us to reach a place that seemed impossible to scale. We often didn't return to our lodgings for several days at a time. (*IS*, 277; translation modified)]

It is interesting to note that hammer and chisel, the trademark tools of the geologist, are employed here in a mountaineering context: they serve to secure climbing routes. This dual iconic functionality illustrates the fusion of science and sport. In this same segment of text Heinrich criticizes the mentality of conquest that has, historically, often accompanied Alpinism (see 4,2:185; *IS*, 277). Although he is a fanatical and now hardened mountaineer, a true *Bergfex* (mountain fanatic) in the parlance of the region, Heinrich displays a nuanced attitude toward the object of his passion. Primarily, he is a geologist whose livelihood depends on rocky terrain. Second, he is drawn to the mountains for reasons of health and vitality, or in modern terms "sport." As will become apparent later in the novel, his intellectual and physical attributes are supplemented by a spiritual component, such that he becomes the consummate nineteenth-century mountaineer, one who exists in a "Spannungsverhältnis zwischen Wissenschaft, Sport und Spiritualität" (tension between science, sport, and spirituality).[9] As often in Stifter, harmony prevails over strife.[10] A healthy equilibrium of these diverse and potentially conflicting motivations underlies Heinrich's Alpine enterprises, many of which are based on the accomplishments of Friedrich Simony.

As a nature enthusiast, mountaineer, and scientist, Friedrich Simony (1813–96) was a prime practitioner of nineteenth-century Alpinism.[11] Like Stifter, who was eight years his senior, Simony hailed from Bohemia, was born into the lower-middle class, rose to fame as an autodidact, and became a talented prosaist and landscape illustrator. He was the first person to carry out systematic meteorological studies in the eastern Alps after the example set by Horace-Bénédict de Saussure in the western part of the range. Thanks to his early scientific pursuits and publications, which were often financed by Austrian nobles such as Metternich, Simony eventually became the first professor of geography at the University of Vienna (in 1851). This emerging and still broadly defined discipline encompassed diverse physiognomies of the earth: geology, mineralogy, glaciology, botany, limnology, and meteorology. In a word, one might sum up Simony's scientific orientation as "geomorphology," a notion whose wide-ranging implications Stifter exploits in *Der Nachsommer*. In addition to his many achievements in the professional arena, Simony was also a serious Alpinist who accomplished a number of pioneering feats. His name is especially associated with the Hohe Dachstein (2,995 m/9,826 ft.), the highest, most glaciated peak in the eastern Alps. He was the first to spend the night on its summit (September 1843), laid on its rocky pinnacle the first

Fig. 1. Friedrich Simony after having spent the night on the summit of the Hohe Dachstein in September 1843. The inscription below reads: "Der Gipfel des Hohen Dachsteins, aufgenommen nach meiner ersten Uebernachtung auf dem Gipfel, 16–17 Septbr 1843. Fr. Simony" (The summit of the Hohe Dachstein, taken after my first overnight stay on the summit, 16–17 September 1843. Friedrich Simony). Österreichische Nationalbibliothek. (In the background and indicated in the upper margin are other major peaks of the Austrian Alps, including, on the left, the Großglockner, Austria's highest mountain.)

secured route or *Klettersteig* in Austria (also in September 1843), and made its first winter ascent (January 1847). He furthermore erected a permanent stone shelter below the peak's main glacier and in 1862 co-founded the Austrian Alpine Club. Simony was thus instrumental in advancing Alpinism as a recreational sport. His name survives in both the Dachsteingebirge and Hohe Tauern. Whereas in the former region one finds the "Simonyhaus" (Simony Hut) and "Simonyscharte" (Simony Notch), the latter boasts of two "Simonyspitzen" (Simony Peaks), the "Simonyschneide" (Simony Ridge), and the "Simonykees" (*der Kees* is a regional term for glacier), all in proximity to the Großvenediger, Austria's fourth highest peak at 3,662 m/12,014 ft.[12]

Heinrich Drendorf's mountaineering projects culminate in a mid-January glacier expedition. Stifter's narrative of this trek is largely based on, if not copied from, Simony's article "Drei Dezembertage auf dem Dachsteingebirge" (Three December days on the Dachstein), which appeared in the *Wiener Zeitschrift für Kunst, Literatur, Theater und Mode* (Viennese Journal for Art, Literature, Theater, and Fashion) in 1843.[13] Stifter himself published some of his tales in this journal. More significantly, he had already capitalized on Simony's essay — along with a later text "Zwei Septembernächte auf der Hohen Dachsteinspitze" (Two September nights on the High Dachstein Pinnacle) from 1844 — for his famous portrayal of the ice cave and rock shelter in *Bergkristall* (Rock crystal, 1845/53).[14] To Stifter's credit, he is paying homage to his geologist friend rather than simply appropriating images to which he, a less hearty outdoorsman who never set foot on a glacier, was not privy. The main impetus for *Bergkristall* stemmed from a hike that Stifter and Simony took together in the lower reaches of the Dachstein massif, and the story can to some degree be viewed as a product of their friendship.[15] Nonetheless, Stifter's vivid evocations of this winter landscape — whether in *Bergkristall* or *Der Nachsommer* — seem all the more astounding given the paradox that his literary version comes across as restrained and objective compared to Simony's emotionally charged and putatively scientific report.[16]

Stifter displays a fundamental empirical orientation toward the world. This orientation increases throughout his writing career, which began under the spell of Romanticism, and reaches its height in *Der Nachsommer*, a work in which the discipline and method of science itself are dominant. Granted, this novel may seem excessively poeticized by our current standards of realism; the artificiality of character interaction and the quasi-aristocratic veneer that tends to transfigure the narrative on other levels are cases in point. Stifter's descriptions of nature, particularly of mountains, are however hyperrealist and at least as empirically scrupulous as Simony's nonfictional accounts. Again, this superlative act of mimesis seems paradoxical, given that the staid and corpulent Stifter was more at home in forests and Alpine meadows than on rock and ice. Nonetheless, the idea of experience is critical throughout the novel; Heinrich learns infinitely more through immediate outdoor exposure than through second-hand knowledge. It is symptomatic of this attitude that he tends to lead more a *vita activa* than *vita contemplativa*. When, for instance, he reveals his winter climbing plans to the locals, they try to talk him out of his endeavor, claiming that no one has ever visited the high country in winter and that the cold at such an elevation is too extreme for humans to endure. Heinrich's response is based on pure logic and empiricism: If no one has yet been up there, then how can anybody know how cold it really is? Then follows a laconic dialogue in direct discourse:

"Aber man kann es sich denken," erwiederten viele.
"Erfahrung ist noch besser," sagte ich. (4,3:100)

["But you can imagine it," many replied.

"Experience is better," I countered. (*IS*, 376)]¹⁷

Here Heinrich succinctly expresses his scientific view: only through unmediated experience can we hope to arrive at a proper understanding of nature. Physical immersion in the environment and careful observation of its data are necessary steps in this approach. But the human being has its sensory limits and must therefore also rely on technical devices to explore reality in full. Heinrich takes along an assortment of instruments in order to record the meteorological conditions that prevail at higher elevations. These include a thermometer, a barometer, and a hygrometer. He and his partner, Kaspar, also equip themselves with technical mountaineering gear such as alpenstocks, crampons, ropes, and snowshoes. Stifter depicts all the stages of this journey in minute detail: the approach through dense woods and boulder-strewn gorges, the high plateau where they spend two nights in a wooden shelter, the steep upper slopes and towering rock faces, and finally the glacier, whose permanent ice lies buried under a thick blanket of snow. Again, all these scenes can be found in Simony's "Drei Dezembertage auf dem Dachsteingebirge." One notable difference between the two texts is that Simony and his companion Wallner suffer "einen kleinen Unfall, der aber leicht von höchst tragischem Ausgang hätte werden können" (a minor accident that could, however, have had a highly tragic result).¹⁸ That is, they become caught in an avalanche and Wallner is trapped beneath the snow for some fifteen minutes before Simony is able to dig him out. Stifter, more a believer in the "gentle laws" of nature, chooses to omit this occurrence, simply suggesting: "der Schnee *konnte* ins Gleiten gerathen" (4,3:109; the snow *could* begin to slide, *IS*, 381; my emphasis). Yet, as always in this novel, the non-Alpinist Stifter cannot plead ignorance of mountaineering practices or protocol: unlike Simony and Wallner, Heinrich and Kaspar are roped together during their traverse. A similar procedure in the real-life scenario might have prevented the near death of Wallner.¹⁹

Beyond these specific mountaineering points, Heinrich takes several measurements in his greater effort to piece together the larger puzzle of nature. On this outing he gathers new information, determining that the air at a higher elevation can actually be warmer than in the valley below. Heinrich thus discovers for himself, though concrete experience and careful experimentation, the phenomenon of inversion. As a result of this climatic effect, cold and fog tend to accumulate in low-lying basins while the mountain air remains clear and is even warmed a few degrees by the sun. Ultimately, though, Heinrich gains more from this trip than scientific knowledge and a new climbing venture. He is also overwhelmed by "ein erhabenes Gefühl" (a sublime feeling) and offers an "Andacht gegen Gott den Herrn, der so viel Schönes geschaffen und uns so glücklich gemacht hat" (4,3:111; a prayer to our Lord, Who had created so much beauty and granted us happiness, *IS,* 382 and 383). Elsewhere in the novel, Heinrich often employs "die Schöpfung" (creation) as a kind of theological synonym for the natural history that he otherwise pursues so empirically. This attitude is symptomatic of the physicotheological current in the mid-nineteenth century. Physicotheology blends philosophy and religion with the natural sciences such that that all physical manifestations of nature are interpreted in connection to a superior and divine order. In the specific province of mountaineering, this view can be considered a kind of "metatheory" that enabled climbers to reconcile undeniable scientific laws with their own spiritual needs.[20] Even in our secularized age, climbers often wax religious on summits. In Europe, enormous crosses (so-called *Gipfelkreuze*) were erected on countless peaks during the early twentieth century, which only reinforced this sacred dimension in the midst of modernity.[21] As outlined in the introduction, mountains have long been imbued with spiritual meaning across the diverse cultures of our world. In Stifter's novel, a sense of this religiosity exists alongside the more dominant nineteenth-century incentives of science and sport.

Given that *Der Nachsommer* predominantly takes place in the Alps and is profoundly immersed in the discourse of mountaineering, it remains a curious work in German letters. It has been classified under a number of diverse genres and subgenres: as a utopian novel and an idyll; more specifically as a "Geologenroman" (geologist novel), "Roman der Wissenschaft" (novel of science),[22] and "pädagogischer Roman" (pedagogical novel).[23] Early on in its genesis Stifter himself referred to it as a "socialen Roman" (social novel),[24] though he eventually settled on the generically nondescript subtitle "Eine Erzählung" (A tale). Most often, however, *Der Nachsommer* has been categorized and canonized as a Bildungsroman.

The Bildungsroman is a much-touted literary form that, upon deeper scrutiny, remains fraught with generic problems. It has even been argued that *Wilhelm Meisters Lehrjahre* (Wilhelm Meister's apprenticeship, 1795/96), the widely accepted epitome of this tradition, does not meet all the requirements of the genre.[25] Yet definitive classification of any given novel can be an academic if not futile enterprise. "Bildungsroman" is oftentimes merely a label affixed a posteriori by the vicissitudes of literary canonization. If one takes the approach of Jeffrey Sammons, who regards "genre categories as instrumental, not ontological," then a more productive discussion can take place.[26] As Sammons argues: the Bildungsroman emerged in the eighteenth century (for example, Wieland's *Agathon*, 1766/67), flourished during the Age of Goethe and Romanticism (for example, Goethe's *Wilhelm Meister*, Novalis's *Heinrich von Ofterdingen*, 1802, and Eichendorff's *Ahnung und Gegenwart* [Presentiment and presence, 1815]), largely disappeared throughout most of the nineteenth century, then reemerged in the early twentieth thanks to authors like Hermann Hesse and Thomas Mann, who consciously revived and modified the genre for their own modernistic purposes.[27] Sammons accords special status to *Der Nachsommer*, which was written in the 1850s, as a kind of missing link in nineteenth-century realism. He calls it "an oblique anti-*Meister*" and "a very eccentric novel," one that still however fits the pedigree. As he concludes, the essential difference with Stifter's text is that the "term *Bildung* is . . . undergoing a semantic change; it is no longer an acculturation of active potentialities of the self, but the passive acquisition of culture by exposure to aesthetic and natural objects."[28] Mountains, I would add, are the prime "natural objects" that promote Heinrich's self-formation: without them he would be utterly *verbildet* or *de*formed.

Heinrich thus develops according to an alternative model of *Bildung*. To draw on Goethe's paradigmatic novels, he seems less a Meister than a Montan; that is a geomorphologist who dwells among crags, striving to decipher the hidden alphabet embedded in the ancient stone.[29] Even though Wilhelm — himself dubbed "der Wanderer" — lives in peregrination and flirts with geology, his evolution is not immediately connected to mountains. While part of *Wilhelm Meisters Wanderjahre* (Wilhelm Meister's journeyman years, 1821/29) takes place in what appear to be the Swiss Alps, this realm constitutes only one of several phases and facets of the hero's education. Heinrich's development, by contrast, occurs in continual correlation to the geological formations among which he roams. His *Bildungsreise* (educational journey) toward the end of the novel exemplifies his anomalous path of maturation. Despite its purported length of nearly two years, this episode takes up only one-half page of text. And although he visits several countries in Western Europe, he is primarily focused on their respective mountain ranges: the Alps, the Italian volcanoes Vesuvius and Etna, the Sierra Nevada of southern Spain, the Pyrenees, and the Scottish Highlands (see 4,3:255; *IS*, 463). When he finally returns to Austria, the implied upshot of his edifying voyage is that "alles . . . fand mich sehr gebräunt" (4,3:256; everyone . . . found me quite tanned, *IS*, 463). It is safe to say that this pedagogical trajectory, exploring mountains and earning a tan in the process, is unique not solely within the history of the Bildungsroman but in all of non-mountaineering literature.[30] Some readers may find this outcome unsatisfyingly superficial for a canonical literary text, but the role of mountains in Stifter's novel cannot be underestimated. Nonetheless, Heinrich still has one final step to take toward self-completion, a step that oddly enough does not occur in Alpine terrain.

As Sammons further insists, a true Bildungsroman must in some fashion deal with the concept of *Bildung* on a thematic level.[31] Regardless of results in the realm of plot — that is, whether the protagonist fails or succeeds at social integration — the fundamental idea of self-cultivation should inform such novels.[32] The fact is that after the mid-nineteenth century most protagonists fail miserably at assimilation, but this shortcoming has more to do with shifting social structures than disqualifying generic conventions. The consequence of Heinrich's own evolution, as idealized by Risach, is less socially, artistically, or even scientifically oriented than readers might expect, given all his foregoing activities. It is, in other words, unclear whether Heinrich truly becomes a functioning member of society by the end of the novel. Risach, who has readily admitted to his own social inadequacy when reminiscing about his past, proclaims in view of Heinrich's engagement to Natalie:

> "Die Familie ist es, die unsern Zeiten noth thut, sie thut mehr noth als Kunst und Wissenschaft als Verkehr Handel Aufschwung Fortschritt, oder wie alles heißt, was begehrungswerth erscheint. Auf der Familie ruht die Kunst die Wissenschaft der menschliche Fortschritt der Staat." (4,3:263)
>
> ["Our times need the family, more than art, science, transportation, commerce, prosperity, or anything else that seems desirable. Art, science, human progress, the state are all, in the final analysis, based on the family." (*IS*, 467)]

One might call this ideal the apotheosis of the Biedermeier. At the very least, it seems that the domestic sphere — the "Häuslichkeit" indicated by the title of the first chapter — suddenly wins out over the natural-Alpine domain that has shaped Heinrich throughout most of the novel. This abrupt turn seems forced, if not dogmatic, on Stifter's part, almost a bourgeois corrective of Heinrich's wanton mountaineering ways. Whether this familial imperative signals the end of his scientific career and concomitant obsession with climbing remains open to debate, for here the narrative ends.

Just as Heinrich has been molded by mountains, these have in turn been sculpted by geological and meteorological forces. The symbolic analogy between the novel's two principal *bildsame Gestalten*, Heinrich Drendorf and the mountains that further his development, is perfectly summarized by Goethe, the master morphologist:

> Das Gebildete wird sogleich wieder umgebildet, und wir haben uns, wenn wir einigermaßen zum lebendigen Anschaun der Natur gelangen wollen, selbst so beweglich und bildsam zu erhalten, nach dem Beispiele mit dem sie uns vorgeht.[33]
>
> [That which is formed is immediately reformed, and if we wish to arrive at a reasonably dynamic contemplation of nature, we ourselves ought to be equally flexible and formable, according to the example that nature sets for us. (my translation)]

This implicit Goethean notion of *Bildung*, whether the formation of landscape or character, is made explicit throughout the book. It is imbedded in the language, "moves" through the textual fabric like a true "motif," and bolsters the broader thematic web of this distinctive Bildungsroman. While there are those who exclude *Der Nachsommer* from the genre because of its pronounced scientific orientation,[34] I counter that the solid scientifico-geological bedrock of Stifter's novel makes it the most thematically genuine representative of this literary tradition.

Notes

[1] Broch's parabolic novel of 1935 about the origins of fascism carried various working titles during its genesis, including *Bergroman*. True to this title, it is set in the Austrian Alps, contains numerous evocations of the Alpine landscape, and harbors a central metaphor involving a mountain. It has, however, now been definitively published as *Die Verzauberung*.

[2] Adalbert Stifter, *Der Nachsommer: Eine Erzählung*, in *Werke und Briefe, Historisch-Kritische Gesamtausgabe*, vol. 4, books 1–3, ed. Wolfgang Frühwald and Walter Hettche (Stuttgart: Kohlhammer, 1997–2000), 4,1:21. For the English version, see Adalbert Stifter, *Indian Summer*, trans. Wendell Frye (New York: Peter Lang, 1985), 16. Further references to the German text are given using the volume and page number of the historical-critical edition, while references to the English translation are given using the abbreviation *IS* and the page number. I occasionally modify Frye's translation in order to highlight salient points of my argument. I have noted this in each instance.

[3] On the importance of the summit perspective for Humboldt's and Stifter's holistic views of nature, see Franziska Schößler, "Der Weltreisende Alexander von Humboldt in den österreichischen Bergen: Das naturwissenschaftliche Projekt in Adalbert Stifters *Nachsommer*," in *Ordnung — Raum — Ritual: Adalbert Stifters artifizieller Realismus*, ed. Sabina Becker and Katharina Grätz (Heidelberg: Winter, 2007), esp. 275–77. For Goethe's thoughts on the sublime and the interconnectedness of nature from a summit block, see Johann Wolfgang Goethe, "Granit II," in *Schriften zur allgemeinen Naturlehre, Geologie und Mineralogie*, ed. Wolf von Engelhardt and Manfred Wenzel, vol. 25 of *Sämtliche Werke: Briefe, Tagebücher und Gespräche* (Frankfurt am Main: Deutscher Klassiker Verlag, 1989), 312–16. Thoreau, for his part, states: "We could see how ample and roomy is nature. . . . Wachusett [Mountain] is, in fact, the observatory of the State. There lay Massachusetts, spread out before us in its length and breadth, like a map." Henry David Thoreau, "A Walk to Wachusett," in *Collected Essays and Poems* (New York: The Library of America, 2001), 52–53. Muir writes in more rhapsodic and ecological terms about the panorama from atop Mt. Dana on the Sierra Nevada crest: "The views from the summit reach far and wide. . . . How interesting everything is! Every rock, mountain, stream, plant, lake, lawn, forest, garden, bird, beast, insect seems to call and invite us to come and learn something of its history

and relationship." John Muir, *My First Summer in the Sierra* (Boston: Houghton Mifflin, 1916), 239–41.

[4] Reminiscing on his days as a private tutor, Risach describes his pupil Alfred in the following terms: "Sein Wesen war nicht verbildet. Er war körperlich sehr gesund, und dies wirkte auch auf seinen Geist" (4,3:179; His character wasn't deformed. Physically, he was very healthy, and this had its effect on his mind, *IS*, 419–20). Frye's translation of *verbildet* as "spoiled" is misleading. Translations in this chapter not otherwise attributed are my own.

[5] The schematic *Einbildung — Bildung — Ausbildung* is discernable in both novels. During his dilettantish artistic phase, Wilhelm relies on *Einbildung* or imagination, but he also has illusions (*er bildet sich ein*) that he is in fact destined to be an artist. He must therefore continually work on his self-formation (*Bildung*) and eventually learn to externalize this inward development by channeling it into a specialized and practical occupation (*eine Ausbildung*).

[6] Robert Macfarlane, *Mountains of the Mind* (New York: Pantheon, 2003), 44.

[7] For some studies that do explore the connections between geology and Stifter's view of human history, see Tobias Bulang, "Die Rettung der Geschichte in Adalbert Stifters *Nachsommer*," *Poetica* 32 (2000): 373–405; Sabine Schneider, "Kulturerosionen: Stifters prekäre geologische Übertragungen," in *Figuren der Übertragung: Adalbert Stifter und das Wissen seiner Zeit*, ed. Michael Gamper and Karl Wagner (Zurich: Chronos, 2009), 249–69; and Peter Schnyder, "Schrift — Bild — Sammlung — Karte: Medien geologischen Wissens in Stifters *Nachsommer*," in Gamper and Wagner, *Figuren der Übertragung*, 235–48.

[8] Martin Scharfe, *Berg-Sucht: Eine Kulturgeschichte des frühen Alpinismus, 1750–1850* (Vienna: Böhlau, 2007), 120.

[9] Peter Grupp, *Faszination Berg: Die Geschichte des Alpinismus* (Vienna: Böhlau, 2008), 62.

[10] Although one should not ignore the darker if not demonic side of existence that punctuates Stifter's works, *Der Nachsommer* is completely lacking in conflict and irrational elements. The worlds of Heinrich and Herr von Risach are purely Apollinian, clear and harmonious, without any trace of disruptive Dionysian chaos.

[11] For more detailed discussions of Simony's life and work, see Albrecht Penck, *Friedrich Simony: Leben und Wirken eines Alpenforschers*, Geographische Abhandlungen 6, no. 3 (Vienna: Ed. Hölzel, 1898); August Böhm von Böhmersheim, *Zur Biographie Friedrich Simony's* (Vienna: Lechner, 1899); J. Neunlinger, "Adalbert Stifters Roman *Der Nachsommer* geographisch betrachtet," in *Alpengeographische Studien aus dem Geographischen Institut der Universität Innsbruck, zum 50. Geburtstag Hans Kinzl's* (Innsbruck: Wagner, 1950), 205–10; and Fritz Krökel, "Stifters Freundschaft mit dem Alpenforscher Friedrich Simony," *Vierteljahrsschrift des Adalbert-Stifter-Instituts des Landes Oberösterreich* 4 (1955): 97–117.

[12] In *Der Nachsommer* Stifter pays his own geographical homage to Simony by renaming the Hallstätter Glacier, the largest ice sheet in the Dachstein range, the "Simmieis."

[13] For a systematic comparison of corresponding, and at times verbatim, passages between the two accounts, see Stefan Braun, *Naturwissenschaft als Lebensbasis? Adalbert Stifters Roman "Der Nachsommer" und weitere Schriften Stifters als Dokumente eines Versuches der Daseinsgestaltung auf der Grundlage naturwissenschaftlichen Forschens* (Linz: Adalbert-Stifter-Institut, 2006), 104–8. On a side note, the title of Simony's article may be misleading. Simony did not actually climb to the top of the Dachstein during this mid-winter outing but spent three days on its upper reaches and glacier. As mentioned above, he would later make the first winter ascent in 1847.

[14] For a detailed comparison of Simony's mountaineering account and Stifter's fictionalization, see Hugo Schmidt, "Eishöhle und Steinhäuschen: Zur Weihnachtssymbolik in Stifters 'Bergkristall,'" *Monatshefte* 56 (1964): 321–35. This article is especially interesting from a geographical standpoint, for Schmidt demonstrates that Stifter created a hybrid literary landscape, one that blends the topographies of the Dachsteingebirge and his own native Bohemian Forest.

[15] For the intriguing details of this hike, including an exhaustive inventory of Simony's climbing equipment and scientific instruments, see the geographer's letter of 19 August 1871 to Emil Kuh, reprinted in Kurt Gerhard Fischer, ed., *Adalbert Stifters Leben und Werk in Briefen und Dokumenten* (Frankfurt am Main: Insel, 1962), 147–52.

[16] On this narrative discrepancy between "subjective" writer and "objective" scientist, see Neunlinger, "Adalbert Stifters Roman *Der Nachsommer* geographisch betrachtet," 209.

[17] Martin Scharfe briefly discusses this scene within the historical context of Alpinism, specifically as testimony of the differing mentality between ambitious mountaineers and unadventurous locals. See Scharfe, *Berg-Sucht*, 70.

[18] Friedrich Simony, *Auf dem Hohen Dachstein* (Vienna: Österreichischer Schulbücherverlag, 1921), 32.

[19] It can also be argued, however, that Simony would have been dragged to his death beneath the sliding snow mass. Such is the inherent danger of simul-climbing: both unbelayed partners run an equal risk of being killed.

[20] See Scharfe, *Berg-Sucht*, 189.

[21] Martin Scharfe has, however, put forward the bold thesis that these summit crosses do not testify to a deep-seated religious sensibility but are in large part a twentieth-century gesture that seeks to compensate for the loss of God. See Scharfe, *Berg-Sucht*, 268–75.

[22] Braun, *Naturwissenschaft als Lebensbasis?* 85, 124 and 125.

[23] Wolfgang Matz, *1857: Flaubert, Baudelaire, Stifter* (Frankfurt am Main: S. Fischer, 2007), 305.

[24] Adalbert Stifter, *Briefwechsel*, vol. 2, in *Sämtliche Werke*, vol. 18 (Prague: Calve, 1918), 147.

[25] See Kurt May, "*Wilhelm Meisters Lehrjahre*, ein Bildungsroman?" *Deutsche Vierteljahresschrift für Literaturwissenschaft und Geistesgeschichte* 31 (1957): 1–37.

[26] Jeffrey L. Sammons, "The Mystery of the Missing *Bildungsroman*, or: What Happened to Wilhelm Meister's Legacy?" *Genre* 14 (1981): 230. Sammons has tackled this issue of categorization with greater insight and nuance than previous scholars, though the classic study by Jürgen Jacobs is also subtle in its approach. See Jürgen Jacobs, *Wilhelm Meister und seine Brüder: Untersuchungen zum deutschen Bildungsroman* (Munich: Fink, 1972). With specific respect to *Der Nachsommer* and its relation to the Bildungsroman, see Otto Friedrich Bollnow, "Der *Nachsommer* und der Bildungsgedanke des Biedermeier," in *Beiträge zur Einheit von Bildung und Sprache im geistigen Sein, Festschrift zum 80. Geburtstag von Ernst Otto*, ed. Gerhard Haselbach and Günter Hartmann (Berlin: de Gruyter, 1957), 14–33; and Klaus-Detlef Müller, "Utopie und Bildungsroman: Strukturuntersuchungen zu Stifters *Nachsommer*," *Zeitschrift für deutsche Philologie* 90 (1971): 199–228.

[27] See Jeffrey L. Sammons, "The Bildungsroman for Nonspecialists: An Attempt at a Clarification," in *Reflection and Action: Essays on the Bildungsroman*, ed. James Hardin (Columbia, SC: U of South Carolina P, 1991), 32.

[28] Sammons, "The Mystery of the Missing *Bildungsroman*," 236.

[29] See for instance the description of Montan's geological endeavors in Johann Wolfgang Goethe, *Wilhelm Meisters Wanderjahre*, vol. 10 of *Sämtliche Werke: Briefe, Tagebücher und Gespräche*, ed. Gerhard Neumann and Hans-Georg Dewitz (Frankfurt am Main: Deutscher Klassiker Verlag, 1989), esp. 292.

[30] Compare Sammons's remark that "there is perhaps nothing else resembling it [*Der Nachsommer*] in European literature." Sammons, "The Mystery of the Missing *Bildungsroman*," 236.

[31] Sammons, "The Bildungsroman for Nonspecialists," 41.

[32] Compare for instance the fruitful thematic study, not restricted to the literary genre of the novel, by W. H. Bruford, *The German Tradition of Self-Cultivation: "Bildung" from Humboldt to Thomas Mann* (London: Cambridge UP, 1975).

[33] Johann Wolfgang Goethe, "Die Absicht eingeleitet," in *Schriften zur Morphologie*, ed. Dorothea Kuhn, vol. 24 of *Sämtliche Werke: Briefe, Tagebücher und Gespräche* (Frankfurt am Main: Deutscher Klassiker Verlag, 1987), 392.

[34] See for instance Schößler, "Der Weltreisende Alexander von Humboldt in den österreichischen Bergen," 278.

"An Apparition from Another World": The Mountains of the Moon and Kilimanjaro from the Perspective of Nineteenth-Century Germany

Christof Hamann

MY NOVEL *USAMBARA* (2007) deals with Kilimanjaro and the Usambara violet, with Hans Meyer, whose ascent of the mountain in 1889 was most likely the first, and with his secretary and botanist Leonhard Hagebucher. In my book I alternately employ "Mountains of the Moon" and "Moon Mountain" as synonyms for Kilimanjaro, but at the same time I emphasize that these are in the end misnomers. When, in February of 2004, I took part in a trekking tour to the top of the highest peak on the African continent for the purposes of researching my novel, I was unaware of these outdated geographical designations. However, in the course of my hike, the associations with our lunar satellite became readily apparent: the vast wasteland of rock above 5,000 meters reminded me, in its barrenness, of photos taken of the moon's surface. I incorporated this observation into my novel, for instance when one of the other main characters, Fritz Binder, who intends to climb Kilimanjaro one hundred years after his great-grandfather Hagebucher, notes: "So stelle ich es mir auf dem Mond vor. Trostlos. Hässlich. Eine Geröllhalde" (This is how I picture it on the moon. Desolate. Ugly. A huge pile of scree).[1]

While composing *Usambara* I came upon another, far less personalized, use of the term "Mountains of the Moon." This appellation dates back to antiquity and was for instance propagated by Claudius Ptolemaios (Ptolemy), whose principal work *The Geography* (circa 160 CE) synthesizes the geographical knowledge of the era. In the section concerning Inner Africa, Ptolemy writes:

> Aethiopia, which is below this land and all of Libya, is terminated toward the north by the indicated southern boundary lines of the land which we have treated, which extends from the Great Bay of the Outer Sea to Rhaptum promontory as we have said, and is located in 73*50, 8°25 S, then by a part of the Western Ocean which is near the Great Bay; by the unknown land toward the west and the south; toward the east by the Barbarian Bay, which near the shallow sea is

called Breve, from the Rhaptum promontory even to the Prasum promontory and the unknown land. . . . Around this bay the Aethiopian Anthropophagi dwell, and from these toward the west are the Mountains of the Moon, from which the lakes of the Nile receive snow water; they are located at the extreme limits of the Mountains of the Moon, 57*00, 12°30 S and 67*00, 12°30 S.[2]

The project of localizing the landscape within a greater geographical coordinate system is thus inextricably linked with the act of ascribing cultural characteristics and differences — for example, barbarian ("Barbarian Bay") or cannibalistic ("Anthropophagi") — especially between the familiar and unfamiliar. Even if the Mountains of the Moon are invoked in precise numerical terms, they still seem situated on the margin of "unknown land." This frontier between the familiar and unfamiliar will remain porous for centuries. While the Mountains of the Moon often appear in atlases throughout the Early Modern era — for instance on the map of Africa designed by the Nuremberg cartographer Johann Baptist Homann (1664–1724) — no one was ever able to determine their topography (they are usually represented as a cluster of similarly drawn hills) or their exact location on the African continent based on Ptolemy's records.

The indistinct line between known and assumed reality, or more broadly between geographical fact and fiction, seems to take solid shape by the nineteenth century, given the increased "measuring of the world" — to quote the title of Daniel Kehlmann's bestselling novel of 2005, *Die Vermessung der Welt*. Scientific progress not only enables us to pinpoint landscapes but also affords insight into their botanical and geological features. Fictions are relegated to the province of literature. I realized that this separation was highly problematic, that fact and fiction are closely intertwined in the discourse about Kilimanjaro and the Mountains of the Moon. This realization was decisive for my (fictional) novel and will be demonstrated in this (factual) essay through exemplary texts from the period between 1850 and 1900. First I will examine the debate around 1850 concerning the existence of glaciated mountains south of the equator; then I will analyze Hans Meyer's travel account *Ostafrikanische Gletscherfahrten* (Journeys across East African glaciers), published in 1890 after his successful first ascent of Kilimanjaro. Finally, drawing on Wilhelm Raabe's novel *Abu Telfan oder die Heimkehr vom Mondgebirge* (Abu Telfan, or, The return from the Mountains of the Moon, 1867), I intend to show that this legendary mountain range can be thematized in a completely different fashion.

The Mountains of the Moon: Between Fact and Fable

Ptolemy's reference to the Mountains of the Moon was significant for European geographical inquiry during the nineteenth century, largely because of his claim that this range harbors the source of the Nile. Many explorers of Africa were determined to solve the riddle of the longest river in the world, a river that has practically no tributaries but that nevertheless bears an enormous volume of water. These so-called "Mountains of the Moon" still enjoyed an ambivalent status in travelogues and scientific writings during the first half of the century: they were perceived as fantastical yet at the same time realistic. This former quality has of course long been attributed to mountains; even the scientifically minded Alexander von Humboldt regarded them as "fabelhaft" or "fabulous."[3]

During the mid-century two missionaries, Johann Ludwig Krapf and Johann Rebmann, challenged this half-fictional, half-factual location of the range, claiming to have seen two snow-covered peaks *with their own eyes* — Mount Kilimanjaro and Mount Kenya. Rebmann reported his discoveries in the *Church Missionary Intelligencer*,[4] a few years later, in 1858, Krapf published his and Rebmann's collective impressions in a book entitled *Reisen in Ostafrika* (Travels in East Africa).[5] These texts sparked a heated scientific debate. The most influential opponent of the two missionaries was the famous English geographer William Desborough Cooley, who in his study *Inner Africa Laid Open* (1852) denied the existence of glaciers south of the equator and dismissed the findings of Krapf and Rebmann as a fantastic tale, declaring "that there is no chain of mountains [i.e. no Mountains of the Moon], no edge of a great table land, running parallel to the coast of Eastern Africa."[6] This controversy came under intense scrutiny in the German-speaking academic world. As early as 1850, Taddäus Eduard Gumprecht summarized the most important theories regarding glaciated mountains in Africa, emphasizing that Rebmann's report had been reprinted in most of the major scholarly journals in Europe. Gumprecht tried to put the nationality of the missionaries in a positive light and thereby mitigate Cooley's critique. In partial support of his claim that these two Germans were better suited to explore Africa than representatives of other nations, he draws various comparisons between Germans and Portuguese. He asserts, for instance, that the latter, during their colonial endeavors in the sixteenth and seventeenth centuries, proved incapable of scientifically exploiting ("ausbeuten") the eastern coast of Africa because of their greediness ("Habgierigkeit"). The intrepid ("kühn-") German missionaries Krapf and Rebmann, on the other hand, had created the preconditions for a successful exploration of the interior thanks to their competent efficiency ("Tüchtigkeit").[7] Here the pursuit of geography reveals itself as the postulation of national stereotypes, an alliance that proves fundamental for the discourse surrounding voyages of discovery throughout the nineteenth century: discovery and appropriation of the foreign, geographical science, and (colonial) politics are all wedded right from the start.

The discussion about the Mountains of the Moon and Kilimanjaro found popular expression in the so-called "family magazines"

(*Familienzeitschriften*), which became the first mass medium in the German-speaking world after 1848. By differentiating between lived experience and the written word, several articles reinforced the "fabulous" character of this legendary mountain range — or of exploratory expeditions in general. A short piece in the journal *Über Land und Meer* (Over land and sea) reports on numbers of people who travel far up the Nile until they disappear from sight, only to then find some bountiful valley on the Abyssinian border, where they lead a comfortable existence worshiping Venus, selling slaves, and hunting game. Readers in Europe, however, are told something completely different:

> Das Publikum zuhaus aber wird mit lächerlichen Fabeln von geschwänzten Njam Njam-Negern, Mondgebirgen und wunderlichen Flußgebieten u.s.w. zu beiderseitiger Zufriedenheit abgespeist.[8]

> [The audience at home, however, is fed with ridiculous fables of tailed Njam Njam negroes, Mountains of the Moon, wondrous river valleys, and so forth, much to the satisfaction of both parties.]

Other texts rely on satriric exaggeration, as is evident in the following excerpt from an article in *Die Gartenlaube* (The summer cottage):

> Mit der Hitze ist's auch nicht zu arg, und die Natur hat bis unter den Aequator hin bereits für umgekehrtes Heizmaterial gesorgt, nämlich für ewigen Schnee auf gigantischen Bergen, von denen man, wo es zu heiß wird, Eis herunterholen wird, um die Zimmer ebenso zu kühlen, wie wir sie heizen.[9]

> [The heat isn't so bad either, and even down under the equator nature has provided for an inverse kind of heating material, namely for eternal snow on gigantic mountains, from whose slopes one can, when it gets too hot, bring down ice so as to cool the rooms of one's home, just as we heat them.]

Yet even articles that at first glance appear to be factual undergo some degree of literary stylization. A case in point is a text bearing the plain title "Die Besteigung des Kilimandscharo" (The ascent of Kilimanjaro), a digest of letters written by Baron von der Decken and Otto Kersten about their attempt to climb the mountain in the 1860s. Here Kilimanjaro and its environs are transformed into the literary topos of a *locus amoenus*, specifically into a landscape consisting of clear streams, beautiful meadows, and delightful strawflowers.[10] The only thing that seems to be missing in this mountain tableau is a frolicking pair of lovers.

The mythical Mountains of the Moon became increasingly disassociated from the empirical investigations surrounding Kilimanjaro in the decades following the latter's controversial "discovery" by Rebmann and Krapf. In the representative words of Hans Meyer, who, after failed attempts in 1887 and 1888, was the first person to reach the summit of Kilimanjaro (on 6 October 1889):

> Nach alledem ist es sehr wahrscheinlich, daß die "Mondberge" des Altertums und des Mittelalters mit keinem äquatorialen Schneeberg, weder mit dem Ruwensori noch mit dem Kilimandscharo etwas zu thun haben.
>
> [Of one thing we may be almost certain, namely that the ancient "Mountains of the Moon" are not to be identified with any equatorial snow-mountain, whether it be Ruwenzori or Kilimanjaro.][11]

This path into the realm of facts is guided by empirical field research; surveying, cataloguing, and the general compilation of data become crucial components of Kilimanjaro travelogues. Conveying all the minute details of an ascent goes hand in hand with the process of selecting and encapsulating these minutiae, as well as with strategies of creating uniform levels of meaning. Furthermore, such putative travel accounts exploit an assortment of literary devices; which is to say that they also contain their share of "fabulous" elements. This key connection between fabling and chronicling becomes especially apparent in Hans Meyer's *Ostafrikanische Gletscherfahrten*.

Narrating Kilimanjaro: Hans Meyer's *Ostafrikanische Gletscherfahrten*

The first European encounter with the colossal snow-capped equatorial mountain results, to some degree, in discursive practices similar to those found in voyages of discovery during the Renaissance. These descriptions, documenting the first contact with native inhabitants on the American continent, are fraught with an anthropological and aesthetic sense of astonishment, wonder, and terror.[12] Such reactions frequently surface in nineteenth-century texts dealing with Africa, whether with nature in general or Kilimanjaro in particular. They manifest themselves most acutely in descriptions of previously unseen natural objects and indeed oddities, transcending the ambit of the observer and entering the domain of the wondrous, holy, and divine.

Curiously, this discursive practice is least pronounced in the account given by the first European known to have laid eyes on Kilimanjaro, the missionary Johann Rebmann. His initial glimpse of the peak prompts him to note in his journal: "At about ten o'clock (I had no watch with me) I observed something remarkably white on the top of a high mountain, and first supposed that it was a very white cloud."[13] Nevertheless, immediately thereafter he uses rational arguments to counter what he dismisses as superstitious notions of the natives. The initial encounter of Otto Kersten, who accompanied and chronicled Baron Claus von der Decken's travels through East Africa during the 1860s, with the mountain more closely approaches the rhetoric of wonder:

> Nach Norden zu war die Ferne größtentheils von Wolken verhüllt. Unter diesen fiel mir eine von blendend weißer Farbe und sonderbarer Bildung auf. Als ich sie dem Baron zeigte, rief er freudig aus: "Das ist ja der Kilimandscharo!" Ich betrachtete den berühmten Berg, welcher sich meinen Blicken so unerwartet bot, mit einem Gemisch von staunender Bewunderung und Begeisterung; er zeigte sich weit großartiger und schöner, als ich mir ihn vorgestellt.[14]

> [To the north, the distant sky was veiled in clouds. Among these I noticed one of a blinding white color and peculiar formation. When I pointed it out to the baron, he let out a joyous cry: "Why, that's Kilimanjaro!" I examined the famed mountain, which so unexpectedly offered itself to my gaze, with a mixture of dumbfounded awe and enthusiasm; it appeared far more magnificent and beautiful than I had imagined it.]

What little Kersten discovers in the cloud-veiled sky eludes precise determination and indeed logic: Kersten is struck by a "blinding" brightness and yet is still apparently able to perceive the "peculiar." Even after the baron identifies the apparition, the narrator fails to deliver a more detailed description of the mountain: he marvels, waxes enthusiastic, and abides by general if not vague observations such as "magnificent" and "beautiful."

Other depictions surpass Kersten's in terms of their symbolic structures, which is to say they employ a language that produces both actual and connotative meanings. In Joseph Thomson's *Through Masai Land* (1885), for instance, one finds a number of religious associations: "The snow-cap shows here to great advantage, forming a close-fitted, glittering helmet artistically laid on the massive head of Kibo, and at times looking not unlike the aureole, as represented in many old pictures of saints, as it scintillates with dazzling effect under the tropical sun."[15] The lexemes "glitter," "scintillate," and "dazzle" not only denote the quality of extreme brightness but, as evinced in the text itself, also have obvious religious connotations. This symbolic subtext has the effect of transporting the mountain away from the observer, as if elevating it to a celestial realm. Indeed, as one soon reads: "For not uncommonly the upper part of Kibo is described away up in mid-heaven, cut off apparently from all earthly connection, shining clear and bright with dazzling effulgence, suggesting a sight of the very heavens opened, a marvel of whiteness, and most fitting emblem of ethereal purity."[16] Hans Meyer is no less captivated by, as he repeatedly stresses, the wondrous and mysterious spectacle of the Kilimanjaro massif, and he relies on narrative practices similar to

Thomson's. The following passage, though lengthy, is highly revealing and, moreover, is crucial for my argument:

> Als aber die ersten Strahlen der Sonne aufglühten, teilte sich schnell der Nebelschleier, und aus Nordwesten strahlte herrlich, groß und überirdisch das Schneehaupt des Kilimandscharo zu uns herüber. Von derselben Stelle hatte ich auch im Juni 1887 den ersten Ausblick auf das wundersame Bergbild, und voll von dem Eindruck schrieb ich damals am Abend in mein Tagebuch: "Man mag tage- und wochenlang das sichere Eintreten eines Ereignisses erwartet haben und noch so gefaßt dem nahenden entgegensehen, es packt uns doch mit unwiderstehlicher Gewalt, wenn es mit einemmal zur Thatsache wird. So ergriff mich hier die plötzliche Erscheinung des sehnlich erstrebten Zieles, des Kilimandscharo. Das Auge war tagelang über die weiten graubraunen Ebenen der Steppen und Savannen geschweift, vergeblich die ersehnte Gebirgslinie am Horizont suchend, und hatte sich an der beständigen Einförmigkeit ermüdet. Da plötzlich öffnet sich vom Kamme eines Höhenzuges ein wundersames Panorama. Einige Meilen vor uns erstreckt sich der schmale, hell schimmernde Dschipe-See nach Süden, dahinter ragen die dunklen, schroffen Mauern der Uguenoberge bis in die grauen Schichtwolken empor; nach rechts hin zieht sich im Mittelgrund der dunkle Streifen der Wälder, welche den Lumifluß umsäumen und Taweta einschließen. Hinter diesen Wäldern steigt die Steppe leicht an und verläuft in dunstiger Ferne zu dem unteren Teil des mächtigen Gebirgsstockes des Kilimandscharo, der nun mit einemmal zu der Riesenhöhe von 6000m unvermittelt aus der Steppenebene emporwächst. Ziemlich deutlich lassen sich unterhalb der breiten Wolkenschicht, welche den mittleren Teil des Gebirges umhüllt, die waldigen Hügel der Dschaggalandschaften erkennen, und über den Wolken strahlt plötzlich aus dem Himmelsblau ein wunderbar erhabenes Bergbild in schneeblendender Weiße hervor wie eine Erscheinung aus einer anderen Welt. Es ist der Kibo, der Hauptgipfel des Kilimandscharo. . . . Welche Gegensätze sind in diesem Bild harmonisch vereinigt! Hier unten die Glut des Äquators und tropisches Leben, neben uns der nackte Neger und vor uns Palmenhaine am Rande des Tawetawaldes; dort oben die Eisluft der Pole; die überirdische Ruhe einer gewaltigen Hochgebirgsnatur, ewiger Schnee auf erloschenen Vulkanen.
>
> Auch diesmal war es wieder für mich und meinen Gefährten ein Moment völligen Vergessens aller Mühen. Wir standen nur und staunten, während der Troß der Karawane an uns vorbeitrottete. Nach der ersten Augen- und Seelenweide begannen wir die Möglichkeit der Ersteigung zu erörtern und schon von hier aus nach Angriffspunkten auszulugen. (*OG*, 71–72)

[With the first rays of the morning sun a magnificent spectacle burst upon us. All of a sudden the veil of mist was rent apart, and to our admiring gaze was revealed the snowy peak of Kilimanjaro, grand, majestic, more than earthly in the silver light of the morning. It was from this same spot that in June 1887 I had my first view of the mountain. For weeks I had thought of almost nothing else — for many weary days I had been journeying to see it. Day after day I had vainly scanned the boundless grey-brown steppes and savannas, longing for a profile of the mountain on the horizon, my eyes growing weary from the constant monotony of the landscape. After all, the spectacle burst upon me almost as a revelation. A streak of silver in the south showed where Lake Jipé glittered in the sunlight beneath the dark, craggy heights of cloud-capped Ugweno; to the right a dark belt of trees marked the course of the Lumi River and the forest fastness of Taveta. Behind the woods lay a stretch of gently rising plain, and on the further side of it, towering up to a height of nearly 20,000 feet, the mighty mountain mass of Kilimanjaro. Beneath the layer of clouds that clung about its central slopes the wooded hills of Jagga showed darkly here and there, and above the clouds there suddenly emerged out of the blue firmament a wondrously awe-inspiring mountain display, blinding in its snowy whiteness, like an apparition from another world. . . . It was a picture full of contrasts — here the swelling heat of the Equator, the naked negro, and the palm-trees of Taveta — yonder, arctic snow and ice, and an atmosphere of god-like repose, where once was the angry turmoil of a fiery volcano.

After our present arduous journey across the steppes, the sublime spectacle once more burst upon us with all the overwhelming charm of novelty. For the moment all our weariness was forgotten. We could only stand and gaze, while the caravan rolled past unheeded and unheeding.

At length, having recovered from our first feelings of awe and wonder, we commenced there and then to discuss the possibility of an ascent, and even at that distance to look out for possible points of attack. (*AG*, 81–82; translation modified)]

In the first sentence of this excerpt, Meyer creates ambiguity through symbolism, thereby recalling his predecessor Thomson: the brightness resulting from the combination of sun and snow is associated with celestial ("überirdisch" / more than earthly) heights. Because the veil of mist parts so abruptly, the observer finds himself all at once confronted with the bright spectacle. This scene practically unfolds like a theatrical event, as if a curtain had been yanked back, revealing a panoply to the spectator's view. Yet here the action on stage, though it appears close and discernible, is imbued with a divine aura and is thus elevated to remote, unattainable heights. Then follows a detailed reminiscence in which the narrator depicts his very first encounter with Kilimanjaro in June 1887. In this extended flashback he directly invokes the mountain a total of four times, the first of which occurs right at the beginning of his retrospect: the sudden presence of the massif contrasts with the drawn-out account of its anticipation ("tage- und wochenlang . . ." / For weeks . . . for many weary days . . .).

The second mention of Kilimanjaro is preceded by an equally drawn-out description of the landscape, whose most striking qualities are "graubraun" (grey-brown) and "Einförmigkeit" (monotony). Before the spectacular view receives its third mention, the author scenically tries to capture the mountain's immediate surroundings, "die dunklen, schroffen Mauern der Uguenoberge" (the dark, craggy heights of cloud-capped Ugweno) and "der dunkle Streifen der Wälder, welche den Lumifluß umsäumen und Taweta einschließen" (the dark belt of trees [that] marked the course of the Lumi River and the forest fastness of Taveta). Finally, Meyer once again refers to a broad layer of clouds before he then evokes the mountain in the same terms used at the beginning of the passage:

> Und über den Wolken strahlt plötzlich aus dem Himmelsblau ein wunderbar erhabenes Bergbild in schneeblendender Weiße hervor wie eine Erscheinung aus einer anderen Welt.
>
> [And above the clouds there suddenly emerged out of the blue firmament a wondrously awe-inspiring mountain display, blinding in its snowy whiteness, like an apparition from another world.]

In its attempt to convey to readers the spectacle of the mountain, Meyer's book contains an astonishing amount of narrative extravagance for a text that is essentially a travelogue. The narrator operates with literary devices of various kinds (symbolic structures, analepsis, variations in narrative tempo, and the technique of narrating a single event — for instance the view of Kilimanjaro — multiple times) and he does so in such concentrated fashion that even explicitly literary prose would pale by comparison. This tactic is all the more surprising given the lines that follow his remembrance. Whereas the bulk of this section is dominated by visual rapture and divine apparition, Meyer now raises the practical question of ascent and seeks out "Angriffspunkt[e]" or "points of attack." These shifts — from religious to military imagery, from a sense of being overwhelmed by the mountain to an empirical understanding of it, from a reminiscence that imagines the mountain as an absolutely unattainable objective to the foreshadowing of an assault upon it — only make sense if one bears in mind that evocations of wonder are part of Meyer's larger narrative strategy.

Stephen Greenblatt, who has studied the category of wonderment with respect to voyages of discovery during the Renaissance, describes this imaginative mode as fleeting and ambiguous; the item of scrutiny only momentarily eludes categorization and systematic comprehension:

> The object that arouses wonder is so new that for a moment at least it is alone, unsystematized, an utterly detached object of rapt attention. Wonder — thrilling, potentially dangerous, momentarily immobilizing, charged at once with desire, ignorance, and fear — is the quintessential human response to what Descartes calls a "first encounter."[17]

Greenblatt argues that these moments, in which the sheer enormity of an object is acknowledged without immediately being neutralized through comparisons, interpretations, and clarifications, hold not only a critical and humanizing but also a colonializing and subjugating potential.[18] Some three hundred years later, European adventurers to Africa such as Hans Meyer make this ambivalence less equivocal, thanks in part to the narrative practices they employ.

Meyer consistently applies the word "Wunder" (wonder/marvel) to the myriad natural phenomena he encounters; related expressions implying incredulity or bafflement also recur, for example: "Geheimnis" (mystery), "Rätsel" (enigma), and "Verborgenes" (secret). Insights into nature, however, are often equated with the opposite revelatory act of "Entschleierung" (unveiling). As Meyer observes upon reaching the summit, for instance: "Das Geheimnis des Kibo lag entschleiert vor uns" (*OG*, 128–29; the secret of Kibo lay unveiled before us, *AG*, 147). This symbolism not only reveals an inherent gender dynamic in explorations of unknown territory; it also points to a clash between two different cultures, the familiar and the foreign, thereby illustrating a hierarchical relationship between (male, European) subject and (female, foreign) object, a relationship that one side uses to gain control over the other. Meyer, accordingly, ascribes to nature feminine attributes, for instance in the observation: "Die Eisfelder des Kibo *funkelten lockend* über den Bachrand herüber (my emphasis; *OG*, 117; the ice-fields of Kibo *sparkled temptingly* above the stream bank, *AG*, 133; translation modified). Beyond such religious-sexual associations, Meyer's text shows scientific exploration to be part of a masculine-military discourse and further suggests that mountain climbing operates not only within the framework of science but also according to the rules of battle. Initially, what counts more than the individual urge to climb a mountain is one's duty toward one's country:

> Es erschien mir deshalb fast als ein Gebot nationaler Pflicht, die gänzliche touristische und wissenschaftliche Eroberung des Kilimandscharo nur Deutschland vorzubehalten, und als ein mit aller Kraft erstrebenswerthes Ziel, diese Eroberung selbst auszuführen.[19]
>
> [I considered it almost a dictate of national duty to reserve the right of touristic and scientific conquest of Kilimanjaro only to Germany, and I aspired with all my powers to carry out this conquest myself.]

The task at hand is thus not a "climb" but a "conquest," and indeed the latter word recurs often enough to function as a leitmotif. Following this logic, the object of conquest is not a mountain but a fortress: "Dagegen blinkte und blitzte über uns der Eishelm des Kibo gleichsam in Kampfeslust um die Verteidigung der Bergfestung."[20] (The ice-helmet of Kibo gleamed and glittered above us, as if in bellicose defense of its mountain fortress). Once the mission is clear, the expedition has to draw up a battle plan, deliberate the "Angriffspunkte" (*OG*, 72; points of attack, *AG*, 82; translation modified); then the soldier can "advance" ("vordringen")²¹ against the enemy and eventually, after much exertion and injury, celebrate the "defeat" of the enemy and look back upon the campaign:

> Der afrikanische Riese war bezwungen, wie schwer er uns auch den Kampf gemacht hatte, und damit eine mehr als vierzigjährige Belagerung und Bestürmung des Kilimandscharo zum Abschluß gebracht. (*OG*, 135)

> [The African giant was defeated, even though it put up a hard fight, and thus a more-than-forty-year siege and onslaught of Kilimanjaro was brought to a close.]²²

After victory comes annexation and, like most victors, Meyer is invested in (re)naming the territory he has conquered. He therefore bestows the name of the German Kaiser upon the highest point of Kibo's crater rim:

> Um ½ 11 betrat ich als erster die Mittelspitze. Ich pflanzte auf dem verwitterten Lavagipfel mit dreimaligem, von Herrn Purtscheller kräftig sekundiertem "Hurra" eine kleine, im Rucksack mitgetragene deutsche Fahne auf und rief frohlockend: "Mit dem Recht des ersten Ersteigers taufe ich diese bisher unbekannte, namenlose Spitze des Kibo, den höchsten Punkt afrikanischer und deutscher Erde: Kaiser-Wilhelm-Spitze." (*OG*, 134)

> [I was the first to set foot on the culminating peak, which we reached at half-past ten o'clock. Taking out a small German flag, which I had brought with me for the purpose in my knapsack, I planted it on the weather-beaten lava summit with three ringing "hurrahs," all seconded by Mr. Purtscheller, and then triumphantly exclaimed: "By virtue of my right as the first person to reach its summit, I christen this hitherto unknown and unnamed point on Kibo — the loftiest spot in Africa and now the German Empire — *Kaiser Wilhelm's Peak*." (*AG*, 154; translation modified)]

This passage is significant insofar as it contains a rare shift from mediated narration to the immediacy of direct discourse. Meyer's pronouncement upon the summit effectively amounts to a baptismal act, which traditionally symbolizes one's acceptance into a religious community. Here, however, this act serves the purpose of assimilating a mountain into the sovereign territory of the German Empire. Defeated and named, Kibo now becomes the highest "German" mountain, its "oberster Stein" (uppermost rock) offered as a gift to the Kaiser, who makes good use of it back home as a "Briefbeschwerer" or paperweight.²³ To pass off this act of name-giving as part of science's service to humanity²⁴ or as a testimony of respect toward the emperor utterly ignores the realistic and authoritative effect of such baptisms. First of all, this conferred identity implies that the "unknown and unnamed point of Kibo" all at once becomes known — and one's own. Furthermore, he who bestows a name inevitably proves to be "master" over that which he names. Indeed, the entire Kilimanjaro massif is signed over to the property of the "victor": streams, notches, glaciers, peaks, and other natural features now bear designations that originate from a distant country. These measures of "de-wonderment," that is, scientific classification and nomenclature, serve to promote a common goal: the Germanization of Kilimanjaro.

Barbaric Storytelling: Wilhelm Raabe's *Abu Telfan oder die Heimkehr vom Mondgebirge*

After the Mountains of the Moon experienced a brief renaissance in Europe during the 1850s, scientific travelogues increasingly relegated them to the realm of fables. This development is reflected in narrative practices of wonderment that consign Kilimanjaro — at first only symbolically, but then also politically — to the property of the German Empire. In this final section of my chapter, I will discuss a literary text whose subject matter does not conform to the above process of appropriation and whose title moreover harks back to Ptolemy: *Abu Telfan oder die Heimkehr vom Mondgebirge*, by Wilhelm Raabe.

The main character of Raabe's novel, a tax inspector's son by the name of Leonhard Hagebucher, has suddenly returned home after a mysterious fifteen-year absence. In contrast to his father, the boy had never been good with numbers; his talent lay, rather, in his incredible speed, and so he sped away from Germany long ago, into the wide world, heading south for Italy, Egypt, then up the Nile into the heart of Africa. At the very beginning of the novel, on his way from Trieste back to his hometown of Bumsdorf, the son is introduced as "ein verwildert[es] und, trotz der halbeuropäischen Kleidung aschanti-, kaffern- oder mandingohaft[es] Subjekt";[25] (a wild-looking individual who, in spite of his half-European attire, resembled some kind of Ashanti, Kaffir, or Mandingo). He left home as an outsider, as a youth who abandoned his studies in theology and did not get along with his father; he now returns to his native land as a barbarian. This development is consistent with a pattern found in other tales by Raabe: characters become affected by a foreign country to such a degree that they return home as foreigners. The transformation in Hagebucher's outer appearance, for instance, is so complete that his face not only looks wild but also "geschwärzt" (*AT*, 21) or "blackened." In the course of the novel, the tax inspector's son is referred to as an "Afrikaner" (African), as "Herr Äthiopier" (Mr. Ethiopian), and even as an "Unmensch" (brute; see *AT*, 28, 53, and 52).

As indicated in the subtitle of *Abu Telfan oder die Heimkehr vom Mondgebirge*, the foreign place from which Hagebucher makes his return is the fabled Mountains of the Moon. The novel presents a few sketches of this terrain, the most detailed of which can be found in Hagebucher's initial description of his wanderings. After stops in Venice and Naples, he arrives in Egypt, where he assists in survey work for the planned Suez Canal. But because the vagabond Hagebucher was not born for "'Lehnstuhl, Schlafrock und Pantoffeln'" (*AT*, 26; armchair, morning-gown, and slippers), he continues his voyage up the Nile, accompanied by a notorious ivory trader, first toward Chartum and from there along the White Nile to Kaka. (As can already be noted above in the case of Hagebucher's hometown "Bumsdorf," Raabe's place names are often sarcastic.) The details then get murky. The text makes mention of a region between Bahr el-Abiad and Bahr el-Asrek, that is between the White and the Blue Nile, and also of the seaway called Bab el-Mandeb or the "Gate of Tears" (see *AT*, 27), a twenty-seven-kilometer-wide channel connecting the Red Sea with the Gulf of Aden. Somewhere in this vicinity lie the Mountains of the Moon, and somewhere here Leonard Hagebucher falls into captivity:

> Ich ging nur als ein Handelsartikel mit variierendem Werte von Hand zu Hand, von Stamm zu Stamm, und wurde zuletzt im Schatten Dschebel al Komris zu Abu Telfan im Tumurkielande einem meiner eigenen Hampelmännern, einem glotzäugigen, grinsenden Kerl mit blauen Hosen, gelben Husarenstiefeln und einer roten Jacke — zugegeben. (*AT*, 28)

> [I passed from hand to hand, from tribe to tribe, like an article of merchandise fluctuating in value and, in the shadow of Jebel al Komris near Abu Telfan in the Land of Tumurkie, was finally handed over to one of my own lackies, a goggle-eyed, grinning fellow clad in blue trousers, yellow corsair boots, and a red vest.]

The vague location of Jebel al Komris — Arabic for the Mountains of the Moon — provided by Raabe seems perfectly in keeping with the contemporary controversies surrounding this range. In the preface to his novel, Raabe himself advises readers not to bother searching any map for Abu Telfan or the Land of Tumurkie, pointing out that:

> Und was das Mondgebirge anbetrifft, so weiß ein jeder ebensogut als ich, daß die Entdecker durchaus noch nicht einig sind, ob sie dasselbe wirklich entdeckt haben. Einige wollen an der Stelle, wo ältere Geographen es notierten, einen großen Sumpf, andere eine ausgedehnte Salzwüste und wieder andere nur einen unbedeutenden Hügelzug gefunden haben, welches alles keineswegs hindert, daß ich für meinen Teil unbedingt an es glaube. (*AT*, 5)

> [And as far as the Mountains of the Moon are concerned, everyone knows as well as I do that their discoverers still cannot agree whether they have truly discovered them. Some claim to have found at this

location, where previous geographers noted the presence of such mountains, a huge swamp, others a vast salt desert, and still others merely an insignificant range of hills, all of which nowise keeps me from absolutely believing in their existence.]

Here Raabe juxtaposes Ptolemy's theory with that of modern geographers, yet he does not choose sides; regardless which theory is correct, his narrator "absolutely believes in their existence." In my view, Raabe is not interested in the age-old geographical question regarding this range. His concern lies, rather, with the Mountains of the *Moon* in a literal sense. This shift from a connotative to a denotative meaning is significant insofar as it points to a broader tradition in which the moon, more than any other natural phenomenon, functions as a central literary motif. In the Age of Goethe, we often find what might be termed a "Mondschwärmerliteratur" (literature of moon enthusiasts), a trend that is especially evident in Empfindsamkeit (sentimentality) and Romanticism, two of the more "inward" literary currents of the era.[26] The popular poem "Abendlied" (Evening song, 1779) by Matthias Claudius is an example of such lunar devotion. Raabe, however, is opposed to this compliant and acquiescent attitude; in *Abu Telfan* he introduces another way of speaking with and about the moon.

This alternative form of articulation is exemplified in chapter 6. Leonhard Hagebucher has just fled a family reunion at which his relatives made it plain to him that he was a useless member of society. Then comes the following scene:

Wie der deutsche Mond höher stieg, fing das Wasser, welches mit dem schon beschriebenen Gegurgel den Graben durchschlich, an, hie und da lieblich zu schimmern, und der leider schon vom ehrlichen Wandsbecker Boten lyrisch verwendete weiße Nebel machte sich ebenfalls auf den Wiesen bemerkbar. Der Mond schien dem Mann aus dem Tumurkielande auf den Kopf, der Nebel stieg ihm in die Nase, und er — Hagebucher — ließ die Schienbeine fahren, schnellte empor, stand hoch aufgerichtet in der holden Nacht, rieb die Hände und hub an — leise vor sich hinzulachen. Er lachte, der Barbar, er wagte sogar, laut zu lachen, der verwilderte Unmensch; und dann schüttelte er sich, er wagte es, sich zu schütteln . . . (*AT*, 52)

[As the German moon climbed higher, the water, which slithered through the ditch with the aforementioned gurgling sound, began to gleam charmingly here and there, and the white mist (which, regrettably, the honorable Wandsbecker Messenger had already made lyric use of) became noticeable on the meadows. The moon shone upon the head of the man from the Land of Tumurkie, the mist rose into his nose, and he — Hagebucher — set his shins into motion, bounded upward, stood tall and straight in the lovely night, rubbed his hands and commenced — to laugh quietly to himself. He, the barbarian, laughed, he even dared to laugh out loud, the wild inhuman; and then he started shaking, he dared to shake in laughter.]

The "Wandsbecker Bote" stands metonymically for Matthias Claudius, who edited a journal under that title during the 1770s. As for the gurgling water, it alerts readers to the absurdity of the "German" moon and other clichéd symbols commonly found in "charming" (read: sentimental, Romantic) poems. Raabe, on the contrary, ushers into being a different kind of poetry, one that is "wild" and "barbaric" — what I would call "Mondgebirgspoesie" (Mountains-of-the-Moon poetry). This particular notion has its ties to a broader symbolism that associates the moon with illness and madness, or what one might more appropriately call "lunacy." Whereas traditional moon poetry validates cultural mores or encourages personal introspection, "Mondgebirgspoesie" has the potential to subvert the familiar. Hagebucher's fits of wild laughter signal a new mode of expression, one that has been made possible through his journey to the Mountains of the Moon. In chapter 18, which Raabe describes as the center of the novel in terms of both structure and content (see *AT*, 183–84), this laughter escalates into a satiric appraisal of German society. Hence there is no use looking for the Mountains of the Moon on any atlas. Raabe's point is that they do not correspond to an actual geographical site but represent an imaginary space of writing that lies beyond one's own cultural parameters and that offers a different perspective — a distant, lunar point of view — through which one can better scrutinize Germany. This imaginary space of writing is something that has always fascinated me about Raabe's novel; many writers no doubt wish to inhabit precisely such a space.

In the course of the novel, Leonhard Hagebucher is often told that he has fallen from the moon. Compare for instance the following quote: "'Sie fallen vom Monde herab, Herr Hagebucher, und haben somit viel zu erzählen'" (*AT*, 78; You have fallen from the moon, Herr Hagebucher, and must therefore have plenty of stories to tell). Through these figures of speech, Raabe self-reflexively alludes to a new form of storytelling, one that does not subordinate the culturally foreign to the culturally familiar but rather transforms the former into the latter. Because the Mountains of the Moon symbolically loom between Hagebucher and the "'süße Vaterland'" (*AT*, 115; sweet fatherland), that is, because he sees his native country through an alien African lens, he is able to tell his stories without inhibition or shame ("unbefangen, ja unverschämt"; *AT*, 186). Like a good barbarian, he can therefore contribute to the ruin of his own culture from within yet at the same time become the torchbearer of cultural renewal.[27] The German audience listening to his exotic tales catches a whiff of freedom, a "Hauch der Freiheit": ". . . verschiedene glatzköpfige Assessoren und zahlenerdrückte Rendanten nahmen sich fest vor, bei der nächsten Begegnung mit dem Vorgesetzten diesen zuerst grüßen zu lassen" (*AT*, 189; Several baldheaded assessors and number-plagued accountants firmly resolved, the next time at the office, to make their supervisors greet them first).

According to this reading, *Abu Telfan oder Die Heimkehr vom Mondgebirge* is not a story about a remote foreign land but about the foreignness within one's own culture. It is also a story about the act of storytelling itself. The barbarian does not dwell in Africa; the actual barbarian is the writer who, through the medium of language, is able to question his national culture. While the ironic reference to assessors and accountants cited above illustrates the limitations of barbaric storytelling, the end of the novel demonstrates all the more that Hagebucher's cultural revolution has reached a (mere temporary?) standstill: "'Wenn ihr wüßtet, was ich weiß, so würdet ihr viel weinen und wenig lachen'" (*AT*, 382; If you knew what I know, you would cry a lot and laugh but little). This Arabic proverb opens and closes the novel, creating a complete circle and suggesting that the time of barbarian upheavals still awaits. How long remains open to debate.

Raabe's absolute belief in the Mountains of the Moon, his faith in a space that eludes assimilation, was also important for my conception of *Usambara*. I wanted to send my own Hagebucher character, and Fritz Binder as well, to the physical heights of Kilimanjaro with the mental concept of *Lunar* Mountains guiding their way. Whereas the Hans Meyer of my novel has only one aim — to scale "his" mountain and appropriate it for himself (and thus for the German Empire) — Hagebucher is interested in a variety of things. Though he, too, has a specific goal, namely to return home with the Usambara violet and thereby find fame, he is also in love (with Theresia, a woman whose name he lends to the precious violet) and furthermore curious about what goes on around him in Africa, including the languages spoken by the natives, the diverse tribal cultures, and the local plant life. Yet the ultimate failure of Raabe's Hagebucher was equally important to me. Despite his enormous gusto for action, my Hagebucher also fails: he slows down, probably grows indifferent, toward both himself and his foreign environment. Hagebucher's great-grandson Binder, who has heard countless stories about his adventure-seeking ancestor, poses the reasonable question whether his forebear had not been inexorably headed for a slipper-clad, hen-pecked existence all along.[28] To both characters, the swift-footed great-grandfather as much as the great-grandson who wants to follow in his footsteps, one can only say in the end: "Slow down!" The narrator (and author?) can still perhaps console himself with the Sisyphean challenge issued by Samuel Beckett: "Ever tried. Ever failed. No matter. Try again. Fail again. Fail better."[29]

— *Translated by Sean Ireton*

Notes

[1] Christof Hamann, *Usambara* (Göttingen: Steidl, 2007), 225. All translations in this chapter are my own, unless otherwise noted (SI).

[2] Ptolemy, *The Geography*, book 4, chapter 7, in http://penelope.uchicago.edu/Thayer/E/Gazetteer/Periods/Roman/_Texts/Ptolemy/home.html (accessed 15 Jan. 2011).

[3] Alexander von Humboldt, *Ansichten der Natur: Erster und zweiter Band*, vol. 4 of *Studienausgabe*, ed. Hanno Beck (Darmstadt: Wissenschaftliche Buchgesellschaft, 1987), 10.

[4] Rebmann's travels during the spring of 1848 are briefly summarized in the *Church Missionary Intelligencer* in 1849. The following year, the journal published excerpts from Rebmann's diaries under the title: "Narrative of a Journey to Jagga, the Snow Country of Eastern Africa." See *Church Missionary Intelligencer: A Monthly Journal of Missionary Information* 1 (1850): 12–23.

[5] See Johann Ludwig Krapf, *Reisen in Ostafrika ausgeführt in den Jahren 1837–1855* (Stuttgart: F. A. Brockhaus, 1964).

[6] William Desborough Cooley, *Inner Africa Laid Open* (New York: Negro Universities P, 1969), 124. Cooley attributes the fantastical elements in the narrative to Rebmann's nearsightedness as well as to the lack of professionalism of both missionaries. Compare for instance his trenchant critique of Krapf: "Miserably poor in facts, he is profuse of theory, his distances are exaggerated, his bearings all in disorder, his etymologies puerile . . ." (125). Cooley sums up his own staunch position as follows: "But the object of our research is Truth, not the Mountains of the Moon" (119).

[7] See Taddäus Eduard Gumprecht, "Die von Rebmann im östlichen Süd-Africa in der Nähe des Aequators entdeckten Schneeberge," *Monatsberichte über die Verhandlungen der Gesellschaft für Erdkunde zu Berlin*, Neue Folge 6 (1850): 285–97.

[8] Anonymous, "Kultur und Wissenschaft," *Über Land und Meer* 13 (1865): 247.

[9] Anonymous, "Der Negerkönig," *Die Gartenlaube* 43 (1853): 473.

[10] See "Die Besteigung des Kilimandscharo," *Westermann's Jahrbuch der Illustrirten Deutschen Monatshefte: Ein Familienbuch für das gesammte Leben der Gegenwart* 15 (Oct. 1863–Mar. 1864): 222–23.

[11] Hans Meyer, *Ostafrikanische Gletscherfahrten: Forschungsreisen im Kilimandscharo-Gebiet* (Leipzig: Duncker & Humblot, 1890), 5. In English *Across East African Glaciers: An Account of the First Ascent of Kilimanjaro*, trans. E. H. S. Calder (London: Longmans, 1891), 5. Further references to this work are given in the text, using the abbreviation *OG* (German original) and *AG* (English translation) and the appropriate page numbers. Though fluidly written and highly readable, Calder's translation is not always faithful to the original and I occasionally modify his prose when it deviates from important arguments that Christof Hamann makes based on Meyer's German (SI). I will note this in each instance.

12 See Klaus R. Scherpe, "Die First-Contact-Szene: Kulturelle Praktiken bei der Begegnung mit dem Fremden," in *Lesbarkeit der Kultur: Literaturwissenschaften zwischen Kulturtechnik und Ethnographie*, ed. Gerhard Neumann and Sigrid Weigel (Munich: Fink, 2000), 151.

13 Rebmann, "Narrative of a Journey to Jagga," 17.

14 Baron Carl Claus von der Decken, *Baron Carl Claus von der Decken's Reisen in Ost-Afrika in den Jahren 1859 bis 1865*, commissioned by the mother of the traveller, Princess Adelheid von Pless; narrative section, vol. 2, *Baron Carl Claus von der Decken's Reisen in Ost-Afrika in den Jahren 1862 bis 1865. Nebst Darstellung von R[ichard] Brenners und Th[eodor] Kinzelbach's Reisen zur Feststellung des Schicksals der Verschollenen, 1866 und 1867*, ed. Otto Kersten (Leipzig: C. F. Winter'sche Verlagshandlung, 1871), 19.

15 Joseph Thomson, *Through Masai Land: A Journey of Exploration among the Snowclad Volcanic Mountains and Strange Tribes of Eastern Equatorial Africa*, new and rev. ed. (London: Sampson Low, Marston, Searle & Rivington, 1987), 117–18.

16 Thomson, *Through Masai Land*, 118.

17 Stephen Greenblatt, *Marvellous Possessions: The Wonder of the New World* (Chicago: U of Chicago P, 1992), 20.

18 Greenblatt, *Marvellous Possessions*, 24–25.

19 Hans Meyer, "Ueber seine Besteigung des Kilimandscharo," *Verhandlungen der Gesellschaft für Erdkunde zu Berlin* 14 (1887): 446.

20 Hans Meyer, *Hochtouren im tropischen Afrika* (Leipzig: F. A. Brockhaus, 1923), 37.

21 See Hans Meyer, "Touristisches von meiner ersten Besteigung des Kilimandscharo," *Mittheilungen des Deutschen und Österreichischen Alpenvereins* 9 (1888): 1.

22 Interestingly, these militaristic lines are not included in Calder's translation.

23 See Meyer, *Hochtouren im tropischen Afrika*, 46.

24 Compare Kurt Schleucher, "Der Erstbesteiger Hans Meyer," in *Salut, Kilimandscharo: Hans Meyers Erstbesteigung und 100 Jahre später* (Darmstadt: Eduard Roether Verlag, 1989), 7.

25 Wilhelm Raabe, *Abu Telfan oder die Heimehr vom Mondgebirge*, vol. 7 of *Sämtliche Werke*, ed. Werner Röpke (Göttingen: Vandenhoeck & Ruprecht, 1951), 7. Further references to this edition of Raabe's novel are given in the text using the abbreviation *AT* and the page number.

26 For an overview of the moon's presence in literature, see, for instance, Elisabeth Franzel, "Der Mond," in *Motive der Weltliteratur: Ein Lexikon dichtungsgeschichtlicher Längsschnitte*, 3rd ed. (Stuttgart: Kröner, 1988), 547–60.

27 See Manfred Schneider, *Der Barbar: Endzeitstimmung und Kulturrecycling* (Munich: Hanser, 1997), 19.

28 Translator's note: In his novel, Hamann employs here the word "Pantoffelheld" (see *Usambara*, 213), which literally means "slipper hero." It is, however, the colloquial German term for "hen-pecked husband." Furthermore, it ties in with

Raabe's remark about Hagebucher not being born for "'Lehnstuhl, Schlafrock und Pantoffeln'" (*AT*, 26; armchair, morning-gown, and slippers). It thus functions as a kind of cipher that reinforces the thematic web connecting the two novels, *Abu Telfan* and *Usambara*. (SI)

[29] Samuel Beckett, *Worstward Ho*, in *Nohow On: Three Novels by Samuel Beckett* (New York: Grove, 1996), 89.

Part III: Modern Expeditions and Evocations: Climbing from the Twentieth into the Twenty-First Century

Leaving the Summit Behind: Tracking Biographical and Philosophical Pathways in Richard Strauss's *Eine Alpensinfonie*

Peter Höyng

WHEN RICHARD STRAUSS conducted his *Eine Alpensinfonie* (An alpine symphony) for the first time in Berlin on 28 October 1915, he offered images of nature through musical means. This, of course, was by no means groundbreaking: Antonio Vivaldi's *Le quattro stagioni* (The four seasons, 1725), Joseph Haydn's *Die Schöpfung* (The creation, 1798), Beethoven's *Pastoral*, his Sixth Symphony (1808), and Bedřich Smetana *Vltava* (Die Moldau, 1882) had already rendered nature in a musical language of its time. But what was innovative on that October night in 1915 was that a symphony presented an extensive mountain tour into the Alps.[1] The musical excursion offered many subplots, all written into the score as follows:

> night, sunrise, the ascent, entry into the forest, wandering by the brook, at the waterfall, apparition, on flowering meadows, in the Alpine pasture, wrong path in the thicket and undergrowth, on the glacier, dangerous moments, on the summit, vision, mists rise, the sun gradually becomes obscured, elegy, calm before the storm, thunder and tempest, descent, sunset, dying away of sound (Ausklang), night.[2]

In order to track this arduous musical journey, including its dark beginning and mysterious, sinister ending, one can choose various pathways, among them biographical and philosophical paths that elucidate why Strauss chose to evoke these images and this narrative of Alpine nature. In this essay, I suggest that multilayered biographical stories and the philosophical concept of Nietzsche's *Antichrist* are prerequisites for explaining how Strauss conceptualized his *Alpensinfonie* as he did, and why he ended in a somber mood, leaving, in the end, the summit behind.

In the summer of 1879, at the age of fifteen, Richard Strauss spent his vacation one hundred miles southwest of Munich (where he was born) in the town of Murnau, located at the edge of the Bavarian Alps. It was also in this same year that the railway system arrived in the small town, making it easier for families like the Strauss's to explore the mountainous region for recreational purposes. Today Murnau proudly advertises that the avant-garde artists of *Der Blaue Reiter* (The Blue Rider), the couples Wassily Kandinsky and Gabriele Münter and Marianne von Werefkin and Alexej von Jawlensky, spent their summer vacations from 1908 to 1914 in this quaint town beside the Staffelsee (Staffel Lake). In reaction to a second wave of rapid industrialization, they escaped the city and utilized nature, thereby revolutionizing modern art in the decade before the First World War, roughly at the same time that Richard Strauss's "ultra-dissonant biblical spectacle" *Salomé* was all the rage.[3]

But in the summer of 1879, the pubescent Richard was far from shocking and wowing his audience. Instead, on 26 August he began a letter to his then close friend Ludwig Thuille that describes leisurely afternoons spent at Staffel Lake with opportunities for bathing, boat rides, and fishing.[4] What triggered this particular letter, however, was the aftermath of an extensive tour into the Alps, a "Bergpartie" (hiking tour in the mountains). In the middle of the night the young Strauss, along with a group of other men, left on a hay cart to the foot of the mountains. Equipped only with a lantern, they hiked for five hours in the pitch-black night before reaching the Heimgarten summit (1,790 m/5,873 ft.), where they were afforded a panorama of various lakes and peaks, including the Zugspitze (2,962 m/9,718 ft.), Germany's highest peak. He goes on to describe their tour in the Alpine region of southern Germany, for instance how they got lost and wandered about for three hours only to be caught in a violent storm that uprooted trees and prevented them from crossing the Kochelsee by boat. As a result, they had to walk around the lake for two hours, becoming drenched by rain and finally reaching the next town, where they were forced to stay overnight. Only the next day did they return to Murnau. Strauss ends his letter as follows:

> Die Partie war bis zum höchsten Grad interressant [sic], apart und originell. Am nächsten Tag habe ich die ganze Partie auf dem Klavier dargestellt. Natürlich riesige Tonmalereien und Schmarrn (nach Wagner).
>
> [The trip was interesting, special, and original to the highest degree. The next day I depicted the whole adventure on the piano. Of course, giant tone painting and [all that] nonsense (according to Wagner).][5]

The letter allows for a number of observations and initial leads. For one, it attests to the phenomenon that in the second half of the nineteenth century climbing mountains and exploring the Alps for personal or recreational experiences instead of scientific adventures had become a somewhat widespread trend for the bourgeoisie, as the *Deutsche Alpenverein*, founded only ten years earlier, indicates.[6] And in the case of Richard Strauss, the letter documents what will eventually become his life-long interest in mountain tours.⁷ Second, in contrast to the dramatic tour it reports, this personal letter is written in a matter-of-fact style. The topographical references outweigh and even dominate any inner personal experiences. By summarizing the tour as "interressant, apart und originell" (interesting, special, and original) the description undermines its very own statement by sounding conventional to the point of being detached. Is it, one wonders, the storm that made the tour "interesting"? Or was it the climbing that made the occurrence special? And what exactly is so "original" about the tour: the storm that caused the additional detour around the lake? If these unexpected events made the excursion unusual, his description from the summit that offered a "wonderful view" certainly is not. Third, this conventional tone is further emphasized when he writes to his friend that, once home, he captured and mimicked the experience on the piano. It is as if Strauss mocks any possibility for becoming too sentimental or carried away by what might have been a formidable experience. Despite using all the tools of expanding the tonal scale on the piano, he trivializes his own musical depiction by invoking the idiomatic word for "nonsense" (*Schmarrn*) when referring to Richard Wagner, the celebrated demigod of the musical world, for whom Strauss's father had a strong dislike and whose taste, for the time being, the son had adopted. Finally, the letter can be understood as an early document that contains some narrative elements that will reappear in his *Alpensinfonie*, such as beginning the tour during the night, or being caught in a storm. Yet Rainer Bayreuther's painstaking documentation and interpretation of the *Alpensinfonie* cautions against the notion that the early rendering on the piano anticipated musical elements of the symphony he finished some thirty-five years later (see *RSA*, 16).

Above all, the letter documents what became Strauss's life-long enthusiasm and familiarity with the Alpine world. His sister Johanna summarizes those early years from 1872 to 1880 as follows:

> [Richards] Liebe für alles, Berg und Wald, Wiesen und Blumen, für alle Tiere, war groß. Er konnte nach den schönen Ausflügen begeisterte Ergüsse an seine Freunde schreiben, die auch seine musikalische Fantasie befruchteten. Meine Eltern verbrachten wegen der Gesundheit meines Vaters . . . den Sommer möglichst im Hochgebirge. . . . Sillian war für uns der Inbegriff aller Wonnen. Schon die Fahrt über den Brenner, die vielen Tunnels, die Kehrtunnels, das war vor siebzig Jahren das reine Wunder. . . . Richard durfte mit dem Vater auch Bergtouren machen, so nach *Heiligenblut* und der *Franz-Josephs-Höhe*.⁸

> [[Richard's] love for everything, mountains and forests, meadows and flowers, for all animals was great. After his wonderful excursions he could pour out his heart to his friends in writing, and these outpourings also fertilized his musical fantasy. Because of my father's health issues my parents spent their summers in the high mountains

as far as possible. . . . Sillian was the embodiment of all blissfulness. Just the trip there itself, over the Brenner pass, the many tunnels, and turns, it was pure magic seventy years ago. . . . Richard was allowed to go on mountain tours with his father, for example to Heiligenblut or the Franz-Joseph heights.]

This excerpt from the late memoir by Strauss's sister not only confirms the obvious, namely her brother's love for and familiarity with mountains and nature, but it also reveals once again a strong link between nature and culture, especially if one considers his need to express subjective impressions both in words and in music.[9]

Whereas these biographical contexts help to explain Strauss's interest in his *Alpensinfonie*, a brief look at a musical piece composed a century earlier further reveals how mountaineering during the second half of the nineteenth century might well be a precondition for conceiving a musical tour into the Alps. One need only think of Ludwig van Beethoven's *Pastoral*, the Sixth Symphony (1808). Like Strauss, Beethoven revered nature throughout his life, and while living in the imperial capital of Vienna he always chose to escape the city in the summer. Yet he never even came close to the Alpine mountains located west of Vienna, let alone to experiencing them through climbing. Hence in his *Pastoral* the subject revels in cheerful sentiments when arriving in the countryside by coach (first movement), takes a walk along a brook (second movement), envisions a "happy gathering" and dance among the country folk (third movement), encounters a thunderstorm (fourth movement), and thereafter hears a shepherd's song, savoring the peaceful scenery (fifth movement). Since no trains were yet available to take one closer to and through the Alps and the mountainous terrain remained, by and large, out of reach, no mountains can be heard in Beethoven's generally serene *Pastoral*.

Looking at Strauss's own life shows how for him the composition emerged out of personal engagement with the Alpine world rather than as an incidental whim. In order to fully translate his experiences into an acoustic narrative, Strauss then needed to utilize a fitting compositional language and form, relying as much on tradition as on inventing his individual ways of musical expression. Further pursuit of *Eine Alpensinfonie* requires continued exploration in the biographical mode, since Strauss was inspired by the life of the Swiss artist Karl Stauffer (1857–91). After all, the beginning of the symphony dates back to sketches for a tone poem entitled *Eine Künstlertragödie* (An artist's tragedy), which Strauss began in 1900 (see *RSA*, 17–18).[10] Stauffer's successful career as a painter in Berlin was marred by the tragic consequences of an adulterous affair, and Strauss explicitly wrote on the back of his sketch book, which contains key motifs of the later *Alpensinfonie*: "Liebestragödie eines Künstlers — dem Andenken Karl Stauffers" (Love tragedy of an artist — in memory of Karl Stauffer; see *RSA*, 18).

Stauffer regularly returned during his summer breaks to his hometown of Bern, and, like Strauss, he enjoyed the mountains as a welcome retreat from his successful career and busy urban life in Berlin. Compared with Strauss, however, Stauffer was a much more accomplished and experienced climber, achieving significant Alpine ascents, including the Wetterhorn (3,692 m/12,113 ft.), an impressive feat for the time (see *RSA*, 151–52). Climbing for Stauffer meant, as it did for Strauss, more than mere recreation or physical distraction; rather it took on a "psychohygienische Funktion" (psycho-hygienic function; *RSA*, 153), because it served as an antidote to modernity, as his biographer Brahm notes.[11] For Strauss and Stauffer, such experiences in the mountains became the inspirational source necessary for their artistic careers in urban settings.

During Stauffer's home-stay in Switzerland after his return from Berlin in August 1885, he met his former schoolmate Friedrich Emil Welti, son of an influential political family and former Swiss president, who was married to Lydia Escher, the daughter of an affluent and highly powerful Swiss family — the Swiss equivalent to the Vanderbilts — which was also heavily involved in the railroad industry and particularly the *Gotthardbahn*.[12] While Friedrich Welti's father was attempting to move the Swiss railroad system from private hands to public, he clashed with Lydia's father, who had brought economic and technical changes to Swiss railroads when he was co-owner of the *Nordostbahn* and the leading entrepreneur of the *Gotthardbahn*. The *Gotthardbahn* eventually replaced the century-old Saint Gotthard pass road, which connects the northern German-speaking with the southern Italian-speaking part of Switzerland via a tunnel. This tunnel, the longest in the world at the time, was celebrated as a masterpiece of engineering, though it also took a heavy toll of human lives.[13]

Stauffer unintentionally became a catalyst in the midst of the political dispute between the two well-known Swiss families after he became friends with Escher and Welti, who sponsored his work by commissioning him to paint Lydia Escher. After Stauffer had decided to leave Berlin for Rome in 1888, Lydia broke out of what she perceived to be a boring and stultifying life by seeking an adventurous affair with Stauffer in Florence. The adultery, which was illegal at the time, resulted in their both being placed in a lunatic asylum. Whereas Lydia managed, after a short period, to leave the hospital and later accepted a divorce forced on her by her husband, it was Stauffer who suffered more from the events, first suffering a mental breakdown and then facing the ensuing legal maneuverings on the part of the Escher family. After he survived one attempted suicide in June of 1890, he died half a year later from an overdose of sleeping pills (*RSA*, 38–46).

For Strauss, Stauffer embodied both a fascinating incarnation of an ingenious artist and a warning signal for transgressing one's artistic boundaries. Stauffer's extreme life allowed Strauss to abstract the specific circumstances and sublimate them into a general narrative of an artist's tragedy, similar to his earlier tone poems *Tod und Verklärung* (Death and transfiguration, 1890) and *Heldenleben* (A hero's life, 1899).

Yet more important in this context is how Strauss, inspired by Stauffer's biography, conceives a triad of nature, human life, and art in the first two sections of the sketches, which are identical to the 1902 draft and ultimately to the beginning of the *Alpensinfonie* as we know it today. Strauss describes his early musical motifs in such detailed fashion as

> Das Gebirge. Nacht. . . . Nebelwallen im Thale . . . allmählich treten die Schneegipel von der aufgehenden Sonne beleuchtet hervor, Licht von oben nach unten beleuchten . . . Aufblitzen der Bergspitzen . . . Zerreißen der Nebel (*RSA*, 60–71)
>
> [The mountains. Night. . . . fog in the valley . . . slowly the snow peaks are emerging, lit by the rising sun, light falls from above, . . . the summits are twinkling, the fog is torn apart]

and finishes with: "nachdem alles von Licht erhellt und von allmählich sanfter Wärme durchdrungen ist, wird auch das kleine Häuschen sichtbar, wo der 'Künstler geboren'" (after everything has been lighted and saturated by mild warmth, the small house where "the artist was born" becomes visible; *RSA*, 371–72). The next set of musical sketches carries the accompanying remarks: "Nach dem Sonnenaufgang Contrast des eigenen schmerzzerissenen Innern" (After the sunrise, contrast of my own pain-riven inner self) (*RSA*, 373).

What is remarkable about this draft is how much Strauss links Stauffer's life to nature. Not only does Strauss sublimate nature through his musical ideas, but he also transcends human life by representing the nature of the Alpine world. Having Stauffer's birthplace emerge from the dark night and into the morning light of the sun-bathed mountains, Strauss's notes project hope, purity, and a visceral bonding between the artist and the natural environment. And it is anything but accidental that Strauss links this beginning to his earlier tone poem, composed in 1896, *Also sprach Zarathustra* (Thus spoke Zarathustra), based on Friedrich Nietzsche's arguably most famous work, written during the mid-1880s. It is not only the beginning in C-major that most obviously connects the two tone poems but also, as Charles Youmans succinctly summarizes, "the majestic unfolding of the C-G-C 'nature' motive" draws on the former composition based on Nietzsche.[14] The more strongly he portrays this idealized union of an awe-inspiring nature and a zealous individual, the stronger becomes the contrast to the subjective pain and disbelief that awaits the artist. This balancing of two opposing forces, "the highest experience of life available to humankind" confronted by the "clear-eyed acceptance of the inevitable periodic return of doubt," reflects, according to Youmans, Strauss's post-metaphysical interest in Nietzsche's *Zarathustra*, which subsequently filtered into all Strauss's tone poems.[15]

The initial musical sketches for the *Alpensinfonie* not only point back to his earlier tone poem but also reflect to some degree the earlier narrative by Strauss's sister, namely that the sublime nature of the Alps infuses the male protagonist with supreme capabilities of experiencing oneself. And it is the male artist who wants to conquer nature through his art, like the engineers whose explosives crush the inner parts of a mountain to build the Gotthard tunnel. And whereas the tunnel connects two ends and makes a man-made shortcut, it is Strauss who couples the prototypical male artist Stauffer with his native environment by way of a philosophical explosion, this time Nietzsche's late polemic *Der Antichrist: Fluch auf das Christentum* (The Antichrist, curse on Christianity, 1888). When Strauss began his drafts in earnest for his new composition in 1902, he called it: "Der Antichrist: Eine Alpensinfonie" (The Antichrist: An Alpine symphony) and retained this title, with some variations, until 1913, shortly before finishing the work in the same year (see *RSA,* ·125, 299).

As I mentioned above, the intertextual and intermusical connections between Strauss's reading of Nietzsche's *Also sprach Zarathustra*, his own musical rendering of the same title, his *Antichrist*, and his *Alpensinfonie* are abundant and have been commented on. What has not been emphasized is that in both works the mountains serve as a metaphor for the ultimate Other, opposing what Nietzsche conceived as the evils of a decadent modernity. In the preface to *Also sprach Zarathustra*, the fictionalized demigod leaves his home and walks off into the mountains, where he lives for ten years. Thanks in part to his solitude, he undergoes a metamorphosis, reaping wisdom that he is now ready to share with ordinary people.[16] Zarathustra announces in his "Buch für alle und keinen" (book for all and none) that he is ready to descend from the summit. Likewise, in the *Antichrist*, Nietzsche frames his critical discourse against Christian morality: "Man muss geübt sein, auf Bergen zu leben, — das erbärmliche Zeitgeschwätz von Politik und Völker-Selbstsucht *unter* sich zu sehen" (You need to be used living on mountains — to seeing the miserable, ephemeral little gossip of politics and national self-interest *beneath* you).[17] In both of these late works Nietzsche sets the mountains against the backdrop of the lowlands, creating a sharp contrast of vision versus blindness, sublime superiority versus ordinary life, solitude versus the masses. In the eyes of Nietzsche, mountains grant an optimal antidote to the low-life of what he conceives as a decadent modernity. The natural heights function as an absolute purity against which everything else is seen as ordinary and impure.

As with Strauss, whose familiarity with Alpine nature directly influenced one of his artistic works, Nietzsche's experiences of the Alps left a mark on his existential philosophy. After 1880 and before his mental breakdown in 1889, Nietzsche lived a nomadic life during which he spent his summers (except for 1882) in Sils Maria,[18] in the southeastern part of

Switzerland, the Engadine, which is located at 5,900 feet and surrounded by mountains nearly 10,000 feet high. In July 1884 he wrote to his friend Resa von Schirnhofer: "Hier ist gut zu leben, in dieser starken hellen Luft, hier, wo die Natur auf wunderliche Weise zugleich mild, feierlich und geheimnißvoll ist — im Grunde gefällt mir's nirgendswo so gut als in Sils Maria." (Here one can live well, in this strong, bright atmosphere, here where nature is amazingly mild and solemn and mysterious all at once — in fact, there is no place that I like better than Sils-Maria).[19] These sublime surroundings inspired his ideas when he wrote in his autobiographical narrative *Ecce Homo*:

> Die Grundconception des Werks [des *Zarathustras*], der *Ewige-Wiederkunfts-Gedanke*, diese höchste Formel der Bejahung, die überhaupt erreicht werden kann, gehört in den August des Jahres 1881: er ist auf ein Blatt hingeworfen, mit der Unterschrift: "6000 Fuss jenseits von Mensch und Zeit."
>
> [The basic idea of the work [*Zarathustra*], *the thought of eternal return*, the highest possible formula of affirmation — belongs to August of the year 1881: it was thrown onto paper with the title: "6,000 feet beyond people and time."][20]

While in Nietzsche's case the linkage between geographic heights and soaring thoughts bears immediacy, Strauss's vacation in Pontresina — approximately ten miles away from Sils Maria — did not result in a juxtaposition between breathtaking nature and an idea.[21] Nevertheless, their shared desire to spend their summers at heights removed from urban crowds indicates a privileged position at a time when tourism was just beginning to burgeon. Furthermore their summer experiences in the Swiss Alps hold the key for opening up some of their respective transcendental concepts.

At this point various paths cross, geographically and biographically: Nietzsche, Stauffer, and Strauss all end up in the Swiss Alps, and all describe their interaction with the natural environment as essential for a sublime, rejuvenating, or purifying experience. In 1900 Strauss began to sketch motifs with the desire to express Stauffer's tragic life after having read his biography. And after reading Nietzsche's *Antichrist* he linked the two texts in order to continue his plan for a larger symphonic work set in the Alps, which became the *Alpensinfonie*. Connecting Stauffer's dramatic and tragic biography with Nietzsche's aggressive refutation of Christianity in the *Antichrist* took an associative reading, free of any analytical concerns, as a brief note in Strauss's calendar on 18 May 1911 shows:

> Ich will meine Alpensinfonie den Antichrist nennen, als da ist: die sittliche Reinigung aus eigener Kraft, Befreiung durch die Arbeit, Anbetung der ewigen herrlichen Natur.

[I want to call my Alpine Symphony the Antichrist as there is the moral purification from within one's own strength, liberation through work, and adoration of glorious eternal nature. (*RSA*, 299)]

Whereas some might regard Strauss's juxtaposition of his symphonic work with Nietzsche's late polemic as the sign of a naive reader, Youmans counters that the commonly held notion of Strauss understanding Nietzsche on "a low intellectual level" is misguided. Youmans demonstrates in detail the extent and capacity of Strauss's reading of Nietzsche, beginning in the late 1890s.[22] Yet Strauss extracts "only" one aspect from the sixty-two mini-essays that comprise *Der Antichrist*. In so doing, he ignores Nietzsche's continuous rampage condemning Judeo-Christianity, in which he argues how theologians, Protestantism, priests, the Apostle Paul, the Gospels, martyrs, and crusaders all established a corrupt ideology of lies that valorized a morality of suffering, sympathy, self-denying love, charity, and the refutation of life's natural rights. In short, it is Christianity's fault that individuals are kept hostage by a moral fabric that prevents them from being set free. This revolutionary attack and its finishing cry, the "Umwerthung aller Werthe" (reevaluation of all values)[23] are muted in Strauss's own distillation. Instead, he focuses on Nietzsche's counter-vision of replacing Christianity by noble and life-affirming values that, without any sense of shame or bad conscience, fully embrace natural instincts. "Das Leben selbst gilt mir als Instinkt für Wachstum, Dauer, für Häufung von Kräften, für *Macht*." (I consider life itself to be an instinct for growth, for endurance, for the accumulation of force, for *power*).[24] Noble spirits, according to Nietzsche, such as one supposedly could find in Roman and Greek antiquity or the Indian sanctified script Manusmriti, celebrate "ein Vollkommenheits-Gefühl, ein Jasagen zum Leben, ein triumphierendes Wohlgefühl an sich und am Leben." (a feeling of perfection, saying yes to life, a triumphant sense of well-being both for its own sake and for the sake of life).[25] It is this subtext in Nietzsche's relentless destruction of Christianity that Strauss translates as the celebration of a liberating self and an adoration of nature — both the nature of the human being with its natural instincts, and the nature by which we are surrounded and on which we depend.[26] Strauss unabashedly exploits these principles, which valorize a powerful male individual, detached from society, and which constitute the individual's value through his prowess and achievements. In his piercing critique of Strauss's programmatic music, Theodor Adorno summarizes this attitude as "Rücksichtslosigkeit, Gewaltsamkeit" (ruthlessness, violence).[27] When Nietzsche authorizes self-centered behavior and propels it to higher grounds, it also boosts the rationale of Stauffer's and Strauss's interest in mountain climbing as an egocentric self-affirmation and quasi-spiritual activity. From this point of view, conquering the mountains becomes not merely a recreational activity but yet another opportunity for a grandiose achievement, and hence appropriating nature for one's own needs. That Strauss ultimately dropped the "Antichrist" as a subtitle from his *Alpensinfonie* makes sense insofar as Nietzsche's writings merely functioned as a catalyst that helped the composer's initial interest in Stauffer's biography transcend into a larger narrative. By utilizing Nietzsche's approach toward a life-affirming philosophy, Strauss's emotional bonding with parts of Karl Stauffer's life allowed the mountain tour to be conceptualized with such points of emphases as natural instincts, boundless energy, and the joy of nature. Yet Strauss equally needed to utilize his critical distance from Stauffer, acknowledging Stauffer's tragic ending, for which Nietzsche's *Antichrist* provided no use — but all the more useful was the philosopher's own insanity, which to some extent echoed in an eerie way that of Stauffer. And once again we can return to Nietzsche's Zarathustra, who not only struggles to attain freedom but also despairs over the recurring existential angst and doubt that Strauss includes in his tone poem of the same name, as Youmans observes: "The inevitable periodic return of pessimism figures decisively in the program, the form, and the succession of moods."[28]

When following Strauss's tour into the Alps, we leave behind Bayreuther's predominant concern about formal composition, a concern that self-consciously oscillates within the discourse of nineteenth-century musical aesthetics, as outlined by Eduard Hanslick in his neo-Kantian treatise *Vom Musikalisch-Schönen* (On the musically beautiful, 1854). Hanslick constructs an opposition between an absolute music that emerges and rests exclusively on its structure, with Beethoven's symphonies as its unsurpassed model, and a programmatic narrative that relies on extra-musical associations as well as mimetic qualities of word-painting, for which Franz Liszt's tone poems and Richard Wagner's dramatic works served as a paradigm.[29] Instead of following Hanslick, I propose to look closer at the "Herstellung von Bildern durch die bilderlose Kunst" (*ZhG* 572; the production of images through imageless art, *RSB*, 20) and the unfolding narrative of *Eine Alpensinfonie*.

The narrative begins with the night giving way to a spectacular sunrise, followed by the gradual ascent: first entering the forest; then wandering by the brook, passing a waterfall and flowering meadows on the Alpine pasture; then arriving on the glacier, where one encounters elements of danger; and finally reaching the summit and experiencing there a sublime vision. However, the symphony does not end at this visionary moment: instead, the sun gradually becomes obscured and a thunderous tempest shows its might, which only hampers the descent. And it all ends as it began: "At night." For this musical journey, Strauss employs a minimum of 107 musicians: 67 string players and 38 wind players and percussionists, adding for the *vision* a doubling of some of the woodwinds. If one considers that the percussionists have to handle such atypical orchestral instruments as a wind- and thunder-machine as well as herd chimes, and furthermore bears in mind that twelve horns, two trumpets, and two trombones are instructed to play off-stage as a distant-sounding hunting group, one might find Adorno's analogy of Strauss's music to that of Franz Liszt as "herrschaftliche Villen von 1910 zu vollgestopften Appartments von 1880" (*ZhG*, 565; lordly villas of 1910 to crammed apartments of 1880, *RSB*, 14; translation adjusted) as something of an understatement. Indeed this orchestral force — only surpassed in Western musical history by Arnold Schoenberg's *Gurre-Lieder* (1911) — indicates, above all, one significant characteristic: Without any further musicological analysis, the sheer size of the orchestra makes abundantly apparent Strauss's mimetic intent and desire to compete against supreme nature by maximizing musical effects. Strauss's assertion that he wanted to compose "wie die Kuh Milch gibt" (like the cow gives milk)[30] both reflects his sheer appetite for showing off and, in a more sincere way, mirrors Nietzsche's notion of an instinctual and unashamed attitude toward life and its artistic rendering. This openly displayed naïveté is, of course, deceptive in view of what Strauss simultaneously asserted at the end of the dress rehearsal: "Jetzt endlich hab' ich instrumentieren gelernt" (Now, I have finally learned to orchestrate).[31]

This self-congratulatory remark on the mastery of his technique points to yet another important characteristic of the composition, namely that the oversized orchestra allows for an extremely varied musical texture, ranging from a thick, dark, and soft string sound with the descending and punctuated Ur-motif of the night,[32] to a spare and intimate-sounding orchestra with a high-pitched oboe before the storm, to the full blast of the storm itself. These mimetic acoustic images and episodes are misleading, insofar as the musical craftsmanship must become highly complex in order to achieve the full effect of sounding like nature, as Adorno stresses when stating: "In Strauss wagt der Aspekt des Gemachten ungescheut, pionierhaft sich vor wie Fabrikschornsteine in frisch eroberter Landschaft" (*ZhG*, 569; In Strauss, the "manufactured" aspect ventures forth boldly, pioneering, like factory smokestacks in freshly conquered country, *RSB*, 17). In this sense Strauss's musical mountain tour can be heard as analogous to the train tunnel that allows for a deeper exploration of mountains than existed before. An industrialized and ever-more differentiated society (like that of the large orchestra) is needed to explore remote, heretofore unknown Alpine regions that for most people were out of reach. For the modern urban individual, the more nature seemed out of reach, the more it increased his or her desire to reach it. The Alps promised a welcome antidote to the very same forces of modernity that facilitated the attainment of new heights. To emphasize this dialectical tension even further, the more complex and demanding the artistic production becomes, the more it reaches for a nature that denies these very means of cultural production. Industrial and cultural productions are synchronized, in that they both become complicit in exploring challenging heights.

Yet this clash of extremes, pinnacles in nature versus the artistic rendition of an apex, is deceptive in another and even more crucial regard. It is telling that Strauss's Alpine tour creates a musical illusion in which the individual climbs alone toward the summit. The music "redet, als spräche aus ihrem Subjekt die Totalität" (*ZhG*, 567–68; talks as though the totality, the whole wide world, spoke directly through its subjectivity, *RSB*, 16). That is, the individual, presumably a male, is one who is allowed to experience an adventurous day in the mountains and overcome hindrances so that he can feel in full control of both himself and nature. In this sense it is noteworthy that passages of the outside world switch to the inner world of the individual, reflecting his experiences in nature.

In any event the story, as noted in the musical score and expressed in musical language, creates for the listener and the audience the illusion that the tour is undertaken in complete solitude. And it is this lacuna that begs some attention. While Strauss has the protagonist hear distant hunting horns, and briefly includes a yodeling motif in the pasture scene,[33] the mountainous region seems for the most part devoid of other humans, or, more precisely, the culture of the Alpine populations. In this regard, it is worthwhile to remember what the mature Nietzsche and young Strauss wrote in their letters about the Alpine surroundings: they admire supreme nature without commenting about the Alpine population and its culture. The indigenous inhabitants do not exist or are not significant enough to become part of Strauss's story, as they did for Beethoven in his *Pastoral*, when he imitates and includes a "simple" folkdance by the people in the countryside. In his symphonic narrative, however, Strauss largely ignores the existing culture in the Alpine mountains. And when he briefly mimics yodeling sounds through woodwinds, their function is purely exotic. The imitative sound assimilates the existing musical practice of the Alps to the extent that it does not interrupt the refined sound of the modern orchestra. From an anthropological point of view, the cultural practice of going to a concert in a city and listening to the most superb and complex orchestral apparatus narrating a tour in an Alpine environment remains artificial and detached from the local musical culture. Long before Strauss's symphony, the various populations of the Alps developed and continued to practice their own musical culture. In contrast, and in the eyes of Nietzsche, urban audiences who quietly listen to music about nature are decadent and prone to be the target of sarcastic criticism. Arguably, Strauss's intention of narrating nature as "naturally" as possible, of portraying a lone mountaineer climbing and descending a mountain in one day is sentimental, which puts his audience into a double bind between nature and culture, and between imitative art and its assumed cultural refinement. It is this artifice of nature presented by a highly unnatural apparatus that motivates Adorno's remark concerning the rotten *Zeitgeist* in Strauss: "Sein Unwahres ist die Wahrheit der Epoche." (*ZhG*, 569; What is untrue in

[Strauss] is the truth of the epoch, *RSB*, 17). For Adorno, Strauss's faux modern music and his attempt in the *Alpensinfonie* to sound like nature mirror the chauvinistic attitude of an imperialism that turned its back on humanity.

A final look at the *Alpensinfonie* discloses yet another story about man and nature, and takes us back to Straus's effort to integrate his natural tour with the tragic biographical elements of Stauffer's artistic life. After all, what makes this composition so unusual, regardless of its grand orchestra and partly mimetic structure, is how the narrative ends. Whereas it is true that Strauss unfolds a day tour that encompasses the outer and inner world of the protagonist, the music ends as it begins, at night. These dark-layered clusters at the end, creating a fearful and mysterious sound, evoke once more Strauss's *Also sprach Zarathustra*. Far from triumphant, Strauss ends his *Zarathustra* as an enigma by leaving a harmonic riddle: the dark basses pluck the nature motif in its original key of C, but the woodwinds and violins respond in the key of B major, in a fading manner. The optimistic beginning is gone. Likewise in the *Alpensinfonie*. Therefore Strauss's climb neither focuses on reaching the natural climax, the summit, nor makes it the only or even exclusive central point of the story. If the goal of mountain climbing is reaching one of its peaks, then it also seems natural to have the story exclusively center on this objective. Yet Strauss chooses otherwise, since the attainment of the summit is followed by an extensive plot that places the blissful moment at the top into a perspective that darkens the inspiring vision from on high. Not only is the harmonious moment immediately followed and disturbed by rising mists that gradually obscure the sun, evoking the sensation of being lost, but furthermore the storm, thunder, and tempest, turn the descent into the true challenge of the climb. Even the sunset after the storm turns out not to be the bittersweet ending of an adventurous day. Rather it is the "Ausklang" (dying away of sound) into the night that figures in the ending of the story, which therefore concludes as it began.[34] The sublime peak is on the one hand even more elevated and visible (or audible), since it is surrounded by its very opposite, the almost indistinguishable sound of the ending. On the other hand, the summit as the center of the work is circumvented precisely because the peripheries, in terms of height and temporal structure, are so pronounced in the narrative. Nevertheless, using the night as a frame for the story, which thus takes place within the temporal structure of one full day, does not create an equilibrium; after all, in the beginning the mysteriously sounding night yields to a sunrise that generates hope, excitement, prospects, and the promise of an adventurous journey and activity for the protagonist that finds its fulfillment on the summit. Ending the story in the dark of night, however, leaves everything behind: fulfillment is gone, and with it any sense of excitement or hope. We are witnessing not a new day but rather a closing night that only imparts a further sense of loss.

Whereas "in the ascent to the summit the individual who masters the challenge of nature through his own efforts is the central focus, it is at the end nature that becomes the dominant power to which the individual has to succumb."[35]

This narrative invites doubts about the interpretation provided earlier, namely that of a male who finds his manhood confirmed by rising to the challenge of mountain climbing, an interpretation that rests on a linear rather than circular narrative mode. Moreover, it also questions the notion of self-affirmative vitalism of Nietzche's *Antichrist*, which Strauss long considered essential for his *Alpensinfonie*. According to a Nietzschean reading, the positive heroic attitude should have ended at, and with, the arrival at the mountaintop. As obvious as the answer to this mystifying — even confusing — ending is, scholars of the work have typically struggled with it, other than stressing that on a formal level it allows for a circular structure. However, when one considers that Strauss initially wanted to create a composition around Karl Stauffer's tragic life, it should come as no surprise that the symphonic narrative does not culminate and end with reaching the summit. Instead, Strauss stayed true to his original plan of portraying Stauffer's life as an artist's tragedy, who after his creative zenith and descent following a tumultuous affair was left with no other choice than to arrive in the dark. In the end, the symphonic narrative presents less of a dialectical twist between the modern man enthralled by nature than an unsettling narrative about the dark side of rising to the challenges of the Alpine world. This darkness at the end, mysterious as it sounds, belies the simple narrative of a man's success in control of Alpine nature. The ending moves the foregoing tour into an uncomfortable zone that stops short of being an abyss, since the recurrence of the beginning sound might give, formally, a sense of comfort, but with regard to meaning, no closure. It is here that Strauss's conception of his last tone poem comes full circle as well: his interest in Stauffer's tragic ending concurs with Nietzsche's and Strauss's *Zarathustra*, in which the cyclic temporality of the natural world surrounds us, and that no matter what summit we might be able to conquer, we have to leave it behind, because we tragically and eternally face the return of nature's all encompassing forces.

Notes

[1] Joachim Raff's seventh symphony, entitled *In den Alpen* (In the Alps, 1875), can claim a first venturing off to the European mountain range. As prolific and successful as the Swiss-born composer was during his lifetime, "his speed of production precluded the creation of significant, deeply felt works." Yet "Raff's influence was wide in his day. . . . The symphonies were of significance for the development of that genre and the symphonic poem in the later 19th century, having an impact

upon such composers as . . . Strauss." James Deaville, "Raff, Joachim," in *Grove Music Online*. Oxford Music Online, http://www.oxfordmusiconline.com/subscriber/article/grove/music/22816 (accessed 31 Oct. 2010).

[2] Richard Strauss, *Eine Alpensinfonie*, op. 64, score, revised by Walter Seifert (Munich: Leuckart, n.d.). All translations in this chapter are my own, unless otherwise noted.

[3] Alex Ross, *The Rest is Noise: Listening to the Twentieth Century* (New York: Farrar, Straus & Giroux, 2007), 3.

[4] Franz Trenner, ed., *Richard Strauss — Ludwig Thuille: Ein Briefwechsel* (Tutzing, Germany: Schneider, 1980), 72.

[5] According to Johanna von Rauchenberger-Strauss's "Jugenderinnerungen" (Memoirs of Our Youth), Richard must have attended the *Götterdämmerung* on 10 August 1879. Johanna von Rauchenberger-Strauss, "Jugenderinnerungen," in *Richard Strauss Jahrbuch, 1959/60*, ed. Willi Schuh (Bonn: Boosey & Hawkes, 1960), 17.

[6] Peter Grupp, *Faszination Berg: Die Geschichte des Alpinismus* (Vienna: Böhlau, 2008), 67.

[7] Rainer Bayreuther, *Richard Strauss' Alpensinfonie: Entstehung, Analyse und Interpretation* (Hildesheim: Olms, 1997), 149. Further references to this work are given in the text using the abbreviation *RSA* and the page number. Cf. Jürgen May, "Wege und Irrwege in und um Richard Strauss' *Alpensinfonie*: Eine Spurenlese," in *Musik und Biographie*, ed. Cordula Heymann-Wentzel and Johann Laas (Würzburg: Königshausen & Neumann, 2004), 366–69.

[8] Rauchenberger-Strauss, "Jugenderinnerungen," 26.

[9] Another record of Strauss's mountain tours can be found in a letter to his parents that he wrote while vacationing in the Swiss Alps in June 1893: "Wolkenlos, strahlend im Sonnenglanz. Monte Rosa, Breithorn, Matterhorn, etc. ringsum lauter Schneeriesen von 4500 Metern und unter mir riesige Gletscher. Es war überwältigend." "No clouds, shining in the sun's glow. Monte Rosa, Breithorn, Matterhorn, etc. all around nothing but snow giants of 14,764 feet and below me giant glaciers. It was overwhelming." Richard Strauss, *Briefe an die Eltern*, 1882–1906, ed. Willi Schuh (Zurich: Atlantis, 1954), 184–85.

[10] Circumstantial evidence suggests that Strauss read Stauffer's biographical account by the well-known theater critic and director Otto Brahm: Otto Brahm, *Karl Stauffer — Bern: Sein Leben, seine Briefe, seine Gedichte* (Stuttgart: Göschen, 1892). Bayreuther, however, relies in his account on the modern biography by Bernhard von Arx, *Karl Stauffer und Lydia Welter-Escher: Chronik eines Skandals* (Bern: Zytglogge, 1991).

[11] "Auf weiten Fußwanderungen vertobte . . . er nervöse Verstimmungen, und eifrig berichtete er uns Berlinern: wie er frühmorgens pfadlos in die Berge marschirt [sic], 'ruppig' aller städtischen Kleidung entsagend; und wie er mit der untergehenden Sonne erst heimgekehrt, mit zerschlagenden Gliedern oft, aber die Sinne freibadet" (On his long wandering tours he acted out his nervous moods, and avidly reported to us in Berlin how he left early in the mornings marching into the

mountains, disregarding pathways, rambunctiously disregarding the urban dress code; and how he only returned at the time of sunset, often with battered limbs, but having purified his senses, Brahm, *Karl Stauffer*, 19).

[12] Cf. Gordon A. Craig, *The Triumph of Liberalism: Zurich in the Golden Age, 1830–1869* (New York: Scribner, 1988).

[13] The nine-mile-long Gotthard rail tunnel replaced the pass road and opened in 1882 for railway traffic at a cost of at least two hundred workers' lives. A second railway tunnel is currently under construction and is scheduled to open in 2016. Cf. Hans Peter Nething, *Der Gotthard* (Thun, Switzerland: Ott Verlag, 1976); Burkhard Bilger, "The Long Dig: Getting through the Swiss Alps the Hard Way," *The New Yorker*, 15 Sept. 2008, 63–73.

[14] Charles D. Youmans, "Strauss's Nietzsche," in *Richard Strauss's Orchestral Music and the German Intellectual Tradition* (Bloomington: Indiana UP, 2005), 108.

[15] Youmans, "Strauss's Nietzsche," 107.

[16] Friedrich Nietzsche, *Also sprach Zarathustra*," in *Werke: Kritische Gesamtausgabe*, section 6, vol. 1, ed. Giorgio Colli and Mazzino Montinari (Berlin: Walter de Gruyter, 1968), 5.

[17] Friedrich Nietzsche, *Der Antichrist*, in *Werke: Kritische Gesamtausgabe*, section 6, vol. 3, ed. Giorgio Colli and Mazzino Montinari (Berlin: Walter de Gruyter, 1969), 165. Friedrich Nietzsche, *The Anti-Christ, Ecce homo, Twilight of the Idols, and Other Writings*, ed. Aaron Ridley and Judith Norman, trans. Judith Norman. (Cambridge: Cambridge UP, 2005), 3.

[18] In 1869 Nietzsche gave up Prussian citizenship and remained a stateless individual with no official citizenship, and he alternated residence between various European countries including France, Italy, and Switzerland.

[19] Friedrich Nietzsche, Brief vom 25. Juli 1884, no. 523, in *Nietzsche Briefwechsel: Kritische Gesamtausgabe*, section 3, vol. 1, ed. Giorgio Colli and Mazzino Montinari (Berlin: Walter de Gruyter, 1981), 516.

[20] Friedrich Nietzsche, *Ecce Homo*, in *Werke: Kritische Gesamtausgabe*, section 6, 3:333. Nietzsche, *The Anti-Christ, Ecce homo, Twilight of the Idols, and Other Writings*, 123.

[21] According to Willi Schuh, Strauss's main biographer, it must have been the Swiss Alps of the Engadine that inspired Strauss's *Alpensinfonie*. Willi Schuh, "Richard Strauss in der Schweiz," in *Straussiana aus vier Jahrzehnten* (Tutzing: Schneider, 1981), 48.

[22] Contrary to Bayreuther, Youmans argues that the *Alpensinfonie*'s connection to Nietzsche "must have been conscious and determined from the beginning," and reasons (1) that Strauss realized the parallels of Stauffer's and Nietzsche's descent into insanity; (2) Strauss was aware that both were "seeking wisdom through contemplation at mountain retreats"; and (3) Strauss's understanding of Stauffer's life shows traces of a Nietzschean interpretation. See Youmans, "Strauss's Nietzsche," 83–113.

[23] Nietzsche, *Der Antichrist*, 251; *The Anti-Christ*, 66 (Aphorism 62).

²⁴ Nietzsche, *Der Antichrist*, 170; *The Anti-Christ*, 6 (Aphorism 6).
²⁵ Nietzsche, *Der Anti-Christ*, 238; *The Anti-Christ*, 56 (Aphorism 56).
²⁶ Strauss reported to Romain Rolland that there is nothing vulgar inside oneself. Cf. Walter Thomas, *Richard Strauss und seine Zeitgenossen* (Munich: Langen Müller, 1964), 88–89.
²⁷ Theodor W. Adorno, "Richard Strauss: Zum hundertsten Geburtstag," in *Gesammelte Schriften*, ed. Rolf Tiedemann, vol. 16 (Frankfurt am Main: Suhrkamp, 1997), 565. In English, "Richard Strauss: Born June 11, 1864," trans. Samuel Weber and Shierry Weber, *Perspectives of New Music* 4, no. 1 (1965): 14–32, and no. 2: 111–29; here 14. Further references to the German essay will be given in the text using the abbreviation *ZhG*, and to the English translation using the abbreviation *RSB*.
²⁸ Youmans, "Strauss's Nietzsche," 106.
²⁹ Bayreuther convincingly argues and demonstrates that Strauss's composition, despite its programmatic content, moves toward a musical texture reminiscent of a symphonic composition, because of its motifs and harmonic structures. He therefore opposes the widely held view according to which Strauss's tone poems are nothing but descriptive music, which is often considered inferior to absolute music. Cf. Bayreuther, 314 and 344–63.
³⁰ Richard Specht, *Richard Strauss und sein Werk*, vol. 1 (Leipzig: Tal, 1921), 332.
³¹ Specht, *Richard Strauss und sein Werk*, 334.
³² Fritz Gysi, *Richard Strauss* (Potsdam: Akademische Verlagsgesellschaft Athenaion, 1934), 67.
³³ Strauss, *Eine Alpensinfonie*, op. 64, section 52.
³⁴ A final comparison with Beethoven's *Pastoral* highlights the difference between the two narratives. Whereas Beethoven portrays "thankful feelings" and an inner peace after the thunderstorm, Strauss descends in terms of both height and time until the subject vanishes into darkness.
³⁵ "Im Anstieg steht das Individuum im Mittelpunkt, das durch eigene Anstrengung die Herausforderung der Natur überwindet; im Abstieg ist die Natur die zentrale Kraft, der das Individuum ausgeliefert ist." May, "Wege und Irrwege," 379.

Elevation and Insight: Thomas Mann's *Der Zauberberg*

Johannes Türk

NINETEEN TWENTY-FOUR, the year Thomas Mann's *Der Zauberberg* (The magic mountain) was published, is an important date in the history of the representation of mountains. In the German tradition, this novel is the most prominent work of literature whose entire plot and structure draw on mountains. It offers an investigation into the repertoire of established tropes of mountain discourses from Petrarchan humanism and the Romantic sublime to the thrill of sport and mountain climbing in modern times. Absorbing literary traditions as well as contemporary travel literature and commonplaces of an emerging bourgeois mountaineering culture, Mann's novel has also shaped the future of mountain literature to the degree that it established itself as a canonical work of German literature. Its publication therefore constitutes a turning point in the way in which the Alpine realm is experienced and represented. After 1924, the mountains would never be the same again.

Few facets of the novel — from the details of contemporary Davos[1] to the allegoric and sociopolitical — have eluded scholarly attention, and since the 1990s the medical dimension of the novel has become a major field of inquiry. But only a handful of interpreters have granted this dimension the importance it deserves. Far from being a subsidiary aspect, it constitutes a major thematic and formal innovation in the text. Although Hans Castorp, the novel's protagonist, experiences the mountains as a place of beauty (or alternatively of the sublime), of humanist reflection, and of sport, these experiences — and with them the reader's expectations — are undermined by irony. But the specific insight the novel produces goes beyond the fact that this layer of meaning is by its very nature illusory. Instead, *Der Zauberberg* conquers new terrain: it depicts the Alpine environment as the locus of a specific "regional epistemology" that allows us to experience and gain knowledge of human physiology — in other words, to gain insight in a literal sense. Acclimatization, mountaineering, skiing, and disease are forms in which the human body enters into intensive processes through which it demands attention and becomes newly accessible. This knowledge gains specific contours in medical discourses that revolve not only around pathology but also the "normal." It is no coincidence, then, that the decisive biographical episode that inspired Mann to write the original novella was a visit to a mountain sanatorium.

What later turned into Thomas Mann's third novel began in 1912 as the sketch for a novella intended as a "humorous sidepiece" to *Der Tod in Venedig* (Death in Venice, 1912).[2] Inspired by a stay in Davos, where his wife Katja was being treated for a catarrh, Mann began to compose a text that accompanied him through the subsequent war and postwar years, a time during which his worldview and politics were transformed; reluctantly abandoning his monarchism, he instead began to voice support for the fragile Weimar Republic. The originally conceived novella grew into a voluminous novel, published in 1924. In its pages, the life of the ordinary citizen Hans Castorp, who has just passed his exams in nautical engineering and is about to start his career in a shipyard, takes a decisive turn when he visits his ailing cousin Joachim Ziemßen at the Berghof sanatorium in the Swiss resort of Davos. The diagnosis of a hitherto undetected tubercular infection that resurfaces under the influence of the bracing Alpine climate allows him to give in to his passion for the Kirghiz *femme fatale* Madame Chauchat, and he stays in the mountains for seven years. The novel never answers the question whether its protagonist is misdiagnosed or whether he instead takes advantage of the medical verdict. The alternative between misdiagnosis and gain from illness establishes a double structure in which the normal and the pathological intertwine.

Although Castorp is, at least initially, not a patient but a tourist, he is a figure that lives in the vicinity of knowledge gained through disease. Through him, the novel places love and acclimatization, tourism and disease, in a relation of contiguity. They are situated on a continuum where they open the question of life anew. This question does not come to a conclusion; rather, it is a process that absorbs Hans's entire life. As a consequence, Mann's novel does not rely on the tripartite structure of ascent, arrival, and descent. Whereas this dramatic linear pattern — most prevalent in mountain-climbing narratives — represents a liminal episode probing life's resilience, reaching for a transcendence of the everyday that is followed by the resumption of normal life, *Der Zauberberg* dilates this structure to the point that it turns into aimless erring and digression. The domesticated experience of sport gives way to a process of existential wandering in which life begins to reflect on death.

Der Zauberberg can still be recognized as a relative of the Venice novella. Both texts share the structure of the episode that prolongs itself against the will of its protagonist, a process that equals the loss of form; and both protagonists meet their destiny in the guise of a disease related to desire. However, crucial elements set them apart. In *Der Zauberberg*, the problem of art that dominates *Der Tod in Venedig* as well as Mann's earlier novella *Tristan* (whose setting is also a sanatorium) is eclipsed by the medical institution and its inhabitants. The narrow thematic scope focused on the figure of the artist is therefore replaced by wider considerations concerning human life and human nature. Art remains a side theme in the novel. The scenes with Doctor Behren's paintings show that the novel is only interested in these topics to the degree that the new medical view of the human body requires new forms of artistic representation. The anatomical and physiological details implied in this perspective translate into a new realism. As the gramophone scenes show, art also comes into focus as a force able to contribute to the ambivalent quest for meaning in life and death. Even more significant in *Der Zauberberg* is that disease no longer plays a primarily symbolic role. Instead, the novel criticizes interpretations of disease that enter tuberculosis into a symbolic register — if through nothing else than the humorous distance Hans Castorp adopts toward all positions claiming death and disease for their cause. This literal understanding is the reason for which *Der Zauberberg* is Mann's first, and maybe also his last, modern novel. In spite of his simplicity, Hans maintains an ironic stance toward the grand debates carried out by Naphta and Settembrini, exploring life instead as something that cannot be detached from the physiological processes underlying it.

What is expected to be a limited episode, beginning with the ascent into the mountains, becomes a turning point after which Hans Castorp's life will never be the same. He plans "to pick up his life again where he had been forced to leave it lying for the moment"[3] (sein Leben genau dort wieder aufzunehmen, wo er es für einen Augenblick hatte liegenlassen müssen).[4] But the ascent is a point of no return: the Alps are represented as a place where the horizon of the protagonist's experience is absorbed in physical exertion, the preoccupation with health and disease, and the sanatorium. As the possibility of return recedes over the course of Castorp's seven-year stay, the frame in which the sojourn could become intelligible as an exception to something like "normal life" dissolves. What appears in the place of a framed episode is the possibility of radical immanence, a life lived without reference to an outside or to its daily preoccupations. The novel that begins as the biography of an engineer turns into the representation of a human life whose main preoccupation is its physical states, their medical significance, and the meaning of this life as a whole. The narrative of *Der Zauberberg* thereby spells out the consequences of the end of metaphysics; no longer can the understanding of life be delegated to transcendent ideas. But transcendence itself is a dimension born out of the terrors of existence, and only the specific experience of Davos opens up this insight.[5]

The conditions that make this experience possible lie in a medical institution that is inseparable from the mountains and forms an important part of their significance around the turn of the century: the sanatorium. In the second half of the nineteenth century this institution emerged as the only cure for tuberculosis, one of the major causes of death at the time. Because of their elevation, mountainous regions were thought to display atmospheric properties that seemed to have the power of healing hitherto incurable diseases. And sanatoria offered a form of life that supposedly cured and at the same time enclosed disease and death. *Der Zauberberg* is therefore the novel of a disease, tuberculosis, and also the novel of a specific institution, the sanatorium.[6] Behind its walls, individuals and collectives faced existential questions, and at the same time their lives were focused on the physiological processes underlying health and disease. They were offered the possibility of gaining insight into the pathological processes that formed their shared existential preoccupation. And this insight acquainted the patients with what was elsewhere taboo: the physiological decay and finitude that are usually hidden under the aesthetic surface of life in the same way that the skin hides the necrosis of lung tissue.

Even before Mann's acquaintance with the Davos sanatorium for pulmonary diseases, the drinking and bathing treatments of spas in northern Germany and the Taunus play a significant role in his first novel, *Buddenbrooks: Verfall einer Familie* (Buddenbrooks: The decline of a family, 1901). As its title suggests, the novel portrays the biological and social waning of a wealthy merchant family. The decline endangers not only the family's business (the history of the Buddenbrooks famously "culminates" in a nervous, weak, and degenerate artist); it also threatens the biological continuation of the patriarchal line. The survival of the family name is not secured, as Thomas Buddenbrook's wife Gerda does not get pregnant. In addition to his brother Christian's failed business and his sister Clara's childlessness, this unfruitful state of affairs forms the third worry of Thomas Buddenbrook, the son on whom the perpetuation of the family legacy depends. Doctor Grabov recommends replacing the spa treatments with dietary measures to help bring about the desired heir:

> "Doktor, unter uns, da muß endlich etwas geschehen, nicht wahr? Ein bißchen Bergluft in Kreuth und ein bißchen Seeluft in Glücksburg oder Travemünde scheint da nicht anzuschlagen. Was meinen Sie . . ." Und Grabov, weil sein angenehmes Recept: "Strenge Diät; ein wenig Taube, ein wenig Franzbrot" in diesem Falle doch wohl wieder einmal nicht energisch genug eingegriffen haben würde, verordnete Pyrmont und Schlangenbad. . . .[7]

> ["Just between us, doctor, something must be done, don't you think? A little mountain air in Bad Kreuth or a little sea air in Glücksburg or Travemünde doesn't seem to have had any effect. What do you suggest?" And since in this case his usual remedy of "a strict diet, a little squab, a little French bread" did not seem to be quite aggressive enough as a treatment, Grabow prescribed a trip to Pyrmont and Schlangenbad.][8]

In a later part of the novel it becomes clear how significant the contrast between the sea and mountains is in the context of a medical understanding of topography. Years have gone by, and Thomas, by now a father, and Christian, who has given up most of his commercial obligations, travel to Travemünde at the bidding of Doctor Langhals, who has recommended sea air for Thomas's worsening nerves. Thomas's reflections on the sea are remarkable:

> Mehr und mehr habe ich die See lieben gelernt . . . vielleicht zog ich ehemals das Gebirge nur vor, weil es in weiterer Ferne lag. Jetzt möchte ich nicht mehr dorthin. Ich glaube, weil ich mich schämen würde. Es ist zu willkürlich, zu unregelmäßig, zu vielfach . . . Gesundheit und Krankheit, das ist der Unterschied. Man klettert keck in die wundervolle Vielfachheit der zackigen, ragenden, zerklüfteten Erscheinungen hinein, um seine Lebenskraft zu erproben, von der noch nichts verausgabt wurde. Aber man ruht aus an der weiten Einfachheit der äußeren Dinge, müde wie man ist von der Wirrnis der inneren. (B, 740–41)

> [I've learned to love the sea more and more — perhaps I preferred the mountains at one time only because they were so much further away. I wouldn't want to go there now. I think I would feel afraid and embarrassed. They are too arbitrary, too irregular, too diverse — I am sure I feel overwhelmed. . . . Health or sickness, that is the difference. A man climbs jauntily up into the wonderful variety of jagged, towering, fissured forms to test his vital energies, because he has never had to spend them. But a man chooses to rest beside the wide simplicity of eternal things, because he is weary from the chaos within. (D, 648)]

The mountains, here a place of vitality and health, shift their meaning in *Der Zauberberg*. If Thomas Mann chose the mountains as a place of disease, then it was due to his acquaintance with an institution, the sanatorium, that changes the topographic valences of the opposition between mountains and sea. The sanatorium was a privileged dwelling place in the early twentieth century. Franz Kafka spent a good third of his life there, and it was also well known to Thomas Mann, whose neurasthenia — a fashionable diagnosis during the *fin-de-siècle* — led him to frequent stays, beginning in 1901 in Mittelbad. During this period, the sanatorium was, to quote Christian Virchov, a "Lebensform" (form of life).[9] It replaced the earlier spas, which were founded on the idea that dry climate was beneficial to those affected by diseases of civilization.

Sanatoria were founded on the concept of an immune space. Hermann Brehmer's 1853 dissertation first claimed that elevation could heal tuberculosis. According to Brehmer, high elevations hold the potential of immunity to the disease. It was widely assumed that a disproportion between an undersized heart and oversized lungs — the so-called "phthitic habitus"— was the cause of tuberculosis. According to Brehmer, geographic altitude can improve this imbalance, because the elevation and Alpine air stimulate the activity of the heart, helping it grow: what Brehmer calls "Gesundheits-Oasen" (health-oases) are places that possess "Immunität der Lungenschwindsucht" (immunity from tuberculosis). The major task for Brehmer is "festzustellen, in welcher Höhe diese Exemption einer Landschaft von der Krankheit beginnt." (to determine at what elevation this exemption of a landscape from the disease begins).[10] Depending on the location of a specific site on the grid of parallels and meridians, it has to have a specific elevation in order to qualify as being "immune." In central Germany, where Brehmer founded the first sanatorium in the Silesian town of Görbersdorf during the 1850s, immunity begins at "an altitude of 2,000 feet."[11] Davos was modeled after this sanatorium and relied on the idea that its Alpine location would make it a place of healing.[12] To "put on protein" (Eiweiß ansetzen) became the major aim of the cure. Brehmer's pupil Dettweiler later added sun exposure and other elements that gave the cure its final outline. It is based on what is taken to be the specific immunity of high altitude.

Throughout *Der Zauberberg* numerous references are made to the quality of the air and the effect of elevation. One of the most interesting scenes that comments on this aspect is the visit of Hans's uncle James Tienappel to the Berghof sanatorium, a scene that mirrors Hans's own arrival with which the novel opens. The uncle

> zog tief die Luft ein, die er für herrlich erklärte. Gewiß, antwortete der andere, nicht umsonst sei sie ja weit berühmt. Sie habe starke Eigenschaften. Obgleich sie die Allgemeinverbrennung beschleunige, setze der Körper in ihr doch Eiweiß an. Krankheiten, die jeder Mensch latent in sich trage, sei er zu heilen imstande, doch befördere er sie zunächst einmal kräftig, bringe sie vermöge eines allgemeinen organischen An- und Auftriebes sozusagen zu festlichem Aufbruch. (*Z*, 647)
>
> [took a deep breath of air and let it out again, declaring it excellent. Certainly, his companion replied, it was not world-famous for nothing. This air had special properties. Although it accelerated the metabolism, the body was still able to store protein. Of course it could heal sickness, but its first effect was greatly to enhance illnesses that everyone carried latent in them, because the impetus and stimulus this air gave the whole organism brought illness to exuberant eruption, so to speak. (*M*, 422)]

This scene underlines the physiological effect of the landscape, through whose impact the body can "put on protein" and work against the disproportion between heart and lungs. It also shows that after more than five years spent at the Berghof sanatorium, Hans Castorp has not only become acquainted with the strict regimen imposed on its ailing inhabitants but has also acquired the medical knowledge underlying the treatment and diagnosis of tuberculosis, enabling him to pass it on to new arrivals such as his uncle.

The healing impact of topography on the physiological constitution is the major trajectory leading to the development of a health industry that prepares the ground for Alpine mass tourism.[13] *Der Zauberberg* reflects these developments and therefore offers, as Claude Reichler writes, an "anthology (and also a typology) of the Alpine landscape."[14] It presents the mountains as a place whose experience is mediated by advertisements that coin stereotypes of the Alpine in the late-nineteenth and early-twentieth century. The real encounter with the mountains takes place in tension with these commonplaces. Thus Hans Castorp has read "Prospekte" (*Z*, 20; brochures, *M*, 9) when he arrives. Through his irony, the narrator distances himself from the landscapes he narrates and presents them at the same time as a mere repetition of what has already been heard and said elsewhere.

Reichler has analyzed this use of landscape as "convention."[15] He places particular emphasis on how the modern Alps are created in a discourse that manifests itself in the first pages of the novel, when Hans Castorp travels up the mountain toward Davos. Without ever having been in this sphere, Hans is already acquainted with a vocabulary able to register it:

> Großartige Fernblicke in die heilig-phantasmagorisch sich türmende Gipfelwelt des Hochgebirges, in das man hinan- und hineinstrebte, eröffneten sich und gingen dem ehrfürchtigen Auge durch Pfadbiegungen wieder verloren. (*Z*, 14)

> [Magnificent vistas opened onto regions toward which they were slowly climbing, a world of ineffable, phantasmagoric Alpine peaks, soon lost again to awestruck eyes as the tracks took another curve. (*M*, 5)]

Both the "großartige Fernblicke" as well as the "ehrfürchtige Auge" are quotes from brochures and travel guides that, according to Reichler, transformed the image of the mountains during this period. As Reichler shows, the arrival is preceded by the acquisition of knowledge. As soon as the cousins arrive at the Berghof sanatorium, Hans is disappointed because these expectations built up through the reading of brochures are not fulfilled. Informed about the sublimity of the mountains, he expected them to be higher:

> "Du siehst Dir die Gegend an?" Das tat Hans Castorp, und er äußerte: "Großartig!" "Findest Du?" fragte Joachim. . . . "Nein, ich finde es offen gestanden nicht so überwältigend," sagte Hans Castorp. "Wo sind denn die Gletscher und Firnen und die gewaltigen Bergriesen? Diese Dinger sind doch nicht sehr hoch, wie mir scheint." (*Z*, 18–19)

> ["Having a look at the scenery, are you?" And indeed that was what Hans Castorp was doing, and he exclaimed, "Magnificent!" "You

think so?" Joachim asked. . . . "No, to be quite frank, I don't find it that overwhelming," Hans Castorp said. Where are the glaciers and the snowcapped, towering peaks? Seems to me, the ones here aren't all that high." (*M*, 7–8)]

The absence of glaciers, firn, and giant mountains relates the scenery to the topoi of health tourism. But as Joachim points out, the glaciers are there: they just look smaller than expected, and Hans has to learn how to see them. Hans is merely incapable of reconciling his actual experience with the words and concepts he already knows. His knowledge has prevented him from perceiving the reality before him:

"Doch, sie sind hoch," antwortete Joachim. "Du siehst die Baumgrenze fast überall, sie markiert sich ja auffallend scharf, die Fichten hören auf, und damit hört alles auf, aus ist es, Felsen, wie du bemerkst." (*Z*, 19)

["Oh, they're high all right," Joachim replied. "You can see the tree line almost everywhere, it's really quite clearly defined; the pines come to an end, then everything else — the end, then rocks, as you can see." (*M*, 8)]

Hans's disappointment is therefore followed by the confidential admission that his premature admiration was more a reflection of the commonplace than of the actual impression.

The experience of disappointment is not limited to the aesthetics of the Alps; it also characterizes Hans's encounter with disease.[16] Upon his arrival, Castorp is introduced to the world of the mountains and to the sanatorium with its strict regimen. He encounters the gruesome reality of the disease at first as an invisible facticity, hidden under the appearance of health that sun exposure and climate bring forth. When Hans Castorp mentions the possibility of returning home together after his brief stay, Joachim's response about having to stay for half a year longer surprises his cousin. What is at stake in this surprise is the nature of medical evidence. It is not the visible reality of Joachim's appearance that forces him to stay, but the symptoms of tuberculosis accessible only through a medical diagnosis relying on X-rays and auscultation:

"Es geht mir ja besser, aber gesund bin ich eben noch nicht. Links oben wo früher Rasseln zu hören war, klingt es jetzt nur noch rauh, das ist nicht so schlimm, aber unten ist es noch sehr rauh, und dann sind auch im zweiten Interkostalraum Geräusche." (*Z*, 17)

["I am feeling better, but I'm not yet entirely well, either. The upper left lobe, where the rattling used to be, there's only a little roughness there now, it's not so bad, but the lower lobe is still *very* rough, and there are also sounds in the second intercostal." (*M*, 7)]

The medical verdict is based on an invisible dimension. It is the contrast between healthy exterior and inner decay that constitutes the discrepancy Hans learns to understand.

The next significant episode in which the Dionysian dimension — the terror of existence described by Nietzsche in *Die Geburt der Tragödie* — of tubercular decay appears is the coughing of the invisible gentleman rider. The cousins hear it when they move into Hans's room, where an American woman had died not long before his arrival. Hans is aware of the newness of this auditory experience: "Es ist ja gerade, als ob man dabei in den Menschen hineinsähe, wie es da aussieht — alles ein Matsch und Schlamm (*Z*, 25; "It's as if you were looking right down inside and could see it all — the mucus and the slime," *M*, 12). It takes a long time until the cough is "understood" and Hans has gained the knowledge necessary for an understanding of the disease. Two trajectories acquaint him with this knowledge. On the one hand, he becomes a patient, even if only a "light case," which changes his life on the mountain significantly. On the other hand, he replaces the book on ocean steamships that accompanied him on his voyage with volumes on physiology and pathology, readings outlined and summarized in the chapter "Forschungen" (research). I will only briefly follow the first trajectory. Initially, Doctor Behrens diagnoses anemia and recommends to Hans that he follow the rules that also apply to the other patients. Then Hans catches a cold and starts to take his temperature on a regular basis (see *Z*, 26 and *M*, 167).

Subsequent visits to the medical cabinet of Doctor Behrens reveal — first through auscultation, then through an X-ray — that he has been infected with tuberculosis, an infection the climate brought to bear again: "'Sie sind ein alter Patient, Castorp, . . . Denn außer den Dämpfungen . . . haben Sie da links oben auch eine Rauhigkeit, die beinahe schon ein Geräusch ist und zweifellos von einer frischen Stelle kommt . . .'" (*Z*, 276–77; "'You are an old patient, Castorp, . . . Because apart from the muffled tones . . . you have some roughness on the upper left, which is almost a rattle and doubtless comes from a fresh area,'" *M*, 178).

The X-ray procedure reveals the interior of the human body in a seemingly immediate way and allows Hans Castorp to access his inner reality visually. Before his own image is captured, he takes a look into his cousin's chest, an experience that anticipates the encounter with his own mortality. This experience also stresses that the medical signs produced by technical means are in need of interpretation, as the disease is nothing but an agglomeration of lines and spots. The irony that characterizes this scene lies less in the questioning of medical language than in the anesthetization of the reader to the cruel realities of disease and diagnostic technology: "Er studierte die Flecke und Linien, das schwarze Gekräusel im inneren Brustraum, während sein Mitspäher nicht müde wurde, Joachims Grabesgestalt und Totenbein zu betrachten, dies kahle Gerüst und

Memento" (*Z*, 332; He studied the spots and lines, the blackish ruffles in the chest cavity while his fellow viewer gazed tirelessly at Joachim's sepulchral form, his dry bones, his bare scaffolding, his gaunt *memento mori*, *M*, 215).

By localizing disease and interpreting it as a correlation of altered tissue in the body, modern medicine gives the experience of death a concrete form that distinguishes it from the experience of mortality known in the tradition of *memento mori*.[17] *Der Zauberberg* is therefore a novel that uses the medical gaze to, as Sara Danius has shown, "cultivate the interior"[18] and make it visible. By gaining access to medical knowledge that bases its statements on clinical signs, Hans learns to inhabit a world in which medicine provides the basis for a new understanding of life. And it is this knowledge — insight in a literal sense — that makes him skeptical when it comes to the battles that Naphta and Settembrini wage over him in the name of ideology.

After his temperature has been measured and found to be high, Hans Castorp has objective evidence that supports his feeling. He tells his cousin that he has been feverish all along. Indeed, habituation to the Alpine climate and altitude does not seem easy, and Hans's stay is accompanied by a permanent sense of excitement that translates into a high temperature. While still on the train that brings him up into the mountains, Hans asks himself if it would not be advisable to ascend at a slower pace and interrupt the voyage in order to acclimatize to the physiologically challenging spheres:

> Vielleicht war es unklug und unzuträglich, daß er, geboren und gewohnt, nur ein paar Meter über dem Meeresspiegel zu atmen, sich plötzlich in diese extremen Gegenden befördern ließ, ohne wenigstens einige Tage an einem Platz von mittlerer Lage verweilt zu haben? (*Z*, 13)
>
> [Was it unwise and unhealthy, perhaps, for him, born only a few feet above sea level and accustomed to breathing that air, to be suddenly transported to such extreme regions without spending at least a few days someplace in between? (*M*, 4)]

High altitudes require a specific adaptation that challenges bourgeois physiology. This challenge marks such heights as the site of a physiological, and by extension a mental, exception.

Once he has arrived, Hans feels his face getting hot. In the ensuing conversation Joachim tells him: "'Manche gewöhnen sich nie'" (*Z*, 24; Some people never get used to it, *M*, 12). From this moment on, "getting used to not getting used to it" is what determines Hans's experience, and acclimatization is one of the most important and widely overlooked leitmotifs of the novel. Acclimatization even serves as the main example introducing the major theoretical chapter on the sense of time. The reflections on variation and immutability, change and stasis, draw on acclimatization as the physiological paradigm of an exceptional period through which the sense of time is renewed and vivified:

> Im Grunde hat es seine merkwürdige Bewandtnis mit diesem Scheinleben an fremdem Orte, dieser — sei es auch — mühseligen Anpassung und Umgewöhnung, welcher man sich beinahe um ihrer selbst willen und in der bestimmten Absicht unterzieht, sie, kaum daß sie vollendet ist, oder doch bald danach, wieder aufzugeben und zum vorherigen Zustand zurückzukehren. . . . Dies ist der Zweck des Orts- und Luftwechsels, der Badereise, die Erholsamkeit der Abwechslung und der Episode. (*Z*, 159 and 160)

> [Ultimately, there is something odd about settling in somewhere new — about the perhaps laborious process of getting used to new surroundings and fitting in, a task we undertake almost for its own sake and with the definite intention of abandoning the place again as soon as it is accomplished, or shortly thereafter and returning to our previous state. . . . That is the reason for every change of scenery and air, for a trip to the shore: the experience of a variety of refreshing episodes. (*M*, 101–2)]

The difficulties of acclimatization that Hans experiences — "'Es fällt mir schwerer, als ich dachte, mich zu akklimatisieren,'" he tells Settembrini (*Z*, 174; I find it much more difficult to get acclimatized than I thought I would, *M*, 111) — do not recede, which is why his recuperation does not come to an end. The initial phase of adaptation never gives way to normalcy. Without the reestablishment of such normalcy, the desired vacation remains ineffective. When Joachim asks about Hans's recuperation, the latter replies:

> Allerdings waren es ja so neuartige Eindrücke hier oben, neuartig in jeder Beziehung, sehr anregend, aber auch anstrengend für den Geist und den Körper, ich habe nicht das Gefühl, mit ihnen schon fertiggeworden zu sein und mich akklimatisiert zu haben, was doch wohl die Vorbedingung aller Erholung wäre. (*Z*, 249)

> [Although there were a lot of novel things to experience up here, novel in every regard, very exciting, but also very taxing to both mind and body, I don't feel that I've quite got used to it all yet and acclimatized myself, although that would be the precondition for any real recuperation. (*M*, 160)]

Acclimatization is a physiological phenomenon in which the psychic and the biological cannot be separated.

In the chapter "Humaniora" the paradox of "getting used to not getting used to it" is acknowledged as such: "Mochte seine Eingewöhnung hier oben nur in der Gewöhnung daran bestehen, daß er sich nicht gewöhnte . . ." (Z, 382; It might well be that getting used to things up here was simply a matter of not getting used to not getting used to them . . ." M, 248). The existential dilemma — according to Behrens an effect of tuberculosis — still plagues the protagonist after years of dwelling in Davos:

> Denn ohnehin stellte die scheinbar so leicht eingehende Atmosphäre strenge Anforderungen an den Herzmuskel, und was Hans Castorp persönlich betraf, so war sein aufgewecktes Wort von der "Gewöhnung daran, daß man sich nicht gewöhnte," in voller Kraft geblieben, und seine Fieberneigung, die Radhamanth von einer feuchten Stelle herleitete, bestand zähe fort. (Z, 713)

> [For although the air seemed to fill the lungs so easily, it made great demands on the heart; and in Hans Castorp's case, his clever remark about "getting used to not getting used" to things was as valid as ever, and his fever, which Rhadamanthus traced to a moist spot, persisted stubbornly. (M, 464)]

The stimulating climate provokes the organism and leads to a permanent irritation in which the inability to reach a homeostasis adequate to the environment is established as normalcy. The renewed activity of the bacteria that remained in his body after a first infection with tuberculosis is the effect of the brisk climate. The episode of transition becomes a permanent state, inducing a physiological pattern that is also the most adequate matrix to describe the formal peculiarity of *Der Zauberberg*. The "Erholsamkeit der Abwechslung und der Episode," (Z, 160; the experience of a variety of refreshing episodes, M, 102), the short voyage, has no marked end and loses its ability to be a pronounced change leading to recuperation from the daily routines. Instead, the work of adaptation becomes permanent and leads to a paradox routine of overexcitation, an ironic commentary on the effectiveness of the cure. The novel calls its final result "Der große Stumpfsinn" (the great petulance).

In more than one regard, the chapter "Schnee" can be seen as a synecdoche of the novel as a whole. It begins as a forbidden adventure born out of the desire for variety in the everyday routine of the sanatorium and forms an episode reflecting on the novel in its entirety. The winter climate does not provide the "meteorologisch[e] Kurmittel, denen die Sphäre ihren Ruf verdankte . . . in dem Umfang, wie der Prospekt es verhieß" (Z, 706; meteorological medicine for which these regions were famous in the quantities promised by the brochure, M, 460). Instead, there is excessive snowfall, the detailed description of which recalls Adalbert Stifter's novella *Bergkristall* (Mountain crystal, 1845/53): "Statt der Sonne jedoch gab es Schnee, Schnee in Massen, so kolossal viel Schnee, wie Hans Castorp in seinem Leben noch nie gesehen" (Z, 708; Instead of sun, there was snow, great, colossal masses of snow, more snow than Hans Castorp had ever seen, M, 461). And this snowfall that restores the world to a state of rare purity makes the inhabitants aware of the "Abenteuerlichkeit und Exzentrizität" (*Z*, 708; bizarrerie and outlandishness *M*, 461, translation modified) of the Alpine sphere. Hans's desire for a "inniger-freier[e] Berührung mit dem schneeverwüsteten Gebirge" (*Z*, 712; a freer, more active, more intense experience of the snowy mountain wilderness, *M*, 464) leads to his acquisition of skis; and, after trying them out a few times, in spite of the "Gewöhnung daran, daß er sich nicht gewöhnte" (*Z*, 713; getting used to not getting used to things, *M*, 464), he leaves Davos for an Alpine adventure.

In the course of this escapade he is caught in a snowstorm, one that he barely survives. He experiences the mountains as a privileged place to perceive the indifference of nature:

> Nein, diese Welt in ihrem bodenlosen Schweigen hatte nichts Wirtliches, sie empfing den Besucher auf eigene Rechnung und Gefahr, sie nahm ihn nicht eigentlich auf, sie duldete sein Eindringen, seine Gegenwart auf eine nicht-geheure, für nichts gutstehende Weise, und Gefühle des still bedrohlichen Elementaren, des nicht einmal Feindseligen, vielmehr des Gleichgültig-Tödlichen waren es, die von ihr ausgingen. (*Z*, 717)

> [No, this world with its fathomless silence did not receive a visitor hospitably. He was an invader who came at his own risk, whose presence was only tolerated in an eerie, foreboding way; and he could sense the menace of mute, elemental forces as they rose up around him — not hostile, but simply indifferent and deadly. (*M*, 467)]

In spite of this indifference, Hans does not give in to the temptation of death, and instead maintains his "Sympathie" with the world and its creatures and their "Würde" (dignity). These characteristics constitute a minimal difference of the human that sets it apart from nature and keeps the question open what the "Stand und Staat des homo Dei" (*Z*, 718–19; state and condition of the *homo dei*, *M*, 468) is without consenting to any particular vision of the human. Even though in the course of his adventure Hans loses orientation and his sense of time — a process analogous to his stay at the Berghof — he perseveres and does not give in to the lure of lying down in the snow. Trying to reach the village again, he ends up wandering in a circle that leads him back to the hut he started from.

The main topic of conversation at the sanatorium is the condition of its patients. Of particular concern are the fever-curve and the so-called Gaffky scale, which indicates the number of bacteria in one's sputum. The patients therefore define the state of their health in "objective" terms, that is with the help of medical technologies such as the thermometer, rather than through their subjective wellbeing. Hans Castorp's continual high temperature and his state of excitement are also a constant topic of conversation between him and his cousin, as well as with other acquaintances. But the novel leaves the causes of the palpitations and high temperature systematically open: it never definitively says whether Hans's perceived ailments derive from an emotional state or a physiological alteration.

After putting his hand on his chest "wie ein Verliebter" (*Z*, 111; like a man in love *M*, 69), Hans reflects on the ambivalence of his state:

> Siehst Du, man hat Herzklopfen, wenn einem eine ganz besondere Freude bevorsteht oder wenn man sich ängstigt, kurz, bei Gemütsbewegungen, nicht? Aber wenn einem das Herz nun ganz von selbst klopft, grundlos und sinnlos und sozusagen auf eigene Hand, das finde ich geradezu unheimlich, versteh mich recht, es ist ja so, als ob der Körper seine eigenen Wege ginge und keinen Zusammenhang mit der Seele mehr hätte. (*Z*, 111)

> [Because, you see, your heart pounds when you're looking forward to some joyous event or if you're afraid — when your emotions are stirred up, isn't that right? But if your heart starts pounding all by itself, for no earthly reason, of its own accord, so to speak, I find that downright bizarre, if you see what I mean. It's as if the body were going off on its own and no longer had any connection to your soul. (*M*, 69)]

The emotion that would have justified and sufficiently motivated the physiological reaction is provided after the fact by Hans's growing desire for Madame Chauchat. This desire — one of the more interesting passions in modern German literature — begins to develop with the noise of the glass door that the slouching Kirghize patient habitually slams shut. The culmination of their relationship is a New Year's Eve spent together, and it has an epilogue when Madame Chauchat returns with Mynheer Peeperkorn after a long absence.

By showing how the motivating emotion is the result or interpretation of a physiological state and not its cause, *Der Zauberberg* reverses the common assumption that psychological reactions induce physical states and shows the primacy of the merely organismic over the psychological:

> Man konnte jetzt nicht mehr sagen, daß es [das Herz] auf eigene Hand, grundlos und ohne Zusammenhang mit der Seele klopfte. . . . eine rechtfertigende Gemütsbewegung ließ sich der exaltierten Körpertätigkeit unschwer unterlegen. Hans Castorp brauchte nur an Frau Chauchat zu denken — und er dachte an sie —, so besaß er zum Herzklopfen das zugehörige Gefühl. (*Z*, 215)

> [One could no longer say that it thudded on its own accord, for no reason, and without any connection to his soul. . . . a justifiable emotion could easily be assigned to his body's overwrought activity. Hans Castorp needed only to think of Frau Chauchat — and he did think of her — and his heart had a suitable emotion to make it pound. (*M*, 138)]

The medical insights into the inner life of his organism that Hans Castrop gains are therefore complemented by the insight into the physiological dimension of love. The two doctors who work at the sanatorium represent two different forms of analysis at work in the novel: one of them, Behrens, reveals the organic interior, its pathological processes of decay, and its micro-processes; the other, Krokowski, ventures to explore the physiological dimensions of psychic life. And not unlike Krokowski, who is called a "Seelenzergliederer" (Z, 20; he dissects the patients' psyche, M, 9) and gives lectures on the different forms of love, the focus of this second investigation of the interior in the novel is amorous. Joachim reports on one of Krokowski's lectures that Hans has missed:

> "Nicht weiter neues . . . Ja, es war die reine Chemie, was er heute verzapfte," ließ Joachim sich widerstrebend herbei, zu berichten. Es handelt sich "dabei" um eine Art von Vergiftung, von Selbstvergiftung des Organismus, habe Dr. Krokowski gesagt. (Z, 286)

> ["Nothing new, really . . . yes, well, he was selling basic chemistry today," Joachim reluctantly and patronizingly reported. It was all about a kind of poisoning, about the organism poisoning itself. (M, 185)]

The Dionysian abyss that opens in *Der Zauberberg* is the physiological reality of life and disease. It is the sanatorium that allows Hans Castrop to access this reality. In the course of his prolonged seven-year stay at the Alpine Berghof, Hans acquires a medical gaze that gives him access to this abyss. At the same time, his own body interacts with the altitude and pushes him to a heightened awareness of the processes he studies. In the immediate vicinity of technologies that turn human life into an assembly of signs for physiological patterns, he begins to perceive life differently. The biographical teleology — Hans's career as an engineer — is interrupted, and although he becomes acquainted with the metaphysical heritage, it is the physiological processes that represent the new image of life he seeks to understand. This is why the young man, who has embraced the profession of a nautical engineer and departs for Davos right after his exams, considers a change of career. To Behrens's question "'Interessieren Sie sich für Physiologie?'" (Are you interested in physiology?), he responds:

> "Sehr! Ja, dafür habe ich mich schon immer im höchsten Grade interessiert. Der menschliche Körper, für den habe ich immer hervorragend viel Sinn gehabt. Manchmal habe ich mich schon gefragt, ob ich nicht Arzt hätte werden sollen, — in gewisser Weise hätte das, glaube ich, nicht schlecht für mich gepaßt. Denn wer sich für den Körper interessiert, der interessiert sich für die Krankheit — namentlich sogar für die —, tut er das nicht?" (Z, 398)

> ["Very much! Yes, I've always taken a great deal of interest in it. The human body — I've always had a singular fondness for it. Sometimes

I've asked myself if I shouldn't have become a doctor. In a certain sense, I think, I would not have done badly at it. Because if a man is interested in the body, he is also interested in illness — particularly in that — isn't he?" (*M*, 258)]

But in the end many professions would have been fitting, and what matters more is that he spends his life in the quest of realities that become readable between the X-rays, the fever-curve, and the charts in which life leaves behind signs that no longer emanate from humanist discourses alone. The palpitations of his heart bring forth a curiosity beyond the human that Hans Castorp follows faithfully. That humanist and Communist-Catholic interpretations — incorporated in Settembrini and Naphta — of this reality try to win back an interpretive sovereignty they lost long ago only underlines the inescapable vitality of the new image of life.[19]

As mentioned above, Hans Castorp remains in the mountains for seven years on the basis of a vague and shifting diagnosis, and returns to the lowlands only when the First World War breaks out and more and more inhabitants of the mountain sanatorium are leaving. He becomes a soldier, and the novel loses him from sight in one of the war's battles. At this point, the battlefields of the plains no longer represent a significant difference to the mountain setting. Instead of returning to the order he left and putting an end to the Alpine "episode," Hans plunges into the chaos of war, in which even the narrator loses his orientation and resorts to deictic gestures instead of maintaining the syntactic order of the narrative, which only gradually regains its orientation:

> Wo sind wir? Was ist das? Wohin verschlug uns der Traum? Dämmerung, Regen und Schmutz, Brandröte des trüben Himmels, der unaufhörlich von schwerem Donner brüllt, die nassen Lüfte erfüllt, zerrissen von scharfem Singen, wütend höllenhundhaft daherfahrendem Heulen, das seine Bahn mit Splittern, Spritzen, Krachen, und Lohen beendet . . . Dort ist ein Wald, aus dem sich farblose Schwärme ergießen, die laufen, fallen und springen. Dort zieht eine Hügelzeile sich vor dem fernen Brande hin. (*Z*, 1080)

> [Where are we? What is that? Where has our dream brought us? Dusk, rain, and mud, fire reddening a murky sky that bellows incessantly with dull thunder, the damp air rent by piercing, singsong whines and raging, onrushing, hellhound howls that end their arc in a splintering, spraying, fiery crash . . . There is a wood spewing drab hordes that run, stumble, jump. There is a line of hills, dark against the distant conflagration whose glow sometimes gathers into fluttering flames. (*M*, 703)]

Although Hans has learned a lot about death and the physiology of life and disease in the mountains, he does not die there. The Alps release him into the flatland, but at a point when the experience of the elevation and the specific insight emerging from a life preoccupied with its own processes has established itself as the only horizon in which he lives. By reducing Hans to a mere speck in the field of forces that constitute a battle, the novel leaves us with an end that affirms his suspicion that life is an assemblage of physiological processes. And yet the fact that readers are not allowed to mourn the protagonist leaves them with the enduring provocation that a human life can disappear and leave nothing behind but the remains of the temporary stability of an assemblage of physiological forces.[20]

Notes

[1] See Thomas Sprecher, *Davos im Zauberberg: Thomas Manns Roman und sein Schauplatz* (Munich: Fink, 1996).

[2] See Thomas Mann, letter of 24 Jul. 1913 to Ernst Bertram, *Briefe I: 1889–1913*, ed. Thomas Sprecher, vol. 21 of the *Große kommentierte Frankfurter Ausgabe* (Frankfurt am Main: Fischer, 2001), 527.

[3] Thomas Mann, *The Magic Mountain*, trans. John E. Woods (New York: Vintage, 1995), 4. Further references to this work are given in the text, using the abbreviation *M* followed by the page number.

[4] Thomas Mann, *Der Zauberberg*, vol. 5 of the *Große kommentierte Frankfurter Ausgabe* (Frankfurt am Main: Fischer, 2002), 12. Further references to this work are given in the text, using the abbreviation *Z*, followed by the page number.

[5] *Der Zauberberg* therefore systematically uncovers an existential dimension outlined in what, according to Michael Neumann's introduction to the critical edition of the novel (see Neumann, "Kommentar," in Thomas Mann, *Der Zauberberg*, 59), is one of the sources of its title, Friedrich Nietzsche's *Die Geburt der Tragödie* (The birth of tragedy, 1872):

> Jetzt öffnet sich uns gleichsam der olympische Zauberberg und zeigt uns seine Wurzeln. Der Grieche kannte und empfand die Schrecken und Entsetzlichkeiten des Daseins: um überhaupt leben zu können, musste er vor sie hin die glänzende Traumgeburt der Olympischen stellen." (Friedrich Nietzsche, *Die Geburt der Tragödie*, in *Sämtliche Werke: Kritische Studienausgabe*, vol. 1 [Munich: dtv/de Gruyter, 1999], 35)
>
> [Now it is as if the Olympian magic mountain had opened and revealed its roots to us. The Greeks knew and felt the terror and horror of existence. That he might endure this terror at all he had to interpose between himself and life the radiant dream-birth of the Olympians. (Nietzsche, *The Birth of Tragedy and The Case of Wagner*, trans. Walter Kaufmann [New York: Vintage, 1967], 42)]

The Olympic world thus opens onto its roots, the terror of existence. In an analogous movement, *Der Zauberberg* explores the Dionysian depths that lie hidden beneath the aesthetic surface of life. In the decay of body tissue caused by tuberculosis, the novel finds the equivalent of a tragic experience. It is this terror that necessitated the invention of the Greek gods.

[6] For more on this function of the novel, see Beat Rüttimann, "Die Lungentuberkulose im Zauberberg," in *Auf dem Weg zum Zauberberg: Die Davoser Literaturtage 1996*, ed. Thomas Sprecher (Frankfurt am Main: Klostermann, 1997), 95–109; Thomas Sprecher, *Davos im Zauberberg*; and Vera Pohland, *Das Sanatorium als literarischer Ort: Medizinische Institution und Krankheit als Medien der Gesellschaftskritik und der Existenzanalyse* (Frankfurt am Main: Peter Lang, 1984), 9.

[7] Thomas Mann, *Buddenbrooks: Verfall einer Familie*, ed. Eckhard Heftrich, vol. 1 of the *Große kommentierte Frankfurter Ausgabe* (Frankfurt am Main: Fischer, 2002), 400. Further references to this work are given in the text, using the abbreviation *B* followed by the page number.

[8] Thomas Mann, *Buddenbrooks: The Decline of a Family*, trans. John E. Woods (New York: Vintage, 1994), 355. Further references to this work are given in the text, using the abbreviation *D* followed by the page number.

[9] See Christian Virchov, "Das Sanatorium als Lebensform: Über einschlägige Erfahrungen Thomas Manns," in *Literatur und Krankheit im Fin-de-Siècle: Thomas Mann im europäischen Kontext*, ed. Thomas Sprecher (Frankfurt am Main: Klostermann, 2002), 183–85.

[10] Hermann Brehmer, *Die chronische Lungenschwindsucht und Tuberkulose der Lunge: Ihre Ursache und ihre Heilung* (Berlin: Enslin, 1869), 91 and 139. My translation.

[11] Brehmer, *Die chronische Lungenschwindsucht und Tuberkulose der Lunge*, 142.

[12] The best recent history of Davos can be found in Susan Barton, *Healthy Living in the Alps: The Origins of Winter Tourism in Switzerland, 1860–1914* (Manchester: Manchester UP, 2008), 19–36.

[13] This is the thesis of Barton, *Healthy Living in the Alps*.

[14] See Claude Reichler, "Le paysage entre convention et envoûtement dans le *Zauberberg* de Thomas Mann," *Colloquium helveticum* 38 (2007): 221.

[15] See Reichler, "Le paysage entre convention et envoûtement."

[16] This section summarizes a part of the Mann chapter in Johannes Türk, *Die Immunität der Literatur* (Frankfurt am Main: Fischer, 2011).

[17] This is why interpretations that try to read the scene as a continuation of a classic topos seem to miss the specific modernity of the novel. See most recently Rodney Stenning Edgcombe, "Mann's *Zauberberg* and Elisabeth Eyberg's 'Röntgenfoto': A Variation on a Topos," *Germanic Notes and Reviews* 1, no. 41 (2010): 30–37.

[18] Cf. Sara Danius, *The Senses of Modernism: Technology, Perception, and Aesthetics* (Ithaca, NY: Cornell UP, 2002), 55–90. Danius analyzes how the novel, by using medical technology such as the X-ray, redefines the perception of the human body.

[19] This layer of the novel has for a long time been neglected or only accepted as one of its many dimensions, because interpreters found it difficult not to share in

the humanist vision offered by Mann. It is also the result of reading *Der Zauberberg* as a novel of ideas in which the plot and the descriptions are secondary and only matter insofar as they can be read as exemplifying the problems of spiritual nature.

[20] Some of this essay draws on or summarizes parts of two chapters — "Der immune Ort als Privileg der Geographie" and "Stille Feiung: Die immunologische Inititation des *Zauberbergs*" — of my book *Die Immunität der Literatur*.

"The Essence of the Alpine World Is Struggle": Strategies of *Gesundung* in Arnold Fanck's Early Mountain Films

Wilfried Wilms

"Die Filme," Siegfried Kracauer claimed in 1927,

sind der Spiegel der bestehenden Gesellschaft. . . . Um die heutige Gesellschaft zu erforschen, hätte man also den Erzeugnissen ihrer Filmkonzerne die Beichte abzunehmen. . . . In der unendlichen Reihe der Filme kehrt eine begrenzte Zahl typischer Motive immer wieder; sie zeigen an, wie die Gesellschaft sich selber zu sehen wünscht. Der Inbegriff der Filmmotive ist zugleich die Summe der gesellschaftlichen Ideologien, die durch die Deutung dieser Motive entzaubert werden.

[Films are the mirror of the prevailing society. . . . In order to investigate today's society, one must listen to the confessions of the products of its film industries. . . . In the endless sequence of films, a limited number of typical themes recur again and again; they reveal how society wants to see itself. The quintessence of these film themes is at the same time the sum of the society's ideologies, whose spell is broken by means of interpretation of the themes.][1]

As a genre that comes to the fore in the 1920s, the successful German *Bergfilm* lends itself to an analysis or critique of ideology according to the criteria set by one of Weimar Germany's leading cultural critics. A number of possible lines of inquiry present themselves: What does the classic *Bergfilm* confess vis-à-vis Germany's postwar society? What are the archetypal motives present in a transient genre that, generally speaking, begins with Arnold Fanck's first mountain film with a dramatic plot, *Der Berg des Schicksals* (The mountain of destiny, 1923/24), and ends with his cinematic version of the first ascent of Mont Blanc in 1786, *Der König vom Montblanc* (The king of Montblanc; also *Der ewige Traum*) and with Luis Trenker's *Der verlorene Sohn* (The prodigal son), both released in 1934?[2] If the movies, in particular as an industry of consumption and distraction, merely reflect and play into the audience's (sub)conscious desires, as Kracauer claims, we ought to wonder what the audiences perceived or judged as attractive, honorable, moral, strong, appropriate, or as its direct opposites. We can investigate what idols and ideals the *Bergfilm* projects onto the silver screen, and what demons the genre castigates. Recognizable conflicts and models appear in tandem with packaged ideologies in the projected solutions or disasters.

Two decades after his perceptive analyses of Weimar Germany, Kracauer provided an examination of Weimar cinema in general, and of the *Bergfilm* in particular. Not surprisingly given its title, Kracauer's seminal study *From Caligari to Hitler* (1947) linked the mountain film of the 1920s and early 1930s primarily to the looming Third Reich. The mountain film's oft-depicted heroism, Kracauer now claimed, was "rooted in a mentality kindred to the Nazi spirit." "The idolatry of glaciers and rocks was symptomatic of an antirationalism on which the Nazis could capitalize" — a rationale since then shared and propagated by many critics.[3] More recent research has broadened our understanding of the many facets the mountain film offers. Eric Rentschler, for instance, recognizes that Kracauer (and others in his wake) overemphasized how mountain films pointed ahead to the Nazi movement and at the same time underestimated how they functioned within the Weimar Republic. Rentschler focuses much of his analysis on the mountain film's gender economies.[4] Nancy P. Nenno discusses the genre as a self-conscious appeal to, and reflection on, the history and practices of tourism at a time of rapid urban modernization.[5]

In the present essay I read the *Bergfilm* as a product that owes much of its beginnings to the experience, (in)visibility, and trauma of a lost war as well as the ensuing affect of defeat that plagued Germany's first experiment with democracy well beyond the critical years of 1918 to 1923. In the following, I will concentrate on three early examples of the *Bergfilm*, all of them products of the inventor of the genre, Dr. Arnold Fanck. I will discuss *Im Kampf mit dem Berge* (Struggle with the mountain, 1921), *Der Berg des Schicksals*, and *Der heilige Berg* (The holy mountain, 1925/26) as vehicles of aesthetic and discursive strategies of *Gesundung* aimed at the individual, (mass) society, and the German nation as a whole.[6] Anton Kaes's recent exemplary study, *Shell Shock Cinema* (2009), argues compellingly that "the experience of trauma became Weimar's historical unconscious."[7] In his analysis of the aesthetic stratagems of some of Weimar's most recognized films, Kaes reverses the pre-fascistic emphasis that Kracauer promoted in the 1940s for an audience eager to understand the Hitler phenomenon. Kaes's post-traumatic focus also guides my reflections on a genre that centers on a remarkably coherent set of themes: exploration and triumph, survival and perseverance, loss and downfall, purification and renewal, death and sacrifice, fraternal masculinity and camaraderie — all notions that determined the front experience of the modern soldier fighting the First World War. Postwar Germany's culture and affect of defeat provided the perfect breeding ground for a film genre that exhibits psychological mechanisms for coming to terms with defeat.[8] We can look at German (speaking) climbers and explorers, eerily similar to Ernst Jünger's worker-soldier in their often passionate yet ice-cold demeanor, as "avengers of national honor,"[9] who perform rituals of mobilization and restoration for an excited German audience bogged down by defeat and massive loss of life in the Great War. The films provide codes of conduct for a society in poor health — for a society scarred by the bitter wounds of war.

Gesundung through Struggle and the Sublime: *Im Kampf mit dem Berge*

By January 1919 seven million men in uniform had been demobilized. For some two million German soldiers this demobilization meant nothing, because they were already dead. A further 4.2 million returned home wounded, many of them missing limbs or facial parts, blind, or shell-shocked. Physically and emotionally scarred by the world's first industrial war, they became the enduring aide memoire of both the national euphoria that accompanied the soldiers' departure in August of 1914 and the collective despair that ensued later in the war and upon their return.[10] Virtually every family was affected one way or another by the slaughter. The wounds of war, according to Eric Weitz, were visible "everywhere on the streets of Germany's cities and towns in the postwar decade."[11] Some injuries, however, were not as readily discernible. High among these we have to consider the shame, humiliation, and loss of confidence that accompanied the defeat and disintegration of the Wilhelmine Empire, including the crisis of masculinity it triggered.[12] The collapse of the authoritative social voices and patterns that had hitherto provided a mooring pushed the door wide open for diagnoses of decline, disease, and degeneration, and most of these attestations ultimately grappled with explanations of defeat. They ranged from the more masculine "stab-in-the-back" myth to the quasi-feminized scenario of an epidemic that had sapped the nation's will to fight. Both the back-stabbing traitor as well as the contamination had their origins in a bygone society that was now recognized on both the Right and Left (and of course for different ideological reasons) as inauthentic, mercantile, superficial, and materialistic. In short, defeat was increasingly understood as the direct result of the empire's frivolity and hollow pomp.

With the attestation of disease and decline came, of course, the recipes for recuperation. The average "faint-hearted" German on the home front, "the pale, frightened, oppressed young people with no self-confidence" who allowed the nation to experience what Schivelbusch calls "one of the most unheroic capitulations in military history"[13] had to be reeducated. And if they were too old, then at least the next generation had to be reached and trained. The Alps, and by extension the *Bergfilm*, were mobilized as vital players in the gradual return to German strength and heroic dedication, the nation's *Gesundung*. The mountains were to serve as a corrective and as an agent of purification for a nation considered to have gone off course. Some of the mountains' tonic lay simply in their sublime natural settings, in particular in their "Entferntheit vom Leben," (detachment from life) as Georg Simmel had already put it in 1905.[14] The mountains, and in particular the *Firnlandschaft* (regions of permanent snow and ice), offered the antidote to modern urban bourgeois life that appeared hectic and disenchanted, random and oppressive — according to Simmel a form of existence devoid of individualism, heroism, purpose, and redemption. A first form of national *Gesundung* thus appears immediately after the war as a recommended escape into the Alpine world, in the (Kantian) hope that the icy peaks might evoke sublime ideas in the one who perceives it and thereby trigger a stirring of its soul.

For Simmel, the majestically towering rocks, the glittering walls of ice, and the crowning snow "der keine Beziehung mehr zu den Niederungen der Erde hat" (which is no longer connected in any way to the lower regions of the earth) are symbols of the transcendental. They guide the soul's gaze upward toward the Absolute, an experience that Simmel sees particularly at work in the firn. The observer, unable to give this Absolute a containing form, instead finds himself "verwebt" (woven into) the landscape's atmosphere.

The ocean, according to Simmel, stands in stark contrast to this Alpine encounter. Generally experienced as a symbol of life, the ocean is marked by its "ewig formwandelnde Bewegung, die Unergründlichkeit seiner Tiefen, der Wechsel zwischen Glätte und Aufgewühltsein, sein Sichverlieren am Horizont und das ziellose Spiel seines Rhythmus" (eternally form-changing movement, unfathomable depths, the ebb and flow between tranquility and uproar; by losing itself on the horizon and by the aimless play of its rhythm) — qualities that, he claims, enable the soul to project the awareness of its own existence into the vastness and flux of this environment. While the ocean, too, can thus provide liberation and redemption from the mere relative quantity of life itself, it does so from the opposite direction than do the mountains — as Simmel puts it, "statt aus der stilisierten Fülle der Leidenschaft des Lebens vielmehr aus einer Ferne von ihm" (not via the artificial richness of life's passion, but rather through a distancing from it).[15]

In the mountains, or better yet in the uppermost regions of snow and ice, Simmel finds an existence removed from all dynamic forces of life, in particular those that communicate temporality and decay. Here life is woven into something that is more peaceful and permanent, more pure and elevated than the life we know. And with reference to the art historian Wilhelm Worringer, his contemporary, he concludes: "Das Meer wirkt durch Einfühlung des Lebens, die Alpen durch Abstraktion vom Leben" (The ocean's effect lies in its becoming one with life, that of the Alps in their abstraction from life). Simmel's juxtaposition of the respective qualities of mountains and the ocean will concern us again below in our discussion of *Der heilige Berg*.

Seemingly untouched by the unraveling of time, the *Firn* zone appears as the absolute ahistorical landscape, severing all associations with life's temporality and relativity. The regions of snow and ice are sublime not because they crown the Alpine landscape as depicted by Romantic painters; they are sublime only where they are entirely "fertig" (complete). And by that Simmel means disconnected from anything below. Only when the valley floors have vanished completely "stellt sich die reine Beziehung nach oben her" (does the unadulterated connection to what lies above present itself). This experience is a quasi-religious one that centers on redemption and deliverance and manifests itself in a general "Gefühl des Erlöstseins" (feeling of salvation) and in a "Gegenüber-vom-Leben" (being opposite to life itself).

Simmel's laborious effort to capture verbally the sublime experience that awaits the climber in the high Alpine regions unwittingly describes the aesthetics that made Fanck's early *Bergfilm* such a phenomenal success.[16] Fanck attempted to capture the Alpine sublime (and beauty) with a new visual language in order to give it form, to represent the non-representable. But already in one of Fanck's earliest cinematic explorations of high Alpine regions, *Im Kampf mit dem Berge: Eine Alpensymphonie in Bildern* (An Alpine symphony in images), the mountain seemingly opposes the climber; indeed, the latter finds himself battling it. It premiered on 22 September 1921 in Berlin's Tauentzien-Palast and carried the added title "1. Teil: In Sturm und Eis" (First part: In storm and ice). *Kampf mit dem Berge* captivated the audience with breathtaking images of the Valais Alps and the area around the Matterhorn and Monte Rosa. Filmed above 13,000 feet, the film depicts and celebrates the world of near-impenetrable seracs and snowy, storm-blasted peaks, a landscape through which two tiny figures work their way to the top of Monte Rosa. The ascent is represented as a dogged search for a safe passage. Repeatedly the climbers have to turn back. Progress in this world of snow and ice is slow and arduous. In fact, for most of the time the audience is left without any sense of clear direction and cannot recognize where the protagonists are relative to the summit or the hut they had left earlier that morning. Frequently the action on the screen itself or the accompanying intertitles make the audience aware of the dangers that surround the two lonely mountaineers, dangers that they will have to overcome if they want to reach their target. Another quality of the film is undeniably its instructional component: it takes great care to display various mountaineering skills, ranging from general rope work to rappelling, anchoring, navigating crevasses, ice pick and crampon techniques in close-up. Surviving in this majestic yet life-threatening landscape requires skill, control, and tenacity, in particular when an unexpected storm forces the mountaineers to take refuge in a rock and ice cave where they huddle together for the night. The intertitle explains that the ascent requires hours upon hours of labor, chiseling steps into the ice on which the climbers work their way up meter by meter. But ultimately there is triumph. The battle with the mountain is finally won when they approach the peak. The last steps are presented after an intertitle reads "Ein Gang durch die Luft" (a walk through the air). And indeed, the next shots show the dark silhouettes of the two climbers on a gentle white slope with nothing but clouds beneath them. The grandiose images perfectly illustrate Simmel's ruminations about the region's complete detachment from a world below. All connections to time and space seem severed; the world below does not exist. What is left is Simmel's unadulterated connection to what lies above.

The glowing reviews Fanck's film garnered bespeak the audience's receptiveness and its fascination with the purity of the Alpine world. Various critics speak of a deeply moved and enraptured audience that applauded enthusiastically. The film, writes a critic of the *Lichtbildbühne*, "erschüttert und ergreift nun im Tauentzienpalast die Herzen der Zuschauer" (deeply stirs and captures the hearts of the audiences in the Tauentzienpalast) and shows "den Triumph des menschlichen Mutes" (the triumph of man's courage). Similarly, in Berlin's *Sportblatt*: "Wie erschütternd . . ., wie hinreißend . . ., wie klar und rein und groß da oben in diesen sturmdurchtobten und sonnendurchglühten Regionen alles ist" (how deeply stirring, how captivating, how pure and pristine and great everything is up there in these regions ravaged by storms and set brightly aglow by the sun). Numerous references stress human triumph and the pleasure of its consumption.[17] Particularly the *Film-Kurier* accentuates the pedagogical importance of an education toward national recovery rooted in the sublime and in struggle, to be carried out by the next generation:

> Die photographische Festhaltung der alpinen Majestät, die nahezu verworfen anmutende Überheblichkeit der schwachen menschlichen Kreatur über die Wolken hinaus, die stolze Siegesempfindung des zitternden Menschenherzens, wenn es viertausend Meter über allen grauen Sorgen pochen darf, — das alles sind . . . läuternde Emanationen unverfälschter Erhabenheit. . . . Ein Film ist das, der an düsterer und klärender Eindringlichkeit zur Weihe und Einkehr zwingt, der eine Predigt ist an die Menschheit in den Städten — und eine Andachtsstunde für die Jugend und die, die zu ihr gehören.[18]
>
> [The way the film captures the Alpine majesty; the seemingly depraved haughtiness of the puny human creature above the clouds; the proud

sense of triumph of the trembling human heart when it is allowed to beat four thousand meters above all common uncertainties — all that is the ... purifying emanation of a genuine sublimity. ... It is a film that pushes us toward solemnity and reflection with gloomy and elucidating urgency. It is a sermon that addresses mankind in the cities — and it is an hour of prayer for the youth and for those that belong to it.]

The reason for this emphasis on struggle might very well lie in the militarization of the Alps during and after the Great War.[19] Gustav Müller's 1922 essay "Die Berge und ihre Bedeutung für den Wiederaufbau des deutschen Volkes" (The mountains and their meaning for the recovery of the German nation), which appeared in the *Zeitschrift des Deutschen und Österreichischen Alpenvereins*, can be considered representative of this trend.[20] Whereas Simmel, around the turn of the twentieth century, attempted to capture or perhaps even safeguard the sublime experience of Alpine grandeur in the face of developing mass tourism,[21] writers like Müller had to come to terms with different demons. His were not only modernity per se, whose values he wholeheartedly rejected as soulless; more particularly, Müller's demons stemmed from postwar life in defeat. As the title of his essay suggests, the rebuilding of the German nation takes center stage. Müller sets out to identify what precisely the mountains had to offer in this process of national *Gesundung*. Most of his musings seem directly inspired by Simmel and others; for instance, the promised elevation of man's spirit to the eternal, unalterable, and unrivaled greatness and power that await the Alpine visitor. Other aspects seem to be more his own (albeit shared by many in the 1920s); for instance, his fervent derision of life in the modern metropolis, where everything is "überintelligent" (2; overly intelligent) and where "Hingabe an das Edle um des Edlen willen" (2; devotion to what is noble for nobility's sake) are lost along with "höheres Menschentum" (2; higher humanity). While Müller deems himself at the height of reflection he is of course only sowing the ominous seeds of a cultural criticism that will be harvested by the National Socialist Party in the decade to follow. He scoffs at the so-called ideals of his contemporaries, who pursue economic advantages and sensual pleasures, both of which he perceives to be indicators of a rotting culture. It comes as little surprise that the mountain climber is stylized as the Other of modernity's decay. The climber's heart, Müller writes, seeks to escape the "Moderdünste einer faulenden Kultur" (3; smell of putrefaction that accompanies a rotting culture). "Der Ekel vor der Hohlheit ... und Leere der Zivilisation läßt uns fliehen. Wir wollen ... wirkliche Menschen sein" (3; disgusted with the hollowness and emptiness of civilization, we seek escape. We want to be authentic people).

It is the little word "heute" (today) that betrays how much of Müller's position is rooted in his personal sense of defeat living in a Weimar Germany deeply traumatized by the lost war and the punitive Treaty of Versailles. "Today" appears in a number of crucial passages in his text. For

Müller, too, the sublime has its merits in the recovery of the German nation. To become aware of the presence of the eternal and infinite is an invaluable advantage today, he writes, because "solche Erkenntnis bedeutet richtige Einschätzung des eigenen Ichs" (5; such an understanding means the correct appraisal of one's Self). However, being in the presence of the Absolute does not adequately capture the essence of the mountains and their instructional potential for Müller. Their lure for the climber, as well as their pedagogical value for Germany's national rejuvenation, lies elsewhere. For him the essence of the mountains is struggle, and their educational worth rests ultimately in embracing that supposed truth: "Kampf ist überall in den Bergen. . . . Das Wesen der Bergwelt ist Kampf. . . . Wir suchen den Kampf und freuen uns, ihn in den Bergen zu finden" (7; struggle is everywhere in the mountains. . . . The essence of the Alpine world is struggle. . . . We seek the battle and are glad to find it in the mountains). *Gesundung* for "today's" mankind, softened by civilization and an effeminate political system — and Müller leaves no doubt that in 1922 he is writing as a German for Germans — thus means nothing less than the creation of a new human type in and through struggle. "Hätte unser Volk nur weniges von der Zähigkeit, der Kampfgeduld und der Kampfkraft der alpinen Pflanzenwelt, es stünde anders mit ihm *und nichts hätte es beugen können*" [my emphasis] (7; *nothing could have bent our Volk if it only had a little of the Alpine flora's tenacity, its perseverance, and its energy to struggle on*). Only when the German people, "ein krankes Volk" (8; a sick nation), rediscover the duty and value of struggle for struggle's sake "nur dann werden wir Deutsche uns wieder ein großes Volk nennen dürfen und unbesiegbar sein" (8–9; only then will we Germans again be permitted to call ourselves a great nation, and only then will we become unconquerable).

It thus seems that an early "nature film" like Fanck's *Im Kampf mit dem Berge*, outwardly apolitical in its display of nature's designs and forces, resonated with the Weimar audiences at least in part because it was able to stir emotions that were acutely rooted in, or permeated by, trauma and defeat. The mountains (and by extension those who successfully navigated their challenges or perished while trying) served as a corrective and purification for a nation in need of renewal. The pristine snowscapes, whether experienced in person or on the screen, might very well have had the capacity to cleanse a dirtied and deficient society mired in greed, corruption, and decadence. What for the conservative nationalists and revanchists became the clichéd baptism by fire, a rite of passage mysterious to those on the home front, the mountain films reinvent in the form of an icy sacrament.[22] In nearly all the mountain films that follow, the protagonists have to pass through ice, snow, and storm on their journey to *Gesundung*.[23] And depending on their conduct, they will either emerge ennobled and hardened, or they will die.[24]

It is difficult to ascertain how conscious Fanck was of the inherent strategies of *Gesundung* that his films entailed. Yet shortly before his death in 1974 Fanck himself claimed that he was struck hard by the negative verdict of a Wurttemberg film office that deemed his Greenland film *S.O.S. Eisberg* (1933) unsuitable for the youth of the newly established Federal Republic of Germany: "Daß ein Film von mir nicht für Jugend geeignet sein solle — ein solches amtliches Zeugnis traf mich besonders hart, weil ich mein ganzes Filmschaffen weitgehend für die Jugend gedacht hatte. Für ihre Ertüchtigung im Kampf gegen Naturgewalten" (That one of my films was supposed to be inappropriate for young people — such an official judgment hit me especially hard since I had intended all my cinematic work by and large for young people. For their training in their struggle against the forces of nature).[25] In the years that followed *Kampf mit dem Berge*, Fanck would make numerous mountain films that transported the audience to the sublime regions of Alpine snow and ice. Increasingly, however, he would experiment with dramatic scenarios that were as much a concession to the audience's need for entertainment and tragedy as they were vehicles to engage further with the trauma of war and the hope for redemption.[26]

Gesundung through Revanche and Affective Stabilization: *Der Berg des Schicksals* and *Der heilige Berg*

The next films by Fanck provide two variations or strategies of recovery. *Der Berg des Schicksals* (1923/24) became Fanck's first Alpine feature film; it centers on individual and national *Gesundung* by means of generational revanche.[27] Two years later, with *Der heilige Berg*, the audience was offered another model of *Gesundung* — one that might best be described as an emotional healing of the film's protagonist in the form of an internal affective stabilization.[28]

Der Berg des Schicksals tells a story of redemption. Obsessed with reaching the top of the majestic Guglia del Diavolo, Tyrol's best climber ("Der Bergsteiger," portrayed by Hannes Schneider) ultimately loses his life in his single-minded pursuit of his goal to be the first to conquer the mountain's steep rock face. Unable to control his infatuation, he eventually falls to his death, leaving behind his wife (Erna Morena), young son, and aging mother (Frida Richard). Many years later, his son, now grown up, repeats his father's quest, despite the fact that he (Luis Trenker in his first role) had vowed (at his mother's request) never to attempt the mountain. At the height of the three-act drama it will be up to the son to rescue his childhood playmate and future wife, Hella, who herself has been inexplicably drawn to the phallus-shaped Guglia and gets trapped on this mountain that seems so deeply woven into the family's fate. In the midst of a violent thunderstorm, and with the blessing of his mother, the son not only reaches the peak but also successfully descends from it, rescuing Hella. As a result, he tames the demons that have haunted his family for so long.

Various aspects of Fanck's first feature allow us to read this *Bergfilm* as an allegorical commentary on the affect of defeat and the yearning for triumph in revanche. The dramatic structure of the father's repeated attempts to scale the overhang — "sein Berg" (his mountain) is evocative of the pointless back-and-forth movements of soldiers of later war films and their depiction of trench warfare. Traumatized by his repeated failure to ascend, a peculiar stationary mobility the film captures cinematically, the battle with the mountain enters the home of the family; in fact, it enters the bed he shares with his wife, in the form of nightmares, as we hear his wife explain to a friend. The father's harrowing obsession with the Guglia remains unexplained and devoid of any rationale — unless, of course, we pay attention to the many visual hints the film has in store for us with regard to the father's self-esteem and masculinity. Repeatedly, and at critical narrative junctures, the Guglia is placed into the frame as a massive phallus that towers over the family, in particular the father. His self-worth is inextricably linked to scaling the mountain. In the first act, after an initial foray up the face, which ends with the father yelling at the mountain and angrily shaking his fist at it, we see him at the open window of his home. Spellbound, he stares at the pillar that reaches into the sky. It is *his* mountain, and he seems destined to achieve triumph, yet it remains unattainable to him. He has his back to his wife, who approaches him from behind, caressing his hair in an attempt to comfort him, but he is unreceptive and absent. The next scene shows him standing by the door, still staring at the mountain, his wife sunk on her knees with her eyes closed, while she clutches his arm. The audience sees what he sees: a close-up of the ever-luring, ever-challenging dome-shaped mountain. Almost the entire second act is dedicated to his final attempts to scale the Guglia, emphasizing his single-minded determination to either succeed or die trying. Ultimately, when he falls to his death, nature comments on it with thunder and lightning. Close-ups of his tiring grip on the overhanging rock capture his imminent demise. Despite his superhuman efforts, he cannot keep the promise he had given his wife in a preceding departure scene: that his strong hands would hold on to whatever they have in their grip. It will be up to the next generation to honor and redeem his promise.

The third and final act establishes the youth as the tool through which deliverance can be had. The character of Hella evokes the *Wandervogel* movement. Exuberant, close to nature, and a climber herself, she introduces the possibility of a different future gender dynamic. The film juxtaposes the two generations in a sequence of shot/counter-shot. One set of frames shows young Trenker and his female counterpart climbing toward each other on the steep rock face, Hella in shorts, her hair flying wildly in the wind, both of them playfully sharing the same passion and seemingly in tune with their natural surroundings. The opposing set of frames shows mother and grandmother at home in their traditional female garb; with their hair in a bun, they are sitting together at the table, reading and knitting.[29] "Das wilde Mädel" (the wild girl) is nevertheless to the liking of the mother, as an intertitle indicates. But Hella seems in need of the heroic deed. It is her improper teasing "Bist du feige?" (Are you a coward?) regarding her friend's refusal to attempt the mountain, and in particular her immature and ill-prepared effort to try it herself, that sets in motion the required rescue (and near death) of all involved. Her Siegfried-like friend, implored to rescue her by Hella's worried father with the words "Du bist der Einzige, der hinauf könnte!" (You are the only one who could make it to the top!), accomplishes the deed after his mother permits him to break his oath. It is here that the film reveals most visibly its narrative organization around a generational (and by extension national) *Gesundung* by means of redemption. "Wenn du durch deine Kunst das Mädchen rettest," his mother says, "hatte das Sterben deines Vaters einen Sinn" (If you can save the girl by means of your art, the death of your father had meaning). The associations that such a line delivered in a German movie theater during the first half of the twentieth century must have had, a theater frequented by more than the occasional postwar widow and orphan, do not need to be explained. A little later, while awaiting the outcome of the daring rescue mission, she calmly reassures her own mother-in-law: "Was der Vater erstrebte, wird der Sohn vollenden" (What the father strove for, the son will complete). When the son finally battles his way to the top of the Guglia, the intertitle explains that he is now "auf dem Gipfel, der seines Vaters Sehnsucht war" (on the peak that was his father's yearning).

The next generation is thus identified as the stronger and healthier one, but also as the one that carries within itself the calling for, and promise of, future triumph — a new zenith. This generation is superior not only in a physical sense; in fact, the son is not superhuman but succeeds in part because of the new climbing techniques and tools that he uses, such as ropes and pitons. The film highlights their implementation with several close-ups during the last act. However, he is healthier first and foremost emotionally. He does not betray any of the irrational and obsessive qualities that ultimately killed his father, never mind the latter's chivalrous (or shall we say Langemarckian?) purity regarding the Guglia. This generation, while strong, is also fully functional and more self-controlled. The taming of Hella is shown as a key ingredient for keeping the future family intact and functioning. Both the grandmother (who pushed her son to succeed or die trying) and Hella are female figures depicted as motivated by questionable forces. The remaining moments of the film then also limit the next generation's emancipation by literally reining in Hella. During the rescue she is shown as clearly inferior in physical strength, skill, and will compared with her friend. When the latter, after reaching the top of the Guglia, finally arrives on the ledge where she had been helplessly trapped, he towers above her and orders her down the mountain. "Mach, daß du hinunterkommst!" (Now see to it that you get down!). Her morose expression leaves no doubt that she had overextended herself in her desire to be like her hyper-masculine dragon-slayer friend.[30] Should her strength be elsewhere? Should she heed her father's earlier request and stop her infatuation with the mountains? While we see a powerful Trenker downclimb, Hella is struggling, repeatedly hanging in the rope that Trenker holds in his vice-like grip. When they finally reach the bottom, he is shown standing with Hella kneeling before him, and they are holding hands. The image was meant to assure Weimar's audiences that a new order and stability between man, woman, and nature had been found.

In light of the above discussion, I will conclude this analysis by briefly considering Fanck's next *Bergfilm*, the commercially available and thus better known *Der heilige Berg*. With the appearance of Leni Riefenstahl as the dancer Diotima, the triumvirate of the German *Bergfilm* would be complete. In the coming years Fanck, Trenker, and Riefenstahl would expand the genre in various directions.[31] In the mid-1920s, however, the strategies of individual and national *Gesundung* seemingly concentrate on undisciplined gender economies that manifestly threaten any future health of postwar German society.

In his piercing analysis of the gender dynamics of Fanck's *Bergfilm*, Rentschler observes that female players "represent and embody a spirit potentially inimical to male images, be they Fanck's imposing vistas or the inner landscapes of his heroes. . . . Mountains and women represent . . . unpredictable and autonomous natural forces that attract and overwhelm." Understood as a disruptive energy that sidetracks her male audiences to the point of death, the dancing Diotima (Leni Riefenstahl), representing the forces of the ocean, has to undergo a rite of passage best described as an act of exorcism.[32] Rentschler determines correctly that one aspect of the mountain film's gender economy addresses the crisis of masculinity that accompanied the lost war in the years that followed. The analysis of *Der Berg des Schicksals* has already made obvious the interconnections between mountains and the climbers' (sexual) identity, self-worth, and possible redemption. *Der heilige Berg* lays further emphasis on what Rentschler calls the genre's "inherently gendered quality," putting on display patterns that ultimately enact "male fantasies of a shattered and distraught postwar nation."[33] In the end, such an analysis criticizes the female as the unruly and disquieting force jeopardizing a higher male mission rooted in the harmonious bond between all men. Reading Diotima as the *Bergfilm's* version of a femme fatale rooted in male projection is undoubtedly correct; postwar Germany's dialogue on gender provides the wider socio-cultural frame. I would suggest, however, that we complicate this notion and investigate the interplay of male and female presented in the *Bergfilm* further, in order to appreciate which aspects of postwar recuperation might have been addressed in this film. One such *Gesundung* clearly targets the female dancer Diotima, who openly yearns for the male gaze and the attention of our climbing comrades Robert and young Vigo, thereby setting in motion their confused and fatal quest for the murderous north face of Santo. Her flirtatious demeanor and generous attention to the other sex, whether ultimately a misunderstanding or simply a lack of restraint on her part, preordain her to be identified as responsible for the ensuing dilemma. Once it is already too late, Robert's mother asks her: "Was one man not enough for you?" The customary reading interprets the icy death of Robert and Vigo on the mountain, in particular Robert's unwillingness to cut the rope that links them ("Vigo — I would never do anything to harm you!"), as the promotion of a future *Gesundung* through comradeship and self-sacrifice. This interpretation implies a reaffirmation and the promised, or at least demanded, anachronistic return of a hyper-masculine bond rooted in the male fantasies of the fabled front community. In particular the last intertitle, if read as a moral lesson for Weimar Germany, could support such a reading: "Above it all looms a Holy Mountain, a symbol of the greatest values humanity can embrace — fidelity — truth — loyalty — faith."[34]

However, we ought to ask why Diotima's rather innocent actions can so easily bewilder and derail Robert (played by Luis Trenker; fig. 1). In fact, his action — to throw himself at Santo's north face and to drag his friend Vigo along — is utterly irrational and even irresponsible. His entire character is designed, I would argue, not to be adored but rather to be looked at skeptically. There is something dysfunctional and unheroic about Robert that requires a surprising strategy of *Gesundung* — one that can be described as a necessary internal affective stabilization pertaining in particular to the male. Robert's acute collapse of self-worth upon finding his friend Vigo in Diotima's lap — with all that follows — lies in his inability to function in the social world of others. He lacks the tools to regulate his emotions regarding the other sex largely as a direct result of his introspective quest high up in the mountains above everyone else. His mother even warns him, pointing out repeatedly that he ought not to seek gods (in and through the mountains) but people, expressing her doubt that her son (the male, representing "Stone") and Diotima (the female, representing the "Sea") will ever find together. From the very beginning, however, the film stresses the desirability of this union, and here we ought to recall Simmel's ruminations about the liberating and redeeming qualities of both mountains and ocean for the modern soul. Any future national *Gesundung* necessitates a healthy individual. Robert, albeit physically strong, is still in

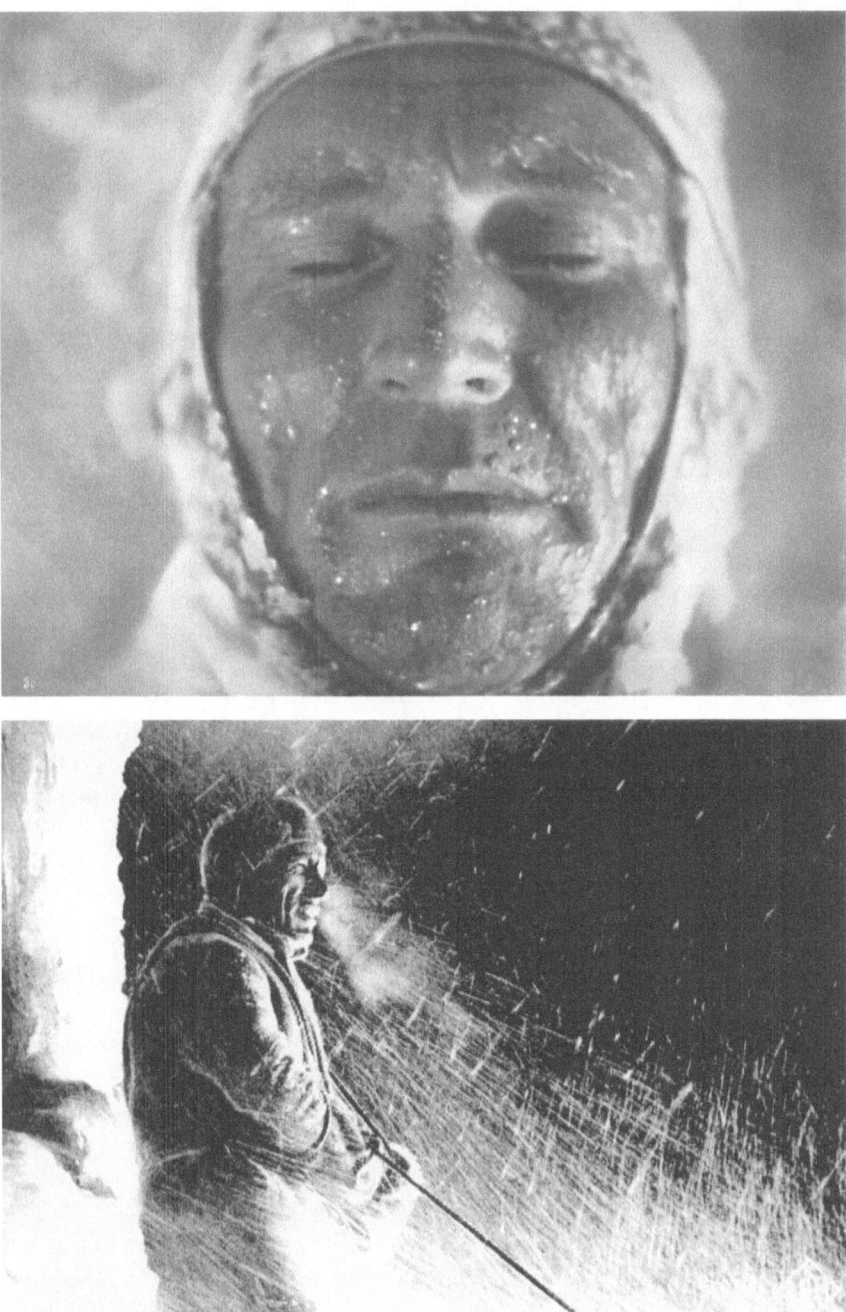

Fig. 1. Luis Trenker in Arnold Fanck's Der heilige Berg *(1925/26).*

search of himself emotionally. He even says so to Diotima when they encounter each other for the first time, an encounter that takes place, not coincidentally, halfway between his snowy Alpine peaks and her green valley. When Diotima asks him "What does one search for up there?" Robert says "One's Self." One is immediately reminded of Müller's "correct appraisal of one's Self" that, presumably, is the desired result of mountain climbing. In *Der heilige Berg*, however, we seem to meet a male model that has yet to transform itself into a "functional ego." Robert is lacking the tools of internal affective self-stabilization.[35] He could be looked at as an example of a required male recuperation that might, by the mid-1920s, show the influences of the sober codes of conduct of New Objectivity. In their current status, mountain (male) and ocean (female) cannot find any middle ground. But identifying only the woman as the source of disruption and danger overlooks the clearly dysfunctional nature of Robert and his "Männerbündnis"[36] (male bond), for the latter does not restore a positive value, at least not for audiences in post-expressionist mid-1920s Germany. Even though his seemingly heroic death evokes the front community and the fabled loyalty among soldiers, it ultimately points back to a detrimental lack of affective control.

Instead of reading Fanck's *Der heilige Berg* as an overly anachronistic tale that pitches this soldierly ideal of *Gesundung* in comradely death, we ought to contemplate whether this *Bergfilm* is instead utterly modern, insofar as it demands more sobriety, that is, the development of an affectively stable and functional ego — a development, perhaps, toward cool conduct so as to avoid a freezing death. By focusing on seemingly apposite gender identities, *Der heilige Berg* sheds light on Fanck's understanding of a receptive *Gesundung* for both genders. Over the next five to seven years, other mountain films — now produced and directed by the Fanck pupils Trenker and Riefenstahl — would supply a variety of responses to Fanck's early diagnoses and strategies of recuperation.

Notes

Throughout the essay I use the multi-faceted German term *Gesundung* in the sense of recovery, recuperation, healing.

[1] Siegfried Kracauer, "Die kleinen Ladenmädchen gehen ins Kino," in *Das Ornament der Masse: Essays*, with an afterword by Karsten Witte (Frankfurt am Main: Suhrkamp, 1977), 279 and 282; in English, "The Little Shopgirls Go to the Movies, in *The Mass Ornament: Weimar Essays*, trans. and ed. Thomas Y. Levin (Cambridge, MA: Harvard UP, 1995), 291 and 294.

[2] In January 1938 Luis Trenker's *Der Berg ruft!* (The mountain calls) appeared. It is a remake of the 1928 silent movie *Der Kampf ums Matterhorn* (Fight for the Matterhorn). Robert von Dassanowsky extends the genre by more than a decade

with his analysis of Leni Riefenstahl's *Tiefland* (1945–54). See von Dassanowsky, "A Mountain of a Ship: Locating the *Bergfilm* in James Cameron's *Titanic*," *Cinema Journal* 40, no. 4 (2001): 18–35.

[3] Siegfried Kracauer, *From Caligari to Hitler. A Psychological History of the German Film* (Princeton, NJ: Princeton UP, 1947), 112.

[4] Eric Rentschler, "Mountains and Modernity: Relocating the *Bergfilm*," *New German Critique* 51 (1990): 137–61.

[5] Nancy P. Nenno, "'Postcards from the Edge': Education to Tourism in the German Mountain Film," in *Light Motives: German Popular Film in Perspective*, ed. Randall Halle and Margaret McCarthy (Detroit: Wayne State UP, 2003), 61–84.

[6] One of the most insightful comments on the *Bergfilm* is a mere side-note in Nenno's analysis of Thomas Mann's *Magic Mountain*, where she writes that the "central unifying subtext of all of Fanck's dramatic mountain films is undoubtedly the defeat of Germany in the First World War." Nancy P. Nenno, "Projections on a Blank Space: Landscape, Nationality, and Identity in Thomas Mann's *Der Zauberberg*, *German Quarterly* 69, no. 3 (1996): 312.

[7] Anton Kaes, *Shell Shock Cinema* (Princeton, NJ: Princeton UP, 2009), 2.

[8] The focus on the early *Bergfilm* in this essay prevents the discussion of some of the most potent links between the *Bergfilm* and defeat, crisis, perseverance, and a possible rebirth.

[9] Wolfgang Schivelbusch, *The Culture of Defeat: On National Trauma, Mourning, and Recovery*, trans. Jefferson Chase (New York: Metropolitan Books, 2003), 10.

[10] See Robert Weldon Whalen, *Bitter Wounds: German Victims of the Great War, 1914–1939* (Ithaca, NY: Cornell UP, 1984).

[11] Eric Weitz, *Weimar Germany: Promise and Tragedy* (Princeton, NJ: Princeton UP, 2007), 9.

[12] See Ernst Hanisch, *Männlichkeiten: Eine andere Geschichte des 20. Jahrhunderts* (Vienna: Böhlau, 2005); Klaus Theweleit, *Male Fantasies*, vol. 1, *Women, Floods, Bodies, History*, trans. Stephen Conway in collaboration with Erica Carter and Chris Turner (Minneapolis: U of Minnesota P, 1987). With specific regard to the *Bergfilm*, see Jutta Menschik-Bendele on climbing as narcissistic regulation of self-worth: "Psychoanalytisches zum Bergfilm: Heldinnen und Helden in den 30er Jahren," in Aspetsberger, *Der BergFilm, 1920–1940* (Innsbruck: Studien-Verlag, 2002), 85–99.

[13] Schivelbusch, *The Culture of Defeat*, 202 and 246.

[14] Georg Simmel, "Die Alpen." Reprinted in Georg Simmel, *Philosophische Kultur: Über das Abenteuer, die Geschlechter und die Krise der Moderne; Gesammelte Essais* (Berlin: Wagenbach, 1983), 115.

[15] See also Georg Simmel, "Alpenreisen," *Die Zeit: Wiener Wochenschrift für Politik, Volkswirtschaft, Wissenschaft und Kunst*, 13 July 1895, 22–24.

[16] See also Carsten Strathausen, "The Image as Abyss: The Cinematic Sublime in the Mountain Film," *Peripheral Visions: The Hidden Stages of Weimar Cinema*, ed. Kenneth S. Calhoon (Detroit: Wayne State UP, 2001), 171–89.

17 See reviews collected by *Berg- und Sportfilm GmbH*, "Pressestimmen über den Film *Im Kampf mit dem Berge*, available in the "'Schriftgutarchiv" of *Deutsche Kinemathek*, Berlin.
18 *Film-Kurier*, 23 September 1921.
19 On the First World War in the Alps, see for example Tait Keller, "The Mountains Roar: The Alps during the Great War," *Environmental History* 14 (2009): 253–74. See also, and in particular, Mark Thompson, *The White War: Life and Death on the Italian Front, 1915–1919* (New York: Basic Books, 2008); Michael Wachtler, *The First World War in the Alps* (Bolzano, Italy: Athesia Spectrum, 2006).
20 Gustav Müller, "Die Berge und ihre Bedeutung für den Wiederaufbau des deutschen Volkes," *Zeitschrift des Deutschen und Österreichischen Alpenvereins* 53 (1922): 1–9. Further references to this work are given in the text using page numbers alone.
21 See, for instance, his essay "Alpenreisen" where he explores the consequences of mass tourism as a result of railway extensions.
22 A recent essay on the mountain films' hypermasculination and hyperfeminization discusses the "cult of the cold" in connection to gender politics. See Ingeborg Majer-O'Sickey, "The Cult of the Cold and the Gendered Body in Mountain Films," in *Spatial Turns: Space, Place, and Mobility in German Literary and Visual Culture*, ed. Jaimey Fisher and Barbara Mennel (Amsterdam: Rodopi, 2010), 363–80.
23 As a child, Fanck was sent to Davos with asthma problems, where he fully recovered. Fanck's autobiography, *Er führte Regie mit Gletschern, Stürmen und Lawinen: Ein Filmpionier erzählt* (Munich: Nymphenburger Verlagshandlung, 1973) is littered with references to *Gesundung*: his own "Abhärtung" (10; toughening up) in the mountains; climbing as "eine äußerst harte, so doch wirksame Schule (30; an extremely hard and therefore effective schooling); the demands of his many dangerous high Alpine tours helped him overcome his "ursprünglich zu weiche Veranlagung" (45; originally too soft disposition), making him more resilient, and so on.
24 The dichotomy of movement and standstill is important in this context, a dichotomy whose allegorical potential ought to be examined elsewhere. In his analysis of the various but patterned responses to defeat, Schivelbusch observes the apparent importance for the vanquished of reclaiming motion after the end of the war whose loss is experienced as a sudden or deadly halt. In mountain films we strive upward, we ascend or descend and are in constant motion through a cold climate. Falling means death, standing still; standing still means freezing to death. A film like Fanck's *S.O.S. Eisberg* (1932/33), for example, makes the forward motion through icy waters, from iceberg to iceberg, the key to survival. The many aerial shots provided by Ernst Udet further associate movement with survival and success.
25 Fanck, *Er führte Regie*, 315.
26 According to Rentschler, the genre soon evolves "into a precarious balance between expressive shapes of nature and the romantic triangles of melodrama. . . .

The *Bergfilm* abides as a blend of striking images and insidious stories." Rentschler, "Mountains," 142 and 149.

[27] See Schivelbusch on the role of revanche, revenge, ressentiment for defeated Germany in his introduction to *The Culture of Defeat*, 1–35.

[28] Here I loosely follow Helmut Lethen's ideas in *Verhaltenslehren der Kälte: Lebensversuche zwischen den Kriegen* (Frankfurt am Main: Suhrkamp, 1994); in English, *Cool Conduct: The Culture of Distance in Weimar Germany*, trans. Don Reneau (Berkeley: U of California P, 2002).

[29] A similar juxtaposition of mobility (Hella; son) and immobility (grandmother; mother; Hella's father) is seen later during the rescue. Movement and therefore rescue lie with the young.

[30] On "hypermasculinity" and the imagination, production, and consumption of adventure images, see Susan Frohlick's "'That Playfulness of White Masculinity': Mediating Masculinities and Adventure at Mountain Film Festivals," *Tourist Studies* 5, no. 2 (2005): 175–93.

[31] One of the very few available academic studies of the genre is Christian Rapp's *Höhenrausch: Der deutsche Bergfilm* (Vienna: Sonderzahl, 1997). Rapp's study contains many good observations but at times appears hasty in its brevity. See also Aspetsberger, *Der BergFilm, 1920–1940*; and Klaus Kreimeier, ed., *Fanck — Trenker — Riefenstahl: Der deutsche Bergfilm und seine Folgen* (Berlin: Stiftung Deutsche Kinemathek, 1972).

[32] Rentschler, "Mountains," 153–55.

[33] Rentschler, "Mountains," 160–61. See also Weitz, *Weimar Germany*, 26 and 328.

[34] See Rapp, *Höhenrausch*, 105–18. With focus on the ethnographic and Riefenstahl, see Rebecca Prime, "A Strange and Foreign World: Documentary, and the Mountain Films of Arnold Fanck and Leni Riefenstahl," in *Folklore / Cinema: Popular Film as Vernacular Culture*, ed. Koven Sherman (Logan: U of Utah P, 2007).

[35] Lethen, *Cool Conduct*, 6.

[36] Rapp, *Höhenrausch*, 110.

"Mountain of Destiny": The Filmic Legacy of Nanga Parbat

Harald Höbusch

IN ADDITION TO BEING physical forms, mountains — as Robert Macfarlane writes in the introduction to his 2003 study *Mountains of the Mind* — are "the products of human perception; they have been *imagined* into existence down the centuries."[1] By the end of the nineteenth century, the focus of this imagination in the minds of European, and especially British, mountaineers had shifted from the Alps to the highest mountain ranges in the world. Macfarlane observes: "The imaginary potency of these greater peaks . . . was formidable, and they frequently became the objects of obsession within the minds of their individual admirers" (16). And not just individuals: while Mount Everest (8,850 m/29,035 ft.) became the obsession of the British, Nanga Parbat (8,125 m/26,658 ft.) fired the imagination of the German nation. Between the early 1930s and 1950s it would become their "Schicksalsberg" (mountain of destiny), and it would be onto its slopes that German mountaineers would project, both figuratively and literally, not only their sporting aspirations but also some of the most pressing social and political concerns of their times.

What exactly were these concerns? In purely sporting terms, the German efforts on Nanga Parbat during the 1930s were motivated by an attitude of competition fueled by British attempts on Everest and their success in consistently pushing upward the world altitude record. But these German expeditions were also the visible expression of a deeply felt desire among German mountaineers for the reconstitution of their nation as a recognizable European, even world, power following the defeat of the empire in the First World War. In 1919, at its first general assembly after the war, the German and Austrian Alpine Club drew up the so-called "Nürnberger Leitsätze" (Nuremberg principles), which identified mountains as key to German national recovery: "Eines der wichtigsten Mittel, um die sittliche Kraft des deutschen Volkes wiederherzustellen, ist der Alpinismus, und zwar in der Form der bergsteigerischen Arbeit." (One of the most important means of rebuilding the moral strength of the German people is Alpinism, and especially the act of mountaineering).[2] In this process of national renewal, expeditions into the high-mountain regions of the world were perceived to play a central role, as Julius Gallhuber, owner and editor of the journal *Der Bergsteiger* (The mountaineer), made clear in 1928:

> Sie sind ein eindrucksvoller Baustein, dem deutschen Volke wieder zur alten Größe, zu altem Ansehen zu helfen, denn das Geheimnis deutscher Macht war und ist die deutsche Tat! Die Expeditionen sollen ein Stützpunkt mehr sein, unser Vertrauen in die deutsche Kraft, unser Selbstbewußtsein wieder zu erobern, unser Ansehen in fremden Ländern zu stärken.[3]

> [They are an impressive step toward once again elevating the German people to their former greatness and standing, since the secret of German power was and is German action! These expeditions are intended to serve as one more way of regaining our trust in German strength, of rebuilding our self-confidence, of strengthening our reputation in foreign countries.]

Responding to increasing calls for an engagement beyond their traditional area of activity in the European Alps, German Alpine organizations soon launched expeditions to various high-mountain ranges around the globe, including the Himalayas. While initial efforts in 1929, 1930, and 1931 focused on Kangchenjunga (8,586m./28,169 ft.), this was soon replaced by Nanga Parbat, perceived to be the easiest of all 8,000-meter peaks. Originally attempted in 1932 by Willy Merkl as part of a German-American expedition, Nanga Parbat would be visited five more times: 1934, 1937 (twice), 1938, and 1939. The mountain, however, did not yield readily to its visitors. German expeditions, now supported by various NS government agencies, were struck by two major disasters, in 1934 and 1937, that resulted in a body count of twenty-six: eleven German and Austrian mountaineers and fifteen local porters. From now on, Nanga Parbat would be referred to as Germany's "mountain of destiny."[4]

Of the six expeditions to Nanga Parbat between 1932 and 1939, four were documented on film. The first of these "documentaries,"[5] *Nanga Parbat: Ein Kampfbericht der Deutschen Himalaja Expedition 1934* (Nanga Parbat: A battle account of the 1934 German Himalaya expedition), premiered in Munich at the conclusion of the 1936 Olympic Winter Games. Rated "staatspolitisch wertvoll, kulturell wertvoll, volksbildend" (of political and cultural value, educational)[6] by the *Filmprüfstelle* (censorship office) of the Ministry of Information and Propaganda, it opened with a lengthy foreword by Reich Sports Leader Hans von Tschammer und Osten. It was brought to the attention of its potential audiences via a centralized advertising campaign coordinated by the Department of Mountaineering and Hiking in the German *Reichsbund* for Physical Education and was widely distributed in both Germany and Austria. The second "documentary" of interest to this investigation, *Kampf um den Himalaja* (Struggle for the Himalayas), was filmed during the two Nanga

Parbat expeditions of 1937. Consisting of footage from both the original, ill-fated, 1937 attempt and the rescue expedition of the same year, it was produced under the aegis of the newly founded German Himalaya Foundation.[7] The film received the highest official predicate awarded by the *Filmprüfstelle*: "staatspolitisch und künstlerisch wertvoll, volksbildend, Lehrfilm" (politically and artistically valuable, educational, instructional film).[8] Following its premiere in Munich on 4 March 1938, it was widely distributed in German and Austrian movie theaters. "Documentary" film material was also produced during the 1938 expedition to Nanga Parbat. This footage, however, would not make it onto German movie screens until after the end of the Second World War, as part of a production titled *Deutsche Himalaja-Expeditionen* (German Himalaya expeditions), a short educational film. Along with this production, the German Himalaya Foundation pursued plans to turn the footage of the 1934, 1937, and 1938 expeditions into a feature-length film. Despite intense and prolonged efforts, this project never came to fruition.

How, then, do the two feature-length expedition films produced under National Socialist rule imagine Germany's recovery as a nation? In *Nanga Parbat: Ein Kampfbericht der Deutschen Himalaja Expedition 1934* the path to national renewal is identified immediately in the opening sequence of the film: with blaring fanfares, the film's title sequence introduces the production as a "battle account." With that, it ties — both musically and semantically — the German mountaineering effort on Nanga Parbat and, by extension, the future of the German nation, to the notion of military combat. This connection is reinforced in a foreword by Reich Sports Leader von Tschammer und Osten, who claims:

> So kommen im Kampf um die Hochgipfel die vornehmsten Mannestugenden zum Einsatz: Einordnung in den militärischen Geist der Gemeinschaftsleistung, Kameradschaft, Kampfesmut und selbstlose Hingabe an das Ziel.
>
> [In the struggle for Earth's highest mountains man's most noble virtues are being employed: submission to the military spirit of collective achievement, comradeship, courage to fight, and selfless dedication to the goal.]

For von Tschammer und Osten, the military mindset finds its clearest expression in the act of mountaineering, and it is Germany's youth for which this particular mindset is being propagated. They are expected to take up both the struggle on the mountain and, by implication, any future military fight.

These early leitmotifs are reinforced via a number of narrative strategies in the film proper. The "documentary" introduces the members of the 1934 expedition as Merkl's "Mannen" (men), but does not identify them individually. It thereby puts the expedition members at the disposal of their leader, diminishes the role of the individual in favor of the communal effort, and stresses von Tschammer und Osten's principle of "collective achievement." Furthermore, it describes the expedition, its members and their progress on the mountain in strictly military terms, thereby underscoring for the viewer the link between mountaineering and military combat established in the foreword to the film. Finally, it ties the expedition to the National Socialist movement by repeatedly depicting its quintessential emblem, the swastika.

Nanga Parbat reaches its dramatic climax in the portrayal of the expedition's ultimate failure. Alfred Drexel, one of the mountaineers, falls ill and dies, despite the desperate efforts of his fellow mountaineers to save his life. The "Angriff" (attack) on the mountain is halted in order for all expedition members to pay their final respects. The film spends considerable time depicting Drexel's burial. The flag pole in the main camp is lowered, the Nazi standard removed from it, and Drexel's body wrapped into the swastika — an image intensified via a close-up depicting the flag-draped body together with the mountaineer's trusty tool of trade, the ice axe. The lengthy depiction of Drexel's burial serves as a vehicle for reinforcing some of the key concepts addressed previously in the film. By showing the expedition leader Willy Merkl delivering Drexel's eulogy, the film sets the stage for presenting its own interpretation of Drexel's death soon after. Drexel, as one intertitle states, is laid to rest in a "nordisches Hünenmal" (Nordic megalithic grave), a description that ties him to the Nazistic version of a Germanic mythological realm, thus elevating him above mere mortal status. In addition, via the reference to a thundering "Salut der Lawinen" (avalanche salute), Drexel's death is militarized and tied to the larger fate of the German nation: "Alfred Drexel, gefallen für Deutschland" (Alfred Drexel, fallen for Germany).

But — as the next intertitle announces — "Das Leben geht weiter" (life goes on), and so the remaining expedition members return to their goal of scaling Nanga Parbat. Their struggle continues to be narrated with the help of military terminology; not only does life go on, but the "attack" on the mountain continues as well. The foundation for this renewed effort, as the film suggests by depicting the swastika flying over camp 4, is provided by the National Socialist idea.

However, the euphoria of the mountaineers — and with it the carefully built anticipation of their success on the part of the audience — is quelled by a sudden turn of events on the mountain. The final minutes of the film reveal the magnitude of the ensuing disaster, chronicling how the mountain has repulsed the "attack" and claimed the lives of nine mountaineers. *Nanga Parbat* concludes by honoring the men who lost their lives on the mountain, listing the names of the six Sherpas and the three German mountaineers who died there in 1934. A final series of intertitles, strategically placed over shots of the very threshold to success on Nanga

Parbat, the "Silbersattel" (silver saddle), explains one last time the meaning of their deaths to German audiences, linking their ultimate sacrifice to the nation's fate at large and calling upon a new generation of mountaineers to continue the struggle on Nanga Parbat: "Sie kämpften für ein hohes Ziel. Sie kämpften für Deutschland. Ihr Kampf geht weiter" (They fought for a noble goal. They fought for Germany. Their struggle continues).

Nanga Parbat: Ein Kampfbericht der Deutschen Himalaja Expedition 1934, in its militaristic and nationalistic portrayal of the German 1934 Nanga Parbat expedition, closely adheres to the official National Socialist theory of sport and its purpose. As Hajo Bernett has documented,[9] Hitler's *Mein Kampf* identified sport as a tool to regenerate the atrophied sense of power for a *Volk* defeated in the First World War and to aid the German nation in "regaining its faith in the invincibility of [its] whole people."[10] On the individual level, this process was to culminate in the transformation of "a young man who has already received flawless physical preparation into a soldier."[11] For the sport of mountaineering, this very purpose, repeatedly propagated during the 1920s and 1930s at the annual general assemblies of the German and Austrian Alpine Club and publicized in various mountaineering journals, was officially confirmed in a series of articles published between 1935 and 1939 by Meinhard Sild, personal referent to Dr. Arthur Seyß-Inquart, the new *Führer* (leader) of the now German Alpine Club. In a programmatic article entitled "Bergsteigen als Rüstung" (Mountaineering as a form of mobilization),[12] Sild wrote:

> Die kriegerischen Maßstäbe, Ordnungen und Gesetze, die in der totalen Mobilmachung sichtbar und wirksam werden, haben durchwegs Gültigkeit für das Bergsteigen;.... Kameradschaft und Führertum, Pflichtbewußtsein und Verantwortlichkeit, Einsatzbereitschaft und Entschiedenheit, Disziplin, Härte, Mut, Tapferkeit —: all das zusammen gibt eine Grundlage, die wesentlich ist nicht allein dem typischen Bewußtsein des Kriegers und des Bergsteigers, sondern in steigendem Maße einem umfassenden neuen bejahenden Lebensbewußtsein.

> [The military standards, orders, and laws that manifest themselves in the act of total mobilization are equally valid in regard to mountaineering;.... Comradeship and leadership, a sense of duty and responsibility, initiative and decisiveness, discipline, toughness, courage, bravery —: all these qualities together form a foundation essential not only for the typical attitude of the warrior and mountaineer, but increasingly also for a new, all-encompassing affirmation of life.][13]

The "most noble virtues" and military "qualities" stressed by Hans von Tschammer und Osten and Meinhard Sild in their respective comments on the role of mountaineering in the renewal of the German nation would continue to play an important part in the film of the 1937 Nanga

Parbat expedition entitled *Kampf um den Himalaja*. But above all it is the notion of legacy, evoked already at the conclusion of *Nanga Parbat*, that forms the conceptual core of this second "documentary" produced under National Socialist rule. At first glance, *Kampf um den Himalaja* seems to do nothing more than simply chronicle the events of the 1937 expedition. A second, closer, look, however, reveals a highly sophisticated arrangement and interplay of image and narrative designed to celebrate — and thereby propagate — such "virtues" as honor, comradeship, and, ultimately, self-sacrifice (to the death). These "virtues," however, were essential elements of the National Socialist movement's mythology.

The themes of comradeship, self-sacrifice, and death are present from the very beginning of *Kampf um den Himalaja*. The film opens with a brief visual reference to those killed on Nanga Parbat in 1934 and subsequently identifies one key motivation for the 1937 expedition: the legacy left by the deceased. By listing the members of the 1937 expedition and marking the names of its dead with crosses in the beginning, the film establishes a type of comradeship that reaches beyond life and into death. In addition, the repeated use of the term "Vermächtnis" (legacy) suggests an almost legally binding contract or at least a strong moral obligation and an honorable task to be performed. Furthermore, the reference to Nanga Parbat as "mountain of destiny" in this opening sequence creates mythical overtones, overtones which, like the previously discussed concepts, continue throughout the narrative and combine with them to form an almost inescapable ideological web.

The quasi-religious nature of the German mission to Nanga Parbat is suggested not through the use of traditional Christian symbols but rather through several references to religious practices indigenous to the region. The narrator twice draws a parallel between a group of Muslim Hajjis, who cross paths with the expedition on their long journey back from Mecca, and the German mountaineers, who are still at the beginning of their own "Pilgerfahrt" (pilgrimage). This reference suggests three things. First, that, much like the Islamic mandatory journey to Mecca, the German trip to Nanga Parbat is of an obligatory nature. Second, it foreshadows the fate awaiting some of the climbers. Indeed, only a few of them would return to their home country, while the majority — like those who came before them in 1934 — would be killed on the mountain. And finally, it implies that religion may be replaced with a different kind of heroic quest for eternity — a view quite in the spirit of National Socialist ideology.

Even more important regarding the overall message of the film is the relationship between the deceased of 1934 and those traveling to Nanga Parbat in 1937. Indeed, it can be argued that this message of "legacy" — and thereby of obligation — marks the very center of this "documentary," and not only metaphorically. Exactly halfway through the film, the members of the 1937 expedition arrive at the gravesite of Alfred Drexel, the first mountaineer to succumb during the 1934 attempt. After depicting them adorning the cairn marking Drexel's grave with freshly cut branches, thereby commemorating their fallen comrade, the film image slowly dissolves into footage from 1934, depicting Drexel's actual burial. Against this background, we read the following words:

> Drei Jahre zuvor:
> Am 11. Juni 1934 wurde Alfred Drexel zu Grabe getragen.
> An seinem Grabe standen:　　　　　　　Willy Merkl †
> 　　　　　　　　　　　　　　　　　　　Willo Welzenbach †
> 　　　　　　　　　　　　　　　　　　　Uli Wieland †
>
> Der Nanga Parbat behielt auch sie.
>
> [Three years earlier:
> On 11 June 1934 we buried Alfred Drexel.
> At his grave stood:　　　　　　　　　　Willy Merkl †
> 　　　　　　　　　　　　　　　　　　　Willo Welzenbach †
> 　　　　　　　　　　　　　　　　　　　Uli Wieland †
>
> Nanga Parbat kept them, too.]

The film, then, literally revolves around death and the continuity of the mission embarked upon in 1934, a conclusion further substantiated by the fact that this notion of continuity is reinforced several times throughout the film. While looking for a possible campsite in order to move the "Hauptlager" (base camp) higher up the mountain, the Sherpas lead the German mountaineers to the site of the 1934 base camp. Intertitles inform the viewer that this is where the current new "Hauptlager" will be erected, and the use of wooden planks left behind from the 1934 expedition emphasizes that the 1937 expedition is literally built upon the foundation of those who labored before — and lost their lives in that effort. At the end of the film the camera once more shows us Nanga Parbat and, against this background, inserts the names of those who died in 1937 as well as the following sentence: "Eingegangen in den Nanga Parbat: Ein unsterbliches Sinnbild ewiger Sehnsucht und männlicher Tat" (Ascended into Nanga Parbat: an immortal symbol of eternal desire and manly deed). The last shot, however, positions the memorial for the deceased of 1934 directly in front of Nanga Parbat, the resting place of those killed in 1937. This final visual connection establishes irrefutably what had been suggested throughout the film: the continuity between the 1934 and 1937 expeditions and, by extension, any future ones. As in 1934, lives were lost in 1937, thereby creating a new "legacy" for those who would follow. Ultimately, the film itself becomes an extension of the obligation extending from the original 1934 expedition via the ill-fated 1937 attempt to the present. Again, it is the term "legacy" that calls to duty not only the survivors but also a new generation of German mountaineers. Part of that duty, it is implied, is to tell the story —

through films, diaries, and scientific reports — of the struggle and ultimately the defeat on Nanga Parbat.

By depicting the 1937 expedition to Nanga Parbat as a sort of pilgrimage and thereby injecting it with mythical overtones, *Kampf um den Himalaja* relies heavily on a strategy that had characterized the National Socialist movement from its very beginning. The 1920 program of the Nazi party (the so-called "25 Punkte" [25 points]), for instance, would later be characterized by Hitler as the "Gründungsurkunde unserer Religion, unserer Weltanschauung" (founding document of our religion, our worldview),[14] thereby reflecting the intention of the Nazis to portray their movement in a quasi-religious light. This intention manifested itself, among other things, in the phenomenon of the National Socialist "Totenkult" (cult of death), the mystification of those who had given their lives for the movement and thereby contributed to its legacy of struggle. This "cult of death" or legacy of struggle, as Jay W. Baird has documented, can be traced all the way back to the death myth of the First World War and is connected to such events as the "martyrdom" of Albert Leo Schlageter, the saga of Horst Wessel and, above all, the "immortals" of the abortive Hitler putsch of 9 November 1923.[15] Several of these "martyrs" had been immortalized in films: the early fighters in *Hitlerjunge Quex* (Hitler boy Quex) and Horst Wessel in *Hans Westmar* (both 1933). Elevating the death of eleven German mountaineers on Nanga Parbat to the level of national martyrdom in *Kampf um den Himalaja* fits squarely into this "cult of death" and its continuing need for symbolic figures. Furthermore, the portrayal of German mountaineering efforts on Nanga Parbat as a "legacy" handed down by one's deceased comrades amounts to what Eric Hobsbawm has characterized as "the invention of tradition," that is, practices "which establish their own past by *quasi-obligatory repetition*."[16] Their purpose lies in either "establishing or symbolizing social cohesion or the membership of groups, real or artificial communities" or in the "socialization, the inculcation of beliefs, value systems and conventions of behaviour."[17] *Kampf um den Himalaja* fulfills both of these purposes.

With the collapse of the Third Reich, Germany, for the second time in less than thirty years, was faced with the challenge of reinventing itself, of redefining its identity as a nation. While some Germans looked to the brief democratic tradition of the Weimar Republic for guidance in this process, many of them chose alternative strategies. They opted either not to deal with the recent past at all, to characterize themselves as having been apolitical and therefore unknowing (with the implication that one was innocent), or to focus on the challenge that lay immediately ahead: rebuilding Germany in a physical and economic sense.

As Helmuth Zebhauser has shown, the German Alpine Club (DAV) applied on an institutional level what many German citizens practiced in private. German mountaineering officials wasted no time declaring that their organization — despite clear evidence to the contrary submitted to the Bavarian Ministry of the Interior in July 1946 — had been "apolitical," thereby denying any link to and involvement in the schemes of National Socialism and absolving themselves of any responsibility for acts committed in that name.[18] To be fair, the influence of individuals such as Fritz Schmitt, Hans Ackermann, Paul Hübel, and Albert Heizer led to a clearly democratic reorganization of the DAV, but there is no denying the fact that politically tainted former functionaries such as Adolf Sotier, Paul Nuber, Hans von Bomhard, and others were able to continue to serve in official roles for the club.[19]

As far as the role envisioned for post–Second World War Alpinism was concerned, old notions of loyalty, comradeship, and fatherland continued to pervade official discourse.[20] In a 1950 draft outlining the statutes of the so-called "Jungmannschaft," the youth branch of the DAV, we find for instance the following:

> Die Jungmannen sollen im Sinne der Satzungen des Alpenvereins das gute, alte Bergsteigertum pflegen und "auf dem Boden des Heimat- und Vaterlandsgedankens" stehen. Sie sollen gute Bergsteiger werden; sie sollen aber ihre Weiterbildung nicht nur als Einzelpersönlichkeit, sondern auch weiterhin in einem möglichst engen Gemeinsamkeitsverband im Sinne der richtigen bergsteigerischen Entwicklung und Vertiefung erfahren, je nach Neigung, Veranlagung und Können zu den höchsten Zielen des tätigen Alpinismus, zur Hochtouristik, heranreifen. Über diese persönliche Ausbildung hinaus sollen sie die Kameradschaft bis hin zur unbedingten Treue gegen den Gefährten pflegen. Sie sollen Sinn für die Reinhaltung der Alpenwelt und des Alpinismus erhalten und bewahren.[21]
>
> [The *Jungmannen* are expected to preserve, in the spirit of the statutes of the [German] Alpine Club, the traditional forms of mountaineering and to ground themselves in the "notion of the home- and fatherland." They are expected to become capable mountaineers; however, they ought to grow not only as individuals but also as part of a close community, thereby practicing and improving the appropriate mountaineering skills and, according to their preference, natural talent and ability, develop toward the highest goal of Alpinism, high-altitude mountaineering. Beyond their individual training they are expected to practice comradeship, including total loyalty and dedication to their peers. They are to develop and maintain a feeling for the purity of the Alps and Alpinism.]

With its call to prepare the youth for the most difficult challenge in mountaineering, that is, to enable them to climb the highest peaks in the world, German mountaineering officials placed an important part of German post–Second World War Alpinism in the tradition of prewar Himalaya expeditions to summits such as Kangchenjunga and, especially,

Nanga Parbat. Expeditions to the latter mountain, however, had clearly been used (and abused) for propagandistic purposes after the National Socialist ascent to power in 1933. Even if this attempt at reclaiming a "memorable" German Alpine tradition was shared by those who themselves had no use for old nationalistic concepts such as loyalty, struggle, heroism, and sacrifice, this legacy was still problematic: it required a clear distancing of one's own enterprise from previous National Socialist efforts. For others, of course, the old ideas posed no problem; they still held on to militaristic "qualities" and ideals that dated all the way back to the trenches of the First World War.[22] This split became clearly visible in the months preceding the 1953 *Deutsch-Österreichische Willy-Merkl-Gedächtnis-Expedition* (German-Austrian Willy Merkl Memorial Expedition) to Nanga Parbat. Headed by the half-brother of Willy Merkl, Dr. Karl Maria Herrligkoffer, this undertaking marked the first expedition launched without the financial backing provided to previous (National Socialist) Nanga Parbat expeditions by the German Himalaya Foundation. In fact, Herrligkoffer had been successful in securing the single annually available expedition permit for Nanga Parbat against strong competition and interference from the Foundation. Herrligkoffer was criticized repeatedly by Dr. Paul Bauer, the leader of the 1937 and 1938 expeditions, for his lack of organization and, especially, the selection of team members. Whereas Herrligkoffer simply tried to recruit the best climbers of the post–Second World War period, Bauer favored (as he had on previous expeditions) the idea of an already familiar group of mountaineers or "Bergkameraden."[23] While Bauer insisted on the sole right of representation of the German Himalaya Foundation regarding expeditions into the Himalayas, Herrligkoffer ignored this "right" and pointed instead to the questionable National Socialist past of the Foundation. In the end, Herrligkoffer emerged victorious from this extended struggle for the right to travel to Nanga Parbat[24] and would carry on with his expedition, one that would ultimately lead to the singular solo ascent of the mountain by the Austrian climber Herrmann Buhl on 3 July 1953.[25]

But how — and this is the crucial question — would this final chapter in the struggle for Nanga Parbat be depicted to audiences in a newly democratized Germany? Hans Ertl,[26] director and cameraman of *Nanga Parbat 1953*, the film of the 1953 *Deutsch-Österreichische Willy-Merkl-Gedächtnis-Expedition*, clearly found it necessary to distance himself from previous German Himalaya expeditions. Referencing the difficulties encountered during the organizational phase of the expedition, he lets his audience know immediately that these problems were in no small part due to the interference of several members of previous National Socialist expeditions to Nanga Parbat, most notably Dr. Paul Bauer. Ertl, therefore, early on draws a clear line between the 1953 expedition and those conducted under National Socialist rule.

As an alternative to the extremely nationalistic orientation — and portrayal — of these previous expeditions, Ertl offers a different way of seeing Nanga Parbat, in that he does not present it as the German "mountain of destiny" but rather as an international mountaineering challenge. Immediately after the opening credits, a brief introductory narrative concludes by stating that altogether thirty-one individuals, mountaineers as well as porters from various nations, had succumbed to Nanga Parbat over the years. A subsequent list then mentions the eleven Germans who died on the mountain in 1934 and 1937 respectively, but it also includes — and this is a significant difference from the 1938 production *Kampf um den Himalaja* — the fifteen Sherpas who had died alongside the Germans. In this way the film reflects an awareness of the new role of post–Second World War Germany; it downplays the nationalist element in favor of a more international self-understanding and self-representation. It is also telling that the summit flag selected for the possibility of a successful ascent is not the West German or, for that matter, the Austrian flag but rather that of the host country, Pakistan. The film thus denies viewers the possibility of reading the expedition in a colonialist context, as an attempt to conquer the mountain for either West Germany or Austria and thereby prove their respective national (or even racial) superiority.[27]

Instead, Ertl's documentary favors the notion of being among equals. This intention, which had manifested itself already in the *In Memoriam* section immediately following the opening credits, is evident in two additional sequences. For one, there is the reaction of the German and Austrian climbers to the news of the British success on Mount Everest. Far from being disappointed, the three men voice respect for the achievement of the British climbers, toast their success with a can of *Löwenbräu* beer, only to move on to their own mountaineering goal. The British Everest expedition is referenced a second time, at the very end of the film. Ertl closes his documentary with a series of telegrams congratulating the joint German-Austrian expedition on the successful summit ascent by Hermann Buhl. The last document presented in this sequence is of British origin, a message from Colonel John Hunt, leader of the British Everest expedition. It is at this moment that the German and Austrian mountaineers have closed the gap with their British counterparts; they are now on equal terms with them.

A second major characteristic of Ertl's documentary is the prominent role assigned to emblems of West Germany's growing economic power, its *Wirtschaftswunder* (economic miracle). While the "documentaries" of the 1934 and 1937 Nanga Parbat expedition featured, albeit in small doses, the swastika as a symbol of inclusiveness, Ertl's 1953 film replaces this political emblem with economic symbols no less representative of the times: he employs what is commonly referred to as "product placement." Items that feature prominently in the film are tents by *Deuter*, beer by

Löwenbräu and, most importantly, radio equipment by *Telefunken*. Their prominence in the film not only reflects the financial support provided by these companies for the 1953 expedition; it is also representative of the key development associated with West Germany during the 1950s, the Economic Miracle. It is with the help of German products, thus at least the implication, that German and Austrian mountaineers succeed in reaching the summit of Nanga Parbat.

Closely connected with this display of German products and their pivotal role in reaching the summit of Nanga Parbat is the attention given to the individual mountaineer. This is, once more, already evident at the beginning of the film. Whereas the 1938 documentary introduces the expedition members grouped together on board a ship with a swastika flag flying over their heads, thereby favoring the group over the individual, Ertl features each participant of the 1953 expedition individually via a still photo and a brief description of his responsibilities. The importance of the individual is further emphasized by the extensive coverage given to Hermann Buhl's *Alleingang*, his solo summit attempt. Preceded by a narrative outlining the events — Ertl, the cameraman and director, did not venture above camp 5 (6,900 m/22,638 ft.) — the film spends almost nine minutes recreating what nobody else could see: Buhl's painful but triumphant journey to the top of Nanga Parbat.

This prominence of the individual effort, however, is of key importance within the larger context of West Germany's reemergence after the Second World War. Like this expedition that from the beginning was more interested in the individual achievements of each mountaineer rather than their group chemistry, the young West German republic with its newly capitalist economic system would have to favor individual initiative and risk-taking over group identity. As Hermann Buhl would later state:

> Es macht mir unbändige Freude, so allein höher zu turnen, ohne hemmendes Seil und ohne schweren Ballast. Das ist wirkliches Klettern! Ich will mich selbst auf die Probe stellen, möchte meine eigenen Grenzen kennenlernen.[28]
>
> [It is an extreme delight to ascend this way, without a restricting rope and without a heavy load. This is real climbing! I want to test myself, want to get to know my personal limits.]

Buhl, in his mind, did not conquer the summit for Germany or Austria, but rather for himself.[29]

While the previously discussed features of Ertl's documentary link the film to post–Second World War Germany and its concerns regarding its new role within the international community, two important elements reflect the influence of an earlier era. For one, there is the indebtedness of Ertl's visual language in *Nanga Parbat 1953* to that of Arnold Fanck, the father of the German *Bergfilm* (mountain film).[30] Sequences such as clouds moving against mountain backdrops, snow blowing over mountain ridges, avalanches thundering down mountain faces, climbers backlit by the sun, and night scenes illuminated by flares combine to form the visual backbone of Ertl's documentary. Fanck had used these elements in masterful combination — for instance the famous night search scene in the depths of a glacier in his 1929 feature *Die weiße Hölle vom Piz Palü* (The white hell of Piz Palu) — in order to depict the mountain as a mystical entity standing opposed to the efforts of man. In *Nanga Parbat 1953* Ertl picks up on this mystification of the mountain, and by extension the mountaineer who throws himself against it, in an extended sequence depicting Hermann Buhl's successful journey to the summit of Nanga Parbat. It is here that the visual elements (described above) combine to make a sequence of great intensity, suggesting simultaneously the vast expanse of the mountain, that is, the challenge; and the dreamlike state of Buhl's mind, the one individual meeting that challenge. All the viewer gets to see is a shadow moving up (and later down) the snowy mountain, sometimes in full contrast against a ridge, sometimes in close-up as a figure on the snow, sometimes just as moving feet; the person himself is never shown in close-up. With this sequence, Ertl visually elevates Buhl into another realm, a mystical realm of other-worldliness where the human being is transformed from body to spirit.

A second element in the film can also be linked to a previous era. Although Ertl had introduced the expedition members individually at the beginning of his film, he inserted a sequence that is somewhat at odds with his original intention. It is a scene that once more conjures up the close relationship among mountaineers of the old school, the *Bergkameradschaft* which may be interpreted as a continuation of the *Grabenkameradschaft* (trench comradeship) not only of the First World War, but also of the Second World War. In this sequence the expedition members are depicted standing together on a rocky knoll above their camp, taking an oath in which they vow to obey the laws of comradeship, give their all in the fight against the mountain, and do so for the honor of their fatherland. In this scene, Ertl's narrative descends into a realm of language and ideas that, in other parts of his film, he had worked very hard to avoid: the sphere of fascist ideology. This ideology of course, was not altogether unfamiliar to Ertl. Besides his work on Fanck's films, Ertl had collaborated with Leni Riefenstahl on *Tag der Freiheit — Unsere Wehrmacht* (Day of freedom — our armed forces, 1935) and *Olympia* (1938) and contributed to National Socialist propaganda efforts on several occasions with his own productions, most notably with *Tag der Deutschen Kunst 1937* (Day of German art 1937) and *Glaube und Schönheit* (Faith and beauty, 1939).[31]

From these combined observations, *Nanga Parbat 1953* emerges as a fascinating hybrid of a documentary. Ertl, in trying to distance himself from the troublesome history of previous German Nanga Parbat expeditions and the subsequent appropriation of its "documentary" film material for propaganda purposes, can do so only with the help of a cinematic language that today is recognized as (pre-)fascist. In addition, Ertl, in trying to present the first successful ascent of Nanga Parbat in an international context through repeated references to British mountaineering as well as the shared format of the Western free-market economy, can only do so via a mystification of the mountain; that is, a uniquely national, German concept. Ertl's film, therefore, marks a position that has repeatedly been identified as symptomatic of the years of the West German Economic Miracle; a position at once characterized by the partial adoption of the new (the new economics, the new role of the individual, the new power of the product) and the partial retention of the old (the old relationships, the old language, the old ways of seeing).[32] Viewed from this angle, *Nanga Parbat 1953* documents not only the successful ascent of one of the world's highest mountains in 1953 but also the central identity problem of West Germany during the time of the Economic Miracle: despite focusing on the present, it simply cannot escape the past. Or, to put it more radically, revealing its most troubling legacy and Ertl's ultimate blind spot: it sees nothing wrong with perpetuating fascist ideas into a democratic future.

Ertl's *Nanga Parbat 1953*, together with *Nanga Parbat: Ein Kampfbericht der Deutschen Himalaja Expedition 1934* and *Kampf um den Himalaja*, is proof positive of the almost unrivaled "imaginary potency"[33] of the German "mountain of destiny," Nanga Parbat, and its enduring place in the German public imagination. As it turns out, Ertl's production would not be the last film thematizing the German "Schicksalsberg." Joseph Vilsmaier's 2010 feature *Nanga Parbat*, a film that claims to retell the story of Reinhold and Günther Messner's 1970 attempt to scale the mountain's then unclimbed Rupal face and their fateful descent on the Diamir side that resulted in the death of Reinhold's younger brother, has been repeatedly criticized for favoring Reinhold Messner's version of events to the exclusion of the views of his former team members. Nanga Parbat, it seems, is still being "imagined" today.

Notes

[1] Robert Macfarlane, *Mountains of the Mind* (New York: Pantheon, 2003), 19.
[2] Quoted in Ralf-Peter Märtin, *Nanga Parbat: Wahrheit und Wahn des Alpinismus* (Berlin: Berlin-Verlag, 2002), 104. See also Rainer Amstädter, *Der Alpinismus: Kultur — Organisation — Politik* (Vienna: WUV-Universitätsverlag, 1996), 322. Over the next two decades German mountaineers and mountaineering officials, at the annual general assembly of the German and Austrian Alpine Club as well as in numerous essays in various German and Austrian mountaineering journals, would

elaborate on the exact dynamic and nature of this envisioned recovery. All translations in this chapter are my own, unless otherwise noted.

[3] Julius Gallhuber, "Die Expeditionen des DÖAV und die alpine Öffentlichkeit," *Der Bergsteiger* 19 (1928): 1.

[4] Paul Bauer, *Auf Kundfahrt im Himalaja: Siniolchu und Nanga Parbat — Tat und Schicksal deutscher Bergsteiger* (Munich: Knorr & Hirth, 1937), 114.

[5] Both *Nanga Parbat: Ein Kampfbericht der Deutschen Himalaja Expedition 1934* and *Kampf um den Himalaja* are best categorized as "Kulturfilme" (cultural films), that is, as belonging to a film genre that Hilmar Hoffmann has described as a "one-sided propaganda device." Hilmar Hoffmann, *The Triumph of Propaganda: Film and National Socialism, 1933–1945* (New York: Berghahn, 1996), 130.

[6] Quoted in Helmuth Zebhauser, Maike Trentin-Meyer, eds., *Zwischen Idylle und Tummelplatz: Katalog für das Alpine Museum des Deutschen Alpenvereins in München* (Munich: Bergverlag Rudolf Rother, 1996), 308.

[7] The German Himalaya Foundation was founded on 28 May 1936 by Dr. Paul Bauer, Reich Sports Leader Hans von Tschammer und Osten, and Fritz Bechtold. Its declared goal was to exclusively organize, execute, and market all German mountaineering expeditions to the Himalayas. For detailed information on the foundation, see Peter Mierau, *Die Deutsche Himalaja-Stiftung von 1936 bis 1998: Ihre Geschichte und ihre Expeditionen* (Munich: Bergverlag Rudolf Rother, 1999).

[8] Quoted in Peter Mierau, *Nationalsozialistische Expeditionspolitik: Deutsche Asien-Expeditionen, 1933–1945* (Munich: Herbert Utz, 2006), 229.

[9] Hajo Bernett, *Nationalsozialistische Leibeserziehung: Eine Dokumentation ihrer Theorie und Organisation* (Schorndorf bei Stuttgart: Verlag Karl Hofmann, 1966), 19.

[10] Adolf Hitler, *Mein Kampf* (Boston: Mariner, 1999), 411. The German original reads: "den Glauben an die Unbesiegbarkeit seines ganzen Volkstums wiedergewinnen." Adolf Hitler, *Mein Kampf* (Munich: Zentralverlag der NSDAP. Franz Eher Nachf., 1938), 456.

[11] Hitler, *Mein Kampf*, 413. The German original reads: "den körperlich bereits tadellos vorgebildeten jungen Menschen nur mehr in den Soldaten verwandeln." Hitler, *Mein Kampf*, 459.

[12] Meinhart Sild, "Bergsteigen als Rüstung," *Österreichische Alpenzeitung* 1195 (1938): 160–64.

[13] Sild, "Bergsteigen als Rüstung," 162.

[14] Quoted in Peter Reichel, *Der schöne Schein des Dritten Reiches: Faszination und Gewalt des Faschismus* (Frankfurt am Main: Fischer, 1993), 208.

[15] Jay W. Baird, *To Die for Germany: Heroes in the Nazi Pantheon* (Bloomington: Indiana UP, 1992), xi.

[16] Eric Hobsbawm and Terence Ranger, eds., *The Invention of Tradition* (Cambridge: Cambridge UP, 1992), 2.

[17] Hobsbawm, Ranger, *The Invention of Tradition*, 9.

[18] For detailed documentation of this process, see Helmuth Zebhauser, *Alpinismus im Hitlerstaat* (Munich: Bergverlag Rudolf Rother, 1998), 205–9.

[19] For details, see Zebhauser, *Alpinismus*, 216.
[20] On this subject, see Märtin, *Nanga Parbat*, 304.
[21] Quoted in Zebhauser, *Alpinismus*, 221.
[22] On this connection see Mierau, *Die Deutsche Himalaja-Stiftung*, 159.
[23] Bauer formulated his position in a letter to the Federal Ministry of the Interior (Bundesinnenministerium) dated 7 March 1953: "Herrligkoffer hat nicht erkannt, dass man für einen Angriff auf einen Achttausender eine fest geschlossene Mannschaft braucht." (Herrligkoffer does not understand that for an attack on a 8,000m peak one needs a unified team). Quoted in Mierau, *Die Deutsche Himalaja-Stiftung*, 159.
[24] For a detailed discussion of this conflict between Herrligkoffer and Bauer, see Mierau, *Die Deutsche Himalaja-Stiftung*, 158–81, and Märtin, *Nanga Parbat*, 255–64.
[25] It is worth noting that in his effort to free his enterprise from the legacy of the German Himalaya Foundation and its expeditions to Nanga Parbat, Herrligkoffer adopted another, more personal legacy: that of his half-brother Willy Merkl, the leader of the 1934 attempt. Merkl's expedition, however, had already been contaminated by the militaristic ideology of the 1930s. Trying to apply Merkl's mountaineering philosophy and leadership principles to a post–Second World War expedition built upon the strengths and achievements of individual mountaineers was a severe mistake on Herrligkoffer's part and resulted in major tensions between Buhl and the expedition leader. On this subject see most recently Ralf-Peter Märtin, *Die Messner-Brüder am Nanga Parbat: Zwei Brüder, ein Berg, ihr Schicksal; Offizielles Buch zum Film von Joseph Vilsmaier* (Munich: Südwest-Verlag, 2010), 29.
[26] For detailed biographical information on Hans Ertl see http://www.herrligkoffer-stiftung.de/bedeutende-persoenlichkeiten/hans-ertl.
[27] It was exactly this notion of German superiority that had driven earlier German efforts on Nanga Parbat. This is once more part of a larger National Socialist strategy regarding the use of sports events and is evident in the comments of several individuals connected to the expeditions themselves. In Peter Reichel's words: "Die sichtbare Überlegenheit der Deutschen in vielen sportlichen Wettkämpfen verdichtete sich zur allgemeinen, 'rassischen' Überlegenheit" (The visible German dominance in various sporting events was condensed into a general "racial" superiority). Reichel, *Der schöne Schein des Dritten Reiches*, 270.
[28] Quoted in Zebhauser, *Alpinismus*, 132.
[29] Buhl's motivation stands in stark contrast to that of the expedition leader, Dr. Karl Maria Herrligkoffer, who, in his official expedition report titled *Nanga Parbat 1953*, identified "das Vermächtnis aller Toten vom Nanga Parbat" (the legacy of all who died on Nanga Parbat) as the driving force for his expedition. Quoted in Horst Höfler and Reinhold Messner, *Karl Maria Herrligkoffer: Besessen, sieghaft, umstritten* (Zurich: AS Verlag, 2001), 71.
[30] Ertl first came in contact with Fanck and his famous Freiburg school of cinematography in 1932, when he joined the production of *S.O.S. Eisberg* as a camera

assistant and mountain guide. Ertl continued to develop his craft under Fanck's tutelage during the production of *Der ewige Traum* in 1933. After collaborating with Leni Riefenstahl on *Tag der Freiheit — Unsere Wehrmacht* (1935) and *Olympia* (1936), and with Luis Trenker on *Liebesbriefe aus dem Engadin* (1937/38), both of whom had learned their craft from Fanck by starring in his films before actually producing their own, he returned as cameraman in charge of exterior shots for Fanck's 1938/39 production *Ein Robinson: Das Tagebuch eines Matrosen*, a propaganda film retelling the trials and tribulations of the German cruiser *Dresden* and her crew during the First World War. It is therefore not surprising that Ertl's cinematic language employed in *Nanga Parbat 1953* is strongly influenced by Fanck's.

[31] For a detailed account of Ertl's work as related to National Socialist propaganda efforts, see Hans Ertl, *Meine wilden dreißiger Jahre: Bergsteiger, Filmpionier, Weltenbummler* (Munich: Herbig Verlag, 1982), 128–29, 185, 194, 203, 209, 240, 242, 248, 253, and 315–17.

[32] See for instance Georg Seeßlen, "Durch die Heimat und so weiter: Heimatfilme, Schlagerfilme und Ferienfilme der fünfziger Jahre," in *Zwischen Gestern und Morgen: Westdeutscher Nachkriegsfilm, 1946–1962*, ed. Hilmar Hoffmann and Walter Schobert (Frankfurt am Main: Deutsches Filmmuseum, 1989), 140.

[33] Macfarlane, *Mountains of the Mind*, 16.

Spatial Orientation and Embodied Transcendence in Werner Herzog's Mountain Climbing Films

Roger Cook

> *Es ist offenbar viel schwieriger, den Berg auf die Leinwand als den Menschen auf den Berg zu bringen.*
> —Reinhold Messner, *13 Spiegel meiner Seele*
>
> [It is apparently much more difficult to bring a mountain to the movie screen than to put a person on the mountain.]

IN 1984 HERZOG ACCOMPANIED the famous South Tyrolean mountain climber Reinhold Messner on an expedition to the central Karakoram mountain range in northeastern Pakistan to film the latter's attempt at an unprecedented climbing feat. Messner and his fellow climber Hans Kammerlander were seeking to become the first to ascend two 8,000-meter peaks (Gasherbrum I and Gasherbrum II) in succession without returning to base camp. In a voiceover during an extended panning shot of the Karakoram at the beginning of the film, Herzog lays out what he wanted to explore in the resulting television documentary, *Gasherbrum — Der leuchtende Berg* (Gasherbrum — the glowing mountain, 1985):[1]

> Uns interessierte nicht so sehr einen Film über die bergsteigerische Tat oder über Klettertechnik zu machen. Was wir wissen wollten, war: was geht in Bergsteigern vor, die so etwas Extremes unternehmen?
>
> [We weren't so much interested in making a film about mountain climbing *per se*, or about climbing techniques. What we wanted to find out was what goes on inside mountain climbers who undertake such extreme endeavors.]

In the same voiceover he establishes a working thesis that will guide the film's investigation into what motivates the climber: "Was ist die Faszination, die sie wie Süchtige auf die Gipfel treibt? Sind diese Berge und Gipfel nicht etwa eine Eigenschaft im Innersten von uns allen?" (What is the fascination that drives them to the summits like addicts? Aren't these mountains and summits perhaps something deep within us all?) The clear connotation here is that it is not necessary to risk one's life climbing to the top of these mountains in order to experience what they have to offer. He is also implying that they can provide us with something profound that is missing in our modern lives.

Whatever that something might be, the other question lurking here as the camera slowly tilts and pans along the ridges and summits is whether film can offer the viewer this profound experience. One answer would be that the film images present this environment in such a way that the viewer projects an inner experience onto mountains. Referring to the long take of a mountain landscape at the beginning of *Lebenszeichen* (Signs of life, 1968),[2] Herzog himself suggests that the shot has such an effect: "It gives you time to really climb deep inside the landscapes, and for them to climb inside you. It shows that these are not just literal landscapes you are looking at, but landscapes of the mind too."[3] In exactly this vein, Eric Ames describes how Herzog's strategy for depicting landscapes relies "on the spectator's powers of visualization and projection." He offers as an example the slow pan of the Karakoram in *Gasherbrum*, claiming that by flattening out the image with the strong telephoto lens, Herzog transforms "the physical environment into a graphic pattern, resignifying the depicted mountains and ravines as the 'highs' and 'lows' of an inner world."[4]

Without denying that the landscape images in *Gasherbrum* may well have this effect on viewers, I want to argue that Herzog also pursues another strategy to convey the experience of the mountain climber. Instead of reading the images either as signs or as icons of a sublime experience,[5] I explore how they exert a physical effect on the viewer and, in doing so, reveal a different likeness to the majestic peaks of the Karakoram. The film induces an embodied mode of viewing, not by representing the environment as landscape, but rather by simulating particular physical circumstances to which the climber must react. To establish how this is possible, my analysis will take something of a circuitous route through physiological questions about the body's systems for establishing spatial orientation (during climbing, in particular) and theoretical questions about the viewer's embodied perception of film space (also with respect to mountain climbing). Drawing on this discussion of spatial orientation, I will show how *Gasherbrum* situates the viewer with respect to the physical environment in a fundamentally different manner than Herzog's other film about mountain climbing, the 1991 feature *Cerro Torre: Schrei aus Stein* (Cerro Torre: Scream of stone). Building on this distinction, I will then suggest how the alternative construction of space in *Gasherbrum* enables the viewer to participate in a body-mind state of the climber and to experience that within us which is like the mountains of the Karakoram.

Spatial Orientation: Cognitive Mapping and Proprioception

To explain how *Gasherbrum* can simulate a certain mind-body-set of the climber I begin with the body's two systems for establishing spatial orientation: *cognitive mapping* (CM) and *proprioceptive spatial orientation* (PSO). Our ability to create cognitive maps and then situate ourselves within a visually represented three-dimensional space is the more dominant system in most human activities and has been the main subject for studies of spatial mapping. CM relies on visual cues to reference one's position within an imagined spatial grid. Recently more attention has been given to the role that the proprioceptive system plays in our ability to move effectively within our immediate environment. Responding to the pure movement of the body through an indeterminate space, PSO does not employ the visual referencing of objects in relation to each other. Dependent solely on internal feedback, proprioception continually reworks neuronal flows marking the movement of parts of the body into a continuous information feed about the position of the body as a whole. While CM depends on one's position within a visually inscribed layout, proprioceptive orientation "*inverts the relation of position to movement.* Movement is no longer indexed to position. Rather, position emerges from movement, from a relation of movement to itself."[6]

For the purposes of this article, the key question is how proprioception works together with cognitive mapping. Even though the viewer remains largely stationary during a film, CM and PSO cofunction with respect to film space in the same basic way that they do in real environments. Although they are never mutually exclusive, the deployment of one system often requires that the other be largely deactivated. For example, if I am walking through an area that I know from past outings I may "lose myself" in the physical activity and suddenly discover that I am not sure where I am. In order to determine my position I have to stop, look for known landmarks, and situate myself within a cognitively mapped mental picture of the area. I turn off the automatic pilot that has been guiding me largely via PSO and engage my powers of CM. But this "takes effort — an effort that interferes with the actual movement of orientation. *Cognitive mapping takes over where orientation stops.*"[7]

It is necessary to stop when one shifts modes, not simply because CM depends on visual cues, but also because it requires the visualization of space. PSO also relies on visual input. Indeed, the argument I will make about the alternative construction of filmic space in *Gasherbrum* depends precisely on the role that vision plays in PSO. To establish how this works, let us consider the following scenario. You are walking down a sidewalk that consists of separate concrete slabs that do not always abut evenly, but rather occasionally form an edge that you might stumble over. You do not need to assess each one cognitively in order to walk smoothly down the sidewalk. Your peripheral vision in conjunction with the unconscious memories stored from all your past experience with irregular sidewalks enables you to negotiate these minor obstacles, even if you have never been down this particular sidewalk before. Only when you actually trip and stumble do you stop, look down at the cause and make a microlevel cognitive map that will help you avoid stumbling in the future. This account indicates that PSO and CM operate in a *hinged* relationship. When one becomes dominant, the door swings toward closing on the other. However, they do not work in exclusion of each other or according to a two-step process, but rather function in an integrated codependency.[8] For example, we could say that the ability to walk down an unfamiliar sidewalk using PSO without stumbling *hinges* on the experience of cognitively mapping the topography of sidewalks after having tripped in the past. This relationship between the two also accounts for the dominant role of CM in spatial orientation. As in the scenario described here, all our movements guided by PSO are subject to a cognitive overcoding that puts this more intuitive system to service in the context of possible future environments that have been mapped out by past experience.

This hinged interplay is at work in the simulated spatial orientation that occurs during film viewing as well. However, the principles and rules for the filmic construction of space in mainstream narrative cinema promote the dominance of CM. Classical editing techniques create a temporal and a spatial continuity, both within each scene and across all the scenes of the film. As a result, viewers can situate and orient themselves within the three-dimensional virtual space of the film.[9] The "eye of the camera" produces an anthropocentrically organized image and an imagined adult body that is its phenomenological correspondent. This invisible body schema, which I call the *embedded viewer*, enables the viewer to cognitively map the spatial environment of the film world.

As the rules of classical narrative cinema promote CM, they also suppress the potential of the embedded viewer to stir simulated proprioceptive responses in the spectator. Camera movements that could generate proprioceptive tactility are reduced to a minimum.[10] Movement between fixed camera shots is largely eliminated, thus carving up the narrative space into compartmentalized segments observed from clearly established points of view. As camera movement has become more prevalent in narrative film, dollies, cranes, tracking, and more recent inventions such as the Steadicam have provided a stable sense of balance and evenness. In contrast to the real world, where proprioception works in conjunction with all the senses to maintain a sense of balance, in mainstream narrative film visual orientation serves as the almost exclusive source of balance.

The basic aesthetic and narrative strategies of classical cinema pose a particular problem to the filmmaker who wants to convey the climbing experience. In contrast to film viewing, climbing demands a continuous activation of proprioception. Indeed, the climber attempting to negotiate a steep ascent is perhaps more dependent on PSO than a person in almost any other situation. Even those who have never scaled a mountain can imagine how more than a minimal interruption of the proprioceptive orientation according to movement could pose a mortal risk. Advice commonly given the novice climber — "Don't look down" — illustrates this. The shift from physical concentration on climbing to looking down restores a dangerous moment of CM. The climber suddenly envisions the location of the body within a cognitively mapped larger space, namely perilously perched high up the mountainside. The danger involved in this situation leads to a chain of cognitive and emotional states that interfere in the sustained and concentrated work of proprioception needed to negotiate the task of climbing.

At the same time, the value of CM is diminished during climbing. The visual sighting of landmarks that are essential in finding our way around a city or a less demanding natural landscape is normally of little use on the side of a mountain. This is not to say that they are not essential for mountain climbing as well. There, too, they are an important part of the cognitive overcoding that always works in a hinged conjunction with PSO. In the case of climbing, this overcoding of CM is in fact often quite complex and extensive. However, it is usually established well ahead of time, when the climbers plan out the route up the mountain, the often long and arduous task of getting to the starting point for the ascent, and the schedule for executing it while the conditions are right. Once the actual climb begins, it usually plays a much smaller role. The important landmarks on the path up the mountain have been mapped by earlier expeditions (the Hillary Step on Mt. Everest, to give a well-known example) and are integrated into the planning such that the mountaineer needs only to note them as they appear along the route. And the most prominent landmark of all, the summit, is seldom visible during the climb. Rather, the climber is often fooled into thinking that the last visible point, the so-called "false summit," is the peak. In other words, CM shifts into automatic pilot on the mountain.

Spatial Orientation and Feature Films:
Schrei aus Stein

Given this fundamental opposition in terms of spatial orientation, film — and narrative film in particular — would seem to be poorly equipped to convey the climbing experience. The construction of narrative space in conventional feature films tends to lock the viewer into the cognitive mode of spatial orientation more firmly and inhibit participation in the climber's attention to proprioceptive self-movement. Herzog's attempt at a Hollywood-style narrative film about mountain climbing, *Schrei aus Stein*, is a case in point.

After his experience making *Gasherbrum*, Herzog gave up on his idea of shooting a feature film in the Karakoram, declaring the conditions simply too rough for filming. Messner suggested that he make instead a film based on the disputed first ascent of Cerro Torre (3,133 m/10,280 ft.), "a frightening, mile-high spike of vertical and overhanging granite . . . once thought (though no longer) to be the world's hardest mountain."[11] Imposing and difficult because of its sheer faces, almost constant strong winds, and the mushroom-shaped rime ice that sits atop its thin summit, Cerro Torre lies in the Southern Patagonian Ice Field in Argentina and does not pose the same problems for filming as the high-altitude Himalayas. The production designer and Herzog collaborator Walter Saxer wrote the script for *Schrei aus Stein* together with a colleague, and Herzog agreed to direct the film because he liked the idea, even though he thought "the script had many weak points, particularly the dialogue."[12] The final product suffers from bad acting as well as bad dialogue and has not been well received. Herzog has also said that he has never really considered the film to be his own.[13]

The film fictionalizes the 1959 attempt at a first ascent of Cerro Torre by Cesare Maestri and Toni Egger. After introducing the basic story of the 1959 climb, *Schrei aus Stein* tells the fictional tale of how the heightened media focus on the disputed ascent leads to a televised race up Cerro Torre between an Alpinist and a sport climber. When the pressure of the highly publicized event spurs the competing climbers to participate despite bad weather, it ends tragically. Martin (Stefan Glowacz), the sport climber, loses his hold near the summit and ends up unconscious, dangling from his rope in a hopeless position. The film ends with a circular helicopter shot of the successful Roccia (Vittorio Mezzagiorno), the Alpinist, standing on the summit. During this shot we also see the dangling Martin as a sign that the two climbers had been lured into participating in a travesty of the climbing experience. The circular camera movement is reminiscent of the final shot of Aguirre alone and crazed on his raft in *Aguirre, der Zorn Gottes* (Aguirre, the wrath of God, 1972).[14] Just as that final scene marks the madness not merely of Aguirre but also of Spain's Catholic-Imperial colonial venture, the closing shot of *Schrei aus Stein* condemns the influence that the media and commercial world have on mountaineering.

In addition to this more obvious message, *Schrei aus Stein* also reveals something about the ability to depict mountain climbing in film. In the long final sequence of the race up Cerro Torre, Herzog provides a visual account that enables the viewer to accompany Martin and Roccia simultaneously on their respective ascents. He employs helicopters and cameras placed on the mountain to film the ascent of the fictional climbers all the way up to the summit. Despite these brilliantly filmed scenes, the film does not capture the climbing experience as effectively as does *Gasherbrum*, in which there are almost no sequences depicting the historic climb. Perhaps aware of film's limits in this regard, Herzog couches the climbing sequences of *Schrei aus Stein* in a plot that seems to suggest that film cannot do them justice. One could argue in fact that the entire film story is an ironical indictment of the film itself. Its harsh critical view of the media's attempts to turn mountain climbing into a competitive sport could just as well be directed at Herzog's effort to make a successful feature film about it.

There is another climber in the film whose role supports this reading. Fingerless (Brad Dourif) is a strange, solitary figure with an obsession for Mae West, who appears out of nowhere and tells Roccia coincidentally that he had, unbeknown to everyone, already climbed Cerro Torre. He explains that he calls himself Fingerless because he had "left" four fingers and his name on the mountain. Roccia writes him off as an intriguing, but ultimately deluded, eccentric. But when he pulls himself up onto the summit, Roccia finds an ice axe implanted in the snow with a picture of Mae West attached to it. This obsessed loner who had scaled Cerro Torre for the first time with no fanfare and without even documenting the climb is a clear, if obviously exaggerated, facsimile of the Messner that Herzog showcases in *Gasherbrum*. The four missing fingers allude to Messner telling Herzog with an impish smile that he only has four remaining toes. Also, the name left on the mountain recalls Messner's account in *Gasherbrum* of his own death and rebirth on Nanga Parbat in 1970. And the fact that Fingerless's ascent was not filmed (or even publicized) corresponds to Herzog's inability to accompany and film Messner and Kammerlander on any part of their double climb in 1984 as he had originally planned. The fact that Fingerless's ascent remains completely offscreen also reveals a perspective that I think Herzog had gained while making *Gasherbrum*. It represents his ideas about film's limited ability to capture the mountaineering experience. As dynamic and masterful as the filmic depiction of the two climbers ascending Cerro Torre is, it gives a distorted sense of the actual experience. I would argue that for Herzog this holds for any filmic depiction of a climb, whether it is a fictional episode in a feature film or a documentary reenactment of an actual ascent. This might also explain why he has not made another film about mountain climbing since *Schrei aus Stein*.

Alternative Construction of Space in *Gasherbrum*

I turn now to *Gasherbrum* and contrast the way space is constructed there as opposed to the later feature film. Even in the dramatic climbing episodes on the side of the mountain in *Schrei aus Stein*, the spectator occupies a cognitively mapped space in the position of what I described above as an embedded viewer. This engagement with the action of the film enables the viewer to share in some of the physical sensations related to the on-the-mountain experience of the characters. However, the narrative context for the climbing scenes also detracts from the film's ability to evoke the underlying state of body-mind that the climber assumes on the mountain.

Herzog is able to convey the climbing experience with more success here because he has no footage that he himself shot while accompanying Messner and Kammerlander on their climb. This was not by choice. Herzog quickly discovered that the harsh conditions in the Karakoram would not allow them to film the climbers once they left base camp.[15] The film includes brief clips shot by Kammerlander with their small 8-mm Bell and Howell camera, but these merely document that they encountered difficult weather conditions and did in fact reach both summits. Herzog could have reenacted the climb in more accessible areas, filmed so as to simulate the ascent of the Gasherbrum peaks. Kevin Macdonald took this approach in *Touching the Void* (2003), which tells the compelling true story of two British climbers' attempt to scale Siula Grande (6,344 m/20,814 ft.) in the Peruvian Andes.[16] Herzog is one who normally relishes the physical challenges of such a shoot rather than shying away from it, as is evidenced in the spectacular footage of the climbers on and atop Cerro Torre in *Schrei aus Stein*. But in this case he chose not to.

Whatever the reason, his decision not to depict the climb itself enables, almost paradoxically, a construction of filmic space in *Gasherbrum* that elicits the proprioceptive orientation of the mountain climber. As the film begins to document in loose narrative form the course of the expedition, Herzog employs alternative film techniques to evoke this spatial relationship in the viewer. In mainstream narrative film, the classical system overcomes the limits of the frame in order to create a full three-dimensional film world. In direct contravention to this method, Herzog employs various techniques to restrict the visual scope provided by the camera. He isolates individual body parts and random stretches of the gorge and river without situating them within a larger filmic space. To let this alternative approach work its effect, Herzog must actively counter the ingrained tendency of the moviegoer to piece together a self-contained filmic space. He does this for example by eschewing conventional establishing shots. The opening shots of Gasherbrum I and Gasherbrum II during the credits serve as establishing shots in the sense that they introduce the mountains to be climbed. But they also present the Karakoram as a location that cannot be mapped visually as a whole. The true establishing shot for the film follows the first brief interview with Messner and Kammerlander. It is an almost two-minute long slow pan in which the camera also tilts so as to follow the outline of the range's ridges and summits. Imparting a physical sense of presence, this shot does not situate the viewer in a narrative space defined by the course of the expedition. Rather it situates the viewer directly in relation to the Karakoram as place. And it also signals that the relationship between humans and the natural environment in this region does not follow familiar patterns.

The frequent shots of the physical setting in *Gasherbrum* also do not offer a landscape view of the region. Nor are they even pictorial shots. On the contrary, they suggest that no expansive, single view can portray the Karakoram, and in doing so they steer away from interpretations of symbolic meaning. In fact, they are not even representational. Rather, they render the natural movement of the region in passages that — as Siegfried Kracauer says about cinema's ability to capture motion — redeem physical reality.[17] These shots exhibit movement in several ways. There are panning shots that slowly sweep the surrounding mountains, and camera tilts that emphasize the dramatic cliffs and slopes rising or dropping off from the camera position. The region itself is also full of movement. In shots reminiscent of *Schrei aus Stein* and *La Soufrière* (1977)[18] clouds swirl around the peaks, always threatening and then actually collecting swiftly into a powerful snowstorm. At another point there is a two-shot sequence of a huge avalanche crashing down through a valley. The first long shot reveals how large it is, the second zooms in to capture up close the movement and power of the cascading snow. Although inserted between two extreme long shots of Messner and Kammerlander as they climb away from base camp, the avalanche does not affect the expedition or their ascent. Rather the shot gives the viewer a physical sense of the movement and force that abound in the Karakoram.

In perhaps the most dynamic sequence of the film, Herzog strings together a series of shots along the expedition's trek up a craggy canyon toward the Baltoro Glacier. The sequence begins and is interspersed with close-ups of the swirling and crashing currents of the Braldu River. As the team works its way up to the base camp, the porters struggle to maintain their footholds in the scree on the slopes above the river, occasionally setting off small rockslides that threaten to send the team members below tumbling down into the river. In close-ups the camera is isolated on the feet of the porters as they cross a narrow plank above a deep gorge and later as they contend with the loose rock. Unframed by establishing shots, these close-ups defy the viewer's attempts to map out spatially the progress of the expedition. Given the lack of such a stable spatial orientation, the close-ups of the churning water, the tumbling rocks, the feet of the porters, and the packs on their backs as well as the tilts and pans of the camera that capture the natural environment of the Karakoram all tend to evoke proprioceptive sensations.

Yet it remains to be shown how film can engage proprioception at all. When feature films show exciting climbing sequences they clearly evoke physical sensations in the viewer, often those associated with either the risk of falling or an actual fall. However, such effects typically aim for kinesthetic responses. The opening sequence of *Cliffhanger* (1993) contains a trademark example of this technique.[19] Various shots leading up to the climactic tragic moment of Sarah's (Michelle Joyner) fall accentuate the sense of danger: from horizontal shots of the steep rock column on which she and her climbing partner are perched, to the vertigo-inducing shots directed downward, to a simple shot of Gabe's (Sylvester Stallone) feet precariously balanced on a tower atop the column. The most dramatic and sensational (in the sense of arousing physical sensations) are the shot/reverse shot subjective views between Gabe and Sarah, culminating in her slow-motion fall from his perspective after her hand slips out of the glove and Gabe's grasp. This stirring of kinesthesia through the representation of movement in film is accentuated by the cognitive mapping that enables the spectator to enter the scene as an embedded viewer. The latter then serves as a conduit through which the physical sensation is conveyed to the moviegoer.

However, proprioception is not activated in this way, nor is it easily engaged in film viewing at all. Although often confused or seen as overlapping with kinesthesia, it depends on feedback from different sensory systems. Kinesthesia functions on the basis of sensory data gained from the surface of the body. Proprioception is stimulated by the nervous system as a whole, that is, by internal sensory data and, in particular, by input from receptors located in the joints and muscles. Because kinesthesia responds to external data, it can be activated by the construction and manipulation of a cognitively mapped narrative film space inhabited by the viewer. The stimulation of proprioception, on the other hand, is heightened when this conventional spatial construction falls apart. Proprioception serves to offset that loss and even to restore it in some alternative fashion. This moment of reconstitution exhibits the hinged relationship between CM and PSO.

Other filmic elements can work in concert with spatial deconstruction to spur proprioception. In *Gasherbrum* the effects of the close-ups of movement in the journey along the Braldu are intensified by sound. The dynamic sounds of the water, the footsteps in the loose scree, and the rocks rolling down the slope, are all accented so as to reinforce the active engagement of the viewer's proprioceptive system aurally. Throughout this sequence the roaring sound of the Braldu River is constantly present, at times foregrounded, at other times forming an almost seismic backdrop to the procession's efforts to negotiate the difficult terrain. When the scene cuts to the traditional resting spot along the approach to base camp, the roar of the river gives way to the gentle babbling of a thermal spring in which Messner and Kammerlander soothe their aches. This transition lets the viewer share in the physical rhythm of the journey as experienced by the climbers, thus extending the proprioceptive involvement in the film in a more tranquil mode as well.

The kinesthetic effect created by falling or the risk of falling depends on the viewer being oriented with respect to horizontal. Proprioception on

Fig. 1. Messner and Kammerlander filmed from base camp on the first leg of the ascent.

the other hand may become engaged when that orientation is withheld, particularly in relation to moving figures. In *Gasherbrum* the massive size and rugged terrain of the mountains enable medium and even extreme long shots that fail to provide the viewer with a clear spatial orientation. At one point in the trek up to the glacier a medium long shot, reminiscent of the opening sequence of *Aguirre*, shows Messner leading the line of porters down a narrow trail between canyon boulders. The episode is filmed from an opposing slope so that the entire shot is enclosed within the narrow canyon walls. As a result the viewer cannot clearly determine the horizontal plane in this scene. The inability to establish this orientation disrupts the sense of balance in the viewer and engages proprioception in an instinctive attempt to restore it. The same effect occurs in the shot of the porters descending the steep slope above the river. As they struggle to maintain their balance, the close-ups of their feet slipping on the loose rock are also set within an image devoid of a secure horizontal frame of reference. This effect reaches its dramatic highpoint when Messner and Kammerlander leave base camp to begin their climb. The first shot of them climbing shows two small figures against a white backdrop of snow. They are almost six kilometers away and 1,000 meters higher than the camp, as Herzog relates in a voiceover, even though they seem to be at the same height as the camera. Herzog then cuts to a shot some time later, their figures still set against snow, but much smaller. Although they must be even higher now, the shot creates the optical illusion that the camera is looking down on them from an even steeper angle. It is not until the camera slowly tilts upward, tracing their route up the mountain, that we get the sense that we were actually looking up at them. The unexpectedly long duration of this tilt before it reaches the summit underscores the magnitude of the climb awaiting them. It also gives the viewer a sense of the restricted spatial orientation available to the climber on the mountain. Only when the camera reaches the summit are we able to see the sky behind the peak. The massive size of the mountain blocks it and until the very end of this extended shot denies visual access to the feature that can establish horizontal orientation. This shot thwarts the viewer's ability to become oriented via cognitive mapping, activates through simulation the proprioceptive system of the spectator, and links this effect to the situation of the mountain climber, all in one.[20]

The Body-Mind Hinge of the Mountain Climber

In *Gasherbrum* the aesthetic strategies that shut down CM and activate PSO serve to convey aspects of the state of body-mind assumed by the mountain climber. The film also explores a deeper link between the physical state required for climbing and the mental make-up that drives the climber to risk everything on the mountain. As he interviews Messner along the way, Herzog discovers something about this connection that he considers key to Messner's motivation for climbing. He asks the kind of existential questions that are often posed to mountain climbers, such as "Why do you do it?" Messner offers clear, well-considered answers that go beyond the common clichéd responses of "Because it is there" (George Mallory) or to "Knock the bastard off" (Edmund Hillary). In something of a philosophical vein he says that it is only in the harshest conditions of great peril on the mountain that one can find the true measure of oneself.[21] Or he assumes the position of social or cultural critic when he declares that mountain climbing is a symptom of the degeneration in human existence.[22] But the most interesting responses occur when Messner begins talking more freely, almost as if he were verbalizing his train of thoughts to an analyst.

The film ends with such a sequence, one where Messner's mental vision correlates with the mode of spatial orientation the film generates. It is part of a longer interview that took place before the climb. The fact that Herzog chooses to end the film with this piece points to its significance for what he is trying to say about mountain climbing. Even though he is about to set off on a perilous venture that will tax the body's limits for pain and exhaustion, Messner asserts that mountain climbing is no longer so important for him. By this he must mean that his desire to accomplish great climbing feats or to find the measure of himself has waned. And yet he is

Fig. 2. Messner in interview sequence voicing the words: "Heute stelle ich mir manchmal vor, oder wünsche ich mir, dass ich über Jahrzehnte, ja vielleicht für immer, einfach nur weiter gehe, nur gehen, . . . bis die Welt aufhört."

preparing to attempt something never done before — to climb two 8,000-meter peaks in succession. In light of this contradiction, Herzog presses Messner for what is driving him. He seems to think he has found a partial answer in the passage he reserves for the end of the film. There Messner says he has a desire to just keep walking without getting anywhere, with no destination:

> Heute stelle ich mir manchmal vor, oder wünsche ich mir, dass ich über Jahrzehnte, ja vielleicht für immer, einfach nur weiter gehe, nur gehen, . . . bis die Welt aufhört
>
> [I imagine sometimes now, or I have the wish, that I just keep walking for decades, or perhaps even forever, . . . simply walking until the world ends.]

Herzog indicates how closely this part of the climber's mental make-up resonates with him when he chimes in here to say that he too has this same wish.[23]

The *Wunschvorstellung* Messner describes here has little to do with the drive to push the limits of human capacity that motivates most mountain climbers, including himself. He says as much: "Das Klettern ist mir schon nicht wie das Hinaufsteigen, sondern das Ziehen, weiter ziehen" (For me now climbing is not like ascending, but rather moving on, moving forward). He is expressing here the desire to remain permanently in the state the climber attains on the mountain in which the proprioceptive system takes over the body almost to the exclusion of cognitive oversight. In the scenario he envisions, his location in the world no longer matters. He would never need to stop and reassess through CM where he is and where he is going: "Ich habe hinten nichts mehr, ich brauche auch hinten nichts mehr, ich gehe auf nirgends hin, ich habe gar kein Ziel, ich gehe nur" (I have nothing left behind me, I don't need anything behind me, I am not headed anywhere, I have no goal, I just keep walking). In a state of pure embodied presence CM would give way completely to the body simply moving through the world, guided solely by the continuation of that movement.

The explanation of how this wish relates to his psychological frame of mind is revealed in a pivotal moment in the film. In the tent shortly before they embark on the climb Herzog asks Messner about his brother's death and how it has affected him. Messner launches into a description of the 1970 ascent of Nanga Parbat (8,126 m/26,668 ft.) on which his brother died.[24] He explains that after his brother had disappeared, apparently swept away by an avalanche, he just kept going out of pure habit, no longer thinking, no longer feeling pain even though he could not get his feet into his boots and had to continue barefoot. When he woke up in the valley and discovered that he had made it down the mountain and was still alive, it was, he says, as if he had died and a new life had begun. At the end of this account, Herzog, in an emotionally exploitative fashion for which he has been criticized,[25] asks how he broke the news to his mother. As Herzog continues to film, Messner begins to sob and is only able to stammer amidst tears that his mother understood better than anyone else. He then buries his face in his arm as he keeps crying.

Herzog's probing question restores the link in Messner back to the past that had been largely severed by what he calls his own "death" and "rebirth" on that tragic climb. Messner's reaction to it also suggests that the need to get back on the mountain stems from the desire to close oneself off from memory and even cognition itself. Herzog cuts from the shot of Messner crying with his face buried in his arms to another shot in the tent apparently only shortly later. Messner and Kammerlander are sorting out what needs to be done in case they do not return. A steely determinedness has returned to him, and the sequencing of these two discussions reinforces his earlier admission that climbing is an addiction. When paired with the wishful fantasy he reveals in the final sequence, this emotional interlude in the tent suggests that he is seeking a pure engagement in the present that leaves little room for cognition, and even less for memory. But in contrast to his fantasy of walking unendingly, leaving everything behind, mountain climbing provides only a temporary reprise from cognition and memory. Messner's responses shed light on his description of climbing as an addiction. Only in the most extreme life-and-death situations on the mountain, when the body must block out cognitive operations connected with the self as being, can memory be held at bay so effectively. Just as the high produced by drugs often serves to obliterate the addict's haunting past, Messner seems to be drawn to mountain climbing now in part because he is trying to slam the door on the past, at least on everything that preceded his "rebirth" after the death of his brother.

The futility of this desire to escape from cognition and its requisite constituent, memory, is evident in the bodily system for spatial orientation. The hinge that connects CM and PSO as cofunctioning parts of a unified operating system — where one never functions without input from the other — exists whenever cognition occurs. Thought can never disengage itself from the sensory responses of the physical organism, and cognitive overcoding interfaces with all physical responses. In other words, the notion of a mind-body duality is a fallacy. Nonetheless, as the basis of the Cartesian subject, this duality is a constituent element of the modern world and responsible for what Messner calls the degeneration in human existence that causes the climber to risk everything for no tangible reason. Conversely, Messner's attempt to escape from this "degeneracy" through mountain climbing reflects a utopian longing to reverse the body-mind split and to return to a harmonious state where the two exist in perfect unison, without the hinge, as it were.

In this regard, Messner's compulsive need to climb mountains belongs to the Romantic turn away from modernity. Herzog's own fantasy of walking forever until all the paths have ended reveals that he shares this Romantic tendency with Messner.[26] It is a tendency that surfaces throughout his films. Critics agree on this point but differ as to the stance he takes toward Romantic fantasizing and mystification. Is he self-indulgent or ironic? Does he cultivate it or deconstruct it?[27] Without suggesting a definitive answer for his work as a whole, I would argue that what Herzog does in *Gasherbrum* is a common maneuver found in many of his films (*Aguirre* and *La Soufrière*, among others). He leads the viewer up to the brink of a sublime, or possibly catastrophic, encounter with natural or primitive cultural forces that might provide a transcendental experience. But Herzog takes the viewer to the threshold of Romantic mystification only to restore the simple truth that there is nothing more there than what meets the eye. The signature example of this tactic is in *Grizzly Man* (2005).[28] The camera fixes on the face of a bear, trained directly into its eyes, while Herzog declares in an emphatic voiceover: "I see only the overwhelming indifference of nature. To me, there is no such thing as a secret world of the bears. This blank stare speaks only of a half-bored interest in food." The reality expressed here asserts itself in *Gasherbrum* when Messner and Kammerlander return to base camp untransformed. There is no escape, no transcendence, only Messner's fantasy of such an experience. Human existence is shown to be as firmly entrenched in its being as the mountains of the Karakoram are in theirs. This is the answer to the central question posed during the establishing shot of the Karakoram: "What is the fascination that drives them to the peaks like addicts? Aren't these mountains and peaks like something deep within us all?" The film suggests that this essential nature within us is found neither in the superhuman endeavor to climb them, nor in the transcendental rapture felt by standing in awe of them, but rather in living our lives in simple coexistence, as the peoples of the Karakoram have done for centuries without feeling the need to ascend its peaks.

Notes

[1] *Gasherbrum — Der leuchtende Berg*, dir. Werner Herzog (Vienna: Werner Herzog Filmproduktion, 1985).

[2] *Lebenszeichen*, dir. Werner Herzog (Vienna: Werner Herzog Filmproduktion, 1968).

[3] Paul Cronin, ed., *Herzog on Herzog* (London: Faber & Faber, 2002), 39.

[4] Eric Ames, "Herzog, Landscape, and Documentary," *Cinema Journal* 48, no. 2 (Winter, 2009): 50.

[5] I think it is debatable to what extent the images can function as signs or icons and still exert the kind of physical effect I detect in *Gasherbrum*. Brad Prager, for example, contends that Herzog's images of mountains and fog "run the risk of losing their impact, or becoming what Noël Carroll refers to as 'icons of the sublimes.'" Brad Prager, *The Cinema of Werner Herzog: Aesthetic Ecstasy and Truth* (London: Wallflower, 2007), 84.

[6] Brian Massumi, *Parables for the Virtual: Movement, Affect, Sensation* (Durham, NC: Duke UP, 2002), 180.

[7] Massumi, *Parables for the Virtual*, 180.

[8] See John J. Rieser, "Dynamic Spatial Orientation and the Coupling of Representation and Action," in *Wayfinding Behavior: Cognitive Mapping and Other Spatial Processes*, ed. Reginald G. Colledge (Baltimore: Johns Hopkins UP, 1999), 176. For a good summary and analysis of the neuroscientific evidence of how conscious visual perception (vision-for-perception) and visuomotor systems (vision-for-action) interact, see Andy Clark, "Visual Experience and Motor Action: Are the Bonds Too Tight?" *The Philosophical Review* 110, no. 4 (Oct. 2001): 495–519.

[9] See David Bordwell, Janet Steiger, and Kristin Thompson, *The Classical Hollywood Cinema* (New York: New York UP, 1985), 214–15; Noël Burch, *Life to Those Shadows*, trans. and ed. Ben Brewster (Berkeley: U of California P, 1990); Tom Gunning, "'Primitive' Cinema: A Frame-Up? Or, The Trick's on Us," in *Early Cinema: Space, Frame, Narrative*, ed. Thomas Elsaesser (London: British Film Institute, 1990), 95–103; and Lev Manovich, *The Language of New Media* (Cambridge, MA: MIT Press, 2001), 107–8.

[10] Joseph D. Anderson makes this point when he claims that because vision dominates the spatial cognitive system "it is possible to enter the diegetic space of a motion picture effortlessly by way of the visual system without the necessity of proprioceptive confirmation." *The Reality of Illusion: An Ecological Approach to Cognitive Film Theory* (Carbondale: Southern Illinois UP, 1996), 113. I would only caution that his wording here seems to suggest a cleaner break between the two than ever actually occurs. See for example Jonathan Crary on this point: "Perception is always an amalgam of information from 'immediate' tactile receptors and 'distant' optical and auditory receptors, and distinctions between the optical and the tactile cease to be significant (or could only have significance for an impossibly motionless subject with no live relation to an environment). Vision as an 'autonomous' process or exclusively optical experience becomes an improbable fiction." Jonathan Crary, *Suspensions of Perception: Attention, Spectacle, and Modern Culture* (Cambridge, MA: MIT Press, 1999), 352.

[11] Jon Krakauer, *Into Thin Air: A Personal Account of the Mt. Everest Disaster* (New York: Willard, 1997), 25.

[12] Cronin, *Herzog on Herzog*, 223.

[13] Cronin, *Herzog on Herzog*, 223.

[14] *Aguirre, der Zorn Gottes*, dir. Werner Herzog. (Vienna: Werner Herzog Filmproduktion, 1972).

[15] Cronin, *Herzog on Herzog*, 195.

[16] *Touching the Void*, dir. Kevin Macdonald (London: Pathé, 2003).

[17] Siegfried Kracauer, *Theory of Film: The Redemption of Physical Reality* (Princeton, NJ: Princeton UP, 1997), 41–42.

[18] *La Soufrière — warten auf eine unausweichliche Katastrophe*, dir. Werner Herzog (Vienna: Werner Herzog Filmproduktion, 1977).

[19] *Cliffhanger*, dir. Renny Harlin (Beverly Hills: Carolco Pictures, 1993).

[20] Scott B. Watson hints at this aspect of the shot when he writes that the landscape "fills the screen and dominates the image, a landscape in which dimension and distance are difficult to determine and in which perspective is almost illusory." Scott B. Watson, "Herzog's Healing Images: Mountain Climbing and Mankind's Degeneration," *Aethlon: The Journal of Sports Literature* 10 (1992): 178. See also Prager, *Cinema of Werner Herzog*, 110.

[21] "Ich glaube, es gibt keine bessere Möglichkeit für einen Menschen im generellen, sein Maß zu finden, als gerade beim großen Bergsteigen."

[22] "Ich glaube, das ganze Bergsteigen ist eine Degenerationserscheinung der Menschheit. Der Mensch, solange er Mühe hat, seinen Lebensunterhalt zu verdienen, . . . denkt gar nicht daran, auf die Berge zu steigen."

[23] Herzog described his propensity for this mode of walking in his conversations with Cronin: "I like the idea of just disappearing, walking away, turning down the path and just carrying on until there is no path to follow. I would like to have Huskies with leather saddle bags and just walk and walk on until there is no road left" (Cronin, *Herzog on Herzog*, 193). See also his diary of his journey on foot in

1974 from Munich to Paris to visit Lotte Eisner in the hospital, *Vom Gehen im Eis* (Munich: Carl Hanser, 1978).

[24] In recent years other climbers on the expedition have challenged Messner's account of what happened and suggested that he was responsible for his brother's death. In part because Messner and his brother were alone on the climb, the dispute remains unsettled. However, the find of his brother's boot in 2004 and then his remains in 2005 tend to corroborate Messner's version. The dispute did not become full blown until years after Herzog's film, and the idea that Messner may have been at fault does not come up in the film.

[25] Prager writes about Herzog's lack of mercy when he places Messner before the camera in this scene (*Cinema of Werner Herzog*, 109) and relates it to two similar situations where Herzog "unblinkingly monitors his protagonists."

[26] Herzog has declared that he rejects Romanticism, which is not to say that his films are void of Romantic tendencies (Cronin, *Herzog on Herzog*, 135–36). Prager examines these Romantic tendencies at length, but does not argue that he actually fits into this tradition (*Cinema of Werner Herzog*, 11–15 and 82–119). Cronin denies outright that Herzog belongs to the Romantic tradition (*Herzog on Herzog*, viii).

[27] For a discussion of the irony question with respect to the mythologizing of landscape, see Ames, "Herzog, Landscape, and Documentary," 56–61 and 65. Alan Singer argues that Herzog's appeal to the "natural sublime" always includes the ironic awareness that reconciliation between nature and human existence is impossible. See Alan Singer, "Comprehending Appearances: Werner Herzog's Ironic Sublime," in *The Films of Werner Herzog: Between Mirage and History*, ed. Timothy Corrigan (New York: Methuen, 1986), 183–205.

[28] *Grizzly Man*, dir. Werner Herzog (Santa Monica: Lion's Gate Films, 2005).

W. G. Sebald's Magic Mountains

Scott Denham

MOUNTAINS ARE EVERYWHERE in W. G. Sebald's prose, from the very first image of the Grand St. Bernard, which appears even before the opening words of the text of the story "Beyle oder das merckwürdige Faktum der Liebe" (Beyle, or the strange fact of love), to "Die Alpen im Meer" (Alps in the sea).[1] The former image, in "Beyle," introduces the story of Napoleon's army's march across the Col-St.-Bernard in 1800, and, rather than the obvious image that comes to mind for us in that context — Jacques-Louis David's equestrian portrait of Le Premier Consul pointing the way ahead over the pass, painted that same year — we find in Sebald's story instead a poor reproduction of an unattributed etching that depicts thousands of miniscule soldiers and riders trekking up the pass toward the massive and imposing mountain in the distance.

> Fast vierzehn Tage lang bewegte sich ein unabsehbarer Zug von Menschen, Tieren und Material von Martigny aus über Orsières durch das Tal von Entremont und sodann in endlos scheinenden Serpentinen hinauf auf die zweieinhalbtausend Meter über dem Spiegel des Meeres liegende Höhe des Passes (7)
>
> [For almost a fortnight, an interminable column of men, animals and equipment proceeded from Martigny via Orsières through the Entremont valley and from there moved, in a seemingly never-ending serpentine, up to the pass two and a half thousand metres above sea level. (3)]

This poorly reproduced, almost gestural image is combined with an iconic description of humans confronting nature, here militarized, an image that in this specific case serves to prepare the context for Sebald's semi-fictional biographical story of Henri Beyle, that is, Stendhal, and his own tribulations both as a participant — one of those tiny figures climbing the mountain — and later as a memoirist who cannot remember correctly these momentous events from nearly two decades earlier. The latter, "Die Alpen im Meer," is the title of a brief essayistic reflection on the demise of nature at the hands of humans. The example is Corsica, and Sebald describes first the natural history of the island, with special attention to the decline of the forests and the practice of the inhabitants of hunting game in these nearly depleted woodlands. Sebald (both narrator and author here) ponders the senselessness of the modern hunt in Corsica as he finds Flaubert's "Legend of St. Julian" in the nightstand table at the hotel where he is staying; the text serves to reinforce for him the pointlessness of killing and violence, "die Verruchtheit der Menschengewalt" (48; the despicable nature of human violence, 44). At this point Sebald looks up and sees through the window the "alps in the sea" of the title; the scene reminds him of an apocalyptic conflagration, the island mountains seeming to be on fire, a kind of auto da fé:

> Die im Verlauf von Jahrmillionen von Wind, Salznebel und Regen aus dem Granit geschliffenen, dreihundert Meter aus der Tiefe emporragenden monströsen Felsformationen der Calanches leuchteten in feuerigem Kupferrot, als stünde das Gestein selber in Flammen und glühe aus seinem Inneren heraus. Manchmal glaubte ich in dem Geflacker die Umrisse brennender Pflanzen und Tiere zu erkennen oder die eines zu einem großen Scheiterhaufen geschichteten Volks. Sogar das Wasser drunten schien in Flammen zu stehen. (49)

> [The monstrous rock formations of Les Calanques, carved from granite over millions of years by wind, salt mist, and rain, and towering up three hundred meters from the depths, shone in fiery copper red as if the stone itself were in flames, glowing from within. Sometimes I thought I saw the outlines of plants and animals burning in that flickering light, or the shapes of a whole race of people stacked into a great pyre. Even the water below seemed to be aflame. (45)]

These are iconic representations of mountains: mountains to be conquered; mountains as the end of the world. In both cases the relationship of people to the mountains is anonymous, either thousands upon thousands of faceless soldiers laboring over the pass, or the figure of a whole people burned up in what is in this context unavoidably an image from the Holocaust. Mountains in both instances are the fundamental backbone of the earth, an elemental component of existence, and in both examples they are the backdrop for humans in extreme situations. Humans — readers, authors, narrators, characters — can and should learn from these extremes and from experiences in mountain extremes. But learn what? And to what end? Sebald suggests answers that point toward irony, ambiguity, and the fleeting, irretrievable experience of the sublime.

Another example from among many depicts the narrator's mountain hike in "Il ritorno in patria," the last of the four stories in *Schwindel*, in November 1987, when he decided to return from Verona to England by way of his childhood village of "W." in the Allgäu.[2] The very first sentence of the story invokes a mountain as a sign . . . of promise? of warning? and some kind of talisman. Sebald makes the decision to depart Verona "als der Großvenediger auf eine besonders geheimnisvolle Weise aus einer grauen

Schneewolke auftauchte" (187; when the Großvenediger emerged from behind a grey snow cloud in an especially ominous way, 171). The mountain creates a feeling of foreboding that remains throughout the rest of the narrative. Sebald takes the night train to Innsbruck, then the early-morning bus to the border crossing at Oberjoch, and spends the day walking the eight miles or so down the mountain pass and through a gorge to approach his childhood home and to recollect the memories of the places of his childhood. The memories are generally unpleasant, often filled with uncanny characters and events. The story's centerpiece is Sebald's memory of the village hunter's death — in the mountains of course, far from his normal stalking routes — brought on somehow because of an improper sexual liaison. Some of Sebald's characteristic photographic images in this story are mountains, too: a postcard of Vesuvius puffing away, a double-page spread from an atlas showing all the longest rivers and highest mountains of the world, which he would study for hours as a child. The author continues on toward home in England across the tidy German landscape, through Heidelberg, then Bonn. The story meanders more or less toward its end with descriptions of the train trip down the Rhine Valley; Sebald's arrival in London and scenes of wandering, as if seeking bearings, through the National Gallery; bookshops; and a long walk through London to Liverpool station. Then, with the narrative ever more sluggish and inward, Sebald sits on the train, thumbing through Samuel Pepys's diary, when he has a dream, which it is important to quote at some length.

> Dann träumte mir, daß ich durch eine bergige Gegend gegangen bin. Lang zog sich die mit feinem weißem Schotter bedeckte Straße in endlosen Kehren durch die Wälder hinan und hinauf und führte zuletzt auf der Höhe des Passes durch einen tiefen Einschnitt auf die andere Seite des Gebirges hinüber, das, wie ich im Traum wußte, die Alpen gewesen sind. Alles, was ich von dort oben aus sah, war einerlei kalkfarben, ein helles, gleißendes Grau, in dem Myriaden von Quartzsplittern schimmerten. Dieses machte mir seltsamerweise den Eindruck, als zerstrahle der Stein. Von meinem Aussichtspunkt aus führte die Straße bergab, und in der Ferne erhob sich ein zweites, zumindest ebenso hohes Gebirge, das ich, wie ich ahnte, nicht mehr würde überwinden können. Zu meiner Linken ging es in eine wahrhaft schwindelerregende Tiefe hinab. . . . Als ein fast vergangenes Echo kehrten sodann in diese atemlose Leere die Worte zurück — Fragmente aus dem Bericht über das große Feuer von London. . . . Ist dies die letzte Stunde? (286–87)

> [And then I dreamed I was walking through a mountainous terrain. A white roadway of finely crushed stone stretched far ahead and in endless hairpins went on and up through the woods and finally, at the top of the pass, led through a deep cutting across to the other side of the high range, which I recognised in my dream as the Alps.

Everything I saw from up there was of the same chalky colour, a bright, glaring grey in which a myriad of quartz fragments glimmered, as if the rocks, by a force deep inside them, were being dissolved into radiant light. From my vantage-point the road continued downward, and in the distance a second range of mountains at least as lofty as the first one arose, which I feared I would not be able to cross. To my left there was a drop into truly vertiginous depths. . . . Into that breathless void, then, words returned to me as an echo of the Great Fire of London. . . . Is this the end of time? (261–62)]

The author's return *in patria* ends, then, both where it began, with the image of the Napoleonic crossing of the Alps that begins the book, by way of Stendhal and the drawing of the army's thousands climbing up and up; but also with an imagined image of a kind of apocalyptic conflagration, by way of Pepys. Dreams of hell, death, and destruction, inspired somehow by these mountain experiences. There is homage in this passage, not only to Stendhal, Pepys, and Stifter (one of Sebald's favorite authors) but also to Hans Castorp's experiences of the sublime and his visions of hell in the "Snow" chapter of Thomas Mann's novel *Der Zauberberg* (The magic mountain).[3] Any dream in the context of mountains in German literature brings Mann's novel and its protagonist, Hans Castorp, to mind. In fact, there is for readers of German an intertextual imperative when it comes to mountains. No mountains without Castorp "up there"; no mountains without Mann's atmosphere of exception from the norm, liberation from constraint; no mountains without the potential for danger that invigorates the mind and the spirit; no mountains without Castorp nearly freezing to death in the snow. And, perhaps most importantly, we can have no mountains without the irony that informs Mann's commentary on the Romantic sublime. All of Sebald's mountains must be read with irony because of Hans Castorp's amateurish trek through the snow high above Davos that day, five years before the beginning of the great conflagration of the First World War. Here I am interested mainly in the relationship between Mann's ironic commentary on the Romantic sublime and Sebald's melancholic memories of mountains. While Sebald invokes other mountain vistas, experiences, and dreams in the other two stories in *Schwindel*, "All'estero" (Abroad) and "Dr. K's Badereise nach Riva" (Dr K. takes the waters at Riva), as well as in the first section of *Nach der Natur: Ein Elementargedicht* (After nature: an elemental poem),[4] I choose here to examine only a few representative examples of memories of mountains.

Beyond themes of toil and destruction and beyond a dream of the end of the world, there is also the sublime experience of expansive grandeur and unlimited desire that is prompted or set free by the view of an Alpine panorama. This experience, familiar to everyone who has climbed a mountain or even just parked at a highway overlook, recurs in ways that always stand at the precipice of cliché, but it remains at the same time transformative for those people who have what we can call the *mountain experience*. This mountain experience causes the sublime; it initiates the state of the sublime. The emotional events that come about through the mountain experience and then also in a dream for the Sebaldian narrator in "Il ritorno in patria" happen for other, non-authorial, characters in Sebald's stories, too. Sebald uses the Romantic sublime — and our standard expectations of how it works in art and literature, for example in Caspar David Friedrich's 1818 painting *Wanderer über dem Nebelmeer* (Wanderer above the sea of fog) — to produce irony. In fact, given the unavoidable intertextual presence of Mann's transfiguration of the Romantic sublime into ironic pathos in Castorp's mountain experience, Sebald is always working with a topos that is doubly ironic and can thus lead only to melancholy.

A mountain experience invokes the sublime and brings about a kind of transfiguration for Mme Lucy Landau in "Paul Bereyter" in the collection *Die Ausgewanderten* (The emigrants).[5] Mme Lucy describes to the Sebaldian narrator her association with the melancholic Paul Bereyter from the time she met him in 1971 in Salins-les-Bain, recounting her first meeting and many subsequent conversations, walks, and excursions with him. She is surprised, she says, as she remembers and tells the narrator about Paul, at how present the images of their shared time together are in her memory, since she had believed that they were "von der Trauer um Paul verschüttet" (67; buried beneath grief at the loss of Paul, 45). Significant here is the word "verschüttet" (buried), which does not mean simply buried but specifically being buried alive, as in an avalanche, rockslide, or some other unanticipated, often natural event. "Buried" here is a mountain word. It leads immediately in the next sentence to a description of how the experience of being high on the Montrond above Lake Geneva — the clearest image of all the images in her memory — brought to her a new emotional and philosophical understanding of herself and her life.

> Von allen am schärfsten aber sehe sie diejenigen [Bilder] des trotz Sessellift nicht ganz unbeschwerlichen Ausflugs auf den Montrond, von dessen Gipfel sie eine Ewigkeit auf die um ein Vielfaches verkleinert wirkende, wie für eine Spielzeugeisenbahn gebaute Genfer Seelandschaft hinabgeblickt hätten. Diese Winzigkeiten einerseits und zum anderen das sanft sich auftürmende Massiv des Montblanc, die in der Ferne fast verschimmernden Glaciers de la Vanoise und das den halben Horizont einnehmende Alpenpanorama hätten ihr zum erstenmal in ihrem Leben ein Gefühl vermittelt für die widersprüchlichen Dimensionen unserer Sehnsucht. (67–68)

> [Clearest of all, though, were the memories of their outing — a somewhat laborious business despite the chair lift — up Montrond, from the summit of which she [they] had gazed down for an eternity at Lake Geneva and the surrounding country, which looked considera-

bly reduced in size, as if intended for a model railway. The tiny features below, taken together with the gentle mass of Montblanc towering above them, the Vanoise glacier almost invisible in the shimmering distance, and the Alpine panorama that occupied half the horizon, had for the first time in her life awoken in her a sense of the contrarieties that are in our longings. (45)][6]

The Romantic sensibility of the sublime, with its contradictory and imprecise invocation of emotions and feelings, is alive and well here, inspired by the view from the top of a mountain. What the experience *means* exactly for Lucy Landau remains unclear to her. Our longing and desires are present; they can be unleashed by the experience of a mountain vista. But perhaps they are not paths to enlightenment but only to ambiguity. And in memory, that experience is one of melancholy, even "buried beneath grief."

The inevitable ironic sublime of the mountain experience in Sebald's fiction occurs again in "Max Aurach" ("Max Ferber" in the English version), the fourth and final story in *Die Ausgewanderten*, in which a brief mountain moment serves to mark a transformative change in the life of the secondary narrator, Max (as usual, a Sebaldian narrator retells another character's tale). Max Aurach's father was interned for six weeks in Dachau following the Kristallnacht in November 1938; after his return, having said not a word to Max about his experiences in the concentration camp, he went skiing with his family at Lengries. There is a photograph in the text at this point, presumably of Aurach's father at the top of Brauneck, skis nearby, snow and mountains all around (278; 186). Then, right after the ski trip, he procures a visa for young Max to emigrate to England. The skiing story has nothing causal to do with what follows, but stands there, Alpine vista in the distance, as a caesura, a marker between the father's experience at Dachau (and subsequent death in 1941) and the son's new life in Manchester. The image of the man on the mountain inscribes the moment between life and death, between staying in one place to be killed and moving on to a new place to survive. Thus the image of Aurach's father, who we know from Aurach's story is deported to Riga in 1941 and dies there, depicts for us a man already condemned at this moment in 1939. This man, portrayed full of life in the snow, with the majestic mountain peaks and valleys behind him, stands on top of the world and is at the same time nothing if not a picture of "the contradictory dimensions of our longings." The sublime and the macabre, life and death, past and future: the mountain experience is like Celan's breathturn here, the moment of grace between before and after, of stillness between movement and change.[7]

Hans Castorp's near-death experience in the high mountain snow above Davos seems to have both formalized and ritualized the modern version of the sublime mountain experience for all literary representations that follow. The literary mountain experience requires certain formal characteristics and contains elements of ritual. There is the view of the mountain, the decision to climb, the vastness and greatness of the mountain compared to the smallness and insignificance of the person, the perception of being lost, then of being found; there is the aesthetic bliss of the vista, the sense of accomplishment at the climb, of surviving the elements, the sense of dialectical relationships in nature — permanence and change, life and death, geological time and human time, and so on.

Castorp's existential trek is well known. In the chapter "Schnee" ("Snow") in book 6 of *Der Zauberberg* Hans Castorp decides to try out what we would call now cross-country skiing. He has been at the sanatorium for nearly two years and his second winter "up there" is marked by more snow than anyone can remember. His motivation is twofold: first, to be alone with his thoughts and in control of them; second, to enjoy an "inniger-freier[e] Berührung mit dem schneeverwüsteten Gebirge, für das er Teilnahme gefaßt hatte" (498; a freer, more active, more intense experience of the snowy mountain wilderness, for which he felt a great affinity, 464). Castorp acquires skis, is encouraged by his humanist mentor Settembrini, and learns his way around the local landscape. His path took him

> entlang der linken Lehne gegen Clavadel oder rechtshin an Frauenkirch und Glaris vorüber, hinter denen der Schatten des Amselfluhmassivs im Nebel spukte; auch in das Dischmatal oder hinter dem "Berghof" empor in Richtung auf das bewaldete Seehorn, von dem nur die schneeige Spitze über die Baumgrenze ragte, und den Drusatschawald, hinter dem man den bleichen Schattenriß der tief verschneiten Rhätikonkette erblickte. (501)

> [along the slope on the left in the direction of Clavadel or to the right on past Frauenkirch and Glaris, the shadowy ghost of the Amselfluh massif looming up out of the fog behind them; he also skied the valley of the Dischma and the hills rising behind the Berghof, in the direction of the wooded Seehorn, only the very tops of its two snow-clad peaks visible above the tree line, and toward the Drusatscha woods, behind which he could see the pale, murky outline of the Rhätikon chain buried under snow. (466)]

This sort of geographical litany occurs in many Alpine descriptions. The reader is supposed to know what is being invoked and see the breathtaking scenery along with the narrators and protagonists. Or, if the mountains and vistas are unfamiliar, more often than not careful and curious readers reach for the atlas or crank up Google Earth (and the temptation here and elsewhere to embed a hyperlink to each mountain peak mentioned is real). As Castorp learns about the Alpine terrain to the west and north of the Berghof, readers, too, get a sense of the adventure that awaits him. There follow descriptions of the stunning beauty of the landscape — also commonplace in such literary descriptions — and, most importantly, the dangers that accompany this sort of expedition into the extremes of nature. For Mann, and for Castorp, the intimate brush with death that comes from exploring the mountains makes for ultimate meaning, and that brush with death demands — or creates — courage. From Castorp's childhood experiences in the surf at Sylt he knew of the adrenaline rush of engaging with the power of nature up close, "das Berührungsglück leichter Liebesberührungen mit Mächten, deren volle Umarmung vernichtend sein würde (502; the exhilarating thrill of brushing up against powers whose full embrace would destroy you, 467). Castorp's courage derives from a kind of empathy with the deadly elements of nature and the understanding that being alone in those deadly quiet and dangerous mountains allowed him to think for himself, really for the first time ever, freed of his obsessions with Pribislav Hippe and Clawdia Chauchat, and from his teachers Settembrini and Naphta. Castorp is of course not an organized thinker, and much of what he comes to understand when up in the mountains seems to have faded away when he comes back down to civilization. Mann's irony allows for the potential for change and understanding, but Castorp, like his contemporaries who also head off to the trenches in the fall of 1914 at the novel's end, has a hard time realizing that potential.

Castorp's experience trekking and skiing in the high Alps culminates in a dramatic and traumatic near-death moment. A storm comes up and he is nearly trapped, suffers hypothermia, begins to hallucinate, and finally, on the verge of freezing to death, has his sublime dream of love and death. It is a vision full of now-clichéd images of fin-de-siècle youthful eroticism in a neoclassical vein, as well as infanticidal, cannibalistic witches, all of which he finds deeply meaningful, concluding, "Ich weiß alles vom Menschen" (521; I know everything about humankind, 486). The experience of the mountains, of his brush with death, of his extreme experience, leads him finally to his famous pseudo-philosophical conclusion: "*Der Mensch soll um der Güte und Liebe willen dem Tode keine Herrschaft einräumen über seine Gedanken*" (523; *For the sake of goodness and love, man shall grant death no dominion over his thoughts*, 487, Mann's emphasis). But Castorp, upon his safe return to the Berghof, seems to forget quickly his conclusions about life and love and death, reverting instead to his old intellectually lethargic ways. For Mann, then, the extreme mountain experience comes to stand for potential philosophical and moral enlightenment, but the moment of understanding is transitory. Death can bring complete understanding, and a brush with death opens up the possibility of gaining some sense of that understanding; but life, for Castorp at least, requires the tedium of daily existence. Castorp wants to ban those tantalizing visions of death from his own existence, but in so doing he also erases his own autonomy and even his own memory of the dreams and thoughts he had up on the mountain.

Sebald's Dr. Henry Selwyn in *Die Ausgewanderten* follows in Hans Castorp's footsteps up and down the mountain in more profound ways than do Henri Beyle in *Schwindel*, Sebald's autobiographical narrators in "Il ritorno in patria" and "Die Alpen im Meer," Lucy Landau in "Paul Bereyter," or Max Aurach's father in "Max Aurach." Selwyn's experience climbing mountains liberates him from a difficult past of childhood emigration and grinding schooling and, by way of an evidently profoundly meaningful, though brief, relationship with a mentor for his mountain climbing, Johannes Naegeli, marks him for the rest of his life. The exhilaration and enlightenment that comes from experiencing the world in high places lets Selwyn come to understand, in Lucy's words, the "contradictory dimensions of our longing," precisely what Castorp found and lost on the magic mountain. Only in Selwyn's case he remains aware of what he has lost and lives a life of ever increasing melancholy, until he finally kills himself.

Selwyn's story, as is so often the case in Sebald, is one of reconstruction through a frame narrative, of an odyssey of displacement and emigration, memories that perhaps explain something but are ambiguous and ironic, a narrative that ends in death. Selwyn's sad life is marked by just this one short period of pleasure: some months of mountain climbing under the tutelage of the Alpinist Naegeli in the Bernese Oberland between the conclusion of his studies in the summer of 1913 and the beginning of the war in August 1914. Selwyn relates his biographical tale to the Sebaldian narrator in two parts, first one evening at a dinner with a friend Edwin Elliot along with Sebald and his wife Clara, who are renting rooms from Selwyn and his estranged wife, Hedy. The dinner takes place in late April 1971, some eight months after Sebald and Clara move into the eccentric, strange, decaying Selwyn house, Prior's Gate. Prompted by his friend Edward (Edwin in the English version), Selwyn describes his experiences mountain climbing in 1913 and 1914. Then, after dinner, following a slide show of Selwyn's and Edward's trip to Crete in 1960, where an image of the vista from the heights of Lasithi transfixes the four viewers, the evening ends with the ironic destruction of the mountain vista.

After finishing university in 1913 Selwyn continued his studies in Bern, but instead of attending university began mountain climbing, and spent most of his time in the Bernese Oberland, getting addicted to mountaineering — "der Bergsteigerei verfallen" (23; taking more and more to mountain climbing, 13) — and then meeting the then sixty-five-year-old Naegeli. They climbed everything together, were together at the top of "dem Zinggenstock, dem Scheuchzerhorn und dem Lauteraarhorn, dem Schreckhorn und dem Ewigschneehorn" (24). All the peaks that Selwyn names are between 9,564 ft. and 13,380 ft. (2,915 and 4,078 meters), serious enough mountains for anyone, especially in 1913. This climbing experience with his Alpinist mentor Naegli was the singular moment of contentment in all of Selwyn's long life, or as he says: "Er habe sich nie in seinem Leben, weder zuvor noch später, derart wohl gefühlt wie damals in der Gesellschaft dieses Mannes" (24; And never in his life, neither before nor later, did he feel as good as he did then, in the company of that man, 14). When the war started, Selwyn was called back to England. He says that parting from Naegeli was deeply painful. He learned shortly thereafter, in the first letter he received as a uniformed soldier, that Naegeli had met with an accident and disappeared on the Aar glacier shortly after the start of the war in August 1914. Selwyn says his ensuing depression at this news made him feel as if he were "begraben unter Schnee und Eis" (25; buried under snow and ice, 15). At this point in the text is a photo of the Aar glacier, looking imposing and dangerous, as well as beautiful (25; 14).[8] A German reader cannot ever, of course, be "buried under snow" without also calling up Hans Castorp intertextually. Whereas Hans was actually covered under fallen snow halfway up the Großer Schiahorn above Davos, and hallucinated his way from there to temporary existential, erotic, and religious enlightenment, Henry imagines himself buried under snow as the profound expression of loss of friendship and freedom, and as a kind of empathetic, vicarious Alpinist death. No enlightenment, just loss (though perhaps enlightenment for Sebald's readers, just maybe). Selwyn's introduction to mountain climbing, his feelings of comfort and well-being through Naegeli's mentorship, then Naegeli's disappearance and loss, Selwyn's subsequent depression, the Aar photo — this brief account takes up only a couple of pages, but it marks a point in Selwyn's life against which all his more complicated and difficult biography is framed.

After the tale of climbing these peaks with Naegeli, Selwyn and the others move to the drawing room to see the slides from Henry's and Edward's trip to Crete some ten years before. One of the slides, an image of Selwyn with a butterfly net, reminds the Sebaldian narrator of a similar picture of Nabokov that he had cut from a Swiss paper just that past week. The photo is presented in the text and shows Nabokov high in the mountains in the springtime, net and boots and hiking shorts and cap, looking off into the distance. Sebald here again invokes the Alps as a place for seeking knowledge and enlightenment, or of liberation from day-to-day cares, or simply as an overwhelming cliché. Then Selwyn pauses on the next slide that the narrator describes thus:

> Auf dem letzten der Bilder breitete sich vor uns die von einer nördlichen Paßhöhe herab aufgenommene Hochebene von Lasithi aus. Die Aufnahme mußte um die Mittagszeit gemacht worden sein, denn die Strahlen der Sonne kamen dem Beschauer entgegen. Der im Süden die Ebene überragende, über zweitausend Meter hohe Berg Spathi wirkte wie eine Luftspiegelung hinter der Flut des Lichts. (28)

> [In the last of the pictures we saw the expanse of the Lasithi plateau outspread before us, taken from the heights of one of the northern passes. The shot must have been taken around midday, since the sun was shining into our line of vision. To the south, lofty Mount Spathi, two thousand meters high, towered above the plateau, like a mirage beyond the flood of light. (17)]

The slide stays up so long that the glass in the slide's frame overheats and breaks, destroying the sublime image with a dark crack across the screen, a quotation of Selwyn's enlightened mountain experience, shattered by memory.

The Sebaldian narrator of this dense plot hears the second part of Selwyn's life story some weeks later after Sebald and Clara have moved into their own house. Selwyn recounts briefly, prompted by his own question to Sebald whether or not he is ever homesick, his emigration as a child from Lithuania to England, then his schooling and studies, anglicizing his name, and after his mountain climbing in the Alps, the years in the 1920s and 1930s as a doctor who married into money, lived a life of luxury with motoring trips throughout Europe and tennis in the back garden. Selwyn describes his ever-more-lonely and sad existence, a result, apparently, of increasing estrangement from his wife, his lack of money, reconsidering his hidden Jewish heritage, and — as the reader already knows — the impossibility that anything "here below," as Castorp would say, could ever be as sublime and exhilarating and enlightening as his experience of mountain climbing with his mentor those many years ago. In between the views of the Aar glacier and the Lasithi plateau lies the wreckage of the twentieth century, the end of the Enlightenment project, and the homesickness of Hersch Seweryn — Henry Selwyn — for all that he has lost. This loss is made clear to Selwyn, to Sebald — and by Sebald the narrator and author — through the experience of mountains and all that we know about literary mountains from the inverse experience of Hans Castorp, who, only a few years before Selwyn was climbing his own mountains, was just about seventy-five miles to the east and seeing visions of his own, then forgetting them. Castorp, naive as ever in the summer of 1914, totters off to war and a likely violent end. In the summer of 1914 Selwyn already knows what loss means, and as he remembers more and more of his mountain experiences over the years, he brings about his own violent end by shooting himself in the head in 1971.

In a kind of coda or epilogue, Sebald's narrator describes the return of Johannes Naegeli — and thus what must have prompted his telling of this story. In the summer of 1986 he is in Switzerland (of course), on a train crossing the Aar (of course), looking out of the window at the mountains that both Selwyn and Naegeli had climbed seventy-two years before. He glances at the paper and sees in a story that Naegeli's remains have just been found. The newspaper page is reproduced in the text and shows "le glacier de l'Aar qui vient de rendre un guide décédé en 1914" (37; 22). The final words of Sebald's tale:

> So kehren sie wieder, die Toten. Manchmal nach mehr als sieben Jahrzehnten kommen die heraus aus dem Eis und liegen am Rand der Moräne, ein Häufchen geschliffener Knochen und ein Paar genagelter Schuhe. (36–37)
>
> [And so they are ever returning to us, the dead. At times they come back from the ice more than seven decades later and are found at the edge of the moraine, a few polished bones and a pair of hobnailed boots. (23)]

Castorp shows readers the potential for experiencing the sublime and for enlightenment at the top of a mountain, on the edge of danger, tasting death, though he retreats to the drudgery of the sanitarium and wanders blindly into the deadly twentieth century. Selwyn knows more of mountains and their potential to liberate one from the cares of history, biography, and daily life, more than Lucy Landau and more than Sebald's implied author returning to his village, but Selwyn's inability to come to terms with the memory of his losses — both the loss of his mountaineering mentor and the loss of his own sense of rootedness and place — force him to look back across the twentieth century and say no. If Mann ironically questions the potential of mountain experiences to expand human understanding, then Sebald affirms that potential, but questions the potential of humans to live with the understanding of themselves that they have gained from the experience at the top of the mountain.[9]

Notes

[1] W. G. Sebald, "Beyle oder das merckwürdige Faktum der Liebe," in *Schwindel: Gefühle* (Frankfurt am Main: Fischer, 1994); in English, "Beyle, or the strange fact of love," in *Vertigo*, trans. Michael Hulse (New York: New Directions, 2000). W. G. Sebald, "Die Alpen im Meer," in *Campo Santo* (Munich: Hanser, 2003); in English, "Alps in the Sea," in *Campo Santo*, trans. Anthea Bell (New York: Random House, 2005). Further references to all works discussed give first the page number of the German edition, then that of the English edition.

[2] The various and variable relationships between Sebald's narrators, Sebald the actual author and Sebald the implied author, are well known and too complicated to discuss here. The status of "Sebald" as author or narrator — the Sebaldian narrator — should be clear enough for the purposes of this essay and are in general interchangeable.

[3] Thomas Mann, *Der Zauberberg* (1924; repr., Frankfurt am Main: Fischer, 1984); In English, *The Magic Mountain*, trans. John E. Woods (New York: Vintage, 1996).

[4] W. G. Sebald, *Nach der Natur: Ein Elementargedicht* (Nördlingen: Greno, 1988); W. G. Sebald, *After Nature*, trans. Michael Hamburger (New York: Random House, 2002).

[5] W. G. Sebald, *Die Ausgewanderten* (1992; repr., Frankfurt am Main, Fischer, 2002); in English, *The Emigrants*, trans. Michael Hulse (New York: New Directions, 1996).

[6] Hulse's translation, which captures Sebald's tone well but contains several inaccuracies, has one error in this passage and one phrase that loses more than it should. The error, reading the second "sie" as "she" instead of the plural "they" in the first sentence, manages to revoke the memory of the two of them together, Lucy Landau *and* Paul Bereyter, taking in the Alpine vista. Lucy Landau's realization of the "contrarieties of our longings," on the other hand is correctly rendered as her realization alone, but "contrarieties" loses the spatial aspect of the "dimensions" in the original. A more accurate translation of Lucy Landau's description of her experience would be to say that it "brought about a feeling of the contradictory dimensions of our longing." It is precisely the extreme aspect of the dimensions visible in taking in the world far below from up on the mountain that causes Lucy to understand the world in a new way.

[7] Paul Celan, *Atemwende* (Frankfurt am Main: Suhrkamp, 1967); *Breathturn*, trans. Pierre Joris (Los Angeles: Sun & Moon Press, 1995). Celan's concept here is that of a moment of transformative, potent silence at the moment of stillness between breathing in and breathing out. He refers to this in his 1960 speech "Der Meridian," which he gave on the occasion of his receipt of the Büchner Prize in Darmstadt, Paul Celan, *Der Meridian und andere Prosa* (Frankfurt am Main: Suhrkamp, 1983), 52; "The Meridian," trans. Jerry Glen, in Jacques Derrida, *Sovereignties in Question: The Poetics of Paul Celan*, ed. Thomas Dutoit and Outi Pasanen (New York: Fordham University Press, 2005), 179–80.

[8] The photograph is misplaced and misformatted in the New Directions edition (14–15), another of the few minor errors in Michael Hulse's otherwise excellent translation.

[9] Scholars have discussed landscape in Sebald's works, but no one to my knowledge has looked exclusively at mountains in Sebald. Jo Catling comes the closest to a sustained analysis of mountain experiences in her important essay on the function of Sebald's landscapes for his wandering protagonists and narrators. Jo Catling, "W. G. Sebald's Landscapes of Memory," in *The Anatomist of Melancholy: Essays in Memory of W. G. Sebald*, ed. Rüdiger Görner (Munich: iudicium, 2003), 19–50; there she examines the "artist-wanderer's precarious existence" between past and present or dream and reality in various geographical settings, such as the Alpine crossings in *Schwindel*, noting that "the Alps which form the principle landscape of the book, uneasily criss-crossed by the respective protagonists of the four sections, become a symbolic watershed between past and present lives" (40). Further on landscape, see Anne Fuchs, "'Ein Hauptkapitel der Geschichte der Unterwerfung': Representations of Nature in W. G. Sebald's *Die Ringe des Saturn*," in *W. G. Sebald and the Writing of History*, ed. Anne Fuchs and J. J. Long (Würzburg: Königshausen

& Neumann, 2007), 121–38. On photographs, specifically including those of mountains, see J. J. Long, "History, Narrative, and Photography in W. G. Sebald's *Die Ausgewanderten*," *Modern Language Review* 98, no. 1 (Jan. 2003): 117–37. Gisela Ecker, in "'Heimat' oder Die Grenzen der Bastelei," in *W. G. Sebald: Politische Archäologie und melancholische Bastelei*, ed. Michael Niehaus and Claudia Öhlschläger (Berlin: Erich Schmidt Verlag, 2006), 77–88, pays some attention to the effects of a mountain experience but in the broader context of Heimat landscapes. Deane Blackler discusses in passing the opening mountain scene of *Vertigo* in *Reading W. G. Sebald: Adventure and Disobedience* (Rochester, NY: Camden House, 2007), 150–51.

Conflicting Ascents: Inscriptions, Cartographies, and Disappearance in Christoph Ransmayr's *Der fliegende Berg*

Olaf Berwald

> *All hell didn't break loose, it was like a rising psalm materializing like snow on an unseen mountain. All that was underfoot was good, but lost.*
> — John Ashbery, *Where Shall I Wander* (2005)

CAN EXTREME MOUNTAINEERING provide helpful allegories for the risks of vertiginous reading? Can a literary work of art, and in turn its reader, temporarily be understood to undergo tectonic shifts that continuously uplift, submerge, and reassert ultimately unmappable epistemic terrain? Avoiding coarsely grained philological quicksand and leaving behind fixations on omniscient methods at hermeneutic base camps, expeditions in reading fiction can still face the challenge of telling apart the climber from the gorge, and untraceable narrators from posthuman landscapes. Could the solitary or synergistic process of reading connote a free-climbing experience, comprising tentative conceptual ascents that navigate across or around petrified dichotomies of conquest and selflessness, of conceptual control and self-abandon? The novel under discussion in this chapter at once thematizes these epistemic conflicts and offers itself as a territory that invites intersecting inscriptions of reading routes.

Rather than signifying sublime permanence in contrast to the vulnerable human body, the mythical Phur-Ri, a fictional, roughly 7,000 meter high Tibetan mountain that is the target of two Irish brothers' expedition in Christoph Ransmayr's *Der fliegende Berg* (The flying mountain, 2006) emerges as a transient phenomenon. Phur-Ri temporarily disappears and is believed by natives to occasionally fly upward until it descends and becomes visible again.[1] Organized around this evasive topos, or rather operating with disappearance and self-dissolution of man and mountain as its organizing metaphor, Ransmayr's lyrical novel interweaves scientific invasiveness and mystical immersion as two seemingly irreconcilable methods of conquering and dissolving into nature.

The novel is composed in a hybrid style. Its lyrical prose in free verse and its precise visual imagination, which have been excessively praised by Uwe Wittstock,[2] prestructure the reading experience as a cognitive serpentine ascent that mirrors the ethical and aesthetic conflict between intuitive self-surrender to nature on the one hand, and epistemic mastery of the hitherto undiscovered on the other. In his poetological "Notiz am Rand" (marginal note) that precedes the novel, Ransmayr asks the reader not to label the text a poem. Positing that the ragged margin that is used throughout the book does not exclusively belong to the realm of poetry and should be instead considered "frei" (free), the author encourages a reading praxis that lets go of rigid genre fixations. The work's left-justified typeface destabilizes the reader's gaze and undermines any clear genre assignment.

Ransmayr's works have been described as "Aufbrüche in den Mythos" (departures into myth).[3] The expedition whose anatomy is presented in *Der fliegende Berg* is irreducible to one particular conflict. One can read the novel as a post-mortem dream-diary. Both brothers perish in climbing accidents. The dead first-person narrator remembers the interwoven stories of their two deaths, and the reader is even at interpretive liberty to consider the two brothers as one figure, despite or rather because of their sharp complementary differences. The conflicted bond between the deceased narrator — the first two words of the novel are "Ich starb" (I died) — who announces that he survived his brother for a while only to mourn his death throughout the text, manifests itself in their radically divergent methods of cognitive and unconscious ascent.

This chapter provides preliminary soundings of the extent to which vertical progress and visual technological mastery are at once codependent and in competition with unmappable ecstatic immersions into nature. Staging this fluid dialectic as the core drama of his novel, Ransmayr assumes that the reader draws connections to textual terrain unearthed by German Romanticism that present conflicted approaches to disappearing into or gaining conceptual control of nature. These texts include Ludwig Tieck's *Der Runenberg* (Rune mountain, 1802), Karoline von Günderrode's *Magie und Schicksal* (Magic and destiny, 1805), and Friedrich Wilhelm Joseph Schelling's *Die Weltalter* (The ages of the world, 1809–11). Ransmayr can be read as an author who continues German Romanticism's project of providing soundings of various modes of violence that inform the way humans appropriate nature and each other. One of the preliminary findings of Tieck's, Günderrode's, and Schelling's fictional and philosophical undertakings is the inversive mutability of power relations between man and nature, and the porosity of cognitive control. Protagonists in these early nineteenth-century texts are exposed to madness (*Der Runenberg*), inadvertent fratricide (*Magie und Schicksal*), and the unconscious of nature and of God (*Weltalter*). Like Ransmayr's novel, these precursors also describe and evoke mourning processes and are organized around a central loss.

Inspired by his lover, the Tibetan guide Nyema, a widowed mother who is portrayed as strong and independent, the narrator immerses himself in language and nature in a playfully erotic and spiritual manner. In contrast, his brother Liam, a geologist, is obsessed with the need for epistemic appropriation. Liam rushes to become the first to conquer the unmapped mountain, which he had discovered while composing geodetic computer programs on his liquid crystal display monitors in Ireland. In the following two sections, I will examine more closely these two competing but codependent methods of conceptual ascent.

The Cartographic Drive and Its Limits

Describing his brother Liam as an expert "einer auf Erdsatelliten und Lasertechnik / gestützten Landvermessung" (in land survey that is based on / satellites and laser technology) who designs "geodätische Computerprogramme" (geodesic computer programs) in order to compose virtual landscapes, the narrator wonders whether he obsessively compares everything he sees in the mountains "gerahmt / vom offenen Eingang seines Kuppelzeltes" (framed by / the open entry of his dome tent) with the digital bits and pieces on the computer-simulated images that he had generated back in Ireland on his liquid crystal display monitors (see 40, 202). But the narrator's supposed insights into the mind of his brother are not verifiable. During their lifetime, the siblings fail to comprehend one another's motivations and desires as much as their own.

The narrator reflects on the correspondence between physical self-exposure to the mountain's challenge and scientific predictions and premappings of the geological formations that await him and Liam. In his mind, the conflicted simultaneity of computer-generated images and corporeal experiences of an unmapped, shape-shifting mountain is linked to a question of power and submission. The narrator speculates as to whether Liam is driven by a desire to be the first to enter and "baptize" what he envisions as "ein unversehrter, namenloser weißer Fleck" (an untouched, nameless blank space) that "vielleicht nur darauf wartete, von uns, von *ihm* / erstmals betreten, vielleicht getauft zu werden" (203; perhaps only waited to be entered, perhaps baptized / by us, by *him*, italics in original). But at the same time, the narrator concedes to the overwhelming power of the sublime evoked by the mountain and posits that neither rational definitions nor unconscious projections can be employed to confine the overpowering sight of the mountain's material reality, the "ungeheuerlichen ... Anblick / der Wirklichkeit" (203; enormous aspect / of reality). Earlier in the novel, the narrator already points to the ultimately irrational core of the epistemic desire for complete conceptual coverage, referring to the seemingly rational imperative to render the unknown transparent as a fictitious undertaking:

> Vielleicht ist jenes Bedürfnis
> tatsächlich unstillbar,
> das uns selbst in enzyklopädisch gesicherten Gebieten
> nach dem Unbekannten, Unbetretenen,
> von Spuren und Namen noch Unversehrten suchen läßt —
> nach jenem makellos weißen Fleck,
> in den wir dann ein Bild unserer Tagträume
> einschreiben können.
> . . .
> Noch Liams astronomische Beobachtungen,
> die er mit computergesteuerten Teleskopen betrieb,
> erinnerten mich manchmal daran,
> daß selbst mit Präzisionsinstrumenten
> nach Welten Ausschau gehalten wurde,
> die vielleicht nirgendwo anders zu finden waren
> als in unserem Kopf. (43)
>
> [Perhaps that need
> is really unquenchable
> that makes us search for the unknown, the untrodden
> for that which is still undamaged by traces and names —
> for that pristine unmapped spot
> into which we can then inscribe
> an image of our daydreams.
> . . .
> Even Liam's astronomical oberservations
> that he conducted with computerized telescopes
> sometimes reminded me
> that even with precision instruments
> we are on the outlook for worlds
> that perhaps cannot be found anywhere
> but inside our head.]

This passage both captures the voracity of epistemic hunger that continues to drive modernity even in its postmodern versions and raises the question of the illusory quality of scientific mastery. Back in Ireland, during their preparations for their expedition, the narrator and his brother discuss the limitations of science. Running Liam's computer simulation programs in order to examine the physiological aspects of climbing, they are astonished by a radical epistemic helplessness that they think persists at the core of science, unmaskable even by the latest technological equipment. The brothers express a fascination with what they call "Mysterien des Organismus" (mysteries of the organism), and Liam is frustrated with the relatively primitive state of current technology. Even something as seemingly simple as the biological process involved in taking one step strikes the brothers as being far more complex than the binary processes of Liam's computers (353–54). Ransmayr's aesthetics of the sublime continues a rich eighteenth- and nineteenth-century tradition. Rather than merely ironicizing uses of the sublime in the wake of postmodernism, Ransmayr's protagonist experiences it as a life-altering phenomenon, while always linking it to optical instruments or questions of visual perspective. The narrator's experience of the sublime is not fueled principally by the mountain's immensity. The object of his awe is, rather, the surprising precision and aesthetic impact of an almost invisible thread, "eine Linie, so hauchzart, so unendlich fein" (a line, so very delicate, so infinitely fine), an unassuming yet insurmountable line of demarcation that is capable of "trennen" and "abschneiden" (separating and cutting off) virtual images from tangible reality (349).

Immersive Inscriptions

Nature and acts of writing are constantly juxtaposed and interwoven in Ransmayr's work. At the end of his early Ovidian novel, *Die letzte Welt* (The last world, 1988), Ransmayr radicalizes the medieval topos of the world as book.[4] The novel culminates in a posthuman scenario. Continuing cycles of metamorphoses in Ovid's work, the protagonist Cotta, in search of the exiled Ovid's manuscripts and of the "Schrift" (scripture) of his own identity, disappears into nature, transformed into an "unverwundbarer Kiesel" (invulnerable pebble), a bird, or moss "auf dem letzten, verschwindenden Mauerrest einer Stadt" (254; on the last, disappearing remnant of a city wall). As one critic points out, *Die letzte Welt* presents "das allmähliche Verblassen der Schrift, deren Überwucherung und endliche Bedeutungslosigkeit in einer versteinernden Welt" (the gradual fading of scripture that is overgrown and finally becomes meaningless in a petrifying world).[5]

Whereas "Schrift" is overgrown by nature and succumbs to universal petrification in Ransmayr's early novel, the praxis of writing in *Der fliegende Berg* represents erotic joy and spiritual hope. During the climbing expedition, the narrator falls in love with Nyema, who is part of the Tibetan team of guides and porters. Through Nyema, who once saves him from falling from the steep banks of a raging river and who is presented as a strong, independent woman and equal partner (indeed the more balanced and self-sufficient one in their short relationship), he discovers the physicality of the spoken and written word, as well as its sensual and spiritual dimensions. Unfamiliar with each other's native language, they use gestures and mimic expressions before they engage in erotic language acquisition, "den Beginn eines gegenseitigen

Unterrichtens" (213; the start of mutual instruction). Temporarily oblivious to the expedition and their fellow mountaineers, Nyema and the narrator are immersed in ludic language acquisition, practicing "Sprechenlernen, Lesen, Schreiben als Liebesspiel" (215; learning to speak, reading, writing as amorous play):

> . . . während sie sprach, schrieb sie mit ihrem Zeigefinger
> manchmal schnelle, fliegende Zeichen
> auf meinen Arm, meinen Handrücken —
> Spiralen, Wellenlinien, Kreise.
> . . .
> (So beschrieb sie nach und nach
> . . .
> meinen ganzen Körper mit sanften,
> von Mal zu Mal lesbareren Großbuchstaben.) (12 and 213)
>
> [While she was talking
> she sometimes wrote quick, flying signs
> with her index finger
> on my arm, the back of my hand —
> spirals, wiggly lines, circles.
> . . .
> Gradually
> . . .
> she inscribed my whole body with gentle
> capital letters that became more and more legible.]

Insisting on the interwovenness of the spiritual and the erotic through acts of reading and writing, Nyema considers inscribing letters onto a body, a stone, or a river as a method of alleviating the painful awareness of human fragility and mortality. For Nyema, loving acts of writing, and making love as a ritual of inscriptions that unite the beloved with the universe by incessantly spreading his or her name across various manifestations of nature, embody temporary transcendence and offer a small dose of an existential pain reliever,

> . . . einer Arznei gegen die Sterblichkeit,
> die zwar nicht heilen,
> aber doch lindern konnte
> . . .
> Die Kunst zu schreiben, die Kunst zu lesen,
> sagte Nyema, sei wohl das größte Geschenk,
> das Menschen einander bereiten könnten,
> weil nur diese Fähigkeit ihnen endlich erlaube,
> sich nicht nur über Meere und Gipfel,
> sondern über die Zeit selbst zu erheben
> und aufzufliegen wie der Phur-Ri. (212)

[a medicine against mortality
that, while not capable of healing,
was nevertheless powerful enough to alleviate pain
. . .
The art of writing, the art of reading,
Nyema said, was probably the greatest gift
that humans could offer one another,
because only this ability finally allowed them
not only to transcend oceans and mountain peaks
but time itself
and to fly upward like the Phur-Ri.]

The narrator remembers taking turns sharing stories with his Tibetan lover as an exploration characterized by radical reciprocity and equality. They familiarize themselves with the differences between their cultural upbringings and life experiences, listening to each other's memories and stories (207). In effortless alternation, they share and switch the roles of storyteller and "aufmerksamer, sprachloser Zuhörer" (209; attentive, speechless listener). The language in which the narrator remembers erotic playfulness is inextricably connected to the way he recaptures the Buddhist practice of engaging mountains in tactile language games of meditative inscriptions. He draws the image of Buddhist pilgrims who turn themselves into spiritual "printers." Using rocks, pebblestones and the flowing water of a river as imaginary paper, such "*Drucker*" (210, italics in original) ceaselessly produce reminders of the inevitability of transformation, "ein fließendes Zeugnis, / daß, was ist, nicht bleiben kann" (211; flowing testimonials / that that which is cannot remain). The narrator playfully imitates the Buddhist name-spreading ritual. He wishes the lake to carry Nyema's name.

The narrator and his lover, as well as the Buddhist monks they encounter, practice their worldly and spiritual pursuits by means of rhythmic repetitions of inscriptive acts on bodies, stones, and water. Their physical embrace of writing enables them to experience and evoke the paradoxical simultaneity of preservation and disappearance, recovery and obliteration. The narrator notices an old monk who spent his life inscribing Buddhist mantras on rocks (see 206). The monk and his Western observer imagine scriptural characters as entering the cycle of nature and temporarily appearing as semiotic rain, snow, and hail:

Mauern, errichtet allein aus beschrifteten Steinen,
die ihre Worte dem Regen und Wind darboten,
damit sie ans Meer geschwemmt
und bis an den Himmel geweht würden.
. . .

mit Schriftzeichen behauene Steine
am Grund erkennbar geworden:

Tausende, Hunderttausende Steine . . .
. . .
damit der Strom die dem Stein anvertrauten Gebete
ans Meer trage und so jedes Wort bewegt, gebetet
und unter der Sonne wieder zu Wasserdampf werde,
und die Schwaden des Dampfes wieder zur Wolke,
aus der dann Zeichen für Zeichen zurückregne,
zurückschneie oder selbst als Hagel zurückschlage
auf das allein den Göttern gehörende Land. (209–10)

[walls made of nothing but inscribed stones
that offered their words to the rain and wind
so that they would be carried to the sea
and blown up to the sky.
. . .
stones smoothed with characters
had become recognizable at the bottom:

Thousands, hundreds of thousands of stones
. . .
so that the stream would carry the prayers that were consigned
to the stone to the sea and each word would be moved and prayed,
turning into vapor again under the sun,
and the vapor again would become the cloud
out of which each single character would rain back,
snow back or even smash down again as hail
on the land that belonged only to the gods.]

In contrast to the serial inscriptive acts of eroticism and spiritual devotion committed by Buddhist pilgrims and the two lovers, the narrator's brother Liam inscribes signs into the mountain for a solely pragmatic purpose. He is mapping out difficult shortcuts for possible solo attempts at first ascents, leaving his marks of epistemic appropriation (see 204). The novel invites a thought-experiment that takes several questions as its point of departure: How stable and irreconcilable are the two brothers' approaches to nature, and how static is the dichotomy between the kinds of experience they both try to attain? Can Liam and the narrator, who are bound together by mutual misreadings of each other, be understood as the very same figure? Can their separate identities be read as the hallucination of a dead narrator who inhabits a shifting time that the stage directions in Ransmayr's most recent play, *Odysseus, Verbrecher: Schauspiel einer Heimkehr* (Odysseus, criminal: Drama of a return, 2010) announce as "in der Schwebe zwischen Gegenwart, Zukunft und einer unauslöschlichen Vergangenheit" (hovering between the present, the future, and an indelible past)?[6] A discussion of the novel's visual dynamics will help to elucidate the unattainability of transparent images of self, other, and their interwovenness.

Photography and Mourning

Ransmayr's novel revolves around the visual dynamics of mourning. The narrator's memories evoke his brother by implicitly asking himself and the reader disquieting questions: Can absence be captured in an image? Can loss itself become freeze-framed? The narrator remembers his return to Ireland, where he spread the photographs from the Tibetan expedition on the floor in his deceased brother's office. He had taken numerous portraits of his brother, and he now compares them with "einigen stumpfen Ansichten des Abgrunds" (several dull views of the abyss), and a blurry picture, taken with "Selbstauslöser" (312; autotimer), shows him and Liam in a triumphant pose on the mountain peak. The richly ambiguous semantic field of "auslösen" deserves a closer look in this context. "Auslösen" can denote "to trigger," as in triggering a catastrophe, and "eine Geisel auslösen" means to pay ransom for a hostage. "Auslösen" also connotes "erlösen" (to redeem), as well as "Los," a noun that plays a central role in Hölderlin's and Celan's poetry as well as in Broch's stream-of-consciousness novel, *Der Tod des Vergil* (The death of Vergil, 1951) and that denotes both fate and lottery ticket. Like the English "-less," it can also be a suffix that indicates negation (for example, "endless" / endlos). Ransmayr's word choice of "Selbstauslöser" alludes both to autonomy and self-dissolution. The men who conquer a mountain ultimately obliterate themselves. Every word and every pause in Ransmayr's lyrical prose demands slow and repeated reading, inviting a carefully receptive approach. The narrator remembers the breakdown he underwent while laying out the photographs:

> Das entstehende Bild . . .
> . . . erst Monate nach Liams Tod
> aus dem Entwicklungsbad gezogen . . .
>
> . . . ich stand inmitten der Leere, als ich endlich wagte,
> den Umschlag mit Negativen und Abzügen
> . . . zu öffnen.
> Schon das erste Bild zwang mich auf die Knie.
>
> Ich erinnere mich, daß ich plötzlich
> auf dem nackten Bretterboden kniete,
>
> . . . den Aufschlag meiner Tränen
> auf den matten Oberflächen der Fotos. . . .
>
> die ich ordnete, neu und noch einmal neu gruppierte,

> und dabei auf den Knien umkroch
> wie in der Hoffnung, Bild für Bild
> würde sich dadurch aus der Erinnerung,
> aus der Zweidimensionalität erheben und protestieren
> gegen die unumkehrbare Richtung der Zeit. (312–14)
>
> [The emerging picture . . .
> taken out of the developing bath
> only months after Liam's death . . .
>
> I stood in the midst of the void when I finally dared to
> . . . open . . . the envelope with negatives and prints.
> Even the first time forced me onto my knees.
>
> I remember that I suddenly
> kneeled down on the naked wooden floor,
>
> . . . my tears falling
> on the matte surfaces of the photographs. . . .
>
> that I arranged and rearranged,
> crawling on my knees
> as if I was hoping that this would trigger each single image
> to emerge from memory,
> from its two-dimensional limits, and protest
> against time's irreversible direction.]

The nexus of mourning and photography, a shifting dialectic whose contours are outlined in Roland Barthes's late work, is encapsulated in this scene of the grieving narrator crawling on his knees with his tears falling onto the pictures of his brother.[7]

In *Der fliegende Berg*, Ransmayr operates repeatedly with the topos of disorientation and despair, picturing himself in absolute physical and mental helplessness. After his brother's death, the narrator's obsessive fascination with photography triggers his fall into a crevasse. He blames himself for having kneeled too long at the crevasse's edge in order to capture his surroundings with a digital camera right before his fall (246). After plunging into the crevasse, he attempts to examine the icy cavity with his bare hands, crawling on his knees. The recurrent narrative act of gesticulation suggests a multilayered perspective of regressive gestures in the face of emotional breakdowns, displaying unconscious traces of religious and erotic impulses beyond the binary logic of conquest and surrender. Ransmayr's narrative exploration of conflicting psychological layers not only echoes early nineteenth-century texts such as Tieck's *Der Runenberg* but also continues the unfinished project of German modernism as manifested in the works of, among others, Alfred Döblin and Hermann Broch. Another thematic thread that interweaves Ransmayr's novel with the works of these authors is that interpretation itself becomes an object of observation. The effort of understanding one's own conflicts becomes itself a protagonist who is constantly exposed to self-erasure and overwriting.

At times the narrator self-critically describes his anger toward and alienation from Liam. However this disabling psychological disposition undergoes a transformation into feelings of solidarity and ecstasy under the benign supervision of Liam's eyes and the lens of his camera:

> Und so verwandelte ich mich
> unter dem Objektiv seiner Leica, unter seinen Augen,
> von einem wütenden Nachläufer
> in einen freiwilligen Gefährten, (317–18)
>
> [And so I changed
> under the lens of his Leica, under his eyes,
> from an angry follower
> into a voluntary comrade,]

Subjected to the fraternal gaze and captured within the scope of Liam's Leica, the narrator revels in expectations of oneness, crafting euphoric images of triune harmony between his Tibetan lover, his brother, and himself. Dream sequences, euphoric projections, and scenarios of irretrievable loss alternate and often blur into each other: the realms of what is real and what is virtual converge into different degrees of disappearance.

Virtuality and Disappearance

In a recent interview with Wittstock, published in January 2010, Ransmayr suggests that his main characters pursue a straightforward epistemological and psychological itinerary:

> Meine Figuren gehen ihren Weg aus der Virtualität in die Realität entlang einer vertikalen Linie, von ganz unten nach ganz oben. . . . Solche Wege, ob sie nun in die extreme Höhe oder in die extreme Weite führen, sind immer auch Wege in die eigene Geschichte, ins Innere des Gehenden, Reisenden.[8]
>
> [My characters follow their path from virtuality into reality along a vertical line, from the very bottom to the very top. . . . Whether they lead into extreme heights or into extremely wide open spaces, such paths are always also ways into one's own story and history, into the inner world of the one who walks, the traveler.]

Does this authorial self-interpretation help the reader embrace the complexities of the novel? On a surface level, the statement seems accurate. After all, Liam and the narrator start their journey in Ireland, topographically hardly above sea-level, and their lives end on unmapped heights in the

Himalaya. However, while partially a fitting description of the directions the characters take in *Der fliegende Berg*, Ransmayr's statement distracts from movements and fluctuations in the novel that do not fit this teleological route and rather one-dimensional explanatory pattern.

The inner worlds of the obsessive explorers in Ransmayr's novel cannot be assigned one clear direction. They instead carve out, and are haunted by, cyclic and spiraling psychic routes. The narrator admits to often experiencing a vortex of dreams within dreams that prevent him from "endlich dort anzukommen, wo ich wirklich bin" (359), a passage that presents a palimpsest of two competing layers of meaning. Depending on where one puts the stress when reading the sentence out loud, the translations arrive at two different if related destinations, "finally arriving where I really am," or "finally arriving where I am real."

Sketching a narrative anatomy of terror ("Grauen"), the narrator admits to himself that an uncontrollable ambiguity constitutes his relationship to death. In his self-diagnosis, he describes his addictive drive to overcome boundaries in order to mitigate his fear and temporarily transform it into ecstatic joy. At once attracted and repelled by an inescapable fear that inexorably pushes him onward, any difference between the two vertical directions, up the mountain and climbing downward, has lost any meaning. They have become indistinguishable for the narrator. No matter whether he ascends or descends, at any given moment he awaits the onset of psychic terror ("erfaßte mich dieses Grauen") whether he is on his way "in die nackte Höhe" (into the naked heights), into "das Tal" (the valley), "die Tiefe" (the depths), or inhabiting their "fliegende Grenze" (flying boundary; all quotes from 239).

In a recent monograph, Dana Pfeiferová discusses Ransmayr along with other contemporary Austrian writers as an author of apocalyptic prose. Her study offers only a sparse analysis, which nevertheless contains the nucleus of a fruitful contradiction. According to Pfeiferová, humans have to perish in all of Ransmayr's novels, and posthuman nature is endowed with positive connotations.[9] A fascination with dystopia and the posthuman sublime is constitutive of Ransmayr's entire oeuvre, beginning with his first novel, *Die Schrecken des Eises und der Finsternis* (The terrors of ice and darkness, 1984), which both tells and undermines superimposed stories of a polar expedition.[10]

Repeatedly transfixed by the correspondence between Liam's computer-generated images of mountains and the non-virtual, tangible terrain that he and his brother experience, the narrator reiterates this central visual and conceptual obsession throughout the novel. Identifying with Liam, the narrator expresses his epistemic satisfaction with semi-religious undertones, reporting "eine erfüllte Prophezeiung, / die auf den Bildschirmen meines Bruders erschienen war" (282; a fulfilled prophecy, / that had appeared on my brother's monitors). Continuously alternating between memories of Liam's liquid crystal display monitors and the mountains they now experience physically, the narrator witnesses the sudden opening of "eine Kluft, ein Fenster, / in dem nun ein seltsam ruhiges Bild stillstand" (276; a crevice, a window, / in which now a strangely quiet image stood still). This reassuring still image defies the swirling "Splitter und Bruchstücke" (splinters and fragments) of the competing petrified and vanishing worlds, "einer beständigen steinernen und einer verfliegenden Welt." The mysterious ridge emerges as "die Wirklichkeit, / die zum Abbild auf Liams Schirmen gehörte" (the reality / that was linked to the image on Liam's screens, all quotes from 276):

> Der nächtliche Anblick hatte mich gebannt,
> als wäre eine jener virtuellen Landschaften,
> die sich in Liams digitalen Atlanten
> zu tektonischen Wellen erhoben und abrollten,
> in einem elektronischen Schöpfungsakt
> *wirklich* geworden;
>
> ... einen Berg, der sich aus der bloßen Vorstellung
> zur Wirklichkeit aufwarf.
> ...
>
> dazu entschlossen, diesem Grat nachzugehen,
> dem fliegenden Berg, und so einer Spur zu folgen,
> die aus Liams matt leuchtenden virtuellen Welten
> in die Wirklichkeit führte. (283 and 291)
>
> [I was spellbound by the nocturnal view
> as if one of those virtual landscapes
> that emerged and unrolled
> in Liam's digital atlases
> in an electronic act of creation
> had become real
>
> ... a mountain that raised itself from mere imagination
> to reality.
> ...
> determined to follow this ridge,
> the Flying Mountain, pursuing a trace
> that led from Liam's dimly luminescent virtual worlds
> into reality.]

In a fleeting moment of ecstatic epistemic fulfillment, the narrator celebrates the perception that his brother's virtual constructions match a hitherto unmapped part of the world. But far from providing conventional tales of science's triumph over the threats of nature, Ransmayr's novels confront the reader with the process of dying related by narrative voices that speak from beyond life. Undergoing contradictory premonitions, the narrator alternates between the euphoric hope of being rescued by Nyema, whom he temporarily imagines as a meticulous and impeccable reader of the signs ("Zeichen") he inadvertently left behind and as a powerful listener capable of hearing his breath, and the fear that his traces may have become indecipherable, covered by snow, and that he might be irrevocably untraceable ("alle meine Spuren / verschwanden") even for his lover (see 255–57).

The novel rejects the installment of rigid boundaries between mapping the unknown and immersing oneself in it, only to disappear into it. Neither scientific conquest nor mystical submission are offered as viable options. Love as the mutual teaching of a new language remains a fantasy in Ransmayr's novel, an ephemeral snapshot in the narrator's pictorial arsenal of melancholia. What offers itself as the imagery of ascent in *Der fliegende Berg* can more precisely be read as the vertiginous and ultimately inescapable self-encircling of its narrative voice.

Ransmayr's novel *Der fliegende Berg* implicitly posits that the act and process of dying remain unmappable and inaccessible to scientific attempts to define and demarcate them. The mountaineering expedition, whose internal dynamic is under constant scrutiny in the novel, passes a point of no return, entering a lethal zone that is marked by communicative failures, irrevocable misreadings that are masked by fantasies of universal oneness through pansemiotic immersion. The narrator yearns to become nothing but a sign that is free of referential meaning, like the nymph Mnemosyne, the lyrical speaker in Hölderlin's eponymous poem from 1803: "Ein Zeichen sind wir, / Deutungslos" (We are a sign, / Pointing nowhere [Void of interpretation / interpretation's destiny]).[11] The dying narrator achieves neither a longed-for harmonious self-dissolution into nature nor a sustainable equilibrium of loving familiarity with another human being, be it his Tibetan lover or his brother. Unable to descend back to the shelter of a communicative base camp, the narrative voice cannot be recovered anymore by the world before the flying mountain. It begins, rather, to inhabit a posthuman crevasse that is irretraceably covered in snow. The competing yet complementary methods of scientific mastery and meditative immersion turn out to be equally incapable of overcoming existential helplessness. Beyond the reach of recovery and ready-made reintegration into a mappable social order, the dissolving narrator is driven to step into the uncontrollable danger of language itself, inhabiting the vortex of its disappearance.

Notes

[1] Ransmayr's novel *Der fliegende Berg* was recently translated into French and Dutch; see *La montagne volante* (Paris: Michel, 2007), and *De vliegende berg* (Amsterdam: Prometheus, 2007). An English translation of the novel has yet to be published. All translations from *Der fliegende Berg* into English are my own, as are

all other translations in this essay. The height of the fictional mountain is not given, but the narrator announces in the second line of the novel that he died "6840 Meter über dem Meeresspiegel" (6,840 meters above sea level), see Christoph Ransmayr, *Der fliegende Berg* (Frankfurt am Main: S. Fischer, 2006), 9. All further references to *Der fliegende Berg* are given in the text, using the page number alone.

[2] For Wittstock's incantatory praise, which temporarily abandons critical ground, see Uwe Wittstock, *Nach der Moderne: Essay zur deutschen Gegenwartsliteratur in zwölf Kapiteln über elf Autoren* (Göttingen: Wallstein, 2009), 133–34 and 136: "rhythmisch durchformt und durchdacht . . . Die Bildphantasie Ransmayrs ist atemberaubend. . . . ebenso poetisch wie präzise . . . eine Sprache von überwältigender, von erschütternder Schönheit." (the rhythm is thoroughly stylized and conceptualized . . . Ransmayr's visual imagination is breathtaking. . . . as poetic as it is precise . . . a language of overwhelming, unsettling beauty).

[3] Wittstock, *Nach der Moderne*, 133.

[4] Christoph Ransmayr, *Die letzte Welt* (Frankfurt am Main: Fischer, 1988).

[5] See Axel Gellhaus, *Schreibengehen: Literatur und Fotografie en passant* (Cologne: Böhlau, 2008), 95.

[6] Christoph Ransmayr, *Odysseus, Verbrecher: Schauspiel einer Heimkehr* (Frankfurt am Main: Fischer, 2010), 9.

[7] On the connection between mourning and photography, see Roland Barthes's autobiographical essay and theoretical outline, *La chambre claire: Note sur la photographie* (Paris: Gallimard, 1980).

[8] See Uwe Wittstock, "'Ich bleibe auch in den Gebirgen lieber Wanderer': Der Schriftsteller Christoph Ransmayr im Gespräch über seinen Freund Reinhold Messner, die gerade verfilmte Nanga-Parbat-Katastrophe und das Abenteuer des Schreibens," *Die Welt*, 9 Jan. 2010, 25.

[9] See Dana Pfeiferová, *Angesichts des Todes: Die Todesbilder in der neueren österreichischen Prosa; Bachmann, Bernhard, Winkler, Jelinek, Handke, Ransmayr* (Vienna: Praesens, 2007), 206–9.

[10] For a cogent examination of the sublime in Ransmayr's first novel, see Torsten Hoffmann, *Konfigurationen des Erhabenen: Zur Produktivität einer ästhetischen Kategorie in der Literatur des ausgehenden 20. Jahrhunderts (Handke, Ransmayr, Schrott, Strauss)* (Berlin: de Gruyter, 2006), 124–44 and 208–22.

[11] See Friedrich Hölderlin, *Sämtliche Gedichte*, ed. Jochen Schmidt (Frankfurt am Main: Deutscher Klassiker Verlag, 2005), 1033. While the suffix "-los" denotes a negation or a "loss," as a noun, "Los" can be translated as "fate" or "destiny."

Works Cited

Abbott, H. Porter. *The Cambridge Introduction to Narrative*. Cambridge: Cambridge UP, 2002.

Addison, Joseph. "Dream of the Region of Liberty." *Tatler*, 20 April 1710, 191–92.

Adorno, Theodor. *Ästhetische Theorie*. Frankfurt am Main: Suhrkamp, 1973.

———. "Richard Strauss: Zum hundertsten Geburtstag." In *Gesammelte Schriften*, edited by Rolf Tiedemann, 16: 165–606. Frankfurt am Main: Suhrkamp, 1997. In English, "Richard Strauss: Born June 11, 1864." Translated by Samuel Weber and Shierry Weber. *Perspectives of New Music* 4, no. 1 (1965): 14–32, and no. 2 (1965): 111–29.

Aguirre, der Zorn Gottes. Directed by Werner Herzog. Vienna: Werner Herzog Filmproduktion, 1972.

Albritton, Claude C. *The Abyss of Time: Changing Conceptions of the Earth's Antiquity after the Sixteenth Century*. San Francisco: Freeman, Cooper, 1980.

Ames, Eric. "Herzog, Landscape, and Documentary." *Cinema Journal* 48, no. 2 (Winter 2009): 49–69.

Amstädter, Rainer. *Der Alpinismus: Kultur — Organisation — Politik*. Vienna: WUV-Universitätsverlag, 1996.

Anderson, Joseph D. *The Reality of Illusion: An Ecological Approach to Cognitive Film Theory*. Carbondale: Southern Illinois UP, 1996.

Arnold, David. *The Tropics and the Traveling Gaze: India, Landscape, and Science, 1800–1856*. Seattle: U of Washington P, 2006.

Arx, Bernhard von. *Karl Stauffer und Lydia Welter-Escher: Chronik eines Skandals*. Bern: Zytglogge, 1991.

Asher, Lyell. "Petrarch at the Peak of Fame." *PMLA* 108, no. 5 (1993): 1050–63.

Ashfield, Andrew, and Peter De Bolla. "Introduction." In *The Sublime: A Reader in British Eighteenth-Century Aesthetic Theory*, edited by Ashfield and De Bolla, 1–16. Cambridge: Cambridge UP, 1996.

Aspetsberger, Friedbert, ed. *Der BergFilm, 1920–1940*. Innsbruck: Studien-Verlag, 2002.

Atherton, Geoffrey. "'Poetische Mahlerey': Placing Albrecht von Haller's 'Enzian' Portrait in a Georgic Gallery." *German Quarterly* 71, no. 4 (1998): 353–76.

Atkins, Stuart. *Essays on Goethe*, edited by Jane K. Brown and Thomas P. Saine. Columbia, SC: Camden House, 1995.

Baird, Jay W. *To Die for Germany: Heroes in the Nazi Pantheon*. Bloomington: Indiana UP, 1992.

Barthes, Roland. *La chambre claire: Note sur la photographie*. Paris: Gallimard, 1980.

Barton, Susan. *Healthy Living in the Alps: The Origins of Winter Tourism in Switzerland, 1860–1914*. Manchester: Manchester UP, 2008.

Bauer, Paul. *Auf Kundfahrt im Himalaja: Siniolchu und Nanga Parbat — Tat und Schicksal deutscher Bergsteiger*. Munich: Knorr & Hirth, 1937.

Bayers, Peter L. *Imperial Ascent: Mountaineering, Masculinity, and Empire*. Boulder: U of Colorado P, 2003.

Bayreuther, Rainer. *Richard Strauss' Alpensinfonie: Entstehung, Analyse und Interpretation*. Hildesheim: Olms, 1997.

Beattie, Andrew. *The Alps: A Cultural History; Landscapes of the Imagination*. Oxford: Oxford UP, 2006.

Beckett, Samuel. *Worstward Ho*. In *Nohow On: Three Novels by Samuel Beckett*, 87–116. New York: Grove, 1996.

Bender, John, and David Wellbery. "Introduction." In *Chronotypes: The Construction of Time*, edited by Bender and Wellbery, 1–18. Stanford, CA: Stanford UP, 1991.

Berman, Russell A. *Enlightenment or Empire: Colonial Discourse in German Culture*. Lincoln: U of Nebraska P, 1998.

Bernett, Hajo. *Nationalsozialistische Leibeserziehung: Eine Dokumentation ihrer Theorie und Organisation*. Schorndorf bei Stuttgart: Verlag Karl Hofmann, 1966.

Bernhard, Thomas. *Frost*. Frankfurt am Main: Suhrkamp, 1972.

Bersier, Gabrielle. "Goethe's Geology in Flux: Vulcanism and Neptunism in the Translation of Richard Payne Knight's *Expedition into Sicily* and the *Italian Journey*." In *Goethe, Chaos, and Complexity*, edited by Herbert Rowland, 35–45. Amsterdam: Rodopi, 2001.

"Die Besteigung des Kilimandscharo." *Westermann's Jahrbuch der Illustrirten Deutschen Monatshefte: Ein Familienbuch für das gesammte Leben der Gegenwart* 15 (October 1863–March 1864): 222–23.

Bialek, Edward, and Jan Pacholski, eds. *"Über allen Gipfeln . . .": Bergmotive in der deutschsprachigen Literatur des 18. bis 21. Jahrhunderts*. Dresden/Wroclaw: Neisse, 2008.

Bilger, Burkhard. "The Long Dig: Getting through the Swiss Alps the Hard Way." *New Yorker*, 15 September 2008.

Blackler, Deane. *Reading W. G. Sebald: Adventure and Disobedience*. Rochester, NY: Camden House, 2007.

Blamires, David Malcolm. *Herzog Ernst and the Underworld Voyage: A Comparative Study*. Manchester: U of Manchester P, 1979.

Boase, T. S. R. "English Artists and the Val d'Aosta." *Journal of the Warburg and Courtauld Institutes* 19, nos. 3–4 (July-December 1956): 286–88.

Boccaccio, Giovanni. *Dizionario geografico: De montibus*. . . . Translated by Nicolò Luburnio. Preface by Gian Franco Pasini. Turin: Fògola Editore, 1978.

Bohls, Elizabeth A. *Women Travel Writers and the Language of Aesthetics, 1716–1818*. Cambridge: Cambridge UP, 2004.

Böhme, Gernot. "'Mir läuft ein Schauer übern ganzen Leib': Das Wetter, die Witterungslehre und die Sprache der Gefühle." *Goethe Jahrbuch* 124 (2007): 133–41.

Böhme, Hartmut. "Berg." In *Wörterbuch der philosophischen Metaphern*, edited by Ralf Konersmann, 46–61. Darmstadt: Wissenschaftliche Buchgesellschaft, 2007.

———. "Romantische Adoleszenzkrisen: Zur Psychodynamik der Venuskult-Novellen von Tieck, Eichendorff und E. T. A. Hoffmann." In *Literatur und Psychoanalyse*, edited by Klaus Bohnen, Sven Aage Jørgensen, and Friedrich Schmoë, 133–76. Copenhagen: Text & Kontext, 1981.

Böhmersheim, August Böhm von. *Zur Biographie Friedrich Simony's*. Vienna: Lechner, 1899.

Bolívar, Simón. "Mi delirio sobre el Chimborazo" [1822]. In *Papeles de Bolívar*, edited by Vicente Lecuna, 233–34. Caracas: Litografía del Comercio, 1917; in English, "My Delirium on Chimborazo" in *Writings of Simón Bolívar*, translated by Frederick Fornoff, edited by David Bushnell, 135–36. Oxford: Oxford UP, 2003.

Bollnow, Otto Friedrich. "Der *Nachsommer* und der Bildungsgedanke des Biedermeier." In *Beiträge zur Einheit von Bildung und Sprache im geistigen Sein: Festschrift zum 80. Geburtstag von Ernst Otto*, edited by Gerhard Haselbach and Günter Hartmann, 14–33. Berlin: de Gruyter, 1957.

Bordwell, David, Janet Steiger, and Kristin Thompson. *The Classical Hollywood Cinema*. New York: New York UP, 1985.

Boschung, Urs. "Ein Berner Patriot: Hallers Lebensstationen." In Elsner and Rupke, *Albrecht von Haller im Göttingen der Aufklärung*, 21–46.

———. "Leben und Umfeld." In Steinke, Boschung, and Proß, *Albrecht von Haller: Leben — Werk — Epoche*, 21–22.

Boyle, Nicholas. *Goethe: The Poet and the Age*. Vol. 1, *The Poetry of Desire*. Oxford: Oxford UP, 1992.

Brahm, Otto. *Karl Stauffer — Bern: Sein Leben, seine Briefe, seine Gedichte.* Stuttgart: Göschen, 1892.

Brant, Sebastian. *Das Narrenschiff.* Stuttgart: Reclam, 2006.

Braun, Stefan. *Naturwissenschaft als Lebensbasis? Adalbert Stifters Roman "Der Nachsommer" und weitere Schriften Stifters als Dokumente eines Versuches der Daseinsgestaltung auf der Grundlage naturwissenschaftlichen Forschens.* Linz: Adalbert-Stifter-Institut, 2006.

Brehmer, Hermann. *Die chronische Lungenschwindsucht und Tuberkulose der Lunge: Ihre Ursache und ihre Heilung.* Berlin: Enslin, 1869.

Brévart, Francis B., ed. *Das Eckenlied: Sämtliche Fassungen.* Altdeutsche Textbibliothek 111. Tübingen: Niemeyer, 1999.

Brown, Jane. *Goethe's* Faust: *The German Tragedy.* Ithaca, NY: Cornell UP, 1986.

Bruford, W. H. *The German Tradition of Self-Cultivation: "Bildung" from Humboldt to Thomas Mann.* London: Cambridge UP, 1975.

Buell, Lawrence. *Writing for an Endangered World: Literature, Culture, and Environment in the U.S. and Beyond.* London: Belknap, 2001.

Bürkli, Johannes. *Gedichte über die Schweiz und über Schweizer.* Vol. 1. Bern: Galler, 1793.

Bulang, Tobias. "Die Rettung der Geschichte in Adalbert Stifters *Nachsommer.*" *Poetica* 32 (2000): 373–405.

Burch, Noël. *Life to Those Shadows.* Translated and edited by Ben Brewster. Berkeley: U of California P, 1990.

Burckhardt, Jacob. *Die Kultur der Renaissance in Italien.* In vol. 3 of *Gesammelte Werke.* Basel: Benno Schwabe, 1955.

Burke, Edmund. *A Philosophical Enquiry into the Origin of Our Ideas of the Sublime and Beautiful.* New Edition. London: J. Dodsley, 1787.

Burn, A. R. "Helikon in History: A Study in Greek Mountain Topography." *Annual of the British School at Athens* 44 (1949): 313–23.

Burnet, Thomas. *The Sacred Theory of the Earth.* Fourth Edition. Vol 1. London: John Hooke, 1719.

Butler, E. M. *The Tyranny of Greece over Germany: A Study of the Influence Exercised by Greek Art and Poetry over the Great German Writers of the Eighteenth, Nineteenth, and Twentieth Centuries.* London: Cambridge UP, 1935.

Buxton, Richard. "Imaginary Greek Mountains." *Journal of Hellenic Studies* 112 (1992): 1–15. Reprinted in revised form in *Imaginary Greece: The Contexts of Mythology*, 80–96. Cambridge: Cambridge UP, 1994.

Calder, Alex, Jonathan Lamb, and Bridget Orr, eds. *Voyages and Beaches: Pacific Encounters, 1769–1840.* Honolulu: U of Hawaii P, 1999.

Carus, Carl Gustav. *Nine Letters on Landscape Painting*. Introduction by Oskar Bätschmann. Translated by David Britt. Los Angeles: Getty Research Institute, 2002.

Catling, Jo. "W. G. Sebald's Landscapes of Memory." In *The Anatomist of Melancholy: Essays in Memory of W. G. Sebald*, edited by Rüdiger Görner, 19–50. Munich: iudicium, 2003.

Celan, Paul. *Atemwende*. Frankfurt am Main: Suhrkamp, 1967.

———. *Breathturn*. Translated by Pierre Joris. Los Angeles: Sun & Moon Press, 1995.

———. *Der Meridian und andere Prosa*. Frankfurt am Main: Suhrkamp, 1983.

Cerro Torre: Schrei aus Stein. Directed by Werner Herzog. Germany: Sera Filmproduktion, 1991.

Cilano, Cara, and Elizabeth DeLoughrey. "Against Authenticity: Global Knowledges and Postcolonial Ecocriticism." *ISLE* 14 (2007): 71–87.

Clark, Andy. "Visual Experience and Motor Action: Are the Bonds Too Tight?" *Philosophical Review* 110, no. 4 (October 2001): 495–519.

Classen, Albrecht. *The German Volksbuch: A Critical History of a Late-Medieval Genre*. Studies in German Language and Literature 15. Lewiston, NY: Edwin Mellen Press, 1995.

———. "Medieval Travel into an Exotic Orient: The *Spielmannsepos Herzog Ernst* as a Travel into the Medieval Subconsciousness." In *Lesarten: New Methodologies and Old Texts*, edited by Alexander Schwarz, 103–24. Frankfurt am Main: Peter Lang, 1990.

———. "Multiculturalism in the German Middle Ages? The Rediscovery of a Modern Concept in the Past: The Case of *Herzog Ernst*." In *Multiculturalism and Representation: Selected Essays*, edited by John Rieder and Larry E. Smith, 198–219. Honolulu: U of Hawaii P, 1996.

———. *The Poems of Oswald von Wolkenstein: An English Translation of the Complete Works (1376/77–1445)*. New York: Palgrave Macmillan, 2008.

———. "Schwellenphänomen, Paradigmenwechsel, Popularitätserfolg: Hybridisierung und Konkretisierung des spätmittelalterlichen Liebeslieds als Erfolgsrezept beim Mönch von Salzburg." *Studia Neophilologica* 81 (2009): 69–86.

———. "Travel Space as Constructed Space: Arnold von Harff Observes the Arabic Space." *German Studies Review* 33, no. 2 (2010): 375–88.

Cliffhanger. Directed by Renny Harlin. Beverly Hills: Carolco Pictures, 1993.

Connochie-Bourgne, Chantal. "Quelques notes sur l'orogenèse chez les encyclopédistes de langue française au XIIIe siècle." In Thomasset and James-Raoul, *La montagne dans le texte médiévale: Entre mythe et réalité*, 53–60.

Cook, E. T., and Alexander Wedderburn, eds. *The Works of John Ruskin*. 39 vols. London: George Allen, 1903–12.

Cooley, William Desborough. *Inner Africa Laid Open*. New York: Negro Universities P, 1969.

Coxe, William. *Sketches of the Natural, Civil and Political State of Swisserland*. London: J. Dodsley, 1779.

———. *Travels in Switzerland and in the Country of Grisons*. 2 vols. Basel: Decker, 1802.

Craig, Gordon A. *The Triumph of Liberalism: Zurich in the Golden Age, 1830–1869*. New York: Scribner, 1988.

Crary, Jonathan. *Suspensions of Perception: Attention, Spectacle, and Modern Culture*. Cambridge: MIT Press, 1999.

Cronin, Paul, ed. *Herzog on Herzog*. London: Faber & Faber, 2002.

Crosby, Alfred W. *Ecological Imperialism: The Biological Expansion of Europe, 900–1900*. Cambridge: Cambridge UP, 1986.

Danius, Sara. *The Senses of Modernism: Technology, Perception, and Aesthetics*. Ithaca, NY: Cornell UP, 2002.

Das Nibelungenlied. Middle High German / New High German. Translated into New High German from the text by Karl Bartsch und Helmut de Boor, with a commentary by Siegfried Grosse. Stuttgart: Reclam, 1997.

Deaville, James. "Raff, Joachim." In *Grove Music Online. Oxford Music Online*. http://www.oxfordmusiconline.com/subscriber/article/grove/music/22816 (accessed 31 October 2010).

De Capitani, François. "Hallers Bern." In Steinke, Boschung, and Proß, *Albrecht von Haller: Leben — Werk — Epoche*, 83–97.

Decken, Baron Carl Claus von der. *Baron Carl Claus von der Decken's Reisen in Ost-Afrika in den Jahren 1859 bis 1865*. Commissioned by the mother of the traveller, Princess Adelheid von Pless. *Erzählender Theil, Zweiter Band: Baron Carl Claus von der Decken's Reisen in Ost-Afrika in den Jahren 1862 bis 1865; Nebst Darstellung von R[ichard] Brenners und Th[eodor] Kinzelbach's Reisen zur Feststellung des Schicksals der Verschollenen, 1866 und 1867*. Edited by Otto Kersten. Leipzig: C. F. Winter'sche Verlagshandlung, 1871.

Dedner, Burghard. "Vom Schäferleben zur Agrarwirtschaft: Poesie und Ideologie des 'Landlebens' in der deutschen Literatur des 18. Jahrhunderts." In *Europäische Bukolik und Georgik*, edited by Klaus Garber, 347–90. Darmstadt: Wissenschaftliche Buchgesellschaft, 1976.

DeLoughrey, Elizabeth. "Quantum Landscapes: A 'Ventriloquism of Spirit.'" *Interventions* 9 (2007): 62–82.

DeLoughrey, Elizabeth, Renée K. Gosson, and George B. Handley, eds. *Carribean Literature and the Environment: Between Nature and Culture*. Charlottesville: U of Virginia P, 2005.

de Saussure, Horace-Bénédict. *Voyages dans les Alpes: Précédés d'un essai sur l'histoire naturelle des environs de Genève*. 4 vols. Neuchâtel, Switzerland: Fauche, 1779–96.

de Selincourt, E., and E. Darbishire, eds. *The Poetical Works of William Wordsworth*. Vol. 1. Oxford: Oxford UP, 1963.

de Staël, Germaine. *Considérations sur les principaux événemens de la Révolution françoise*. Vol. 3. Paris: Delaunay, Bossange & Masson, 1818.

Der Berg des Schicksals. Directed by Dr. Arnold Fanck. Freiburg/Breisgau: Berg- und Sportfilm GmbH, 1923/24.

Der heilige Berg. Directed by Dr. Arnold Fanck. Berlin: Universum Film AG, 1925/26.

Der König vom Montblanc. Directed by Dr. Arnold Fanck. Berlin: Cine-Allianz Tonfilm GmbH, 1933/34.

Der Stricker. *Daniel von dem Blühenden Tal*. Edited by Michael Resler. Altdeutsche Textbibliothek 92. Tübingen: Niemeyer, 1995.

Der verlorene Sohn. Directed by Luis Trenker. Berlin: Deutsche Universal-Film AG, 1933/34.

Derrida, Jacques. *Sovereignties in Question: The Poetics of Paul Celan*. Edited by Thomas Dutoit and Outi Pasanen. New York: Fordham UP, 2005.

Deutsche Himalaja-Expeditionen. Directed by Frank Leberecht. FRG: Institut für Film und Bild in Wissenschaft und Unterricht (FWU), 1950/51.

Die Besteigung des Chimborazo. Directed by Rainer Simon. GDR/FRG/Ecuador: DEFA, 1989.

Die weltlichen Lieder des Mönchs von Salzburg: Texte und Melodien. Edited by Christoph März. Münchener Texte und Untersuchungen zur deutschen Literatur des Mittelalters 114. Tübingen: Niemeyer, 1999.

Dietrichs Flucht: Textgeschichtliche Ausgabe. Edited by Elisabeth Lienert and Gertrud Beck. Tübingen: Niemeyer, 2003.

Dorst, Tankred. *Auf dem Chimborazo*. Frankfurt am Main: Suhrkamp, 1974.

Ducos, Joëlle. "Entre terre, air et eau: la formation des montagnes." In Thomasset and James-Raoul, *La montagne dans le texte médiévale: Entre mythe et réalité*, 19–51.

Dzialas, Ingrid. *Auffassung und Darstellung der Elemente bei Goethe*. Berlin: Ebering, 1939.

Eck, Reimer, ed. *Albrecht von Haller in Göttingen*. Exhibition catalogue. Göttingen: Institut für Wissenschaftsgeschichte, 2008.

Ecker, Gisela. "'Heimat' oder Die Grenzen der Bastelei." In *W. G. Sebald: Politische Archäologie und melancholische Bastelei*, edited by Michael Niehaus and Claudia Öhlschläger, 77–88. Berlin: Erich Schmidt Verlag, 2006.

Edgcombe, Rodney Stenning. "Mann's *Zauberberg* and Elisabeth Eyberg's 'Röntgenfoto': A Variation on a Topos," *Germanic Notes and Reviews* 1, no. 41 (2010): 30–37.

Edmond, Rod. *Representing the South Pacific: Colonial Discourse from Cook to Gaugin*. Cambridge: Cambridge UP, 1997.

Elsner, Norbert, and Nicolaas A. Rupke, eds. *Albrecht von Haller im Göttingen der Aufklärung*. Göttingen: Wallstein, 2009.

Emrich, Wilhelm. *Die Symbolik von Faust II*. Bonn: Athenäum, 1957.

Engel, Claire-Eliane. *La littérature alpestre en France et en Angleterre aux XVIIIe et XIXe siècles*. Chambéry: Dardel, 1930.

Engelhardt, Wolf von. *Goethe im Gespräch mit der Erde: Landschaft, Gesteine, Mineralien und Erdgeschichte in seinem Leben und Werk*. Weimar: Böhlau, 2003.

Enzensberger, Hans Magnus. "A. v. H. (1769–1859)." In *Mausoleum: Siebenunddreißig Balladen aus der Geschichte des Fortschritts*, 56–58. Frankfurt am Main: Suhrkamp, 1975; in English, "A. v. H. (1769–1859)," in *Mausoleum: Thirty-seven Ballads from the History of Progress*, trans. Joachim Neugroschel, 62–66. New York: Urizen, 1976.

Ertl, Hans. *Meine wilden dreißiger Jahre: Bergsteiger, Filmpionier, Weltenbummler*. Munich: Herbig, 1982.

Euripides. *The Bacchae and Other Plays*. Oxford: Oxford UP, 2008.

———. *Bacchae*. In *Euripides V*. Translated by William Arrowsmith. Chicago: U of Chicago P, 1959.

Ewton, Ralph W. "Life and Death of the Body in Tieck's *Der Runenberg*." *Germanic Review: Literature, Culture, Theory* 50 (1975): 19–33.

Fanck, Arnold. *Er führte Regie mit Gletschern, Stürmen und Lawinen: Ein Filmpionier erzählt*. Munich: Nymphenburger Verlagshandlung, 1973.

———. "Die Zukunft des Naturfilms." 1928. In *Berge, Licht und Traum: Dr. Arnold Fanck und der deutsche Bergfilm*, edited by Jan-Christopher Horak and Gisela Pichler, 143–46. Munich: Bruckmann, 1997.

Fehn, K. "Alm." In *Aachen bis Bettelordenskirchen*, vol. 1 of *Lexikon des Mittelalters*, 443. Munich: Artemis, 1980.

Felfe, Robert. *Naturgeschichte als kunstvolle Synthese: Physikotheologie und Bildpraxis bei Johann Jakob Scheuchzer*. Berlin: Akademie Verlag, 2003.

Fichte, Johann Gottlieb. "Einige Vorlesungen über die Bestimmung des Gelehrten." In *Gesamtausgabe der Bayerischen Akademie der Wissenschaften*, vol. 1,3:1–74. Stuttgart: Frommann-Holzboog, 1966. In English, "Several Lectures on the Vocation of the Scholar," in *Fichtes Early Philosophical Writings*, 137–84. Edited and translated by Daniel Breazeale. Ithaca, NY: Cornell UP, 1988.

Fiennes, Ranulph. *Race to the Pole: Tragedy, Heroism, and Scott's Antarctic Quest*. New York: Hyperion, 2005.

Finley, Gerald E. "The Genesis of Turner's 'Landscape Sublime.'" *Zeitschrift für Kunstgeschichte* 42, 2–3 (1979): 141–65.

Fischer, Kurt Gerhard, ed. *Adalbert Stifters Leben und Werk in Briefen und Dokumenten.* Frankfurt am Main: Insel, 1962.

Fisher, Jaimey, and Barbara Mennel, eds. *Spatial Turns: Space, Place, and Mobility in German Literary and Visual Culture.* Amsterdam: Rodopi, 2010.

Forster, George. *A Voyage round the World.* Edited by Nicholas Thomas and Oliver Berghof. Honolulu: U of Hawaii P, 2000.

Foucault, Michel. *Discipline and Punish: The Birth of the Prison.* New York: Random House, 1995.

———. *Madness and Civilization: A History of Insanity in the Age of Reason.* New York: Random House, 1988.

Franzel, Elisabeth. "Der Mond." In *Motive der Weltliteratur: Ein Lexikon dichtungsgeschichtlicher Längsschnitte*, 547–60. 3rd edition. Stuttgart: Kröner, 1988.

Fraser, James. *The Golden Bough.* London: Penguin, 1996.

Freud, Sigmund. *Elemente der Psychoanalyse.* Volume 1 of *Werkausgabe in zwei Bänden.* Edited by Anna Freud and Ilse Grubrich-Simitis, Frankfurt am Main: Fischer, 1978.

———. *Das Unheimliche: Aufsätze zur Literatur*, edited by Klaus Wagenbach. Hamburg-Wandsbek: Fischer doppelpunkt, 1963. In English, *The Uncanny.* Translated by David McLintock. London: Penguin, 2003.

Frohlick, Susan. "'That Playfulness of White Masculinity' — Mediating Masculinities and Adventure at Mountain Film Festivals." *Tourist Studies* 5, no. 2 (2005): 175–93.

Fuchs, Anne. "'Ein Hauptkapitel der Geschichte der Unterwerfung': Representations of Nature in W. G. Sebald's *Die Ringe des Saturn.*" In *W. G. Sebald and the Writing of History*, edited by Anne Fuchs and J. J. Long, 121–38. Würzburg: Königshausen & Neumann, 2007.

Füssel, Stephan. *Kaiser Maximilian und die Medien seiner Zeit: Der Theuerdank von 1517; Eine kulturhistorische Einführung.* Cologne: Taschen, 2003.

Galeano, Eduardo. *Memoria del fuego*, vol. 2: *Las caras y las máscaras.* Montevideo: Chanchito, 1987.

Gallhuber, Julius. "Die Expeditionen des DÖAV und die alpine Öffentlichkeit." *Bergsteiger* 19 (1928): 1.

Gamper, Michael, and Karl Wagner, eds. *Figuren der Übertragung: Adalbert Stifter und das Wissen seiner Zeit.* Zurich: Chronos, 2009.

Garbarino, Giovanna. "Secum peregrinari: Il tema del viaggio in Seneca." In *De tuo tibi: Omaggio degli allievi a Italo Lana*, 263–85. Bologna: Pàtron, 1996.

Garrard, Greg. *Ecocriticism*. London: Routledge, 2004.

Gasherbrum — Der leuchtende Berg. Directed by Werner Herzog. Vienna: Werner Herzog Filmproduktion, 1985.

Gearey, John. *Goethe's Other* Faust: *The Drama, Part II*. Toronto: U of Toronto P, 1992.

Gellhaus, Axel. *Schreibengehen: Literatur und Fotografie en passant*. Cologne: Böhlau, 2008.

Gelzer, Florian and Béla Kapossy. "Roman, Staat und Gesellschaft." In Steinke, Boschung, and Proß, *Albrecht von Haller: Leben — Werk — Epoche*, 156–81.

Gerbi, Antonello. *La disputa del Nuovo Mondo: Storia di una polemica, 1750–1900*. Milan: Riccardo Ricciardi, 1983.

Gérard, François. *L'Amérique relevée de sa ruine par le commerce et par l'industrie* (1814). In *Atlas géographique et physique des régions équinoxiales du Nouveau Continent*, frontispiece. Paris: Gide, 1814–38.

Gerwald, Mattias. *Der Entdecker: Historischer Roman über Alexander von Humboldt*. Bergisch Gladbach: Lübbe, 2001.

Gesner, Conrad. *On the Admiration of Mountains, the Prefatory Letter Addressed to Jacob Avienus, Physician, in Gesner's Pamphlet "On Milk and Substances Prepared from Milk."* Translated by H. B. D. Soulé. San Francisco: Grabhorn, 1937.

Gilpin, William. *Observations, Relative Chiefly to Picturesque Beauty, Made in the Year 1772, on Several Parts of England; Particularly the Mountains and Lakes of Cumberland and Westmoreland*. 2 vols. Second Edition. London: R. Blamire, 1788.

———. *Three Essays: On the Picturesque Beauty; On Picturesque Travel; and On Sketching Landscape; To which is added a Poem, on Landscape Painting*. Third edition. London: T. Cadell & W. Davies, 1808.

Girdlestone, Cuthbert. *Poésie, politique, Pyrénées: Louis-Francois Ramond, 1755–1827*. Paris: Minard, 1968.

Glotfelty, Cheryll, and Harold Fromm, eds. *The Ecocriticism Reader*. Athens: U of Georgia P, 1996.

Goethe, Johann Wolfgang. "Die Absicht eingeleitet." In *Schriften zur Morphologie*, edited by Dorothea Kuhn, vol. 24 of *Sämtliche Werke: Briefe, Tagebücher und Gespräche*, 391–95. Frankfurt am Main: Deutscher Klassiker Verlag, 1987.

———. "Brief an Charlotte von Stein, 3.10.1779." In *Das erste Weimarer Jahrzehnt: Briefe, Tagebücher und Gespräche vom 7. November 1775 bis 2. September 1786*, edited by Hartmut Reinhardt, in *Sämtliche Werke: Briefe, Tagebücher und Gespräche*, volume 2:29, 196–98. Frankfurt am Main: Deutscher Klassiker Verlag, 1997.

———. *Faust: A Tragedy*. Translated by Walter Arndt. Edited by Cyrus Hamlin. New York: Norton, 2001.

———. *Faust: Texte*. Edited by Albrecht Schöne. Frankfurt am Main: Deutscher Klassiker Verlag, 1994.

———. "Granit II." In *Schriften zur allgemeinen Naturlehre, Geologie und Mineralogie*, 312–16.

———. "Höhen der alten und neuen Welt bildlich verglichen." *Allgemeine Geographische Ephemeriden* 41 (1813): 3–8.

———. "Karlsbad, Anfang September 1819." In *Schriften zur allgemeinen Naturlehre, Geologie und Mineralogie*, 210–12.

———. *Die Leiden des jungen Werther*. Vol. 12 of *Goethes Werke*. Stuttgart: J. G. Cotta, 1817.

———. *Schriften zur allgemeinen Naturlehre, Geologie und Mineralogie*. Edited by Wolf von Engelhardt and Manfred Wenzel. Vol. 25 of *Sämtliche Werke: Briefe, Tagebücher und Gespräche*. Frankfurt am Main: Deutscher Klassiker Verlag, 1986.

———. *The Sorrows of Werter* [sic]*: A German Story*. Translated by Daniel Malthus. London: J. Dodsley, 1784.

———. "Über die Ursache der Barometerschwankungen." In *Schriften zur allgemeinen Naturlehre, Geologie und Mineralogie*, 255–64.

———. *Wilhelm Meisters Wanderjahre*. Edited by Gerhard Neumann and Hans-Georg Dewitz. In vol. 10 of *Sämtliche Werke: Briefe, Tagebücher und Gespräche*. Frankfurt am Main: Deutscher Klassiker Verlag, 1989.

———. "Witterungslehre 1825." In *Schriften zur allgemeinen Naturlehre, Geologie und Mineralogie*, 274–300.

———. "Wolkengestalt: Nach Howard." In *Schriften zur allgemeinen Naturlehre, Geologie und Mineralogie*, 214–34.

Greenblatt, Stephen. *Marvelous Possessions: The Wonder of the New World*. Chicago: U of Chicago P, 1992.

Grizzly Man. Directed by Werner Herzog. Santa Monica: Lions Gate Films, 2005.

Groote, Eberhard von, ed. *Die Pilgerfahrt des Ritters Arnold von Harff von Cöln durch Italien, Syrien, Aegypten, . . . wie er sie in den Jahren 1496 bis 1499 vollendet*. Cologne: J. M. Heberle, 1860.

———, ed. *Rom — Jerusalem — Santiago: Das Pilgertagebuch des Ritters Arnold von Harff (1496–1498)*. Translated from the text of the Eberhard von Groote edition. With a commentary and introduction by Helmut Brall-Tuchel and Folker Reichert. Cologne: Böhlau, 2007.

Grupp, Peter. *Faszination Berg: Die Geschichte des Alpinismus*. Vienna: Böhlau, 2008.

Gumprecht, Taddäus Eduard. "Die von Rebmann im östlichen Süd-Africa in der Nähe des Aequators entdeckten Schneeberge." *Monatsberichte über die Verhandlungen der Gesellschaft für Erdkunde zu Berlin*, Neue Folge 6 (1850): 285–97.

Gunning, Tom. "'Primitive' Cinema: A Frame-Up? Or, The Trick's on Us." In *Early Cinema: Space, Frame, Narrative*, edited by Thomas Elsaesser, 95–103. London: British Film Institute, 1990.

Guthke, Karl S. *Die Entdeckung des Ich: Studien zur Literatur*. Tübingen: Francke, 1993.

Gysi, Fritz. *Richard Strauss*. Potsdam: Akademische Verlagsgesellschaft Athenaion, 1934.

"Hadrian." *The Scriptores Historiae Augustae*. Vol. 1. Translated by David Magie. Cambridge: Harvard UP, 1967. 3–81.

Hall, Anja. *Paradies auf Erden? Mythenbildung als Form von Fremdwahrnehmung — Der Südsee-Mythos in Schlüsselphasen der deutschen Literatur*. Würzburg: Königshausen & Neumann, 2008.

Haller, Albrecht von. *Versuch Schweizerischer Gedichte*. 9th ed. 1762. Reprint, Bern: Herbert Lang, 1969.

Hamann, Christof. *Usambara*. Göttingen: Steidl, 2007.

Hammel, Claus. *Humboldt und Bolivar oder Der neue Continent*. Berlin: Aufbau, 1980.

Hanisch, Ernst. *Männlichkeiten: Eine andere Geschichte des 20. Jahrhunderts*. Vienna: Böhlau, 2005.

Hanley, Keith. "Wordsworth's Grand Tour." In *Romantic Geographies: Discourses of Travel, 1775–1844*, edited by Amanda Gilroy, 71–92. Manchester: Manchester UP, 2000.

Hartman, Geoffrey H. "Wordsworth's *Descriptive Sketches* and the Growth of a Poet's Mind." *PMLA* 76, no. 5 (December 1961): 519–27.

Hartmann, Sieglinde, and Freimut Löser, eds. *Kaiser Maximilian I. (1459–1519) und die Hofkultur seiner Zeit*. Wiesbaden: Reichert, 2009.

Hausler, Bettina. *Der Berg: Schrecken und Faszination*. Munich: Hirmer, 2008.

Hegel, Georg Wilhelm Friedrich. "Reisetagebuch Hegels durch die Berner Oberalpen 1796." In *G. W. F. Hegels Leben*, edited by Karl Rosenkranz, 470–90. Darmstadt: Wissenschaftliche Buchgesellschaft, 1963.

———. *Vorlesungen über die Ästhetik III*. Frankfurt am Main: Suhrkamp, 1970.

Heidegger, Martin. *Parmenides*. Translated by André Schuwer and Richard Rojcewicz. Bloomington: Indiana UP, 1992.

Herburger, Günter. *Humboldt: Reise-Novellen*. Munich: A1 Verlag, 2001.

Heringman, Noah. *Romantic Rocks, Aesthetic Geology*. Ithaca, NY: Cornell UP, 2004.

Hermand, Jost. *Im Wettlauf mit der Zeit: Anstöße zu einer ökologiebewußten Ästhetik*. Berlin: Sigma Bohn, 1991.

Herzog, Werner. *Vom Gehen im Eis*. Munich: Carl Hanser, 1978.

Herzog Ernst: Ein mittelalterliches Abenteuerbuch. Published in the Middle High German version B in accordance with the Karl Bartsch edition, together with the fragments of version A, translated, and with notes and an epilogue by Bernhard Sowinski. Stuttgart: Reclam, 1970.

Hill, David. *Turner in the Alps: The Journey through France and Switzerland in 1802*. London: George Philip, 1992.

Hintzsche, Erich, ed. *Albrecht Hallers Tagebuch seiner Studienreise nach London, Paris, Straßburg und Basel, 1727–1728*. Bern: Hans Huber, 1968.

Hinz, Sigrid. *Caspar David Friedrich in Briefen und Bekenntnissen*. Munich: Rogner & Bernhard, 1968.

Hitler, Adolf. *Mein Kampf*. Munich: Zentralverlag der NSDAP, Franz Eher Nachf., 1938. In English, *Mein Kampf*. Translated by Ralph Manheim. Boston: Mariner, 1999.

Hobsbawn, Eric, and Terence Ranger, eds. *The Invention of Tradition*. Cambridge: Cambridge UP, 1992.

Hoffmann, Hilmar. *The Triumph of Propaganda: Film and National Socialism, 1933–1945*. New York: Berghahn, 1996.

Hoffmann, Torsten. *Konfigurationen des Erhabenen: Zur Produktivität einer ästhetischen Kategorie in der Literatur des ausgehenden 20. Jahrhunderts (Handke, Ransmayr, Schrott, Strauss)*. Berlin: de Gruyter, 2006.

Höfler, Horst, and Reinhold Messner. *Karl Maria Herrligkoffer: Besessen, sieghaft, umstritten*. Zurich: AS Verlag, 2001.

Hölderlin, Friedrich. *Sämtliche Gedichte*. Edited by Jochen Schmidt. Frankfurt am Main: Deutscher Klassiker Verlag, 2005.

Homer. *Odyssee*. Translated by Johann Heinrich Voss, ed. Peter Von der Mühll. Zurich: Diogenes, 1980.

Horace. *Odes*. In *Q. Horati Flacci Opera*. Edited by Fredericus Klingner. Leipzig: Teubner, 1970.

Howorth, J. *The Poems of Baron Haller*. London: J. Bell, 1794.

Huggan, Graham. "'Greening' Postcolonialism: Ecocritical Perspectives." *Modern Fiction Studies* 50 (2004): 701–33.

Huggan, Graham, and Helen Tiffin. "Editorial." *Interventions* 9 (2007): 1–11.

Humboldt, Alexander von. *Ansichten der Natur: Erster und zweiter Band*. Vol. 4 of *Studienausgabe*. Edited by Hanno Beck. Darmstadt: Wissenschaftliche Buchgesellschaft, 1987.

———. *Atlas géographique et physique des régions équinoxiales du Nouveau Continent, fondé sur des observations astronomiques, des mesures trigonométriques et des nivellemens barométriques*. Paris: Gide, 1814–34.

———. *Essai sur la géographie des plantes, accompagné d'un tableau physique des régions équinoxiales. . . . avec une planche*. Paris: Schoell, and Tübingen: Cotta, 1807.

———. *Kleinere Schriften*. Vol. 1, *Geognostische und physikalische Erinnerungen: Mit einem Atlas, enthaltend Umrisse von Vulkanen aus den Cordilleren von Quito und Mexico*. Stuttgart: Cotta, 1853.

———. Letter to Wilhelm von Humboldt, dated Lima, 25 November 1802. *Annales du Muséum national d'histoire naturelle* 2 (1803): 322–37.

———. *Nova genera et species plantarum*. 7 vols. Paris: Librairie Grecque-Latine-Allemande, 181[6]–2[6].

———. *Ueber einen Versuch den Gipfel des Chimborazo zu ersteigen*. Edited by Oliver Lubrich and Ottmar Ette. Berlin: Eichborn, 2006.

———. "Ueber zwei Versuche den Chimborazo zu besteigen." In *Jahrbuch für 1837*, edited by H. C. Schumacher, 176–206. Stuttgart: Cotta, 1837.

———. *Vues des Cordillères et monuments des peuples indigènes de l'Amérique*. Paris: Schoell, 1810–13.

Hussey, Christopher. *The Picturesque: Studies in a Point of View*. London: Frank Cass, 1967.

Im Kampf mit dem Berge: Eine Alpensymphonie in Bildern. Directed by Dr. Arnold Fanck. Freiburg/Breisgau: Berg- und Sportfilm GmbH, 1921.

Isserman, Maurice, and Stewart Weaver. *Fallen Giants: A History of Himalayan Mountaineering from the Age of Empire to the Age of Extremes*. New Haven, CT: Yale UP, 2008.

Iwańczak, Wojciech. *Die Kartenmacher: Nürnberg als Zentrum der Kartographie im Zeitalter der Renaissance*. Translated by Peter Oliver Loew. Darmstadt: Primus, 2009.

Jacobs, Jürgen. *Wilhelm Meister und seine Brüder: Untersuchungen zum deutschen Bildungsroman*. Munich: Fink, 1972.

Jacobs, Michael. *The Painted Voyage: Art, Travel, and Exploration, 1564–1875*. London: British Museum Press, 1995.

Jameson, Anna. *Visits and Sketches at Home and Abroad*. Vol 1. London: Saunders and Otley, 1834.

Jantzen, René. *Montagne et symboles*. Lyon: Presses Universitaires de Lyon, 1988.

Johnson, Claudia L. "'Giant HANDEL' and the Musical Sublime." *Eighteenth-Century Studies* 19, no. 4 (1986): 515–33.

Joost, Ulrich. "'Trübselige kleine Stadt in einem trübseligen Land'? Hallers Göttingen." In Elsner and Rupke, *Albrecht von Haller im Göttingen der Aufklärung*, 71–105.

Joppien, Rüdiger, and Bernhard Smith. *The Art of Captain Cook's Voyages.* 2 vols. New Haven, CT: Yale UP, 1985.

Kaes, Anton. *Shell Shock Cinema.* Princeton, NJ: Princeton UP, 2009.

Kaiser Maximilian I. *Theuerdank, 1517.* Dortmund: Harenberg Kommunikation, 1979.

Kampf um den Himalaja. Directed by Frank Leberecht. Germany: Tobis-Melofilm, 1938.

Kant, Immanuel. *Kritik der Urteilskraft.* Volume 10 of *Werkausgabe.* Edited by W. Weischedel. Frankfurt am Main: Suhrkamp, 1957. In English, *Critique of Pure Reason*, translated by F. Max Müller. London: Macmillan, 1881.

Kehlmann, Daniel. *Die Vermessung der Welt.* Reinbek: Rowohlt, 2005.

Keller, Tait. "The Mountains Roar: The Alps during the Great War." *Environmental History* 14 (2009): 253–74.

Kelley, Theresa M. *Wordsworth's Revolutionary Aesthetics.* Cambridge: Cambridge UP, 1988.

Koerner, Joseph Leo. *Caspar David Friedrich and the Subject of Landscape.* 1995. 2nd edition, London: Reaktion, 2009.

Kopp, Peter F. "Natur und Berge — erforscht, erlebt und angebetet." In *Natur: Ein Lesebuch*, edited by Rolf Peter Sieferle, 278–93. Munich: C. H. Beck, 1991.

Koselleck, Reinhart. "Historische Kriterien des neuzeitlichen Revolutionsbegriffs." In *Vergangene Zukunft: Zur Semantik geschichtlicher Zeiten*, 67–86. Frankfurt am Main: Suhrkamp, 1988.

Kracauer, Siegfried. *From Caligari to Hitler: A Psychological History of the German Film.* Princeton, NJ: Princeton UP, 1947.

———. "Die kleinen Ladenmädchen gehen ins Kino." In *Das Ornament der Masse: Essays*, 279–94. Frankfurt am Main: Suhrkamp, 1977. In English, "The Little Shopgirls Go to the Movies." In *The Mass Ornament: Weimar Essays.* Translated, edited, and with an introduction by Thomas Y. Levin, 291–304. Cambridge, MA: Harvard UP, 1995.

———. *Theory of Film: The Redemption of Physical Reality.* Princeton, NJ: Princeton UP, 1997.

Krakauer, Jon. *Into Thin Air: A Personal Account of the Mt. Everest Disaster.* New York: Willard, 1997.

Krapf, Johann Ludwig. *Reisen in Ostafrika ausgeführt in den Jahren 1837–1855.* Stuttgart: F. A. Brockhaus, 1964.

Kreimeier, Klaus, ed. *Fanck — Trenker — Riefenstahl: Der deutsche Bergfilm und seine Folgen*. Berlin: Stiftung Deutsche Kinemathek, 1972.

Krökel, Fritz. "Adalbert Stifters Freundschaft mit dem Alpenforscher Friedrich Simony." *Vierteljahresschrift des Adalbert-Stifter-Instituts des Landes Oberösterreich* 4 (1955): 97–117.

Kuchenbuch, Ludolf, and Joseph Morsel. "Naturräume." In *Enzyklopädie des Mittelalters*, edited by Gert Melville and Martial Staub, 2:246–48. Darmstadt: Wissenschaftliche Buchgesellschaft, 2008.

Kudrun. Nach der Ausgabe von Karl Bartsch herausgegeben von Karl Stackmann. Tübingen: Max Niemeyer, 2000.

Kühnel, Harry, and Peter Dinzelbacher. "Natur/Umwelt: Mittelalter." In *Europäische Mentalitätsgeschichte: Hauptthemen in Einzeldarstellungen*, edited by Peter Dinzelbacher, 648–68. Stuttgart: Kröner, 2008.

"Kultur und Wissenschaft." *Über Land und Meer* 13 (1865): 247.

Kunz, Edith Anna. "'Luftige Welten'— Zur Poetik von Rauch und Wasserdampf in Goethes *Faust*." *Colloquia Germanica* 39, no. 1 (2006): 43–56.

Landow, George. *The Aesthetic and Critical Theories of John Ruskin*. Princeton, NJ: Princeton UP, 1974.

Landsberg, Sylvia. *The Medieval Garden*. Toronto: U of Toronto P, 2003.

Larson, Edward J. *An Empire of Ice: Scott, Shackleton, and the Golden Age of Antarctic Science*. New Haven, CT: Yale UP, 2011.

La Soufrière — warten auf eine unausweichliche Katastrophe. Directed by Werner Herzog. Vienna: Werner Herzog Filmproduktion, 1977.

Le Alpi porta d'Europa: Scritture, uomini, idee da Giustiniano al Barbarossa; Atti del convegno di studio. Edited by Laura Pani and Cesare Scalon. Spoleto, Italy: Editoriali Fondazione Cisam, 2009.

Lebenszeichen. Directed by Werner Herzog. Vienna: Werner Herzog Filmproduktion, 1968.

Lecouteux, Claude. "La Montagne d'Aimant." In Thomasset and James-Raoul, *La montagne dans le texte médiévale: Entre mythe et réalité*, 167–86. In German, "Die Sage vom Magnetberg." In *Burgen, Länder, Orte*, edited by Ulrich Müller and Werner Wunderlich, 529–39. Constance: UVK Verlagsgesellschaft, 2008.

Lethen, Helmut. *Verhaltenslehren der Kälte: Lebensversuche zwischen den Kriegen*. Frankfurt am Main: Suhrkamp, 1994. In English, *Cool Conduct: The Culture of Distance in Weimar Germany*. Translated by Don Reneau. Berkeley: U of California P, 2002.

Liebersohn, Harry. *The Traveler's World: Europe to the Pacific*. Cambridge, MA: Harvard UP, 2006.

Lionarons, Joyce Tally. "The Otherworld and Its Inhabitants in the *Nibelungenlied*." In *A Companion to the Nibelungenlied*, edited by Winder McConnell, 153–71. Columbia, SC: Camden House, 1998.

Loetscher, Hugo. "Humboldt und die Rehabilitierung eines Kontinentes." *Du* 30 (1970): 666.

Long, J. J. "History, Narrative, and Photography in W. G. Sebald's *Die Ausgewanderten*." *Modern Language Review* 98, no. 1 (January 2003): 117–37.

Lubrich, Oliver. "Alexander von Humboldt: Revolutionizing Travel Literature." *Monatshefte* 96, no. 3 (2004): 360–87.

———. "In the Realm of Ambivalence: Alexander von Humboldt's Discourse on Cuba." *German Studies Review* 26, no. 1 (2003): 63–80.

———. "Postcolonial Studies." In *Literaturtheorien des 20. Jahrhunderts*, edited by Ulrich Schmid, 351–76. Stuttgart: Reclam, 2010.

———. "Welche Rolle spielt der literarische Text im postkolonialen Diskurs?" In *Archiv für das Studium der neueren Sprachen und Literaturen* 157, no. 242 (2005/1): 16–39.

Macfarlane, Robert. *Mountains of the Mind*. New York: Pantheon, 2003.

MacPhee, Ross D. E. *Race to the End: Amundsen, Scott, and the Attainment of the South Pole*. New York: Sterling Innovation, 2010.

Majer-O'Sickey, Ingeborg. "The Cult of the Cold and the Gendered Body in Mountain Films." In Fisher and Mennel, *Spatial Turns: Space, Place, and Mobility in German Literary and Visual Culture*, 363–80.

Mann, Thomas. *Briefe I: 1889–1913*. Vol. 21 of the *Große kommentierte Frankfurter Ausgabe*, edited by Thomas Sprecher. Frankfurt am Main: Fischer, 2001.

———. *Buddenbrooks: Verfall einer Familie*. Vol. 1 of the *Große kommentierte Frankfurter Ausgabe*, edited by Eckhard Heftrich. Frankfurt am Main: Fischer, 2002. In English, *Buddenbrooks: The Decline of a Family*. Translated by John E. Woods. New York: Vintage, 1994.

———. *Der Zauberberg*. Frankfurt am Main: Fischer, 1984.

———. *Der Zauberberg*. Vol. 5 of the *Große kommentierte Frankfurter Ausgabe*, edited by Michael Neumann. Frankfurt am Main: Fischer, 2002. In English, *The Magic Mountain*. Translated by John E. Woods. New York: Vintage, 1995.

Manovich, Lev. *The Language of New Media*. Cambridge: MIT Press, 2001.

Marold, Werner. *Kommentar zu den Liedern Oswalds von Wolkenstein*. Edited and revised by Alan Robertshaw. Innsbrucker Beiträge zur Kulturwissenschaft. Innsbruck: Institut für Germanistik, 1995.

Martin, Alison E. "Natural Effusions: Mrs J. Howorth's English translation of Albrecht von Haller's *Die Alpen*." In *Translation Studies* 5.1 (2012): 17–32.

Märtin, Ralf-Peter. *Die Messner-Brüder am Nanga Parbat: Zwei Brüder, ein Berg, ihr Schicksal; Offizielles Buch zum Film von Joseph Vilsmaier*. Munich: Südwest-Verlag, 2010.

———. *Nanga Parbat: Wahrheit und Wahn des Alpinismus.* Berlin: Berlin-Verlag, 2002.

Mason, Stanley. *The Alps: An English Translation.* Dübendorf, Switzerland: Walter Amstutz De Clivo Press, 1987.

Massumi, Brian. *Parables for the Virtual: Movement, Affect, Sensation.* Durham, NC: Duke UP, 2002.

Mathieu, Jon. *Geschichte der Alpen, 1500–1900: Umwelt, Entwicklung, Gesellschaft.* Vienna: Böhlau, 1998.

Matteson, Lynn R. "The Poetics and Politics of Alpine Passage: Turner's Snowstorm; Hannibal and His Army Crossing the Alps." *Art Bulletin* 62, no. 3 (September 1980): 395–96.

Matussek, Peter, ed. *Goethe und die Verzeitlichung der Natur.* Munich: Beck 1998.

Matz, Wolfgang. *1857: Flaubert, Baudelaire, Stifter.* Frankfurt am Main: S. Fischer, 2007.

May, Jürgen, "Wege und Irrwege in und um Richard Strauss' *Alpensinfonie*: Eine Spurenlese." In *Musik und Biographie*, Festschrift für Rainer Cadenbach, ed. Cordula Heymann-Wentzel and Johannes Laas, 364–80. Würzburg: Königshausen & Neumann, 2004.

May, Kurt. "*Wilhelm Meisters Lehrjahre*, ein Bildungsroman?" *Deutsche Vierteljahresschrift für Literaturwissenschaft und Geistesgeschichte* 31 (1957): 1–37.

Mazzolini, Renato G. "Haller and the Swiss Scientific Movement." In Steinke, Boschung, and Proß, *Albrecht von Haller: Leben — Werk — Epoche*, 381–414.

McCarthy, John. *Remapping Reality: Chaos and Creativity in Science and Literature (Goethe — Nietzsche — Grass).* Amsterdam: Rodopi, 2006.

Meiners, Christoph. *Briefe über die Schweiz.* Berlin: Spener, 1785–91.

Mendelssohn, Moses. "Über das Erhabene und Naive in den schönen Wissenschaften." In *Schriften zur Philosophie, Aesthetik und Apologetik*, 169–209. Hildesheim: Olms, 1968.

Menschik-Bendele, Jutta. "Psychoanalytisches zum Bergfilm: Heldinnen und Helden in den 30er Jahren." In Aspetsberger, *Der BergFilm, 1920–1940*, 85–99.

Messner, Reinhold. *13 Spiegel meiner Seele.* Munich: Piper, 1994.

Meyer, Hans. *Hochtouren im tropischen Afrika.* Leipzig: F. A. Brockhaus, 1923.

——— *Ostafrikanische Gletscherfahrten: Forschungsreisen im Kilimandscharo-Gebiet.* Leipzig: Duncker & Humblot, 1890. In English, *Across East African Glaciers: An Account of the First Ascent of Kilimanjaro.* Translated by E. H. S. Calder. London: Longmans, Green, 1891.

———. "Touristisches von meiner ersten Besteigung des Kilimandscharo." *Mittheilungen des Deutschen und Österreichischen Alpenvereins* 9 (1888): 1–4.

———. "Ueber seine Besteigung des Kilimandscharo." *Verhandlungen der Gesellschaft für Erdkunde zu Berlin* 14 (1887): 446–54.

Meyers, Amy R. W., and Margaret Beck Pritchards, eds. *Empire's Nature: Mark Catesby's New World Vision*. Chapel Hill: U of North Carolina P, 1998.

Mierau, Peter. *Die Deutsche Himalaja-Stiftung von 1936 bis 1998: Ihre Geschichte und ihre Expeditionen*. Munich: Rudolf Rother, 1999.

———. *Nationalsozialistische Expeditionspolitik: Deutsche Asien-Expeditionen, 1933–1945*. Munich: Herbert Utz, 2006.

Milton, John, *Paradise Lost*. Edited by Alastair Fowler. London: Longman, 1972.

Montiglio, Silvia. "Should the Aspiring Wise Man Travel? A Conflict in Seneca's Thought." *American Journal of Philology* 127 (2006): 553–86.

Montúfar, Carlos. "Diario del año de 1802: Biaje de Quito á Lima" [9 June–10 September 1802]. The Lilly Library, Indiana U, Bloomington: Manuscripts Department, Latin American Mss. — Peru.

Muir, John. *My First Summer in the Sierra*. Boston: Houghton Mifflin, 1916.

Müller, Gustav. "Die Berge und ihre Bedeutung für den Wiederaufbau des deutschen Volkes." *Zeitschrift des Deutschen und Österreichischen Alpenvereins* 53 (1922): 1–9.

Müller, Jan-Dirk. *Gedechtnus: Literatur und Hofgesellschaft um Maximilian I*. Munich: Fink, 1982.

———, ed. *Romane des 15. und 16. Jahrhunderts*. Bibliothek der Frühen Neuzeit 1. Frankfurt am Main: Deutscher Klassiker Verlag, 1990.

Müller, Klaus-Detlef. "Utopie und Bildungsroman: Strukturuntersuchungen zu Stifters *Nachsommer*." *Zeitschrift für deutsche Philologie* 90 (1971): 199–228.

Mummery, A. F. *My Climbs in the Alps and Caucasus*. London: Scribners, 1895.

Nanga Parbat: Ein Kampfbericht der Deutschen Himalaja Expedition 1934. Directed by Frank Leberecht. Germany: Döring-Film-Werke, 1934/35.

Nanga Parbat 1953. Directed by Hans Ertl. FRG: Deutsche London-Film Verleih GmbH, 1953.

Nash, Roderick Frazier. *Wilderness and the American Mind*. 4th edition. New Haven, CT: Yale UP, 2001.

"Der Negerkönig." *Die Gartenlaube* 43 (1853): 472–74.

Nelken, Halina. *Alexander von Humboldt: His Portraits and Their Artists*. Berlin: Dietrich Reimer, 1980.

Nenno, Nancy P. "'Postcards from the Edge': Education to Tourism in the German Mountain Film." In *Light Motives: German Popular Film in Perspective*, edited by Randall Halle and Margaret McCarthy, 61–84. Detroit: Wayne State UP, 2003.

———. "Projections on a Blank Space: Landscape, Nationality, and Identity in Thomas Mann's *Der Zauberberg*." *German Quarterly* 69, no. 3 (1996): 305–21.

Nething, Hans Peter. *Der Gotthard*. Thun, Switzerland: Ott, 1976.

Neumann, Michael. "Kommentar." In Thomas Mann, *Der Zauberberg*, Frankfurt edition, 59.

Neunlinger, J. "Adalbert Stifters Roman *Der Nachsommer* geographisch betrachtet." In *Alpengeographische Studien aus dem Geographischen Institut der Universität Innsbruck, zum 50. Geburtstag Hans Kinzl's*, 205–10. Innsbruck: Wagner, 1950.

Nicolson, Marjorie Hope. *Mountain Gloom and Mountain Glory*. 1959. Reprint, Seattle: U of Washington P, 1997.

Nietzsche, Friedrich. *Also sprach Zarathustra: Ein Buch für Alle und Keinen*. Leipzig: C. G. Naumann, 1899.

———. *Der Antichrist*. In *Werke: Kritische Gesamtausgabe*, section 6, vol. 3, 162–252. In English, *The Anti-Christ, Ecce homo, Twilight of the Idols, and Other Writings*. Edited by Aaron Ridley and Judith Norman. Translated by Judith Norman. Cambridge: Cambridge UP, 2005.

———. *The Birth of Tragedy and Other Writings*. Edited by Raymond Geuss and Ronald Speirs. Translated by Ronald Speirs. Cambridge: Cambridge UP, 1999.

———. *The Birth of Tragedy and The Case of Wagner*. Translated by Walter Kaufmann. New York: Vintage, 1967.

———. *Ecce Homo*. In *Werke: Kritische Gesamtausgabe*, section 6, vol. 3. 253–372.

———. *Die Geburt der Tragödie*. In vol. 1 of *Sämtliche Werke: Kritische Studienausgabe*. 9–156.

———. *Nietzsche Briefwechsel: Kritische Gesamtausgabe*. Section 3, vol. 1. Edited by Giorgio Colli and Mazzino Montinari. Berlin: Walter de Gruyter, 1981.

———. *Sämtliche Werke: Kritische Studienausgabe*. 15 vols. Edited by Giorgio Colli and Mazzino Montinari. Munich: dtv/de Gruyter, 1999.

———. *Werke: Kritische Gesamtausgabe*. 40 vols. Edited by Giorgio Colli and Mazzino Montinari. Berlin: Walter de Gruyter, 1967-.

Nixon, Rob. "Environmentalism and Postcolonialism." In *Postcolonial Studies and Beyond*, edited by Ania Loomba, Suvir Kaul, Matti Bunzl, Antoinette Burton, and Jed Esty, 23–51. Durham, NC: Duke UP, 2005.

O'Brien, Patty. *The Pacific Muse: Exotic Femininity and the Colonial Pacific.* Seattle: U of Washington P, 2006.

O'Brien, Susie. "Articulating a World of Difference: Ecocriticism, Postcolonialism, and Globalization." *Canadian Literature* 170–71 (2001): 140–58.

Oehlschlaeger, Max. *The Idea of Wilderness: From Prehistory to the Age of Ecology.* New Haven, CT: Yale UP, 1991.

Ozturk, Anthony. "Geo-Aesthetics: Venice and the Architecture of the Alps." In *John Ruskin and Nineteenth Century Cultural Travel*, edited by Keith Hanley and Emma Sdegno, 187–211. Venice: Le Bricole: Università Ca' Foscari, 2010.

Pearsall, Derek, and Elizabeth Salter. *Landscapes and Seasons of the Medieval World.* London: Paul Elek, 1973.

Penck, Albrecht. *Friedrich Simony: Leben und Wirken eines Alpenforschers.* Geographische Abhandlungen 6/3. Vienna: Ed. Hölzel, 1898.

Petrarch, *Epistolae familiares*. In English, *Petrarch: The First Modern Scholar and Man of Letters.* Translated by James Harvey Robinson. New York: Putnam, 1898.

Pfeiferová, Dana. *Angesichts des Todes: Die Todesbilder in der neueren österreichischen Prosa: Bachmann, Bernhard, Winkler, Jelinek, Handke, Ransmayr.* Vienna: Praesens, 2007.

Phelps, Leland. "Goethe's Meteorological Writings." *Monatshefte* 48, no. 6 (1956): 317–24.

Phillips, Dana. *The Truth of Ecology: Nature, Culture, and Literature in America.* Oxford: Oxford UP, 2003.

Pimentel, Juan. *Testigos del mundo: Ciencia, literatura y viajes en la ilustración.* Madrid: Marcial Pons, 2003.

Piper, Andrew. "Mapping Vision: Goethe, Cartography and the Novel." In Fisher and Mennel, *Spatial Turns: Space, Place, and Mobility in German Literary and Visual Culture*, 27–52.

Pliny (Gaius Plinius Secundus). *Natural History.* Translated by H. Rackham. Cambridge, MA: Harvard UP, 1949.

Pohland, Vera. *Das Sanatorium als literarischer Ort: Medizinische Institution und Krankheit als Medien der Gesellschaftskritik und der Existenzanalyse.* Frankfurt am Main: Peter Lang, 1984.

Powers, Elizabeth. "The Sublime, 'Über den Granit,' and the Prehistory of Goethe's Science." *Goethe Yearbook* 15 (2008): 35–56.

Prager, Brad. *Aesthetic Vision and German Romanticism: Writing Images.* Rochester, NY: Camden House, 2007.

———. *The Cinema of Werner Herzog: Aesthetic Ecstasy and Truth.* London: Wallflower, 2007.

Pratt, Mary Louise. "Alexander von Humboldt and the Reinvention of América." In *Imperial Eyes: Travel Writing and Transculturation*, 111–43. London: Routledge, 1992.

Prime, Rebecca. "A Strange and Foreign World: Documentary, and the Mountain Films of Arnold Fanck and Leni Riefenstahl." In *Folklore / Cinema: Popular Film as Vernacular Culture*, edited by Koven Sherman, 54–72. Logan: U of Utah P, 2007.

Pritchett, W. K. *Studies in Ancient Greek Topography 1*. Berkeley: U of California P, 1965.

Ptolemy. *The Geography*. http://penelope.uchicago.edu/Thayer/E/Gazetteer/Periods/Roman/_Texts/Ptolemy/home.html (accessed 15 January 2011).

Raabe, Wilhelm. *Abu Telfan oder die Heimkehr vom Mondgebirge*. Volume 7 of *Sämtliche Werke*, edited by Werner Röpke. Göttingen: Vandenhoeck & Ruprecht, 1951.

Ramond de Carbonnières, Louis-François. *Lettres de M. William Coxe à M. W. Melmoth, sur l'état politique, civil et naturale de la Suisse*. New edition. Paris: Belin, 1782.

Ransmayr, Christoph. *Der fliegende Berg*. Frankfurt am Main: Fischer, 2006.

———. *Die letzte Welt*. Frankfurt am Main: Fischer, 1988.

———. *Odysseus, Verbrecher: Schauspiel einer Heimkehr*. Frankfurt am Main: Fischer, 2010.

Rapp, Christian. *Höhenrausch: Der deutsche Bergfilm*. Vienna: Sonderzahl, 1997.

Rauchenberger-Strauss, Johanna von. "Jugenderinnerungen." In *Richard Strauss Jahrbuch, 1959–60*, edited by Willi Schuh, 7–30. Bonn: Boosey & Hawkes, 1960.

Rebmann, Johann. "Narrative of a Journey to Jagga, the Snow Country of Eastern Africa." *Church Missionary Intelligencer: A Monthly Journal of Missionary Information* 1 (1850): 12–23.

Reichel, Peter. *Der schöne Schein des Dritten Reiches: Faszination und Gewalt des Faschismus*. Frankfurt am Main: Fischer, 1993.

Reichler, Claude. "Le paysage entre convention et envoûtement dans le *Zauberberg* de Thomas Mann." *Colloquium helveticum* 38 (2007): 221–40.

———. "Ramond de Carbonnières avec et contre William Coxe." In *Le second voyage ou le déja-vu: Etudes réunies*, edited by François Moureau, 39–48. Paris: Klinksieck, 1996.

Reill, Peter Hanns. "'Planzengarten der Aufklärung': Haller und die Gründung der Göttinger Universität." In Elsner and Rupke, *Albrecht von Haller im Göttingen der Aufklärung*, 47–69.

Rentschler, Eric. "Mountains and Modernity: Relocating the *Bergfilm*." *New German Critique* 51 (1990): 137–61.

Richter, Jean Paul. *Titan*, vol 2. Berlin: Aufbau, 1986.
———. *Vorschule der Ästhetik*. Hamburg: Meiner, 1990.
Rieser, John J. "Dynamic Spatial Orientation and the Coupling of Representation and Action." In *Wayfinding Behavior: Cognitive Mapping and Other Spatial Processes*, edited by Reginald G. Colledge, 168–90. Baltimore: Johns Hopkins UP, 1999.
Rigby, Kate. *Topographies of the Sacred: The Poetics of Place in European Romanticism*. Charlottesville: U of Virginia P, 2004.
Robinson, James Harvey, trans. *Petrarch: The First Modern Scholar and Man of Letters*. New York: Putnam, 1898.
Robinson, Sidney K. *Inquiry into the Picturesque*. Chicago: U of Chicago P, 1991.
Rosenblum, Robert. *Modern Painting and the Northern European Tradition: Friedrich to Rothko*. New York: Harper & Row, 1977.
Ross, Alex. *The Rest Is Noise: Listening to the Twentieth Century*. New York: Farrar, Straus & Giroux, 2007.
Rousseau, G. S., and Roy Porter, eds. *The Ferment of Knowledge: Studies in the Historiography of Eighteenth-Century Science*. Cambridge: Cambridge UP, 1980.
Rousseau, Jean-Jacques. *Julie, or the New Héloïse: Letters of Two Lovers Who Live in a Small Town at the Foot of the Alps*. Translated and annotated by Philip Steward and Jean Vache. In vol. 6 of *Collected Works of Rousseau*. Hanover: UP of New England, 1997.
Rücker, Elisabeth. *Hartmann Schedels Weltchronik: Das größte Buchunternehmen der Dürer-Zeit; Mit einem Katalog der Städteansichten*. Munich: Prestel, 1988.
Rudolf von Ems. *Alexander: Ein höfischer Versroman des 13. Jahrhunderts*. Edited by Victor Junk. Darmstadt: Wissenschaftliche Buchgesellschaft, 1970.
Rudwick, Martin. *Bursting the Limits of Time: The Reconstruction of Geohistory in the Age of Revolution*. Chicago: U of Chicago P, 2005.
Rupke, Nicholas, A. "Caves, Fossils and the History of the Earth." In *Romanticism and the Sciences*, edited by Andrew Cunningham and Nicholas Jardine, 241–59. Cambridge: Cambridge UP, 1990.
Rüttimann, Beat. "Die Lungentuberkulose im Zauberberg." In *Auf dem Weg zum Zauberberg: Die Davoser Literaturtage 1996*, edited by Thomas Sprecher, 95–109. Frankfurt am Main: Klostermann, 1997.
Safranski, Rüdiger. *Romantik: Eine deutsche Affäre*. Frankfurt am Main: Fischer, 2009.
Sahlins, Marshall. *Islands of History*. Chicago: U of Chicago P, 1985.
Sala, Charles. *Caspar David Friedrich: The Spirit of Romantic Painting*. Paris: Terrail, 1994.

Salas, Tito. *Mi delirio sobre el Chimborazo*. Caracas, Casa Natal del Libertador, 1929–30.

Sammons, Jeffrey L. "The Bildungsroman for Nonspecialists: An Attempt at a Clarification." In *Reflection and Action: Essays on the Bildungsroman*, edited by James Hardin, 26–45. Columbia, SC: U of South Carolina P, 1991.

——. "The Mystery of the Missing *Bildungsroman*, or: What Happened to Wilhelm Meister's Legacy?" *Genre* 14 (1981): 229–46.

Saunders, Corinne J. *The Forest of Medieval Romance: Avernus, Broceliande, Arden*. Cambridge: D. S. Brewer, 1993.

Sayre, Gordon M. "If Thomas Jefferson Had Visited Niagara Falls: The Sublime Wilderness Spectacle in America, 1775–1825." In *The ISLE Reader: Ecocriticism 1993–2003*, edited by Michael P. Branch and Scott Slovic, 102–23. Athens: U of Georgia P, 2003.

Schama, Simon. *Landscape and Memory*. London: Harper Collins, 1995.

Scharfe, Martin. *Berg-Sucht: Eine Kulturgeschichte des frühen Alpinismus, 1750–1850*. Vienna: Böhlau, 2007.

Schedel, Hartmann. *Weltchronik: Nachdruck [der] kolorierten Gesamtausgabe von 1493*. With an introduction and commentary by Stephan Füssel. Augsburg: Weltbild, 2004.

Scherpe, Klaus R. "Die First-Contact-Szene: Kulturelle Praktiken bei der Begegnung mit dem Fremden." In *Lesbarkeit der Kultur: Literaturwissenschaften zwischen Kulturtechnik und Ethnographie*, edited by Gerhard Neumann and Sigrid Weigel, 149–66. Munich: Fink, 2000.

Schiller, Friedrich. *On Naïve and Sentimental Poetry*. In *German Aesthetic and Literary Criticism: Winckelmann, Lessing, Hamann, Herder, Schiller, Goethe*, edited by H. B. Nisbet. 177–232. Cambridge: Cambridge UP, 1985.

——. "Über das Erhabene." In *Gedichte, Prosa*, edited by Benno von Wiese, 665–82. Cologne: Kiepenheuer & Witsch, 1959.

——. *Wilhelm Tell*. Edited by Matthias Luserke. In *Werke und Briefe*, 385–504. Frankfurt am Main: Deutscher Klassiker Verlag, 1996.

Schivelbusch, Wolfgang. *The Culture of Defeat: On National Trauma, Mourning, and Recovery*. Translated by Jefferson Chase. New York: Metropolitan Books, 2003.

Schleucher, Kurt. "Der Erstbesteiger Hans Meyer." In *Salut, Kilimandscharo: Hans Meyers Erstbesteigung und 100 Jahre später*, 7–24. Darmstadt: Eduard Roether Verlag, 1989.

Schmid, Wolf. "Event and Eventfulness." In *Handbook of Narratology*, edited by Peter Hühn, John Pier, Wolf Schmid, and Jörg Schönert, 80–97. Berlin: de Gruyter, 2009.

Schmidt, Aurel. *Die Alpen — schleichende Zerstörung eines Mythos*. Zurich: Benziger, 1990.

Schmidt, Hugo. "Eishöhle und Steinhäuschen: Zur Weihnachtssymbolik in Stifters 'Bergkristall.'" *Monatshefte* 56 (1964): 321–35.

Schneider, Christian. *Hovezuht: Literarische Hofkultur und höfisches Lebensideal um Herzog Albrecht III. von Österreich und Erzbischof Pilgrim III. von Salzburg (1365–1396)*. Heidelberg: Winter, 2008.

Schneider, Manfred. *Der Barbar: Endzeitstimmung und Kulturrecycling*. Munich: Hanser, 1997.

Schneider, Sabine. "Kulturerosionen: Stifters prekäre geologische Übertragungen." In *Figuren der Übertragung: Adalbert Stifter und das Wissen seiner Zeit*, edited by Michael Gamper and Karl Wagner, 249–69. Zurich: Chronos, 2009.

Schnyder, Peter. "Schrift — Bild — Sammlung — Karte: Medien geologischen Wissens in Stifters *Nachsommer*." In *Figuren der Übertragung: Adalbert Stifter und das Wissen seiner Zeit*, edited by Michael Gamper and Karl Wagner, 235–48. Zurich: Chronos, 2009.

Schöne, Albrecht, ed. *Johann Wolfgang Goethe: Faust; Kommentare*. Frankfurt am Main: Deutscher Klassiker Verlag, 1994.

Schößler, Franziska. "Der Weltreisende Alexander von Humboldt in den österreichischen Bergen: Das naturwissenschaftliche Projekt in Adalbert Stifters *Nachsommer*." In *Ordnung — Raum — Ritual: Adalbert Stifters artifizieller Realismus*, edited by Sabina Becker and Katharina Grätz, 261–85. Heidelberg: Winter, 2007.

Schuh, Willi. "Richard Strauss in der Schweiz." In *Straussiana aus vier Jahrzehnten*, publication of the Richard-Strauss-Society of Munich 5, 43–54. Tutzing: Schneider, 1981.

Schwarz, Ingo. "Acerca de la historia de la dedicatoria 'Al segundo descubridor de Cuba. La Universidad de la Habana, 1939' en el monumento a Alejandro de Humboldt en Berlín." In *Alejandro de Humboldt en Cuba*, edited by Frank Holl, 103–9. Augsburg: Wissner, 1997.

Sebald, W. G. *Die Ausgewanderten*. 1992. Reprint, Frankfurt am Main: Fischer, 2002. In English, *The Emigrants*. Translated by Michael Hulse. New York: New Directions, 1996.

———. "Beyle oder das merckwürdige Faktum der Liebe." In *Schwindel: Gefühle*, 7–36, 1990; reprint, Frankfurt am Main: Fischer, 1994. In English, "Beyle, or Love is a Madness Most Discreet." In *Vertigo*, translated by Michael Hulse, 1–30. New York: New Directions, 2000.

———. *Campo Santo*. Munich: Hanser, 2003. In English, *Campo Santo*. Translated by Anthea Bell. New York: Random House, 2005.

———. *Nach der Natur: Ein Elementargedicht*. Nördlingen, Germany: Greno, 1988. In English, *After Nature*. Translated by Michael Hamburger. New York: Random House, 2002.

Seeßlen, Georg. "Durch die Heimat und so weiter: Heimatfilme, Schlagerfilme und Ferienfilme der fünfziger Jahre." In *Zwischen Gestern und Morgen: Westdeutscher Nachkriegsfilm, 1946–1962*, edited by Hilmar Hoffmann and Walter Schobert, 136–61. Frankfurt am Main: Deutsches Filmmuseum, 1989.

Seitz, Gabriele. *Wo Europa den Himmel berührt: Die Entdeckung der Alpen*. Munich: Artemis, 1987.

Semmler, Josef, ed. *Der Wald in Mittelalter und Renaissance*. Studia humaniora 17. Düsseldorf: Droste, 1991.

Seneca, L. Annaeus. *Ad Lucilium epistulae morales II*. Translated by Richard M. Gummere. Cambridge, MA: Harvard UP, 1958.

Sild, Meinhart. "Bergsteigen als Rüstung." *Österreichische Alpenzeitung* 1195 (1938): 160–64.

Simmel, Georg. "Die Alpen." In *Philosophische Kultur: Über das Abenteuer, die Geschlechter und die Krise der Moderne; Gesammelte Essais*, 113–18. Berlin: Wagenbach, 1983.

———. "Alpenreisen." *Die Zeit: Wiener Wochenschrift für Politik, Volkswirtschaft, Wissenschaft und Kunst*, 13 July 1895, 22–24.

Simon, Rainer. *Fernes Land: Die DDR, die DEFA und der Ruf des Chimborazo*. Berlin: Aufbau, 2005.

———. "Meine Chimborazo-Tagebücher." In Simon and Schäfer, *Die Besteigung des Chimborazo*, 120–57.

Simon, Rainer, and Paul Kanut Schäfer. *Die Besteigung des Chimborazo: Eine Filmexpedition auf Alexander von Humboldts Spuren*. Cologne: vgs, 1990.

Simony, Friedrich. *Auf dem Hohen Dachstein*. Vienna: Österreichischer Schulbücherverlag, 1921.

Singer, Alan. "Comprehending Appearances: Werner Herzog's Ironic Sublime." In *The Films of Werner Herzog: Between Mirage and History*, edited by Timothy Corrigan, 183–205. New York: Methuen, 1986.

Slovic, Scott. "Editor's Note," *ISLE* 14 (2007): v–vii.

Smith, Bernhard. *European Vision and the South Pacific*. New Haven, CT: Yale UP, 1985.

Soden, Garrett. *Falling*. New York: Norton, 2003.

S.O.S. Eisberg. Directed by Dr. Arnold Fanck. Berlin: Deutsche Universal-Film AG, 1932/33.

Specht, Richard. *Richard Strauss und sein Werk*. Vol. 1. Leipzig: Tal & Co, 1921.

Sprecher, Thomas. *Davos im Zauberberg: Thomas Manns Roman und sein Schauplatz*. Munich: Fink, 1996.

Spufford, Francis. *I May Be Some Time: Ice and the English Imagination*. London: Faber & Faber, 1996.

Stabler, Jordan Herbert. *Bolívar: The Spirit of Chimborazo Speaks.* Caracas: Vargas, 1930.

Stafford, Barbara Maria. *Voyage into Substance: Art, Science, Nature, and the Illustrated Travel Account, 1760–1840.* Cambridge: MIT Press, 1984.

Stein, Alexandra. "Die Wundervölker des *Herzog Ernst (B)*: Zum Problem körpergebundener Authentizität im Medium der Schrift." In *Fremdes wahrnehmen — fremdes Wahrnehmen: Studien zur Geschichte der Wahrnehmung und zur Begegnung von Kulturen in Mittelalter und früher Neuzeit*, edited by Wolfgang Harms and C. Stephen Jaeger, 21–48. Stuttgart: S. Hirzel, 1997.

Steinke, Hubert, Urs Boschung, and Wolfgang Proß, eds. *Albrecht von Haller: Leben — Werk — Epoche.* Göttingen: Wallstein, 2008.

Steinke, Hubert, and Martin Stuber. "Haller und die Gelehrtenrepublik." In Steinke, Boschung, and Proß, *Albrecht von Haller: Leben — Werk — Epoche*, 381–414.

Stepan, Nancy. *Picturing Tropical Nature.* Ithaca, NY: Cornell UP, 2001.

Stifter, Adalbert. *Briefwechsel.* Vol. 2. In *Sämtliche Werke*, vol. 18. Prague: Calve, 1918.

———. *Der Nachsommer: Eine Erzählung.* In *Werke und Briefe: Historisch-kritische Gesamtausgabe*, edited by Wolfgang Frühwald and Walter Hettche, vol. 4, bks. 1–3. Stuttgart: Kohlhammer, 1997–2000. In English, *Indian Summer*. Translated by Wendell Frye. New York: Peter Lang, 1985.

Strathausen, Carsten. "The Image as Abyss: The Cinematic Sublime in the Mountain Film." *Peripheral Visions: The Hidden Stages of Weimar Cinema*, edited by Kenneth S. Calhoon, 171–89. Detroit: Wayne State UP, 2001.

Strauss, Richard. *Eine Alpensinfonie*, op. 64. Munich: Leuckart, n.d.

———. *Briefe an die Eltern 1882–1906.* Edited by Willi Schuh. Zurich: Atlantis, 1954.

Stutzer, Walter. *Jean-Jacques Rousseau und die Schweiz: Zur Geschichte des Helvetismus.* Zurich: Tages-Anzeiger, 1950.

Sullivan, Heather I. "Collecting the Rocks of Time: Goethe, the Romantics, and Early Geology." *European Romantic Review* 10 (1999): 341–70.

———. "Ecocriticism, the Elements, and the Ascent/Descent into Weather in Goethe's *Faust. Goethe Yearbook* 17 (2010): 55–72.

———. "Ruins and the Construction of Time: Geological and Literary Perspectives in the Age of Goethe." *Studies in Eighteenth-Century Culture* 30 (2001): 1–30.

Sulzer, Johann Georg. "Erhaben." In *Allgemeine Theorie der schönen Künste*, 97–114. Leipzig: Weidemann & Reich, 1771–74.

Tantillo, Astrida Orle. "Damned to Heaven: The Tragedy of *Faust* Revisited." *Monatshefte* 99, no. 4 (2007): 454–68.

Tarbell, Ida. M, ed. *Napoleon's Addresses: Selections from the Proclamations, Speeches and Correspondence of Napoleon Bonaparte*. Boston: Joseph Knight, 1897.

Tennyson, Alfred. *Selected Poems*. London: Penguin, 2007.

Texte, Joseph, and J. W. Matthews. *Jean-Jacques Rousseau and the Cosmopolitan Spirit in Literature: A Study of the Literary Relations between France and England during the Eighteenth Century*. London: Duckworth, 1899.

The Nuremberg Chronicle: A Facsimile of Hartmann Schedel's Buch der Chroniken; Printed by Anton Koberger in 1493. New York: Arno, 1979.

Theweleit, Klaus. *Male Fantasies*. Vol. 1, *Women, Floods, Bodies, History*. Translated by Stephen Conway in collaboration with Erica Carter and Chris Turner. Minneapolis: U of Minnesota P, 1987.

Thomas, Walter. *Richard Strauss und seine Zeitgenossen*. Munich: Langen Müller, 1964.

Thomasset, Claude, and Danièle James-Raoul, eds. *La montagne dans le texte médiévale: Entre mythe et réalité*. Cultures et Civilisations Médiévales 19. Paris: Presses de l'Université de Paris-Sorbonne, 2000.

Thompson, Mark. *The White War: Life and Death on the Italian Front, 1915–1919*. New York: Basic Books, 2008.

Thomson, Joseph. *Through Masai Land: A Journey of Exploration among the Snowclad Volcanic Mountains and Strange Tribes of Eastern Equatorial Africa*. New and revised edition. London: Sampson Low, Marston, Searle & Rivington, 1987.

Thoreau, Henry David. "A Walk to Wachusett." In *Collected Essays and Poems*, 42–56. New York: The Library of America, 2001.

Tieck, Ludwig. *Schriften in 12 Bänden*. Vol. 6, *Phantasus*. Edited by Manfred Frank. Frankfurt am Main: Deutscher Klassiker Verlag, 1985.

Tilman, H. W. *When Men and Mountains Meet*. In *The Seven Mountain-Travel Books*, 269–422. Seattle: The Mountaineers, 1983.

Todorov, Tzvetan. "Structural Analysis of Narrative." *NOVEL: A Forum on Fiction* 3, no. 1 (Autumn, 1969): 70–76.

Touching the Void. Directed by Kevin Macdonald. London: Pathé, 2003.

Trenner, Franz, ed. *Richard Strauss — Ludwig Thuille: Ein Briefwechsel*. Tutzing, Germany: Schneider, 1980.

Türk, Johannes. *Die Immunität der Literatur*. Frankfurt am Main: Fischer, 2011.

Turner, Katherine. *British Travel Writers in Europe, 1750–1800: Authorship, Gender and National Identity*. London: Ashgate, 2001.

Unsworth, Walt. *Hold the Heights*. Seattle: The Mountaineers, 1994.

Van Cleve, John. "Social Commentary in Haller's 'Die Alpen.'" *Monatshefte* 72, no. 4 (Winter 1980): 379–88.

van der Laan, J. M. *Seeking Meaning for Goethe's* Faust. London: Continuum, 2007.

Verne, Jules. *Les enfants du Capitaine Grant, voyage autour du monde.* Paris: Hetzel, 1868. In English, *A Voyage round the World.* 3 vols. [No translator is named]. London: George Routledge & Sons, 1876.

Virchov, Christian. "Das Sanatorium als Lebensform: Über einschlägige Erfahrungen Thomas Manns." In *Literatur und Krankheit im Fin-de-Siècle: Thomas Mann im europäischen Kontext*, edited by Thomas Sprecher, 171–98. Frankfurt am Main: Klostermann, 2002.

Virgil. *Aeneid.* In *P. Virgili Maronis Opera.* Edited by R. A. B. Mynors. Oxford: Oxford UP, 1969.

Volk, Winfried. *Die Entdeckung Tahitis und das Wunschbild der seligen Insel in der deutschen Literatur.* Heidelberg: Kranz & Heinrichmöller, 1934.

Von Dassanowsky, Robert. "A Mountain of a Ship: Locating the *Bergfilm* in James Cameron's *Titanic.*" *Cinema Journal* 40, no. 4 (2001): 18–35.

Vredeveld, Harry. "Ludwig Tieck's *Der Runenberg*: An Archetypal Interpretation." In *Germanic Review: Literature, Culture, Theory* 49, no. 3 (1974): 200–214.

Wachtler, Michael. *The First World War in the Alps.* Bolzano, Italy: Athesia Spectrum, 2006.

Wagner, Virginia L. "John Ruskin and Artistical Geology in America." *Winterthur Portfolio* 23 (1988): 151–67.

Warrell, Ian. *Through Switzerland with Turner: Ruskin's First Selection from the Turner Bequest.* London: Tate Gallery, 1995.

Watson, J. R. *Picturesque Landscape and English Romantic Poetry.* London: Hutchinson, 1970.

Watson, Scott B. "Herzog's Healing Images: Mountain Climbing and Mankind's Degeneration." *Aethlon: The Journal of Sports Literature* 10 (1992): 169–81.

Weber, Heinz-Dieter, ed. *Vom Wandel des neuzeitlichen Naturbegriffs.* Constance: Constance UP, 1989.

Wennerhold, Markus. *Späte mittelhochdeutsche Artusromane: "Lanzelet," "Wigalois," "Daniel von dem Blühenden Tal," "Diu Crône"; Bilanz der Forschung, 1960–2000.* Würzburg: Königshausen & Neumann, 2005.

Weitz, Eric. *Weimar Germany: Promise and Tragedy.* Princeton, NJ: Princeton UP, 2007.

Whalen, Robert Weldon. *Bitter Wounds: German Victims of the Great War, 1914–1939.* Ithaca, NY: Cornell UP, 1984.

Whitey, Lynne. *Voyages of Discovery: Captain Cook and the Exploration of the Pacific.* Berkeley: U of California P, 1987.

Williams, Helen Maria. *A Tour in Switzerland, or A View of the Present State of the Government and Manners of Those Cantons*. 2 vols. London: G. G. & R. Robinson, 1798.

Wilton, Andrew. *Turner and the Sublime*. London: British Museum, 1980.

Wilton, Andrew, and Tim Barringer. *American Sublime: Landscape Painting in the United States, 1820–1880*. London: Tate Gallery, 2002.

Wimmer, Clemens. "Die Alpen: Vom Garten Europas zum Stadion Europas." In *Mit den Bäumen sterben die Menschen: Zur Kulturgeschichte der Ökologie*, edited by Jost Hermand, 81–118. Cologne: Böhlau, 1993.

Wittenberg, Hermann. "The Sublime, Imperialism and the African Landscape." PhD. thesis, U of the Western Cape, 2004.

Wittstock, Uwe. *Nach der Moderne: Essay zur deutschen Gegenwartsliteratur in zwölf Kapiteln über elf Autoren*. Göttingen: Wallstein, 2009.

Wordsworth, William. *A Complete Guide to the Lakes, Comprising Minute Directions for the Tourist with Mr Wordsworth's Description of the Scenery*. Kendal, UK: J. Hudson, 1846.

———. *Descriptive Sketches: In Verse; Taken during a Pedestrian Tour in the Italian, Grison, Swiss and Savoyard Alps*. London: J. Johnson, 1793.

———. *Wordsworth: Representative Poems*. Edited by Arthur Beatty. New York: Doubleday, 1937.

———. *The Prelude; or, Growth of a Poet's Mind*. Edited by Ernest de Selincourt. 1805. Reprint, Oxford: Oxford UP, 1970.

Worster, Donald. *Nature's Economy: A History of Ecological Ideas*. Cambridge: Cambridge UP, 1977.

Wu, Duncan. *Wordsworth's Reading, 1770–1799*. Cambridge: Cambridge UP, 1993.

Wyatt, John. *Wordsworth and Geologists*. Cambridge: Cambridge UP, 2005.

Wyder, Margrit. "Goethes geologische Passionen: Vom Alter der Erde." *Goethe Jahrbuch* 125 (2008): 136–46.

Youmans, Richard D. *Richard Strauss's Orchestral Music and the German Intellectual Tradition*. Bloomington: Indiana UP, 2005.

Zagajewski, Karl. *Albrecht von Hallers Dichtersprache*. Strasbourg: Trübner, 1909.

Zebhauser, Helmuth. *Alpinismus im Hitlerstaat*. Munich: Rudolf Rother, 1998.

Zebhauser, Helmuth, and Maike Trentin-Meyer, eds. *Zwischen Idylle und Tummelplatz: Katalog für das Alpine Museum des Deutschen Alpenvereins in München*. Munich: Rudolf Rother, 1996.

Contributors

PETER ARNDS is Professor and Director of Comparative Literature and the Centre of Literary Translation at Trinity College Dublin, where he also teaches in the German and Italian departments. His interests in literature and cultural studies are widespread, from Sophie von La Roche to W. G. Sebald, post-Holocaust literature, magical realism, the satirical visual arts, the wolf-man, travel literature, and translation theory. His publications include two monographs, *Representation, Subversion, and Eugenics in Günter Grass's* The Tin Drum (Camden House, 2004) and *Wilhelm Raabe's* Der Hungerpastor *and Charles Dickens's* David Copperfield: *Intertextuality of Two Bildungsromane* (Peter Lang, 1997), approximately forty articles, and numerous prose pieces and poems. A good part of his work revolves around human rights, with a focus on genocide and its limits of cultural representation and translation. An Alpinist in the true sense of his former home, the Bavarian Alps, he now enjoys promenading through Dublin's parks and taking quick baths in the Irish Sea.

OLAF BERWALD is Chair of Modern & Classical Languages & Literatures and Associate Professor of German at the University of North Dakota. His book publications include *Globalization and Its Apparitions: Intercultural Engagements and Disengagements Seen from the South and the North / La globalización y sus espejismos: Encuentros y desencuentros interculturales vistos desde el Sur y el Norte*, coedited with Michael Handelsman (Editorial El Conejo, 2009); *Der untote Gott: Religion und Ästhetik in der deutschen und österreichischen Literatur des 20. Jahrhunderts*, coedited with Gregor Thuswaldner (Böhlau, 2007); and *An Introduction to the Works of Peter Weiss* (Camden House, 2003). He is the editor of Camden House's forthcoming *Companion to the Works of Max Frisch*. Though he currently admires the Northern Plains, there are sightings of him every summer in the Alps and the Black Forest.

ALBRECHT CLASSEN is University Distinguished Professor of German Studies at the University of Arizona, working on the European Middle Ages and the Early Modern Age. He has published over sixty scholarly books, most recently a monograph entitled *Sex im Mittelalter* (Bachmann, 2011) and a coedited volume called *Friendship in the Middle Ages and Early Modern Age* (de Gruyter, 2011). In 2010 he published the three-volume *Handbook of Medieval Studies*. He is the editor of *Tristania* and

Mediävistik, and most recently also of *Humanities*. He is an aficionado of volleyball and enjoys bicycling as well as the outdoors of the Southwest.

ROGER COOK is Professor of German Studies and Director of the Film Studies Program at the University of Missouri. He has coedited (with Gerd Gemünden) *The Cinema of Wim Wenders: Image, Narrative, and the Postmodern Condition* (Wayne State UP, 1996) and has published extensively on New German Cinema and contemporary German film. He has also written on eighteenth- and nineteenth-century German literature, with a particular emphasis on Heinrich Heine. He is the author of *By the Rivers of Babylon: Heinrich Heine's Late Songs and Reflections* (Wayne State UP, 1998) and the editor of *A Companion to the Works of Heinrich Heine* (Camden House, 2003). His current work engages research in neuroscience and media theory to investigate issues of embodiment and affect in film viewing. He enjoys hiking and backpacking in a variety of terrains, especially the mountains of the western United States.

SCOTT DENHAM is Charles A. Dana Professor of German and Chair of the Center for Interdisciplinary Studies at Davidson College, where he has taught German language and literature, humanities, writing, and cultural studies since 1990. His main areas of interest include German and European literary modernism, translation theory, modernist architecture, and questions of identity, loss, and memory in the central European context. Although no alpinist, he is an avid road cyclist who rides the Clinch and Iron Mountain ranges of Southwest Virginia, and a passionate hunter whose pursuit of elk takes him to the Maroon Bells–Snowmass Wilderness Area in Colorado.

SEAN FRANZEL is Assistant Professor of German at the University of Missouri. His research interests include the history of scholarly culture and the university; histories and theories of media; the eighteenth- and nineteenth-century novel; and the history of science. Recent publications include articles on Karl Philipp Moritz's public lectures in the *Goethe Yearbook*, on Jean Paul and print culture in *Romanticism and Victorianism on the Net*, and on anti-monumental (i.e. anti-sublime) critical style in *Telos*. A native of the Pacific Northwest, he went on frequent backpacking trips while growing up; recent mountain and ocean encounters include forays in the North Cascades and on the West Coast Trail of Vancouver Island.

CHRISTOF HAMANN is a writer of fiction and also currently holds a visiting professorship at the Universität zu Köln. He has published several novels, most recently *Usambara* (Steidl, 2007) and *Nur ein Schritt bis zu den Vögeln* (Steidl, 2012). His areas of research encompass literature from the nineteenth to the twenty-first century, specifically postcolonialism and theories of space. His scholarly publications include a number of edited volumes, a monograph entitled *Grenzen der Metropole: New York in der deutschsprachigen Gegenwartsliteratur* (Deutscher Universitäts-Verlag, 2001), and the coauthored study (together with Alexander Honold) *Kilimandscharo: Die deutsche Geschichte eines afrikanischen Berges* (Wagenbach, 2011). His mountain climbing activities are almost exclusively restricted to the European Alps, though he has also visited the Canadian Rockies and set foot on Kilimanjaro.

HARALD HÖBUSCH is Associate Professor and Director of the Division of German Studies at the University of Kentucky. His research interests include: German and English literature and films about (high-altitude) mountaineering, Thomas Mann, and world language pedagogy. He is currently working on a book-length study of the cultural representation and political appropriation of high-altitude mountaineering expeditions to Germany's "mountain of destiny," Nanga Parbat, between 1932 and 1953. His outdoor pursuits regularly take him to the Rockies, the European Alps, and (hopefully soon) the Himalayas.

DAN HOOLEY is Professor of Classics at the University of Missouri. He has written three books including *The Knotted Thong: Structures of Mimesis in Persius* (U of Michigan P, 1997) and *Roman Satire* (Blackwell, 2007) as well as a number of articles and book chapters on Roman satire and the later reception of Latin poetry. He is currently working on a new monograph about the reception of Persius in Europe. He regularly climbs rock, snow, and ice throughout the United States, especially on the limestone cliffs of Missouri and in the Rockies of Colorado, Wyoming, and Montana.

PETER HÖYNG is Associate Professor of German Studies at Emory University. Focusing on German literature and culture since 1750, Höyng's research centers thematically around three distinct areas: drama within its performative context, German-Jewish topics, and how literature interacts with classical music. Höyng's cross-disciplinary interests are especially evident in his book project on Beethoven as a reader of literature; his edited volume on the Jewish dramatist George Tabori (*Verkörperte Geschichtsentwürfe: George Taboris Theaterarbeit / Embodied Projections on History: George Tabori's Theater Work* (Francke, 1998); and his monograph that interconnects the discourses of history and drama: *Die Sterne, die Zensur und das Vaterland: Geschichte und Theater im späten 18. Jahrhundert* (Böhlau, 2003).

SEAN IRETON is Associate Professor of German at the University of Missouri. He specializes in philosophy and literature from the late eighteenth through the twentieth century. He has published a monograph entitled *An Ontological Study of Death: From Hegel to Heidegger* (Duquesne UP, 2007) as well as diverse articles on Stifter, Nietzsche, Thomas Mann, and others. He has hiked and climbed extensively throughout the United States and Europe, also in Morocco, Canada, Mexico, and Bolivia. His favorite range, however, will always remain the densely forested and heavily glaciated North Cascades of Washington State.

OLIVER LUBRICH is Professor of German and Comparative Literature at the University of Bern in Switzerland. Previously, he was Junior Professor of Rhetoric at the Peter Szondi Institute of Comparative Literature and the Cluster of Excellence "Languages of Emotion" at the Freie Universität Berlin. He has published monographs on Shakespeare's self-deconstruction and postcolonial poetics and also has edited and/or coedited Alexander von Humboldt's *Central Asia*, *Kosmos*, the *Chimborazo Diary*, the first German version of *Vues des Cordillères*, and Humboldt's ethnographic and political essays. In his current research he is documenting international testimonies from Nazi Germany, including *Travels in the Reich, 1933–1945: Foreign Authors Report from Germany* (U of Chicago P, 2010).

ANTHONY OZTURK is Professor of Literature and Art History at Les Roches-Gruyère University, Switzerland. He is the author of works on literary and artistic interactions, including the visual aesthetics of Ezra Pound, Adrian Stokes, and John Ruskin. His current research projects focus on poetic and pictorial responses to eighteenth- and nineteenth-century travel in Switzerland, and he is writing a monograph called *The Invention of Helvetica*. His forthcoming publications include chapters on cultural relations between early geology and Anglo-American literature and painting. He has published poetry and short fiction in Europe and the United States, and enjoys cross-country running and skiing.

CAROLINE SCHAUMANN is Associate Professor of German Studies at Emory University. She is the author of *Memory Matters: Generational Responses to Germany's Nazi Past in Recent Women's Literature* (de Gruyter, 2008) and has published widely on postwar and postwall German literature and culture. Her present research interests include ecocriticism in film and literature. She is currently working on a book-length study that examines the cultural shifts in the perception, meaning, and artistic representation of mountains from the mid-1800s to the present. Schaumann can be found on rock faces throughout the world, but in particular enjoys the granite of California and the sandstone of the South and Southwest.

HEATHER I. SULLIVAN is Professor of German and Chair of the interdisciplinary minor in comparative literature at Trinity University in San Antonio, Texas. Her current research focuses on Goethe and ecocriticism, with a particular emphasis on Goethe's science. She is a contributor to the volume, *Ecocritical Theory: New European Approaches* (eds. Axel Goodbody and Kate Rigby, Virginia UP, 2011), and her essays have appeared in the

Goethe Yearbook; Monatshefte; Ecozon@; ISLE (Interdisciplinary Studies in Literature and the Environment); 1650–1850: Ideas, Aesthetics, and Inquiries in the Early Modern Era; Bulletin of Science, Technology, and Society; Studies in Eighteenth-Century Culture; and the *European Romantic Review*. Her book, *The Intercontextuality of Self and Nature in Ludwig Tieck's Early Works*, was published in 1997 by Peter Lang. Throughout her career, she has been dedicated to the study of nature as explored in texts and in walks amongst all its material manifestations, especially mountains.

JOHANNES TÜRK is Assistant Professor of Germanic Studies and Adjunct Assistant Professor of Comparative Literature at Indiana University, Bloomington. He has published on Freud, Kafka, Musil, Proust, Kleist, and the history of immunology. His book *Die Immunität der Literatur* appeared in 2011 (Fischer). He was born in the vicinity of the Carpathian Mountains and still enjoys the rare opportunities to hike and ski. His most enjoyable experiences include alpine views and the quietude of Portugal's Serra da Estrela.

SABINE WILKE is Professor of German and Chair at the University of Washington. Her research and teaching interests include modern German literature and culture, intellectual history and theory, and cultural studies. She has written books and articles on body constructions in modern German literature and culture, German unification, aesthetics and gender constructions, German colonialism, and the overlapping concerns of postcolonialism and ecocriticism. In 2011 she received the Alexander von Humboldt Research Prize for networking in the environmental humanities. The digital platform that was developed to support the network can be found at www.environmental-humanities-network.org and contains information on participants and their projects, book series, journals, curricular initiatives, and recent scholarship. During the summer months and winter ski season Wilke enjoys the Methow Valley trail system located on the eastern slope of the North Cascades.

WILFRIED WILMS is Associate Professor of German at the University of Denver. He is the coeditor of *German Postwar Films: Life and Love in the Ruins* (Palgrave, 2008) and *Bombs Away: Representing the Air War over Europe and Japan* (Rodopi, 2006) and has published numerous scholarly articles on German intellectual history, literature, and film. His current book project focuses on Weimar mountain film. Living in Colorado, he regularly enjoys all that the Rockies have to offer: mountaineering, rock climbing, hiking, skiing, and fly-fishing.

Index

Aar: Glacier, 329–31; Gorge, 109–10; River, 68–69, 330
Abraham, 3
acclimatization, 14, 248–49, 257–58
Adam and Eve, 3
Addison, Joseph, 83, 94
Adorno, Theodor, works by: *Ästhetische Theorie*, 115; "Richard Strauss: Zum hundertsten Geburtstag," 239, 241–43, 247
Aetna, Mount. *See* Etna
Age of Goethe, 116, 203, 223
Aguirre, der Zorn Gottes (dir. Werner Herzog), 307, 312, 316
Aiguille, Mont, 8, 23
Alexander the Great, 61
Alexandrine, 57, 61
Alpine clubs: Alpenverein, 227, 232, 293, 299; Alpine Club, 92; Austrian Alpine Club, 200; German Alpine Club, 289, 292–93; German and Austrian Alpine Club, 285, 289, 298; Munich Alpine Club, 16; *Zeitschrift des Deutschen und Österreichischen Alpenvereins*, 273, 283
Alpine myth, also Helvetic myth, 11, 58, 74, 79–81
Alpine topography, 68, 73, 80–81, 83–84
Alpinism, 7–8, 10–13, 136, 193–200, 208, 285, 293, 299
Alps, 1–2, 5, 7–10, 13–17, 20, 22–23, 26, 35, 43, 47, 52, 55, 104–6, 134, 136, 193–95, 197, 200, 204, 206, 231–32, 234, 237–38, 240–42, 254–55, 263, 273, 285–86, 289, 327, 330; Austrian Alps, 13, 17, 194, 200, 206; Bernese Alps, 11, 62, 99, 108; Swiss Alps, 18, 58, 104, 106, 204, 238, 245–46
Ames, Eric, 303
Andes, 1, 5, 134, 153, 156–58, 160, 165, 309
Appalachians, 1
Ararat, Mount, 3, 24
Arnold, David, 145
Arnold von Harff, 45
Athos, Mount, 30
Atkins, Stuart, 130, 133
Augustine, 22–23
Ayers Rock, 6

Baboquivari Peak, 24
Baird, Jay W., 292, 299
Balmat, Jacques, 10
Barthes, Roland, 343, 348
Bauer, Paul, 294, 299–300
Bayers, Peter, 135
Bayreuther, Rainer, 233, 240, 245–47
Bear Butte, 24
Bear Lodge (Devil's Tower), 24
Beatty, Arthur, 88, 96
Beckett, Samuel, 225
Beethoven, Ludwig van, 240
Beethoven, Ludwig van, works by: Sixth Symphony (*Pastoral Symphony*), 231, 234, 242, 247
Benzoni, Girolamo, 162
Bergfilm, 15–16, 267–68, 270–71, 276, 278–79, 280–84, 296
Berlin Wall, 169
Berman, Russell, 138
Bern, 58, 60, 63–64, 74–75, 85, 235, 328
Bernese Oberland, 60, 328. *See also* Alps, Bernese
Bernett, Hajo, 289, 299

Bernhard, Thomas, 17
Bible, 3, 18, 128, 186
Biedermeier, 176–77, 179, 205
Bierstadt, Albert, 71
Bildung, 13, 181, 183, 193–96, 204–5, 207
Bildungsroman, 13, 181, 193, 196, 203–5, 209
Blanc, Mont, 10, 81, 91, 95–96, 267, 324–25
Der Blaue Reiter, 232
Boccaccio, Giovanni, works by: *De montibus, silvis, fontibus, lacubus, fluminibus, stagnis seu paludibus, et de nominibus maris*, 52
Böhme, Gernot, 128
Böhme, Hartmut, 2, 185
Bolívar, Simón, 154–55, 157, 163, 171
Bolívar, Simón, works by: "Mi delirio sobre el Chimborazo," 154, 170
Bonaparte, Napoleon, 85–86, 95, 154, 320; crossing of the Alps at the St. Bernard Pass, 86, 320, 323
Bonpland, Aimé, 153–54, 168–72
Botsch, Katharina, 8
Boussingault, Jean Baptiste, 161–62, 173
Brahm, Otto, 235, 245
Brandis, Regina von, 8
Brant, Sebastian, works by: *Das Narrenschiff*, 186
Brehmer, Hermann, 252–53
Broch, Hermann, 343
Broch, Hermann, works by: *Bergroman*, 193, 206, 343; *Der Tod des Vergil*, 342
Brocken, 117–18, 121, 131
Buch, Leopold von, 161–62
Buch, Leopold von, works by: *Physicalische Beschreibung der canarischen Inseln*, 161
Buffon, Georges-Louis Leclerc de, 165
Buhl, Hermann, 294–97, 300
Burckhardt, Jacob, works by: *Die Kultur der Renaissance in Italien*, 7, 18
Bürgerliches Trauerspiel, 66

Burke, Edmund, 20, 29, 78, 88
Burke, Edmund, works by: *A Philosophical Enquiry into the Origin of Our Ideas of the Sublime and Beautiful*, 78, 93, 99–100, 102; *Reflections on the Revolution in France*, 79, 85
Bürkli, Johannes, 80
Burn, A. R., 24
Burnet, Thomas, works by: *The Sacred Theory of the Earth*, 77–78
Butler, E. M., 6
Buxton, Richard, 24–25
Byron, Lord George Gordon, works by: *Alastor*, 81; *Childe Harold's Pilgrimage*, 81; *Manfred*, 81; *Prometheus Unbound*, 81

Cain and Abel, 186
Calpi, 153
Canary Islands, 161, 168
Carguairazo, Mt., 157, 162, 172–73
Carmel, Mount (and range), 3, 24
Carmina Burana, 66
Carus, Carl Gustav, 87–88, 96
Catesby, Mark, 137
Celan, Paul, 325, 332, 342
Cerro Torre, 307–9
Cerro Torre: Schrei aus Stein (film), 17, 303, 306–10
Chimaera, Mt., 27
Chimborazo, Mt., 1, 12, 153–75
Cithaeron, mountain range, 24–25
Claudius, Matthias, works by: "Abendlied," 223–24
Cliffhanger (dir. Renny Harlin), 311
cognitive mapping (CM), 17, 304–6, 308, 311, 313, 315–16
Coleridge, Samuel Taylor, 78, 93
Coleridge, Samuel Taylor, works by: "Hymn before Sun-rise, in the Vale of Chamouni," 81, 96
Confucius, 7
Cook, Captain James, 134–35, 138, 143, 148
Cooley, William Desborough, works by: *Inner Africa Laid Open*, 212, 226

Corsica, 320–21
Coxe, William, 11, 82–85
Coxe, William, works by: *Sketches of the Natural, Civil, and Political State of Swisserland*, 79–80, 85, 87; *Travels in Switzerland*, 80
Crosby, Alfred W., 137
Cyllene, Mount, 24

da Vinci, Leonardo, 8
Dachstein, (also Dachsteingebirge, Dachsteinmassif), 200–202, 207–8
Danius, Sara, 257, 265
Dante, 18
D'Asti, Bonifacio Rotario, 7
David, Jacques-Louis, works by: *Napoleon at the St Bernard Pass*, 86
Davos, 14, 248–51, 253–54, 259, 260, 262, 265, 283, 323, 325, 329
de Saussure, Horace-Bénédict, 10–11, 80–82, 84, 199
de Saussure, Horace-Bénédict, works by: *Voyages dans les Alps*, 10, 81, 91, 94
de Staël, Germaine, 158
de Ville, Antoine, 7–8, 23
Decken, Baron Carl Claus von der, 213, 215
Dedner, Burghard, 58, 74
DeLoughrey, Elizabeth, 145
Denali (also known as Mt. McKinley), 24, 135
Der Berg des Schicksals (dir. Arnold Fanck), 267–68, 275–78
Der heilige Berg (dir. Arnold Fanck, 268), 271, 275, 278–81
Der König vom Montblanc (dir. Arnold Fanck), 167
Der verlorene Sohn (dir. Luis Trenker), 267
Descartes, René, 218
Dhaulagiri, 1
Dicte, Mount, 24
Die Besteigung des Chimborazo (dir. Rainer Simon), 169–70
Die weiße Hölle vom Piz Palü (dir. Arnold Fanck), 297
Dietrich epics, 44, 46, 52

Diogenes, Laertius, 27
Dionysian, 91, 178–81, 184–89, 207, 256, 262, 264
Dionysus, 25, 177–78
Döblin, Alfred, 343
Dorst, Tankred, works by: *Auf dem Chimborazo*, 170, 175
Drexel, Alfred, 288, 290–91

early modern age/era, 7, 23, 36, 46–52, 55–56, 186, 211
Eckenlied, 39
ecocriticism, 11, 12, 116, 118, 130, 132, 136–37
Economic Miracle, 295–96, 298
Eden, Garden of, 3, 59, 64, 77, 92
Edmond, Rod, 134
Egger, Toni, 307
Eichendorff, Joseph von, works by: *Ahnung und Gegenwart*, 203
Eiger, 9, 16, 21
Elijah, 3
Emei, Mount, 6
Empedocles, 27, 29
Emperor Maximilian, works by: *Theuerdank*, 7, 49–52
Engel, Claire Eliane, 84
Enlightenment, 5, 21, 63, 73, 138, 146, 153, 158, 164–65, 176–79, 185, 189, 330
Enzensberger, Hans Magnus, works by: "A. v. H. (1769–1859)," 170, 174
Ertl, Hans, 16, 294–98, 300–301
Escher, Lydia, 235, 245
Etna, Mt. (also spelled Aetna), 27–28, 30, 204
Euripides, 6, 13
Euripides, works by: *Bacchae*, 25, 178, 184, 187, 189
Everest, Mt. (also known as Chomolungma/Qomolangma/Sagarmatha), 1, 24, 135, 285, 294–95, 306

Fanck, Arnold, 15–16, 267–68, 271–84, 296–97, 300–301
Fanon, Franz, 137

Flaubert, Gustave, works by: "Legend of St. Julian," 321
Fichte, Johann Gottlieb, 11, 99, 103
Fichte, Johann Gottlieb, works by: *Einige Vorlesungen über die Bestimmung des Gelehrten*, 105–6, 108
Fichtelgebirge, 190
First World War, 232, 263, 268–69, 282–83, 285, 289, 292, 294, 297, 301, 323
Forster, George, 12, 134–48
Forster, George, works by: *A Voyage round the World*, 134–48
Forster, Johann Reinhold, 134–35, 140, 142–46
Fortunatus, 45–46
Foucault, Michel, works by: *Discipline and Punish*, 176, 185, 188; *Madness and Civilization*, 189
French Revolution, 73, 79–80, 86, 88, 92, 158
Freud, Sigmund, 13, 178; death drive, 181–84, 187–88; ego, 183–84; *eros*, 176, 181–82, 184–85, 188; id, 183–84; pleasure principle, 181–84; reality principle, 181, 183–84; sexual drive, 181–84; *thanatos*, 181–82, 184, 188; *das (Un)heimliche*, 178–80, 189, 191
Freud, Sigmund, works by: "Das Ich und das Es," 183
Friedrich, Caspar David, 19, 79, 86–88, 91, 109
Friedrich, Caspar David, works by: *Kreuz im Gebirge*, 91; *Riesengebirgslandschaft mit aufsteigendem Nebel*, 86–87; *Wanderer über dem Nebelmeer*, 88–91, 324; *Der Watzmann*, 86–87
Fuji, Mount, 5–6, 24

Galeano, Eduardo, 155, 163, 170–71
Galeano, Eduardo, works by: *Memoria del fuego*, 155
Gallhuber, Julius, 285
Garrard, Greg, 59, 74–75, 132
Gasherbrum — Der leuchtende Berg (dir. Werner Herzog), 17, 302–4, 307–19

Gasherbrum I and Gasherbrum II, 302, 309
Gay-Lussac, Joseph Louis, 157
Genesis, 77–78, 87, 95
Geneva, Lake, 60, 73, 324
geology, 1, 10, 77, 80, 86, 91, 93, 113, 126, 132, 161, 193–209
Gérard, François, 158–60
Gérard, François, works by: "L'Amérique relevée de sa ruine par le Commerce et par l'Industrie," 158–59
German Himalaya Foundation, 287–88, 294, 299–300
Gerwald, Matthias, works by: *Der Entdecker*, 169–70
Gesner, Conrad, 8–9
Gesner, Conrad, works by: *De montium admiratione*, 8–9; *Descriptio Montis Fracti juxta Lucernam*, 8
Gessner, Johannes, 57–60, 62–63
Gilpin, William, 78
Girdlestone, Cuthbert, 84
Glaube und Schönheit (dir. Hans Ertl), 297
Glowacz, Stefan, 307
Goethe, Johann Wolfgang, 11, 81–83, 99, 116–33, 155, 160, 172, 194–96, 205; Goethe's science, 116, 119–20, 124–26; meteorological studies, 120–21, 127–31; mountain ascents, 117–19, 121; Weimar, 119, 121, 155
Goethe, Johann Wolfgang, works by: "Die Absicht eingeleitet," 205; *Briefe aus der Schweiz*, 81, 99, 106–8, 111; *Dichtung und Wahrheit*, 81; *Faust*, 11–12, 81, 116–33; "Granit II," 101–2, 106, 111, 206; "Harzreise im Winter," 117; *Die Leiden des jungen Werther(s)*, 81, 83; *Wilhelm Meister* novels, 196, 203–4, 209
Golgotha, 3
Gottfried von Straßburg, works by: *Tristan*, 35
Grand Teton, 5. *See also* Tetons
Grand Tour, 80, 82, 96

Greenblatt, Stephan, 218–19
Grizzly Man (dir. Werner Herzog), 316
Großglockner, 200
Gross-Grünhorn, 9
Großvenediger, 200, 321–22
Grove, Richard, 137
Grupp, Peter, 18, 107, 145
Guglia del Diavolo, 275–78
Gumprecht, Taddäus Eduard, 212
Günderrode, Karoline von, works by: *Magie und Schicksal*, 335

Hadrian, 27, 29
Haemus, Mount, 22–23, 26
Hall, Anja, 138
Haller, Albrecht von, 10, 46, 57–76, 79–84, 94, 136
Haller, Albrecht von, works by: "Die Alpen," 10, 46, 57–74, 81; *Enumeratio methodica stirpium Helvetiae indigenarum*, 68–69; "Sehnsucht nach dem Vaterlande," 59–60
Hamann, Christof, works by: *Usambara*, 12–13, 210, 225, 227–28
Hammel, Claus, 155, 163
Hammel, Claus, works by: *Humboldt und Bolivar oder Der neue Continent*, 154, 171
Handel, Georg Friedrich, 100
Hannibal, 26, 86
Hans Westmar (dir. Franz Wenzler), 292
Hanslick, Eduard, works by: *Vom Musikalisch-Schönen*, 240
Hawaii (also Hawaiian Islands), 1, 134
Haydn, Joseph, 231
Haydn, Joseph, works by: *Die Schöpfung*, 231
Hegel, Georg Wilhelm Friedrich, 115, 165
Hegel, Georg Wilhelm Friedrich, works by: *Reisetagebuch*, 11, 99, 108–12, 115; *Vorlesungen über die Ästhetik*, 177, 181, 190

Heidegger, Martin, 13, 176, 188, 189; *aletheia*, 178–80, 187–89, 187; *lethe*, 178–80, 187–89
Heidegger, Martin, works by: *Parmenides*, 178, 186
Heimat, 112, 293, 333
Heimgarten Summit, 232
Helicon, Mount, 24, 26, 32
Herburger, Günter, 160
Herburger, Günter, works by: *Humboldt: Reise-Novellen*, 172
Herder, Johann Gottfried von, 194
Hermand, Jost, 116, 131
Herodotus, 29
Herrligkoffer, Karl Maria, 294, 300
Herzog, Werner, 15, 302–19
Herzog Ernst, 36–39, 52
Hesse, Hermann, 203
Hillary, Edmund, 306, 313
Himalaya(s), 1, 13–14, 20, 134, 157, 285–301, 302–19
Hinterstoißer, Anderl, 16
Hitler, Adolf, 286, 289, 292
Hitler, Adolf, works by: *Mein Kampf*, 289, 299
Hitlerjunge Quex (dir. Hans Steinhoff), 292
Hobsbawm, Eric, 292, 299
Hodges, William, works by: *Tahiti Revisited*, 144
Hoffmann, E. T. A., 185
Hoffmann, E. T. A., works by: *Die Bergwerke zu Falun*, 178, 188
Hohe Dachstein, der, 199–201, 208
Hohe Tauern, 200
Hölderlin, Friedrich, 342, 347–48
Homann, Johann Baptist, 211
Homer, 10, 29
Horace, 6, 64
Horace, works by: *Epistles*, 29; *Odes*, 26–27
Humboldt, Alexander von, 12, 82, 153–75, 194–95, 206, 212
Humboldt, Alexander von, works by: *Ansichten der Natur*, 156; *Atlas géographique et physique des régions équinoxiales du Nouveau Continent*, 158, 160; *Diary*, 165–68, 174; *Essai*

sur la géographie des plantes, 160; *Jahrbuch für 1837*, 161, 164; *Kleinere Schriften*, 161–65; *Kosmos*, 156; *Nova genera et species plantarum*, 160; *Relation historique*, 156; "Ueber einen Versuch den Gipfel des Chimborazo zu ersteigen," 161–65; "Ueber zwei Versuche den Chimborazo zu besteigen," 160–61; *Vues des Cordilléres*, 156–58, 164, 172–73
Humboldt, Wilhelm von, 156, 164, 194
Hunt, Colonel John, 295

Ida, Mount, 24
Im Kampf mit dem Berge: Eine Alpensymphonie in Bildern (dir. Arnold Fanck), 268–75, 283
Industrial Revolution, 62, 73, 119
industrialization, 136, 186, 189, 232
Isaac, 3
Isserman, Maurice, 13–14

Jacobs, Jürgen, 209
Jacobs, Michael, 140
Jawlensky, Alexej von, 232
Jean Paul (Friedrich Richter), 99
Jean Paul (Friedrich Richter), works by: *Titan*, 102; *Vorschule der Ästhetik*, 102, 114
Jebel al Komris (Mountains of the Moon), 222
Jebel-an-Nur (Mountain of Light), 6
Jünger, Ernst, 269
Jungfrau, 9, 109

Kaes, Anton, 268, 282
Kafka, Franz, 252
Kammerlander, Hans, 17, 302, 308–12, 315–16
Kampf um den Himalaja (dir. Frank Leberecht), 286–87, 289–92, 295
Kandinsky, Wassily, 232
Kangchenjunga, 286, 293
Kant, Immanuel, 11, 20, 82, 89, 90, 99, 101, 103, 106, 115, 270
Karakoram, 302–3, 307, 309–10, 317

Kazantzakis, Nikos, 29
Kehlmann, Daniel, works by: *Die Vermessung der Welt*, 170, 175, 211
Kelley, Theresa, 86
Kenya, Mount, 6, 212
Kersten, Otto, 213, 215
Kibo, 215, 216, 219–21. See also Kilimanjaro
Kilimanjaro, Mount, 1, 6, 12–13, 173, 210–21, 225–26, 381. See also Kibo
Koch, Joseph Anton, 19
Kracauer, Siegfried, 267–68, 310
Krapf, Johann Ludwig, 212–13, 226
Kudrun, 38, 44
Kunlun Mountains, 5
Kurz, Toni, 16

La Condamine, Charles Marie de, 162
La Soufrière (dir. Werner Herzog), 310, 316
Laborde, Jean-Benjamin de, works by: *Tableaux topographiques, pittoresques, physiques, historiques, moraux, politiques, littéraires de la Suisse*, 81
Lacan, Jacques, 21
Laugenspitze, 8
Laurentians, 1
Lebenszeichen (dir. Werner Herzog), 303
Lessing, Gotthold Ephraim, 110
Lessing, Gotthold Ephraim, works by: *Laokoon oder über die Grenzen der Malerei und der Poesie*, 68
Linnaeus, Carl, 138, 141
Liszt, Franz, 240–41
Livy, works by: *History of Rome*, 22–23, 26
Llullaillaco, 5
Longinus, works by: *On the Sublime*, 29
Lucilius, 28–30
Lukács, Georg, 177
Lyell, Charles, 196
Lyotard, Jean François, 21

Macdonald, Kevin, 309
Macfarlane, Robert, works by: *Mountains of the Mind*, 190, 207, 285, 298, 300

Maestri, Cesare, 307
Magnetic Mountain, the, 37–38, 49, 53
Mallory, George, 21, 313
Mann, Thomas, 203, 248–66
Mann, Thomas, works by: *Buddenbrooks*, 251–52; *Der Tod in Venedig*, 249; *Tristan*, 249; *Der Zauberberg*, 14, 188, 203, 248–66, 282, 323–28, 331
Mao Zedong, 6
Matterhorn, 193, 245, 271
Mauna Kea, 1
Mauna Loa, 1
Maximilian I, works by: *Theuerdank*, 7, 49–52
McCarthy, John, 128, 133
Mendelssohn, Moses, 99–100, 103, 111
Merkl, Willy, 286–88, 291, 294, 300
Meru, Mount, 5
Messner, Günther, 16, 298
Messner, Reinhold, 16–17, 298, 302, 307–16, 318–19, 348
Meteora, 30
Metternich, Klemens von, 199
Meyer, Hans, 173, 210, 225
Meyer, Hans, works by: *Ostafrikanische Gletscherfahrten*, 12–13, 211, 213–21
Mezzagiorno, Vittorio, 307
Michelangelo, 157–58
Middle Ages, the, 7, 35–46, 52–55, 186, 189
Milton, John, works by: *Paradise Lost*, 77
mining, 13, 118–19, 125, 136, 165, 186
modernity, 14, 130–31, 158, 177, 189, 203, 235, 237, 241, 265, 273, 316, 337; critique of, 64, 116
Mohammed, 6
Monboso, 8
Mönch, 9
Mönch von Salzburg, der, 43
Mons Inascensibilis, 8
Montiglio, Sylvia, 28–29

Moore, John, works by: *A View of Society and Manners in France, Switzerland and Germany*, 85
Morena, Erna, 275
Moses, 3
Mount of Olives, 3
Mount of Temptation, 3
Mount of Transfiguration, 3
mountaineering, 6, 10–14, 16, 20, 23, 29, 117, 134–37, 141–43, 146, 193, 197–200, 202–5, 208, 234, 248, 271, 285–89, 292–93, 295, 298–300, 307–8, 328, 331, 334, 347
mountains: as barriers, 7, 21, 36–38, 46, 50; in the Bible, 2–3; depths of, 7, 27, 39, 46, 118, 176, 178, 183–87; in Eastern cultures, 2–3, 5–6; as a *locus amoenus*, 10, 62, 81, 176, 213; as a *locus daemonis*, 62, 81, 176–77, 213; as a *locus horribilis* or *topos horribilis*, 7, 10, 25, 62, 81; "mountain experience," 324–27, 330; as objects of conquest, 12, 14–15, 20–21, 44, 92, 135–36, 143, 146, 163, 199, 219–21, 239, 244, 275, 295–96, 321, 334, 336, 342–43, 347; as objects of nationalism, 14–16, 20–21, 219–21, 267–301; as objects of recreation or sport, 15, 20–23, 30, 134, 193, 198–200, 203, 232, 235, 239, 248–50, 285–89, 300, 307–8; as objects of scientific interest, 1, 10, 25, 29, 46, 57–58, 69, 73–74, 76, 112, 117, 160, 163–65, 173, 193–95, 198–99, 202–3, 219, 221, 336–37, 347; as *terra incognita*, 5, 7, 35–56, 163, 186; in Western cultures, 1–3, 5, 11, 18, 136–37, 141
Mountains of the Moon, 12–13, 210–14, 221–26
Montúfar, Carlos, 153–54, 167
Montúfar, Carlos, works by: *Diario del año de 1802: Biage de Quito á Lima*, 167–68
Muir, John, 195

Muir, John, works by: *My First Summer in the Sierra*, 206
Müller, Gustav, 16
Müller, Gustav, works by: "Die Berge und ihre Bedeutung für den Wiederaufbau des deutschen Volkes," 273–74, 281
Mummery, A. F., 30
Münter, Gabriele, 232
Murnau, 231–32

Nanga Parbat, 16, 285–98, 300, 308, 315, 348
Nanga Parbat (dir. Joseph Vilsmaier), 298
Nanga Parbat: Ein Kampfbericht der Deutschen Himalaja Expedition 1934 (dir. Frank Leberecht), 286–90, 298–99
Nanga Parbat 1953 (dir. Hans Ertl), 16–17, 294–98, 300–301
Napoleon. *See* Bonaparte, Napoleon.
Nash, Roderick, 3
Nebo, 24
Nenno, Nancy P., 268, 282
Nibelungenlied, 39, 46, 52
Nietzsche, Friedrich, 13–14, 177–78, 180, 237, 241–42, 246; the Apollinian, 178, 180; the Dionysian, 177–81, 184–89, 256, 262, 264–65
Nietzsche, Friedrich, works by: *Also sprach Zarathustra*, 18, 91, 236–38, 240, 243–44; *Der Antichrist*, 231, 237–40; *Ecce homo*, 18, 238; *Die Geburt der Tragödie*, 256, 264
Nordwand (dir. Philipp Stölzl), 16
Novalis, 187–88
Novalis, works by: *Heinrich von Ofterdingen*, 203

Odysseus, 29, 153, 155
Ol Doinyo Lengai, 6
Olympia (dir. Leni Riefenstahl), 297, 301
Olympus, Mount, 24, 26
Orohena, Mt., 134
Oswald von Wolkenstein, 41–43

Ötzi, 5, 18

Paccard, Michel-Gabriel, 10
Pacific, the, 1, 134–36, 141, 143, 146
Parnassus, 26
pastoral, the, 57–59, 62, 67, 72–73, 81–82
Pepys, Samuel, 322–23
Petrarch, 6–8, 21–23, 29–30, 195, 248. *See also* Ventoux, Mont
Pfeiferová, Dana, 345
Philip of Macedon, 22–23, 26
Phillips, Dana, 119, 132
Picnic at Hanging Rock (dir. Peter Weir), 191
picturesque, the, 78, 80–84, 87–88, 92, 140, 145
Pied Piper (of Hamelin), 178, 186
Pilate, Pontius, 3, 8
Pilatus, Mount, 3–4, 8
Pilot Knob, 24
Pindar, 6, 20
Pindus Mountains, 26
Plato, 21, 27, 29
Pliny the Elder, 27, 53
Pliny the Younger, 27
Polybius, 26
Popocatépetl, 5
postcolonialism, 136–38, 145, 163
Pritchett, W. K., 24
proprioceptive spatial orientation (PSO) (also proprioception, proprioceptive system), 17, 304–7, 309–13, 315–16, 318
Ptolemy, 13
Ptolemy, works by: *The Geography*, 210–11, 221, 223
Pyrenees, 6, 22, 26, 46, 84, 204

Raabe, Wilhelm, works by: *Abu Telfan oder die Heimkehr vom Mondgebirge*, 13, 211, 221–25, 228
Rainy Mountain, 24
Ramond de Carbonnières, Louis-François, 11, 82, 84–88
Ransmayr, Christoph, works by: *Der fliegende Berg*, 15, 334–48; *Die letzte Welt*, 338; *Odysseus, Verbrecher:*

Schauspiel einer Heimkehr, 341; *Die Schrecken des Eises und der Finsternis*, 345
Rauchenberger-Strauss, Johanna von, 233, 245
Rebmann, Johann, 212–14
Reichenbach Falls, 109–10, 115
Renaissance, 23, 52, 157, 214, 218
Rentschler, Eric, 268, 278, 282–84
Rhine, 47, 69, 322
Richard, Frida, 275
Riefenstahl, Leni, 16, 278, 281, 284, 297, 301
Rigaud, Jean Francis, works by: "Ioh: Reinhold Forster und George Forster, Vater und Sohn," 137
Rigby, Kate, 116, 118, 131–32
Ritter, Karl, works by: *Die Erdkunde im Verhältnis zur Natur und Geschichte des Menschen*, 196
Rocciamelone, 7
Rockies, 5
Rohde, Hans, 15–16
Roman Empire, 7, 64
Romanticism (also Romantic literature, Romantic era or period), 7, 11, 20–21, 78–79, 91, 95, 145, 176–77, 179, 185, 187, 189–90, 201, 203, 223, 319, 335
Rosa, Monte, 245, 271
Rosa, Salvator, 145
Rousseau, Jean-Jacques, 58, 73, 79, 82, 84–85
Rousseau, Jean-Jacques, works by: *Confessions*, 82; *Julie, ou la nouvelle Héloïse*, 10, 73, 82–83; *Letter to M. d'Alembert*, 82
Rudolf von Ems, works by: *Alexander*, 44
Ruskin, John, 11, 58, 77, 79, 91–93, 97
Ruskin, John, works by: *Modern Painters*, 79, 91, 97

Safranski, Rüdiger, 180
Salas, Tito, 154–55, 171
Sammons, Jeffrey, 203–4, 209
Saxer, Walter, 307

Scharfe, Martin, 72, 75, 207–8
Schaufelberger, Walter, 15–16
Schedel, Hartmann, works by: *Liber chronicarum*, 47–49, 52
Schelling, Friedrich Wilhelm Joseph, works by: *Die Weltalter*, 335
Scheuchzer, Johann Jakob, 4, 9–10, 19, 57–58, 74
Scheuchzer, Johann Jakob, works by: *Itinera per Helvetiae Alpinas Regiones Facta Annis 1702–1711*, 4; *Natur-Histori des Schweizerlands*, 9
Schiller, Friedrich, 11, 99, 103–6
Schiller, Friedrich, works by: *Die Horen* (editor), 106; "Über das Erhabene," 103–4, 108; *Über naive und sentimentalische Dichtung*, 83; *Wilhelm Tell*, 9, 104–5, 109
Schivelbusch, Wolfgang, 269, 282–84
Schlageter, Albert Leo, 292
Schönberg, Arnold, works by: *Gurre-Lieder*, 241
Schopenhauer, Arthur, 20
Schrader, Julius, 153, 155, 171
Schreckhorn, 9, 68, 328
Schumacher, H. C., 161–62, 173
Scott, Robert Falcon, 21, 31
Scottish Highlands, 204
Sebald, W. G., 14–15, 320–33
Sebald, W. G., works by: "Die Alpen im Meer," 320, 328; *Die Ausgewanderten*, 324–25, 328; "Beyle oder das merckwürdige Faktum der Liebe," 320; "Il ritorno in patria," 321, 324, 328; "Paul Bereyter," 324, 328, 332; *Schwindel*, 321, 328, 332–33
Second World War, 287, 296–97; post-Second World War, 293–96, 300
Seneca, Lucius Annaeus, 6; works by: *Ad Lucilium epistulae morales*, 28–30, 64
Sermon on the Mount, 3
Shaftesbury, 3rd Earl of (Anthony Ashley Cooper), 20
Shelley, Mary, works by: *Frankenstein*, 21, 31

Shelley, Percy Bysshe, 78, 93
Shelley, Percy Bysshe, works by: "Mont Blanc: Lines Written in the Vale of Chamouni," 81, 95
Sherpa(s), 20, 288, 291, 295
Sierra Nevada (California), 5, 206
Sierra Nevada (Spain), 204
Sild, Meinhard, 289, 299
Sils Maria, 237–38
Simler, Josias, 19, 57
Simler, Josias, works by: *De Alpibus commentarius*, 19; *Vallisiae descriptio*, 19
Simmel, Georg, 16, 270–73, 279
Simon, Rainer, 169
Simony, Friedrich, 13, 193, 199–201, 208
Simony, Friedrich, works by: "Drei Dezembertage auf dem Dachsteingebirge," 200, 202; "Zwei Septembernächte auf der Hohen Dachsteinspitze," 201
Simplon Pass, 95
Sinai, Mount, 3, 24, 45
Siula Grande, 309
Skelligs, 30
skiing, 14, 248, 325–27
Smetana, Bedřich, works by: *Vltava*, 231
Smith, Bernhard, 144
Soracte, Mt., 26–27
S.O.S. Eisberg (dir. Arnold Fanck), 275, 283, 300
St. Gotthard Pass, 2, 88–89, 106, 235, 237, 246
Stabler, Jordan Herbert, 154–55, 163, 171
Stafford, Barbara, 140
Staubbach Falls, 71
Stauffer, Karl, 14, 234–40, 243–46
Stendhal, 320, 323
Steuben, Karl von, 153, 155, 171
Stepan, Nancy, 146
Stifter, Adalbert, 193–209, 323
Stifter, Adalbert, works by: *Bergkristall*, 201, 259; *Der Nachsommer*, 13, 193–209
Stoics, 22

Stölzl, Philipp, 16
Strauss, Richard, 14, 231–47
Strauss, Richard, works by: *Eine Alpensinfonie*, 14, 231–47; *Also sprach Zarathustra*, 236–37, 240, 243–44; *Heldenleben*, 236; *Eine Künstlertragödie*, 234; *Salomé*, 232; *Tod und Verklärung*, 236
Stricker, der, works by: *Daniel von dem blühenden Tal*, 39–41, 46, 52
Sturm und Drang, 83
sublime, the, 9, 11, 15, 20–21, 27, 29, 31, 57–58, 69–71, 77–97, 98–115, 117–18, 122, 125, 128, 136, 140, 144–45, 163, 174, 195, 202, 206, 217, 237–38, 240, 243, 248, 269–75, 303, 316–17, 319, 321, 323–25, 327, 330–31, 334, 336, 338, 345, 348
sublimity, 29, 30, 78–82, 86, 91, 93, 99, 102, 106–8, 111, 117, 119, 122, 145, 254, 273
Sulzer, Johann Georg, 101
Switzerland, 3–4, 10, 14, 57, 59–60, 80–87, 235, 238, 246, 330

Tacitus, 27
Tag der Deutschen Kunst (dir. Hans Ertl), 297
Tag der Freiheit — Unsere Wehrmacht (dir. Leni Riefenstahl), 297, 301
Tahiti, 12, 134–49
Tai Shan, 5–6, 24
Tantillo, Astrida, 118, 131
Teide (Mount), 162, 168
Tennyson, Alfred, 29
Tetons, 184. *See also* Grand Teton
Theocritus, 66
Third Reich, 268, 292
Thomson, Joseph, works by: *Through Masai Land*, 215–17
Thoreau, Henry David, 195
Thoreau, Henry David, works by: "A Walk to Wachusett," 206
Thüring von Ringoltingen, works by: *Melusine*, 46
Tieck, Ludwig, works by: *Der getreue Eckart und der Tannhäuser*, 178,

185; *Der Runenberg*, 13, 176–92, 335, 343
Tilman, H. W., works by: *When Men and Mountains Meet*, 20–21, 30
Todorov, Tzvetan, 98–99
Touching the Void (dir. Kevin Macdonald), 309
Trenker, Luis, 275, 277–81, 301
tropicalization, 12, 135–36, 143, 145–46
Tschammer und Osten, Hans von, 286–89, 299
Turner, J. M. W., 79–80, 86–89, 91–92, 94–97, 109, 115
Turner, J. M. W., works by: *The Passage at Mount St. Gotthard*, 88–89; *Snowstorm: Hannibal and His Army Crossing the Alps*, 86

Valais, 19, 60, 82, 85, 271
Van Cleve, John, 65–66, 75
van der Laan, J. M., 130, 133
Venice, 91–92, 222
Ventoux, Mont, 6, 8, 21, 29
Venus Mountain, 178, 184–85, 188, 191
Vergil (also spelled Virgil), 6, 27, 32, 141, 342
Verne, Jules, 168, 174
Verne, Jules, works by: *Les enfants du Capitaine Grant*, 168, 174
Vesuvius, Mt., 27, 155, 204, 322
Vilsmaier, Joseph, 16, 298
Virchov, Christian, 252
Vivaldi, Antonio, works by: *Le quattro stagioni*, 231
Vogel, Jakob, 8–9

Wagner, Abraham, works by: *Merkwürdige Prospekte aus den Schweizer-Gebürgen und derselben Beschreibung* (or *Vues remarquables des montagnes de la Suisse*), 81
Wagner, Richard, 177, 232–33, 240
Walther von der Vogelweide, works by: "Unter der linden," 35, 66
Weaver, Stewart, 13–14

Weimar Germany (also Weimar Republic), 15, 249, 267–68, 273–74, 278–79, 292
Weitsch, Friedrich Georg, 153, 155, 171
Weitz, Eric, 269, 282, 284
Weltli, Friedrich Emil, 235
Welzenbach, Willo, 291
Werefkin, Marianne von, 232
Wessel, Horst, 292
Wetterhorn, 235
Whymper, Edward, 173
Wieland, Christoph Martin, works by: *Agathon*, 203
Wieland, Uli, 291
wilderness, 2–3, 9, 18, 82, 178, 260, 326
Williams, Helen Maria, 11, 84–85, 95
Williams, Helen Maria, works by: *A Tour in Switzerland*, 84–85
Wimmer, Clemens, 136
Wittenberg, Hermann, 145
Wittstock, Uwe, 335, 344, 348
Wolf, Caspar, 19
Wordsworth, William, 11, 58, 78, 82, 86–88, 92–93
Wordsworth, William, works by: *Descriptive Sketches*, 82, 87; *The Prelude*, 82, 87–88
Worster, Donald, 138

Youmans, Charles, 236, 239–40, 247

Zebhauser, Helmuth, 292, 299–300
Zimmermann, Johann Georg, 81
Zoroaster, 6
Zugspitze, 232
Zurlauben, Baron, works by: *Tableaux topographiques, pittoresques, physiques, historiques, moraux, politiques, littéraires de la Suisse*, 81

www.ingramcontent.com/pod-product-compliance
Lightning Source LLC
Chambersburg PA
CBHW022226010526
44113CB00033B/511